Baby Face Nelson

BABY FACE NELSON

PORTRAIT OF A PUBLIC ENEMY

STEVEN NICKEL

WILLIAM J. HELMER

CUMBERLAND HOUSE
NASHVILLE, TENNESSEE

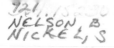
For the grandkids (all our favorite Baby Faces):
Brittany, Dylan, and Jordan; Jessie, Kara, and Blake;
Alyssa and Daniel.

Published by
CUMBERLAND HOUSE PUBLISHING, INC.
431 Harding Industrial Drive
Nashville, TN 37211
www.CumberlandHouse.com

Cover design by Gore Studios, Inc.

Library of Congress Cataloging-in-Publication Data

Nickel, Steven.
   Baby Face Nelson : portrait of a public enemy / Steven Nickel, William J. Helmer.
     p. cm.
   Includes bibliographical references and index. Illustrated.

   ISBN 1-58182-272-3 (Hardcover, alk. paper)
  1. Nelson, Baby Face, 1903-1934. 2. Criminals—Middle West—Biography.
   I. Helmer, William J.   II. Title.
   HV6248.N45 N53 2002
   364.1'523'092—dc21

                                                                2002004675

Printed in the United States of America
1 2 3 4 5 6 7—07 06 05 04 03 02

CONTENTS

INTRODUCTION

THE PUBLIC ENEMY ERA

THE EARLY YEARS OF the 1930s were unique in the annals of American crime, an era producing a succession of colorful, larger-than-life professional bandits who blasted their way into headlines and captured the imagination of an entire nation languishing in the throes of the Great Depression.

Newspapers called them gangsters, a generic title that barely distinguished them from the millionaire mobsters who reigned as the overlords of organized crime. In contrast, the depression desperados were blue-collar criminals, free-lancers who worked for a living. Their favorite targets were the small-town banks dotting the plains and prairies of America's heartland.

Using Tommyguns instead of six-shooters and fast cars instead of horses, they were essentially a revival of the Old West outlaws. Many of the highways they traveled were paved over some of the same trails once used by the Jameses, Youngers, and Daltons. They were sometimes dubbed "auto bandits," a term seldom used since it made them sound like car thieves, although it more aptly described their hit-and-run tactics and fugitive lifestyle. They were nomads, forced to stay mobile, unable to put down roots, dependent more on their vehicles than their weapons. Underworld figures in cities such as Chicago or St. Paul offered protection for a price, but it was usually brief and always costly.

The press chronicled the bandits' exploits in a style that reflected the Saturday matinee serials of the era, a spectacle of daring daylight holdups, tire-screeching getaways, sensational gun battles, and desperate escapes. To provide them with a little extra flash they were labeled with catchy nicknames; "Wooden Gun John" Dillinger, "Pretty Boy" Floyd, "Ma" Barker, Alvin "Old Creepy" Karpis, "Machine Gun" Kelly, and "Baby Face" Nelson.

The public was enthralled. A nation suffering hard times often saw them as underdogs, rugged individualists, and rebels who were driven to crime, thumbing their noses at authority and attacking society's symbols of greed. But before long the bank robbers were branded as "public enemies" and targeted for extinction by a branch of the Justice Department known as the Division of Investigation, officially renamed the Federal Bureau of Investigation in 1935. The bureau's director, John Edgar Hoover, actually helped turn the criminals into celebrities, thereby ensuring greater glory for his agency when his men brought them down.

For a full thirty years after the era ended, the stories of the depression desperados were generally lumped together into a single history that focused on the achievements of Hoover's FBI and their triumph over the public-enemy menace. It was a saga strictly limited in its scope, told and retold in terms of black and white, good guys and bad guys, gangsters and G-Men, fully sanctioned and sanitized by the director's public relations machine. The many books heralded as authoritative accounts—among them Courtney Ryley Cooper's *Ten Thousand Public Enemies*, Hoover's own *Persons in Hiding* (actually ghostwritten by Cooper), and Don Whitehead's *The FBI Story*—never deviated from the Hoover-approved accounts.

It wasn't until the 1960s that a few revisionist writers dared to take a more in-depth and revealing look behind the popularly accepted images drawn from folklore and some carefully crafted FBI fables. Part of this quest for a critical examination of the facts was a result of the times; the counter-culture shift in the sixties led many to challenge the official record, and the revival of the anti-hero in literature and especially films generated fresh interest in the bad guys of bygone days. But the real milestone for serious researchers was the Freedom of Information Act passed by Congress in 1966, which allowed access to formerly classified government documents. Historians for the first time were able to peek at FBI files Hoover and his agents never imagined would be opened to public inspection.

From this unlikely source and others, most of which surfaced after Hoover's death in 1972, a more complete and balanced portrait emerged, providing greater insight into the rise, reign, and fall of the notorious figures of the early depression years. The picture is often intriguing but considerably less conventional. We now know the good guys weren't always so good and the bad guys were not quite the personification of evil, and that many major events used to enhance the bureau's image (the capture of Machine Gun Kelly, the so-called Kansas City Massacre, and Hoover's personal arrest of Alvin Karpis, for example) actually transpired quite differently than the authorized versions promoted for public consumption would lead us to believe.

Over the last four decades numerous written works have revisited those years to provide a more factual retelling of the rise and fall of the depression desperados. Yet there is one figure from the era who has been curiously shunned by the revisionists and kept shrouded in popular clichés. Evidently some legends die harder than others.

Baby Face Nelson remains as vilified and one-dimensional today as he was then, depicted by Hoover-inspired journalists as a vicious, strutting psychotic who killed without a conscience. Contemporary authors seem to have embraced this stereotype without any critical challenge. Jay Robert Nash (*The Dillinger*

Dossier, Bloodletters and Badmen) labeled him "the most blood-thirsty, death-dealing bandit of the Public Enemy Era," claiming that Nelson "mercilessly slaughtered . . . a score of innocent bystanders." In his book *The Bad Ones*, Lew Louderback described Nelson as "something out of a bad dream. . . . Baby Face killed for the sheer hell of it." Carl Safikis (*The Encyclopedia of American Crime*) wrote that Nelson's approach to bank robbery was to come "through the doors shooting," then force "the lucky survivors to hand over the loot," emphasizing that the bandit "often needlessly shot down bank guards and bystanders." Such exaggerations have kept alive the portrait of Nelson as the quintessential trigger-happy punk. No wonder writers have shied away from him as the subject of any serious work on his life.

Nelson might never have achieved the notoriety he did had he not joined forces with Dillinger, the most wanted man in America at the time. Their association ultimately proved to be the main reason Nelson is today shrouded in infamy. To put it simply, Dillinger was a hard act to follow. The Indiana bank robber had an undeniable charisma which attracted a fair amount of public support before Hoover's bureau officially entered the chase and mounted its propaganda campaign against him. Later, when a revival of the Dillinger legend occurred, his biographers and others placing him on a public-enemy pedestal decided that the best way to make Dillinger look good was to portray those around him as considerably worse. Baby Face Nelson, the feral little gangster everyone loved to hate, made an excellent candidate who could be saddled with all the more reprehensible acts attributed to the gang.

In reality, of the seven lawmen slain by the Dillinger gang, Nelson was accountable for only one. But that one was extremely significant. During a bungled FBI raid in Wisconsin, the young outlaw killed one of Hoover's agents. It was the first time Nelson was catapulted into the national spotlight. Hoover, who had learned to use the press to his advantage, did his utmost to ensure that the young gangster was properly reviled.

The press seemed happy to oblige. By the time Nelson hit the headlines the tide was beginning to turn against the bandits and their kind. The widespread dismay and anti-government sentiment that inspired the public to applaud the bank robbers was crumbling, replaced by a fresh spirit of patriotism invoked by a new administration in the White House. Hoover's "War On Crime" came to be viewed essentially as another part of Franklin D. Roosevelt's New Deal.

Crime reporters of the era tended to shape their portrayals of bad men into easily recognizable figures. Thus while some bandits like Dillinger and Floyd were compared to Jesse James, and Ma Barker's boys were viewed as a '30s version of the Daltons, Nelson's press coverage depicted him as a latter day Billy the Kid—a cold-blooded young gunslinger interested only in carving notches on his pistol, although most historians today agree the real Billy was nothing like his notorious legend.

Hollywood also played a part in the way Americans looked at gangsters, and the temptation to judge real-life criminals by what appeared on movie screens was often irresistible. In the 1931 film *Public Enemy*, James Cagney set the standard for the rebellious, amoral, undersized anti-hero with his portrayal of gangster Tommy Powers. Newsmen noted the physical resemblance between Nelson and Cagney and shaped their stories of Baby Face to jibe with the ruthless film role.

All of these factors combined to create a powerful, almost impenetrable aura of infamy which has survived intact these past six decades. The man buried beneath the myths was more complex, difficult to describe in the broad black-and-white strokes with which most have preferred to paint him. He was in fact a tangle of curious contradictions. The side of Nelson rarely seen, but which makes him so fascinating in light of his crimes, reveals a clean-cut young man who didn't drink, smoke, or chase loose woman, the usual vices associated with his brand of criminal. In a surprising departure from the gangster norm, Nelson and his wife were fiercely devoted to each other. Their two children and Nelson's mother often joined them on the road. Between holdups he seemed content to live in a quiet domestic setting with his family, a feat he actually managed to accomplish for the greater part of his time as a fugitive. Those who knew or encountered him when he wasn't robbing banks were mostly unanimous in their description of Nelson as a polite, personable, and generous individual who liked to be surrounded by loved ones and friends.

Ironically, the outlaw Hoover described for the 1930s media as a "vicious lone wolf . . . despised by even his follow criminals" appeared to have partisans almost everywhere, some of whom willingly risked prison to help him in his flight from justice. An FBI report dated October 6, 1934, written at the very height of the Nelson manhunt, listed his known acquaintances and associates. The report ran to ninety-two pages and contained more than 300 names.

His friends rarely saw the public enemy side of Nelson, often finding it impossible to reconcile the young man they knew with the vicious outlaw they read about. Many were made to suffer for their loyalty. Nineteen were prosecuted, and some were able to avoid prison or reduce their sentences by "cooperating" with federal agents. A number of other potential advocates for Nelson were threatened with jail or otherwise intimidated into silence if they disputed the official record. The classic example was the gradual about-face performed by Joseph "Fatso" Negri, a pal and part-time henchman of Baby Face. After his arrest Negri supplied a thirty-eight-page statement documenting his association with Nelson—a fascinating behind-the-scenes look at the private life of a public enemy and the disintegrating relationships between the remaining members of the dying Dillinger gang. It also presents a remarkably fair portrait of Nelson, illuminating a likable side along with his less-admirable qualities. Negri later provided two supplemental statements that painted a notably darker picture of his former crony. When Negri testified against others on trial for aiding the desperado, he described Nelson from the witness stand in increasingly loathsome and violent terms.

In 1940 Negri sold his story to *True Detective Mysteries*, published as an eight-part series entitled "In the Hinges of Hell: How G-Men Ended Crime's Reddest Chapter." Repeatedly contradicting his own original statement, he presented a portrait of Baby Face Nelson that was nothing short of evil incarnate in a wildly exaggerated narrative. Even so, Negri's preposterous tale was regarded as gospel by an entire generation of crime writers and became the basis, or at least a primary influence, for much of the misinformation and many of the misconceptions about Nelson.

※ ※ ※

The principal objective of this work is to present a full, factual chronicle of Nelson's life and times. It is also, to a certain degree, an attempt to set the record straight and discover the real man behind the myth, a journey which often involved sifting through mountains of material—much of it clearly distorted or biased but also much which had been overlooked or ignored in order to keep the stereotype alive. So many falsehoods surround Nelson that if each were addressed, it would slow the narrative and substantially expand the length.

Even without the controversy, and for all his sins, Nelson's story deserves to be told without compromising historical accuracy. Until now, he was the only major criminal figure of the depression era not examined fully in a biographical study, existing primarily in Dillinger's shadow or as merely a secondary character roaming the sidelines of crime. As a result, a great portion of his life has never been told, nor has he been given his proper due among his criminal contemporaries.

He might have been the most resourceful, widely traveled, and well-connected outlaw of his era. It was Nelson who introduced the Barker-Karpis gang to the underworld in Reno, Nevada, where the desperados laundered the ransom money from their kidnappings. Long before they became partners in crime, Dillinger sought out Baby Face for his gangland contacts in Chicago. Dillinger's escape from the Lake County Jail in Crown Point, Indiana—his most celebrated feat and the cornerstone of the Dillinger mystique—succeeded partly through Nelson's help. Despite his youth Nelson was the driving force behind an efficient bank-robbing crew which, thanks to the addition of Dillinger, became the most publicized and relentlessly pursued gang of the period. While there was actually no recognized leader, the notorious group was largely Nelson's creation. Historians, however, have labeled the outlaw band "the Second Dillinger Gang," in the process relegating Baby Face to the role of simply "the trigger-nervous runt" among them.

The record of Nelson's life also provides a dramatic, insightful, unglamorous view of outlaw life in the 1930s underworld. While Nelson and others of his kind prided themselves on being independent free-lancers, it becomes clear how utterly reliant upon gangland connections they really were. Most of all Nelson's tale demonstrates the futility of a life lived outside the law. His four months as the nation's Public Enemy Number One was little more than an aimless odyssey in which Nelson and his companions were forced to keep moving in a desperate attempt to stay one step ahead of the law.

His story also contains a colorful supporting cast—those who loved him, followed him, or hunted him—some of whom at times emerged as central figures in the drama. Foremost was his young wife, Helen, who endured a grueling, often nightmarish existence to remain at her husband's side, and who, briefly and unofficially, was labeled the nation's first female Public Enemy Number One, thanks to Hoover's efforts to portray her as a "gun moll."

There was John Paul Chase, an amiable West Coast bootlegger five inches taller and seven years older than Nelson, whose friendship and loyalty to Baby Face brought him out of criminal obscurity and landed him in Alcatraz with a life sentence.

The two men largely responsible for shaping Nelson's style of bank robbery were Eddie Bentz and Homer Van Meter, the former his chief mentor and the other his principal accomplice, who had a penchant for gunplay which proved infectious. Nelson's association with Bentz, one of the most sophisticated but overlooked bandits of his day, seems to have eluded most writers. His relationship with Van Meter—beginning as the best of friends and ending as bitter enemies—is often absurdly misrepresented.

There were also shadowy background figures such as Jimmy Murray, a Chicago entrepreneur who specialized in protecting criminals and funding their operations, and Father Phillip Coughlan, a maverick Catholic priest whose close ties to Baby Face almost cost him his collar. Both apparently played key roles in the mystery that still surrounds Nelson's final hours.

But the most puzzling and intriguing character in the story is Nelson himself. St. Paul crime historian Paul Maccabee observed that "Baby Face Nelson really is an enigma because he died before a soul interviewed him." The closer one looks at Nelson's progressively violent life—escalating from problem child to public enemy—the more paradoxical he becomes. The fact that he lived his life without offering any apologies, excuses, or explanations for his crimes only generates more speculation—and ultimately more exaggeration—about the forces that compelled him to follow the self-destructive path he chose.

The best any biographer can do is strive to salvage his subject from the realm of myth in order to present the facts and reconstruct an accurate, detailed account of his life. In the end, the reader is left to decide who the real Baby Face Nelson was and what made him tick.

BABY FACE
NELSON

I think he [J. Edgar Hoover] had to have bad guys, and he
specialized not in creating them but illuminating them.
— Ramsey Clark,
U.S. Attorney General, 1967-69

CHAPTER 1

MOST WANTED

THE DYING MAN WAS sprawled facedown at the mouth of the alley, his feet still on the curb. The brim of his straw hat and his wire-framed glasses lay crushed between his forehead and the grimy cobblestones. The sharp cracks of the five gunshots that had brought him down—fired from three separate weapons at point-blank range, so close together that onlookers claimed they heard only two shots—still echoed in the thick, muggy evening air, along with the smell of cordite. A crimson stain spread across the man's white shirt where a slug had ripped into his right side, while a second, larger pool of blood began to form around his shattered head.

A number of startled bystanders, many emerging from the same theater as the victim, screamed, ducked for cover, or ran, unsure if they were witnessing a mob killing or a holdup, for over the past decade Chicago had experienced plenty of both. Quickly the three shooters and their colleagues, all clad in ties and suit jackets despite the sweltering summer night, formed a tight circle around the bleeding figure. There were nearly two dozen of them on the scene, only now flashing badges identifying themselves as government agents.

Two women on the opposite side of the alley continued to shriek. Both had been wounded by federal bullets, one by a stray shot, the other by a slug that had passed through the victim.

It was 10:35 Sunday night, July 22, 1934.

Word of the incident swept along Lincoln Avenue and swiftly spread throughout the entire city. John Herbert Dillinger—Indiana farm boy turned

3

bank robber, the most notorious desperado of the depression era, America's Public Enemy Number One—had been slain outside Chicago's Biograph Theatre by the nation's latest brand of lawmen, J. Edgar Hoover's G-Men.

※　　※　　※

Asked in later years what was the "greatest thrill" of his long and controversial career as director of the Federal Bureau of Investigation, Hoover immediately replied, "The night we got Dillinger."

He was always careful to describe the actions of his agency by using the collective we, as if all of its offices and operatives spread across the nation acted as a cohesive unit—parts of a single body working in conjunction with the undisputed head, who was virtually enthroned as a czar at his headquarters in Washington.

Hoover was a master of manipulating the media, and through a shrewd, carefully orchestrated public relations campaign he managed to redefine the country's cultural perception of its heroes and reshape the very concept of the American lawman. His strategy was to present his bureau as an elite, modern crimefighting force that was far superior to incompetent, corrupt, and outdated local police departments. By promoting an image of his agents as untarnished, efficient warriors against crime, he hoped to win public approval and support, which would in turn generate more legislation and greater funding to empower and establish the bureau as the premier law enforcement agency of the land.

The means Hoover employed to achieve this end were to select specific renowned criminals, vilify them as evildoers and agents of anarchy, then go after them with the resources then at his disposal. The bureau, still in its infancy, was curiously quiet throughout the Roaring Twenties. Gangland figures like Al Capone in Chicago and Waxey Gordon in New York proved too untouchable to target. (Hoover's FBI, even in later years, never mounted any serious attempts to take on organized crime.) The so-called Midwestern crime wave of the early Thirties, however, was exactly what Hoover needed to launch his crusade against lawlessness.

By the summer of 1933 America was ripe for change. With a new president at the helm and the nation trying desperately to emerge from the chaotic gloom of the Great Depression, the popular folk-hero status of the midwestern desperados began to fade. Their bank robberies and defiant escapades, which an embittered public could easily admire if not openly condone, were denounced by the new administration's attorney general, Homer S. Cummings, as more than crimes; they were an assault on society itself. And a critical part of President Franklin D. Roosevelt's road to economic recovery was an appeal for national unity and a restoration of law and order.

Sensing the winds of change and an opportunity to amass power, Hoover moved to position his agency and himself at center stage of the government's "War On Crime." Following the example of his boss Cummings, the director opened fire with scalding rhetoric branding the principal figures of the Midwest's bandit gangs as "public enemies," a label that had been gaining increasing recognition since it was first applied to Al Capone.

Hoover utilized a series of melodramatic metaphors to dramatically present his anti-crime movement in stirring symbolic terms designed to unify public opinion behind the bureau. At times he invoked images of a military campaign, casting his agents as soldiers fighting to defend the nation against the forces of lawlessness, with Hoover presiding over them like a general. He portrayed the conflict as a holy crusade in which the bureau guarded decent citizens and American society from the scourge of immoral gangsters. By far his favorite tactic was to depict criminals as sub-human scavengers encroaching upon peaceful communities. They were denounced as "rats" and "vermin," and the "molls" who ran with them were reviled as "filthy and diseased women." For the good of the nation, "they need to be exterminated," Hoover raged, adding that his agents were the guardians anointed "to carry out this extermination."

Eventually the top priority in Hoover's campaign to disinfect the American landscape became bringing down John Dillinger. There were many outlaws more dangerous and deadly than Dillinger, but none was as celebrated. His smooth, swashbuckling style of bank robbery and his flamboyant flight from justice glorified everything Hoover sought to vilify. Further, Dillinger's highly publicized antics made him a star among his criminal peers, a headliner who, for the moment, had managed to enrapture the public. If the director was to prevail in his quest for power, Dillinger had to die and the bureau must be credited with the kill. Designating the Indiana bandit as "Public Rat Number One," Hoover instructed his men to do whatever it took to get Dillinger.

On the evening Hoover fondly recalled as the night "we" got Dillinger, he was nowhere near Chicago. When the desperado was cut down by the G-Men's bullets, the FBI's thirty-nine-year-old director was at home with his mother in Washington waiting for the call confirming Dillinger's death. When the phone rang he spoke with the two men supervising the stakeout—Melvin Purvis, SAC (special agent-in-charge) of the bureau's Chicago office, and Inspector Sam Cowley. The pair took turns supplying details of the shooting. Hoover congratulated them, then made a series of quick calls to selected reporters, among them Rex Collier of the *Washington Star*, who had previously provided favorable coverage of the director and his bureau.

It was almost midnight when a jubilant J. Edgar Hoover arrived at the Justice Department for an after-hours press conference. He had promised a bombshell and delivered one. After announcing Dillinger's demise, Hoover stressed that the bureau had intended to take the criminal alive (a claim that was later questioned), but he "went for a gun in his pants pocket, and the agents were forced to shoot." To that he added, "Personally, I am glad Dillinger was taken dead. . . . The only good criminal is a dead criminal."

Hoover praised his men for their "almost unimaginable daring" but refused to name the agents who fired the fatal shots. The reason, he stated, was not to put any man "on the spot," making him a possible target for gangland revenge. The truth of the matter, however, is that the director did not want any of his men singled out for individual recognition or personal glory. He wanted Dillinger's slaying to be perceived as an execution by firing squad—as if the entire bureau had collectively pulled the trigger. It was essential that the organization, not individuality, be stressed. The bureau was only big enough for one ego, and that belonged exclusively to J. Edgar Hoover.

One reporter dared to inquire if the bureau would relax its efforts now that it had eliminated Public Enemy Number One. The director replied, "Dillinger was just a yellow rat that the country may consider itself fortunate to be rid of. There are other rats to be gotten, however, and we are not taking any time off to celebrate Dillinger. . . . We're serving notice on underworld figures throughout the country that this agency will not rest until they are rooted out and dealt with to the full extent of the law. This does not mean the end of the Dillinger case. Anyone who ever assisted him in his crimes or aided in his flight from the law will be pursued by our agents."

This was the moment many had been waiting for. The newsmen instantly clamored to find out, "Who moves to the top of the list now?" "Who will succeed Dillinger as Public Enemy Number One?"

The question apparently caught Hoover off guard. Dillinger was dead, the occupant of a cold slab in the Chicago morgue and already enshrined as a part of the evolving FBI mystique. But if the saga of Hoover's G-Men was to continue, the bureau needed to choose a new national menace, a crime figure worthy of inheriting Dillinger's mantle as America's most dangerous desperado. Unable to decide on the spot, Hoover assured the reporters he would make the announcement soon.

The next day was a busy one for Hoover, culminating that evening in a congratulatory dinner at the White House with President Roosevelt. Nevertheless, the director found time that afternoon to fire off a press release naming George "Baby Face" Nelson, as his bureau's new most wanted man. Newspapers immediately responded by touting him as "Public Enemy Number One."

Reporters and lawmen across the country were genuinely surprised by Hoover's choice. Nelson was a relative newcomer to the crime scene. It was only three months earlier that the public had first heard his name when he and other members of Dillinger's gang shot their way out of a bungled FBI trap in the north woods of Wisconsin, killing one agent and making fools of the rest of Hoover's raiding party. There were many notorious criminals plaguing the country, including Charles "Pretty Boy" Floyd and the Barker brothers and their associate Alvin Karpis—desperados who had been at large much longer and were responsible for more deaths.

But, like Dillinger, Nelson was not chosen for the number or the severity of his crimes. Hoover was not interested in bringing down the worst criminal walking the streets; rather, he wanted to target a malefactor whose apprehension would ensure the continuing enhancement of the bureau's image and reputation in the eyes of the public. For a number of reasons—hinted at by Hoover in the days to come—Nelson proved to be the best candidate.

First and probably foremost was his past association with Dillinger. By choosing someone who could be described as "Dillinger's chief lieutenant and trigger man," the director could remind the public of the bureau's latest triumph in every news story pertaining to Nelson.

Second, in contrast to Dillinger, Nelson had never achieved the folk-hero status of his former partner in crime. It was easy for Hoover to portray the little bandit (Nelson stood barely five feet, five inches tall and tipped the scales at 133 pounds) as "a despicable and reprehensible character." In many ways Nelson epitomized the perfect public enemy, for he possessed all of the violent, lawless, anti-social traits that Hoover had sworn to stamp out with his agency. Vain and volatile, undeniably addicted to crime since his youth, he seemed to harbor an almost pathological contempt for law in general and lawmen in particular. Most menacing of all was his obsessive love of guns; he could rarely resist exiting a robbery without spraying the scenery with lead.

While some might argue that Dillinger was forced into a life outside the law by an unjust prison sentence, Nelson simply seemed to be a bad seed who had graduated into big-time bank robbery. And while Dillinger had staged holdups and evaded capture with a flashy, flaunting style of banditry, Nelson's criminal career was more a full-throttle assault upon the forces of law and order. "He's a crazy killer," Hoover declared. "A vicious, half-pint yellow rat who shoots without provocation."

Lastly, Nelson's chief claim to notoriety was not the banks he robbed but the agent he had slain at the Wisconsin resort. "We're not going to let anyone kill one our men and get away with it," Hoover informed the press. Regardless of whether Nelson was actually menacing enough to be proclaimed the nation's most wanted criminal, no one could fault the bureau for wanting to avenge one of its own. In all likelihood, Hoover's main motivation ran deeper than a desire to even the score. A cause as lofty and solemn as his needed martyrs, and the bureau's recent battles had produced two: an agent gunned down in the infamous Kansas City Massacre in June 1933 and the agent killed by Nelson in Wisconsin. In tabbing Baby Face Nelson as the bureau's chief priority, Hoover kept alive the memory of the blood shed by FBI operatives in the line of duty.

Armed with Hoover's quotes and little else, the media went to work. Few photos were found of the new public enemy; most papers printed his mug shots (snapped at the Illinois State Penitentiary three years earlier), which showed a handsome young man with a boyish face radiating a defiant, insolent glare. Aside from his association with Dillinger, newsmen discovered little about the diminutive bandit except that he had been born and raised in Chicago, spent time in a reformatory as a youth, and for the past two and a half years had lived as a fugitive after escaping from a Joliet prison guard while serving a sentence for bank robbery. There seemed nothing to discount Hoover's statement that Nelson was "a cheap small-time crook who would never have been heard of if he hadn't fallen in with Dillinger."

That was the story the press ran with.

Everyone expected a quick resolution to the Nelson manhunt—a few days or a couple of weeks at most, a Chicago agent boasted at the time, which was possibly a factor in Hoover's choice. The general opinion was that Baby Face lacked the savvy and smarts Dillinger had employed to elude lawmen. There seemed no reason to dig any deeper into a subject destined to become yesterday's news as early as tomorrow.

❋   ❋   ❋

At a few minutes past 7 P.M. that Monday, about the same time Hoover was enjoying dinner with the president, the nation's new Public Enemy Number One walked into the Pioneer Restaurant on Grand Avenue in the heart of Chicago's Near West Side.

He was an angry young man whose choirboy face concealed a hair-trigger temper. Loyal and generous to friends, family, and allies, and ruthless and unforgiving to those he considered enemies, Nelson often fluctuated between a pleasant, disarming demeanor and a brooding coldness with flashes of explosive rage.

Those who knew him best insisted his unstable behavior was only a recent development, the inevitable result of life on the run. Others believed it stemmed from his need to compensate for his youthful, mild-mannered appearance in order to bolster his tough-guy image. His habit of wearing layers of clothing often hid his slim physique, and because he always wore a bulky bulletproof vest during robberies, witnesses often described him as stocky. His round, boyishly handsome face made it appear that he was still in his teens, and his thick, wavy blond hair was usually covered by a hat or cap. People generally considered his smile to be charming when he displayed his perfect teeth, or "peculiar" and rather crooked when his thin lips remained pressed together. He spoke in a low-toned, smooth manner except when angry or excited, at which times his voice became shrill and high-pitched.

There were a couple of elements of his otherwise innocuous looks that hinted at the restless, erratic spirit within. His movements conveyed a distinctive panther-like quality—slow, deliberate, and in the words of one FBI informant, "with a slight sway of his body from side to side." He had a curious habit of squinting, but even reduced to narrow slits, his eyes were his most striking feature. They were an icy grayish-blue with tiny flecks of yellow, causing more than one person to remark that his gaze seemed piercing, even predatory, seeing everything but revealing nothing.

His unexpected appearance at the Pioneer that evening generated some startled expressions among the patrons. The restaurant, located near the busy intersection of Grand and Western Avenues, was a well-known hot spot for criminals and was owned and operated by a friend of the underworld named Johnny Bananas. The place was often diligently watched by police and, more recently, by federal agents looking to spot notorious customers. The Pioneer was located in the southeastern corner of the West Side known to locals as The Patch. Over the preceding decade the multi-ethnic area had produced a number of prominent gangland characters, including Anthony Accardo, "Tough Tony" Capezio, "Three-Fingered Jack" White, and Baby Face Nelson. The house where Nelson was born and the streets where he played as a child and prowled as a troubled youth were only a few minutes' walk away.

He had been a frequent patron of the restaurant in times past but for obvious reasons had kept his distance for the last couple of years. Most of the clientele that evening remembered Nelson from his days in The Patch; some had been boyhood chums, and the rest knew him by reputation. They were also aware that, despite the media's portrayal of him as a reckless, demented gangster, he was quite clever and extremely cautious about showing his face in public. With the entire nation hunting him, however, it seemed incredibly foolhardy for Nelson to make a personal appearance at the Pioneer.

Nevertheless, he looked perfectly at ease as he passed among the diners, nodding at several he recognized and behaving like a hometown kid returning to his roots after making a name for himself in the world. He strolled directly to the back where he joined a heavyset figure seated in a booth.

Jack Perkins was probably more surprised than anyone else to see Nelson enter the restaurant and sit across from him. A stocky man with a wide grin, watery blue eyes, and a whispery voice, Perkins had a pot belly and thinning hair that made him look ten years older than his baby-faced crony, but he was actually three months younger.

Pals since grade school, the pair had maintained their friendship over the years with a fierce loyalty and a few joint enterprises. Perkins was a player, a minor figure in the vast Chicago crime scene who managed some syndicate-owned slot machines in the western suburb of Cicero and ran an independent bookie operation with a partner, Arthur "Fish" Johnston, on the side. His gangland connections allowed him to perform favors for his old friend, such as peddling stolen bonds, arranging hideouts, and the acquiring "hardware"—guns, ammunition, bulletproof vests, and, on occasion, cars. Recently Perkins had taken a more active role in Nelson's activities. They met regularly, once or twice a week, usually on a secluded stretch of highway outside the city and always after dark. The fact that Nelson showed up unexpectedly at the Pioneer while it was still light left no doubt he was there on an urgent matter.

"What are you doing here?" Perkins asked.

"Looking for you," Nelson replied coolly. "We're taking a trip to the West Coast, and I wanted to see if you'd come along." He promised to cover all expenses, making the journey sound more like a carefree vacation than what Perkins knew it actually was—an attempt to escape the local "heat" following the death of Dillinger. Nelson even urged him to bring his wife, Grace, and their two children, Patricia and John Jr.

After some questioning, Perkins got him to admit that the presence of the children might help the pair travel without attracting suspicion. "Why don't you take your own kids?" he inquired.

"Don't you think I would if I could?" Nelson threw back. "The cops and feds are watching 'em round the clock. Helen and I can't get anywhere near them."

"I've got obligations I can't just walk away from," Perkins protested, adding that Art, his partner, "will kick my ass into the next county." When Nelson persisted with his invitation, Perkins told him, "I need some time to think it over."

They agreed to meet again at eight o'clock Wednesday evening at a remote spot on River Road, five miles out of Chicago. Perkins promised to have an answer for him at that time.

He spent the next forty-eight hours agonizing over his decision. On the morning of their meeting, July 25, Perkins, a religious reader of the *Tribune*, spotted an article on page two amid all the splashy coverage of the Biograph Theatre shooting. It seemed like a further warning against joining his fugitive pal on the trip west:

Agents Launch Hunt For New Enemy No. 1

Federal agents turned their attention today to fugitive George (Baby Face) Nelson, who became public enemy no. 1 and assumed the risks that go with that title when John Dillinger was slain. A widespread search for Nelson was ordered by Washington.

Nelson, termed a "rat" by Attorney General Cummings and called "kill-crazy" by other authorities, first shared notoriety with the Dillinger gang in the gun battle at the Little Bohemia resort near Mercer, Wisconsin. . . .

In related stories the paper reported that on the previous evening—about the same time Nelson was seated across from him in the Pioneer—the baby-faced desperado was spotted trading shots with highway patrolmen near

Sandusky, Ohio, later staging a holdup outside of Detroit, and then somehow finding time to rob a bank in Kentucky with three accomplices.

Perkins thought of dozens of reasons to decline the invitation, the most compelling being the fact he would place himself and his family in harm's way by traveling with the man every law officer in the land was looking for. But in the end he knew he couldn't refuse Nelson. Decades later when an aged Jack Perkins, reminiscing about his days as an "old time outlaw," was asked why he stuck by his boyhood pal—an act earning him his only time inside a prison—he answered, "Because he stuck by me. He was the best friend I ever had."

He wasn't really a bad kid, not at all like they claim he was. . . . He was normal but terribly obstinate. I don't remember him ever being openly defiant or disobedient to our parents. But the moment you turned your back on him or left him alone, poof—he was gone, off on one of his adventures with friends.
— Juliette (Gillis) Fitzsimmons

CHAPTER 2

THE PATCH

LONG BEFORE HE BECAME the most wanted man in America, Lester Joseph Gillis—the boy who would one day become Baby Face Nelson—seemed always to be running from something. His habit of turning up where he wasn't supposed to be and finding only trouble was the hallmark of his middle-class upbringing on Chicago's Near West Side. It was also a constant source of irritation, and ultimately heartbreak, for his immigrant parents, who believed that the way to tap into the American Dream was through a life of honesty, integrity, and hard work, virtues they strived to impart to each of their children.

His mother, Marie Doguet, was born in the Flemish farmlands around Louvain in central Belgium in 1869, one of eight children in a respected rural family that provided her with the finest education available. A petite, bright, studious girl with a special flair for literature and language, she was able to speak and read Dutch, French, and English by her teens. Friends insisted that the best opportunities—and the promise of a better life—lay in America, so for two years Marie worked as a teacher, saving her money. At age twenty she decided to make the move, becoming one face among the many thousands of European immigrants pouring into the United States at that time.

13

Eventually she settled in Chicago, invited to live with a family from her homeland. Through mutual friends she encountered Joseph Gillis, a young Belgian she had known as a child in Louvain and who was the same age as she. He had arrived in America several years earlier and was boarding with his brother Jules while making a good living as a tanner. After a three month courtship Marie and Joseph were married.

Described as a gentle-spirited man except when he drank, Gillis was most of all an industrious, dedicated worker. A national trade publication once rated him the finest tanner in the country. For her part, Marie—gradually becoming known among her new American friends as Mary—set aside her dreams to further her education and continue teaching in order to keep house and raise a family. The couple's first child died in infancy, but the birth of two daughters— Amelia (Amy) in 1892, named after Joseph's mother, and Eugenia (Jenny) the following year—eased the sorrow of their earlier loss.

With his young family bursting the seems of a three-room apartment on Augusta Street, Gillis devoted the greater part of his paycheck into building a three-story red brick town house at 942 North California Avenue, near Humbolt Park. The family moved into its new home in 1896, just before the birth of a third daughter, Juliette. Next came a son, Edmund, in 1898, then another daughter, Leona, in 1902, each delivered in the Gillises' bedroom.

And it was there, on December 6, 1908, that their seventh and final child entered the world. Mary later insisted that Lester was the most beautiful of her babies, and the brightest. Blond-haired and apple-cheeked, with luminous gray-blue eyes and a radiant smile, he was an active, ebullient, insatiably curious child. The former schoolteacher had high hopes for her little boy.

As the baby of the family, Lester was pampered and doted on, especially by his four sisters. Amy, the eldest, was married about this time, and her first son, born in 1911, was named Lester. Joseph, meanwhile, was promoted to assistant supervisor at the tannery, enabling him to construct a larger, more modern house on the lot next door at 944 North California. By Lester's second birthday the family had moved into the new place. The extra room and broader back-yard allowed the children to acquire an array of pets—dogs, cats, rabbits, even a lamb. Lester seemed to develop a closer affinity with the animals than his brother or sisters did, and almost every photo snapped of the boy shows him clasping one of the family pets. After a visit to his uncle's farm in the country, he begged his parents for weeks to buy a horse.

The youngster was soon bringing home strays found around the neighbor-hood, but Joseph and Mary usually decreed that the animals be returned to the streets. One exception was a straggly terrier Lester called Rags. According to the story he told his parents, he had been attacked in an alley by a snarling bull-dog, when suddenly Rags appeared, engaged the bulldog in a fierce battle, and chased it away. The boy insisted he couldn't leave the terrier after it had come to his rescue. His father voiced some doubts, suspecting that Lester had devised a clever tale in order to keep his latest furry friend. Mary, however, believed every word, later declaring her son "could never abide a lie." In fact, even after all that occurred during Lester's brief, violent life, she remained convinced that he had always told her the truth.

Rags was permitted to remain in the household, and Lester and the dog were inseparable until the terrier was nabbed by a dog catcher. His father refused to pay the fee to redeem Rags, leaving Lester embittered and heartbroken. He soon found a replacement. This time the boy claimed he had been passing a quarry on Grand Avenue when he heard the desperate cries of a puppy that had either fallen or been tossed into the pit. "Momma, I couldn't just leave him there," he explained on the doorstep, the tiny pup shivering in his arms. "Can we keep him a few days until he's better?"

The few days became a months, then years. The puppy, which he named Brucie, grew into a large, friendly mutt, becoming Lester's favorite companion through the greater part of his adolescence.

At the age of six he was enrolled in the Lafayette public school at Augusta and Fairfield Avenue. His first three years passed smoothly, even encouragingly, as there were no reported behavioral problems and he received good grades. When he was nine, approaching his first communion, his parents transferred him to St. Mark's parochial school. Almost immediately Lester had problems adjusting to the more rigid standards and conformity of the Catholic institution, and he also mourned the loss of companionship with some of his neighborhood friends. His parents soon began receiving reports that their son was not attending classes.

Tragedy befell the family about the same time Lester's absences began. Less than a week after her twenty-fifth birthday, Jenny Gillis became gravely ill, a victim of the great influenza epidemic that swept across America at the end of World War I claiming half a million lives. After eight bedridden days, she died on October 19, 1918.

The visitation was held in the Gillises' front room where family and friends gathered around the coffin as a priest conducted a brief ceremony. Mary, noticing her youngest son was not present, searched the house and found him cowering in his bed. The nine-year-old pleaded to remain where he was, terrified at the idea of viewing Jenny in death. His mother pulled him from the bedroom and marched him downstairs. With her hands clasping his slender shoulders, she guided the trembling lad to the casket and said, "See now how peaceful your sister looks?"

Despite her assurances that Jenny was at rest, Mary noticed that from that day on, her boy displayed an unusual dread of anything associated with death. The mere sight of a cemetery from the car window would make him shudder.

After the funeral his parents decided to deal with Lester's dissatisfaction with St. Mark's by sending him to the St. Patrick boarding school in Momence,

15

Illinois, where their youngest daughter, sixteen-year-old Leona, was enrolled. They were confident his sister's presence, along with the school's remote location fifty miles south of Chicago, would discourage his truancy. A month passed with reports that he was doing well and seemed content.

Late one rainy afternoon Lester—drenched, dirty, and clutching a tiny kitten—appeared at his father's tannery. When Joseph demanded an explanation, the boy confessed that he could no longer stand the confinement at St. Patrick's. The previous day he had run off and slept overnight in a cornfield where he found the kitten and did his best to keep the animal warm and dry during a thunderstorm. In the morning the driver of a bakery wagon offered him and his new feline friend a ride, taking them as far South Holland, Illinois. A salesman drove him into Chicago and generously provided the youngster with change for the street car.

At home Lester received a scolding from Mary, who announced he would be taken back to St. Patrick's the next morning. But her husband, usually the strict disciplinarian of the house, was apparently touched by his youngest son's pleadings not to be sent back. "The boy is homesick," he told Mary. "We shouldn't force him to go away if he wants to be here."

A heated discussion ensued between the couple, but Joseph prevailed. Lester was re-enrolled in St. Mark's with the understanding that he would abide by its rules. For a brief time the boy appeared to make an effort, but then he began skipping school again. Evidently Lester had acquired a taste of freedom away from the classroom, and sitting at a desk for half the day made him bored and restless.

Mary began walking her son to school each morning to ensure that he arrived, but by noon on most days she would receive word that he had slipped away again. When she set out to search for him, Lester could usually be found in nearby Humboldt Park playing with Brucie or one or more neighborhood pals—boys almost always older than Lester. Each time he dutifully went home with his mother, freely admitting his guilt, humbly apologizing, and promising not to play hooky any more. The next day the school would call again.

Finally the Sister Superior at St. Mark's notified Lester's parents that the school could no longer keep him as a student. She said she was fond of Lester, explaining that he was always well-behaved in the classroom. The problem was that he was almost never there.

Lester, now eleven, was transferred back to Lafayette, his parents hoping the return to public school might solve his truancy problems. But the former pattern soon began to recur, and when Joseph and Mary resorted to harsher discipline, it had little lasting effect. A thrashing by his father produced only a cold, silent glare from the boy. If Mary administered the spanking, Lester would respond with a stoic shrug or even an understanding smile. He refused to let his parents see him cry.

"Whippings, making him work, punishments of all kinds made no difference," his sister Julie told the press years later. "I don't think he ever wanted to hurt our parents. In fact, he was always very considerate, wanting to help around the house. He just couldn't resist temptation. He figured he didn't need school, so he went his own way and fell in with a bad crowd."

Mary found herself on an almost daily quest to locate her absentee son. Each time he was a little harder to track down.

❋ ❋ ❋

The Patch doesn't appear on any maps of the Chicago metropolitan area. Aside from the people who lived there, few have ever heard the name. Its boundaries seem to fluctuate, enlarging, diminishing, or bending according to the individuals one consults. Among those who have, most agree it encompassed the triangle-shaped area between North and Western Avenues and the diagonal slash of Grand, although some argue that the borders extended slightly north and/or substantially east. Its centerpiece was Humboldt Park, its curving southwest edge sharply marked by the sprawling Western Avenue train yards.

During the early years of the twentieth century the area was populated primarily by immigrant families, attracted by low-cost housing and, more importantly, the opportunity to settle among their own ethnic groups. The Patch was like a patchwork quilt draped across a section of the city's Near West Side, composed of nearly a dozen distinctive European cultural communities coexisting within sight of one another. The Irish and Italians greatly outnumbered the other groups, and all—except for a small number of Jews—shared the bond of Catholicism.

In those days The Patch was a thriving, mostly residential, predominantly middle-class stretch of interlocking neighborhoods dotted with markets and shops and family-owned businesses. While many of the foreign-born parents staunchly observed the cultural divisions within the area, their children for the most part displayed little adherence to Old World taboos and traditions. In the schools and the streets of The Patch a fresh generation of American youngsters intermingled and ignored ethnic barriers.

In 1919 ten-year-old John Alfred Perkins moved with his mother and older sister from St. Louis into an apartment on Chicago's West Side. Tagged a newcomer to The Patch—and even worse, an outsider—he was a shy, chubby boy and quickly became the favorite target of schoolyard bullies and neighborhood ruffians. The abuse abruptly ended when he was befriended by young Lester Gillis, who seemed to take Jack under his wing the way he sheltered the forlorn animals he came across. "Nobody messes with Les," was the word around The Patch.

"He was the toughest kid I ever met," Perkins said in later years. "Tougher than ratshit. He never backed down from a fight, no matter how big, old, or ugly the other kid was."

By the time Perkins came along, Lester had already gained a reputation for being streetwise and self-reliant and had made allies of a gang of local boys (probably the "bad crowd" to which his sister Julie later referred). Lester was smaller, younger, and better groomed than the others, but he had obviously won their trust and respect, earning the right to run with them. When he invited his new friend to tag along, there were no objections from the group, no initiation test required of Perkins—Lester's recommendation was good enough. The central figures in the gang were called "the two Tonys," a pair of Italian teenagers three years older than Lester. Anthony Capezio was a product of The Patch; his best friend, Anthony Accardo, lived a few blocks east on Grand Avenue near Ogdon. The rest of the boys rallied around them. Evidently it was Dominic Capezio, Tony's younger brother, who brought Lester into the group.

The boys never adopted a name for the gang, which never had more than a dozen hard-core members and whose eldest members were still in their mid-teens. It was really little more than a group of youngsters bound together by the thrill of mischief, pulling pranks and generally raising hell as they roamed the streets, rode the trolley cars, or hung around the Western Avenue train yards. Eventually their antics grew bolder and more serious, venturing farther outside the law.

According to Perkins, it was the two Tonys who introduced their followers to crime. Their favorite method of obtaining quick cash was a practice called "ringing registers." The boys would enter a store and cause a commotion. While the employees were distracted, Lester—the fastest and most agile—would slip behind the counter, hit the register's "no sale" button, and sweep the cash drawer clean. George Ackerman, another gang member and close friend of Gillis, later revealed that the boys were also used as "tools" in a local extortion racket. Only Capezio and Accardo knew who was hiring them, and they would lead the youngsters to the intended target, a house or more often a business, where they would hurl bricks through the windows or perform other acts of vandalism.

Lester's role within the gang was usually a prominent one. He was the kid always willing to accept a challenge or take a dare. "He loved danger," Perkins recalled of his childhood chum. Lester's innocent appearance proved invaluable when he was sent ahead to check out a store. His well-mannered behavior around adults often won him favor with the parents of the other boys. He was a frequent guest at the Capezio home, where he developed a love for homemade Italian meals.

Mary Gillis was aware her son had taken up with a gang of local boys but remained ignorant of his delinquent activities. So careful was Lester in concealing his criminal behavior from his family that on days when Mary was unable to locate him, she assumed he was playing games with his pals. His worst offense, other than habitual truancy, was the occasion on which his mother caught him and an older boy smoking in the park. Mary herded her son home where she dealt him a harsher-than-usual spanking. Apparently this was one admonishment that proved effective, for in later life Lester never touched tobacco.

It was no surprise when the principal of Lafayette school informed Lester's parents that he'd had to expel the boy for his repeated absences. Like the sister at St. Mark's, he regretted the decision because Lester was a likable boy and never any trouble on the rare occasions he reported for class. He recommended they place Lester in the Glenwood School for Boys, where his conduct would be more strictly supervised. Mary inquired about enrolling her youngest son, but when the Glenwood interviewers learned the Gillises were Catholics, she was advised to look elsewhere.

Mary next visited the Board of Education where she was counseled to send her son to a special school for boys a few blocks north of the family's home. The principal took an instant liking to the boy, and for the first few days Lester seemed enthusiastic. "But before long it was the same old story," his mother later related. "He just didn't go to school."

This time the education authorities stepped in. Labeling him a repeatedly truant child, Lester was placed in the Parental Boarding School on Montrose Avenue, a home for wayward boys. Rules were rigidly enforced, students were restricted to school grounds, and weekend furloughs were issued for youngsters with records of good behavior and grades. Lester's new classmates were orphans, troubled teens, and unwanted or unsupervised youths. He settled in quickly, accepting the new rules without complaint and easily making friends with other boys and members of the staff. His family was allowed to visit each Sunday.

In late spring 1921 Lester was returned to the custody of his parents. Lester pledged to faithfully attend school and stay out of trouble—but trouble, it seemed, had a way of finding him. As Mary later wrote, "Again we hoped things had been straightened out when he came back. Instead they grew worse."

On July 4 Lester and a neighborhood pal were inside the latter's garage, admiring his father's new automobile. Young Gillis slid behind the wheel and noticed a loaded revolver resting in the side pocket of the door. "Guns always had a terrible fascination for Lester," his mother later confessed, although Joseph Gillis had been "fanatical" about firearms, even refusing to allow his sons to play with toy guns. In Lester's case the prohibition seemed to have the opposite effect.

The two boys took the weapon to a nearby alley. It was, after all, Independence Day, and the neighborhood was crackling with the sound of fireworks. Who would notice a few extra bangs? Several younger boys were already playing in the alley, and Lester suggested they give the kids a scare. Mimicking a western gunfighter, he drew a bead on a fence post and fired. One of the little boys screamed and grabbed his face. The bullet had fragmented when it hit the post, and a piece of it had lodged in the child's jaw.

19

An hour later Mary returned home after babysitting for her daughter Julie and found a crowd gathered outside their house. A neighbor hurried over to declare, "They've arrested Lester."

"My God," Mary gasped. "What has he done now?"

The twelve-year-old appeared in juvenile court a few days later. The Gillis family paid the injured boy's hospital bills, and Mary pleaded for her son before the judge. The shooting, she argued, was a tragic accident, and the owner of the gun was equally at fault for having left a loaded weapon where youngsters could find it. But Lester's record of misbehavior went against him, and he was sentenced to twelve to fifteen months in the Cook County School for Boys.

The old reformatory, located on Harlem Avenue in Berwyn, was similar to the Parental School in its rules and general operation. Once again Lester became a model inmate, as if the restrictions were more a comfort than a punishment. The superintendent and his wife grew fond of the cherub-faced youngster. They later recalled him as an unusually cheerful lad, eager to please them, willing to do extra work, and much more respectful than the majority of their other charges. He was permitted to accompany the couple when they drove to the country to buy milk and fresh food for the institution. On several occasions they even allowed Lester to operate their vehicle outside the city limits.

One day Lester and another boy turned up missing. It was feared the pair had run off until a search located them in the garage, servicing the superintendent's car. The boys did an excellent job, and briefly "Lester was in his element and blissfully happy." Mary later recalled.

After a few months Mary was allowed to take her son from the reformatory on Sundays. The only restrictions were that Lester could not visit the Gillis home and that he be returned to the school each evening by eight o'clock. Mary later described these times as some of the happiest she shared with her son. They would go on picnics in the country or stay in the city and see a movie. Her husband—by this time drinking more often and becoming increasingly despondent with life in general and his youngest boy in particular—refused to accompany them.

One cold rainy afternoon mother and son were on their way back to the reformatory, riding aboard a streetcar which stopped a block away. "Mama, you don't need to come out in this weather to take me back," Lester insisted. "It's only a block away." On the same streetcar was another boy being returned to the school by his parents. Lester said he could walk with them so that his mother could stay aboard and remain warm and dry.

"You're sure you'll go back?" Mary asked.

"Yes, Mother, I'll go back," he assured her, flashing his winning smile.

The next morning Mary received a phone call from the superintendent's wife informing her that Lester and the other boy had not returned. Two hours later he showed up at the Gillises' door, confessing that he and the other boy had decided on the spur of the moment to "beat it to Florida." They had ridden a streetcar to Cicero where they "borrowed" a vehicle and headed south. Only a few miles out of the city they realized it was too far and turned back. After abandoning the car the boys separated. Mary fed Lester breakfast and returned him to the reformatory.

With only this single lapse in an otherwise unblemished record, Lester was permitted to return home after serving a full year in the reformatory. The first few months after his release passed smoothly, and Lester was scheduled to resume his education at another parochial school, St. Malachy's, in the fall. Mary was hopeful her son had learned his lesson and would complete his education without further problems.

In his free time that summer Lester knocked around the neighborhood with a trio of best friends—Jack Perkins, George Ackerman, and Mike Juska. He remained on good terms with the two Tonys but rarely saw them. Now in their mid-teens, Capezio and Accardo were spending most of their days closer to the city running with a rougher crowd, moving up to more serious crimes such as burglary and mugging. Their favorite hangout was the Circus Cafe at 1857 North Avenue, a few blocks east of The Patch. The pack of young toughs who congregated there came to be called the Circus Gang. Like the group the two Tonys had founded in The Patch, the Circus Gang was open to youngsters of all ethnic backgrounds; American-born Irish, Jewish, and Eastern European youths joined the ranks of the Italians and Sicilians.

Their leaders at this early stage were Claude Maddox and Vincent Gebardi, the latter better known as "Machine Gun Jack" McGurn. The son of a South Side "alky cooker" (an illegal distiller of alcohol) murdered by rival gangsters, McGurn abandoned a promising career as a welterweight boxer in order to take up the Tommygun and track down all five of his father's killers. Before the decade was over Chicago police credited him with nearly two dozen slayings, as well as complicity in the St. Valentine's Day Massacre and the throat-slashing of comedian Joe E. Lewis. Through the two Tonys Lester developed some valuable ties with the Circus Gang, which was becoming a notable force among the Chicago mob scene, zealously controlling all illegal operations within the city's Twenty-ninth Precinct. Young Gillis grew to be a great admirer of McGurn.

At the time, however, he was a scrawny thirteen-year-old, while most of his old pals from The Patch were wearing long pants and driving cars. Looking to change his pre-adolescent image, Lester devised a novel way of making money by siphoning bootleg beer from a pipe in the back of a Grand Avenue speakeasy. Aided by Perkins and other pals, he collected the brew in pails, then carried it to a construction site and sold it to the workmen.

One day the speakeasy owner caught the boys and warned them to stay away. According to Perkins, Lester gave the man an icy glare and said, "You gonna call the cops? I'll call 'em for you. We'll come back whenever we damn well please." The owner decided a few pails of beer were cheaper than new windows or a bigger police payoff.

Lester's top priority with his new cash flow was to outfit himself in more suitable attire. "Kids wear knickers, grownups wear trousers," he told Perkins, and from then on they clad themselves according to their own tastes instead of their mothers'. When they found themselves with extra cash, the pair would ride a streetcar into the city and eat at "fancy restaurants."

Merely dressing like an adult wasn't enough—Lester wanted to drive. He had always been enthralled by cars, and although he was only thirteen he repeatedly appealed to operate the family auto. His father adamantly forbade it.

During a trip to his uncle's farm that summer Lester, according to Mary, "talked about nothing but cars," boasting that he was able to recognize every make and model, and how, if he had to, he could take one apart and reassemble it. Most of all he spoke of how much he craved to operate one. Jules Gillis, who was especially fond of Lester, invited his young nephew to slip behind the wheel for a drive along country roads. When they returned hours later the uncle reported to Mary, "He's a better driver than his father. There's nothing wrong with that boy. He has unusual abilities. You just don't know how to handle him. I wish I had that boy."

One afternoon Joseph Gillis discovered his car was missing. So too was Lester. "He collected several of the neighborhood children and took them all for a joy ride," his mother recalled. "They drove until well after dark. We parents were frantic. But they all came back unharmed and bubbling over with the adventure of it all."

Mary regarded the incident as merely a boyhood prank. His father, however, was not so forgiving. Lester's punishment was severe enough to keep him away from the family car, but it did not diminish his compulsion to drive. He looked elsewhere for "available" autos, and neighbors soon began to complain that their cars were being taken by Lester and his pals, then returned undamaged when the gas tank was empty.

There were always other boys involved in these unauthorized excursions, but Lester was invariably the leader. He acted genuinely puzzled when confronted with his crimes. He insisted he wasn't stealing the cars, only borrowing them—and never for very long. His parents couldn't seem to get through to him the serious consequences of his actions.

As usual he had to learn the hard way. When a neighbor notified police of one of his joy rides, he was arrested and escorted back to juvenile court, this time charged with auto larceny. On October 10, 1922, Lester Gillis was sentenced to eighteen months in the Illinois State School for Boys at St. Charles.

❋ ❋ ❋

The original idea behind the reformatory was to create a charitable institution where underprivileged boys trapped in the squalor of cities could escape to experience the quiet, scenic solitude of a rural retreat and breath clean air. Its founder was John B. Gates, a St. Charles native who amassed a personal fortune in business and was renowned for his philanthropy. Near the turn of the century he gave substance to his vision by donating 901 acres of rolling countryside and rich farmland in the Fox River valley forty miles west of Chicago, three miles southeast of St. Charles, four miles southwest of Geneva. Gates poured $20,000 of his own money into the venture, then raised $80,000 more to develop the grounds. In early spring 1901, with the project needing more construction and better management, Gates was advised by others to turn to the state for additional funding, and he eventually convinced legislators to take charge.

Illinois had its own ideas for the institution, seeing a more practical need for a correctional facility for delinquent youth. Over the next three years nearly half a million dollars was appropriated for building expenses, books, tools, maintenance, and supplies. Construction was completed on December 11, 1904, and the first inmates arrived five days later. Gates died in Paris in 1906 without ever seeing the ten-foot-high fence erected around the school's grounds.

When Lester Gillis arrived at the reformatory, two months shy of his fourteenth birthday, there were more than 800 boys between the ages of nine and seventeen housed in the facility's eleven cottages. More than half were from Cook County. Two-thirds were Protestants and, with the exception of several Jewish youths, the rest were Catholics, like Lester, who were required to meet for spiritual consultation with a local priest each Saturday and Mass on Sunday mornings.

A new inmate was assigned to a specific cottage where he was provided with a personal bed and locker. The buildings were two-story, steam-heated structures measuring a hundred feet long by sixty feet wide. Each cottage was supervised by a husband and wife team of "house parents." The parents' living quarters were located on the ground floor along with a sitting area for the boys, a pantry, sinks, and restrooms. The top floor was divided into two dormitories separated by a locker room. Each dorm contained forty iron beds.

In addition to the cottages, the reformatory featured a school building with fifteen classrooms and a library; six barns, the largest 240 feet long and capable of holding more than 100 cows; a gymnasium which, at the time, was the largest in the state; a small hospital overseen by a physician and two nurses; a powerhouse; and an industrial building where the inmates performed the majority of their daily work.

The boys woke each morning at six o'clock and were served breakfast half an hour later. They were assigned cleaning chores around their cottages until 7:45, when half of the inmates were marched to the school building to attend classes and the others were put to work in the various vocational departments. At 11:30 the boys returned to their cottages for lunch, followed by a brief free time for all who had faithfully adhered to the rules. At 1:15 the earlier schedule was reversed, with those who worked in the morning going to classes while the others reported to the manual arts shops.

From 4:30 to 5:30 the boys performed a military-type drill. After supper they were allotted another hour of free time inside their cottages to read, write letters, or play games. Lights out was rigorously observed every evening at 7:30. To discourage any restless youths from sneaking away in the dead of night, each boy was required to undress at his locker, then go to bed clad only in a nightshirt. The house parents and a night guard checked to make sure all clothing was in place before the lockers were sealed until morning.

The institution was overcrowded and understaffed, and there were outbreaks of small pox and diphtheria during its early years. By 1922 four lads had died there, three from illness, one in an accident. Even so, its record of reforming delinquent youngsters was exemplary, and the boys themselves seldom complained about conditions. Corporal punishment was rare. Discipline was mostly maintained by the regimented schedule, rewards for good behavior, and an added workload for those who caused trouble or failed to do their share. The boys were usually kept too busy to allow opportunities for mischief. Along with their daily routine inmates were expected to help maintain the grounds and tend the school's livestock and crops. They were also encouraged to use their "volunteer time" to help in the kitchen or the laundry, work on the school's monthly journal, or participate in baseball, basketball, football, or the school band.

Lester's sentence at St. Charles did not begin well. He was put to work in the tailor shop on the second floor of the industrial building. The first time his mother visited he spoke only about how he hated the place "with a fierceness that scared me when I talked to him." On February 12, 1923, Lester was reported missing. After a brief search he was discovered hiding inside a basement sewer pipe.

A couple weeks later he was transferred to the machine shop, and immediately his brooding subsided, as the work, although difficult, proved to be more to Lester's liking. Unable to go his own way, he made the best of his situation and gradually became the model student he had been at the Parental School and the Cook County reformatory. He became good friends with the shop's chief engineer, who recalled the young Gillis as a good-natured kid who "liked to get his hands dirty" and displayed a special zest for working with machinery and often volunteered to do extra jobs or help fellow students.

Surprisingly, his performance in the daily military drills was rated very high. He openly enjoyed caring for the school's livestock and played a prominent role in the construction of a small zoo on the north side of the grounds that featured local wildlife such as squirrels and raccoons. In the classroom he was an average student, doing what was required but no more. When his sentence at St. Charles was almost finished, Lester lacked only a few weeks of completing the eighth grade, and his mother, after speaking with school officials, suggested that he remain an extra month to receive his diploma. The teenager agreed.

Released on April 11, 1924, Lester returned home "glowing with enthusiasm and excitement," his mother recalled. Each day he helped with chores around the house, proudly showing Mary the "correct" way to make beds, which he had as he learned at St. Charles. But between father and son there was only tension, and each studiously avoided the other."

During Lester's absence his eldest sister, Amy, had divorced. While employed as a salesclerk at Boston Store, she had met Frederick Kenniston, a private detective employed to spot shoplifters and pickpockets. They were married in the fall of 1923, Kenniston moving in with Amy and her four children in their apartment on North Mozart. Both were unhappy with their jobs; Kenniston wanted to be a chef in his own restaurant, and Amy, who worked sporadically as a singer in Chicago nightclubs, aspired to be on the stage full time.

At the urging of their daughter, Joseph and Mary Gillis invested a sizable chunk of their savings in a restaurant, the Culinary Arts Shop on Howard Street, which opened on May 25, 1924. Amy served as hostess, while her mother helped Kenniston in the kitchen. Joseph, still employed at the tannery, assumed the role of business manager; however, over the next few months there was depressingly little business to manage. Finding himself saddled with a failing venture that was sapping the family's finances, Gillis began to drink more frequently.

Occasionally over the summer Lester lived with his sister Julie and her husband, Robert Fitzsimmons, at their apartment above a grocery store on West 22nd Street, possibly to diffuse the strained relations with his father. The mother of two with a third on the way, Julie was happy to have his help. Her little brother proved to be "a terrific babysitter" and once spent an entire afternoon on hands and knees scrubbing all the floors in the six-room dwelling.

Mary wanted her youngest boy—now a skinny fifteen-year-old grown to his full height of five feet, five inches tall—to either find a job or go back to school to get more education. She encouraged Lester to do the latter but thought it wise not to push him. It was summer; she figured by fall he would go one way or the other. But while his mother was preoccupied with a despondent husband and an foundering restaurant, Lester couldn't resist returning to the streets to keep company with his old pals, many of whom were beginning to turn to crime as a profession instead of a mere pastime.

Jack Perkins and others from the old gang were making money stealing car parts and often entire vehicles. Their principal buyer was Albert Van de Houton, who operated a filling station for his father on North Sacramento through which the stolen goods were filtered. It was never determined if Lester became an active participant in the car thefts at this time. What is certain is that he was caught with several others riding in a stolen vehicle on the final day of summer.

His protest that he was unaware the automobile was "hot" really did not matter; his presence alone was enough to prompt the courts to revoke his parole. On September 28 he was sent back to the state school at St. Charles.

Joseph Gillis continued to sink deeper into depression. The return of his youngest son to the reformatory was probably a contributing factor but there were others, mainly financial. Two half-hearted suicide attempts alerted Mary to the seriousness of his worsening condition, but when sober, Joseph stubbornly refused to seek any medical or psychological help. The problem was kept within the family. As the holidays and his fifty-fifth birthday (on November 25) approached, his drinking became heavier.

On Christmas Eve he came home intoxicated. Later that night, Mary smelled gas and discovered her husband slumped lifeless beneath a jet discharging the lethal fumes. The coroner's inquest attributed his death to "asphyxiation due to inhaling illuminating gas, said gas escaping from a ceiling jet turned on with his own hand with suicidal intent while despondent."

On December 27 Lester was taken from St. Charles to attend his father's funeral at St. Joseph's Cemetery in River Grove. Mary—saddened, embittered, and confused—was comforted by her remaining children as her husband was laid to rest beside their daughter Jenny. Although Lester never spoke of it later, Julie reported her brother felt a deep sense of guilt over his father's death and his mother's widowed plight. Joseph's drunken example and tragic end probably played a key part in Lester's later abstinence from liquor.

Back at the reformatory his behavior abruptly improved, and during the next six months he served as adjutant to the military instructor overseeing the school's cadet regiment. He was rated by his house parents as "one of the best boys ever" under their supervision, and as a result he was appointed captain of his cottage. He continued to display enthusiasm and superb skills in the machine shop, where the engineer considered Lester his top student. On July 22, 1925, he was granted a second parole.

By this time Mary was reduced to taking in boarders for extra income to pay bills. Lester vowed to help around the house and, more importantly, stay out of trouble. Within a few weeks the sixteen-year-old was hired as an assistant mechanic at the Park View Motor Company, a Chrysler dealership at Sacramento and Grand. For a brief time he appeared to be doing everything right. He offered to share his modest wages with his mother, but Mary naturally refused, exhorting him to save his money to purchase his own car. But before long Lester again began to pursue illegal activities with his friends. Mary blamed her son's regression on twenty-five-year-old Al Van de Houton, who she described as "an evil man" who exercised a Fagan-like influence over Lester and other boys.

With the promise of making some "fast money" it probably took little convincing for Lester to be recruited; provided with an opportunity, he had never shown any hesitancy to stray beyond the boundaries of the law.

In the summer of 1925 the Twenties were just beginning to roar, especially in Chicago, where successful criminals abounded. The advent of Prohibition five years earlier had transformed mobsters into millionaires, and gangs flourished throughout the city, each vying for a piece of the action. Crime bosses divided Chicago into territories that they ruled like ancient warlords, exacting tribute from their vassals and zealously guarding their turf from outside intruders.

Johnny Torrio, Chicago's preeminent gang boss during the first half of the decade, shrewdly foresaw the financial potential in supplying a thirsty public with illegal alcohol and moved quickly to secure a workable truce among the city's leading mob figures. Unlike his chief lieutenant—a chunky, cigar-chomping young Italian-American named Alphonse Capone—Torrio detested violence, viewing it as wasteful and self-defeating. There was no need to fight, he admonished his rivals, since the Volstead Act— combined with an approving public and a legion of corrupt police, politicians, and judges—offered plenty of opportunities to make them all wealthy.

Despite the uneasy treaties hammered out, there remained a brooding mistrust and active animosity among the crime bosses. This often was because of cultural bad blood—tensions invariably ran high between the Italian and Irish mobsters—territorial squabbles, or envy among the bosses. The feuds were numerous and bloody: Gang wars during the Twenties claimed nearly 500 lives and left a dark stain on the Windy City that remains to this day. "The secret to survival in Chicago," wrote New Yorker Lewis Manford, "was to maim and kill with more expert precision than one's neighbor."

Torrio himself was targeted for assassination and was punctured by a flurry of bullets outside his house on January 23, 1925. Barely surviving the attack, he chose retirement rather than retribution. His colossal criminal empire was inherited by Capone, who demonstrated early, often, and without reservation that he would not abide any interference with his organization.

Capone was only twenty-six when he became the most powerful gang lord in the city. The transfiguration of the mob under his leadership is often described as a youth movement. He appointed men his own age or younger to serve as his chief henchmen and advisors without regard to their ethnic backgrounds. Some of these young Turks were recruited from The Patch, among them Machine Gun Jack McGurn and Tony Accardo. "Tough Tony" Capezio and the Circus Gang remained a faithful Capone satellite on the Near West Side.

Like everyone else in Chicago watching the mob scene that summer, Lester Gillis was on the outside looking in, but his view was a bit more intimate. A number of the older kids he had known in the neighborhood or had encountered in the Cook County or St. Charles reform schools were rising to prominent positions in the Chicago underworld. Many now wore silk shirts, drove the finest new cars, and carried wads of cash in their pockets. Like Henry Hill in Nicholas Pileggi's *Wiseguys*, Lester found himself admiring, even idolizing, the gangsters in his midst—and there were many to choose from.

The West Side neighborhood where Lester Gillis grew up was on the northern edge of the domain belonging to the O'Donnell brothers and their gang, which controlled all the vice between Chicago Avenue and Madison Street. William, nicknamed "Klondike," was the eldest and the recognized leader. He was a tall, handsome Irishman, astute and arrogant, sharper and more cerebral than his two ill-tempered brothers, Myles and Bernard. Klondike tolerated Torrio but loathed Capone, viewing their intrusion into the western suburbs of Cicero, Stickney, and Berwyn as a violation of O'Donnell territory—or at the least a flanking maneuver by the Italians. Over the course of the decade the O'Donnell and Capone factions exchanged insults, threats, and more than a few bullets—Capone and some followers attempted to ambush the brothers with machine guns one night in 1926—but for the most part Klondike wisely realized Torrio was right about violence being bad for business.

Though Gillis was never known to have any active association with the O'Donnell gang—the brothers only trusted and recruited fellow Irishmen—he was regarded as a good friend by Klondike, who probably first encountered him on the streets of The Patch and later proved to be a valuable underworld ally.

Another band of brothers, considerably less powerful and organized than the O'Donnells, was "the Terrible Touhys." There were six Touhy boys, all sons of a Chicago policeman who beat them so often that neighbors frequently intervened. Two brothers were shot to death in gang wars, a third wasted away in prison, and a fourth prudently stayed out of the rackets and lived an honest life. The remaining pair, Roger and Tommy, were rising stars on the West Side crime scene. Roger, the youngest, had the brains while Tommy generated the bluster. Tommy was in and out of jail so often that one official suggested installing a revolving door for him. During one prison stretch he attempted a desperate escape by arranging for nitroglycerin to be smuggled into his cell. When he and a fellow convict, future North Side mobster George "Bugs" Moran, set off the charge, a steel liner inside the concrete prevented the blast from punching through the wall. Guards rushed to the scene and found the two prisoners lying unconscious and bleeding amid the rubble.

The explosion reportedly left Tommy slightly unhinged, and his subsequent boisterous, often bizarre behavior made him a legendary figure in the Chicago underworld. Once when facing arrest, he threatened to blow himself up, taking with him any police who attempted to grab him. Though the Touhys' territory was several miles north of The Patch, young Gillis already was acquainted with several of the brothers and was particularly close to Tommy.

Another up-and-coming mob figure Lester befriended was William White, known in gangland circles as "Three-Fingered Jack." In his youth his right hand had been crushed under a brick at a construction site, resulting in the amputation of his middle fingers. White learned to shoot left-handed, and it was said that he could draw faster and possessed a deadlier aim than almost anyone else in the city. In public he wore gloves with wads of cotton filling the empty fingers. Convicted of robbery and sent to Joliet in 1919, he had been paroled recently and returned to his old neighborhood, selling his talents as a trigger-man and general thug to the highest bidder. He was associated with both the Touhys and the Circus Gang before moving up to a top position within the Capone organization.

But of all the criminal cronies Lester could brag about, the most prominent—and reportedly the most emulated by him—was Jack McGurn. By decade's end McGurn would become Capone's most valued and trusted lieutenant. In many ways he perfectly symbolized the city and the era—flashy, cocky, self-absorbed, and completely callous. With his Valentino looks and expensive, snappy style of dressing, he was a familiar patron of speakeasies throughout Chicago, a lover of jazz and platinum-blond flappers.

But in the summer of 1925 McGurn and the others who would become luminaries of Chicago gangdom were little more than neighborhood chums of Lester's who had moved up to bigger and better criminal lifestyles. Collectively, however, they served as a rogue's gallery of role models for the teenager, making a mockery of the adage "crime doesn't pay."

But while envisioning himself as a future gangster, Gillis quickly learned that he was still a clumsy amateur. Once again—almost a year to the day from his last arrest—he was caught stealing an automobile. This time the authorities offered a deal if he would supply police with the names of his confederates in the car-stripping gang. Lester refused, and on October 1 he was shuttled back to St. Charles.

❈   ❈   ❈

On June 11, 1926, Gillis received his third and final parole from the state institution. Just six months shy of his eighteenth birthday, he was duly warned that his next offense could land him in adult court and possibly prison. Prior to his release, St. Charles officials offered him a job as assistant engineer at the reformatory, a position that provided room, board and a modest salary. The teenager declined, explaining he was eager to get back to his family.

Lester's job at the Park View Motor Company was waiting for him when he returned. He was soon promoted from the garage to the sales floor, and exchanging grimy overalls for a suit and tie seemed to enhance his self-esteem along with his paycheck. He did well, relying on his intimate knowledge of cars to impress customers and close the sale. By year's end, however, the dealership ran into financial trouble, forcing the owner to let Lester go.

Eighteen and unemployed at the beginning of 1927, he grabbed the first thing to come along—a job assembling stoves in a factory on the northwest side of the city. It was dirty, demanding work, and Lester despised it from the start. He began looking elsewhere and ended up back with his old partners in crime Perkins and Van de Houton. The latter now was proprietor of his own tire shop, but his favorite method of obtaining merchandise remained the same. Mary claimed her son applied at Van de Houton's business seeking an honest position, but the owner was only interested in recruiting Lester for his gang of car thieves.

Perkins probably played a key role in luring Gillis back into a life a crime. A few months earlier Jack's girlfriend had discovered she was pregnant and lost her job as a switchboard operator. The couple, both seventeen, eloped to Waukegan, Illinois, and were married under false names. With a new wife, an apartment of their own, and a baby on the way, Perkins was desperate for cash and was no doubt delighted when his best friend agreed to help with the illicit enterprise.

Their main target was tires, either stripped from parked cars or stolen from Van de Houton's competitors. Other items, some specifically requested by Van de Houton and some merely part of what the thieves could carry away, were included. The stolen goods were purchased by Van de Houton and sold through his shop, usually to a special clientele he labeled "individual buyers."

On the evening of March 2, 1927, Lester and an accomplice were arrested for breaking into Larson and Co. in an attempt to steal tires. Charged with burglary, he admitted his guilt but adamantly refused to implicate Van de Houton and others in the "tire-theft ring"—even after his interrogators, according to Gillis, resorted to "rough stuff." Eventually Van de Houton was arrested and charged with receiving stolen property. He pleaded guilty and avoided jail by paying a hefty fine.

Lester's case went to court on March 17. Mary, who had been gradually falling into debt since her husband's death, managed to scrape together enough money to pay restitution on behalf of her son. She pleaded before the judge to show leniency since Lester had been "influenced and misled" by Van de Houton. Gillis was sentenced to a year's probation.

Once a month he reported to his probation officer, Joseph J. Sheehan, who viewed Gillis as "clean-cut and quiet," more polished than his other charges. Even so, Sheehan could see in Lester's eyes that he resented authority, "though he hid it well." The two principal terms of the youngster's probation were that he avoid all association with criminals and that he acquire steady, lawful employment.

Two days after his release he obtained a job in the transportation department at the Commonwealth Edison Co. While his official title was listed as chauffeur, his chief duties were driving a truck and making deliveries. Between assignments Lester employed his mechanical skills to maintain and service company vehicles at the Edison garage on South Throop Street. The pay was just thirty dollars a week, but the young man relished the job after his brief taste of factory work. He remained an Edison employee for the next year and a half, the longest single legitimate job he managed to hold during his short life.

It appeared that Gillis was finally making a concerted effort to reform his ways. He was living rent-free with his mother, who, although struggling, continued to refuse any financial help from him. She was determined to see her youngest son get his life in order and was convinced he was doing his best. That summer Lester bought his first car, a Chrysler roadster, thanks in part to his brother-in-law, Bob Fitzsimmons, co-signing for the loan.

His only problems with the law at this time stemmed from a habitual failure to observe speed limits. He was constantly being pinched, but between 1927 and 1929 only three of his speeding citations ever went to traffic court. Gillis feared that if he lost his license he would lose his job, and he soon discovered that many police officers, when offered a five- or ten-dollar bribe, were happy to tear up a ticket. Once he was caught speeding in a western suburb by a constable who indignantly announced that he did not accept bribes. He ordered Gillis to follow him to his house, where a rusted-out jalopy was parked in the backyard. The constable plucked a headlight from the wreckage, handed it to Gillis, and said, "Here. "I'll sell you that for five dollars." Lester was allowed to go without a ticket.

According to Mary, her son became a favorite target of local police looking to line their pockets, and lawmen began to appear at the Edison garage. The shakedown was always the same: The officers claimed to be investigating some recent neighborhood crime, a burglary or stolen car, and threatened to pull Gills off his job to take him in for questioning or to appear in a lineup. "Les knew that this would cost him his job," Mary claimed, so he would "pay the cops" and they would leave him alone for a while. "They kept this up all the time he was there [at the Edison company]. His money was always going to detectives who appeared to need a five- or ten-dollar bill more than he did."

It was during this period, Mary believed, "that police pushed him over the line into a definitely anti-social life." Whether the fact he was being squeezed for cash by cops was the reason or merely the excuse he was looking for, Gillis swiftly resumed his association with his criminal pals once his year of probation ended in mid-March 1928.

A number of exaggerated tales about Gillis's activities at this time have persisted to this day, the most outrageous claiming that he worked as an enforcer for Capone. Stories alleged that he had killed several men and robbed a few banks, and that he was making big money as an independent bootlegger, but only the latter claim contained even a kernel of truth. That spring Gillis joined his old pals Van de Houton and Perkins in setting up a still on Western Avenue in Evanston. The enterprise lasted just four months. As Van de Houton later explained in an FBI interview, they were forced to shut down because the individual they employed to oversee the still and cook the mash "stole the largest part of the alcohol," leaving almost no profit.

There are unverified but credible reports that Gillis used his contacts with the Touhys to obtain occasional work to supplement his income. These ventures were usually unremarkable—overnight excursions into Wisconsin to transport shipments of bootleg booze to Chicago, with Gillis either driving or riding shotgun. He may have also participated in a few hijackings, a favorite gangland method during Prohibition years to procure product quickly and cheaply while humiliating and hurting one's rivals in the process.

Why Gillis didn't use his friendly relations with underworld figures to secure a permanent position within the Chicago mob scene is anyone's guess. The assumption by most historians is that the gang lords rejected him because of his unstable character. In reality, the evidence indicates that he was highly regarded by his friends in the gangs and that it evidently was Gillis himself who shied away from becoming too deeply involved in the rackets. This doesn't necessarily mean he was doing all he could to live an honest, upright life, as his mother and sisters later insisted. He perhaps recognized that mob life demanded more submission than his independent spirit could allow. Or, more likely, he realized that if he affiliated himself with one gang he would instantly become the enemy of all his other underworld acquaintances throughout the city.

Or it may be that he simply had other priorities at the time, for in the late spring of 1928 Lester Gillis found himself in love.

Her name was Helen Wawrzyniak, a tiny, raven-haired girl with a soft, milky complexion and sapphire-blue eyes. She had turned fifteen on March 23 and was presently dividing her time between classes at Harrison High School, a part-time job as a clerk in the toy department at Goldblatt's on Western Avenue, and a rigid home life in an apartment on North Campbell Avenue, four blocks east of the Gillis household. Like Lester and many youths in the neighborhood, she was the child of immigrants, a German-born couple of Polish descent. The family name, difficult to pronounce and infuriating to spell, was eventually changed to Warwick, although Helen at school and work stubbornly clung to the original rendering.

Small and sickly as a child, she developed a meek, melancholy nature that reflected the recent tragedies in her life. Her mother, Kazmiera, died in 1924 giving birth to the family's third son, Leonard. In 1927 one of Helen's sisters, Marie, died of tuberculosis. Their deaths left her with her father, Vincent, a meat packer at the Fullerton Packing Company, along with three brothers and two other sisters, who often looked to Helen to prepare meals and handle the domestic chores. When her duties were done she invariably sought the seclusion of her room, where she would escape into the pages of a book or magazine. She was still mourning Marie, suffering nightmares about her own precarious health, and feeling trapped at home when a young man known as Les Gillis came into her life.

It's not certain exactly how they met. One version claims he was buying gifts for his nieces and nephews when he spotted Helen behind the counter and invited her out. Another holds that the two knew each other beforehand. Steven Warwick, the eldest of Helen's brothers, was only two years younger than Les and reportedly ran with the Two Tonys' gang on occasion. He was also a close friend of both George Ackerman and Mike Juska, two of Gillis's best pals. Whatever the circumstances, Les and Helen soon became inseparable.

"They were both just youngsters," Mary wrote without mentioning that her son was almost four years older than his sweetheart. "There had never been a girlfriend for Les up to the time of their meeting. He would go out once in a great while with some friend of his sisters', but from the moment he met Helen there was never room for any other girl in his thoughts."

His job and her home duties left them only evenings together. When she worked weekends he visited so often that the management at Goldblatt's asked Helen to encourage her boyfriend to keep away. The two frequently stayed out past two in the morning, generating concern from Les's mother and resentment from Helen's father. Other than the fact it was a chore to wake her son for his job, Mary was pleased he had found a nice girl who might settle him down. And Vincent Warwick couldn't help but notice that his daughter was in brighter spirits and was coming out of her self-conscious shell since she had begun dating Gillis.

Their summer of love ended predictably—by September Helen was pregnant. Without a word to family or friends, the couple planned and saved and finally eloped to Indiana. They were married at the Porter County Courthouse in Valparaiso on October 30, 1928. On their marriage license Gillis listed his occupation as "chauffeur," although he had quit his job at the Edison company two months earlier and stated his age as twenty-one instead of nineteen. His three-months-pregnant child bride added five years to her date of birth.

Back in Chicago the newlyweds lived with his mother until it became evident, due to mounting debts, that she would have to sell the California Avenue house. Mary moved in with daughter Amy and her family; Les and Helen were invited to stay with Julie, her husband Bob, and their four children at their six-room apartment. Leona, the youngest of the three sisters and still unmarried, also resided there. It was a tight fit, but for the next fifteen months it was home for the young couple.

In January Helen, her petite figure swelling with child and often battling a fever, quit her job at Goldblatt's, content to remain inside the steam-heated apartment during one of the worst winters in Chicago history. "She loved to be in the kitchen trying new recipes," reported Julie, happy to let her new sister-in-law do some cooking for the household. Les offered to pay part of the sixty-dollar monthly rent and purchased groceries, toys, and clothes for the expected baby. Julie and her husband often commented to each other how her brother was able to afford such things. "We were fairly sure he was working for bootleggers at the time," Julie later admitted. "We didn't ask, and he never offered any details."

Mobsters were the talk of the town that winter as the majority of frostbitten Chicagoans huddled in their houses and warmed themselves with the gory details of the city's ongoing crime wars. Gangland slayings had sharply accelerated since 1926. The carnage culminated in the wholesale slaughter of seven men, members of Bugs Moran's North Side Gang, in a grimy garage on North Clark Street on February 14, 1929. The so-called St. Valentine's Day Massacre shocked the public and brought international infamy to Chicago's already unsavory image. Even veteran reporters, thinking they had seen it all and growing bored of the repetitive coverage of mob killings, were stunned and sickened at the sight of the bloody, bullet-torn corpses. "Right now I've got more brains on my shoes than under my hat," was the ghoulish remark of one pale-faced journalist leaving the scene.

Since the killers had worn police uniforms, there were rumors that the gunmen were cops. But everyone suspected who was really responsible. "Only Capone kills like that," Moran insisted. Capone, however, had the perfect alibi: At the moment of the massacre he was relaxing at his Palm Island estate in Florida in the presence of the Dade County district attorney.

In the end the killers were never officially identified and no one was brought to trial. It remains one of the great unsolved mysteries of American crime. Exactly what happened and who was involved has been a subject of speculation for the past seventy years. Only a privileged few with access to underworld information ever knew the details. According to some, Lester Gillis was one who had the answers.

He never needed to read the papers or listen to the radio to know what was happening among the city's gangs, and he often learned of their escapades before they occurred. He rarely shared specifics with his family, but he was always dropping hints that he had inside information about mob activities, including the massacre. He probably knew, for instance, that his old pals from The Patch—McGurn, Accardo, and Capezio, along with Circus Gang members Claude Maddox and Gus Winkler—were all intimately involved in the planning of the slayings, and at least some were active participants. Capezio, allegedly the driver of the police car, was injured in an explosion a week after the massacre while attempting to dispose of the vehicle. He was badly shaken but not gravely injured and was thereafter known among underworld denizens as "Tough Tony."

Probably the most indisputable fact was that McGurn was the mastermind behind the massacre. Traditional thinking holds that he acted on direct orders from Capone to exterminate the Moran gang. However, some sources maintain that he might have engineered the entire affair on his own without Capone's consent. McGurn, growing increasingly cocky and volatile with his status inside the Capone organization, had sufficient motivation. The previous year he had been machine-gunned while inside a phone booth; the shooters were brothers Peter and Frank Gusenberg, Moran's top "torpedoes," or hit men. Critically wounded, McGurn crawled from the shattered phone booth swearing revenge. Evidently he got it—both Gusenberg brothers were among the dead in the North Clark Street garage.

Even if Capone had known in advance about the meticulously planned assault on his North Side rivals, he certainly would never have agreed to anything so bloody. Over the years he had learned the hard way that gang killings were better for business if they were carried out quietly, such as a one-way ride, for instance. Seven dead was officially a "massacre," and the slayings ignited the wrath of not only newspapers and lawmen but average citizens as well. The Capone mob had gone too far. For all his vaunted ferocity and callousness, Capone was extremely sensitive about his public image. He was probably the only gangster in history who called his own press conferences and openly relished his relationship with reporters. But the Valentine's Day Massacre hurt him, eroding his popularity with Chicagoans who tolerated gang wars in order to enjoy bootleg liquor. Worse, it attracted the attention of President Hoover himself. The once stagnant federal machinery charged with enforcing Prohibition laws would begin to descend like a hammer on Capone over the next few years.

McGurn suffered as well. While not officially excommunicated from the mob, he was treated as a pariah by its top echelon and never again enjoyed his favored position with Capone. He was tagged "too hot," too unstable to remain a part of the outfit's inner circles. (Years later Gillis was given a similar label by Chicago mobsters.)

Lester's pipeline into gangland activities ran through a number of shady underworld hangouts which he found time to frequent outside his home life. One of his favorites was the Pioneer on West Grand, at various times known as the Pioneer Club, Pioneer Restaurant, and Pioneer Tavern. Other popular haunts included the Hy-Ho Club at 2242 South Cicero Avenue, partly owned by Tony Capezio, who was often present to greet the clientele and circulate among them; the Arabian Nights Club, owned by Rocco De Grazia, another prominent mob figure close to Gillis; the Silver Slipper on South Harlem; and the Rainbo Gardens on North Clark. Whenever Lester made the rounds he was usually accompanied by Jack Perkins, who was developing his own circle of underworld contacts, or other friends from The Patch.

At this time there is no evidence Gillis was actively involved in any other illegal activities, although he was known to consort with some of the city's most notorious gangsters and professional criminals. He felt a special kinship with the fraternity of hoodlums and was welcomed where few were and was trusted with all kinds of gangland gossip. In effect he was living in two worlds, trying his best to walk a line between his family and his criminal acquaintances—being pulled one way, then the other, yet devoted to both.

On April 27 Helen gave birth to a son, Ronald Vincent Gillis. Two months later Les found a job working several nights a week at a Standard Oil station at 800 North Sacramento owned by brothers George and Cliff Johnson. About this time he also became associated with an automobile agency on Fullerton and a garage at 8201 Grand Avenue in River Grove. Both were operated by Howard Davis, yet another old chum from The Patch. Davis used his businesses to provide cars and automotive service to the Touhy brothers. Since Lester's name never appeared on the payroll at either place it seems likely that his time spent with Davis involved activities outside the law.

Despite various sources of income, both legal and illegal, the Gillises suffered a money crunch in the latter half of the year. That fall Helen announced she was pregnant again, and Les became determined to save some cash in order to secure their own home before the baby's arrival.

No one knows exactly how he first encountered either Harry Lewis Powell or Stanton John Randall. At least one source alleged Mike Juska, at the time a part owner of a pool room on California Avenue, made the introductions. But their meeting might have occurred anywhere among the underworld spots Les visited or through any number of mutual contacts. Randall, a stocky figure of forty-three whose friendly basset-hound face concealed a vicious temper, had spent twelve years in an Ohio prison for murder. He was living with his wife, Katherine, in Rogers Park, a residential North Side neighborhood. He reportedly worked on occasion for the Touhy gang, which would have placed him in Gillis's orbit of underworld acquaintances.

Powell, a newcomer to town and recently married, was twenty-six, short, and swarthy, with dark eyes and a weak chin. His real name was Harold Pinsky, and he was the son of a Maryland rabbi. After living for years in Edmonton, Alberta, he joined his older brother Samuel working for a dairy in Seattle before drifting into Chicago.

The three of them—an unlikely trio, with Randall twice the age of Gillis, and Powell a relative novice in the underworld—began to spend time together. They discovered they shared a common desire to better their respective situations through getting their hands on some quick cash. According to George Ackerman, who befriended Powell but never liked Randall, they began discussing pulling off a series of big-time heists.

"You could tell he [Gillis] was hooked," Ackerman reported. "The idea of sticking up people really appealed to him."

Ackerman recounted one conversation in which they joked about wealthy families ruined by the recent stock market crash. Someone remarked that "the high-society rich bitches" were probably doing fine since the bulk of their fortunes was invested in jewelry. Powell immediately revealed that he had once worked in a jewelry shop and knew all about gems and precious metals. He agreed that jewelry never lost its value, even in a shaky economy, and boasted that he possessed the skill to distinguish "the gold from the junk." All they needed, he said, was to find a good fence willing to pay top dollar. Gillis claimed he had several contacts who could peddle the merchandise for them.

On December 6, 1929, Les celebrated a bittersweet twenty-first birthday. His family insisted there was never any tension within the crowded confines of the Fitzsimmons apartment. Years later, Julie described what a proud father and devoted husband her brother had been: "He loved to stay around the house cuddling his little boy and helping Helen in the kitchen." But beneath the cheerful exterior, Les was growing increasingly anxious about changing their circumstances and getting ahead financially. In order to earn some much needed cash, Helen returned to Goldblatt's to work part time over the holiday season. Les promised that once they were on their feet and out on their own, she would never have to work again.

One afternoon Julie and two of her children returned from Christmas shopping. She spotted Les standing beside a car parked near their apartment, conversing with three men who, judging from their attire, were hoodlums. Later she caught her brother alone and asked about the strangers. He told her they were just friends.

"Don't tell me those gangsters are your friends," she said.

His expression hardened, his eyes suddenly becoming steely. "If you really don't want to know, then I won't tell you."

"Well," she fired back, trying not to sound like a preachy big sister, "I guess that's your business. But I don't want those kind of people around our home."

He gave her his wide, reassuring grin. "Don't worry, all that stays outside," he said. "My family is here too."

Weeks later Julie was sorting through their mail and found a letter from an auto dealer bearing their correct address but written to a George Nelson. As Les passed her on his way out, she held up the envelope and asked, "You know who this is?"

He flashed an embarrassed smile. "That's for me."

He plucked the letter from her hand and hurried out, leaving Julie to wonder why in the world he was using an assumed name.

The criminal has no hates or fears—except very personal ones. He is possibly the only human left in the world who looks lovingly on society. He does not hanker to fight it, reform it, or even rationalize it. He only wants to rob it. He admires it as a hungry man might admire a roast pig with an apple in its mouth.
— Introduction to *The Alvin Karpis Story*

CHAPTER 3

CRIME WAVE

AT PRECISELY 7 P.M. on January 6, 1930, a bitterly cold Monday in Chicago, the doorbell rang at 1418 Lake Shore Drive. Inside the twenty-room mansion millionaire Charles M. Richter, vice president of the Consolidation Magazine Corporation, and his wife, Jean, were preparing for dinner. The couple had said good-night to their children, eight-year-old Stephen and six-year-old Mary Pat, who had been fed earlier and were being tucked into bed by their nurse, Nora Roach. In the dining room Katherine Walsh, the parlor maid, left the table she was setting to answer the door.

Two young men bundled in heavy overcoats stood outside, their collars turned up against the wicked lakefront winds. In a pleasant voice the shorter man announced, "Mr. Marshall calling for Mr. Richter."

"He's upstairs dressing, but I'll call him," Walsh replied.

Several minutes later Richter appeared and unlatched the lock to get a look at the pair. The shorter man lunged forward and shoved the muzzle of a pistol into the millionaire's stomach. "Steady now, Mr. Richter," he growled softly. "You know what we want. Turn around and lead us in."

As Richter obeyed, he caught a glimpse of three more men rushing in, one burly figure cradling a shotgun. In the foyer the five intruders pushed Richter and the maid facedown on the floor with a gruff warning not to move. The man

39

with the shotgun stood guard over the pair while his companions fanned out through the first floor. One marched directly to each of the four downstairs telephones and cut the lines. Another discovered the cook, Lucy Smith, and hustled her out of the kitchen at gunpoint. She was ordered to lie down next to her employer. A third man rummaged through the library and took time to open the room's three windows, presumably in case they needed to make a quick exit. The icy night air began to swirl through the mansion's interior.

All this occurred in the span of a minute. Jean Richter, oblivious to the invasion of her home, descended the stairs and halted with a gasp halfway down when she noticed the armed figures huddled around her husband and the two servants. Richter raised his head off the floor and said, "It's a holdup, dear. Now don't get excited. Give these men everything they want."

"Let's get a look at those valuables you keep up there," one bandit said.

She clasped the railing with both hands. "Please, my children are asleep upstairs," she said. "I'll give you anything if you promise not to frighten them."

The short gunman with the cap assured her, "There won't be any shooting as long we get cooperation and there's no alarms." He started up the steps followed by two others. "C'mon, Mrs. Richter, take us up there."

She led the trio to the second floor. One drew a knife and severed the wires of both upstairs phones. A comrade peeked into the children's bedroom. Stephen sat upright in his bed at the sight of the stranger. "He's got a gun," the boy cried out in an excited, wide-awake voice. The nurse stared in shock at the armed man in the doorway. She was warned to stay quiet and remain in the room.

Jean Richter marched over to the gunman. "You're not keeping your word."

"Lady, it was an accident," he apologized profusely, closing the door. "It wasn't our fault. I'm sorry."

They moved to the master bedroom, where Jean surrendered her jewelry. The thieves took three diamond bracelets, her diamond engagement ring, a sterling diamond necklace, a diamond broach, and an emerald ring. "We know the stuff is insured," remarked the young man with the cap, "so it's no loss to you."

Downstairs Richter was relieved of his platinum watch and a ring set with three diamonds before he was tied to a bench and his mouth sealed with a strip of adhesive tape. A bandit jabbed him with his pistol and snarled, "We don't want to have to come back here again. So you might want to think twice about IDing any photos they show you."

At 7:20 the invaders left by the front door, carrying plunder estimated at nearly $25,000.

The looting of the Richter mansion earned front-page headlines and outraged the residents of Chicago's exclusive Gold Coast, reputedly the safest section of the city. Chicago's elite demanded immediate capture of the culprits, and a special task force of detectives was assigned to the case, with an assistant state district attorney personally overseeing the investigation. Richter and his wife studied hundreds of police photos but failed to identify a single member of the bandit team.

Two weeks later the gang struck again. This time its target was the home of Stuart J. Templeton, a wealthy attorney, at 1388 North Green Bay Road in the wealthy suburb of Lake Forest.

January 22 was another bleak, bone-chilling Wednesday, with temperatures near zero. Late that afternoon Mrs. Templeton put down her two-year-old daughter for a nap before going next door to visit her mother, leaving the house in the care of her two black maids. Minutes later eighteen-year-old Selma Wirtals answered a knock at the back door and found three well-dressed young men. One explained that they worked for an interior decorating service and had been called to make some estimates. Selma opened the door.

As they entered, a fourth man appeared and pushed his way inside. Pressing a revolver into the maid's ribs he warned, "Let's not have any trouble and no one will get hurt."

His companions drew their pistols and moved swiftly through the house. They came upon another maid, twenty-two-year-old Birdie Horan, and forced her into the kitchen. As one gunman tied Birdie to a chair, Selma was ordered to lead the others upstairs. In the Templeton bedroom they emptied the jewelry box of rings, bracelets, and necklaces, snatching up an estimated $5,000 worth of valuables.

When they finished, they tied Selma to a chair beside Birdie and placed adhesive tape over their mouths, one bandit apologizing to the maids for having to leave them that way. Less than half an hour later Mrs. Templeton returned home. After freeing the pair of servants, she ran upstairs to her daughter's room. The little girl had slept through the entire robbery.

Neither maid was able to supply detailed descriptions of the quartet except that they were young, very polite, and extremely calm. Lake Forest and Chicago investigators had little need to compare notes—both were certain the two heists that had occurred just sixteen days apart were the work of the same crew. Feeling violated and vulnerable, Chicago society put pressure on police to make arrests and recover the stolen property.

Two months passed with no leads, no suspects, and no solution in sight. Nor were there any new holdups, prompting lawmen to assume the gang had either broken up or relocated outside the area. The wealthy residents in and around Chicago began to feel a little safer in their homes.

At three o'clock on Monday afternoon, March 31, two men arrived at the front door of the Von Buelow mansion at 5839 Sheridan Road along Chicago's North Side lakefront. When Christopher Gross, Mrs. Von Buelow's brother-in-law, answered the doorbell, the pair introduced themselves as census takers.

Gross explained that the owners were not at home, saying the interviewers should come back in a couple of hours.

The Von Buelow household was in a state of turmoil at the moment. While vacationing in Central America ten months earlier, Lottie Brenner, rich widow of manufacturer and politician Nathan Brenner, was swept off her feet by a dashing playboy presenting himself as Count Enrique Von Buelow, a German aviator. Despite two decades' difference in their ages—he was thirty-six, she was in her mid-fifties—they were married. Following an around-the-world honeymoon they returned to Chicago to live off Lottie's inherited fortune. After just three months the romance soured when it became apparent that the count was more interested in spending his wife's millions than spending time with her. Lottie did some checking and discovered that her new husband was neither a count, a Von Buelow, nor a pilot, but in reality was Henry Dechow, a German gigolo. She had recently filed suit for divorce.

The census takers reappeared at five o'clock, and Gross led the pair to an upstairs parlor where Lottie sat with her sister Mae. The unsuspecting brother-in-law failed to notice a third man who had slipped inside behind the others. When they entered the room all three whipped out pistols and barked, "Stick 'em up!"

"What do you want?" Lottie gasped.

One of the intruders was short, slim, blond, and boyishly handsome. Lottie would remember his face. "We know you've got a million bucks, lady. We just want a piece of it," he said.

Gross and his wife were bound with rope and blindfolded with rags, their mouths sealed with tape. While the blond bandit remained with Lottie, his accomplices moved through the house cutting phone lines. They encountered the chauffeur and a maid and tied up both in the kitchen before returning upstairs.

Lottie was marched into the bedroom and ordered to fetch her valuables. As she spilled the contents of her jewelry cases on the bed, a robber snatched a framed photo of her estranged spouse from the dresser. "Hey, look," he called to his partners. "This is her husband, the count. We oughtta stick around and bump him off."

"Oh, no, please!" Lottie cried out.

"Where's all the money then?" snarled another, the oldest and largest of the trio. He wanted cash as well as jewelry. He spotted a wall safe and demanded that she open it. Lottie tried to explain that the safe was emptied after her first husband's death and she no longer had the combination.

"Bullshit!" he raged. "You open it right now!"

"I can't," she insisted, close to tears.

The big bandit worked the tumbler, attempting to hear the clicks. His confederates rummaged through the jewelry and chose pieces to be stuffed into a cloth sack. Lottie stood to the side, praying that they would take their loot and leave.

Suddenly there was a sound from downstairs—the front door opening, then closing. The two bandits at the bed stiffened, one grabbing the pistol he had set down to examine her valuables. The pair moved to the door and crept into the hallway, taking Lottie with them. "For your sake," one whispered fiercely, "this better not be the cops."

The two men waited silently with their hostage, listening to a pair of footsteps ascending the staircase. The newcomer reached the landing, then turned into the hall and found himself staring into the barrel of a .45 thrust into his face. His hands shot upward. The gunman recognized him instantly.

"Evening, count," the handsome young robber greeted him. "Keep those hands in the air."

Von Buelow—or rather Dechow—was preparing to leave for New York and had picked the wrong time to drop by the house to gather some belongings. The gunmen plucked ninety-five dollars from his wallet and stripped him of his wristwatch and a pocket watch. He and Lottie were then herded back into the bedroom where the third bandit was still engaged in his futile assault upon the safe. Exasperated, the big man began to strike the tumbler with his pistol until the weapon's wood stock shattered.

"We got what we came for," a comrade snapped. "We're going."

Gathering the pieces of his broken pistol grip, the heavyset man continued to curse and complain that he intended to find some "big bucks" somewhere on the huge estate. He stormed out of the room, leaving his partners to tie up Lottie and her soon-to-be ex-husband in separate chairs. They heard the big robber ransacking other rooms, and once the couple was securely bound, the two thieves departed. Lottie heard a brief exchange of angry voices before the front door slammed. The robbers were gone.

After several minutes Lottie managed to free herself and untie the others. The police were summoned to the scene from a neighbor's house. It took Lottie hours to complete a full accounting of her missing valuables. In addition to the cash and watches lifted from Dechow, the thieves had taken a $40,000 pearl necklace, a $3,500 diamond ring, a lavaliere with twenty-eight diamonds valued at $3,500, a $5,000 diamond bracelet, four pairs of diamond earrings ranging from $800 to $5,000, a $3,000 pendant and another worth $1,200, and three $300 chains.

Chicago Police Captain John Stege was initially convinced the robbery was an inside job, and his prime suspect was Lottie's counterfeit count. The fact that Dechow had appeared at the house during the robbery, providing a perfect alibi, seemed too much of a coincidence. But Dechow was cleared of any complicity once it became evident the heist was the work of the same crew that had raided the Richter and Templeton homes. Chicago braced itself for a crime wave.

❋ ❋ ❋

Two weeks after the Von Buelow heist a young couple moved into an apartment at 6109 West 25th Street in Cicero. To their new neighbors they introduced themselves as the Nelsons, George and Helen. They were a diminutive pair, looking more like high school sweethearts than a married couple with a little boy about to celebrate his first birthday. Helen, timid and soft-spoken, was close to delivering their second child. Her husband was a sharp dresser who could greet someone with a warm, disarming smile one day and a cold glower the next.

Friends and family of the former Lester Gillis, now George Nelson, were puzzled by his name change and newfound prosperity. He still worked several nights a week at the Johnson brothers' Standard station, his only verifiable income over the past year. Yet he managed to pay cash for a new Chrysler on January 24, two days after the Templeton robbery, having the title issued to him in the name of George Nelson. The couple's move to Cicero obviously required some financing. To those who asked how they were able to afford a place of their own adorned with new furnishings on his part-time wages, Nelson would give differing answers. He told his mother and sisters that Helen's father had loaned them money. Helen told her family that Les's mother had helped with the bills. To those inquiring about his new name, Nelson said he was tired of the police hounding him.

On May 11 Helen gave birth to a baby girl at Garfield Park Hospital. Nelson briefly reassumed his real identity for the event, and the infant was named Darlene Helen Gillis.

That summer Nelson invited his mother to move into their Cicero apartment with them. Mary welcomed the chance to help the couple with their newborn. Nelson, it seems, felt a deep responsibility for her, perhaps to make amends for past behavior. Nevertheless, Mary earned her keep by watching Ronald and his baby sister. When Nelson didn't work nights at the gas station, he and Helen often spent their evenings out.

They visited expensive supper clubs, went to movies, or toured West Side underworld speakeasies and nightspots. A number of friends often tagged along or joined them on the way. The young couple were always a welcome sight. Nelson spent money lavishly, bought rounds of drinks, and was recognized everywhere as a generous tipper. Although he invariably left untouched any glass of bootleg beer placed before him, Nelson's abstinence never put a damper on the party. Helen seemed especially exuberant when out on the town. She would smoke, sip drinks, and share jokes, behavior she never exhibited around family members. On several occasions at the Rainbo Gardens she even participated in the floor show.

During the daytime Nelson devoted himself to a new hobby. With the help of Clarence Lieder, a good friend and owner of Oakley Auto Construction Company at 2500 West Division Street, he built a race car, which he entered in events on the area dirt-track circuit. A small, black-haired man of twenty-four, Lieder had immigrated from Poland with his parents and grown up in The Patch. Like Jack Perkins, he became the object of abuse by bullies, although in his case the scrapes usually centered around anti-Semitic taunting. And, also like Perkins, he was offered friendship and thus a measure of protection by a neighborhood kid named Lester Gillis when few others would do so. Though three years younger than Lieder, Gillis stood up to anyone who dared mistreat or threaten his pal "Clarey."

"He definitely had an iron will," Lieder revealed years later. "You either loved or hated him, and that was the way he wanted it. If he was on your side, you couldn't have a better friend in the world. I never believed half the things the papers said about him."

Lieder also declared that his pal was "one of the best drivers I've ever seen." In the summer and fall of 1930 Nelson competed in a number of races at Robey Speedway at 108th Street and Indianapolis Avenue. Each time Nelson managed a respectable finish but failed to take any prizes. He and Lieder intended to make some improvements and were looking ahead to racing again the next spring.

About this same time Nelson encountered Father Phillip W. Coughlan, a Catholic priest and one of the most enigmatic figures in the saga of Baby Face. Like the majority of Nelson's friends and associates, Coughlan was a product of Chicago's West Side where a goodly share of Irish lads (just like in B-movies) became either hoodlums, cops, or priests. Coughlan chose the latter path, training for the priesthood at St. John's Seminary in Little Rock, Arkansas. He spent the greater part of the Twenties ministering in parishes in Missouri and Oklahoma. In 1929 he returned to Chicago and for the next three years served as chaplain at the Oak Park Hospital.

During this time the good Father cultivated some close ties with gangland characters, including members of the Touhy gang. More than once his friendly relations with criminals were brought to the attention of the church, but he was able to talk his way out of trouble by assuring his superiors that his dealings with the Touhys and other disreputable figures were strictly of a spiritual nature. One source claimed Coughlan was extremely partial to Irish whiskey, and the only spirits involved were of the ninety-proof variety that gangsters supplied to him.

It was Tommy Touhy who, in the late summer of 1930, introduced Coughlan to a polite, well-dressed young man calling himself George Nelson. They were definitely an odd couple, the tea-totaling little gangster and the whiskey-loving priest, but they became fast friends. They obviously enjoyed each other's company and had a number of mutual acquaintances. For Nelson's part, he appeared to value the Father's friendship chiefly because Coughlan was someone he could trust—a quality he counted as precious among friends and difficult to come by.

It is doubtful that either Lieder or Coughlan played any part in Nelson's illegal activities at this time. For the moment, Randall and Powell were his principal partners in crime, although the trio spent the major part of the summer on hiatus from their heists and one another. By fall their proceeds from the house robberies were beginning to wither away. Much of the Von Buelow jewelry was declared too hot to fence, and a portion was sold off for a mere fraction of its actual worth. Nelson kept the rest, searching for a buyer while his two comrades pressured him for their shares.

When the three bandits finally came together in September, it was obvious they had reached a crossroads. Randall voiced his opinion that the jewelry heists were no longer worth the time, energy, or risk involved. Nelson readily agreed, and from then on they focused their efforts on acquiring strictly cash.

❄ ❄ ❄

At 9 A.M. on October 3 the State Bank of Itasca, located in the small Du Page County community fifteen miles northwest of Chicago's city limits, opened its doors for business. Assistant cashier Raymond Frantzen and teller Emma Droegemueller were preparing for the day's transactions. The bank's president, Frantzen's father, had stopped at the post office and was running late.

A pair of well-dressed young men entered. One stopped a few steps inside the door while the other approached Frantzen at the counter and declared, "I'd like to buy a cashier's check."

Frantzen bent down to retrieve the ledger. When he looked up the young man thrust an automatic pistol in his face. "This is a stickup," Harry Powell announced nervously. "Step back."

The second man rushed forward and nimbly vaulted over the railing. Drawing a .45, Nelson marched toward the employees. "Lay on the floor, both of you," he commanded.

Nelson stood guard over the prostrate pair as Powell raided the teller cages, tossing the cash into a white pillowcase. After dropping facedown on the floor beside her co-worker, Droegemueller felt like she was "in a fog," completely numb with fear. She swiftly snapped back to reality when Nelson pressed the muzzle of his gun against her right hand and growled, "Are you touching an alarm?"

The teller realized her hand had slipped beneath the radiator, arousing the gunman's suspicions. She immediately yanked it back, crying out, "No! No!"

A moment later Powell finished cleaning out the cash drawers. "Where's the rest of the money?" Nelson inquired, looking at Frantzen. "Open the vault for us."

Frantzen rose from the floor. A lean, athletic man in his late twenties and a onetime baseball player at Amherst, he took a moment to brush off his suit and then started walking away from the vault. "Where are you going?" Nelson demanded.

"I gotta have the key to let you in the vault," Frantzen replied brashly.

His curt tone surprised the bandits. "What are you so worried about?" Nelson asked. "You're covered by insurance."

"Well," the cashier shot back, "how do I know you two aren't hopped up or something?"

Still hugging the floor, Emma listened to the exchange thinking her co-worker would get them both shot by "acting so fresh with the robbers." Eventually Frantzen, refusing to be hurried or intimidated by the gunmen, opened the vault. Once again Powell gathered the money. When he had finished, the two employees were ordered inside. As Emma followed Frantzen into the vault she looked directly at Nelson. "He had blond hair and the bluest eyes I've ever seen," she recalled later. "I always wondered how someone so innocent-looking could be robbing us."

In hushed voices the bandits discussed locking the pair inside the vault but finally decided against it. Nelson called out, "Give us ten minutes to get out of town."

An elderly gentleman who owned a business next door encountered the young men as they excited the bank. Nelson smiled and said, "Good morning." The pair hustled into a waiting maroon sedan with an older, larger man at the wheel. The vehicle instantly raced north before turning east on Irving Park Boulevard.

Dividing the loot, the trio discovered they had collected $4,678, four times the average yearly income in 1930. Nelson celebrated by once again upgrading his personal vehicle, purchasing an eight-cylinder Imperial sedan eight days after the robbery.

Just over a month later, on November 7, a cool and sunny Friday morning, the maroon sedan resurfaced in the town of Plainfield, Illinois, thirty miles southwest of Chicago. In what began as a replay of the Itasca holdup, the car parked in front of the town's bank and two men stepped out while the third, this time Powell, remained at the wheel.

Inside, Bank President Avery Lambert and cashier Clyde Wolf were standing behind the glass-enclosed counter waiting on a pair of female customers. The bank had been robbed twice during the past year, the last time in July, and special precautions had been taken to prevent any further attempts.

Wolf glanced up from his customer to see two men enter and halt in the doorway, scanning the interior. The pair looked like they didn't belong together. One was young and short, wearing a fedora and an expensive dark suit and tie beneath a gray overcoat. His companion, twice as old and almost twice as big, was clad in grimy coveralls, giving him the appearance of a burly mechanic. Immediately suspicious, Wolf was about to point out the strangers to Lambert when the smaller man whipped out a pistol and shouted, "Stick 'em up!"

The man in coveralls, brandishing his own weapon, forced the two customers back against a wall and kept them covered. His partner approached Lambert, demanding admittance to the cages. When the president failed to move fast enough, Nelson squeezed off an ear-splitting shot, striking the glass a foot over Lambert's head. The slug ricocheted toward the little bandit, almost hitting him. Lambert fought a smile as he tapped on the glass and proudly declared, "Bulletproof."

Enraged, Nelson stepped back and he and Randall fired a volley of seven more shots at the counter. One of the women cringing in the corner screamed as a ricochet creased her forehead above the right eye. Wolf grabbed a shotgun from beneath a cash drawer, ready to return the fire. But the would-be robbers, realizing the futility of their situation and panicked over wounding a bystander, were fleeing out the door. As Lambert hit the alarm, Wolf ran into the street with the shotgun, arriving in time to see the sedan roar off toward Aurora.

Undaunted and no doubt embittered by their failure at Plainfield, the bandits struck again just two weeks later, this time in the suburb of Hillside, several miles west of Cicero. A few minutes past 9 A.M. on Saturday, November 22, three well-dressed men walked into the Hillside State Bank with their guns drawn. One bandit fired a couple of rounds into the ceiling to announce their entrance and to show that they meant business. Cashier Edward W. Heidorn made a move toward the alarm but was instantly covered by a robber who hissed, "Do it and you're dead."

Heidorn and his three co-workers—Bank Director Andrew Yundt, his seventeen-year-old son Howard, and Assistant Cashier Joseph Marik—were herded into the lobby and ordered to face the wall with their hands raised. "Anyone twitches gets drilled," warned the man guarding them. His two companions ransacked the cages, taking $4,155, and confiscated a pair of bank pistols in the process. "Don't move for five minutes," one called out as the trio departed, scrambling to a getaway car where a fourth man sat at the wheel.

Once law enforcement authorities in the three communities compared notes, there was little doubt the Hillside bandits were the same crew which had struck at Itasca and Plainfield. It was evident a Chicago-based gang was targeting small-town banks west of the Windy City. Previously Chicago police had displayed only lukewarm interest in the suburban holdups, but now, because Hillside was within Cook County, they began to take a more serious look.

It was nearly six weeks before lawmen received a break in the case. Pat Roache, chief investigator for the state's attorney's office, heard from an "underworld source" about a young up-and-coming hood named George Nelson who was pulling off stickups with a hand-picked crew. The source could not provide many details other than the fact that some underworld old-timers, resentful of Nelson's youth and cockiness, mockingly referred to him as "Baby Face" or "Big George" behind his back. This struck a chord with Roache; describing one of the bandits at Plainfield, a witness had stated, "He had sort of a baby face." Nelson's right hand man, it was said, was a gangster named Hamilton.

The tip might have gone overlooked if not for a second informer who confided to Police Sergeant Roy Steffen that a man named Hamilton residing in Rogers Park had been involved in some recent robberies. Roache decided the pair of reports taken together warranted further investigation. Steffen and Detectives Charles Touzinsky and Edward Farr were assigned to the case.

Rogers Park was a quiet residential area, the last place one would look for criminals. The mysterious J. H. Hamilton was traced through mail to Apartment One at 6236 North Mozart Street. Curiously the occupants were named Stan and Kathy Randall. Convinced Randall and Hamilton were the same man, the officers tapped his phone and spent a full week monitoring the couple's calls. The most intriguing conversations were with an individual named Harry who lived at the Diversey Arms Hotel in Melrose Park. Randall and Harry spoke at length about a planned bank job at "M," eventually making it clear through a number of references that they intended to hold up the State Bank of Marengo, Illinois. Randall complained that he wanted to "get to it," and was bitterly critical of "George," who he claimed was "dragging his feet" about the M job and also in finding a buyer for their "goods."

Harry proved to be Harry Lewis Powell, also known as Harry Lewis or Harry Parnell. While neither Powell nor his wife, Gloria, were employed, they had lived at the expensive Diversey Arms for nearly a year. A second team of detectives, led by Sergeant Michael Ahern, was assigned to Powell and installed a phone tap and tailed the suspect and his wife wherever they went. On one occasion Powell was contacted by a caller identifying himself as "George." "Everything is OK," he assured Powell. "The stuff will be sold in a few days and the dough will be put on the line. We'll make another spot soon."

Several days later, on February 12, 1931, one of Powell's tails followed him to a telegraph office. When the suspect departed, the detective entered, flashed his badge, and asked to see the telegram. It read, "Wait till I see you downtown. Harry." It was addressed to George Nelson, 6109 West 25th Street, Cicero.

The lawmen were satisfied they had pinpointed the principal members of the robbery ring, although at this stage there was no solid evidence linking the gang with any crime other than the impending Marengo holdup. The seven officers working full time on the case debated whether to move in and arrest the trio in three separate simultaneous raids or wait, keeping them under surveillance until they came together in one place. It was finally decided to round up the gang members individually, lessening the chances for gunplay. The team covering Randall would act first.

The next afternoon, Friday the thirteenth, the officers on the Rogers Park stakeout observed Randall and his wife leave their apartment. Steffen, Touzinsky, and Farr slipped into the building and stationed themselves around Apartment One to make the arrest when the couple returned. Shortly after 6 P.M. a man and woman approached the apartment. The lawmen moved in, realizing too late it was not the suspect and his wife.

Taken aside and questioned, the couple insisted they were innocent acquaintances of the Randalls. The man was identified as Tony Curvan of 931 North Francisco Avenue. His companion—a pale, petite, dark-haired young woman—remained silent at first, then finally gave her name as Mrs. George Nelson.

Touzinsky remained at the scene while his partners escorted the pair to the Detective Bureau. In custody Helen repeatedly pleaded to be released, claiming she needed to return home to care for her two babies. But when asked about her residence, her husband, and what she knew about Stanton Randall, she obstinately refused to answer the officers.

The Randalls, meanwhile, had returned to their apartment. Once Steffen and Farr rejoined Touzinsky, they waited an hour after observing the lights go out. At 1:45 A.M. they crept into the building and Touzinsky knocked on the door. When Katherine answered, clad in a robe and complaining that it was too late for visitors, the officers pushed their way in. Steffen marched to the bedroom where he found Randall naked and bleary-eyed, fumbling for a pistol in a drawer of the bedside table. He froze when Steffen shoved a revolver into his face. The weapon he was reaching for was later identified as one stolen from the Hillside bank.

Once Randall and his wife were deposited behind bars, Steffen and his partners sped to the Diversey Arms and joined the other team in raiding the Powell apartment. Unlike the Randalls, Powell and his young wife had only recently returned and were still awake and dressed when they were placed under arrest, protesting they knew nothing of the Randalls, Nelson, or any robberies.

Touzinsky handled the interrogations while Steffen, Farr, and Sergeant Ahern drove to Cicero to apprehend the final member of the trio. Four detectives—James Zegar, Walter Miller, Leo Anderson, and John Sherping—were keeping the Nelson apartment under surveillance and were certain the suspect was home.

It was approaching 5:30 A.M., and Steffen wanted to take Nelson before sunrise. The seven officers proceeded into the building, but instead of knocking, two detectives put their shoulders to the door, breaking the lock in a single coordinated charge. Nelson was in bed, sitting up, as the men rushed in. Looking more puzzled than alarmed, he asked, "Who the hell are you guys?"

"Detectives," Steffen replied. A .45 pistol rested on the dresser within reach of the suspect. Steffen pocketed the weapon and asked, "Are you George Nelson?"

The young man nodded. Ordered to get dressed for a visit downtown, he complained, "My kids are in the next room. I don't want to wake them and I can't leave them."

"Yes you can," a detective shot back. Nelson cast an angry glare at the speaker. Steffen ordered a pair of men to remain with the children until someone arrived to watch them. Nelson provided the officers with the phone number of his sister Julie.

Convinced they had rounded up "one of the worst stickup mobs in the city's history" but initially lacking any solid evidence, the State Attorney's Office went to work trying to link the suspects to every unsolved jewelry heist and bank holdup over the past year. In addition to the three house robberies, investigators considered nine similar stickups involving jewelry, including the mugging of Chicago Mayor "Big Bill" Thompson's wife the previous October that had netted $17,000. Along with the three suburban bank raids, the gang was credited with robberies in Waukegan and a $1,250 heist in Rockton, more than 100 miles away.

More than sixty witnesses (including Mrs. Thompson) were summoned to the Detective Bureau and paraded past the four men and the three women captured with them. The instant Lottie Von Buelow saw Nelson she cried out, "He's the one who has my jewels." She also identified Randall and Powell as his accomplices. Ray Frantzen stated he was positive Nelson and Powell were the two bandits who entered the Itasca bank. Three witnesses from the Plainfield bank identified Nelson and Randall as the pair of thwarted robbers, and three more from Hillside were certain that Nelson, Randall, and Powell were the holdup trio.

Tony Curvan could not be connected with any of the crimes, though it was suspected he had played a minor role in the gang's scores. He was released along with the three women. Helen rejoined her children at the Fitzsimmons home and was invited by Julie to stay with them. The Cicero apartment was vacated and the bulk of their furniture and possessions, along with Nelson's car, sold off. Helen needed the cash to hire an attorney for her incarcerated husband.

When the story broke, Captain John Stege declared the arrest of the trio was "among the most important in the police history of Chicago." In the official statement identifying the three suspects, someone in the department, evidently aware that the Chicago press liked their criminals colorful, added the nickname "Baby Face" to George Nelson, though at the time it was only an obscure label that had been pinned on him by some unknown underworld character. News accounts appearing the next day portrayed the twenty-two-year-old bank robber as an already-notorious gangster and the obvious leader of the bandit team.

It was the public's first encounter with Baby Face Nelson.

❋ ❋ ❋

On February 20, 1931, Nelson, Randall, and Powell were indicted by the grand jury for the Hillside and Von Buelow robberies. Testifying against the trio was Sergeant Steffen, who related the details of the investigation and arrests; Andrew Yundt and Edward Heidorn, who provided accounts of the Hillside holdup; and Lottie Von Buelow and her sister Mae Gross, who told of their harrowing experience with the three gunmen who robbed them and left them tied up.

Lottie—now divorced from Dechow and insisting that she be called Mrs. Brenner—stunned the courtroom when she revealed that she had received a phone call the previous day. A gruff voice on the line had warned, "If you go before the grand jury and testify against my pals in that stickup job, you'll be taken for a ride." She told the jurors, "But you know, boys, I'm not afraid. I'm here to tell all I know."

Bail was set at $25,000 for each of the defendants. All three remained behind bars as the legal process got under way.

Powell was the first to crack and confess the crimes, once his lawyer had negotiated a deal with county prosecutors. In exchange for his testimony and cooperation in convicting his cronies, he would be ordered to serve only a year's probation. In addition to his roles in the Hillside and Von Buelow affairs, Powell admitted involvement in the Richter and Templeton robberies. He was unable to provide any names or details about the other participants, claiming they were all friends of Nelson.

Informed of Powell's betrayal, Randall cursed him and everyone else in sight. Once he settled down he tried to fight the charges through a series of petitions and motions. His lawyers were granted a number of postponements, but when they filed for a change of venue, it was denied. An attempt to have the Hillside pistol that was found in his apartment ruled inadmissible because it was obtained as the result of an illegal search and seizure also failed. With his trial rapidly approaching and his legal maneuvers exhausted, Randall took the advice of his attorneys and on June 18 pleaded guilty to the Hillside robbery. He was sentenced to serve one to ten years in the Illinois State Prison.

Nelson stood alone, the only one to adamantly maintain his innocence. His lawyer, Charles Dougherty, recommended that he negotiate a deal for a reduced sentence, as his co-defendants had done, but he refused to budge. Detectives repeatedly grilled him, taunting the young bandit over his rigid silence. He was a fool, they insisted, for taking the fall while his friends sold him out and cut deals. Specifically they wanted to know who, other than Randall and Powell, had participated in the holdups. Nelson reportedly answered them with obscenities.

One of the interrogators, speaking to Assistant State's Attorney John Swanson, described Nelson as "a tough little shit."

During his four months in the Cook County lockup, Nelson received regular visits from his wife, mother, and three sisters. He told them the same tale he maintained before the detectives, minus the profanity. As usual, Mary Gillis believed every word her son told her. "Sometimes," she later wrote, "if I asked him about some wrongdoing, he would simply nod and I would know he had done it." But when she confronted him about the Hillside robbery—the charge which the prosecution decided to proceed on—he declared, "Mother, I didn't do this."

According to Mary, she had an opportunity to speak with Powell on the eve of her son's trial, and he confided to her that Nelson indeed was not involved in the holdup. Powell promised that when the time arrived, he would refuse to testify against him.

Nelson's trial began on June 22 before Judge John Prystalski. The selection of jurors occupied the entire first day and part of the second. When the prosecution presented its case only three witnesses were called: Andrew Yundt, Edward Heidorn, and Harry Powell. Mary Gillis, seated in the gallery with one-year-old Darlene on her lap, was shocked to hear Powell take the stand and describe her son as the ringleader of the gang. In his cross-examination, Dougherty managed to get the witness to admit his deal with the state that guaranteed immunity from prosecution in exchange for his testimony, but he was unable to damage Powell's credibility.

The defense's case was embarrassingly flimsy. Several friends of Nelson, including garage owner Howard Davis, risked perjury to testify that on the day of the Hillside robbery, the defendant was in their company and nowhere near the scene of the crime.

On June 25 both sides presented their closing arguments and the jurors retired to decide Nelson's fate. After only two hours they returned with their verdict: "We the jury find the defendant, George Nelson, guilty of robbery in the manner and form as charged in the indictment. And we further find from the evidence that at the time of the commission of said robbery, the defendant was armed with a dangerous weapon. . . . "

Two weeks later, on July 9, Nelson returned for sentencing. Judge Prystalski ordered the prisoner to serve one year to life in the state prison at Joliet.

In a succession of tearful goodbyes before his removal from the Cook County Jail, Nelson kissed Helen, hugged his children, and embraced his mother and sisters. Mary reported, "Les told me it was all up now—there was no use trying to live right. His only thought from that time on was escaping from prison, I believe."

❋ ❋ ❋

The state prison at Joliet had stood since the Civil War, its massive walls capable of containing close to a thousand men. On July 17 Nelson was received as inmate 5437. Before being assigned a cell he endured the standard indoctrination procedure. Once he was photographed and fingerprinted, he was led into an examination room and ordered to strip. While undergoing a physical, a clerk asked him questions from a checklist.

Clerk: "Are you a native or naturalized citizen?"

Nelson: "Native."

Clerk: "Native to Illinois?"

Nelson: "Chicago, yes."

Clerk: "What religion are you?"

Nelson: "Catholic."

Clerk: "Do you smoke?"

Nelson: "No."

Clerk: "Do you chew?"

Nelson: "No."

The questions addressed a wide variety of subjects, including his education and whether his crimes were "attributed to the use of liquor." Asked his occupation, Nelson replied that he worked as an "oiler." The doctor recorded his physical condition as "good." Nelson was asked about past illnesses and injuries and whether there was any family history of hereditary ailments or mental disorders. The latter must have brought to mind his father's suicide, but he answered no to all the queries. Then, provided with a fresh set of prison garb, he was allowed to dress. A guard read the regulations and itinerary of the daily routine all prisoners were expected to observe. Nelson signed a statement that he understood and was handed a copy of the rules to keep.

Stanton Randall had arrived at Joliet a week earlier. Word was relayed among corrections officers that there might be bad blood between Nelson and inmate 5409. Evidently the two avoided contact with each other. A cellmate of Nelson, Wilford Leeson, later said the young convict never spoke of Randall, though it was obvious from the way the pair exchanged glances that they were no longer friends. Leeson added, however, that Nelson often mentioned Powell and had vowed to track down and kill him.

During his first five months at Joliet, Nelson apparently slipped back into the role of model prisoner that he had performed so well during his three stretches in St. Charles. As usual, he made friends easily and readily dropped names of his pals involved in the Chicago underworld. Word spread that he was a man with mighty connections, someone not to be crossed or molested.

While coping with the tedious routine and restrictions of prison life, he confided to his monthly visitors—Helen, his mother and sisters, or an occasional friend like Mike Juska—that the confinement was unbearable. His lawyer visited too, never bearing good news. Nelson's appeal for a new trial was rejected, and authorities in Du Page County were seeking to prosecute him for the Itasca robbery. Despite Dougherty's repeated admonitions to remain positive, his mood grew worse with each contact. He bitterly complained that the police and the courts had singled him out for persecution. Dougherty pleaded with him to give prosecutors the information they demanded to secure a reduced sentence. Nelson stubbornly refused.

His increasingly brooding disposition no doubt played a part in his single recorded incident of misbehavior at Joliet. On December 6—Nelson's twenty-third birthday—he was disciplined for cursing, specifically for calling a corrections officer "obscene names." The offense was judged serious enough to suspend his privileges, including visitation, and he was relocated to a more restrictive wing of the prison for the next three months.

As it turned out, Nelson spent little time there. By the end of the year he received official notification that Du Page prosecutors were proceeding with the Itasca case, and on January 6 he was moved to Wheaton to be formally charged. Pleading not guilty again, he was transported back to Joliet to await his trial, which was set to begin on January 26.

Early one Sunday morning shortly before the trial date, two women came to the home of Raymond Frantzen on South Oak Street in Itasca. Mrs. Frantzen admitted the pair, thinking they were clients of her husband, who was in the process of forming his own business. The women marched to where Frantzen was working at a table. The older of the two introduced herself as Nelson's mother and made a sorrowful plea to the bank cashier not to take the stand against her boy. Her appeal was so dramatic and eloquent that Frantzen and his wife were certain she was actually a Chicago actress hired by the Gillis family. There was no doubt, however, that her younger companion was Helen Gillis. When Frantzen asked them to leave, Helen angrily advised, "You better not testify, if you know what's good for you."

At the trial in the county courthouse in Wheaton both Frantzen and co-worker Emma Droegemueller appeared for the prosecution. Emma provided a vivid account of the holdup but failed to positively identify Nelson. Frantzen, however, expressed no uncertainty at all—the defendant was absolutely the bandit who had leaped over the counter and done most of the talking. At the end of the day, as Nelson was led from the courtroom, he fixed Frantzen with a cold stare and vowed, "I'm gonna get you for this."

The defense was able to produce only a few unconvincing characters who swore that Nelson had been with them at the time of the robbery. The jury took less than an hour to agree on a verdict of guilty.

On February 17 Nelson was sentenced to serve one year to life. After judgment was pronounced, the young convict was led into a conference room where he was allowed a few minutes to say his farewells to his family. When time was up a pair of Du Page deputies frisked him and turned him over to R. M. Martin, a husky corrections officer appointed to return the prisoner to Joliet. Martin snapped a handcuff around Nelson's right wrist and attached the other end to his own left wrist.

The Gillis family followed the pair to the Wheaton depot. It was a blustery, overcast Wednesday, and snow flurries whipped about the platform as Nelson and his guard waited to board the train. The diminutive prisoner, hatless and shivering in a light jacket, seemed dwarfed by the huge Martin. Ordered by the guard to maintain a respectful distance, Nelson's loved ones gathered a few yards away until the passengers climbed aboard the coach. As the train pulled away, Helen and the others walked alongside waving.

It was dusk and turning bitterly cold when Nelson and Martin reached the Joliet station. The handcuffed pair scrambled into the back of a taxi, and Martin instructed the driver, Joseph Candic, to take them to the prison. The ride took only a few minutes. Nelson seemed preoccupied with his own thoughts and stared silently out the window. Suddenly, as the vehicle pulled within sight of the prison gates, Nelson shifted closer to the guard. Martin felt a sharp jab in his ribs. He looked down to discover his prisoner pressing a .45 automatic into his left side.

"Don't give me a reason to shoot you." Nelson spoke the words so calmly Martin was convinced he would not hesitate to pull the trigger. "Nice and easy now, take off the cuffs."

As Martin obeyed, Nelson asked the driver his name. Candic, rapidly understanding what was occurring in the back of his cab, answered. "Well, Joe," said Nelson, his eyes locking on Martin, "just keep driving. Head for Chicago and stay under the speed limit. No stops unless I say."

"I've got a family," Candic said over his shoulder.

"Small world," Nelson replied. "So do I. Don't sweat it, Joe. No one gets hurt if we all behave."

Four miles southwest of Cicero, near the community of Summit, Nelson ordered Candic to turn onto a side road. After a few minutes Baby Face spotted Resurrection Cemetery along a lonely stretch of rural highway. "This looks good," he announced.

As Candic pulled the taxi onto the shoulder and stopped, Nelson asked Martin for his wallet. He plucked ten dollars from the billfold and handed it back. "Take it all," Martin suggested. "You'll need it."

"This is enough," Nelson replied, stuffing the bill inside a pocket. He ordered the pair out of the cab, and once Candic and Martin stepped away, Nelson slid behind the wheel and sped off toward Chicago's brightly lit skyline.

About 2 A.M. determined fists began to pound furiously on the door of Fred and Amy Kenniston's home on South Millard where Mary Gillis—along with daughter Leona, daughter-in-law Helen, and grandchildren Ronnie and Darlene—had moved several months earlier. Roused from their sleep, the adults in the household threw on robes and hurried into the front room. The incessant pounding was punctuated by the bellowed command, "This is the police! Open up!"

When Amy unlocked the door a whole squad of lawmen swarmed inside. Martin, the big Joliet guard, was among them. As the others fanned out and began searching the house, Martin marched directly to the tiny figure of Mary and demanded, "Where's your son?"

Mary blinked at the huge man, obviously bewildered. "Why, I thought he was with you."

Martin's face reddened when he noticed Helen, Amy, and Leona were all wearing wide grins.

A few days later Ray Frantzen, learning that Nelson was at large and remembering the bandit's words to him in the Wheaton courtroom, applied for a permit to carry a gun.

❋ ❋ ❋

A week after Nelson's escape a short, pot-bellied man dressed as a priest called at the Kenniston home for Helen Gillis. The teenage mother accompanied the visitor, who, Amy explained to her curious husband, was a friend of the family. When Helen returned the next day, her mother-in-law discovered her packing a suitcase. "Did you see Les?" Mary eagerly asked.

Helen nodded. "He can't risk coming to see us, but he'll keep in touch. When he finds a safe place he'll send for me. It might take time, but I have to ready to go when he calls."

"What about the children?" Mary inquired.

Helen confessed that she and Les had discussed the matter at length. "Ronnie is going with us," she said, adding that she and her husband had agreed that Darlene, not yet two years old, should stay behind until they were settled. All three of Nelson's sisters had consented to care for their little niece until Les and Helen sent for her.

Several days later Mary was able to speak briefly with her son on the phone. He assured her that everything would "work out fine" and urged her not to worry. "I'm smarter than they are," he boasted. Mary reluctantly suggested that it might be best if Les surrendered to the authorities. "I can never go back there," he told her solemnly, referring to Joliet. "They'd kill me."

Chicago police, meanwhile, attempting not only to track down the young fugitive but also to determine how he obtained the gun, failed to do either. Detectives explored the possibilities that a Du Page County deputy, the cab driver, or even Martin himself had provided Nelson with the weapon in exchange for a payoff. They ultimately concluded that someone—a family member or a criminal crony—had slipped him the .45 somewhere between the courthouse in Wheaton and the taxi at the Joliet station.

Later that year Nelson recounted his escape to a number of individuals, including Alvin Karpis, confiding that "an angel" had planted the gun for him in a rest room aboard the train. Everyone assumed he was talking about Helen, but at least one informant insisted it was actually his sister Leona who had performed the deed. In an FBI review of Nelson's life written years later, Leona was named as the leading suspect in aiding her brother's escape. Perkins, Mike Juska, and Al Van de Houton were also singled out as possible candidates.

Nelson's movements over the next two weeks are also a bit of a mystery. It appears he spent part of the time hiding out in the Chicago home of one Frank Paska at 1526 Berry Street. Paska, a tall German immigrant and ex-con, was a distant relative of Nelson's Joliet cellmate Willy Leeson. Perkins and Juska were frequent visitors to the Paska residence and acted as Nelson's chief messengers to his family and friends. There was an unconfirmed report that Nelson and Juska drove to Iowa and pulled off a series of small-time stickups, including a gas station and several movie theater box offices, in order to acquire some traveling money for the young fugitive.

Back in Chicago Nelson touched base with a number of his gangland chums. Klondike O'Donnell, Tony Capezio, Jack White, and Tommy Touhy all pledged their support by making calls or writing letters of introduction to ensure that their pal from The Patch was set up with "the right people" on the West Coast.

Then, shortly after the first of March, Nelson vanished, not to be seen again in his hometown for almost a year. According to one story, Perkins provided his friend with a ride to St. Louis, where Nelson boarded a train heading west.

Helen waited more than a month, spending a melancholy nineteenth birthday without her fugitive husband. In late April Father Coughlan again visited the Kenniston home and informed Helen that her husband was waiting for her. After a quick round of farewells—the hardest was telling tiny Darlene that "mommy and brother have to go away"—she grabbed Ronnie and her suitcase and followed the priest to a car outside. Fred Kenniston noticed a portly young man—Perkins—behind the wheel.

Perkins drove southwest for more than an hour. Finally, along a back road near a gravel pit, he drew to a stop beside a black Ford. The Ford's door opened and the former Lester Gillis, presently calling himself Jimmie Burnett of Sausalito, stepped out to greet his wife and son.

A few days later the young couple and their little boy arrived on the Pacific coast.

*I met one kid whose company I enjoyed, a sharp young guy with a
teenager's face and good taste in clothes. He was Lester Gillis, who would
one day be the notorious Baby Face Nelson. He was an escapee out of
Illinois, and the Nevada boys were taking care of him. I used to go out to
his place and have meals with him and his wife and two children. They
were a pleasant family.*
— From *The Alvin Karpis Story*

CHAPTER 4

NEVADA BLUES

NELSON'S FIRST STOP ON his journey west was Reno, and his first act after stepping
off the train was to find a phone to call Bill Graham and announce his arrival.

William J. "Curly" Graham and his chief associate, James C. "Red" McKay,
were already living legends in the desert community declaring itself "The
Biggest Little City in the World." When the Nevada Legislature legalized gambling in 1931, Graham was ready with the influence, bankroll, and foresight to
turn Reno into an enticing mecca for tourists hungry for action. They found it
first and foremost at the glitzy Bank Club, which Graham had up and operating
on day one. During the following months he and McKay added the Rex Club
on Virginia Street, the Haymarket Club in Douglas Alley, the Monte Carlo,
and the plush Cal-Neva Lodge within spitting distance of the California border. Graham and his partner also owned a sizable interest in The Stockade, the
city's scandalous red light district.

Thanks in large part to Graham's efforts, Reno was booming in the spring
of 1932, despite the depression. San Francisco was only a little more than 200
miles away, and the Union Pacific's *City of Los Angeles* arrived daily, its coaches
packed with Californians attracted by the gambling, prostitution, and Nevada's

quickie divorce laws. Las Vegas, 450 miles to the south, was fifteen years away from mounting any serious competition.

His remarkable success in Reno left Graham enshrined in Nevada history as the state's great pioneer casino tycoon and McKay as the financial wizard who stood behind him. But they were much more than that, although by their looks one could hardly tell. Graham was tall, rangy, and wavy-haired, resembling an aging cowboy decked out in his city clothes, or somebody's good-natured uncle. McKay was short and squat, his best smile making him appear like a disenchanted frog. Both wore glasses, and both were equally ruthless players within and outside the limits of the law.

In addition to the casinos they owned outright, it was rumored that the pair received a percentage from every gambling joint in the city and many more across the state. Anyone hoping to share in the action around Reno swiftly learned that no one operated in the territory controlled by Graham and McKay unless the pair allowed it and received proper tribute.

Graham also earned a reputation as a crack shot and a tough man to tangle with. In the summer of 1931 an argument with "Blackie" McCracken, one his faro dealers at the Haymarket Club, ended with Graham pulling a six-shooter and emptying it into his employee. When the sheriff arrived on the scene and found a gun lying next to McCracken's corpse, he ruled the killing "justifiable homicide" on the spot.

Incredibly, Graham and McKay managed to operate behind a facade of respectability, presenting themselves as conventional businessmen and civic leaders. Heavyweight boxer Jack Dempsey was a onetime partner in some of their enterprises, helping to draw and promote championship bouts in Reno. Actress Clara Bow was one of their favorite patrons—until she lost $35,000 at the Cal-Neva roulette table one night and refused to pay her debt. The pair were always rubbing elbows with celebrities, sports figures, and prominent politicians, who invariably voted the way Graham and McKay desired on crucial bills.

At first Nelson was enthralled and a bit overwhelmed by the new environment. He was taken more with the sun-drenched scenery—the desert, sagebrush, and rugged slopes of the Sierras—than with the gambling action and other pleasures sought by most newcomers to Reno.

Graham liked him instantly. "Call me Curly," he repeatedly told the young refugee when Nelson persisted in calling him Mr. Graham for the first week or so. "Everyone else does."

People in Reno came to know Nelson as "Jimmie," the alias he adopted after his escape and used—together with a variety of surnames—for the remaining two and a half years of his life. (In his letters he always spelled the name with *ie* instead of the traditional *y*.) According to one source, it was Graham who suggested the name, either because Nelson "looked like a Jimmie" or because he reminded Graham of actor James Cagney.

Using the name James J. Johnson, Nelson spent his first two weeks in Reno at the Anderson Hotel while performing various duties for his hosts, usually errands involving considerable driving. Later he moved to a cottage known as the Log Cabin near Graham's Cal-Neva Lodge on the northeast shore of Lake Tahoe.

The Cal-Neva, so named because the nine-story, 220-room resort actually straddled the state line, had been purchased by Graham and McKay from a San Francisco tycoon a few years earlier. With its magnificent view of Crystal Bay, rustic log exterior, stone vestibule, wood-beamed cathedral ceiling, and massive granite fireplace, the lodge became a favorite attraction and playground for the owners' celebrity friends. (In the 1960's Frank Sinatra purchased it to entertain his "Rat Pack" pals and such notables as Marilyn Monroe, mobster Sam Giancana, and, it was often rumored, President John F. Kennedy.)

For two or three weeks Nelson served as an assistant to the lodge's manager, Henry Orlando Hall, known as Henry O. or simply Tex to his friends. Described as a "Reno sportsman," a onetime cowboy, and the most trusted of Graham and McKay's many associates, Hall was a thick-set man of fifty-one with a square, leathery face and a heavy drawl. During their brief time together, he grew especially fond of the young fugitive.

In early April Graham, evidently feeling that Nelson's talents were not being utilized fully, or perhaps sensing that the baby-faced refugee felt ill at ease in the Cal-Neva's elegant setting, sent him to his underworld affiliates on the West Coast. Nelson checked in at the Andromeda Cafe on Columbus Avenue in San Francisco and was escorted by bartender Freddie Field to a back room to meet James J. Griffin, the proprietor. Griffin, having received a call from Graham, was expecting him.

Over the next few days Nelson was introduced to a parade of local characters living to the left of the law. The most significant was Hans Leon Strittmatter, chief associate of rum-runner Joe Parente. "We hear good things about you from the Touhys," Strittmatter said in his thick Teutonic accent. "Our operation could use an extra hand, if you feel up to it. There's some risk involved."

"From the feds?" Nelson inquired.

"Nah, we pay them off," Strittmatter laughed. "They are more a nuisance than a threat. Our competitors are the real pain in the ass. Hijackings—we got birds almost every night trying to put the snatch on our shipments. We need some boys who are good drivers and can handle a gun if things get dicey."

The offer appealed to Nelson. "Count me in," he said.

Strittmatter took his new recruit back to Sausalito, the Parente outfit's base camp for their smuggling activities. After finding Nelson a place to stay, Strittmatter brought him to his store, the Bridge Cigar Company, one of the gang's many "fronts." It was there that Nelson met another fledgling member of the Parente operation, a tall fellow with intense, sunken eyes and a jutting jaw. His name was John Paul Chase.

Born December 26, 1901, in San Francisco, Chase was the second oldest of five sons. His father worked for the U.S. mint until his death in 1913; his mother died four years later. The five teenage orphans were taken in by Mrs. I. H. Cheney, a family friend living in San Raphael, California. One of the brothers died a few years later, and the surviving four—Frank, John, Charles, and Ambrose—grew up and went their separate ways.

Mrs. Cheney later stated that she regarded Johnny as the most exceptional of the bunch. He was a big, broad-shouldered lad with a slim waist and long legs. His dark, lean, expressive face was Hollywood handsome. More than one person remarked about his Valentino looks, and Chase often wore his coal-black hair slicked back to enhance his Sheik-like features.

Beyond his good looks, however, there was not much there. Johnny proved to be amiable, unambitious, and not terribly bright. After a single year of high school he dropped out and enrolled in night courses to earn a machinist's degree. For a while he was content to work on a dairy ranch outside San Raphael, and his proudest moment was winning the annual Marin County milking championship.

Eventually he obtained a job as an office boy for the Northwestern Pacific Railroad at Tiburon, California. In time he moved up to machinist apprentice, then spent the next four years working in railway shops, the only true period of stability in his adult life. After leaving the railroad he drifted through an array of oddly unrelated jobs: For a year and a half he was the private chauffeur for Archbishop Hanna of San Francisco, then he caught a ship sailing to the Orient, worked briefly as a machinist in the Far East, and upon his return took a job at the California state fish hatchery in Mount Shasta.

About 1930 Chase fell in with bootlegger Ross "Midnight" Turney. From that point on he was connected with one liquor-smuggling operation after another but never rose to a place of prominence within the gangs. By late 1931 he was working exclusively with the Parente outfit.

Nelson and Chase quickly became inseparable friends. For his part, Nelson displayed an unconditional trust in his new pal, revealing that he was an escaped convict from Joliet and sharing stories of his illegal exploits. Chase felt privileged to be taken into the younger man's confidence, and he was genuinely impressed, perhaps even a bit awed, listening to Nelson recount his Chicago crime stories. Before long Chase was introducing Nelson around the Bay Area as his half-brother.

In time Nelson got to meet the rest of the bootlegging mob, including Joseph John Parente himself, the recognized "king of the Pacific Coast rumrunners." He was a shrewd, round-shouldered man, born in Italy in 1889 and raised in Pennsylvania. In his late teens he relocated to San Francisco and rapidly established himself as the Bay Area's premier bootlegger through the latter half of the Twenties. He served a stretch in San Quentin for forgery, and he was indicted twice in 1928 for violating Prohibition laws and was heavily fined. As mobsters go, Parente had some admirable qualities: He abhorred violence, often warning his henchmen that he would not tolerate it, and he also aspired to be an honest citizen. Foreseeing the end of Prohibition, his goal was to amass enough capital to get out of the rackets and finance a respectable business within the limits of the law.

Parente's associates in the smuggling trade were a mixed bag of local businessmen who were using their companies as fronts and an assortment of Runyonesque criminals from the Bay Area. Aside from Strittmatter, his right hand man, there were Frank "Nippi" Constantine, a short, swarthy young *paisan* who served as the gang's chief lieutenant; Anthony "Soap" Moreno, a stocky, neckless figure with a bulldog's face who was a former bodyguard for Jack Dempsey and Parente's main liaison with the Graham-McKay syndicate in Reno; Ralph "Scabootch" Rizzo, a rotund bail bondsman who handled payoffs to police and politicians; and William Schivo, ex-convict and San Francisco manufacturer whose box factory on Davis Street was used for storing and shipping the mob's merchandise. Other notables included Louis "Doc Bones" Tambini, Len "Red" Kennedy, Castro Arverson, and Louis Leonhart.

One of the last members of the operation Nelson met was a recent recruit like himself. Joseph Raymond Negri was twenty-six, chunky, round-faced, wavy-haired, and stood five-feet-nine and weighed 200 pounds. He preferred to be called Joe, but the label "Fatso" had followed him since his teens. Born in San Francisco and raised around the raucous, anything-goes Barbary Coast, Negri's launched his criminal career in his pre-teen years by rolling drunks and stripping cars. By age twenty he had graduated to armed robbery. After serving four years in San Quentin, he was paroled in 1929 and briefly worked as a taxi driver in a token effort to go straight. Like Chase, he had been loosely connected with a many bootleggers before joining Parente.

During his first couple of months in the gang, Negri served in a minor, part-time capacity, driving trucks and helping to load or unload shipments. One evening while awaiting a delivery near Half Moon Bay, Negri noticed a new face among the regulars. "Who is that?" he asked Hans Strittmatter.

"That's Jimmie," was the reply. "He's gonna work with us."

A few days later Negri was called to Strittmatter's cigar store. He was ushered into a back room and told that a shipment had been hijacked and traced to a man named Eddie. Strittmatter wanted Negri to regain the stolen goods and said he would send along "a couple of the boys" to help. Negri agreed to the assignment, and Strittmatter brought in two men, one short and blond, the other tall and dark. "This is Jimmie and Johnny," he said, indicating the pair. "They're gonna help you get our liquor back."

The trio piled into a car and drove to Eddie's house, where the hijacked cases were reportedly stored in the cellar. Once their vehicle pulled to a stop, neither of Negri's companions made a move; they merely stared silently at the front door. "Well, come on!" Negri urged. "Let's go in and get it. What are we waiting for?"

At that moment Eddie emerged from the house and stopped in his tracks at the sight of the three stone-faced men glaring at him from the car. He surrendered the cases without any argument.

Later Strittmatter revealed that the job, though genuine, had been given to both Negri and Nelson as a test. When told the details, Parente was especially pleased that the trio did not resort to any physical violence or gunplay to retrieve the merchandise. "Hell," Negri proudly remarked, "we didn't even have to get out of the car. When he saw us sitting out there, he turned so yellow he couldn't give the liquor back fast enough."

Negri learned that he had made a favorable impression on Nelson as well as Parente. "Jimmie thinks a lot of you," Chase confided one day, explaining that when Negri declared in the car that they should "go in and get it," Nelson had regarded it as "a ballsy move."

From that moment on, Parente and Strittmatter used the trio as their top security team to safeguard the transfer of liquor shipments. The bulk of the gang's merchandise came from Parente's business partners in Vancouver, British Columbia, usually two or three deliveries a week. The "mother ship" would anchor just beyond the five-mile limit, and the smugglers would transfer the cases of rich Canadian liquor to speedboats and ferry them to shore. Their favorite landing spots lay along the rugged coastline of Sonoma County, where countless jagged inlets, coves, and steep craggy cliffs afforded almost perfect protection and seclusion for the clandestine activities. Nelson, Negri, and Chase, armed with pistols, would stand guard while the landing party loaded their truck and one of Parente's lieutenants—Constantine, Moreno, Kennedy, or Tambini—acted as "beach boss" to supervise the transfer.

When the truck was full, Negri would take the wheel while Nelson and Chase followed closely in a car, watching for lawmen and potential hijackers until the truck arrived safely at its destination.

Nelson earned almost $300 a week for his role in the smuggling operation. Within a couple of weeks he was able to afford his own car, a 1930 Ford sedan. A few days after that, he requested some time off, and when he reappeared a week later he had his wife and son with him.

Calling himself Jimmie Burnett, Nelson and his family rented a second-floor apartment in the four-story Mohn rooming house on the corner of Benita and Turney, just three blocks from Strittmatter's cigar store. Ironically, the hilltop apartment building was directly across the street from the house of Sausalito's chief of police, Manuel Menotti, who often exchanged a friendly hello with the young couple and their little boy.

❀ ❀ ❀

Over the next six months Nelson, working with Chase and Negri, continued to serve as a guard for Parente's gang. For the most part the moonlit rendezvous with the cargo boats and the trips along the pre-dawn country roads into the city were uneventful. According to Negri, however, the excursions sometimes became exciting.

One evening Negri and Chase traded places, and Nelson noticed a car following them. "What do you think?" Negri asked from the passenger's side of the escort car. "Chowder men [Prohibition agents] or hijackers?"

"Could be either or neither," Nelson replied. "Let's find out."

Nelson accelerated. As he passed the truck he blinked his lights twice, a signal to Chase to take the next side road. When Chase made the turn, the other car continued to follow. Nelson made an immediate U-turn.

"Back when I was a cabbie, I could get from one end of 'Frisco to the other faster than anyone," Negri boasted. "Want me to take the wheel?"

"Are you kidding?" said Nelson, displaying a wolfish grin. "Just sit back and watch an old dirt-track racer handle the road."

In a matter of seconds Nelson was approaching the rear of the mystery car so rapidly that Negri braced himself for a collision. Pulling within inches of his quarry, Nelson abruptly swerved into the opposite lane, pulling alongside the vehicle and forcing it onto the shoulder. When the driver attempted to fight his way back onto the road, Nelson managed to deftly lock the right side of his rear bumper onto the other car's front bumper. Then, veering sharply back toward the shoulder, he sent the other auto crashing into a fence.

Two days later Negri noticed an article about a carload of federal agents that had been run off the road by suspected smugglers.

On another evening Negri and Nelson were discussing guns, the latter's favorite subject along with cars and his family. Negri mentioned that he was keeping a machine gun at his place for a friend who had used it in a robbery six months earlier. Nelson's narrow eyes suddenly became the size of silver dollars. He eagerly asked to see it.

Negri was reluctant to show off the weapon, fearing that if he were ever caught with it he might be implicated in the holdup. Nelson persisted and gradually wore him down. They drove to Negri's apartment above a restaurant in Half Moon Bay, and when Negri showed the machine gun to his friend, he recalled later that Nelson "looked like a little kid with a new toy."

"This is a honey, one of the good ones," Nelson remarked, admiring the weapon as if it were a priceless artifact.

"Careful, Jimmie," Negri warned. "It's loaded to the gills."

"Hey, don't sweat it, Fats. I'm a Chicago boy, I know all about these babies."

A second after he spoke the words, the gun accidentally fired a shot into the floor. Minutes later there was a fierce knocking at the door. Negri, fearing it was the police, frantically concealed the weapon. But it was only the enraged owner of the restaurant below, complaining that the bullet had embedded itself in a kitchen counter just inches away from where his cook was mincing onions. The terrified cook had run off, leaving the owner to prepare the remaining meals. The two young men apologized and promised it wouldn't happen again.

Negri later insisted (in his highly exaggerated account, "In the Hinges of Hell") that Nelson talked him into bringing along the machine gun on their midnight runs, but that claim contradicts his statement to government agents that Nelson never carried anything but a pistol during working hours. Many writers accept Negri's story and its ridiculous sequel—in which Nelson captured a quartet of hijackers and almost massacred them before Negri boldly interceded on their behalf—simply because so little is known about Nelson's six-month sojourn in Sausalito.

The scarcity of information from this period suggests that Nelson was conducting himself in a moderate fashion, doing little to call attention to himself other than riding shotgun behind the delivery trucks. Brandishing a machine gun in the presence of Parente's lieutenants (as Negri asserted) would have infuriated Parente and led to Nelson's banishment from the mobster's prodigious sphere of protection.

The fact that Nelson confided to just two people—Strittmatter and Chase—that he was an escaped convict is further evidence he was keeping a low profile. When not performing his nocturnal duties for Parente, he lived quietly in his hilltop apartment with his wife and son, presenting a picture-perfect image of a modest young family. They visited the beach, went to movies, often took Ronnie to a neighborhood ice cream parlor, and regularly attended Mass at a nearby Catholic church.

Late that summer Helen fell gravely ill, complaining of severe stomach pains. Nelson went to Strittmatter, who recommended a hospital which assured the privacy of its patients.

Thomas C. Williams was general manager and part owner of the Vallejo General Hospital. Serving in that capacity for over a decade, he had established himself as one of Vallejo's leading citizens, a pillar of the community acclaimed for his philanthropic deeds. But behind the veneer of respectability existed a man no one in the bayside town could have imagined. His real name was Tobias William Cohen, and some thirty-five years earlier he had committed a string of burglaries across the Northwest and spent years languishing in a Montana prison. Upon his release he scraped together the profits from his crimes—which he had shrewdly deposited in a series of bank accounts to earn interest while he served his time—and arrived in Vallejo under the assumed name of Williams, presenting himself as a businessman.

Now, three and a half decades later, the underworld still knew him as "Tobe," a "right guy," and his squeaky-clean position in the community enabled

eanwhile, was growing increasingly restless. He was eager to get back
ness of banditry, and the steady stream of underworld characters pass-
Reno brought stories of the explosion of crime currently sweeping
t. Conditions were ripe for plunder.

d of unique social elements had combined to produce an unprece-
of lawlessness in the nation's heartland. Foremost was the advent
Depression, now in its third full year and becoming bleaker with
ght. Family fortunes were obliterated, individual savings erased,
property seized, and the economy was in the midst of a seemingly
osedive. More than twelve million persons—a fourth of America's
were unemployed. Embittered and desperate, many blamed
or their misfortunes.

al level much of the discontent was directed at banks. The gen-
was that greedy bankers—an image long nurtured among the
in the Midwest and Southwest—had squeezed, drained, and
ows, orphans, and common folk; thus, it was widely believed,
e fat with foreclosure cash. The millions who were suffering and
ecially the more destitute in bread lines or soup kitchens—
kers as symbols of evil and avarice.

prise, then, that banks became the main targets of depression-
etween 1931 and 1934 they were plundered at a rate of two per
ith three of every four such robberies occurring in the Midwest.
era Americans found a lot to admire in the bank robbers who,
mobsters with foreign names and foreign ways, were "all-
who were only "stealing from the banks what the banks stole
The outlaw thus became a new breed of folk hero, represent-
ntempt for banking institutions.

ee Prohibition paved the way for the public's nodding accep-
and its disdain for lawmakers and law enforcers. The major-
garded the Volstead Act with obvious scorn and open defi-
wonder that gangsters—whether big-city mobsters or
ers—and their underworld associates were viewed more as
nd justifiable, if not legitimate, businessmen rather than as
Al Capone, who often went to great lengths to promote his
eated by many in Chicago as a celebrity, admired for the
thumbed his pudgy nose at the law. When the government
own in 1932, it wasn't for murder or bootlegging but for
taxes—another offense the public could easily excuse.
dered Capone a thug and a threat to society felt the gov-
rue justice by creating a case out of a legal loophole.
public's perception of right and wrong was particularly

him to fund illegal activities. He had become the unofficial financier for much of the West Coast's bootlegging business and at times—and for the right price—was known to assist criminals in need or on the run. Through a network of gangland connections, including Bill Graham and Joe Parente, he used his investment in the hospital to provide specialized services—the occasional illegal operation for a girlfriend or patching up incriminating gunshot wounds.

When Nelson arrived at the hospital asking to see the chief administrator, he was led into an office and greeted by a rather startling figure. A few months shy of his sixty-third birthday, Tobe Williams stood six-foot-seven and his lanky frame was topped with fluffy snow-white hair. He moved about stiffly, leaning on a polished ebony cane to compensate for a wooden left leg. Two fingers were missing from his right hand, the digits—along with the absent limb—blown off in a bungled attempt to dynamite a safe during his second-story days.

After introducing himself, Nelson—as instructed by Strittmatter—announced, "I was told to see the Goniff from Galway."

"That would be me, my boy," Williams answered with a wide, snaggletoothed grin. The phrase served as a password letting Williams know the visitor had been sent by underworld confederates. Nelson explained his situation and was assured by Williams that his wife's treatment would be held in strict confidence.

On September 12 Helen was admitted to the hospital under the name Mrs. James Burnett of Sausalito and immediately scheduled for an appendectomy. Asked to list his wife's nearest relative, Nelson penciled in "William Graham, 548 California Avenue, Reno, Nev., telephone—Reno 5215."

For the next five days Nelson resided at the Casa de Vallejo Hotel while spending the greater part of his time at the hospital. Helen's attending physician, Dr. Edward Peterson, and several nurses later remarked how impressed they were with the young man's obvious devotion to his wife, especially after he told them he had been granted time off from work in order to remain almost constantly at Helen's bedside. The staff made allowances for him to remain after visiting hours to continue his vigil. On two occasions Mrs. Burnett and her husband were visited by a curious pair, one described as tall and lean (John Paul Chase), the other as short and dumpy (Fatso Negri).

Evidently Nelson made a favorable impression on Williams as well. Whenever he wasn't doting over his ailing wife he could be found in Tobe's office. The pair frequently sent out for coffee and sandwiches and talked for hours. Williams was fascinated by the fugitive's stories about Chicago mobsters.

Upon Helen's release from the hospital on September 17, the couple returned to their Sausalito apartment. A few days later Helen received a surprise when she was reunited with their daughter. Hoping to brighten his wife's spirits during her recovery, Nelson arranged for his sister Leona to bring Darlene to the West Coast, along with letters, gifts, and get-well wishes from the Warwick and Gillis families.

Leona had some good news of her own to share: The only unmarried Gillis sibling had recently become engaged. Leona's fiancee, William McMahon, was serving with the Coast Guard and expected to be relocated to a station on the West Coast within a year. They were planning a spring wedding.

Nelson took Leona to dinner in San Francisco, showing her the sights and even introducing her to some of his fellow smugglers in the Parente gang. Leona shared the latest family news from home: Julie and her husband were expecting their sixth child and had moved into a larger apartment on South Marshfield. Their mother, having shifted from one family location to another, had finally settled at the new Fitzsimmons home. Amy and her second husband, Fred Kenniston, had separated briefly, then reunited and moved to Indiana where they were hired to manage a posh, exclusive hotel. Jack Perkins, who dutifully acted as the go-between in delivering the letters Nelson and Helen sent to family members, had been constantly harassed by the police and arrested for a variety of offenses—but the charges never stuck.

Nelson, now in his seventh month of exile, confided to Leona that he was growing homesick. He missed all of them, especially their mother. But while he ached to be back, he told her it was better for the moment to be living by the bay instead of being hunted back in Chicago.

Once Helen was well enough, Nelson returned to the graveyard shift, trailing liquor trucks along the back roads of Sonoma and Marin Counties. A month passed uneventfully, then one day in late October one of Parente's men was flipping through a recent copy of *True Detective Line-Up* and spotted a familiar face. "Hey, Fatso," he called to Negri. "Ain't this Jimmie?"

There on the page, appearing with the caption "escaped convict/notorious bank robber," was the Joliet mug shot of Lester Gillis, alias Baby Face Nelson. Negri was stunned, for despite his close association with Nelson over the past few months he had never heard him speak of his past. By the time Negri reached Chase with the news it was too late. "He's already gone," Chase told him.

Apparently others in the Bay Area had picked up the magazine and noticed the resemblance, too. A source within the Sausalito police phoned Strittmatter to tell him the department had received a report from a citizen "fingering Jimmie as a wanted fugitive." Strittmatter immediately alerted Nelson, and within a few hours the young fugitive and his wife had gathered their kids and all they could carry and had taken to the road.

Their destination was Reno, where Bill Graham once again received Nelson with open arms and assured him that he could rest easy now that he was back in Graham's town. "No one goes to the slammer round here less I say so," he said.

Graham arranged for the family to move into a furnished bungalow at 126 Caliente Street. Nelson, now calling himself Jimmie Burnell, was put back on

the payroll as Graham's personal chauffeur and [...] sisted primarily of running errands, servicing [...] jobs." Among his duties was providing his boss [...] was happening around Reno and who was inv[...] casinos and clubs, chatting amiably with bar[...] patrons, and he frequently came away with use[...] ming profits, winning too much, or not doing [...]

Graham trusted him implicitly, and whe[...] affiliation arrived in Reno he often solicite[...] gangland figures flocking to Reno that fall ca[...] where temperatures were dropping. Seekin[...] Reno's promised protection and twenty-f[...] lance criminals of all kinds converged or[...] personally check on or keep track of. He [...] and who were potential troublemakers. S[...] ers he knew only by reputation. Anyone[...] automatically accepted by the gambling [...]

Overseeing the maintenance and [...] Graham-McKay vehicles brought Ne[...] Cochran, owner and operator of the [...] Street. The two became friends. Co[...] pilot with an angular face and a narr[...] young man's knowledge of mechanic[...] known close affiliation with Bill Gr[...]

In time Cochran's wife, Anna[...] often visited each other for backya[...] One night Cochran spoke of his e[...] Jimmie the chance to fly with h[...] inside a plane, responded with a [...] notorious, you can fly me out of [...]

Now it was Cochran's turn[...] young man who preferred soft [...] and kids ever becoming a dan[...] and McKay.

Evidently Helen found R[...] spent considerable time wi[...] Graham and Mrs. McKay e[...] brought her along on sho[...] domestic role. The bunga[...] apartments.

Nelson, m[...]
to the busi[...]
ing throug[...]
the Midwe[...]

A myria[...]
dented wav[...]
of the Great[...]
no end in s[...]
homes lost, [...]
irreversible n[...]
work force—[...]
Washington f[...]

At the loc[...]
eral consensus[...]
impoverished [...]
preyed on wid[...]
their vaults we[...]
struggling—esp[...]
viewed the ban[...]

It was no su[...]
era desperados. [...]
day nationally, w[...]
Many depression[...]
unlike big-city [...]
American" boys [...]
from the people. [...]
ing the public's co[...]

To a great deg[...]
tance of criminals[...]
ity of Americans r[...]
ance. It was littl[...]
backwoods bootleg[...]
public benefactors a[...]
a national menace. [...]
public image, was t[...]
garish, cocky way he[...]
finally brought him [...]
failing to pay incom[...]
Even those who cons[...]
ernment sidestepped [...]

The change in th[...]

him to fund illegal activities. He had become the unofficial financier for much of the West Coast's bootlegging business and at times—and for the right price—was known to assist criminals in need or on the run. Through a network of gangland connections, including Bill Graham and Joe Parente, he used his investment in the hospital to provide specialized services—the occasional illegal operation for a girlfriend or patching up incriminating gunshot wounds.

When Nelson arrived at the hospital asking to see the chief administrator, he was led into an office and greeted by a rather startling figure. A few months shy of his sixty-third birthday, Tobe Williams stood six-foot-seven and his lanky frame was topped with fluffy snow-white hair. He moved about stiffly, leaning on a polished ebony cane to compensate for a wooden left leg. Two fingers were missing from his right hand, the digits—along with the absent limb—blown off in a bungled attempt to dynamite a safe during his second-story days.

After introducing himself, Nelson—as instructed by Strittmatter—announced, "I was told to see the Goniff from Galway."

"That would be me, my boy," Williams answered with a wide, snaggletoothed grin. The phrase served as a password letting Williams know the visitor had been sent by underworld confederates. Nelson explained his situation and was assured by Williams that his wife's treatment would be held in strict confidence.

On September 12 Helen was admitted to the hospital under the name Mrs. James Burnett of Sausalito and immediately scheduled for an appendectomy. Asked to list his wife's nearest relative, Nelson penciled in "William Graham, 548 California Avenue, Reno, Nev., telephone—Reno 5215."

For the next five days Nelson resided at the Casa de Vallejo Hotel while spending the greater part of his time at the hospital. Helen's attending physician, Dr. Edward Peterson, and several nurses later remarked how impressed they were with the young man's obvious devotion to his wife, especially after he told them he had been granted time off from work in order to remain almost constantly at Helen's bedside. The staff made allowances for him to remain after visiting hours to continue his vigil. On two occasions Mrs. Burnett and her husband were visited by a curious pair, one described as tall and lean (John Paul Chase), the other as short and dumpy (Fatso Negri).

Evidently Nelson made a favorable impression on Williams as well. Whenever he wasn't doting over his ailing wife he could be found in Tobe's office. The pair frequently sent out for coffee and sandwiches and talked for hours. Williams was fascinated by the fugitive's stories about Chicago mobsters.

Upon Helen's release from the hospital on September 17, the couple returned to their Sausalito apartment. A few days later Helen received a surprise when she was reunited with their daughter. Hoping to brighten his wife's spirits during her recovery, Nelson arranged for his sister Leona to bring Darlene to the West Coast, along with letters, gifts, and get-well wishes from the Warwick and Gillis families.

Leona had some good news of her own to share: The only unmarried Gillis sibling had recently become engaged. Leona's fiancee, William McMahon, was serving with the Coast Guard and expected to be relocated to a station on the West Coast within a year. They were planning a spring wedding.

Nelson took Leona to dinner in San Francisco, showing her the sights and even introducing her to some of his fellow smugglers in the Parente gang. Leona shared the latest family news from home: Julie and her husband were expecting their sixth child and had moved into a larger apartment on South Marshfield. Their mother, having shifted from one family location to another, had finally settled at the new Fitzsimmons home. Amy and her second husband, Fred Kenniston, had separated briefly, then reunited and moved to Indiana where they were hired to manage a posh, exclusive hotel. Jack Perkins, who dutifully acted as the go-between in delivering the letters Nelson and Helen sent to family members, had been constantly harassed by the police and arrested for a variety of offenses—but the charges never stuck.

Nelson, now in his seventh month of exile, confided to Leona that he was growing homesick. He missed all of them, especially their mother. But while he ached to be back, he told her it was better for the moment to be living by the bay instead of being hunted back in Chicago.

Once Helen was well enough, Nelson returned to the graveyard shift, trailing liquor trucks along the back roads of Sonoma and Marin Counties. A month passed uneventfully, then one day in late October one of Parente's men was flipping through a recent copy of *True Detective Line-Up* and spotted a familiar face. "Hey, Fatso," he called to Negri. "Ain't this Jimmie?"

There on the page, appearing with the caption "escaped convict/notorious bank robber," was the Joliet mug shot of Lester Gillis, alias Baby Face Nelson. Negri was stunned, for despite his close association with Nelson over the past few months he had never heard him speak of his past. By the time Negri reached Chase with the news it was too late. "He's already gone," Chase told him.

Apparently others in the Bay Area had picked up the magazine and noticed the resemblance, too. A source within the Sausalito police phoned Strittmatter to tell him the department had received a report from a citizen "fingering Jimmie as a wanted fugitive." Strittmatter immediately alerted Nelson, and within a few hours the young fugitive and his wife had gathered their kids and all they could carry and had taken to the road.

Their destination was Reno, where Bill Graham once again received Nelson with open arms and assured him that he could rest easy now that he was back in Graham's town. "No one goes to the slammer round here less I say so," he said.

Graham arranged for the family to move into a furnished bungalow at 126 Caliente Street. Nelson, now calling himself Jimmie Burnell, was put back on the payroll as Graham's personal chauffeur and bodyguard. His dual role consisted primarily of running errands, servicing vehicles, and performing "odd jobs." Among his duties was providing his bosses with verbal reports on what was happening around Reno and who was involved. He regularly cruised the casinos and clubs, chatting amiably with bartenders, pit bosses, dealers, and patrons, and he frequently came away with useful information—who was skimming profits, winning too much, or not doing their jobs.

Graham trusted him implicitly, and when new faces claiming underworld affiliation arrived in Reno he often solicited Nelson's opinion. Many of the gangland figures flocking to Reno that fall came from Chicago and the Midwest where temperatures were dropping. Seeking to escape the cold while enjoying Reno's promised protection and twenty-four hour action, mobsters and freelance criminals of all kinds converged on the city—too many for Graham to personally check on or keep track of. He needed to know who could be trusted and who were potential troublemakers. Some were well-known to Nelson; others he knew only by reputation. Anyone receiving Nelson's seal of approval was automatically accepted by the gambling czar and his associates.

Overseeing the maintenance and occasional repairs of the small fleet of Graham-McKay vehicles brought Nelson into frequent contact with Frank Cochran, owner and operator of the Air Service Garage on South Virginia Street. The two became friends. Cochran—a slender, square-shouldered ex-pilot with an angular face and a narrow, dimpled chin—was impressed with the young man's knowledge of mechanics, as well as his generous tips and his widely known close affiliation with Bill Graham.

In time Cochran's wife, Anna, grew close to Helen, and the two families often visited each other for backyard barbecues and an evening of playing cards. One night Cochran spoke of his experiences as a pilot and offered his new pal Jimmie the chance to fly with him sometime. Nelson, who had never been inside a plane, responded with a hearty laugh, "Maybe one day when I become notorious, you can fly me out of the country."

Now it was Cochran's turn to laugh. He couldn't imagine the clean-cut young man who preferred soft drinks to beer and seemed so devoted to his wife and kids ever becoming a dangerous criminal, despite his close ties to Graham and McKay.

Evidently Helen found Reno to her liking. Along with Anna Cochran she spent considerable time with the wives of Nelson's employers. Both Mrs. Graham and Mrs. McKay entertained the teenage mother at their homes or brought her along on shopping trips. But most of all Helen enjoyed her domestic role. The bungalow seemed more like a home than their previous apartments.

❊ ❊ ❊

Nelson, meanwhile, was growing increasingly restless. He was eager to get back to the business of banditry, and the steady stream of underworld characters passing through Reno brought stories of the explosion of crime currently sweeping the Midwest. Conditions were ripe for plunder.

A myriad of unique social elements had combined to produce an unprecedented wave of lawlessness in the nation's heartland. Foremost was the advent of the Great Depression, now in its third full year and becoming bleaker with no end in sight. Family fortunes were obliterated, individual savings erased, homes lost, property seized, and the economy was in the midst of a seemingly irreversible nosedive. More than twelve million persons—a fourth of America's work force—were unemployed. Embittered and desperate, many blamed Washington for their misfortunes.

At the local level much of the discontent was directed at banks. The general consensus was that greedy bankers—an image long nurtured among the impoverished in the Midwest and Southwest—had squeezed, drained, and preyed on widows, orphans, and common folk; thus, it was widely believed, their vaults were fat with foreclosure cash. The millions who were suffering and struggling—especially the more destitute in bread lines or soup kitchens—viewed the bankers as symbols of evil and avarice.

It was no surprise, then, that banks became the main targets of depression-era desperados. Between 1931 and 1934 they were plundered at a rate of two per day nationally, with three of every four such robberies occurring in the Midwest. Many depression-era Americans found a lot to admire in the bank robbers who, unlike big-city mobsters with foreign names and foreign ways, were "all-American" boys who were only "stealing from the banks what the banks stole from the people." The outlaw thus became a new breed of folk hero, representing the public's contempt for banking institutions.

To a great degree Prohibition paved the way for the public's nodding acceptance of criminals and its disdain for lawmakers and law enforcers. The majority of Americans regarded the Volstead Act with obvious scorn and open defiance. It was little wonder that gangsters—whether big-city mobsters or backwoods bootleggers—and their underworld associates were viewed more as public benefactors and justifiable, if not legitimate, businessmen rather than as a national menace. Al Capone, who often went to great lengths to promote his public image, was treated by many in Chicago as a celebrity, admired for the garish, cocky way he thumbed his pudgy nose at the law. When the government finally brought him down in 1932, it wasn't for murder or bootlegging but for failing to pay income taxes—another offense the public could easily excuse. Even those who considered Capone a thug and a threat to society felt the government sidestepped true justice by creating a case out of a legal loophole.

The change in the public's perception of right and wrong was particularly evident in the films coming out of Hollywood. Gangster movies such as *Little Caesar* (1930) with Edward G. Robinson, *Public Enemy* (1931) starring James Cagney, and *Scarface* (1932) with Paul Muni were extremely popular, creating a whole new genre for filmmakers. Prior to the depression Hollywood was careful to provide a noble, responsible hero for filmgoers to applaud and identify with, but in the early Thirties the grim, gritty crime flicks became the first screen stories to present a villain as the lead character, the advent of the anti-hero. The protagonist was usually portrayed as an outsider and a rebel—tough, mean, amoral, clawing his way to the top through sheer ruthlessness. In the end he always paid for his sins, but along the way audiences were treated to a display of open defiance of conventional society through his exploits.

The moviegoing public obviously loved the ride. The film gangster represented to some extent the angry, resentful social climate that existed within the nation. Without condoning the actions of these anti-heroes, audiences could applaud their anti-social behavior. In the midst of a stifling economic depression, it was invigorating to watch a screen character brutally brush aside customary mores and laws to get ahead.

At a time when Americans desperately needed national heroes, there were few traditional ones to be found. With faith in the country's leaders at a low ebb and a notable drought among dynamic sports figures—Babe Ruth and Red Grange were approaching the end of their careers and foreigners like Max Schmeling dominated the boxing arena—there also was widespread disenchantment and sometimes outright contempt for the once valiant figure of the American peace officer, another byproduct of the Prohibition era. Saddled with the Herculean task of upholding an unpopular and virtually unenforceable law, many lawmen at the local, county, state, and federal level lapsed into either apathy or corruption. This fact was also reflected in the early crime films, which often portrayed policemen as incompetent, crooked, and hopelessly ineffective.

Sadly the picture of corruption and inefficiency among law officers was not merely the product of Hollywood screenwriters. By 1930 every major metropolitan area in the Midwest had earned a reputation among criminal elements as a "safe city" or a "right town." The phenomenal growth and organization of the underworld during the preceding decade had resulted in a system of protection for crooks on the lam provided by the existing municipal powers. Often it was no more than a handful of elected officials or a few men in uniform, but there were always individuals in key positions to ensure that the fix was in. Visiting criminals needed only to check in with the local underworld boss or one of his associates to be granted a safe haven and, for the right price, supplied with valuable contacts inside the city—doctors, lawyers, fences, women, whatever was needed or desired.

This network of gangland-sponsored protection for criminals rendered the efforts of honest cops utterly useless. To make matters worse, most police forces were woefully understaffed, under-funded, and under-equipped to combat the machine gun-toting marauders of the era. Few departments had automatic weapons or even decent vehicles. There was a total lack of cooperation and communication among lawmen in different cities or states. Thus a gang that robbed a bank in Kansas needed only to cross the state line into Oklahoma or Missouri to be home free.

America's penal system at the time was archaic, often mismanaged, and shockingly overcrowded. Conditions were notably bad in state institutions, such as Lansing in Kansas, which was constructed to accommodate up to 900 inmates but whose cells were crammed with twice that number. Jefferson City in Missouri was almost as terrible, and McAllister in Oklahoma was worse. The much-quoted axiom that prisons are breeding grounds for crime was never more true than in the early Thirties. An incarcerated criminal usually made his most valuable contacts while doing time, and many of the major bank-robbing gangs of the depression were actually formed inside the walls of a state penitentiary.

Escapes were alarmingly frequent and, thanks to the crowded conditions and the susceptibility of guards and officials to bribes, not as difficult as one might think. More patient, less daring inmates pursued paroles and could obtain them in a variety of ways. At Lansing, for instance, a prisoner could shave years off his sentence by volunteering to work in the state's coal mines. Good behavior often ensured an early parole—prisons needed the room—and payoffs to state officials virtually guaranteed one.

All of these factors—economic despair, animosity toward banks, an absence of traditional heroes, Hollywood's glamorization of the gangster, the public's infatuation with real-life desperados and the press's exploitation of their escapades, inefficiency and corruption of police and public servants, urban sanctuaries for on-the-lam criminals, the failure of state prison systems—combined to create an ideal climate for the bands of bank-robbing outlaws descending on the Midwest.

One component rarely mentioned was the fact that, like the rest of the country, crime as a business suffered during the depression. When profits from bootlegging and other mob-controlled vices sharply plummeted, many underworld figures had to explore new avenues to augment their sagging incomes. In 1932 the situation worsened with the election of Franklin Roosevelt, who vowed to repeal Prohibition, the cornerstone on which underworld figures had built their criminal empires. Thus, many gangs no longer could afford to employ such affiliates as bootleggers, bodyguards, and drivers.

One of the great myths about the depression-era desperados was that they were primarily honest individuals who were forced into a life of crime by the hard economic times. While a few amateurs did gain notoriety, the vast majority of the successful bandits of the early Thirties were established criminals long before the depression struck. Many, in fact, were already skilled, seasoned bank robbers with years of experience.

In the first few years after the 1929 stock market crash a number of audacious, expert criminals rose to the front ranks of American thievery. The undisputed dean of bank robbers was Harvey John Bailey. Forty-seven years old in 1932, with dark eyes and bushy hair tinged with gray, he wore a perpetually phlegmatic expression on his square, distinguished face, looking more like a banker than a bandit. Between 1925 and 1929 he engineered and participated in nearly a dozen major Midwest bank holdups from Ohio to Kansas whose combined take amounted to almost a million dollars. Bailey had invested the greater part of his share, at least $100,000, in the stock market and was looking forward to retiring with his wife and two sons to a dairy farm in Wisconsin when the October 29 crash on Wall Street wiped out his fortune, driving him back to crime.

Bailey's methodical way of "casing a jug" became the standard blueprint for the new wave of bank robbers. Blessed with uncanny recall and an eye for detail, he often spent weeks planning a heist until every conceivable angle was laid out on paper and burned into his memory. Not only did the targeted bank's layout, alarm systems, schedules, and employees come under his meticulous scrutiny, he also studied the entire town and surrounding countryside. He developed and mastered the technique of "running the cat roads," designing a detailed and carefully measured escape route that traversed rural roads and avoided major highways and towns.

Bailey carefully picked his accomplices for each holdup and made sure each man was well rehearsed in all the particulars and knew his specific role. He was never the leader of one specific gang; his robbery team changed with each heist. He preferred to work with professionals like himself—men who approached the business of bank robbery with cool, quiet efficiency and were not prone to gunplay. It was a rare occasion when any shots were fired during a Bailey-arranged holdup.

Contemporaries who joined Bailey as partners from time to time included such legendary figures as Frank "Jelly" Nash, dubbed "the Gentleman Bandit" for his polite manner and meek appearance while staging nearly one hundred holdups during a quarter-century outlaw career; Eddie Bentz, renowned as one of gangland's best setup men, who helped Bailey and Nash engineer a $2.6 million bank heist in Lincoln, Nebraska; and Francis Keating and Thomas Holden, an inseparable pair of Chicago-bred bandits who were convicted of a train heist, sentenced to Leavenworth, and in 1930 escaped to embark on a remarkable two-year bank-robbing spree.

More than any others, these five—Bailey, Nash, Bentz, Keating, and Holden—were regarded as the elite bandits of the era, the consummate professionals that others looked up to, learned from, or strove to emulate. Each was a uniquely cerebral criminal who went out of his way to avoid violence, and each was a devoted husband and avid golfer. When not robbing banks they dedicated their time and energy to simple but comfortable lifestyles which made them seem like anything but master bandits. Nash read classic works like

Dickens and Shakespeare; Bentz owned a library of rare books and an impressive coin collection.

By 1932 a new breed of younger, distinctively more violent bank robber started to appear. Most came from the South and lower Midwest, where the depression had hit the hardest and the roots of the old outlaw traditions of Jesse James and the Daltons ran deep, still embraced by the simple, struggling inhabitants of the impoverished land.

Out of eastern Texas came the Barrow gang, which by year's end had a score of holdups and half a dozen killings credited to them. Clyde Barrow and his sweetheart Bonnie Parker were the nucleus around which a small band of followers, including Clyde's older brother Buck, gathered. What the Barrows lacked in organization and skill they made up for with sheer ferocity. For the most part, however, they were small-time bandits who targeted gas stations, grocery stores and the occasional bank, often stealing from the poor as well as from the rich. As a result, they were regarded with disdain by most of the 1930s' crime establishment. Cast out by their fellow criminals and the rest of society, the "Texas screwballs," as Alvin Karpis once called them, spent the majority of their days roaming the highways. Still, they achieved folk-hero status among a small but fiercely loyal contingent of sharecroppers and migrant families along the Texas-Oklahoma border.

Crisscrossing paths with the Barrow gang over many of the same rural roads was a broad-shouldered, somber-eyed outlaw named Charles Arthur "Pretty Boy" Floyd. He was adored by the inhabitants of his native terrain—the Cookson Hills of eastern Oklahoma—and vilified almost everywhere else. Like the Barrows, he was basically a loner who rarely worked with more than one or two accomplices. Floyd, however, had the savvy to remain in the good graces of the big-city hoods and court their protective services when on the run outside his home state.

If Floyd had had his way, he never would have left the rugged hill country and dusty back roads of his youth. By 1932 he was being hailed as "the Bandit King of Oklahoma," a prolific holdup artist who eluded posses like a phantom. Families in the close-knit communities of the poverty-stricken region preferred to call him "the Robin Hood of the Cookson Hills." While cheering his daring exploits, they provided him with food, shelter, and warning if lawmen came around. According to local lore, Pretty Boy showed his gratitude by taking time to burn mortgage records during his bank raids, or leaving behind a few dollars for a needy household.

The manhunt for Floyd grew so intense that at times he was flushed from the hills. Beyond Oklahoma's borders and out of his element, he manifested a dramatically different personality, one less flamboyant and self-assured, and notably more prone to violence. In Kansas City and Cleveland, two of his favorite locations for laying low, he displayed an affinity for liquor and prostitutes and squandered the greater part of his time and cash in brothels. Though he paid for protection he eyed everyone with suspicion and when cornered, he would erupt with guns blazing. Ten killings already had been credited to Pretty Boy, although the actual total was probably less than half that.

By the end of 1932 Floyd was back in Oklahoma looking for a new partner. His two previous sidekicks, William Miller and George Birdwell, were both in the graveyard, the former shot down in a gun battle with Ohio police in which Floyd escaped after killing an officer, the latter during a bank robbery. Pretty Boy recruited a diminutive, timid-looking crook named Adam "Eddie" Richetti, who had never robbed anything larger than a gas station. Floyd took his new protégé under his wing and schooled him in the art of plundering banks.

From western Tennessee came a husky, blue-eyed, beefy-faced bandit calling himself "Machine Gun" Kelly, a Memphis bootlegger with a knack for earning too little and getting caught too often. Kelly, whose real name was George Barnes, eventually landed in Leavenworth, where he made the acquaintance of Francis Keating and Thomas Holden. After helping the pair escape, Kelly was allowed to join the elite bank robbing crew they assembled. On July 15, 1930, the trio teamed up with Harvey Bailey and three others to rob a bank in Wilmar, Minnesota, of $142,000.

A novice working with seasoned pros, Kelly found himself highly regarded in the exclusive circles of big-time bank bandits and hired out his talents to only the best in the trade. He worked with Bailey and Frank Nash on an April 8, 1931, strike on the Central State Bank of Sherman, Texas, that scored $40,000, and he joined Eddie Bentz for a $71,000 holdup of the First Savings and Trust Bank in Colfax, Washington, on September 21, 1932. Kelly later boasted that his participation in these and other robberies netted him an average annual income of more than $100,000.

His closest friend during this period was Verne Miller, one of the era's most enigmatic and notorious figures. His blond hair, Nordic features, sleepy eyes, and passive expression masked a particularly vicious and paranoid personality. Miller was a decorated hero in World War I (where he learned his proficiency with a machine gun) and was elected sheriff in his hometown in South Dakota. Within a couple of years he tarnished his badge by falling in with bootleggers and ultimately was convicted of embezzlement. Upon his release from prison, the disgraced war hero and ex-peace officer slipped into the underworld in St. Paul, Minnesota, and established himself as a hired gun, working with Bailey, Nash, Keating and Holden, Kelly, and the Barker-Karpis gang. Miller drifted from one gang to another, one bank job to the next, almost never establishing close ties. His friendship with Kelly was one of the few exceptions, probably due in large part to Kelly's easygoing nature. Many of his occasional confederates like Bailey and Karpis were instinctively distrustful of Miller because of his background as a lawman. Others were simply repelled by his penchant for violence. Miller's dark side became the basis for much macabre and perhaps exaggerated underworld gossip that credited him with a string of unsolved gangland killings.

Eventually Kelly concluded that Miller had a bit of twisted wiring in his head and, after a two-year association, went his own way. Kelly simply lacked the stomach for bloodshed. He liked to drink and brag about his skill with a machine gun, but behind all the bravado he was really a mild-mannered and basically unambitious criminal. Kelly probably would not have amounted to much of an outlaw had it not been for the driving force of his wife, Kathryn, who was always in the background urging her husband to seek out bigger and better scores.

The list of rising underworld stars would not be complete without mention of the Barker-Karpis gang, which by the end of 1932 had established itself as a formidable force among its gangland contemporaries. The Barkers came from simple, dirt-poor obscurity, Missouri born and Oklahoma bred. According to folklore and FBI tradition, the four sons of Kate Barker ran afoul of the law almost from the moment they were able to walk. It seemed Herman, Lloyd, Arthur (called "Doc"), and Freddie were destined to go bad, but their reasons for turning to crime remain murky and mostly unverified. Once his bureau had killed or caught the gang's major members, J. Edgar Hoover insisted that Ma Barker was a "she-wolf" who schooled her boys in crime and shrewdly oversaw their careers. Evidence recently gleaned from the FBI's own files reveals that the director's vehement allegations against the old woman were mostly unsubstantiated nonsense.

Herman had some scrapes with the law while the family was in Missouri, but the Barkers' true descent into crime began after they moved to Tulsa, Oklahoma, about 1916. The four boys joined (some claim they formed) a band of rowdy street toughs called the Central Park Gang and rapidly graduated from misdemeanors to felonies. The worst that can be reliably said of Kate Barker is that she was fiercely protective of her wayward sons, refusing to believe they were guilty of any of the accusations against them. Even in later years, when Doc and Freddie were the most wanted men in America, Ma stubbornly stuck by them, perhaps choosing to remain ignorant of their misdeeds.

In at least one instance her indignation at the way her boys were treated by the authorities might have been justified. Doc was sent to McAlister to serve a life sentence for killing a night watchman at a Tulsa hospital—a murder to which a man in California confessed years later. Guilty or not, by that time all of Doc's brothers were deep into crime. Lloyd was captured robbing the U.S. Mail and sentenced to twenty-five years in Leavenworth. In 1927 Freddie was convicted of burglary and landed in Lansing. That same year Herman—who had moved away, married a Cherokee girl, and joined outlaw Ray Terrill in a series of holdups—ran into police near Newton, Kansas. During the ensuing shootout an officer was killed and Herman was seriously wounded. Either realizing he was dying or dreading capture, the eldest Barker boy turned his gun on himself.

The Barker-Karpis gang actually was conceived in 1930 when Freddie, still languishing in Lansing, received a new cellmate. The only son of a Lithuanian couple living in Canada, Francis Albin Karpaviecz began calling himself Alvin as a young boy when the family moved to Topeka, Kansas, and later, at the suggestion of a teacher, he shortened his surname to Karpis. As a youngster, he enjoyed a fleeting moment of wholesome fame when he became Topeka's marbles champion. But even in his pre-teen years, Karpis enjoyed the company of criminals and other shady characters, and he made it his life's goal to become an accomplished thief.

When he was fifteen his family moved to Chicago, settling into an apartment in the northwestern section of the city near The Patch. After two honest and uneventful years working as an errand boy and retail clerk, he struck out on his own and returned to Kansas where he became a bootlegger and pulled burglaries on the side. In 1926 he was caught and sentenced to five to ten years in the state reformatory at Hutchinson. He escaped three years later with fellow con (and future Barker-Karpis gang member) Lawrence DeVol. The pair swept through Oklahoma staging a string of small-time holdups until DeVol was apprehended. Karpis fled to his parents' home in Chicago and found work in a North Side bakery until the stock market crash forced his employer to dismiss him. Karpis drifted west again and was arrested at Kansas City in March 1930.

He was returned to Hutchinson and was soon transferred to Lansing, where he became friends with the youngest of the Barker boys. Freddie, working on his fourth year inside, treated Karpis like a welcome guest, sharing his stock of contraband, including a generous supply of marijuana. The pair behaved themselves, reduced their sentences by working in the state's coal mines, and in the spring of 1931 were rewarded with paroles.

The two young men—Karpis was twenty-three, Barker five years older—embarked on a crime spree, robbing gas stations, grocery stores, and jewelry shops throughout Oklahoma, Missouri, Nebraska, and Minnesota, while collecting a small band of followers and a sizable arsenal along the way. By fall they were knocking over banks and gaining a reputation. In 1932 the gang, dividing its time between hideouts in Kansas City and St. Paul, confined its activities exclusively to bank jobs. Bailey, Nash, Keating, and Holden—always looking for young, efficient talent—joined the gang on occasion or recruited its members for robberies. One of their joint ventures, the plunder of the Citizens National Bank at Fort Scott, Kansas, on June 17, netted the participants $47,000. On July 26 the Barker-Karpis bandits, operating alone, took $240,000 in cash and bonds from the Cloud County Bank of Concordia, Nebraska.

Along for the ride—and not much else—was Freddie's beloved mother. Kate Barker was sixty, a plump, frumpy, woman with stringy dark hair who stood barely five feet tall. Feeling responsible for her, Freddie brought her along on the gang's travels, and her presence provided excellent cover when the bandits moved into a new location posing as honest citizens. She was surely aware of what her youngest son and his pals were doing, but despite the legends and Hoover's outlandish allegations labeling her "the most vicious, dangerous, and resourceful criminal brain of the last decade," Ma was never the mastermind of the gang. According to Bailey, Ma "couldn't plan breakfast. When we'd sit down to plan a bank job, she'd go in the other room and listen to *Amos and Andy* or hillbilly music on the radio."

Freddie was not only a good son, he was a faithful brother. A sizable chunk of his loot was slipped into the pockets of several Oklahoma officials who showed their gratitude by paroling Arthur in September 1932. Doc immediately joined the gang in St. Paul. The Barker boys celebrated his release by robbing a bank in Redwood Falls, Minnesota, of $35,000 on September 23, and a week later by knocking over another in Wahpeton, North Dakota.

Up to this point the gang's heists had been uncommonly professional and mostly bloodless affairs, although Freddie had a tendency to pistol-whip tellers who moved too slowly. Then, on December 16, the crew descended on the Third Northwestern National Bank, which occupied one of the busiest street corners in downtown Minneapolis. As the bandits collected almost $20,000 in cash and $100,000 in securities, an employee triggered the alarm. Police arrived on the scene, forcing the gang members to shoot their way to freedom, in the process cutting down two officers and an innocent bystander.

The triple homicide turned the chilly climate of the Twin Cities into a very hot place for the gang. Within twenty-four hours the Barkers pulled up stakes and were on the move. Most of the gang members headed west.

❋ ❋ ❋

They arrived in Reno in two cars—Freddie, Doc, and Ma in one, two other gang members, William Weaver and Jess Doyle, in the other. Karpis stopped briefly in Chicago, caught a plane, and showed up a few days later. Shaken and sleepless from his first time flying, he climbed into a cab and went immediately to Bill Graham's Rex Club on Virginia Street. He found the others waiting for him in the casino's back room, already settled in and planning a big Christmas party.

For two months they relaxed and enjoyed the pleasures Reno had to offer. "We played keno at the clubs, went to movies, sat around the Rex, and generally killed time," Karpis later recalled. "Whores were legal in Nevada and they were a diversion." Most of all, the outlaws appreciated the mild climate and Graham's assurances of protection.

According to Karpis, "There were plenty of people in our line of business around taking it easy, and there was a lot of socializing." Among the many gang-land characters, both notorious and obscure, that he encountered, there was one "whose company I enjoyed," Karpis recalled, "a sharp young guy with a teenager's face and good taste in clothes." The snappy dresser was Nelson, who, upon hearing that the Barkers were in town, rushed to the Rex to welcome them and clue them in to all the hot spots around Reno and what joints to avoid. Gradually, as they grew to know and trust one another, they exchanged valuable inside information, Nelson sharing all he knew about his California contacts and Chicago pals while listening to the Barkers sing the praises of St. Paul and recount their recent adventures with such premier bank robbers as Harvey Bailey.

Karpis, one year older and a couple inches taller than Nelson, hit it off right away with the young fugitive. "Nelson and I hadn't known each other as kids," he wrote, "but when we found out we had lived in the same neighborhood in Chicago, we developed a kind of bond. We both hung out around West Division and Sacramento and even knew the same kids. We saw each other a lot . . . " He was a frequent guest at the Nelson bungalow, enjoying Helen's home-cooked meals and quiet evenings of card playing and chatting. "They were a pleasant family," according to Karpis, who described Nelson as "a stern but understanding father."

In their private conversations Nelson repeatedly confided that he was itch-ing to leave Reno and return east. As Karpis later said, "He wanted to get to work, sticking people up," and he was starting to resent that "he was more or less being looked after financially by Graham and McKay . . . He hated being dependent on the whims of those two guys." Nelson's escalating bitterness over his stagnant situation was sharpened by the fact that he was grateful to Reno's dynamic duo. He not only liked and trusted Graham but deeply respected him. "I'd do anything for Bill Graham," Nelson once told Fatso Negri, ominous words in light of subsequent events.

Nelson's goal was to work with pros, and he particularly wanted to hook up with an outfit that knew how to handle big-time bank jobs. Karpis informed him that the gang had all the men it needed but promised that once he returned east, he would see what he could do for him. He provided Nelson with the names of key people and good contact spots in St. Paul.

At this point the only thing stopping Nelson was his fear of being spotted again as an escaped convict. The close call in California and the fact that his picture had appeared in a nationally sold magazine left their marks on him.

Shortly after New Year's Karpis, suffering from an increasingly nagging sore throat, took Nelson's advice and visited Tobe Williams' hospital in Vallejo where his tonsils were removed. Kate Barker, whom Karpis described as "a good sport" who "put up with our gypsy way of living," accompanied him to the Bay Area. There was great affection between the two, and when Freddie or Doc wanted to spend time with women, it was Karpis who usually offered to get Ma out of the way, taking her to movies, county fairs, or on shopping excursions. After his operation, they spent a few days seeing the sights in San Francisco and visiting some of Nelson's former associates, such as Soap Moreno. There is a persistent rumor that Ma had grown especially fond of Tobe Williams during their stay and that the aged pair later spent a weekend together at Lake Tahoe.

On returning to Reno, Karpis discovered Nelson had resorted to a radical method to conceal his identity by "rubbing his fingertips with some powerful solution." A local hood guaranteed the acid-based mixture would obliterate all traces of his fingerprints. "But from what I could see it was just raising blisters," Karpis declared. The pain was constant, at times excruciating, and while the results were minimal, Nelson persistently applied the substance each day for several weeks. At the time, Karpis viewed his friend's grueling ordeal as bizarre and unnecessarily desperate, but two years later he would submit to very painful operations to have his own prints removed.

Nelson refused the offer of another underworld ally to provide shots of morphine to relieve his agony. Instead he devoured bottles of aspirin and relied on Helen to comfort him and help with the simplest acts, such as picking up a fork when he sat down to a meal. Frank Cochran later recalled that during Nelson's last couple of months in Reno in 1933, he had a habit of "hiding his hands," keeping them shoved into his pockets. Occasionally he caught a glimpse of Nelson's bandaged fingertips but refrained from asking questions, sensing that "Jimmie didn't want to talk about it." The garage owner also noticed Nelson was growing a mustache, though his beard was so light "you really had to look close to see it."

Cochran, among others, observed a subtle change in the young man's behavior at this time. He seemed moody, edgy, and less talkative. "His fingers were always paining him," Karpis explained, aware that the perpetual anguish Nelson put himself through also must have taken a psychological toll. "But worse than the pain was the restlessness. Nelson wanted out of Reno."

By mid-February Karpis and the rest of the Barker gang were ready to move on as well. They left Nelson with an open invitation to look them up when he returned to the Midwest.

He remained in Reno another month, then one spring day he showed up at the Air Service Garage announcing that he was leaving town. He shook hands with Cochran and told him he hoped to be back the following winter. Both Graham and McKay were sorry to see their young protégé depart. One underworld source said Graham bestowed a bonus of several thousand dollars on Nelson for his dedicated service. Another version claims the money was actually a loan that Nelson later repaid by performing a valuable service for his former protector.

*If a fellow was going into the bank robbery business . . . I'd say the
first thing to do would be to get a place to work from. That was
always my system.*
— Eddie Bentz

CHAPTER 5

SUMMER RENTAL

U.S. ATTORNEY GENERAL HOMER S. Cummings called it "a poison spot of crime." Alvin Karpis fondly referred to it as "a crook's haven" where the nation's most notorious criminals could congregate in a congenial atmosphere unhampered by the local authorities. As Karpis described it, "St. Paul was a good spot for both pleasure and business. You could relax in its joints and speakeasies without any fear of arrest, and when you were planning a score, you could have your pick of all the top men at all the top crimes."

It was the perfect place for Nelson to find the people he needed to form a band of select bank robbers—veterans who could teach him their trade and young Turks like himself to recruit as partners. Thanks to Karpis, he knew exactly where to go and who to see.

At the time of Nelson's arrival in mid-April 1933, the control of St. Paul's underworld was almost evenly divided between two men, neither of whom looked or lived like a mobster. Harry Sandlovich, known around town as Harry Sawyer ("Dutch" to his friends), and John "Jack" Peifer appeared to be friendly rivals who sometimes looked after the other's interests while trying to outdo him. Both exercised considerable influence over the city's politicians and key figures within the Police Department. Both were guardians of the time-honored "O'Connor system," which guaranteed local and out-of-town criminals that they would be accorded absolute protection if they behaved and pursued their illegal activities outside the St. Paul city limits.

Police Chief John L. O'Connor, dubbed "the Big Fellow," came to power at the turn of the twentieth century. Instead of wasting his department's resources by waging a war against crime, O'Connor chose to strike a deal with the city's hoodlums. The arrangement worked remarkably well, for although criminals of all kinds from across the nation swarmed into St. Paul, the city remained virtually crime free. On those rare occasions when an independent or impulsive crook accosted a woman, became too rowdy, or robbed a business, the underworld personally dealt with the culprit or handed him over to O'Connor's men. Thus the streets of St. Paul were kept safe, O'Connor remained in power for two decades, and local commerce prospered as the visiting criminals spent their loot freely in the city. Unlike Chicago and almost every other American city, there were no beer wars and few gang killings. Illegal establishments offering gambling or prostitution could operate only with the consent of the police chief, who received a share of the profits.

O'Connor had considerable help in implementing and overseeing his protection system. His younger brother, Richard "the Cardinal" O'Connor, a city alderman and later Democratic party boss, used his prodigious influence to make sure elected officials and local judges all played their parts and were kept happy with bribes and political favors.

Less respectable but equally important were men like Daniel "Dapper Dan" Hogan, an underworld fixer who served as O'Connor's middleman to the network of criminals, both residents and tourists, within the city. One of Hogan's chief duties was to welcome visiting hoods, set them up with a place to stay, let them know the rules, and graciously accept a small or large (depending on the notoriety or recent success of the criminal) donation as part of the "layover agreement." Hogan also used his gangland resources to provide such services as fencing stolen goods or laundering hot securities.

When O'Connor died in 1924 his system, like a well-oiled machine, continued to operate under the efficient supervision of Hogan, reaching a new and higher level of influence during Prohibition. But one chilly December morning in 1928, Hogan started his car and was blown to bits by a dynamite charge wired to the accelerator. His successor and (according to gangland rumors) probable killer was Harry Sawyer.

A notably less feared and flamboyant figure than Dapper Dan, the stocky, flabby-faced Sawyer developed a more intimate rapport with the police but was less liked and generally mistrusted by local hoodlums. In time Sawyer gravitated more toward the out-of-town criminals, who by the early Thirties included a remarkable assemblage of elite interstate bank robbers, among them Bailey, Nash, Keating, Holden, and Bentz. Sawyer received them all as friends and went to considerable lengths to ensure their comfort and that their needs were met. He expanded Hogan's role as supplier to include such services as underworld banking and providing physicians, automobiles, "clean" license plates, and firearms.

While Sawyer was preoccupied with tending to the out-of-towners, a number of individuals moved in to take charge of the local rackets. Jack Peifer was the most notable. A native of rural Minnesota, Peifer's major enterprise was running swank gambling joints, although he also held interests in prostitution, bootlegging, and drug trafficking in Hennepin County. In contrast to the slow, methodical manner of Sawyer, Peifer was full of boundless energy, bright-eyed, and witty. Although Sawyer was the main contact for the many gangs and free-lancers drifting into the city, a number of the visitors preferred the company of Peifer.

After depositing Helen and the kids in a hotel, Nelson went directly to the Green Lantern Saloon on North Wabasha, a few blocks from the state capitol. The establishment was not only the downtown headquarters for Sawyer but also the favorite meeting place for the rank and file of the city's criminals, especially visiting gangsters. The patrons were often a rogues' gallery of the most wanted men in the United States. Whenever celebrity criminals such as Bailey or Nash were in town they dropped by the Green Lantern almost daily. Even Karpis, who liked to slip into a booth and sip beer while socializing, admitted he was dazzled by the heavyweights who showed up to mix and mingle with their own kind.

The Lantern's criminal clientele rarely used the front entrance. Most entered through a back door in the alley behind the building that led directly to the Blue Room, which was separated from the front room by a false wall. Here, in a smoky speakeasy atmosphere, Sawyer entertained his gangland guests with food, liquor, music, and on special occasions professional strippers.

Karpis was on hand that day to vouch for his friend Jimmie and introduce him to Sawyer. The Lantern's owner greeted Nelson with his usual gusto, informing the newcomer that if there was anything he wanted, he only needed to ask. A Lithuanian Jew by birth, Sawyer had black doll-like eyes, a blustery voice that could be heard above often raucous noise filling his place, and a pot belly that proceeded him as he worked his way among the tables shaking hands and chatting with customers. Despite his almost constant presence at the Lantern, Sawyer was much too busy to be bothered with the operation of the business. Those duties were delegated to Thomas Gannon, the saloon's unofficial manager, and Pat Reilly, its chief bartender.

As it turned out, Karpis was extremely busy himself and unable to spend much time with Nelson. The gang, working with Frank Nash, had recently returned to St. Paul after pulling one of its biggest heists: the April 4 robbery of the First National Bank at Fairbury, Nebraska, in which the robbers collected $151,000 in cash and securities. The bank alarm was set off and the bandits were forced to shoot their way out of town through a gauntlet of police and armed citizens. Gang member Earl Christman caught a bullet in the chest, died several days later, and was secretly buried by the Barkers near Kansas City.

Nelson inquired if the loss of Christman might provide an opening for him with the gang. But Karpis revealed the next score was already in the works, some sort of "specialty job" Freddie Barker had worked out with Jack Peifer and a pair of ex-Chicago hoods, Fred Goetz and Byron Bolton, whom Nelson knew by reputation. Karpis was not at liberty to furnish any details and said only that it was going to be big.

Baby Face was probably glad they had no place for him when he later learned the job was kidnapping St. Paul brewery baron William Hamm Jr. Although he never lost respect for Karpis, Nelson once stated that "snatching people is a dirty way to make a living." It's not known whether his objection stemmed from his curiously uneven code of criminal ethics or merely indicated a preference. Kidnappings rarely involved gunplay or any action, the very things which seemed to attract him to daylight holdups.

The Barkers, however, were ready for a change of pace. Their last two bank raids were marred by bullets, bloodshed, and alarmingly narrow escapes. A "nice quiet kidnapping" with a $100,000 payoff sounded like an ideal score. Karpis and other gang members were already working out the details of the abduction while also struggling to unload thousands of dollars' worth of stolen securities around town. On a more personal note, Karpis was dating a new sweetheart, a cute seventeen-year-old brunette named Dolores Delaney, and was attempting (with Sawyer's help) to find a safe apartment they could share.

Despite the demands on his time, Karpis occasionally was able to devote a few hours to Nelson, showing off the sights of St. Paul in much the same way that Baby Face had acted as host in Reno. The pair dropped in on Ma Barker, who was temporarily residing in elegance at the Commodore Hotel. Several times Nelson, Helen, and their children visited Freddie and other gang members living with their girlfriends in cottages along White Bear Lake.

Nelson spent most of his time at the Green Lantern hoping either to hook up with a team of professionals or find enough experienced people to form his own gang. But much to his chagrin, Nelson discovered that virtually all the big name talent was elsewhere. Bailey, Keating, and Holden were in prison, Nash was hiding out in Hot Springs, Eddie Bentz was vacationing in Texas, Verne Miller was in Kansas City, and Machine Gun Kelly had temporarily returned to his native Tennessee. All were expected to return to St. Paul by summer, but Nelson had neither the funds nor the patience to wait that long. He was forced to work with what was available.

With Karpis preoccupied, Nelson sought the advise of others. Both Gannon and Reilly were quickly won over by his easy, talkative manner and generous tips. Gannon grew notably attentive when Nelson unveiled his intention to put together a bank-robbing gang. One day Gannon invited him to lunch at McCormick's Town Talk Sandwich Shop, where they discussed

Nelson's proposed crime spree. Gannon said he wanted to be counted in, whatever the risks or demands.

A slender, sallow hoodlum of thirty-two, Gannon looked considerably more sinister than his past would indicate. He had cold blue eyes and a thin pockmarked face, with one jagged scar on his forehead and another across the bridge of his nose. A tattoo of a heart pierced by a dagger decorated his right forearm. Like Nelson, he had grown up around an assortment of nefarious characters destined for gangland stardom. Irish mobsters like Dapper Dan Hogan and William "Reddy" Griffin were his role models. Despite a long history of drifting along the fringes of the Twin Cities underworld and his intimate affiliation with Sawyer, Gannon had never participated in any major projects offering an opportunity for excitement—until now.

Also like Nelson, when Gannon left the Green Lantern he preferred to live quietly with his wife, Clara, and their two children in their home on the eastern edge of Minneapolis. Over the next couple of weeks the two families visited one another. Ronnie Gillis, who had just turned four, was about the same age as Gannon's son Thomas Jr.

Bartender Pat Reilly proved to be a willing and valuable ally as well, although by his own admission he wasn't cut out to play an active role in holdups. Albert William Reilly, age twenty-six, was once a mascot for St. Paul's double-A baseball team. Pale and prone to nervousness, his introduction into the local underworld scene came about in large part through his marriage, in 1927, to Helen "Babe" Delaney. Thanks to his in-laws and friends of the family, Reilly found himself in the company of the city's most notorious figures. He was intrigued enough to become an errand boy for Sawyer and eventually worked his way up to waiter, then chief bartender at the Green Lantern.

Babe's two sisters also maintained loose connections to the underworld. As already noted, Dolores, the youngest, had moved in with Alvin Karpis. The middle sister, Jean Angela Delaney Crompton, had recently divorced and was dating a local hood named Tommy Carroll. Reilly told Nelson that Carroll was a competent stickup man looking to break into the big time, exactly the kind of material Baby Face was seeking. The bartender arranged a meeting at the Lantern.

Thomas Leonard Carroll was a young-looking thirty-six, a square-jawed, muscular, ruggedly handsome man who seemed to have endured hard times throughout his life while straying back and forth across the line separating lawfulness from crime. Born in Montana of partly Native American, mostly Irish stock, he was orphaned at nine and on his own by his mid-teens, wandering through an array of odd jobs—boxer, bartender, boilermaker, taxi driver—across the Midwest. His efforts to earn an honest living were usually halfhearted and brief, even after he took a wife, Viola, in 1925. He was repeatedly arrested for possession of stolen property, auto theft, armed robbery, and burglary throughout Iowa, Missouri, Nebraska, Kansas, Illinois, Oklahoma, and

Minnesota, and served four prison terms, including seventeen months in Leavenworth. Viola faithfully followed her man and waited for him each time he was put behind bars. Upon his release from Leavenworth in October 1931 they moved to St. Paul, where Carroll went to work in a restaurant. Within a few months he abandoned both the job and his wife.

Carroll found a new sweetheart—Sally Bennett, a local nightclub singer known around town as "Radio Sally." During the greater part of 1932 they lived together in a second-floor apartment on the west side of St. Paul. Needing more income than Sally's earnings as an entertainer provided, Carroll hooked up with a local bandit named Charles Fisher. Using St. Paul as their staging ground and working with a few trusted accomplices, they pulled off almost forty holdups and burglaries in small towns across Minnesota and parts of Wisconsin and Iowa. Their favorite scores were post offices, and among the ones they looted were those in Ogena, Turtle Lake, Elmore, Gibbon, and Lakeville, Minnesota, and one in Superior, Wisconsin. The take was never very big—over the course of a year the pair had split only about $20,000. Carroll, disillusioned and anxious by the spring of 1933, constantly read the newspaper accounts of bank heists and yearned to use his talents as part of a professional crew.

His relationship with Sally began to deteriorate. The singer was growing tired of Carroll's "gangster friends" always coming around and of his sometimes abusive behavior. Carroll was described as considerate and well-mannered, but frequently when he drank his mood soured and he turned belligerent. After separating, the couple continued to occasionally see each other. Carroll, in fact, rented a room from Sally's brother on South 16th Avenue in Minneapolis. About this time he met Pat Reilly's sister-in-law Jean, a buxom blond who had been working as a waitress in St. Paul since her divorce from a Chicago musician. Over the next few months Carroll darted back and forth between both women, something neither Sally nor Jean realized until later.

It was an evening in late April when Carroll and Chuck Fisher arrived at the Green Lantern to meet Baby Face Nelson. Reilly made the introductions and served their drinks as the three slid into a booth and were joined by Gannon. Carroll and Fisher talked about their recent stickups. In appearance they were an odd couple. Carroll sat ramrod straight and square-shouldered, his powerful arms crossed on the table's edge. His fling as an amateur boxer had left him with a trim, husky physique, while his face was marred by a flattened nose, a scared chin, and a mouth that twisted distinctly downward on the right. Fisher, eight years younger, was a stocky, slouch-shouldered, slow-moving bandit who wore a perpetual scowl. When they finished boasting about their robberies, Nelson asked, "You boys ready to move up to something meatier?"

Both said they were. Carroll was especially impressed when Nelson mentioned that he planned to acquire some heavy-duty weapons and bulletproof vests to use on their bank heists.

Before leaving the Twin Cities Nelson heeded the advise of Karpis and others who suggested that he call upon Jack Peifer. Just as his rival Harry Sawyer operated out of the Green Lantern, Peifer's home base was the Hollyhocks, a three-story mansion near the banks of the Mississippi where the river loops below St. Paul. Despite its reputation as a notorious gambling den, the Hollyhocks—reflecting its owner's style—was notably more fashionable and high-toned than Sawyer's downtown speakeasy. The nightclub attracted a high-class clientele that included some of St. Paul's most prominent citizens. Wealthy couples attired in tuxedos and expensive gowns attended dinner parties with gangsters, then hung around to shoot craps or play roulette.

Nelson's visit to the Hollyhocks turned out to be profitable. Peifer—a short, mercurial mobster with a round, friendly face and dimpled chin—welcomed the young hood and escorted him into his office at the rear of the first floor. Peifer remarked they had some "mutual friends." He was referring principally to Karpis, whose recommendation of Nelson he didn't dare take lightly. Karpis had recently spent considerable time and money at the Hollyhocks, using the nightclub for romantic interludes with Dolores and meetings with Peifer to plot the impending Hamm abduction. Knowing that he needed Karpis to keep the Barkers involved, Peifer was ready to accord Nelson every courtesy. "I hear you're tight with the Touhys," Peifer said at one point.

"Quite a bit," Nelson replied proudly. "Tommy has always been a good pal of mine."

Peifer revealed that Tommy and his wife, along with brother Roger and others of their gang, had all been guests at the Hollyhocks from time to time. Eventually Peifer got to the point: "I understand you're looking for some of the big boys. Could be I've some information you can use."

Peifer revealed that Frank Nash was to return to town the following month, much sooner than anyone else expected. The update on Eddie Bentz—described by Peifer as "a good friend" and "a real gentleman"—was even better. Bentz had had a close encounter with lawmen in Texas but managed to slip away. He was presently back in the Midwest and was looking to spend the summer along northern Indiana's lakefront. Peifer supplied the names of several contacts who might be able to put Nelson in touch with the bank robber.

Elated, Nelson asked, "How good is your information?"

"Good as gold," Peifer claimed, confiding that he had spoken to Bentz by telephone just a few days earlier.

※ ※ ※

Of all the colorful criminals gaining notoriety in the 1930's, none looked more and acted less like a public enemy than Edward Wilhelm Bentz. He was a solidly built six-footer with a tendency to talk out of the right side of his mouth. His sloping forehead (bearing a triangular birthmark), wide jaw, apish arms, and massive shoulders gave him a brutish, Neanderthal-like appearance. Yet many on both sides of the law spoke of his refined tastes, dignified behavior, impeccable manners, shrewd intelligence, and abhorrence to violence. Even J. Edgar Hoover, who delighted in portraying gangsters as vermin, had to admit that Bentz easily outclassed all other bank robbers of his era.

❦ Now thirty-nine, Bentz's remarkable outlaw career stretched back two decades. His father, a Nebraska rancher, was killed by a horse when Eddie was nine. His mother, left with five daughters and four sons, moved the family to Tacoma, Washington. Eddie was a habitual criminal and as a youth frequently arrested for stealing bicycles and scrap metal. His first serious offense was auto theft in 1914, which landed him in the state penitentiary at Walla Walla. Released after two years, Bentz worked his way to the Midwest, more often blundering than succeeding as a small-time thief and burglar. Between 1916 and 1926 he was captured and incarcerated six more times, in Illinois, Wisconsin, and Michigan. Behind bars he developed a love for classic literature and intently studied photography and architecture. Outside his cell Bentz sought out the best criminal minds among his fellow inmates and implored them to share their expertise and techniques with him.

Gradually learning from past mistakes while absorbing the advice and admonitions of the old masters in the prison yard, Bentz was able to perfect the science of bank robbery. Early on his favorite method was to break into banks at night and cut his way into the vault with an acetylene torch. Since the necessary equipment included a tank weighing over 150 pounds, he quickly tired of the procedure.

"I'm through," he reportedly declared to his partners following a clumsy, ponderous getaway. "From now on I'll take these joints in daylight during business hours."

He soon established himself as one of the pioneers of modern bank robbery. Not as prolific as Bailey or Nash, nor as celebrated, Bentz chose his targets and henchmen with meticulous care. He rarely worked with the same people twice. A Bentz-orchestrated holdup was never performed unless each minute detail was worked out to his satisfaction, a process that usually took at least six weeks. Once a bank was decided upon, Bentz would dissect the floor plan and security systems and study the employees to determine who might panic or try to be a hero and who could open the vault. He spent days figuring the best getaway route and diligently logged every turn and bump along the route, which was never less than 300 miles.

Realizing that he actually looked like a thug, Bentz went to great lengths to ensure that his lifestyle reflected respectability. He ate in the best restaurants, wore the finest clothes (except during a robbery, when he often donned a farmer's bib overalls), stayed in the best hotels, and never associated with known criminals in public or let himself become too attached to any one group of confederates. He was a maverick who cherished his independence, his wife, Verna, playing golf, and reading good books. He limited himself to no more than three holdups a year, recognizing that most criminals were caught because they were too greedy, too self-confident, and too sloppy in their approach to crime, or because they simply spent too much time around other crooks.

Bentz passed the early months of 1933 touring the Southwest, making contacts and casing banks. His arrest by a pair of deputy sheriffs outside his hotel in Dallas was a complete fluke. Bentz shrewdly talked his way out of custody before the Dallas officers realized just who they had nabbed. By the time they did, Eddie and Verna were on their way back to the Midwest.

For a number of years Bentz preferred to spend his summers along the shores of Lake Michigan in Indiana. Since wedding the former Verna Freemark in 1930 the practice had become a ritual. The couple's favorite vacation location was Long Beach, a lakefront community at the northeastern tip of Michigan City. Both husband and wife had relatives in the area, and Bentz greatly appreciated the local underworld contacts who were able to provide services and guarantee security. Ironically, since it was located within a few miles of the Indiana State Prison, Long Beach was widely recognized as a long-time hoodlum retreat. The late great Legs Diamond (recently rubbed out by rival Dutch Schultz) had come all the way from New York for rest and recreation. In a 1934 FBI report a Michigan City police captain complained to agents that law officers in the community were "notorious for catering to criminals." The report estimated that at any given time "90 percent of the cottages were leased to gangsters."

By mid-May Bentz had secured a lakeside cottage and moved in with his wife, her sister Leona, and Leona's six-year-old son. Calling himself Ed Dewey, a Detroit oil company executive on vacation with his family, he traveled about the area freely, visiting bookstores and coin shops and perfecting his golf game (he was rumored to shoot in the low eighties) on the finest courses he could find. Business more often than pleasure brought him to Chicago, forty-five miles to the west, where he kept in contact with a carefully selected array of fences and arms dealers. On the way he frequently stopped at Indiana Harbor, the lakefront section of East Chicago at the western end of Indiana's arcing shoreline, to touch base with another batch of underworld friends who inhabited the district.

On May 19 Bentz dropped by the Inland Hotel on Block Avenue, one of the Harbor's favorite meeting places for local criminal talent. Roy Dahlien, the proprietor, called Bentz aside to inform him that a young hood was looking for him.

"What do you know about this guy?" Bentz inquired.

"Seems like a good kid," Dahlien said. He added that visitor had registered at the Inland as "Jimmie Williams" three days earlier and had been asking how to contact Bentz. Suspicious, Dahlien had checked on him. "His real name is Gillis. He's hot. Busted out of Joliet about a year ago. The Touhys vouch for him. He's got family in Chicago. In fact he told me his wife and kids are staying with relatives while he finds a safe spot to live around here."

"What's he want with me?"

"You'll have to ask him."

Bentz proceeded to Art's Army Store, a short walk from the Inland. Art Stross, the owner and operator, was another friend of the bank robber, renowned for his ability to obtain anything his customers requested, and for being a reliable fence and bookmaker. Bentz spotted Stross standing at the curb by his store speaking to a man seated in a Ford. The shop owner motioned for Bentz to come over. "I want you to meet someone, Ed," Stross called out. "This is Jimmie. He was just asking about you."

A boyishly handsome face peered out of the car window, smiling brightly. Bentz, who prided himself on his acumen in sizing up people, was certain Jimmie was twenty, twenty-one at the most. His eyes were a striking steely blue. Nelson thrust a small hand out the window, and it vanished as Bentz clasped it.

"It's a genuine pleasure to meet you, Mr. Bentz," Nelson said with obvious enthusiasm.

Bentz instructed him to call him Ed, adding "for the time being, the last name is Dewey." Then he asked, "Is there something I can do for, Jimmie?"

Nelson revealed that he was searching for a summer place for himself, his family, and maybe some friends arriving later. "I was hoping to find a spot where the fix was in. I hear the setup is real sweet over at Long Beach where you're staying. Can you get me in by you?"

Bentz shrugged. "I know for a fact there's a few vacant cottages by mine. But I'm afraid real estate isn't my racket, and I don't pull any strings with the leasing company. As far as I know, they're strictly legit. If you're as hot as I hear you are, you might want to be discreet."

Nelson said he understood. He invited Bentz to a nearby coffee shop. The wily veteran agreed, intrigued by Jimmie's affable manner and sensing that he was after more than just a place to stay. But for the next hour the pair only discussed general topics, such as their families and living out west. Bentz left their first meeting wishing Nelson luck in his quest to lease a summer place and regarding him as a likable and sharp young man.

Later that day Nelson appeared at the Vesley Motor Company on Ogden Avenue in Chicago. He traded his Ford for a dark blue Essex Terraplane, which was quickly becoming the preferred vehicle of bank bandits due to its rapid acceleration and capacity to reach a breathtaking eighty-three miles per hour. Through Jack Perkins he sent word to Helen at the Fitzsimmons apartment, where she and the kids had stayed since Darlene's birthday on May 11, letting her know he would have a place for them within a week.

The next day he stopped at the Willard Cafe in Michigan City and met an old friend. Father Phillip Coughlan had overseen a chapel in the area since January, his transfer, it was rumored, arranged by church superiors concerned about his association with Chicago crime figures like the Touhys. Evidently the change and any chastisement he received had little lasting effect. In northeastern Indiana he once again found a flock among local hoodlums, and on May 20 he renewed his friendship with the young man he knew as George Nelson, now calling himself Jimmie Williams. Coughlan later insisted to government agents that his reunion with Nelson at the Willard Cafe was merely a chance encounter. The evidence, however, suggests that the two had kept in contact and their meeting was prearranged.

Accompanied by Coughlan, Nelson visited the Long Beach Reality Company and asked to see some cottages available for summer rental along the lake. A salesman drove the pair out to Lake Shore Drive where Nelson displayed particular interest in the Higgins cottage between Stops 17 and 18. The roomy two-story brick structure was some 500 feet from the shoreline and located directly beside the cottage leased by Bentz. The salesman said the home was available for $100 a month. Nelson paid $400 in advance.

On May 25 Nelson checked out of the Inland Hotel and moved into the cottage along with Helen, their two children, and his mother, Mary. A few days after settling in, Nelson wandered over to his neighbor's home. Bentz was swaying peacefully in a backyard hammock, paging through a rare edition of *The Pilgrim's Progress*. "I don't mean to interrupt your siesta, Ed," Nelson apologized sheepishly. "I was hoping we could talk."

"Sure." Bentz set aside his book and swung his huge frame out of the hammock. "What's on your mind?"

"Some friends and I are thinking of doing a job in Gary."

"You're talking about knocking off a bank?"

"Absolutely."

Bentz suggested they take a walk. They strolled along the dunes between the cottages and beach, the only sounds the screeching of gulls and waves lapping the shore. Nelson openly admitted that he was looking to pick up some tricks of the trade. Bentz, believing it was his duty to advise young talent, as the old-timers had tutored him, readily consented. He later recalled significant parts of their conversation in a feature article in *Argosy*:

"You want me to share some of my expertise?" Bentz began. "So here it is. It includes a lot of do's and don'ts you might not care to hear."

"No, that's fine. We want your help. Hell, we need it."

"Okay, then. An area like Gary is too congested. That's a major don't. You want to stay away from big cities. They're nice to hole up in but hell to get out of. You run into a traffic backup and you're done for. You might get away with more money, but chances are you won't be going far.

91

"You see, Jimmie, any idiot or bunch of idiots can walk into a bank, pull out guns, and grab the cash. It's the ones who are smart and careful enough to make a clean escape and do it again a month, a year later, whatever—those are the real pros.

"Small-town banks are your best bet. They're the only kind of scores I'll even consider. Fewer cops, less traffic, lots of countryside to lose the heat in. If you do your homework right, you can find some pretty ripe banks in hick towns. You just have to know what to look for."

Nelson frowned. "That's our problem. None of us know shit about casing a job—which bank to pick, which ones to stay away from. We figured you could help us out."

"You mean recommend a mark?"

"I'm talking about setting us up all around. You pick the jug, you do the casing, you work out the getaway chart, the whole thing. You don't have to be along when we take it, and we'll cut you in for an even share."

Bentz gave the offer serious thought and finally agreed to be their setup man. "Tell me about your gang."

"I've got some people lined up in St. Paul. I'll head over there next week and get them over here."

"How many?"

"At least three for sure. They're all good holdup men. Kinda raw but very reliable."

Bentz massaged his wide jaw. "Any experience with bank jobs?"

"Not a one, unless you count me. I was in a couple small capers a few years back. Nothing to brag about. How many men will we need?"

"You can take a bank with three, if they're all pros and you want to live dangerously. Four or five is ideal. Since you boys are just starting out, I'd suggest no fewer than six. Three inside, three covering the outside."

"I should be able to come up with a couple more men," Nelson announced confidently. "What else do we need?"

"Money. At least a thousand, probably more. There's certain essentials you'll need. A clean getaway car is the top priority because you're just gonna abandon it later unless you're a fool. You can use a hot car if you want, but it only increases the risk. Better to buy one like any businessman, as long as you make sure it can't be traced back to you."

"I can work that out through some people in Chicago. You got a particular score in mind for us?"

"As a matter of fact, I was thinking of one not far from here. A little town in Michigan called Grand Haven. I cased it last year, but my people thought it was too small. I've got the notes in my files, but they'll have to be updated."

"What's the estimated take?"

"If I remember right, about fifty G's. Sound okay?"

"Sounds great. If you say it's the right job for us, that's all I need."

On June 7 Nelson and his wife, leaving the kids in Mary's care, departed for St. Paul. Traveling with the young couple in their new Terraplane was Father Coughlan, who had jumped at the invitation extended by Nelson to tag along. The trio stopped overnight at Louie's roadhouse along the Northwest Highway in Fox River Grove. The place had become a favorite gathering spot for gangsters over the years. The owner was Louis Cernocky, whose enormous weight (in excess of 300 pounds) was matched only by the gracious way he treated his notorious patrons like celebrities. His wife and two sons, Eddie and Louis Jr., helped run the establishment, along with a small staff of waitresses.

Exactly when Nelson first began patronizing the roadhouse is unknown. According to Caroline Corder, a twenty-year-old waitress hired in April, the couple she knew only as "Jimmie and Helen" seemed to be regulars by the time she encountered them. She also revealed that during her first five months three members of the Barker-Karpis gang were present almost nightly. Kate Barker was often accompanied by Helen Ferguson and Myrtle Eaton, two of the gang's molls. (Corder later told FBI agents she had never heard the old woman addressed as "Ma"; it was always "Mother.") She identified photos of Karpis, whom everyone called "Ray," his girlfriend Dolores, Freddie Barker, and Volney Davis. Freddie, who once took her to lunch and offered her rides, was described as polite and too timid to directly ask her for a date.

Among the Barkers' friends observed at Louie's were two men Nelson was very anxious to meet. One, called "Jelly" by the others, was short and sported a thick mustache, glasses, and a "bad toupee." This was Frank Nash, who was accompanied by his wife, Frances, and his young stepdaughter. The other was Eddie Green, who with his longtime mistress, Bessie Skinner, had recently returned from a fishing excursion to northern Wisconsin.

Barker and Karpis were still too busy to engage in any lengthy socializing. The scheduled date for the Hamm kidnapping was just a week away, and the two were preparing a hideout in nearby Bensonville where the victim would be held until the ransom was paid. Nash and Green weren't involved in the caper, so Nelson was able to get acquainted, hoping to solicit them for future projects. Green seemed especially interested in working with the young hood. Long regarded as one of the Midwest's premier "jug markers" (someone who investigates and selects the best banks to plunder), he had worked with some of the biggest names in the business and played a prominent part in the Fairbury heist. Green was currently looking to make some connections in Chicago and find a temporary place there. Nelson supplied a detailed list of where to go and who to see.

Arriving in St. Paul on June 9, Nelson, Helen, and Father Coughlan checked into the Commodore Hotel on Western Avenue. The six-story edifice sporting an art deco bar and a magnificent ballroom was easily the most elegant establishment in the Twin Cities. Socialites from near and far, among them

F. Scott Fitzgerald and wife Zelda, had patronized the Commodore since its opening in 1920. In more recent years guests had included such notorious figures as Al Capone, bank robber Jimmy Keating, and Kate Barker.

Over the next few days Nelson showed Father Coughlan the city. Their tour included a stop at the Green Lantern, where Nelson introduced the priest to Tommy Carroll. On several occasions Nelson visited Carroll's Minneapolis apartment where, joined by Chuck Fisher, they discussed the proposed score at Grand Haven, the pledge of Eddie Bentz to assist them, and the setup at Long Beach. Fisher, formerly a chef in Michigan City and familiar with the area, displayed great enthusiasm for the project and declared he was ready to start immediately.

Carroll announced he had some issues to resolve before joining the crew. On May 18 he had been arrested in St. Paul on suspicion of burglary. Released only days earlier, he was presently negotiating through Harry Sawyer to get the charges dropped, hoping to see the matter finalized before leaving town. Another headache was brewing in his prolific love life. Both Sally and Jean, still unaware of each other's presence, were screaming for attention now that he was back on the streets. He intended to chose one as a traveling companion but was unable to decide which, or what to tell the other.

Tom Gannon, who showed up for several meetings at Carroll's place, reported that he also would be delayed, thanks to his duties at the Green Lantern. It would be at least a week, possibly two, before he could reach Long Beach.

As Nelson was struggling to line up recruits for the Grand Haven job, the city was buzzing over the latest gangland developments. On June 15 the Barkers snatched William Hamm off a St. Paul street and whisked the wealthy brewer away to their Illinois hideout while ransom negotiations were worked out. The story rapidly became the most publicized kidnapping since the Lindbergh abduction the previous year. Just two days later Frank Nash was dead, slain along with four lawmen, including one of Hoover's agents, in the so-called Kansas City Massacre. Nash, with numerous ties to the city, had been in St. Paul just the week before. Verne Miller, also a longtime associate of the Twin Cities underworld, was named one of the suspected perpetrators.

In the midst of all the furor Nelson, Helen, and Father Coughlan left St. Paul on June 22 and arrived in Long Beach the next day. Nelson immediately met with Bentz, promising that his St. Paul people would show over the next couple of weeks. The veteran, never known to rush into a job, seemed delighted to have some extra time to put all the pieces together. He asked Nelson, "How you boys fixed for firearms?"

Nelson replied that the gang had a shotgun and some pistols. "You'll need some heavier hardware," Bentz told him. "At least one machine gun, preferably two. I'll talk to a fellow I know in Chicago and see what he can do."

In the meantime Bentz drew up a list of items they would need, including several sets of Michigan license plates, a keg of roofing nails (tossed onto high-ways to puncture the tires of pursuing police cars), extra ammunition, a shovel, an ax, a medical kit, and several gas cans. Nelson and Bentz drove to Indiana Harbor where they acquired most of what they required from Art Stross. The pair also purchased a sawed-off 12-gauge riot gun with a pistol grip, two Remington rifles, and several .38 pistols mounted on .45 frames, a special model designed for the Pennsylvania State Police.

Stross later revealed it was at this time that Nelson encountered a band of hoods that had recently appeared in East Chicago. The five men, all ex-cons from Michigan City, were frequent visitors to Art's Army Store as well as the Inland Hotel, where several stayed from time to time. Bentz, who had met two of the men while Nelson was in St. Paul, presented the pair to his young pal. "This is Johnnie and Wayne, both fresh from the joint." Their three friends were introduced as Harry (Copeland), Sam (Goldstein), and "Whitey" (Clarence Mohler).

All seven, accompanied by Stross and a local fence named Fred Breman, retired to the Three Sisters, a waterfront tavern operated by Breman's brother. Johnnie, Wayne, and a couple of the others ordered gin fizzes. The entire group laughed when Nelson asked for his fizz without the gin.

Johnnie was obviously the leader of the five newcomers. His full name was John Herbert Dillinger. He was short, barely three inches taller than Nelson, with a narrow, roguishly handsome face, a high forehead, a cleft chin, and a cocky, crooked grin. A product of central Indiana, Dillinger had spent the last nine years incarcerated for a single crime—a bungled assault and robbery of a grocer. Paroled from Michigan City just a month earlier and presently a month shy of his thirtieth birthday, Dillinger was deeply embittered at the injustice of his lengthy sentence, and his goal was to pull off a series of profitable robberies to raise enough money to arrange a prison break for a small circle of friends he'd left behind bars.

Thus far Dillinger had tallied only one bank score, a $10,000 heist in New Castle, Ohio, with Copeland on June 10. Otherwise, working with an inept band of local criminals around Muncie and Indianapolis, he had robbed a string of supermarkets and drugstores, once striking an old man who got in his way. Just the previous day he had shot an assistant manager in the leg during a botched attempt to rob a factory. The reason for his recent visits to East Chicago was to recruit more professional accomplices, as well as looking up his old prison crony, Wayne, who was paroled two weeks after Dillinger.

Wayne's real name was Homer Van Meter. Tall and lanky, with sleepy eyes and slouching shoulders, he was more handsome than his scowling prison pho-tos indicated. Since his release he had grown a thin mustache, detracting from a slightly flattened nose. Two years older than Nelson, Van Meter had run away from his home in Fort Wayne as a teenager and hitchhiked to Chicago. Working as a bellhop and a busboy, his first brush with the law came in 1922 when he was arrested for being drunk and disorderly. The charge was dropped, but less than a year later he was arrested again for the same offense and spent forty-one days in jail. That same year he was caught stealing a car and was sentenced to serve one to ten years in Menard.

Paroled after thirteen months, he returned to Indiana and took up armed robbery. He narrowly escaped during a shootout at South Bend in which his partner was killed by police. Six days later, on March 12, 1925, lawmen captured him at Crown Point. This time the sentence was ten to twenty years. His best pal for the next seven years was fellow inmate John Dillinger.

Contrary to the popular belief that Nelson and Van Meter never liked each other, they in fact became instant friends. Their companions either departed or wandered off to other parts of the bar, leaving the two locked in conversation at a table. They spoke at length about one of Nelson's favorite subjects— Chicago. During his years in the Windy City Van Meter, like Karpis, had frequented many of the same hangouts and knew some of the same characters that Nelson did.

Gradually they discovered they shared a number of common interests, chiefly an insatiable obsession with firearms. They would constantly kid each other about who was the better marksman; Van Meter, known for his rowdy, often wicked sense of humor, was usually the instigator. Both possessed uncanny quickness and accuracy with guns, and some thought their respective bragging went beyond good-natured competition. "They were like two kids," recalled Marie Conforti, Van Meter's mistress. "One was always trying to out-do the other, especially in holdups. If one fired five shots, the other fired six, then the first had to top that."

It was a friendly rivalry but a harrowing experience for anyone caught standing on the sidelines. Each tried to be the toughest, the most menacing, with the volatility of the one igniting a worse response in the other. The inevitable result of their yearlong association would prove explosive.

Nelson confided that Bentz and he were staging a bank job in Michigan, and since they needed an extra man, he urged Van Meter to join them. But the ex-con was reluctant to commit himself. He felt a special loyalty to Dillinger and feared disappointing him by switching to another gang. But despite their close bond, Van Meter did not share Dillinger's agenda. He wanted no part of the proposed prison break at Michigan City, which he viewed as reckless and unrewarding. If the plan succeeded, Van Meter believed, it would mean the end of his relationship with Dillinger, for Harry Pierpont, one of the four convicts Dillinger had vowed to free, detested Van Meter and would surely bar him from the gang.

Nevertheless, Nelson extended an open invitation to Van Meter to visit him at Long Beach, whatever his decision might be.

The next day, June 26, Chuck Fisher arrived from St. Paul. After meeting Bentz and spending the night at Nelson's cottage, the portly bandit drove to Michigan City and rented a room above the Willard Cafe. At about the same time, another recruit reached Long Beach, a short, stocky, stubby-legged criminal in his late thirties named Earl Doyle. Nelson had met him either in St. Paul, where one of Doyle's brothers lived, or possibly in Chicago. Originally from Kansas City, Doyle had been a successful bootlegger along the Oklahoma-Missouri-Kansas borders before Prohibition agents caught him in 1927. Sentenced to two years in Leavenworth, he was released in 1930 and participated in several bank holdups, including a 1932 Kansas City robbery with Eddie Green in which a lawman was killed.

He was accompanied by his wife, Hazel Angleton Doyle, an attractive blond almost ten years younger. She brought along her beloved "babies," a pair of Pekinese dogs. Hazel, a close friend of Nelson's sister Amy, may have put Baby Face in contact in Doyle to recruit him for the Grand Haven heist. The couple leased a cottage not far from those occupied by Bentz and Nelson.

On the night of June 27 Bentz called a meeting at Nelson's place. He informed the others that his weapons supplier in Chicago had reported it would take at least three months to deliver a pair of Tommyguns. "That's not going to help us if you're planning to go through with this before the end of summer," Bentz told them. "I put in a call to a gun dealer I met a few months ago in San Antonio. He says he can get what we need. All we have to do is pay cash and pick 'em up in person, if a couple of you don't mind making the long drive down there."

Nelson and Fisher volunteered to make the trip. In their absence Bentz and Doyle planned to visit Grand Haven, re-case the bank, and work out the getaway route. Bentz wrote down for Nelson instructions for contacting his San Antonio source: "Lebman Sporting Goods, 111 South Flores Street. Ask for Hymie."

Early the next morning Nelson, Helen, their son Ronnie, Nelson's mother, and Fisher piled into the Terraplane and started for Texas. Darlene was left in the care of Hazel Doyle. Just hours after they departed Tom Gannon reached Long Beach. He was invited to move into the Doyle cottage.

❋ ❋ ❋

On the afternoon of June 30 Hyman Saul Lebman, proprietor of a San Antonio sporting goods shop specializing in saddlery and second-hand guns, glanced out his store window and noticed a dark sedan with California plates parking in front. Two men stepped out along with a young woman and a small boy. An elderly woman with gray hair remained in the car.

Entering Lebman's shop, the younger of the two men asked for Hymie and introduced himself as Jimmie Williams. He was well dressed, about five-foot-five, no more than 135 pounds, with sandy hair combed straight back, a neatly trimmed mustache, and light blue, almost grayish eyes. His companion was a burly fellow who said little and seemed curiously out-of-place with the dapper, talkative Jimmie and the young woman and boy he proudly introduced as his family.

"You folks from California?" Lebman asked.

"Truth is," answered Jimmie, "we just drove down from Indiana. We've got a mutual friend back there who says you're a helluva gunsmith."

Lebman realized then that the party was expecting to pick up the order placed by Bentz. He regretfully informed the visitors there had been a snag in the delivery of the machine guns. The weapons had been shipped disassembled by a distributor in Fort Worth, and for some reason all the parts had not yet arrived. Lebman said it might be another few days before the merchandise would be ready. Jimmie assured him there was no problem; in fact, he was looking forward to spending some time in the city and taking in the sights with his family.

Nelson and his companions spent a full week in San Antonio. Each day, except for July 4, Nelson dropped by the store, sometimes with his wife and son or Fisher, other times alone. Lebman was impressed by the young man. Like so many others, he found it difficult to visualize Nelson as a gangster, although he knew, since he was associated with Bentz, that must be the case. He also suspected Nelson's real name was not Jimmie—several times the shop owner overheard Helen calling her husband "Les."

Lebman was no saint, either. A Russian Jew born in Odessa in 1903, he became a naturalized U.S. citizen at the age of nine and worked hard to be accepted in Texas society and to build a reputable business. While developing his trade as a gunsmith and store owner, Lebman discovered the handsome profits that could be realized from wholesaling exotic weaponry, especially machine guns. In years past he had made extra money by smuggling guns, primarily into Mexico, often selling to the highest bidder among several opposing factions. More recently, with the increasing demand for machine guns by American gangsters, Lebman had resorted to smuggling weapons back across the border to re-sell in the States.

Nelson—whom Lebman regarded as bright, easygoing, and a great conversationalist—was the kind of customer he preferred. The young man talked endlessly about his native Chicago, fascinating Lebman with inside stories about the city's most famous mobsters. He also spoke fondly of living in California the previous year, declaring San Francisco to be "a great town."

But most of all they discussed guns. According to Lebman, Jimmie "really knew his stuff." Nelson was particularly interested in Lebman's current pet project—converting a standard automatic pistol into a "baby machine gun." Lebman got the idea from a design patented by a West Coast arms company for the Los Angeles Police Department, specifically for use by motorcycle and patrol car officers. The original model—advertised as the "Steady Fire and Multi-Shot Riot and Anti-Bandit Gun," with "the handiness of a pistol, the accuracy of a rifle, and the rapidity of a machine gun"—came in two versions, a .45 automatic and a .38 super-automatic modified to fire on full auto. Both were fitted with a shoulder stock and an extra-long clip containing eighteen rounds for the .45 model, twenty-two for the .38. Lebman's design discarded the bulky shoulder stock and added a vertical foregrip (taken from a Thompson machine gun) and a Cutts-type compensator to improve accuracy. A single sustained press of the trigger emptied the eighteen- (or twenty-two-) shot magazine in a mere five seconds.

On July 6 Lebman reported that their order was ready. In addition to two submachine guns—for which Lebman charged $300 apiece—Nelson and Fisher purchased four automatic pistols. Baby Face promised to return in a couple of months to buy some of the shop owner's machine-gun pistols.

❋ ❋ ❋

That same day Eddie Bentz and Earl Doyle left Long Beach in Bentz's 1932 Buick to make the 100-mile trip to Grand Haven on Highway 31 along Lake Michigan's shoreline. Bentz had delayed the trip because his wife wanted to entertain friends and relatives over the July Fourth holiday, and because he needed at least several days to properly re-case the bank and chart an escape route back to Long Beach.

Shortly after noon the pair entered the sleepy town of about 10,000 nestled along the lake at a point almost equidistant from Muskegon to the north, Grand Rapids due east, and Holland directly south. Bentz parked on Washington Avenue near the People's Savings Bank and instructed Doyle to go inside and discreetly look over the layout.

Bentz walked to the post office across the street and stood by the window, where he spent the next twenty minutes sketching a diagram of the bank's exterior and street setup. The bank occupied the southeast corner of Washington and Third next to a furniture store. There were two entrances: the main portal on Washington and a door in the rear of the building that opened onto Third near the alley behind the bank. Finishing his drawing, Bentz walked to the bank and leisurely strolled through the lobby, scanning the interior and studying each employee. There were four teller windows. Bentz went to the one affording the best view of the vault and made a mental note of everything as he exchanged a twenty-dollar bill for singles.

Back at the car Bentz and Doyle compared notes and drew up a design of the bank's interior. They also discussed the seven employees—five men and two women—they had observed. "Can you pick out the one most likely to give us trouble?" Bentz asked.

Doyle shrugged. "I don't believe I can."

Bentz had identified him immediately—the tall, muscular teller who changed his twenty. "The guy looks like he's been in the service at some time. You want to make sure you cover him right away and keep him covered, 'cause he's definitely the type who might try to pull some hero shit if he gets the chance."

The two remained in town overnight, staying at separate hotels, Bentz at the Hotel Ferry. The next morning he visited the library and checked the Bankers Directory, which provided the People's Bank's latest financial report and the names of its principal employees. He was able to identify the tall teller as Assistant Cashier Arthur Welling. The head cashier was Frederick Bolt, the man Bentz deemed most likely to open the vault. Before leaving town Bentz returned to the bank, this time changing a fifty-dollar bill as he reexamined the interior and the employees.

The pair spent the next three days charting and driving their getaway route. Bentz's customary method was to depart in the opposite direction he intended to flee, then work his way along country roads in a sweeping circle to bring him back to his destination. However, the only road north out of Grand Haven was U.S. 31, which crossed the Grand River on a swing bridge that could be raised, leaving the bandits trapped. Bentz worked out a route that would take them ten miles south, then seven miles east, then twenty north, avoiding towns in the process. At that point the route zigzagged southeast, going north of Lansing, northeast of Jackson, and west of Adrian to Highway 20 in Ohio, and from there into Indiana. They reached Long Beach on July 10 and located Nelson and Fisher, who had returned the night before.

For the remainder of the month Bentz met with the others—Nelson, Fisher, Doyle, and Gannon—almost daily to school them in the fine art of bank robbery. He took them to a secluded beach and demonstrated how their new machine guns should be held, fired, and swiftly reloaded.

After all had mastered the technique, he gave them with his special sermon on the use of the Tommygun: "Make sure you never actually shoot anyone. It's not worth it. It'll only make the cops come after you with everything they got. Plus, if you grab any securities in the holdup they'll be worthless, too hot to handle if there's a killing attached to them.

"Remember," Bentz said, "the object is to scare the hell out of people. Blast the glass in store windows or shoot the shit out of some parked cars. The noise will drive the people off the street and out of your way, which is really all you want. I've been knocking off banks for the last ten years and I've never shot a single soul."

They repeatedly reviewed the plan and each man's assigned duties. Bentz explained that a good robbery team consisted of five key roles. The "wheelman" occupied the driver's seat of the getaway car at all times, keeping the motor running and a machine gun ready in case an alarm sounded before the robbery was completed. The "tiger" was stationed at the bank's entrance as a lookout; once in position, he prevented anyone from entering or leaving the building. The "center fielder" covered the customers and employees with a second machine gun while standing in the lobby. The remaining two bandits were the money collectors; the "skimmer" grabbed the cash from the teller cages while the other cleaned out the vault.

Bentz emphasized that as long as each man knew his specific role and held his position, the holdup should go smoothly and take no more than five minutes. He continued to stress that, because of their inexperience and the particular setup of this bank, the robbery team should consist of six men. The extra man could act as a second tiger, guarding the rear door while the front lookout helped the center fielder secure the lobby. Each time he inquired who would fill the other two spots, Nelson assured him there were more men on the way—at least one from St. Paul (Carroll) and a hood from Chicago who wanted to participate.

Finally Nelson awkwardly told Bentz, "The boys and I were thinking we almost have to have you along on this job."

"That wasn't our deal, Jimmie," the older criminal replied grimly.

"I know. But we'll botch it for sure if you're not there to make sure things go right."

Bentz shook his head. "I've got other things to do. Besides, I already earned my share of the take. Our agreement was I set you boys up with a score and teach you how to pull it off like professionals. My work is done. The rest is up to you."

"Think it over, please," Nelson insisted. "Along with your share of the cash, we'll let you have all the securities we snatch, if you go with us."

Gannon, Doyle, and Fisher appealed to the veteran as well, but it took several days before Bentz wore down and agreed to assist in the robbery. There were two conditions: First, he would take the role of wheelman. And second, since he had "another venture" to attend to, the date for the holdup—set for late July—would be rescheduled for mid-August. Nelson and his pals eagerly accepted the terms.

❋ ❋ ❋

With the plan for the Grand Haven heist basically set, the outlaws had little else to do but relax and enjoy the next several weeks of summer along the lakefront. Nelson's cottage seemed to be the focal point for most of the activity, as someone was always dropping by or staying over. Nelson and his wife entertained their friends with cookouts and conversation that frequently lasted into the morning hours.

By the last week of July Tommy Carroll and girlfriend Sally Bennett showed up, registering at a hotel near East Chicago. To the disappointment of his cronies, Carroll seemed more preoccupied with keeping Sally pacified with numerous trips into Chicago to visit the World's Fair and tour the nightclub scene (where she hoped to find work and leave the less glitzy St. Paul circuit) than discussing the upcoming robbery.

Another familiar face at the cottage was Jack Perkins, often accompanied by his wife and two children. When Bentz was able to obtain just two bullet-proof vests through Art Stross, Nelson had turned to his boyhood buddy, who promised to deliver the needed body armor for a price of $200 apiece. Perkins was also enlisted to secure the getaway car several days before the robbery. Despite Bentz's objections, Baby Face declared, "We'll have to take our chances with a hot car on the job."

About this same time Homer Van Meter joined the group, moving into the cottage as Nelson's guest. Occasional callers, no doubt attracted by the congregation of fellow criminals, included Barker-Karpis gang member Volney Davis, veteran bank robber Eddie Doll, and ex-con Jack Liberty.

Among the parade of visitors that summer were a few not affiliated with the underworld. Bentz introduced a number of his relatives, in-laws, and friends to his neighbor Jimmie, who was usually hosting a huge gathering next door. One of these was Bentz's younger half-brother Theodore, who occasionally helped Eddie dispose of stolen bonds and securities. Ted, who was destined to pay a dreadful price for his association with his brother, later admitted to meeting Nelson, Van Meter, Fisher, and Doyle there and learning that they were planning a robbery. Several days before the holdup Eddie warned him to leave Long Beach, saying they would soon have some "paper to peddle."

On three occasions Nelson's sister Julie and her husband made the trip to Long Beach. As Bob Fitzsimmons later explained, the day before each visit Helen would come to their apartment and arrange a specific time to rendezvous at the Willard Café, and from there she would follow Nelson's car to the cottage. Fitzsimmons said both he and his wife often "felt uneasy" at the cottage due to the "tough-looking characters" who were always present. Although Nelson and Helen urged them to stay over, the couple each time chose to return to Chicago by nightfall. During one of their visits, Fitzsimmons noted that "a Catholic priest dropped in" and appeared to know all of Nelson's guests by name.

The presence of Father Coughlan among the outlaws and their women was frequently puzzling to observers outside the criminal clique. A year later, under FBI interrogation, the priest claimed he had no idea that any of the visitors were involved in illegal activities. At Nelson's cottage he was introduced to Van Meter, who called himself Wayne Huttner, and became reacquainted with Carroll, who introduced Radio Sally as his wife. Coughlan also spent time with

Chuck Fisher and on July 31 accompanied him to a Michigan City car dealership where Fisher, using the name H. L. Keith, purchased a new Dodge sedan.

Of Nelson's friends the one who most easily impressed Coughlan that summer was the suave, refined Eddie Bentz. The priest visited Bentz's cottage almost as often as he visited Nelson's. Bentz proudly displayed his collection of rare coins and his library of more than three thousand books, including first editions of Stevenson, Hugo, Cooper, Voltaire, and Washington Irving. Bentz's favorite subject was golf, and he once requested that Coughlan sign, as a reference, his membership application for the Long Beach Golf Club. The priest agreed, although he didn't understand why Bentz, whom he knew as Ed Dewey, used the name Mulheim on the form. Bentz showed his appreciation by inviting Coughlan to join him on the links. Another time, during a meal at their cottage, Bentz and his wife revealed that they were unable to have children and inquired if Coughlan could adopt a baby for them.

Despite Coughlan's professed naivete, there is powerful evidence suggesting that he not only knew he was associating with outlaws but was also aware a major robbery was in the works. In any case, the priest, perhaps unknowingly, played a role in the preparation for the holdup. Two weeks before the robbery he drove to Oak Park at Nelson's request and returned the next day with a young couple who rented a room near the Father's residence on the outskirts of Michigan City. Later that day Coughlan brought them to Nelson's cottage where they were introduced to Bentz as Mr. and Mrs. Freddie Monahan. Nelson proudly reported that he and Monahan had worked together in the Touhy gang and vouched for his reliability.

Bentz later described Monahan as about thirty years old, six feet tall and 190 pounds, with a slender build, narrow face, and small, shifty hazel eyes. The two middle fingers of his right hand were missing. Monahan's wife looked much younger.

For reasons mostly instinctive, Bentz—who had met Monahan just three times prior to the day of the heist—took an instant disliking to him. The veteran had always trusted his intuition, but this time he let it go. In the ten weeks he had known Nelson, Bentz had come to regard him as "a perceptive kid," and therefore accepted his enthusiastic support of Monahan, although he suspected Nelson's fierce loyalty to friends might hinder his judgment.

Shortly after Monahan's arrival the principal figures—Nelson, Bentz, Fisher, Gannon, Doyle, Carroll, Van Meter, and Monahan—assembled around the kitchen table at Nelson's cottage to finalize their plans. According to one version, Father Coughlan was also present and even took part in some of the discussion. The key debate at the outset centered around who would be the sixth member of the holdup team. While Bentz favored Van Meter, the majority were persuaded by Nelson to select Freddie after what Bentz termed "considerable talk." Van Meter and Carroll were encouraged to remain available in case any of the six dropped out or were unable to participate. A date was set for the holdup: Friday August 18.

Three days before the robbery Nelson drove to Chicago and contacted Perkins. The next day Jack delivered a freshly stolen seven-passenger Buick sedan with only 1700 miles on the odometer. Nelson gave his friend fifty dollars for his service, promising a sizable bonus after the holdup. As Bentz, Gannon, and Van Meter looked on, Nelson subjected the vehicle to a thorough inspection to make certain everything was in perfect running order. A pair of Indiana plates—ordered by Bentz through a cousin working for a Michigan City car dealer—were substituted. That evening Nelson took the getaway car to Father Coughlan's home, Bentz following in his own vehicle. The Buick was placed in the garage for safekeeping. The priest later explained that "Jimmie and Mr. Dewey asked me to temporarily store the car for them as they did not have room for it at the cottages."

On Thursday, August 17, the gang members collected their equipment and placed in the basement of Nelson's cottage. That evening a line of savage thunderstorms rumbled through the region. Although exhorted by Bentz to get plenty of rest, Nelson, Fisher (who stayed at the cottage that night), and Gannon remained awake past midnight, too anxious to sleep. They sat on the porch watching the flashes of lightning and the torrential rain that swept over the lake in sheets.

By morning the storms subsided. When Bentz and Doyle came over shortly after sunrise, Nelson greeted them with a wide grin and observed, "Looks like great weather for a bank robbery."

Father Coughlan and Monahan were the last to arrive, driving the Buick. As the hardware and weapons were loaded inside, Bentz consulted a checklist to be sure nothing was left behind. The supplies included the twenty-five-pound keg of roofing nails, several five-gallon cans of gas, a gallon of oil, two water jugs, three pink-and-blue laundry sacks to hold the loot, six bulletproof vests, extra license plates, and a first-aid kit that had been augmented with a syringe and vials of morphine. A stack of maps and the notebook containing Bentz's getaway chart were shoved into the Buick's glove compartment. A picnic basket filled with sandwiches and snacks prepared by Helen and Verna was placed in the back seat.

The gang's arsenal was packed in the trunk. In addition to the pistols each man carried there were the pair of machine guns, two shotguns, two Remington riles, five extra pistols and a dozen backup clips, and boxes of assorted ammunition.

Bentz had suggested the others dress in worn, loose-fitting clothes, and he set an example by wearing a shabby pair of blue-and-white farmer's coveralls. Nelson was the one exception, putting on an expensive blue suit, a tie, and straw hat.

He waited until the last moment to dart inside for a quick farewell to his wife and children. Although upbeat and excited, he told Helen, "Better have the kids and our stuff ready to go when I get back. We might have to leave in a hurry."

The six bandits climbed into the Buick and, with Nelson at the wheel, were approaching Grand Haven on U.S. 31 by one o'clock. Three miles outside town Bentz spotted a side road on the left and instructed him to turn off. Parking in a patch of woods between the highway and the beach, the bandits stepped out and stretched before donning the bulky bulletproof vests beneath their shirts and rechecking their weapons. Bentz set out the picnic basket and encouraged the others to eat. Aside from Bentz, only the skinny, scar-faced Gannon displayed any appetite.

As Bentz leaned against the car devouring a sandwich, Nelson approached with an uneasy expression. Suspecting he would hear something he wouldn't like, Bentz snapped, "Now what?"

"Sorry, Ed, but we were thinking we'll miss the big money with you staying in the car."

"I agreed to come along as the wheelman, Jimmie. What the hell? You wait till you get me all the way up here before you drop this on me? If I go into the bank, who do want to drive?"

"Freddie can handle the driving."

"Freddie's got some fingers missing," Bentz pointed out.

"That's exactly the reason he should stay outside. It's the kind of thing witnesses will notice and remember."

Grudgingly conceding that Nelson made sense, and realizing this wasn't the time or place for an argument, Bentz consented to the switch. He called the others together to discuss the change in plans and review everyone's position using the diagram he'd sketched of the streets and bank's interior. After outlining their approach to the bank in two separate groups, he instructed Monahan to park the car near the post office where he could observe both of the bank's doors. "Stay behind the wheel, keep the motor running, and be ready to use the Tommy to clear the street if there's trouble," Bentz ordered.

Doyle would station himself outside the rear door to ensure that Monahan didn't miss any action on the street. Gannon was positioned at the front entrance to help secure the lobby. Nelson, armed with the second machine gun, was appointed center fielder. Fisher would "skim" the cages while Bentz emptied the vault.

The veteran had a few extra points to emphasize. He reminded the others to speak as little as possible and try not to leave any fingerprints. He told them to order the employees and customers to lie on the floor but cautioned, "Don't tell anyone to raise their hands. A pedestrian or a motorist spots that and we'll have the whole town down on us." He also warned against treating women rudely or abusively, for they might scream, turn hysterical, or—worse—inspire men to come to their defense.

When he finished, Nelson and Doyle replaced the Buick's Indiana plates with a set of Michigan tags. While Doyle and Monahan topped off the gas tank with a couple of gallons of reserve fuel, Nelson emptied the picnic basket and placed his machine gun inside. Bentz took the three sacks, handed one to Fisher, and stuffed the others inside his coveralls.

At a few minutes past two o'clock all was ready.

❄ ❄ ❄

It was a pleasant, peaceful afternoon in Grand Haven. A steady, cooling wind from the lake blew along the small town's streets, holding the temperatures to the low 80s beneath the scorching mid-August sun. The storms of the previous night had moved on, and the ground had dried sufficiently to allow the area's two major events that day—the Ionia Free Fair and the finals of the Spring Lake Women's Golf Tournament—to resume without delay.

The clock in the tower of the First Reformed Church read 2:25 when the Buick sedan pulled into town. None of the residents noticed anything odd about the vehicle as it cruised in lazy yet deliberate circles around the business district like a cautious predator. In the alley behind the People's Savings Bank three boys with wooden pistols played cops-and-robbers, blithely unaware of the much more realistic version of the game that would soon erupt in Grand Haven's streets.

At precisely 2:40 the Buick stopped at the corner of Franklin Avenue and Fourth Street, dropping off two men who marched north toward Washington. The car moved west along Franklin, depositing three more figures at the corner of Third. The driver, alone now, proceeded to Second Street, turned right, then right again on Washington, positioning the car near the post office.

By that time the first two men had rounded the corner and briskly approached the bank from the east, passing the Addison, Pellegrom, and Colson Furniture Store. They must have appeared a curious pair. One was big and husky, dressed in coveralls, and his companion was half a foot shorter, looked half his age, and was smartly attired in a dark suit and carrying a picnic basket.

Their three confederates were moving up Third Street. Doyle halted beside the rear door while Fisher and Gannon continued walking, reaching Washington at the same moment Bentz and Nelson came abreast of the bank. The front door, set back between the building's two ornamental pillars, was propped open to allow the afternoon breeze inside. Bentz glanced in, make a quick survey of the street, then touched his hat—the signal to proceed—and entered with Nelson directly behind him. Fisher and Gannon slipped inside moments later.

Almost from the moment the bandits stepped through the door things began to go wrong. On the positive side, the six employees—head cashier

Frederick "Ted" Bolt, assistant cashier Arthur Welling, auditor John Lindemulder, tellers William Pellegrom and Martha Meschke, and bookkeeper Vera Correll—were immersed in various duties, trying to finish before the bank's 3 P.M. closing and too busy to notice the four suspicious figures entering in single file. The only other person present was a Mrs. Van Dyke, who was doing custodial work at the rear of the building. Though the lobby was empty of customers, a pair of local businessmen, Peter Van Lopik and Lawrence Dornbos, were approaching and saw Gannon struggling to shut the front door. Thinking the bank was about to close, they hurried inside.

Bentz immediately headed straight for the office of Ted Bolt. According to the plan, the others were to wait until he brought the head cashier into the lobby at gunpoint. But Bentz froze at the office door when he found Bolt at his desk speaking on the phone. Instead of drawing his pistol, Bentz stood in the doorway like an impatient customer until Bolt finished his call.

Nelson took up his assigned position in front of Art Welling, the man Bentz had designated as the person most likely to attempt heroics. When Bentz failed to reappear from the office, Nelson, cradling the picnic basket, seemed unsure what to do when Welling looked up and asked, "Can I help you?"

To buy some time Nelson asked to exchange a couple of dollars for nickels. Welling had a roll within reach and instantly tossed it onto the counter. Fisher, standing just behind Baby Face, was unable to stifle a croaking laugh. Nelson glared indignantly at his companion, then started to chuckle himself.

Welling, a star football player at the University of Michigan a decade earlier, didn't see what was so funny and wondered, *What's wrong with these fools?* Naturally suspicious—as Bentz had feared—he worked the tip of his shoe beneath the floor alarm, a foot pedal which had to be raised, rather than depressed, to be activated. When Bentz brought Bolt out of the front office, Nelson whipped out the machine gun and cast aside the basket. No longer looking amused, he ordered Welling, "Step back and lie on the floor, damn you!"

The cashier set off the silent alarm with his foot as he obeyed.

Bentz barked a command for everyone to drop. Gannon covered the two customers, echoing the order to hit the floor. As Van Lopik and Dornbos complied, he locked the door and pulled down the front shades. Fisher intercepted the two women coming out of an office and directed them to where Nelson was holding his weapon on Welling and Pellegrom. Bentz growled at Bolt and Lindemulder to "worm" their way across the floor to the others.

Leaving Gannon to watch the lobby, Nelson scampered around the counter and stood guard over the prostrate employees. Fisher started collecting cash from the cages while Bentz marched to the rear door and opened it. Doyle stepped inside, nodding that all was clear on the streets. Bentz returned to the front, leaving Doyle standing beside a maintenance closet.

Unknown to Doyle and his comrades, Mrs. Van Dyke had heard the commotion and ducked into the closet seconds before Bentz stomped down the hall. Standing in the dark, cramped interior clutching her broom, she peeked through the partially open door at the pudgy Doyle. The thought flashed through her mind she could easily crack the broom handle over the robber's skull. But remembering that she had four young daughters at home, she decided to remain a concealed spectator.

❄ ❄ ❄

One might have thought it was a remarkably bad day for Grand Haven to experience a bank robbery. Police Chief Lawrence DeWitt had taken the day off to attend the Ionia fair with his family, and Sheriff Ben Rosema was in nearby Leeland on business. As a result, the response to the bank's silent alarm probably wasn't as rapid or organized as it might have been. When the klaxon sounded at the Sheriff's Office, Undersheriff Edward Rycenga and Deputy Maurice Rosema—the sheriff's son—decided to answer the call, taking shotguns despite their certainty that it was a false alarm.

In addition to sounding at the Sheriff's Office, the Grand Haven Police Station, and the State Police Post north of town, the remote alarm also began to blare in the furniture store next door to the bank. Edward Kinkema, the proprietor and a cousin of Ted Bolt, snatched a Remington repeating shotgun from a wall rack and rushed outside. Approaching the bank he noticed a large, dark sedan parked near the post office, its engine idling. Positive it was the getaway car, Kinkema raised his shotgun and aimed at the driver. The bandit instantly slumped down, then threw the Buick into reverse and vanished down the street.

A few curious pedestrians, attracted by the car's screeching departure and the sight of the gun-toting Kinkema, began to cluster around the bank. The furniture dealer frantically waved his arms and warned them to get off the street. Instead the crowd of onlookers began to swell.

❄ ❄ ❄

After leaving Doyle inside the rear door, Bentz hurried back to the others and ordered Bolt to accompany him to the vault. The head cashier repeatedly fumbled the combination and complained he was unaccustomed to opening the safe. In an irritated voice Bentz told Bolt to go back and lie down with the others, then shouted to Nelson, "Bring Welling over here."

"Get moving," Nelson snarled, prodding the cashier with his machine gun. Warned by Bentz not to "try anything foolish," Welling stalled, working the tumbler with methodical slowness while the big bandit persistently grumbled, "Hurry it up or we'll shoot you. Come on, come on!"

After delaying as long as he could, Welling finally opened the safe and was directed to get back with the rest. At that moment Gannon, peering out the front window, spotted Kinkema lurking on the sidewalk with his shotgun and saw people gathering across the street. He immediately alerted Nelson, who dashed to the vault and cried, "Hurry, we got a rank (alarm)."

Bentz trotted out of the vault and looked toward the windows. "What's our move?" Nelson asked the veteran.

"Get everyone to the back door."

"The women too?"

At the front Gannon called out, "Looks like things are warming up out there."

"Everyone," Bentz told Nelson. "Get 'em all back there."

✶ ✶ ✶

Minutes earlier Charles Bugielski, twenty-one-year-old assistant manager of the McClellan Five and Ten Cent Store, had strolled across Third Street with the afternoon deposit. It was part of his daily routine to arrive at the bank's rear door and tap on the glass to be admitted. But today there was no reply, even after repeated knocking. Stepping back into the street to check the clock in the church tower—it was a couple of minutes past three o'clock—Bugielski heard someone call out, "Hey, Charlie!"

It was Ed Kinkema, standing in a low crouch near the corner of the bank, clutching a shotgun to his chest. He motioned at the building and exclaimed, "Bank robbery!"

Bugielski hurried back across the street to his convertible parked behind McClellan's, retrieving a .38 revolver he kept in the glove box. Kinkema joined him at the rear of the store, and both trained their weapons on the bank's back door.

✶ ✶ ✶

The five robbers herded their eight hostages down the narrow hallway until the entire group was pressed around the exit. Nelson slipped behind Bolt, jabbed the banker's spine with the muzzle of his Tommygun, and ordered, "You lead the way, baldy." Bolt opened the door and stepped out, the baby-faced gunman hunkering behind him. Doyle, using Welling as his shield, came next, followed by Bentz, his huge arm encircling one of the women. The other prisoners, shoved together and moving as one, squeezed through the doorway, with Fisher and Gannon bringing up the rear.

As the procession emerged shots rang out from the opposite side of Third Street. Kinkema and Bugielski fired high, hoping to throw a scare into the bandits. Nelson immediately answered with his machine gun, firing a quick burst into the air, then sending a stream of slugs across the side of the store. The pair of would-be ambushers threw themselves down. Inside McClellan's, customers screamed and ran for cover as several of Nelson's bullets chewed through the walls.

At that moment the county patrol car arrived, unwittingly turning the corner onto Third Street and pulling almost directly into Nelson's line of fire. Abruptly realizing the call was not a false alarm, Rycenga and Rosema grabbed their shotguns and scrambled out the car's right side.

Nelson swung his machine gun toward the new target, strafing the vehicle with a blizzard of bullets. A side window shattered, a tire blew, and gas splattered onto the street from the punctured fuel tank. The two lawmen took cover near Kinkema and Bugielski, and all four began returning fire.

Confusion and raw panic erupted among the robbers and their captives. Some of the hostages tried to retreat into the bank, only to be pushed back out by Fisher and Gannon who had to fight to get through the door. When Doyle opened fire with his pistol, Welling broke away and dove under a parked car. The woman Bentz was using as a shield dropped to the pavement. Others followed her example or tried to run. To make matters worse, within seconds of the first shots being fired the air on both sides of the street grew thick with gunsmoke.

In the midst of all this, Bentz stood dumfounded as he scanned the intersection for the Buick. Fisher, right behind him, screamed, "Car! Car! Where the hell is our car?"

Seeing they were in a bad situation that was growing worse by the second, Bentz called to his comrades to follow him. First colliding with one hostage, then almost tripping over another, he ran south toward Franklin. Nelson was close behind him, scuttling sideways as he squeezed off short, sporadic bursts at the rear of McClellan's.

With Nelson's machine gun slugs shrieking over their heads and partly blinded by the gunsmoke, the officers and businessmen poured a hail of bullets and buckshot at the figures scattering outside the bank. Unfortunately, the indiscriminate firing took a greater toll on their fellow citizens than it did on the outlaws. Pellegrom, trying to flee toward Washington, crumpled to the sidewalk with a pellet embedded in his foot. Lindemulder dropped facedown to escape the barrage but was grazed across his back by a volley of slugs. Van Lopik was sprawled a few feet away with buckshot wounds in his neck, arms, back, and thighs. Dornbos, the other customer, managed to dart into the alley and escaped injury.

On the west side of the street the only casualty was Julian Pleinies, a retired army sergeant employed as a custodian at the Elks Club next to McClellan's. He was performing some yardwork when the shooting erupted. A stray .45 slug, undoubtedly from Nelson's weapon, plowed into his lower back and lodged in his groin.

Gannon raced after Bentz and Nelson; Fisher paused long enough to fire a couple shots across the street, then followed his partners. Lagging behind and not so lucky, Doyle reeled as a load of buckshot creased his forehead. The stunned bandit groped about for a new human shield. (His original, Welling, was still beneath the car, untouched by the gunfire.) Doyle latched on to Bolt, who had been cast aside by Nelson when the gun battle began.

But Bolt was in no mood to be dragged away as a hostage. He seized Doyle's gun hand, trying to pry the weapon from his grasp. As they struggled the pistol fired and Doyle screamed. The bullet had blown a hole through his left hand.

With the other robbers on the run, the two officers moved into the street, firing at the fleeing quartet. Kinkema, his shotgun empty, saw Bolt grappling with the remaining bandit for the pistol. With Bugielski behind him, the furniture dealer charged across the street to aid his cousin.

He arrived just in time. Despite his bleeding head and hand, Doyle turned the pistol toward Bolt, but before he could pull the trigger, Kinkema swung his shotgun like a club, smashing the stock over the gunman's skull. Doyle toppled over, pulling Bolt down on top of him.

Doyle's misfortunes continued. As he fell his left leg twisted awkwardly beneath him, the femur snapping in two places. Still he continued to fight. When Bolt struggled free, Doyle fired toward the banker, Kinkema, and Bugielski, but the bullet remarkably missed all three. Kinkema hit him again with the shotgun as the others battered him with their fists and feet. Even after Kinkema wrested the pistol from his grasp, Doyle fought and cursed, attempting to crawl away from his assailants with his broken leg dragging behind. "Shoot him! Kill him!" someone shouted.

Bugielski, aware that his pistol was empty, pressed the muzzle against Doyle's head and cocked the hammer. The robber froze. "Don't kill me," he pleaded. "My leg is broke. I'm not going anywhere."

Meanwhile, his fellow bandits continued their frantic retreat along Third Street. Every few seconds Nelson's machine gun chattered as he sprayed lead into plate glass windows to drive curious spectators away and discourage pursuit. "Go easy on the soup," Bentz called to him. "All our extra ammo is in the car."

Bentz spotted a figure crouching behind a parked car and fired—the first and only shot he took that day. The bullet broke a side window and sent the onlooker scurrying away. Gannon, too busy running, had not fired at all. It was then that Bentz realized the sack, containing more than $100,000 in securities and several hundred dollars in cash, had slipped from his grasp during the commotion around the bank's rear door.

Fisher had dropped his cash-filled bag several times, but in each instance he stopped and picked it up. Some cash had spilled out, leaving a trail of money behind them. Stories persisted for some time in Grand Haven that some residents, mostly kids, darted into the street and filled their pockets, adding to the pandemonium and slowing efforts to pursue the bandits. Bugielski and other merchants reported that youngsters seemed to have plenty of extra money to spend on candy over the next few days.

❄ ❄ ❄

Reaching Franklin Street the stranded desperados looked for an accessible vehicle. Bentz spotted an oncoming Chevrolet with two women in the front seat and immediately ran into the street waving his arms. As the car screeched to a halt he yanked open the driver's door and shoved his pistol inside, threatening to "plug" the occupants if they didn't get out. When the woman at the wheel failed to move quickly enough, Bentz—forgetting his own rule about mistreating ladies—gruffly pulled her from the car, tearing her dress. "Wait," she cried as Bentz squeezed his bearish frame into her seat. "Don't take our babies!"

Four small children—the three sons of one woman and the daughter of another—were huddled in the back seat. Fisher and Gannon quickly lifted them out and took their places.

Nelson fired a last blast into the air to keep the spectators back, or perhaps as a final exasperated farewell to the inhabitants of Grand Haven, before leaping into the front seat beside Bentz. "We gotta go back for Doyle," he said as they sped away.

"Not a chance," Bentz retorted. "We don't have the ammo. Hell, we don't even have our get (getaway chart), thanks to your pal Freddie. I'm afraid Doyle is on his own."

"He's right," Gannon added. "We can't go back in there."

Bentz turned right on Second Street and headed south until reaching U.S. 31, leaving Grand Haven and Earl Doyle behind. The outlaws were almost a mile out of town before they noticed the gas gauge was bouncing on empty.

❄ ❄ ❄

Once Doyle was fully subdued, Rycenga and Bugielski leaped into the latter's convertible and took off after the bandits. The trail was easy to follow inside the city limits—townspeople were clustered at almost every street corner excitedly pointing out the path of the hijacked Chevrolet. But when the pursuit changed to country roads it turned into a hapless guessing game.

Back in town the people of Grand Haven—angered by the raid on their bank and elated by the rude welcome dealt the robbers—mounted a colossal effort to search for the fleeing culprits, swiftly forming a posse composed of 150 citizens and volunteers from the Coast Guard cutter *Escanaba*. A local pilot took to the air in the hopes of spotting the fugitives.

The State Police were a late addition to the town's mobilization. When the bank alarm had sounded at their post north of town a squad of troopers was dispatched. Unfortunately, the attendant at the swing bridge, hearing of the robbery, had raised the bridge to prevent any escape to the north. The State Police vehicle had been trapped on the opposite side of the river.

While many of the townfolk prepared to hunt down the gang, others looked after the wounded. Bank employees Pellagrom and Lindemulder had suffered only minor injuries; Pleinies and Van Lopik were more seriously injured, but both eventually recovered. The worst off by far was Earl Doyle. In addition to a broken leg, a bullet-shattered hand, and a buckshot-torn scalp, the robber had sustained severe bruises and lacerations about his face and arms. His bulletproof vest no doubt had prevented some fractured ribs and lessened his overall injuries. The prisoner was removed to the county jail, where his wounds treated in his cell. Under questioning Doyle gave his name as Harry Harris of Chicago. He refused to speak about his partners other than cursing someone named Freddie, who had ruined everything by skipping town with their car.

❄ ❄ ❄

Five miles south of Grand Haven the bandits were almost out of gas when they passed a Chrysler parked near a farm on the left side of the road. The car belonged to Oscar Varneau of Grand Rapids, who had stopped at the farm of Ernest Behm purchase strawberries, leaving his wife and son inside the vehicle with the family dog. Mrs. Varneau glanced up to find three "nervous-looking fellows" approaching. One yanked open her door and barked, "Get out of the car."

Her husband was near the farmhouse some 500 feet away. Hearing her call out, "They're taking our car!" he rushed toward the strangers. Nelson raised his machine gun in Varneau's direction, a gesture menacing enough to bring the would-be rescuer to an instant stop. It took a few moments to entice the dog to leave the back seat and join the family, then the gunmen piled into the vehicle and started away, pausing beside the Chevrolet to allow the fourth bandit to climb aboard. In his haste Fisher left another $300 scattered on the back floorboard. The Behms attempted to phone police in Grand Haven but discovered all lines were busy.

Again Bentz took the wheel, assuring the others he could drive most of the getaway route by memory. A few miles south of Sparta they stopped for gas. About ten o'clock that evening, just as the four were starting to relax and think they were safely away, a tire blew, causing Bentz to lose control and smash the Chrysler into a tree near Hudson, about 160 miles southeast of

Grand Haven. They flagged down a passing Ford containing four teenage boys. Nelson once again used his almost-empty machine gun to persuade the youths to surrender their vehicle. This time Gannon drove while Bentz directed him from the passenger seat.

At eight o'clock the next morning the gang arrived in Long Beach, exhausted, disillusioned, and angry. Gannon remained at the wheel while the others retrieved their own cars. Then, with Fisher following him, he drove off to dispose of the Ford. Nelson and Bentz, in separate vehicles, headed to Michigan City to find Monahan. It was no surprise when they learned the ex-Touhy mobster and his wife had disappeared the night before.

A half-hour later the outlaws reassembled to divide the loot. Not including money and securities recovered in the streets, bank records put the loss at $2,568 in currency and $6,410 in bank checks and seven Pacific Railway bonds. Bentz claimed the cash take was closer to $3,500, still a major disappointment in light of the anticipated $50,000. The money was split six ways, with Doyle's share set aside for his wife. Bentz insisted that Nelson take Monahan's cut since he had covered most of the costs out of his own funds. As previously agreed, Bentz pocketed the checks and bonds.

Fisher and Gannon voiced their disgust over the spoils and criticized Nelson for overriding Bentz's objection to Monahan as the wheelman. Baby Face humbly admitted his error, then laughed and said, "I sponsored Freddie, so I'll make sure he never runs out on anyone again. He'll get what's coming to him."

Saying farewell with a round of handshakes, Bentz retired to his home and caught a brief nap while Verna packed their belongings. The couple left Long Beach late that afternoon and moved into another lakeside cottage at Union Pier, Michigan.

Accompanied by Helen, Nelson visited Hazel Doyle and broke the news of her husband's capture. The woman wept for a full hour, clutching her two precious Pekinese dogs to her bosom as the young couple did their best to comfort her. Nelson gave her Earl's share of the loot plus a couple of hundred extra. He offered to help her in any way he could and vowed to do everything possible to secure her husband's freedom.

But Doyle was already beyond help. On August 21 he was arraigned in his cell, his condition still too serious for a trip to court. He was charged with bank robbery, possession of firearms, and felonious assault on Bolt, Welling, and Pellegrom. Bond was fixed at $25,000. Doyle raised his swollen, battered head and croaked, "You might just as well have made that $150,000, Judge."

The next day Doyle, still insisting his name was Harry Harris, pleaded not guilty. A court appearance was set for September 5. (On September 9 Doyle changed his plea to guilty and was sentenced to life imprisonment. Twenty-four hours later, hobbling on crutches, he entered the Michigan State Prison at Jackson.)

After repeated invitations from Nelson and his wife, Hazel moved into their cottage several days later. She was already known to Ronnie and Darlene as "Aunt Hazel" and was greatly loved. When Jack Perkins returned to Long Beach, Nelson confessed that he was unable to give him the promised bonus from the Grand Haven proceeds. Perkins was willing to shrug off the debt, but Nelson, intent on compensating him for his services, offered the use of his cottage. He said that he, Helen, and the others were pulling up stakes and moving to St. Paul by the first of the month, just a few days away. Nelson asked only that Perkins look after Hazel and eventually get her settled in an apartment back in Chicago.

On August 29 Nelson, Fisher, Gannon, and Van Meter met Bentz near a Michigan City riding academy at the far east end of Lake Shore Drive. They talked for nearly two hours at this final gathering about how the Grand Haven job could have gone so sour after all their meticulous planning. Each could now joke about the frantic Wild West shootout they had survived.

"Don't let it discourage you," Bentz exhorted Nelson. "Bank robbing is a business, and in every business there's an element of risk. Just consider this a learning experience. Next time you can avoid the mistakes we made."

Nelson assured him he had already taken care of one mistake. "Freddie is no more," he said without further elaboration.

It was the last time Bentz saw his young protege, except in photos accompanying newspaper accounts of the exploits of Baby Face Nelson. Regarding the demise of Freddie, Bentz said he later learned that Nelson had staked out Monahan's house in Melrose Park on Chicago's West Side for two days before he caught his former friend and gunned him down.

The actual identity and ultimate fate of Freddie Monahan remains one of the most perplexing pieces in the puzzle of Nelson's life. Three years later Grand Haven Police Chief Lawrence DeWitt, hoping to close the books on the robbery by determining that all the major participants were either in prison or the graveyard, prompted FBI agents and Chicago police to conduct a thorough inquiry into the Monahan matter. They reported there was no record of a Touhy gangster or any other Chicago-area criminal by that name. An examination of homicide cases failed to turn up any that fit the details of Nelson's alleged slaying of Monahan.

The authorities agreed the only individual even remotely resembling the description of the mysterious Monahan was Three-Fingered Jack White, not only a former associate of the Touhys but also a friend of Nelson. White's age and general features roughly matched the description of Monahan, notably the missing fingers on the right hand. And just weeks prior to the Grand Haven heist White had married a young Chicago actress in Indiana—the bride reportedly bore a striking similarity to Monahan's wife. Along with being an ex-con, a cop killer, and a ruthless racketeer, White also had a background in armed robbery and was implicated in Chicago's $80,000 International Harvester pay-roll holdup in 1926.

While all of this might seem to indicate that White and Monahan were the same person, it would require a rather vivid stretch of the imagination to believe that a mobster of White's status and reputed toughness would join an inexperienced band of bank robbers and then run away at the first sign of trouble. By 1930 Three-Fingered Jack had left the Touhys far behind on his way to becoming a major figure in the Capone organization. By 1933 he was sitting at the right hand of Capone "enforcer" Frank Nitti and was regarded as one of the most powerful and feared mobsters in Chicago. It is unlikely that such a man would involve himself in a high-risk venture like the Grand Haven robbery.

Nevertheless, the abrupt end of White's gangland career at the hands of "persons unknown" has prompted some to make the connection and credit Nelson with White's killing. The facts, however, tells a different story.

On January 23, 1934, a full six months after the Grand Haven robbery, Three-Fingered Jack welcomed two visitors into his home on Wesley Avenue in Oak Park. Since White was known to be an obsessively cautious individual, the pair must have been close friends or trusted associates. Drinks were poured and all three sat a table conversing for several minutes. Without warning the men whipped out pistols and opened fire on their host. Hit twice, White staggered into the bedroom in an attempt to reach a pair of pistols in a dresser drawer. A final shot smashed through the back of his skull, killing him instantly.

Although the gunmen were never identified, their cool professional style left little doubt the hit was the work of a mob-sponsored assassination team. Years later Alvin Karpis implicated Fred Goetz, a Barker affiliate and former Capone torpedo, in White's death, taking part as a hired gun or for personal reasons. Goetz himself was gunned down outside a Cicero tavern two months later, perhaps in retaliation for White.

One thing is certain: Baby Face Nelson took no part in White's slaying and in fact had the perfect alibi. According to reliable witnesses, at the very moment White was being murdered, Nelson was almost 2000 miles away in San Francisco—purchasing a vehicle that, ironically, would later place him at the scene of another killing.

Since virtually all that remains of Monahan is a name—and probably an alias, at that—the fate of the underworld pal who failed to live up to the trust Nelson displayed in him may never be known. It may have been the occasion on which, as Nelson later boasted to Bentz, he killed his first man. One scenario suggests that he disposed of Monahan's body, thus leaving no record of his death—not an outlandish contention considering that in a later murder attributed to Nelson the victim's body was never found.

But there is no hard evidence to indicate that Nelson ever caught up to Monahan, or even tried. Nelson vowed numerous times to "get" certain individuals—turncoat Harry Powell or bank cashier Ray Frantzen, among others—without ever once carrying out the threat.

On August 30, the day after his final meeting with Eddie Bentz, Nelson left Long Beach, a little wiser if not significantly richer. Over the course of the summer he had been schooled in the business of bank robbing by one of the recognized masters of the trade and managed to cultivate a working relationship with a small force of aspiring criminals like himself. He was ready for bigger and bolder escapades.

My conscience doesn't hurt me. I stole from the bankers. They stole from
the people. All we did was help raise the insurance rates.
— Harry Pierpont

CHAPTER 6

THE GUNS OF AUTUMN

WHILE BABY FACE NELSON spent the summer of 1933 holding a small-scale crime convention at his Long Beach cottage, a much higher-profile series of events was grabbing headlines and throwing the midwestern underworld scene into turmoil.

There was also a shift in the public's attitude toward the depression desperados that summer. As long as the outlaws preyed on banks and avoided bloodshed, their crimes were generally regarded with a fair amount of sympathy, if not total approval. The Kansas City Massacre on June 17— depicted by the press as "gangland's machine gun challenge to American society" and condemned as a defiant assault upon the forces of law and order—sent shock waves throughout the nation. The slaughter at Kansas City's Union Station was viewed as far more reprehensible than its St. Valentine's Day predecessor since four of the five victims were lawmen. (Information recently obtained from the FBI's files indicates the so-called massacre may have been triggered by a ghastly mishap, with the prisoner Frank Nash and at least two officers killed by an agent whose weapon accidentally discharged.)

In Washington, Attorney General Cummings and FBI Director Hoover seized on these incidents as justification for launching a war against crime, especially since one of the slain officers was a federal agent. Hoover vowed that "no time, money, or labor will be spared toward bringing about the apprehension of the individuals responsible for the cowardly and despicable act . . ." All he lacked was the necessary authority and funding to turn his bureau into the "super police force" he had long envisioned.

Toward that end Cummings unveiled his Twelve Point Program and called on President Roosevelt to help ram Cummings's host of anti-crime bills through Congress, broadening the powers of Hoover's agents. The key element in the attorney general's proposed legislation was defining certain acts as "interstate crimes," thus allowing the FBI to ignore local police jurisdiction and fight the forces of gangdom wherever Hoover chose to go. Some of the proposals were greeted with stiff resistance from lawmakers who feared Hoover's "briefcase-toting cops" might become a secret police force rather than a super police agency. Ultimately it would take the much-publicized exploits of John Dillinger and Baby Face Nelson the following spring to motivate Congress to accede to Cummings's demands.

That summer Verne Miller, the only participant in the Kansas City Massacre whose guilt was certain, became the most hunted man in the nation. He was not only targeted by lawmen but also by underworld denizens enraged by the media frenzy surrounding the carnage and the death of Nash, the man he had intended to free. The maverick ex-sheriff managed to stay at large a full five months, but in the end it was his fellow gangsters who caught up with him first. His body, bludgeoned and stabbed with an ice pick, was discovered in a ditch outside Detroit on November 29.

Pretty Boy Floyd also found himself the object of federal pursuit after the massacre. While Floyd's involvement has long been a subject of controversy and is seriously doubted by many, Hoover had been looking for an excuse to go after the celebrated Oklahoma bandit for some time. The director was able to scrape up enough evidence to implicate Pretty Boy in the Union Station ambush, and Floyd, as a result, was forced to go into deep hiding with his timid-looking sidekick, Adam Richetti. It would be almost a year before Floyd resurfaced—and not without more controversy—in the company of Dillinger and Nelson.

It didn't help that the massacre occurred just two days after the Hamm kidnapping and four weeks prior to the abduction of Oklahoma oil magnate Charles Urschel by Machine Gun Kelly on July 22. While bank robbery was seen as an act against an institution, kidnapping was a direct assault upon an individual, even if the victim was a millionaire. Abduction for ransom was viewed as particularly repugnant, recalling for most Americans the outrage surrounding the still-unsolved (at the time) kidnap-murder of the Lindbergh baby. The public applauded the efforts of Hoover's agents to track down the perpetrators.

Realizing too late that he had bitten off more than he could chew, and regretting that he didn't stick to bank holdups, the amiable Kelly, like Floyd, went underground with his wife, Kathryn, who reportedly prodded him into the kidnapping. Eventually the trail led to Memphis, where he was captured by agents and city detectives in an early morning raid on his bungalow on September 22. Clad in pajamas, Kelly seemed almost relieved when he saw the officers, calmly remarking, "I've been waiting for you."

Although the arrest was a cooperative effort, the bureau took credit for cracking the case and bringing about the downfall of the ruthless outlaw. Details of Machine Gun Kelly's capture were later revised by Hoover's hand-picked historians to make it appear the gangster had blubbered, "Don't shoot, G-Men!" when he first caught sight of the federal agents.

Many other desperados were also experiencing hard times. By late July the Barrow gang was close to extinction after drifting too far north and being forced to shoot its way past a posse of Iowa lawmen. Buck Barrow was mortally wounded and his wife, Blanche, captured. Miraculously Bonnie and Clyde, both wounded, managed to escape on foot. The pair made it back to their native Texas and began forming a new gang.

Meanwhile, Nelson's old pals in the Touhy mob became the focus of an FBI crusade. Heading the investigation was Melvin Purvis, the dapper, diminutive SAC of the bureau's Chicago office. Declaring that he had an "iron-clad case," Purvis accused Roger Touhy and three henchmen of executing the Hamm kidnapping. While being interrogated, Touhy alleged later, he refused to confess to a crime he didn't commit and was beaten, starved, and denied sleep. The fact that he lost twenty-five pounds, seven teeth, and suffered three fractured vertebrae in his upper back tends to support his story. The four gang members were delivered to St. Paul and on August 12 were indicted by a federal grand jury. During the subsequent trial Touhy and his companions were found innocent. Nevertheless the government refused to release the gangsters, charging them with another kidnapping back in Chicago.

At the same time, the members of the Barker-Karpis gang—the actual perpetrators of the Hamm abduction—were discovering that their eagerly awaited ransom money wasn't stretching as far as they'd anticipated. Once the cash had been laundered in Reno through Graham and McKay, who charged the gangsters $7,500 for the service, the Barkers had been obliged to pay $25,000 for their St. Paul police protection. After spending almost $20,000 on expenses and various underworld associates, the seven gang members had been left with less than $50,000 to divide among themselves. Within two months their wallets were growing thin.

On August 30, the same day Nelson and his family left Long Beach, the gang snatched a $30,000 payroll on the steps of the South St. Paul Post Office. Two police officers guarding the payroll were swiftly removed by the Barker brothers—Doc callously executed one with a shotgun while Freddie used his machine gun to mow down the other, who somehow survived with more than two dozen wounds to his body. Freddie then swept the street with bullets, narrowly missing a score of innocent bystanders.

A few days later Nelson contacted Eddie Green in Chicago where the jug marker was residing on Kedzie Avenue. Disgusted by the brutal, cold-blooded tactics employed in the South St. Paul payroll heist, Green announced that he was through with the Barkers. With Frank Nash dead, Verne Miller a marked man, and Bailey and most of his former associates in prison, Green was actively seeking a new crew. Nelson confessed that his people were raw but eager to pull off some grand-scale bank jobs. Green decided to join them.

Harold Eugene "Eddie" Green was a short, slim, scowling man with a pockmarked face, squinty eyes, and a razor-thin mouth. He was born November 2, 1898, in Pueblo, Colorado. His father died when Eddie was just three. His mother Margaret was described as a saintly woman, but Eddie and his two brothers, James and Frank, all went into crime. He served prison terms in Wisconsin and Iowa for grand larceny before drifting into St. Paul where in 1922 he was convicted of robbing a $2,000 payroll and sentenced to a term at Stillwater. He was an unruly inmate, constantly at the center of fights and disturbances that landed him in solitary confinement. Prison officials tagged him as incorrigible, citing his hair-trigger temper and habitual defiance of authority.

After his parole Green worked sporadically in Twin Cities iron mills. But like Pat Reilly—who became a friend and admirer of Eddie—Green got a thrill out of touring St. Paul's underworld hangouts and rubbing elbows with big-name gangsters. In time he became a disciple of Bailey and Nash, learning a more cerebral approach to crime.

While recognized as one of the premier jug markers in the Midwest, Green—still the insolent rebel—yearned to play a more active role in his heists. He told Nelson he'd selected six or seven fat banks in Minnesota, Iowa, Nebraska, Wisconsin, and South Dakota and was eager to get back to work. He promised to meet him in St. Paul in a couple of weeks.

In no particular hurry, Nelson took time in Chicago to look up old friends and make some new ones. Most notable among the latter was James Murray, an almost legendary character on the local gangland scene, a stout figure with a beefy face, bull neck, thin mustache, soft blue eyes, and a jagged scar across his left temple.

Born in Chicago on March 31, 1887, Murray studied law, worked as a clerk in the Chicago court system, and dabbled in politics, serving as a precinct captain in "the old bloody 19th Ward." His political and police connections proved to be numerous and especially valuable at the outset of Prohibition. Foreseeing (as did so many others) the fantastic potential in bootlegging, Murray invested in breweries around Chicago and in Wisconsin, re-licensing them to manufacture "near beer." The profits from the legal low-alcohol beverage were minimal compared to those that could be realized from diverting the potent alcohol used to make it and selling it at inflated prices to speakeasies. Over the next few years Murray and his "$10 million operation," as the press termed it, became a major supplier to the O'Donnells and other Chicago gangs.

Soon Murray was living the good life. He moved his wife and three daughters into a plush new home in Oak Park and bought summer cottages in Michigan, Wisconsin, and Wauconda, Illinois. His underworld dealings prompted him to become involved in a number of other nefarious enterprises. Word spread around town that Murray was the man to see if you needed a safe hideout to cool off, were looking to move stolen merchandise, or were seeking a loan or financial backing for any kind of illegal project.

It was in this context that Murray became a principal behind-the-scenes participant in one of America's last great train robberies. The actual bandits were the four Newton brothers and a pair of confederates, lured all the way from Texas for their holdup talents. Murray was labeled the mastermind behind the heist. Whether true or not, he played a central role in planning and bankrolling the caper and in recruiting the "inside man," a postal inspector who supplied essential details. The robbers struck on the evening of June 12, 1924, stopping the mail train at the Roundout crossing thirty-two miles outside of Chicago. The guards and clerks inside the express car were flushed out with homemade formaldehyde grenades. In minutes the bandits collected nearly two million dollars. Things went smoothly until one robber, choking on the noxious fumes, spotted movement in the gloom outside and fired, wounding another member of the crew.

Instead of returning immediately to Texas after the heist, the Newtons were forced to remain in Chicago until their companion could travel. Murray set them up in a house on the Northwest Side where they were observed by the inevitable overly curious neighbor. Police were alerted, and within forty-eight hours of the robbery the main characters were rounded up. Eventually the trail led to one James Maloney who, it turned out, was none other than Jimmy Murray. He was sentenced to twenty-five years in Leavenworth.

After serving five years Murray cut a deal with officials to obtain his release, a practice at which—both before and after the Roundout affair—he was uncommonly skilled. In return for surrendering $385,000 in stolen bonds, he was granted a full parole. By 1931 Murray was back in business, maintaining a considerably lower profile but once again renowned throughout Chicago's underworld as a man with powerful connections. To provide himself with a respectable front he opened a restaurant, the Rainbo Barbecue at 7190 West North Avenue, which soon became a favorite meeting place for local criminals.

But there may have been more to Murray's bid for freedom than simply exchanging the stolen bonds for a parole. The exact terms of the arrangement are not known; however, some believe the deal stipulated that Murray would from time to time use his intimate gangland connections to provide authorities with information. If he did in fact serve as a pipeline to the police (and perhaps later to the FBI), he may have done so completely voluntary in order to enhance his own position and secure continued protection. It's also possible that he supplied only insignificant details, amounting to little more than an occasional bone tossed to police hounds, or that he deliberately fed authorities misinformation. In any event, if Murray was playing both sides against the middle to achieve his own ends, he was involved in a very dangerous game.

Just when or how Murray and Nelson crossed paths is not known. Both were Chicago West Siders with roots and numerous connections in The Patch. It's possible they encountered each other before the Roundout train robbery, but Nelson would have been just a teenager starting out in small-time crime. No doubt Nelson had heard of Murray and was probably the one who initiated their meeting, figuring that the one-time politician, former beer baron, and ex-con could be a useful contact.

What is known is that Murray and Nelson, despite their twenty-year age difference, developed a friendly relationship by the end of summer 1933. They discovered they had some mutual friends, including the enigmatic Father Coughlan. The past association between Murray and Coughlan is most interesting if certain information is to be believed. Years later a woman named Mary Henderson claimed that Coughlan, during his ministry in Oklahoma, had acted as a conduit to the Newton brothers and recruited them for the Roundout robbery on Murray's behalf. Similarly, the priest may have served as Murray's link to Nelson.

When he arrived in St. Paul on September 5 Nelson found his comrades facing a minor crisis. The day before, Tommy Carroll had been in an auto accident at the corner of Rice Street and Wheelock Parkway and was arrested after police discovered a loaded .45 automatic in his car. Although there were several outstanding warrants for the bandit, both locally and in Wisconsin, Harry Sawyer's influence at the police station secured his release. "No one gets pinched in this town except you, Tommy," Gannon ribbed him in front of the others at the Green Lantern that evening.

At the same meeting the gang discussed preparations for upcoming heists. The most pressing need at the moment was weapons. When Freddie Monahan fled with the getaway car at Grand Haven he took with him the greater part of the arsenal. (The Buick was later found abandoned in southern Michigan with some of the guns still inside; the rest, including a machine gun, shotgun, rifle, and several pistols were evidently taken by Monahan and presumably sold.) Among them, the five outlaws possessed a single machine gun. Shotguns and rifles were no problem to replace, but Nelson insisted they needed more "machinos," as he called them, before tackling any big jobs. He volunteered to drive to Texas to see what he could acquire from Lebman; the others donated cash toward the purchase of new weapons.

After a brief stopover in Chicago, where Ronnie and Darlene were deposited with the Fitzsimmons family, Nelson and his wife arrived in San Antonio on September 10. Sporting goods store owner Hymie Lebman enthusiastically welcomed the young couple. Nelson said he had "a big order" for Lebman, adding, "I'll pay top dollar for all the machine guns you can get your hands on."

"That is a big order," Lebman replied. "How long will you be in town?"

"Only a couple of days." Nelson explained that if Lebman needed longer he would pay for the weapons in advance and furnish an address where they could be shipped.

The gunsmith promised to do all he could. In the meantime he proudly displayed several of the machine-gun pistols he had finished modifying. Nelson bought two, a .45 and .38 model. He also purchased four other pistols—a .38 super automatic, a pair of .380 automatics, and a .25 automatic—and two rifles.

The next day Lebman told Nelson that a contact in El Paso could provide five machine guns but delivery would take a couple of weeks. He also put in a call to his brother-in-law, Louis Schwartzman, in Corpus Christi, Texas. Schwartzman occasionally located weapons for Lebman through a friend named "Izzy" who bought second-hand guns from a source inside the local sheriff's department. When Izzy reported that he had obtained a Thompson, Lebman immediately drove to Corpus Christi and purchased it for $150.

The machine gun, a rare Model 1927 Thompson, was delivered to Nelson on September 13. After paying Lebman $300 Baby Face examined the weapon and noted that there was no full-auto lever. Lebman said he hadn't test-fired the gun and offered to give it a complete inspection.

Nelson shook his head. "We're leaving tonight," he told the gunsmith. "If there's any problem I'll send it back."

The young outlaw offered to pay for the remaining five Thompsons, but Lebman said a $200 deposit would be sufficient. Nelson promised to notify him within a week where the weapons could be shipped C.O.D.

With their business completed, Nelson announced he would be returning to Texas in a couple months, emphasizing that Helen and he wanted to find a more moderate climate before winter arrived. Lebman invited Nelson and his family and friends to join him for Thanksgiving dinner.

✳ ✳ ✳

At 7:50 A.M. on the same day Nelson left San Antonio, assistant cashier Clifford Olson entered the Union State Bank in the small town of Amery in northwestern Wisconsin to prepare for the nine o'clock opening. Olson immediately discovered he was not alone; four masked figures materialized from the shadows and surrounded him. One invader was armed with a sawed-off shotgun, another brandished a rifle, the other two held pistols. "That's right, lock that door," a gunman hissed. "Now get away from that window!"

Warned not to make any false moves, Olson was marched to the back and ordered to open the vault. As the nervous cashier fumbled with the combination, missing on the first try, he received several sharp kicks from a tall, nervous bandit. Moments after the vault was finally opened, head cashier Vincent Christenson walked through the bank's rear door, calling out to Olson that the lock looked as though it had been jimmied. "That's all right," a robber declared, aiming a pistol at Christenson's head. "Come in and lie down on the floor."

The man with the shotgun stood guard over the captives while two of his companions loaded $11,000 in cash and $35,000 in securities into a pair of black satchels. The fourth bandit removed his mask and slipped outside, pulling the crew's getaway car into the alley beside the rear door as his three partners emerged. The robbers were last spotted speeding toward the Minnesota border less than fifteen miles outside of Amery.

The quartet consisted of Carroll, Fisher, Gannon, and Van Meter, the latter of whom had used his favorite method of persuading bank employees to do his bidding—prodding them with the tip of his shoe. The robbery was reportedly the brainchild of Carroll, who had passed through Amery numerous times and thought the bank looked like an easy target.

Nelson's return to St. Paul a few days later, after retrieving his children in Chicago, was not a pleasant one. He was bitterly disappointed at having missed the Amery holdup, although he had left the others with the understanding that they would find a way to grab some quick cash. The fact that he showed up with just one machine gun was bad enough; when they tested the weapon in some woods near White Bear Lake they learned to Nelson's embarrassment that it fired only in single-shot mode, as he had suspected it might. Baby Face absorbed a considerable amount of ridicule from Van Meter for trusting "a Jew peddler."

Nelson assured his partners that Lebman was an honorable man and the error would be rectified. After some discussion it was decided to have the anticipated machine guns shipped to a private residence rather than an apartment or hotel room. Carroll suggested his place on South 16th Avenue in Minneapolis, a duplex he was renting from Radio Sally's brother John.

The unsatisfactory Thompson was dismantled, crated up, and mailed back to San Antonio. Nelson included $400—$300 in checks from a Chicago bank and a $100 money order—along with the following letter:

September 25, 1933

Dear Pal

Could not write sooner the address here is

Mr. Joseph Bennett
3242 Sixteenth Ave. So.
Minneapolis, Minn.

Enclose my personal letter in another envelope addressed to "Jimmie."
Hope to hear some good news from you soon. Don't get me any more outfits like the last one. It was "one way" like I thought it was. I'm sure you understand what I mean. But don't let it worry you.

As ever your pal,

Jimmie

Ten days later a shipment of five Thompson submachine guns was delivered to the Bennett duplex with C.O.D. charges of $825. This time all of the weapons functioned perfectly. Nelson wrote Lebman a letter acknowledging receipt of the "merchandise," adding that the weather in Minnesota was already growing cold and once again promising that he would see him soon.

By that time Eddie Green, accompanied by girlfriend Bessie Skinner, had joined the others in the Twin Cities. Posing as Theodore J. Randall, a shoe salesman, he rented Apartment 207 in the four-story Charlou Apartments building on South Freemont Avenue in Minneapolis, a few blocks west of Carroll's duplex. Green's new apartment quickly became the favorite meeting place for the gang and the primary storage facility for its growing arsenal, with one room set aside exclusively for stockpiling weapons, bulletproof vests, and assorted ammunition.

The bandits were in the process of sizing up the first of Green's major scores—a large, reputedly impregnable bank in the town of Brainerd, 135 miles north of the Twin Cities in the heart of north-central Minnesota's scenic, tranquil, densely forested lake region. Nelson and his partners settled on a date to strike, October 23, Chuck Fisher's twenty-ninth birthday.

A week before the robbery a pair of black Buick sedans with North Dakota plates pulled into the parking area of the Sebago Resort, fourteen miles outside

Brainerd on the north shore of Round Lake. Two men, Homer Van Meter and Tom Gannon, climbed from one car and stretched. The other vehicle contained a small, narrow-eyed man and a red-haired woman.

Lester Penny, the resort's owner, hurried outside to welcome the visitors. Leaving Bessie in the Buick, Eddie Green stepped forward as spokesman for the group. "Got any cabins to rent?"

Grateful for the off-season guests, Penny said he could provide two cabins at a weekly rate of ten dollars apiece. Green handed over twenty dollars, then stuffed an extra ten-dollar bill in the owner's hand and asked, "Anyone else staying here?"

"Not a chance," Penny replied. "After Labor Day it's pretty dead around here."

"We like it quiet," said Green. "We don't like blabbermouths. Get it?"

"I hear you," answered Penny, pocketing the cash. He had no illusions about reporting the quartet's presence to the law after Green's not-so-veiled threat. He figured they were probably crooks of some kind who had chosen his resort to cool off for a while. During their week's stay Penny furnished his guests with fresh milk and vegetables, once receiving five dollars for fifty cents' worth of goods.

A few days earlier three other strangers had appeared at Louge Lake, fifteen miles north of Brainerd. Baby Face Nelson, Tommy Carroll, and Chuck Fisher were staying at a cabin owned by Charles Layman, a former Minneapolis police officer. Neighbors often spotted the trio making trips into town. Nelson seemed the most sociable of the three, usually stopping to chat while his two companions kept to themselves. The folks around Louge Lake later reported that Nelson often spent his evenings hiking through the woods with a rifle, shooting small game.

The six gangsters met daily in Brainerd to closely monitor the First National Bank on the corner of South Sixth and Front Streets during working hours. They kept a diligent record of the names, descriptions, and routines of the nineteen employees. Claiming to be a buyer interested in local real estate, Green hired plumber Mitch DeRosier to show him around town and the surrounding countryside. At the time DeRosier thought nothing of the fact that the routes Green wanted to scout always centered around the bank.

On the morning of October 23 the neighbors at Louge Lake rose to find that the three men occupying the Layman house had departed, apparently well before dawn. Lester Penny made a similar discovery at the Sebago Resort.

❄ ❄ ❄

Brainerd was a peaceful, colorful community of slightly more than 10,000 residents, known principally for logging and the local lore about Paul Bunyan. Six decades later Joel and Ethan Coen, a pair of native Minnesota filmmakers, would bestow a quirky homage upon Brainerd in their film *Fargo*.

The First National seemed a large bank for such a small town, but it was one of the few financial institutions serving the vast region south of Duluth and north of St. Croix.

At six o'clock Monday morning bank custodian George Fricker, a small man with a bushy mustache, arrived at the front entrance. A voice behind him called, "Hey, hold on a minute." He turned to find a chubby figure dressed in a hunting cap and a plaid jacket over blue coveralls hurrying toward him. The stranger's shoes scuffed the sidewalk, prompting Fricker to notice that he wore black dress oxfords, an odd contrast to the rest of his clothing.

Chuck Fisher rammed a pistol into the custodian's ribs and ordered him to unlock the door. Fricker tried to bluff the gunman, complaining that he didn't have the key. "Like hell you haven't," Fisher snarled. "You've been opening that door for the past ten days."

As Fricker obeyed the command, two more men approached, each awkwardly attempting to conceal a machine gun beneath his jacket. Tommy Carroll was outfitted almost identically to Fisher, and Baby Face Nelson wore his blue suit, a tie, and a gray cap. Once inside, the trio covered the bottom half of their faces with bandannas.

Fricker was led to an office in the back and instructed to sit on the floor and relax. Minutes later Fricker's wife arrived to assist her husband in his duties. She was taken to the office where one bandit graciously provided a chair for her. Christine Peterson, an elderly cleaning woman, entered next. Nelson greeted her at the door with a friendly "Hello, Grandma."

She looked at the masked man, noticing his sparkling blue eyes above the bandanna. "Do you know me?" she gasped.

"Grandma, I've seen you every morning for the past couple of weeks." He encouraged her go about her normal routine.

Almost ninety minutes later the bank's guard, Robert Titus, stepped inside and saw Mrs. Peterson cleaning the counters with a feather duster, just as she did every morning. Nelson sprang from behind a pillar beside the entrance, his machine gun aimed at the guard's chest as he warned, "Don't move!" Fisher appeared, snatched the revolver from Titus's holster, then shoved him toward the office where the Frickers were being guarded by Carroll.

Baby Face was alone at that moment when seventeen-year-old Zane Smith, a collection clerk, walked in carrying the day's mail. Nelson pounced on the youth, punching him in the face, then grabbed him by his coat collar and dragged him across the lobby to the office. Forcing Smith to sit next to Fricker and Titus, Nelson crouched down and growled, "Now you're going to tell me everything I need to know, right?"

Stunned from the blow to his jaw, the teenager nodded. But when Nelson asked how much money was in the vault, Smith insisted that he had no idea. Nor could he provide any information about the time lock. Fisher suggested that sticking a lighted cigarette into the youth's ear might produce better answers, but Smith finally convinced his inquisitors he was telling the truth.

The next arrival, teller Ben Lagerquist, was able to provide a few details. Menaced by the gunmen and admonished not to "tell us any fables," Lagerquist said the time lock was set to deactivate at precisely 8:50 A.M.

Between 8:15 and 8:30 the remaining employees arrived in a steady stream. The men were prodded or pushed, the women more politely guided, into the back office until the room was crammed with fourteen nervous prisoners. The robbers not only addressed the employees by name but also seemed to know their duties and usual time of arrival. As the minutes dragged by, one bandit offered cigarettes to the captives, warning them not to reach in their pockets for matches. He returned to each and provided a light.

Finally, at 8:45, Nelson selected Vice President C. W. Boteler to accompany him to the vault. Boteler protested that he might not be able to work the combination. In a calm, flat voice Nelson responded, "You'll open it or get killed."

When cashier George C. Flaata volunteered to open the vault, Boteler was allowed to sit down. At that point Nelson and Fisher herded Flaata and three other cashiers—Al Mroz, Russell La Course, and Arthur Drogseth—out of the room, leaving Carroll to stand guard over the rest.

The instant the time lock snapped off, Flaata opened the heavy door. Each cashier was then instructed to unlock his or her individual safe within the vault. As Fisher started filling a pair of canvas sacks with cash, Nelson marched the cashiers back to the office. The baby-faced gunman ordered Fricker to come with him. After sitting on the floor for nearly three hours, the custodian rose and walked stiffly into the lobby where Nelson directed him to tape an NRA poster over a specific window.

The poster was a signal to Nelson's confederates outside. Van Meter, wearing denim coveralls and a mackinaw and clutching a bushel basket covered by a blanket, loitered near the main entrance. Upon spotting the poster he moved to the curb and motioned to Gannon, who sat chain-smoking behind the wheel of a black Buick parked down the street. Gannon started the engine.

Fisher returned to the office lugging the two sacks bulging with $32,000 in cash. One bag was handed to Carroll, who immediately walked out the front door and joined Gannon in the front seat of the car. Nelson and Fisher ordered the captives to march single-file out the office. All fourteen were forced into the cramped confines of the men's room. Nelson warned, "I'll blow off the first head I see come through this door."

It was exactly 9 A.M. At that moment S. H. Gregg, an insurance agent from Chicago, approached the front door. An hour earlier Gregg had left the Ransford Hotel, directly across from the bank, to go to breakfast. He had observed "a tall, gangling country youth, shabbily dressed and carrying a basket" pacing the sidewalk. To his surprise, the young man was still there.

Gregg walked to the bank entrance and discovered it was locked. He checked his watch, then tried to peer inside. Rattling the door, he noticed the "country youth" had slipped directly behind him, as if he also expected to be admitted. "They must be running a few minutes late," Gregg remarked over his shoulder.

The figure muttered something about the bank opening "later than usual today." As Gregg peered through a window, the door burst open and two men rushed out. One was a short young man with a machine gun who passed the startled Gregg without a word. His stocky companion paused, then pressed the barrel of his pistol against Gregg's chest. "Brother," Fisher told him, "get in there and get in quick."

The insurance man noticed that Van Meter, now grinning maniacally, had pulled a machine gun from his basket and was aiming at the entrance. Gregg scrambled inside, lunging for cover behind a pillar an instant before a shrieking barrage of bullets vaporized the glass in the doors.

Seconds after Van Meter began blasting the entrance, Nelson halted at the curb, turned, and opened fire on the building, shattering several windows. The Buick pulled up, and the three bandits piled into the back seat, Fisher in the middle, Nelson and Van Meter poking their Tommyguns out the windows on either side, both muzzles spitting fire and lead at the rows of shops and businesses along Brainerd's streets as Gannon drove off. Bullets punctured parked cars, smashed windows, chewed away chunks of concrete, and sent dozens of bystanders dashing for cover. Ernest Butler, owner of the Ransford Hotel, threw himself to the ground when a slug barely missed his right ear. A few doors away, the front of the YMCA was riddled by eighteen rounds.

"They wanted to let folks know they were here," one lawman surmised. The citizens of Brainerd were not as infuriated by the plundering of their bank as they were by the gang's blazing exit from town. Remarkably the only injury reported was Zane Smith's aching jaw. Years later, after becoming the bank's vice president, Smith was able to joke about the robbery. "It's my one claim to fame," he declared. "I can tell people I was socked in the mouth by Baby Face Nelson."

❄ ❄ ❄

Before noon, after driving a serpentine route over the region's back roads, the bandits reached Eden Valley, Minnesota, twenty-two miles southwest of St. Cloud, where they rendezvoused with Green and Bessie Skinner. The men, money, and weapons were transferred to Green's Buick and Fisher's Auburn sedan. The getaway car, stolen in North Dakota the previous month, was abandoned.

Three hours later the bandits arrived at a roadhouse on the outskirts of Minneapolis owned by Pete Doran, a local underworld figure. The six celebrated their profitable venture and Fisher's birthday with a private party and were joined by Helen, Clara Gannon, and professional auto thief Claire Lucas, who reportedly received a share of the loot for supplying the getaway car. Following the festivities Van Meter left for Chicago to rekindle a romance with a plucky, petite twenty-year-old brunette named Marie "Mickey" Conforti, whom he had met during the summer.

Nelson and his family had rented a cottage on the east edge of White Bear Lake in the resort community of Mahtomedi, a locale most likely suggested by Alvin Karpis, who had spent the summer of 1932 there with the Barkers. From late September to early November the young couple presented a friendly, familiar demeanor to their neighbors and local merchants. The children—the chestnut-haired, dark-eyed boy favoring his mother and the blond little girl resembling her father—were always well-behaved. Except for a two-week period in mid-October when the husband was away on business, the family feasted on pizza and spaghetti virtually every night at Vince Guarnera's Italian restaurant.

During this time they made at least one trip back to Chicago. While Helen and the kids visited family, Nelson met with Van Meter, who was living at the Lincoln Park Arms Hotel. In addition to spending time and money on Mickey Conforti, the skinny hood had re-contacted his prison buddy John Dillinger, who was hiding out in the Windy City with his partners.

The Dillinger gang, currently composed of seven members, was rapidly acquiring considerable notoriety. Most of the publicity centered on Dillinger, who, while not the actual leader, was easily the most flamboyant, a characteristic played up in media coverage throughout Ohio, Indiana, and Illinois.

Since his last encounter with Nelson, probably in late July, Dillinger had participated in a string of at least four bank robberies that netted him enough money to buy and smuggle a cache of pistols to his friends inside the walls of the Indiana State Prison. Then, four days before the scheduled breakout, Dillinger's remarkable luck in evading the law failed and he was nabbed by police in Ohio.

On September 26 ten inmates armed with Dillinger's weapons forced their way out of the Michigan City prison. Five—Harry "Pete" Pierpont, John "Red" Hamilton, Charles "Fat Charley" Makley, Russell Clark, and Edward Shouse—broke from the rest and contacted Harry Copeland. After staging a quick bank holdup in Makley's hometown of St. Mary's, Ohio, the six descended on Lima, Ohio, some thirty miles away, where Dillinger was being held. On October 12 they raided the jail and freed their friend. In the process Pierpont shot and killed Sheriff Jess Sarber when the lawman reached for his gun.

On the same day Nelson and his partners struck the Brainerd bank, Dillinger and company pulled into Greencastle, Indiana, and scored a $75,000 holdup. Since then the gang had been laying low in Chicago, scattered amid an array of North Side apartments, living unobtrusively with their girlfriends.

Dillinger had taken up with Evelyn "Billie" Frechette, a part-Indian beauty from Wisconsin. The couple shared an apartment on North Clarandon with Pierpont and his sweetheart Mary Kinder.

Van Meter told Nelson "the boys" were attempting to make connections with the local underworld but were not having much success, and he had suggested to Dillinger that "Jimmie could help."

A meeting was arranged at one of the gang's apartments. Nelson was received as an old friend by Dillinger and Copeland, who introduced him to the others. Predictably, Nelson and Pierpont seemed to take an instant dislike to each other, Baby Face having already formed his opinion based on Van Meter's sarcastic comments. Pierpont's disdain for the young visitor was probably sealed when he heard that Nelson was a pal of Van Meter. Their mutual animosity could also be attributed to a clash of too-similar personalities. Both were described as vain, temperamental, and authoritative, and both harbored the same pathological hatred for lawmen.

Apparently Nelson got along fine with the rest of the gang, especially Makley and Shouse, who he told Jack Perkins were "great guys." With the exception of Hamilton, who, like Nelson, never touched alcohol, Dillinger and his pals sipped bottles of Schlitz as they shared stories about their recent adventures. "You know," Dillinger remarked at one point, "they've already hung that Grand Haven job on me, along with every other damn thing over the last couple of months."

"You're welcome to take the credit for that one," Nelson joked.

Eventually the conversation turned to Nelson's Chicago contacts. He asked, "What kind of services you shopping for?" A sizable chunk (over $100,000) of the combined loot from the St. Mary's and Greencastle holdups comprised securities and bonds which they hoped to unload for a fair price. They also needed sources that could provide cars, license plates, and auto repairs.

The principal name Nelson supplied was his newest best friend, Jimmy Murray, who he guaranteed could "move the paper" for the best price. Baby Face recommended Murray's restaurant, the Rainbo, as a safe meeting place, along with Louie's roadhouse, The Seafood Inn in Elmhurst, and many others. He also provided a list of trustworthy auto dealers around the city, including his pal Clarence Lieder. For anything else they required—small arms, ammunition, vests—he suggested Jack Perkins and his partner Art Johnston. The pair were currently operating a bookie joint out of a pool hall on Sheridan Road, just a few blocks from the gang's apartments.

At the end of their meeting Nelson announced that he was determined to head south before he spotted "a single snowflake" and promised to stop back and see how things had worked out before his departure. Dillinger confided that he and his associates also intended to find a warmer climate in a month or so and were hoping to spend Christmas and New Years in Florida. They were presently casing three banks to acquire some traveling money. One in Racine, Wisconsin, was scheduled to be hit in a couple of weeks.

Nelson returned with his family to White Bear Lake. A few days later Van Meter arrived back in St. Paul and met with the others at the Green Lantern. Green suggested they get to work right away setting up another robbery. All the rest agreed—all, that is, but Nelson, who proposed they wait until spring.

On November 11 the debate was abruptly resolved for them. That morning Minneapolis Police Detectives Adam Smith and Clarence McClaskey stormed the Bennett residence after receiving a tip that a man involved in the Brainerd holdup was hiding there. The officers caught Tommy Carroll—shirtless and barefoot, half his face covered in shaving lather—before he could escape out a back window.

Once Carroll's hands were cuffed, Smith and McClaskey searched the premises. They discovered two shotguns, an automatic pistol, a submachine gun hidden inside a suitcase, and $1,582 in mostly crisp new bills, none of which supported Carroll's claims that he was a law-abiding salesman. While Smith continued to rummage through the room, his partner escorted the suspect outside and ordered him into the back seat of their car. As he climbed in, Carroll suddenly flung himself backward onto the seat and kicked McClaskey in the face with his bare feet. The dazed officer collapsed on the curb. Carroll leapt on him, snatching McClaskey's revolver and, after a frantic search through his pockets, the handcuff key.

Inside the duplex Smith heard the commotion and rushed to a window in time to see the barefoot bandit scampering down the street. By the time Smith reached the sidewalk, Carroll was nowhere in sight. Several blocks away the fugitive stole a truck and drove to the St. Paul apartment of Pat Reilly.

That evening when Carroll's cronies came together to discuss his latest close encounter with the law, they could not resist poking fun at him after hearing how he had arrived at Reilly's place shoeless and half-shaven. On a more serious note, they agreed that since Carroll and anyone associated with him were being sought in connection with the Brainerd job, the Twin Cities had become too dangerous for them at the moment. This time when Nelson declared it was time to leave, there were no objections. Only Green elected to remain behind to continue his jug marker duties with the help of Reilly, who by now was recognized as a fringe member of the gang and a general errand boy for Green and Gannon.

On November 13 the gang left town in four groups—Nelson and his family riding in their Terraplane; Van Meter and Mickey Conforti in a Terraplane with Illinois plates; Gannon, his wife, Clara, and their five-year-old daughter, Ruth, in a Buick coach; and Carroll and Fisher in the latter's Auburn. The travelers reassembled outside Chicago and spent the next few days in a tourist camp. At least one visit was arranged with Nelson's sister Julie, during which it was decided that Darlene would remain in Chicago over the winter with her grand-mother and aunts.

Nelson and Van Meter dropped in on Dillinger to see if his gang had made use of Nelson's recommended contacts. The Indiana desperado gratefully acknowledged that each of the names had proved valuable, especially Murray, who had paid a handsome price for the bonds. Baby Face mentioned he had a source in Texas for automatic weapons and said he would be willing to purchase merchandise on their behalf, if they were interested. The Dillinger crew, which had brazenly raided two police armories the previous month in their quest for artillery and ammo, found the offer intriguing. Dillinger was particularly fasci-nated when Nelson described Lebman's modified machine-gun pistol and said he wanted one "as long as the price is right."

The day after Nelson's people arrived in Chicago a blustery wave of frigid weather pushed through the Midwest, sending temperatures plummeting into single digits. Nelson, probably spoiled by his sojourn out west over the previous winter, voted to leave immediately. However, the others, including Helen, wanted to remain in the Chicago area another week.

But as the mercury dropped, Nelson's hometown became a very hot place. On November 15 Dillinger narrowly escaped when he unwittingly drove into a police ambush on Irving Park Boulevard managing to lose his pursuers only after a furious chase through the streets. Two days later Copeland was arrested. Dillinger and the rest fled to Wisconsin, where they robbed the Racine bank four days later. Nelson's group headed south.

Sunny skies and seventy-degree temperatures greeted the four-car caravan when it arrived in San Antonio on November 19. Nelson and the rest stopped by Lebman's shop to announce their arrival. The gunsmith, pleased to see his friend and favorite customer "Jimmie Williams," was introduced all around.

Nelson and Van Meter checked into a tourist camp on the southeast side of town, and Gannon and his family rented a place close by. Carroll registered at the downtown Bluebonnet Hotel as James C. McLarken. Fisher, using his favorite alias, Harold L. Keith, took a suite in the Aurora Apartments on the city's north side. Scattered throughout the city, they frequently got together at a cafe on South Presa Street for meals and planning sessions. The one excep-tion was Carroll who, within a matter of days, was dating at least two local women, a manicurist and a clerk at a pharmacy near Lebman's shop.

The rest generally acted like tourists, relaxing, seeing the sights, going horseback riding by day and to restaurants and movie theaters at night. They often visited Lebman's home on Evergreen Street where the gunsmith's wife, Mollie, and their two children came to know Jimmie, Helen, their son Ronnie, and most of their friends. The women shopped and the children played while the men talked endlessly about firearms during card games. On one occasion Lebman and his wife accompanied the group on a daylong trip to Laredo. On

November 30 Lebman, keeping his promise, hosted a Thanksgiving feast at his home that was attended by Nelson and his family, Van Meter and Mickey Conforti, and Chuck Fisher.

In the midst of all the rest and recreation, the gang managed to squeeze in some business at Lebman's shop. Nelson purchased a .38 machine-gun pistol for Dillinger and selected a pair of .380 automatics for himself. He also obtained Texas plates for his Terraplane. Carroll bought a .380, and Fisher traded in an old .45 for a .38 super automatic. Van Meter decided he, too, wanted one of the gunsmith's specially crafted baby machine guns. When Lebman said he had sold his last available model to Nelson, "Wayne" presented him with a Colt .45 and requested that he convert the weapon to fire on full auto. Lebman agreed but said it would take time. Van Meter said there was no hurry; he would return for it in the spring.

Lebman informed Nelson that the Thompson he'd previously purchased and sent back had been repaired to fire in automatic mode. Explaining that he planned to be on the move for the next few months, Nelson asked the gunsmith to ship him the weapon later. Lebman, however, wanted to get rid of it as soon as possible, for just a month earlier, on October 25, Texas had passed a law banning the sale or possession of machine guns except by lawmen, with violators subject to a hefty fine and two to ten years' imprisonment. Lebman offered to mail the repaired Thompson to the Bennett address in Minneapolis.

"No, not there," Nelson responded. He promised to send the gunsmith a new address where the weapon could be shipped.

On December 6 Nelson celebrated his twenty-fifth birthday with an overnight trip to Mexico, accompanied by Helen, Van Meter, and Mickey Conforti. Three days later Nelson, Van Meter, and Gannon stopped by Lebman's shop to say goodbye. Fisher and Carroll decided to remain in town another week or so.

Outside San Antonio the three cars went their separate ways. Gannon continued north toward St. Paul, while Van Meter turned east, planning to meet the members of the Dillinger gang in Daytona, Florida. Nelson steered his Terraplane west.

❀ ❀ ❀

Their departure turned out to be fortuitous in light of Carroll's uncanny knack for attracting lawmen along with the ladies. For the past two weeks San Antonio police had been looking into reports that a group of suspicious out-of-towners, "at least five men, three women, and two children" traveling in vehicles with either Illinois or Minnesota plates, was spending large amounts of cash in the area. Convinced the visitors were members of some midwestern gang that had chosen the Texas town as a place to cool off, officers set out to locate and question them.

Shortly after noon on Monday, December 11, police received a tip that one of the visitors, a man called McLarken, was to meet a woman named Bobbie at her apartment in the 300 block of South Street that day. The call reportedly was made by one of Carroll's other San Antonio sweethearts, embittered after learning the bandit was seeing another woman.

A trio of detectives was dispatched, and the three parked a few doors away to await the suspect's arrival. Alfred Hartman, a craggy-faced veteran, was at the wheel, and fifty-six-year-old Henry Perrow, holding a sawed-off shotgun on his lap, sat beside him. A native Virginian who had fought in the Spanish-American War and in China during the Boxer Rebellion, Perrow was already a living legend among lawmen. After military service he'd joined the Texas Rangers and survived a gun battle with Mexican revolutionaries that had left left a bullet embedded in his jaw. Lee Jones, a handsome young detective half the age of Hartman and Perrow, occupied the back seat.

Watching for a car with out-of-state plates, they were caught off guard when a taxi pulled up at 4:30 and a man hopped out and entered the building before they were able to get a good look at him. Minutes later Blanche "Bobbie" Bowman, a pretty brunette, emerged from the doorway, quickly surveyed the street, then signaled behind her. Carroll, attired in brown riding breeches and cowboy boots, came out and climbed into the cab with her.

Hartman started the motor and slipped into traffic behind the taxi, which turned north on Water Street. When the cab stopped at the intersection of East Commerce Street, Hartman pulled the detectives' vehicle directly alongside. At the sight of the lawmen, Carroll swiftly leapt from the cab and began running down East Commerce.

Jones jumped out and raced after the suspect, his partners following until their car became snarled in traffic. Abandoning the vehicle, the two veterans joined the chase. When Perrow fired his shotgun in the air as a warning, Carroll darted into what turned out to be a blind alley. Finding himself trapped, the desperado, in true Wild West fashion, pulled a pair of pistols, a .380 and a .38, and prepared to shoot it out. Hartman halted beside the mouth of the alley, with Perrow stationed a few yards behind him. Drawing his old-fashioned six-shooter, Hartman barked, "Throw up those hands and step out here."

Jones scrambled through a Jewish market next door and emerged on the opposite side of a high board fence where the alleyway dead-ended. The young detective impetuously scaled the fence, but Carroll spotted him and aimed at the figure perched above him. The two fired at the same time. Both missed, but Carroll's slug came uncomfortably close, ripping a hole through Jones's jacket. The officer lost his balance and toppled into the alley.

At the sound of the shots Hartman lunged around the corner and fired. Carroll turned on him, both pistols blazing. A bullet struck the lawman in the right wrist, tore along his forearm, and shattered his elbow, knocking the revolver from his grasp. Hartman clutched his arm and fell against the wall.

Carroll ran past him to the mouth of the alley. Peering around the corner he saw Perrow standing by the curb, his shotgun trained on the alleyway. The outlaw took careful aim and fired twice. Perrow reeled as a slug slammed into his left temple, exiting from the right side of his head. The shotgun boomed, its pellets striking the sidewalk as the officer crumpled.

The instant Perrow went down, Carroll dashed from the alley. Jones, recovering from his fall, fired at the fleeing man but missed. Carroll jumped on the running board of a passing vehicle, but the driver, undaunted by the pistol Carroll shoved in his face, gruffly pushed the gunman off. Carroll hit the pavement, sprang back to his feet, and sprinted down the street.

Jones came to Hartman's aid, helping the wounded veteran stand. The pair lurched out of the alley in time to see Perrow being loaded into the back of a bystander's car to be taken to the nearest hospital.

A few blocks away, on North Center Street, Carroll clambered into the cab of a pickup truck that had stopped at a traffic sign. Flashing his pistol he commanded the owner to "drive and drive fast." With the gunman directing, they proceeded to the corner of Nueva and South Flores where Carroll ordered him to stop. The driver watched Carroll walk briskly down the street and enter Lebman's Sporting Goods. When police later questioned Lebman, the shop owner told them Carroll had said nothing of his battle with the detectives, though he appeared to be in a hurry. He had asked to borrow a pair of denim trousers "to wear hunting," then slipped them on over his conspicuous riding pants and ducked out the back door.

An hour later Lebman received a phone call from Fisher asking him to meet the outlaw on Broadway near Brackenridge Park. When Lebman arrived he spotted the bandit seated in his Auburn sedan. Fisher asked if he'd heard about the shooting. Lebman replied that he had—the girl at the pharmacy who dated Carroll had phoned with details of the bandit's frantic escape after wounding the two detectives. She pleaded with the gunsmith not to mention her involvement with Carroll if police questioned him.

Fisher apologized for "the mess" and said he intended to retrieve his belongings and "get the hell out of town." He said he hated to "cut out on Tommy," but the local heat left him no choice.

At the same moment Fisher and Lebman were meeting, Gus T. Jones, SAC of the FBI's San Antonio office, was finishing dinner with his wife in a downtown restaurant. As the couple walked to their car they heard newsboys crying reports of the shooting. Jones, a heavy-set man with a round face and glasses, raced to the police station to find out more. The Detective Bureau was crowded with officers, some of them deputy sheriffs and Texas Rangers, many openly shedding tears. The news from the hospital was grim: Perrow was not expected to live and the doctors might have to amputate Hartman's right arm.

Jones spoke with Detective Captain Aubrey Hopkins about the manhunt for the mysterious "McLarken" and offered to bring in his G-Men to assist. Hopkins confided that information was sparse—other than a general description of the gunman the only lead they had was that McLarken often visited another suspicious character who lived at the Aurora Apartments, which was presently under surveillance. As they discussed the possibility that McLarken and his cronies were kidnappers on the lam, a call came into the station advising the detectives that the man McLarken had been visiting at the Aurora was now in his room.

More than two dozen officers rushed from the room and headed for the apartment house. One of them was Jones, whose wife, patiently working a crossword puzzle, awaited him in their car. The SAC snatched his submachine gun from the trunk and handed her the weapon as he slid behind the wheel. When they arrived at the building, Jones took the gun and ordered her to remain in the car. This time, however, she followed him inside and helped the apartment manager, who had been warned of possible gunfire, clear some children from the hallways.

Moments after lawmen reached the scene Fisher, dressed in an expensive suit and carrying a small bag, walked out his suite. Before he could step into the elevator a team of detectives led by Captain Hopkins surrounded him. The suspect indignantly refused to raise his hands and resisted when officers attempted to seize him. His struggle ceased the instant Jones moved in and rammed the muzzle of his machine gun into his ribs.

Fisher was carrying a .380 automatic and two full spare clips, along with a money belt containing more than $1,100. A search of his car produced boxes of rifle and pistol ammunition, nearly 400 rounds. Under interrogation he insisted his name was Harold Keith and admitted nothing. After grilling the suspect for over two hours Police Commissioner Phillip Wright told reporters, "All I got out of him you could put in your eye and not get hurt."

Lebman was also brought in for questioning and freely acknowledged that the men he knew as McLarken and Keith had visited his shop many times, purchasing several handguns and a quantity of ammunition. He said he had no idea they were wanted men.

His answers failed to satisfy Jones, who had been allowed to sit in on the sessions with the gunsmith. He was convinced Lebman was dealing weapons to the gangsters and knew much more than he was saying. In statements to others, Jones made it clear that since Lebman was a Jew he was "a natural liar." The SAC's anti-Semitic arguments for detaining the gunsmith were in vain. After spending a day and a night in police custody Lebman, thanks largely to the efforts of his lawyer, was released.

At 4:45 P.M. on December 13, almost exactly forty-eight hours from the moment he was shot, Detective Henry Carrington Perrow died in his hospital bed.

By that time fingerprints had revealed the man arrested at the Aurora was Charles W. Fisher, who was wanted in connection with a series of post office holdups throughout Minnesota and Wisconsin, all federal crimes. The prisoner was promptly turned over to Jones and his G-Men. On December 21 agents escorted Fisher back to Minnesota to be indicted and tried for robbing the U.S. Mail.

Photos of Fisher's known associates were sent to San Antonio. Witnesses to the fatal shooting—including Detectives Hartman and Jones—identified Thomas Leonard Carroll as the killer. Despite a massive statewide search, no trace of the fugitive was found after he slipped out the back door of Lebman's shop. Texas lawmen finally assumed he must have escaped into Mexico.

In reality Carroll had hitchhiked his way back to the Midwest and eventually, dressed as a hobo, hopped a freight that took him into the Twin Cities. Arriving a full three weeks after his gunfight with the San Antonio detectives, he learned that Fisher was in federal custody, Detective Perrow had died, and he, Carroll, had been branded as the murderer.

Red [Hamilton] got busy right after the cops grabbed us down at
Tucson. . . . [He] got in touch with Van and Jimmie, who were doing
some casing around St. Paul, and asked to borrow some money. . . . They
were planning that Sioux Falls heist then, and Red tells Van that if he can
get me out of jail in time, we could kick it back to him out of our share.
— John Dillinger

CHAPTER 7

THE FIX

FOLLOWING A LEISURELY TOUR of the Southwest and a few days' stay near the Grand Canyon, Nelson and his wife and son pulled into Reno on December 16, a week after their departure from San Antonio. At some point during the journey Nelson had shaved off his blond mustache, making him appear even younger. Many mistook him for a youth in his late teens.

One of his first stops was the Air Service Garage, where he visited with Frank Cochran while leaving his vehicle for some minor repairs. Invited to dinner at the garage owner's home, Jimmie and Helen brought early Christmas presents for the Cochrans' children, including an expensive radio for their son.

Anna Cochran was happy to see the young couple, but she was immediately alarmed by Helen's appearance. The tiny twenty-year-old looked thinner, more frail than she had the previous spring. When Anna found a private moment to share her concern Helen confided that she was suffering from anemia and not sleeping well. Jimmie, she added, intended to have her see some doctors over the next few weeks.

While in Reno Nelson met with his former bosses Graham and McKay and their associate Tex Hall. He learned from them that the Parente mob had broken up, abandoning its once-lucrative liquor-smuggling operation. The repeal of Prohibition on December 5 was the chief reason, along with increased interference from federal agents and Parente's own desire to earn an honest living. The gang members had scattered—some were now in Sausalito, most were across the bay in San Francisco.

Graham and McKay had problems of their own. They, along with six others, were under federal indictment, charged with using the U.S. Mail to commit fraud. Investigators and prosecutors working with the U.S. Postal Inspectors' Bureau had exposed a nationwide scheme that had swindled dozens of victims through the operation of a phony out-of-state racetrack service and bilked numerous investors by peddling bogus stock in a Nevada mining company. The government intended to prove Graham and his partner received fifteen percent of the profits. The key witness for the prosecution was Roy John Frisch, who had been a cashier at the Riverside Bank in Reno until it closed a year earlier and now was an assistant to the federal receiver for the bank. Frisch was scheduled to testify at the April 2 arraignment of Graham and McKay. He was also expected to appear before a U.S. Senate subcommittee investigating George Wingfield, owner of the Riverside and six more failed Nevada banks and a key associate of Graham.

Graham made it clear that without Frisch's testimony the government's case against them would collapse. No one knows what arrangement—if any—was discussed, although it is evident Nelson came away from the meeting with the understanding that he was in a position to repay his former bosses for their generous services to him. Nelson's role in the upcoming removal of the witness—whether volunteered, solicited, or pressured—was apparently agreed upon.

One week before Christmas Nelson brought his wife back to the Vallejo General Hospital. While there are no records to confirm her ailment, sources within the Gillis family later indicated she was experiencing complications from a third pregnancy that had ended in a miscarriage. As before, Tobe Williams oversaw all the paperwork and assured Nelson of complete confidentiality. Helen was scheduled to enter the hospital on January 8.

The couple traveled to Sausalito where, after a bit of searching, Nelson found John Paul Chase managing the Oasis, a restaurant-bar on Water Street. Chase was elated to see his friend and former rumrunning partner. While talking over old times Nelson inquired about Fatso Negri, the third member of their trio. Chase revealed that shortly after Nelson's flight from Sausalito, "the feds and local cops made a big bust on us at Point Sur." Negri and several others had been nabbed and brought to trial. "Fats pulled a six-month stretch in the county joint," Chase said.

He added that he was disgusted with Parente, Strittmatter, and Ralph Rizzo for failing to help Fatso fight the charges, saying it was one reason he had quit the gang. (Another account claimed Chase left after the federal bust because he feared capture.) Following his release, Negri took a job as a bouncer at Spider Kelly's, a San Francisco nightclub partly owned by Rizzo.

The next evening Nelson and Helen visited the nightclub on Pacific Street—part of the booming Barbary Coast revival and packed every night since repeal. Negri was stunned when he spotted the diminutive couple edging through the crowd. After a round of enthusiastic hellos he ushered them into the first available booth. Joining them during a break, Negri noticed his young pal was sipping a glass of plain seltzer.

"Still not drinking, Jimmie, even though it's legal now?"

"'Fraid not."

"What brings you back to town?"

Nelson explained that Helen was scheduled to go into the hospital, adding, "Looks like we'll be here for a spell."

"I hear you're pretty hot back east," Negri remarked.

"What've you heard?"

"Nothing specific. Just some of the old gang talking, saying Jimmie broke into the big time. Stuff like that. The cops after you?"

"Cops don't bother me," Nelson boasted. "I bother them."

Eventually Baby Face inquired about Negri's finances, asking, "How's the hay here?"

"Not so hot," Negri admitted. "I'm only getting thirty-five dollars a week."

"Hell, Fats, that won't even keep you in cigarettes."

Nelson suddenly pulled out a wad of cash and laid seven hundred-dollar bills on the table. "That should tide you over a while," Nelson said, smiling brightly as he and Helen slipped out of the booth. "I'll be back in touch with you later."

During the next two weeks Nelson moved back and forth between Reno and the coast, using his old alias Jimmie Burnell in Nevada and calling himself Jimmie Rogers in California. Christmas Day was spent with the Cochrans. Chase, who had abruptly quit his job at the Oasis, was also in attendance.

On January 7 Nelson brought his wife to the Vallejo hospital where she was admitted under the name Helen Williams. Each day for the next two weeks he stayed dutifully at Helen's side. After visiting hours he spent his evenings with Chase, circulating around the Bay Area and visiting old associates like Tony "Soap" Moreno, Louis Tambini, and Jim Griffin.

He also made another appearance at Spider Kelly's, this time with Chase tagging along. Negri found time to sit with his former comrades and inquired about Helen. "She's doing well," Nelson reported. "You should come by the hospital. She'd like to see you, and so would old Tobe. How's your cash holding out?"

When Negri confessed he had already spent the $700, Nelson laughed. After about fifteen minutes of conversation, Negri announced he should return to work.

"You like this job?" Nelson asked.

Fatso shrugged. "Like I said, it ain't so hot. But I got nothing else at the moment."

"Let it go."

Negri looked puzzled, asking what his friend meant.

"Quit, walk away. Come with Johnny and me. We got big things lined up. I can use a guy like you, someone I can count on."

The invitation made Negri squirm. "I don't know, Jimmie. I want to stay out of hot water."

Nelson acted insulted. "Well, I guess our friendship doesn't mean anything to you, then."

"Hey, don't get sore, Jimmie. I don't want to argue with you. I'll help you out. Just tell me what you need."

Nelson said he would get back to him. The next night Negri received a call from a bartender asking him to come to a tavern on Commerce Street. When Fatso arrived he spotted Nelson and Chase at a table. "I didn't mean to rattle you," Baby Face apologized. "Stay where you are for the time being. Later on, when I need you, Johnny will be in touch."

Over the next few nights Nelson and Chase continued to drop by and chat with their friend. On January 16 Negri followed the pair to Vallejo. Stopping at a florist's shop, Nelson handed Fatso ten dollars, saying, "She'd really appreciate something from you." Negri purchased a huge bouquet of flowers, which he presented to Helen in her hospital room.

Later that day, after Negri departed, Nelson and Chase stopped at a car dealership on Marin Street in Vallejo where they picked out a new Plymouth sedan. The vehicle was registered in the name of John Paul Chase, although the salesman, Ray Hitchcock, distinctly recalled later that it was Nelson who paid for the car in cash.

The next day Chase walked into Spider Kelly's and beckoned for Negri to follow him outside. On the street Chase proudly showed off his new automobile. "All paid for, every penny," he crowed, displaying the receipt.

"Looks like you're really in the dough," remarked Negri.

"Jimmie is. I will be, too, now that I'm going away with him."

Admiring the Plymouth, Negri confided that he was sorry he'd balked when Nelson asked him to come along. "Don't worry, Fats, you'll get your chance," Chase promised. Privately Negri felt torn between remaining in San Francisco or going on the road with his pals. It occurred to him that it might be better if Nelson did not offer a second chance to join them.

❋ ❋ ❋

Throughout this period Nelson vigilantly monitored events back in the Midwest, scanning newspapers, listening to radio broadcasts, and on rare occasions making phone calls to Green and Van Meter in the Twin Cities or to one of his contacts in Chicago. He heard about the San Antonio shootout and the capture of Chuck Fisher. At present no one knew the whereabouts of Tommy Carroll, and rumors circulated throughout the underworld claiming the outlaw had died of thirst wandering the vast ranges of Texas.

Nelson had to face the fact that he had lost one, possibly two valuable confederates. Realizing the gang needed replacements, he looked to his former bootlegging cronies and found Chase an eager recruit. Negri voiced reservations about moving up to big-time crime but indicated he would consent if Baby Face forced the issue. But after his experience with Freddie Monahan, Nelson apparently had no desire to enlist anyone who was not willing and ready to join.

Meanwhile, John Dillinger and his band of not-so-merry men continued to grab headlines. The Racine robbery on November 20 had netted the gang $27,000. In the process Charley Makley had shot and wounded an assistant cashier and a policeman, then sprayed the street with machine-gun fire as the bandits emerged from the bank.

The gang returned to Chicago. On December 14 John Hamilton was approached by police in a garage on North Broadway. Questioned as a suspicious person, Hamilton—a la Tommy Carroll—drew a pistol and blasted his way past the lawmen, killing police Sergeant William Shanley. Two days later Captain John Stege (whom Nelson had encountered after his 1931 arrest) announced the formation of a special forty-man "Dillinger Squad," headed by Sergeant Frank Reynolds and devoted exclusively to tracking down the Indiana bank robber and his henchmen. "We'll either drive the Dillinger mob out of town or bury them," Stege vowed before the press. "We'd prefer the latter."

A week after Shanley's death Ed Shouse was captured. During his apprehension another policeman was killed, shot accidentally by a fellow officer. It turned out that Shouse, a month earlier, had been ejected from the gang by Dillinger and Pierpont, reportedly because he had become too friendly with Billie Frechette, Dillinger's girlfriend. Shouse promised to cooperate and ultimately provided volumes of information about his former partners.

By that time the gang members had split up and reunited in Daytona where, joined briefly by Van Meter, they celebrated New Year's by firing their Tommyguns into the surf. Back in Chicago police descended on the associates they had left behind, including Nelson's friends Perkins, Johnston, and Jimmy Murray, whose ties to Dillinger were exposed by Shouse. All were relentlessly interrogated and threatened with prosecution, but eventually they were released.

Federal agents helping Chicago police in an unofficial capacity questioned Shouse about Dillinger's interstate bank-robbing spree. Asked about the Grand Haven heist, Shouse denied reports that Dillinger was behind the holdup. He said the actual perpetrator was a young hood known to him only as "Jimmie," who claimed to possess numerous connections inside the Chicago underworld and was a close friend of Van Meter.

On December 28 Illinois issued a list of the state's top twenty-one public enemies. Dillinger was placed at the top, with his fellow gang members Pierpont, Hamilton, Makley, and Clark occupying the next four spots on the list. Largely because of his rumored ties to Dillinger, Van Meter was ranked eighteenth. The name appearing at the bottom of the list, Illinois public enemy No. 21, was George "Baby Face" Nelson, "a convicted bank robber and escaped convict." Police had not yet connected him with the Grand Haven or Brainerd holdups, nor had they identified him as Shouse's mysterious Jimmie who visited Dillinger.

On January 15, with the gang's funds depleted after several weeks of living high in Florida, Dillinger made a brief but dramatic return to the Midwest in a desperate bid to seize some quick cash. That afternoon Dillinger and Hamilton entered the First National Bank of East Chicago. A third bandit, never identified, remained at the wheel of the getaway car. It is possible the wheelman was Van Meter, who, because of Pierpont's absence, may had consented to help his old prison buddy plan and execute the holdup. Another suspect was Fred Breman, the East Chicago fence who was present when Nelson first met the Dillinger crowd. Informants later asserted that Breman was the chief setup man for the robbery.

Armed with a machine gun, Dillinger secured the lobby while Hamilton looted the teller cages and vault of more than $20,000. The bank's vice president, Walter Spencer, tripped a silent alarm, summoning almost a dozen policemen to the scene. Dillinger spotted the uniformed figures gathering out front and alerted his partner. "But don't hurry," Dillinger reportedly added. "Get all that dough. We'll kill these coppers and get away. Take your time."

The pair emerged from the bank using two hostages as shields. Dillinger fired a burst from his Tommy into the air. Most of the officers, not daring to shoot back, scurried for cover. One, however, Patrolman William O'Malley, bravely stood his ground. When Dillinger's hostage broke free, giving O'Malley a chance to fire, he pumped several slugs into the bandit's steel-reinforced vest. Dillinger swiftly replied with a machine gun blast that left the patrolman dead.

O'Malley's fellow officers started shooting. Hamilton fell with a wound near his groin, but Dillinger kept the lawmen at bay long enough to help his comrade into the car. After a brief pursuit and exchange of gunfire, the robbers outdistanced the police and worked their way to Chicago.

The moment they hit town Dillinger contacted Perkins and Johnston frantically seeking a doctor and a safe place for his wounded companion. The bandits were taken to the house of Johnston's aunt on North Homan Avenue where Hamilton spent the next six weeks recovering, nursed by his mistress, Patricia Cherrington, and tended by an underworld doctor who charged $5,100 (one-fourth of the East Chicago take) for his services. Some accounts claim the physician was Dr. Joseph Moran, a well-known scalpel-for-hire in the Chicago underworld and, in recent months, senior health-care provider for the Barker-Karpis gang. Perkins evidently knew Moran through Nelson, who, according to an FBI report, had befriended the doctor in Joliet while Moran served a sentence for performing abortions. Once Dillinger paid the doctor's hefty fee and was assured that Hamilton was receiving proper treatment, he departed to rendezvous with the rest of the gang and their girlfriends in Tucson.

The day after the East Chicago holdup Charles Fisher appeared in federal court at Mankato, Minnesota. The chubby outlaw pleaded guilty to the string of post office robberies and was sentenced to serve eight years in Leavenworth. Fisher, like Earl Doyle, was out of the picture indefinitely.

The following day, January 17, big news came out of the Twin Cities. The Barker-Karpis gang had pulled off another kidnapping. Their victim was Edward Bremer, a wealthy Minneapolis banker. This time they demanded $200,000, twice the Hamm ransom. Federal agents swarmed into the Twin Cities like hungry locusts. It was going to be a long hot winter, Nelson decided, glad to be far away and in no hurry to get back.

Helen was released from the hospital on January 20 and told by her doctors to rest for the next four weeks. Nelson took her to Reno, where their son had been staying for the past few days with the Cochrans. Two days later Nelson was back in the Bay Area with Chase. Using the name James Rodgers of 154 Eastwood Drive in San Francisco, he purchased a Hudson sedan from the Earl E. Anthony Sales Company on Van Ness and was told it would take several days to prepare the vehicle. Nelson introduced Chase as his business partner and left Chase's phone number (Sausalito 404) so the manager could notify them.

Four days later, on January 26, Chase called Nelson in Reno to say the Hudson was ready. Nelson and Helen were on their way to San Francisco when the radio crackled with the news that Dillinger and his gang had been captured by police in Tucson the day before. Baby Face listened to the report with equal measures of disbelief, amusement, and genuine concern since the law had caught up to the desperados just one state away from his Nevada hideout. Later, poring over the newspaper accounts with Chase, Nelson wondered how "a bunch of hick cops in a two-horse town" had managed to round up the entire Dillinger gang without firing a shot. "The idiots must've been wearing name tags," he commented sarcastically.

Actually, a fire had broken out in the hotel where Makley and Clark were staying. Firemen retrieving their luggage had become suspicious of the pair due to the unusually heavy weight of their cases—packed with weapons and ammunition—and the huge tips they handed out. Alerted by the firefighters, police had placed the out-of-towners under surveillance and soon discovered the presence of Pierpont and eventually Dillinger. The Tucson officers had been patient and efficient, waiting to make their move until the suspects were alone and nabbing them one at a time. Pierpont and Clark had put up a fight but had been subdued before they reached their guns. Cursing and spitting as he was dragged into a cell, Pierpont had vowed to return some day and kill them all.

Three states—Wisconsin, Indiana, and Ohio—became embroiled in a legal battle over which would claim the prisoners.

Under his alias Jimmie Rodgers, Nelson was issued a pair of 1934 California license plates (G-H-475) for his new Hudson. Cochran consented to store Nelson's Terraplane at his home garage. Nelson repeatedly brought the Hudson and Chase's Plymouth back to Cochran's business, accumulating repair bills of more than $200. In addition to standard servicing he ordered new, more powerful radios installed in each vehicle along with such special features as a switch that allowed the driver to extinguish the taillights while keeping the headlights on.

Cochran later claimed "Jimmie was fanatical about the state of his cars." Each vehicle had to be fine-tuned and maintained in peak condition for acceleration, speed, and durability. Cochran recalled, "He was tough on his cars but never let them run down." Others remembered Nelson was just as meticulous about caring for his personal cache of weapons.

Near the end of January Nelson asked Chase to drive to Chicago and contact some people for him. He provided his sister Julie's address, saying Chase was welcome to stay there, and also requested that he bring back Mary Gillis to visit and help out with Helen.

Chase left Reno on February 1 and arrived in Chicago two days later. At the Fitzsimmons apartment he introduced himself as "Johnny from California, a friend of Les and Helen." The entire family was impressed by his affability and manners, even Julie's husband, who usually disapproved of his brother-in-law's gangland pals. Chase reported that Helen was out of the hospital and recuperating under her husband's care in Reno. He told Mary her son was eager to see her and that she was welcome to accompany him on his return trip. But first he needed to deliver some messages from Nelson to certain other people.

Exactly whom Chase saw and what he told them was never revealed. Jack Perkins, back on the streets after being grilled about his alleged association with Dillinger, is a likely candidate. It's also possible that he met with Hamilton and perhaps Van Meter at Louie's roadhouse. Each gave Chase a note to take back to Nelson. Chase later insisted that he wasn't privy to any of the information he was conveying, although he suspected "something big" was in the works.

Chase left Chicago with Mary Gillis on February 5. Just outside the city limits the Californian, unaccustomed to driving on icy roads, ran his Plymouth into a ditch. Neither was injured, and the vehicle was towed to a garage where it was determined that repairs would take several days. Chase took Mary, who was anxious to reach her youngest son and ailing daughter-in-law, to Union Station, purchased a ticket for Reno, and gave the sixty-four-year-old widow some extra cash as she boarded the train. He then sent a telegram to the Cochrans to alert Nelson to his mother's impending arrival. A few days later Chase reclaimed his car and again headed west.

When he arrived in Reno he was informed that Nelson and his family had left town the day after Mary's arrival and had left word for Chase to contact them through "Blondie." He immediately drove to San Rafael, California, where he contacted Eugene Mazet, a short, sandy-haired friend who operated a service station. Mazet directed Chase to a bayside cottage between San Rafael and Sausalito that Nelson had rented for his family.

Over the next two weeks Nelson lived quietly with his mother, son, and recovering wife. His sister Leona and her five-month-old son, Timothy, traveled down from their home in Bremerton, Washington, and stayed with them for a few days. Chase was a frequent visitor to the cottage. Nelson told his mother that he and Johnny were partners in a business venture, marketing used cars and automobile parts. "It's strictly legit," he swore to her, no doubt hoping to put her mind at ease about his source of income. Chase, he explained, handled all the visible dealings of their enterprise, thus sparing Nelson the risk of exposure for his past misdeeds. Mary, as always, believed every word.

Several times Chase accompanied Nelson to San Raphael, usually waiting in the car while his friend exchanged cash for a fistful of coins, which he took to the nearest pay phone. Nelson had lectured Chase on the dangers of communicating sensitive information over the telephone lines, and the fact that he placed more than a dozen long-distance calls convinced Chase there was some sort of emergency back east.

Suddenly, on February 21, Nelson announced it was time to leave. Helen, whom he considered leaving behind in the care of his mother, assured him that she was well enough to travel and was eager to return to the Midwest. Before departing, Nelson and Chase stopped at the home of Gene Mazet and left a small trunk in his care. Mazet eventually grew curious and peeked inside. Among the contents, mostly family photos and letters, was a shoebox containing $2,000. There was also a note addressed to Mazet saying, "If you need any money, help yourself." Mazet later admitted he took $500.

The group left in two cars—Nelson and his wife in the Hudson, Chase, Mary, and Ronnie in the Plymouth. Evidently Nelson was in no hurry or, for Helen's sake, decided not to push it. They arrived in Reno and spent two nights there before resuming their journey on February 23. Nelson, who often would drive all night on the open road at speeds exceeding 80 mph, took it slow and stopped frequently.

They arrived in St. Paul on February 26 and checked into the Commodore Hotel. Leaving his family in Chase's care, Nelson met Eddie Green at the Charlou Apartments. The pair walked across South Fremont Avenue to the Josephine Apartments where Van Meter and Mickey Conforti were living in

Number 201 as Mr. and Mrs. John L. Ober. Tommy Carroll, who had been hiding out in Wisconsin for the past month, was also there.

The four outlaws engaged in a long discussion that night. Green reported he had targeted three banks, one in South Dakota and two in Iowa, all high-profile jobs. The probable take from all three, Green boasted, might come close to a quarter-million dollars. With Van Meter's help, the jug marker had recently revisited the banks, sketched diagrams of their interiors, and made maps of getaway routes.

The main obstacle at the moment was a lack of manpower. Tom Gannon was becoming increasingly nervous about taking an active role in robberies, and his status in the gang from this point on would become vague. With Green insisting the scores were six- or seven-man jobs, Van Meter claimed to have the answer. The others knew what was coming, even Nelson who had discussed the matter with him on the phone. The skinny bandit had spoken of little else over the past weeks.

❋ ❋ ❋

Extradited from Arizona a month earlier, John Dillinger was incarcerated in the reputedly "escape proof" Lake County Jail at Crown Point, Indiana, to await trial for the murder of Patrolman O'Malley during the East Chicago bank heist. (Pierpont, Makley, and Clark were sent to Ohio and charged with the slaying of Sheriff Sarber.) For the duration of Dillinger's celebrated stay, dozens of additional armed guards were brought in to patrol the grounds. Thus the stage was set for one of the most sensational and audacious jailbreaks in modern history.

In order to pull it off, however, Dillinger needed a little help from his friends.

On February 15 he was visited by his attorney, the bombastic, snowy-haired Louis Piquett, and his assistant Arthur O'Leary. Dillinger managed to slip a note to the pair, asking them to deliver it Billie Frechette, who called daily at Piquett's office in Chicago. Upon leaving Crown Point the pair decided to read the message. They were startled to find that Dillinger had instructed Billie to forward the note to Hamilton. On one side was a crudely sketched diagram of the jail; on the other was a plea for Hamilton to engineer his escape. Dillinger outlined a reckless scheme that called for Hamilton and some recruits to dynamite a section of the building in order to free him.

Piquett reluctantly gave the note to Billie, voicing his opinion that the dynamite plan was too desperate and doomed to fail. The attorney was relieved to hear that Hamilton felt the same way and was still too incapacitated to attempt such an ambitious plan. Nevertheless, Piquett was eager to see his client freed; Dillinger had explained it was the only way he could get his hands on the $50,000 he'd promised to pay Piquett.

An alternate plan was devised. O'Leary had contacts in the East Chicago underworld whose influence extended to the Crown Point jail. For the right price, guards would look the other way while a gun was smuggled into Dillinger's cell. Piquett apprised his client of the proposal, and Dillinger heartily approved. The only problem was cash. The "boys" in East Chicago wanted $25,000 to arrange the fix.

A shroud of secrecy surrounds most of the arrangements, and many of the key participants remain unidentified. Dillinger had numerous ties to Chicago's gangland characters, and most of his contacts—including such operators as Roy Dahlien, Fred Breman, and Art Stross—apparently came through underworld kingpin Sammy Sheetz or Sheetz's right hand man, Hymie Cohen. Sheetz's tentacles reached into City Hall through political fixers like James Regan and into the Police Department through corrupt officers such as Captain Timothy O'Neil and Sergeant Martin Zarkovich. Sheetz and Cohen also wielded considerable influence in judicial circles. Judge William Murray, who was presiding over Dillinger's case, had links to the East Chicago gang lords. When prosecutor Robert Estill attempted to have Dillinger transferred to Michigan City to await trial, Murray ruled the prisoner should remain at Crown Point.

At least some of these played a part in the behind-the-scenes action that ultimately would result in freeing Dillinger. O'Leary and ex-Michigan City inmate Meyer Bogue acted as liaisons between Piquett and the East Chicago fixers. Piquett relayed the information to his client and Billie Frechette, who passed along details to Hamilton, who stayed in contact with Van Meter.

After some negotiating the East Chicago crowd agreed to accept partial payment for the job, probably half, with the balance to be paid once Dillinger had been sprung and was back in business. Word came from Hamilton that "Van and Jimmie" had some big scores lined up, and the banks would be knocked off as soon as Dillinger joined them.

To get the ball rolling Piquett managed to borrow $5,000. Hamilton, his funds drained over the past month, donated what he had and appealed to Van Meter for the balance.

On February 26, the same day Nelson arrived in St. Paul, Piquett and Billie visited Dillinger at the Lake County Jail. While the blustery attorney distracted the guards with idle chatter, Billie whispered to her lover that Red had spoken to both Van Meter and Nelson and the pair had agreed to advance the needed cash as long as Dillinger agreed to "kick it back" out of his share from their first score together. The prisoner, in no position to do otherwise, consented to the terms.

❋ ❋ ❋

In Minneapolis that evening the four outlaws dipped into their pockets and put together enough cash to finance the East Chicago fix, Nelson and Van Meter contributing the largest sums. They realized there were no guarantees—Dillinger might be recaptured or killed in the attempt—but after lengthy discussion all viewed the risks as acceptable. With Pierpont out of the way and facing a probable death sentence for the Sarber killing, Van Meter was looking forward to being reunited with his old friend. For his part, Nelson was eager to join forces with the Indiana desperado. His addition would be a major step toward what Baby Face envisioned as the creation of a supergang. Finally he was on the verge of the big time. Even Alvin Karpis would take notice.

Green was the only one with serious reservations about linking up with Dillinger. He feared the bandit's presence might bring an undesirable amount of publicity to their exploits. Nelson, privately craving notoriety, was probably the first to scoff at the objection. They concluded that if the heists proved as big as Green had promised, there would be plenty of cash to buy all the protection they needed. In the end, Green, anxious to get under way with their plans, conceded it was the right move.

Early the following morning Carroll was dispatched to deliver the bribe money to Hamilton in Chicago. The envelope was passed to the East Chicago mob, but there was a problem. Deputy Ernest Blunk, the inside man designated to smuggle the gun to Dillinger, was getting cold feet. O'Leary offered a solution: Instead of giving the prisoner a real gun, Blunk could give him a wooden pistol instead. That way, if Dillinger failed to escape, they could claim he carved it in his cell. Blunk agreed.

The breakout was set for Friday, March 2. If all went well Dillinger could reach Minneapolis either late Saturday or early Sunday and would be ready to join Nelson and his partners the next day to strike their first target, the Security National Bank and Trust Company in Sioux Falls, South Dakota.

As the gang prepared for the heist, Nelson took time to hunt for a new place to live. On March 1 he moved his family into Apartment 106 in a rental complex at 1325 West 27th Street near Hennepin Avenue, a few blocks south of the apartments of Van Meter and Green. Nelson used his alias Jimmie Williams; Chase identified himself as John Rodgers, a friend of the family.

That evening two of the gang set out in search of a vehicle, something fast, roomy, dependable, and disposable to use in the robbery. The pair strolled into the garage of the Joy Brothers Motor Car Company on Pleasant Avenue in downtown St. Paul and informed the attendants, Sidney Ricketts and Clifton Lowell, they were looking for a distributor. After spending considerable time eyeing a new dark green Packard, one of the bandits abruptly turned on the two employees with a drawn pistol and said sharply, "Let's take her for a test spin."

Outside the city, along the banks of the Mississippi and a good hike to the nearest phone, the Packard stopped. Ricketts and Lowell, certain they would be shot, were ordered out. One gunman handed them a dollar for "cab fare," and apologized for stranding the pair "in the sticks." "Nice car," his companion commented as they sped away. "We'll take it."

The next morning the Packard was brought to a garage on University Avenue. Eddie James, the mechanic on duty, often worked on the cars of gangland friends. Tom Gannon, one of his favorite "special" customers, was accompanied by a young man Eddie had met on several occasions, known to him only as Jimmie. They wanted the Packard fully inspected and re-tuned if necessary, an absurd request since the mechanic noted the vehicle appeared as if "it just came off the showroom floor." While Eddie worked, Nelson bolted a pair of Kansas license plates onto the car.

Later that day word came from Chicago that O'Leary had been late delivering the wooden gun, pushing back Dillinger's escape another twenty-four hours. Green acted disgusted, but his partners viewed the news as merely a minor setback. At worst, depending on when Dillinger arrived, the scheduled holdup might be delayed a day or two.

Early Saturday the quartet piled into the Packard and drove the 235 miles southwest to Sioux Falls. Van Meter and Carroll shot a few games of pool while Nelson, escorted by Green, got his first look at their target. The Security National Bank occupied the first floor of a huge granite building on the southwest corner of Ninth and Main. Baby Face explored the outside and casually peered through the window at the sprawling rectangular lobby that dominated the interior. Green's diagram included everything—the cages, vault area, offices, even restrooms.

Reviewing their getaway route late that afternoon, the news they were waiting for finally came over the radio: John Dillinger had broken out of the Crown Point jail, stealing a pair of submachine guns and the sheriff's car in the process. He was last seen speeding toward Chicago.

After a brief meeting with Piquett, Dillinger was reunited with Billie and spent the night at her sister's apartment on North Halsted. His whereabouts were relayed to Minneapolis, probably through Hamilton. Early the next evening—Sunday, March 4—Tommy Carroll arrived at the address. O'Leary and Bogue, on their way to visit Dillinger, spied the husky outlaw waiting behind the wheel of a green Ford and identified themselves. "Johnnie won't be able to see you," Carroll told them. "He's leaving right now, sooner that he expected."

Minutes later Dillinger and Billie came out carrying a pair of suitcases and the two machine guns. As they climbed into the back seat, Dillinger apologized to O'Leary and Bogue for being unable to chat, saying "I haven't a moment to lose."

Carroll immediately drove away, having no time to explain that they had people to meet and places to rob.

❄ ❄ ❄

Shortly after dusk that Sunday evening—about the same time Carroll was chauffeuring Dillinger and his mistress out of Chicago—residents along Alabama Avenue in St. Louis Park, a western suburb of Minneapolis, noticed a large Hudson sedan cruising up and down their street. The vehicle's occupants appeared especially interested in the house at 4055, the home of Ted and Verna Kidder. One neighbor later claimed he'd seen a spotlight or flashlight beam directed at the house as the Hudson crept past. The Kidder place was dark; no one was at home.

While their house was being watched, the couple and Verna's mother, Effie, were attending a birthday party for the twin teenage sons of some friends, the Comforts, in Minneapolis. At 10:20 the Kidders said their goodbyes and departed, Ted at the wheel, his pretty wife of eight years beside him, his mother-in-law in the back seat. As they drove along Lake Street near the intersection of Chicago Avenue, a Hudson suddenly pulled alongside and attempted to force the Kidder vehicle to the curb. Ted accelerated quickly and soon left the other car behind. "What was that about?" Verna asked.

"Must be drunks," her husband replied with a bewildered shrug.

Three miles later and just a few blocks from their house the mystery car reappeared behind them. Glancing nervously in his rearview mirror, Kidder continued past their home and circled the block. The Hudson continued to stalk them.

Finally Kidder pulled to the curb on Excelsior Boulevard near a small corner diner, the Brookside Inn. It was almost 10:45. Telling his wife he would be right back, he stepped out of the car, intending either to confront the occupants of the Hudson or go into the restaurant to phone for help. The big sedan swerved in directly behind them, bathing the thin, thirty-five-year-old salesman in its headlights. Verna heard a car door open, then slam shut. Kidder had gone a few paces when someone from the Hudson strode toward him calling, "Hey, Teddy."

Kidder halted and spoke with the stranger, their voices too low to be heard by the women. In Verna's words the man "looked like a gangster." Attired in a Fedora and long overcoat, he appeared to be of medium height and build, although it was difficult to tell beneath the bulky coat. He kept his hands shoved inside his pockets. Verna looked back at the Hudson and clearly saw four more men seated inside. She caught a glimpse of the driver's face, noticing that he was clean shaven and seemed very young.

After about thirty seconds the man in the overcoat moved a couple steps away from Kidder. At that moment one of the men inside the Hudson fired three quick, crackling shots. Verna saw her husband clutch his chest and collapse in the street.

"My God! They've shot him!" she screamed as she sprang from the car and dashed to Ted's side. "What have you done?" her mother cried from the back seat.

"Keep your damned mouths shut or we'll give it to you too!" the man in the overcoat shouted at the frantic women.

Hearing the gunfire, several customers rushed from the diner in time to see the man plunge into the Hudson's back seat. An instant later the sedan roared off into the night, but not before one witness observed that the vehicle had California plates. Three men carried Kidder into the diner. An ambulance was called but arrived too late. Kidder, shot twice in the chest and once in the stomach, died within minutes.

Verna and her mother remained at the scene over an hour, telling and retelling their stories to police. When they were allowed to return home the pair found their ordeal was far from over. Despite the late hour, well after midnight, newsmen besieged the house in hopes of obtaining more details about Ted Kidder and his sudden, violent death. The women fought their way inside and locked the doors. One reporter attempted to climb in through the bathroom window until Verna's mother, armed with a mop handle, persuaded him to retreat.

The killing caused a momentary sensation in the Twin Cities and was played by the press as an innocent citizen callously gunned down by gangsters—yet another example of Twin Cities lawlessness, another reason why Minneapolis and St. Paul needed to purge their communities of gangland elements. The police declared themselves baffled. The only theories that made sense were that the five men in the Hudson had mistaken Kidder for someone else, or that Kidder had somehow enraged them earlier when the two cars almost collided.

While the slaying was never officially solved nor a satisfactory motive determined, by the end of 1934 the St. Louis Park police and the Hennepin County Sheriff's Office announced they were satisfied that Kidder's death was the work of Baby Face Nelson. Their conclusion was based primarily on the fact that FBI agents by that time had identified the Hudson sedan used by the killers as the same one Nelson had purchased in San Francisco some six weeks before the slaying.

Aside from the car, however, the G-Men were unable to learn any further details relating to the murder, although they grilled every one of Nelson's associates they found, including his mother. The closest they came were a few tidbits supplied by Fatso Negri, who admitted hearing comments about the killing but nothing about a motive. But seven years later, in his highly embellished account of the Nelson gang, Negri alleged that Baby Face personally boasted about the murder:

". . . I and two or three of the boys were driving it [the Hudson] in Minneapolis a few days ago, and we happened to cut in ahead of another car.

155

The driver, one of those fresh guys, cut right back in front of us. He stopped his car, got out and came back towards us, and said to me:

"'What the h—— do you mean? Get out of that car and I'll slap your face for you.'

"He had taken a step or two toward us when I leveled on him and hit him. Then we had to tear out of that place. But we made it. . . ."

Negri's version, which claims to be Nelson's firsthand account of the murder, supports the early theory that Kidder's encounter with his killers was a totally random event and his shooting a savage response to the salesman's unwise decision to leave his car and confront the other motorist.

Despite some glaring inaccuracies and the fact that he contradicts his own sworn statement to the FBI, Negri's rendition of the Kidder affair generally has been embraced as genuine. However, even a casual examination reveals that Negri cites the wrong date (he places the murder in mid-April) and the wrong location (he says the slaying occurred in Minneapolis, where the cars first came close to smacking bumpers, not later in St. Louis Park). Alta Johnson, a niece of Ted Kidder, claims the account is "all wrong," especially the description of her uncle storming over to the other car to give the driver a piece of his mind. "He would never have done anything like that," she said. "He was much too mild-mannered a man. I don't believe he even had a temper."

The most powerful argument against Negri's widely accepted version is the fact that Kidder's slayers addressed him by name at the murder scene—a vital detail reinforced by the claims of neighbors who saw the Hudson prowling the street outside the Kidder home, strongly suggesting that Kidder was being hunted.

This only deepens the mystery. How did Theodore W. Kidder, a meek collector of antique furniture and a paint salesman for the National Lead Co., become a target for gangsters?

Gradually a few tantalizing facts have surfaced indicating that Kidder had developed some unsavory associations in the Twin Cities. There is evidence that he was affiliated with a Minneapolis sporting goods shop specializing in guns and that Kidder even sold wholesale ammunition out of his home. It was suspected, but never substantiated, that his principal clientele were local gangsters. Years later Verna confessed that her husband often played golf with some notorious underworld figures, a practice she apparently frowned upon. There was also a persistent but unverified report claiming that Kidder used his intimate dealings with Twin Cities hoods to supplement his income by feeding facts to police as a paid informant. In conjunction with this theory was a rumor implying that Kidder was put on the spot by one of Harry Sawyer's corrupt cops.

Precisely how any of this relates to Nelson and his comrades is a matter of conjecture. There is absolutely nothing linking any of the bank robbers to

Kidder prior to the night of his death. Mystery surrounds not only the motive but also the identity of the five occupants of the Hudson and the man who fired the fatal shots. Since it was his car, Nelson was almost certainly the young driver glimpsed by Verna; his four companions that evening might have included Van Meter, Green, Gannon, or even John Paul Chase, Pat Reilly, or someone else. (Chase, while confessing that Nelson had introduced him to Van Meter, Green, and Carroll at this time, later insisted that he knew nothing of the Kidder affair or anything about the robberies the gang had planned.)

Nelson, it should be noted, had returned to town just a week earlier after a three-and-a-half-month absence. The others, except for Chase, had been living in the area much longer, and thus were more likely to have had dealings with Kidder, if indeed his murder was the result of a suspected betrayal.

At the morgue it was discovered that two of the three bullets which took Kidder's life were still embedded in his body. They proved to be a rare brand of copper-jacketed slugs fired from a .32 pistol, a weapon Nelson was never known to carry. "Jimmie had a thing for .45s," gunsmith Hymie Lebman once remarked. "He wouldn't look at much else for personal use." While this in no way exonerates Nelson, it does suggest that one of the others in the car was the shooter.

The only one of Nelson's associates known to have used a .32 was Eddie Green. A month later, on his deathbed surrounded by federal agents he mistook for friends, Green would groan, "Get my .32 out of the dresser drawer so I can put it in my pocket." The government men searched Green's apartment and found a partial box of .32 bullets and two loaded clips for a .32 pistol. (It was never determined if this ammunition or the fatal slugs came from the stock Kidder sold out of his home.) The pistol, however, was never found.

❋ ❋ ❋

Whether Nelson pulled the trigger, acted as a willing accomplice, or was merely there, the Minneapolis slaying marks the first time he was directly involved in a murder. Kidder's death evidently left him rattled, for when he returned to his apartment in the early morning hours of March 5 he woke his family and ordered them to pack, announcing they were leaving at first light. Apparently Nelson deemed the location as unsafe or somehow connected to the murder.

FBI documents attempting to chronicle his movements at this time say Nelson and his family immediately fled Minneapolis and returned to the West Coast. In truth, they moved just ten blocks north, renting another flat on the second floor of an apartment building on 17th Street near LaSalle Avenue. Once they were settled in, Nelson departed, saying he would be away the next couple of days.

Dillinger arrived in town early that morning. By noon America's most wanted man and his girlfriend, calling themselves Mr. and Mrs. Irving Olson, had moved into the four-story Santa Monica Apartments on South Girard Avenue, just one block north of the Fremont Avenue apartments of Van Meter and Green. Billie was left to unpack while Dillinger hurried to a meeting at Green's place.

The gang was all there—perhaps. There is conjecture regarding the presence of John Hamilton. According to one source Hamilton rode with Carroll and Dillinger; another alleges he traveled separately. Yet another account insists he was unable to reach the Twin Cities until *after* the Sioux Falls robbery, and his place as the sixth member of the holdup team was filled by someone else, possibly Gannon or even Chase.

Dillinger studied Green's diagram of the bank as they discussed their assigned positions and the plan. None of the six had had much rest over the past twenty-four hours, so they forced themselves to grab some sleep, several staying with Green, the others retiring to Van Meter's apartment across the street.

They had a long drive and a big day ahead of them. Green, intent on being there when the Security National Bank opened its doors, wanted to be on the road well before dawn.

I thought Baby Face Nelson was better dressed than the others.
I said to Mother, "I don't believe he's been with them very long.
He doesn't look hard like them. . . ."
— Dorothy Ransom

CHAPTER 8

THE BIG FELLOW AND THE LITTLE BIRD

TUESDAY MORNING MARCH 6 was a clear, crisp 35 degrees in Sioux Falls, South Dakota's largest city, nestled in the southeast corner of the sprawling state. The bandits were running late and had missed the bank's 9 A.M. opening. One suggested that they take the time to cruise the streets and look things over.

At 9:50 a couple driving north on Dakota Avenue found themselves behind a new, large dark green Packard with Kansas plates. The car was "filled with men" and was creeping along the street at an infuriatingly slow speed. At the intersection with Ninth Street the Packard stopped and sat there. The husband honked until the vehicle finally inched its way around the corner and proceeded at its former ponderous pace toward the Security National Bank.

Two dozen employees and a handful of customers were inside the bank. Several among a group of stenographers sipping coffee beside the windows on the building's north side noticed the big Packard crawling up Ninth. "I thought right away the men looked funny," recalled Emma Knabach. "They were all alert, ready to jump out." One of the other women jokingly remarked, "This looks like a bank holdup."

Don Lovejoy, speaking in a more serious tone, said, "If it is, I'll stand right here by the alarm button."

159

The car turned onto Main and drew to a stop. Five men sprang out. All wore long heavy overcoats with the collars turned up and had their hats pulled down low. Four of the five carried bulky objects beneath their coats.

Nelson led the way inside, followed closely by Green. Carroll took a position in front of the doors. Dillinger and Van Meter waited until the getaway car pulled a short distance down the street before they started toward the entrance.

Bessie Dunne, working on her books in the savings department, looked up to find "a young, smooth-shaven fellow, well dressed" stepping up to her window. Nelson pulled a machine gun from under his coat and said, "This is a holdup. Lie down."

As she instantly obeyed, Nelson hurdled a waist-high railing and landed a few feet from her face. Lying on her stomach Bessie saw the little gunman strutting around the desks in her department, peering into offices, ordering everyone he encountered—including the bank's vice president—to "get down" or "hit the floor" with a menacing gesture of his weapon. When he noticed an assistant cashier staring up at him, Nelson snapped, "Get your head down or I'll blow you to hell!"

Within seconds an explosion of voices came from the lobby. Dillinger and Van Meter strode through the doors shouting and waving their weapons, threatening to kill anyone who failed to do as they were told. Patrolman Peter Duffy, passing through the bank at that moment, wisely chose not to go for his gun. Van Meter disarmed him before punching the officer in the face.

Bookkeeper Alice Blegen was in a conference room on the bank's south side when she heard the shouting. "My first thought was that someone [had] started a fight." She hurried to the door and found herself staring into a machine gun held by Green. He calmly told her to raise her hands and turn to face the lobby.

"They were screaming so loud we couldn't hear another thing," Emma Knabach recalled. Beside her, Lovejoy, still standing within reach of the alarm and suddenly realizing it was a holdup, pressed the button setting off a bell whose persistent clanging was heard throughout the rest of the robbery. Just moments after Lovejoy hit the alarm, Nelson marched up to the stenographers and ordered them to drop to the floor.

For the first few minutes there was considerable confusion over what to do with the employees and customers. It was obvious that the bandits, each of whom had his own ideas, had failed to discuss the matter. Nelson, a graduate of the Eddie Bentz school of bank robbery, swept through bank's north side directing everyone to lie on the floor. At the same time Green was ordering people on the south end to raise their hands and turn toward the lobby. Dillinger and Van Meter, enraged to find half the bank's occupants staring at them, started barking for everyone—including those cringing on the floor—to move back and face the walls with their hands upraised. Nelson became infuriated when he saw people standing against the north wall (which was almost entirely windows) with their hands in the air. He immediately shouted at them to "get those arms down" and "get back from those windows!"

"I think they were trying to confuse us or scare us to death," Miss Knabach later declared.

"It was as though they were putting us through calisthenics to wear us out," another witness reported.

By that time Green had singled out teller Fred Anderson and forced him to unlock the door to the money cages. Dillinger latched onto bank President C. R. Clarke and persuaded him to lead the way to the vault with a swift kick in the seat of his pants, drawing a cackling laugh from Van Meter. When Clarke was unable to work the combination head teller Robert Dargen was brought over to perform the task. Dargen was then directed to open the reserve vault. Dillinger handed Clarke a white sack and ordered, "Drop all that dough in there."

Meanwhile, Nelson and Van Meter engaged in a brief hushed conference, agreeing on a method to oversee their captives. Using what Alice Blegen termed "descriptive language" the pair herded everyone into the center of the lobby and stood guard over them. The catlike Nelson climbed atop a marble counter and paced back and forth, cradling his machine gun. Van Meter, the only bandit armed with a pistol, circled the group, snarling, "If any of you wants to get killed, just make some move."

In the confusion the gang overlooked the switchboard operator, who was crouching beneath her station, still wearing her headset and connected with central. "Notify everybody," she said, keeping her voice low. "They're holding up the Security National Bank."

❄ ❄ ❄

The first policeman to answer the bank's alarm was Patrolman Homer Powers. At the entrance a man in a dark overcoat and Fedora shoved the muzzle of a machine gun into the officer's ribs. As Powers raised his hands and faced the bank's wall as Carroll had commanded, he realized he had seen the man in local restaurants and pool halls during the past few weeks and considered him a suspicious person. Once disarmed the officer was allowed to put his hands down.

An employee of the city's newspaper, the *Argus-Leader*, glanced out a window overlooking the intersection of Ninth and Main at that moment and witnessed Powers being taken captive. "The bank is being held up," he shouted, starting a stampede of reporters, photographers, and even clerks and secretaries rushing for the doors. The clanging alarm drew pedestrians, merchants, and shoppers like a magnet. Within minutes nearly a thousand spectators lined the sidewalks and spilled into the streets. At one point Carroll, feeling the crowds were pressing too close, stepped to the curb and fired several short bursts into the air. "Get back there or I'll blow the daylights out of you!" he screamed.

Half a block south of the bank's entrance the sixth bandit—either Hamilton or his substitute—stood beside the getaway car with a machine gun. Several times he moved into the middle of the streetcar tracks and directed traffic. Any automobiles moving too slowly or stopping to watch were promptly motivated to move on by a threatening gesture from the bandit and his weapon.

The next policeman to reach the scene was Roy Donahue, the department's fingerprint expert. Seeing Powers standing by another man near the entrance, Donahue pulled his car to the curb and asked what was happening. Carroll marched over and demanded, "Come out of that car." When Donahue failed to respond, the outlaw fired a blast at the front of the vehicle, puncturing a tire. "I said get your ass out here," Carroll sneered. This time Donahue obeyed.

As Carroll was inviting Donahue to join the party, a car carrying another officer parked along Ninth Street. Motorcycle Patrolman Hale Keith, off-duty but in uniform, jumped out and hurried toward the bank, his hand atop his holstered revolver.

Hearing the staccato crackle of Carroll's machine gun, Nelson sprang from the marble counter and hopped across desktops to the reach the windows looking north onto Ninth. As he stood on the desk of trust officer Adolph Lodmell surveying the scene outside, more shots were heard. Then, as he spotted Keith hustling down the sidewalk toward Carroll's position at the front, Nelson fired from the hip, blasting a cluster of holes through the plate glass and sending four slugs ripping into the officer's right side. When Keith crumpled to the concrete, the little gangster proudly shouted, "I got one, I got one."

A bystander on Ninth Street heard the shots and saw the policeman fall no more than ten feet away. A voice yelled "Flop!"—it might have been Keith, another pedestrian, or even Carroll who, attracted by the gunfire, stared down Ninth with his machine gun ready. The bystander dropped to the sidewalk.

Seconds later Carroll's attention was diverted by the arrival of another police car, this one containing Chief of Police Monty Parsons and a detective. The machine gunner had both men covered immediately. "Don't make a move if you want to live," he warned as he swiftly disarmed the pair and forced them to join his other captives by the wall.

The bystander, meanwhile, crept closer to Keith and asked, "How bad are you hurt?"

"Pretty bad, I guess," the officer gasped. He dragged himself to the curb, leaving behind a trail of blood. One slug had pierced his abdomen, another was buried in his right thigh, a third was in his upper right arm, and a fourth had shattered his right wrist.

✸ ✸ ✸

After gunning down the patrolman, Nelson swaggered back to the lobby, casting a triumphant glare at Van Meter. From that moment on, according to Alice Blegen, "the tall, dark-haired bandit . . . seemed bent on killing someone." Showering the group with profanity, Van Meter demanded to know "who the hell set off that alarm?" Receiving no reply he bellowed, "I'm gonna shoot the living shit out of everyone here if I don't get an answer."

Just then a bandit in the back, probably Dillinger, called for him, either because he needed help collecting the money or simply to calm the jittery gunman. Van Meter stomped away, leaving Nelson to guard the captives. "No more threats were made," recalled Mrs. Blegen, who believed the interruption in Van Meter's tirade was "a lucky break" that averted bloodshed.

The switchboard operator, still undiscovered, had patched herself into a local radio station and was providing a play-by-play account of the events transpiring inside the bank. The broadcast sent more curious spectators and lawmen racing to the site. Among the latter was Sheriff Melvin L. Sells, who had been summoned from the courthouse by an urgent call to "bring some guns down to Ninth and Main." With a reporter tagging along, Sells arrived with a machine gun and a riot gun. He backed his car into an alley a block south of the bank, then worked his way through the crowds. "They shot Hale Keith," someone shouted. "He's lying on the sidewalk."

Sells was able to see the gang's two sentries, each clutching a machine gun, but the intersection was so jammed with people the sheriff didn't dare fire. Sells and the reporter rushed toward the Lincoln Hotel hoping to reach a second-story window that might provide a clear shot at the bandits.

By that time Dillinger, Green, and Van Meter had emptied the cages and the bank's four vaults of over $49,000 and returned to the lobby where Nelson was separating about a dozen hostages to act as shields. Van Meter immediately took over, directing the terrified group to form a circle around the four bandits. As he booted the backsides of several men to keep them in line, the elevator doors on the south side opened. Gus J. Moen, a retired banker from Canton, Minnesota, who had assumed the alarm was only a routine fire drill, stepped out and strolled toward the entrance, completely unaware of the robbery in progress.

Nelson spotted him and shouted a command to halt. With the alarm ringing, Moen didn't hear the order and started through the door. Baby Face fired a quick burst, blasting out the glass above the banker's head. Dazed and covered with shards of glass, Moen staggered outside only to face the machine gun-wielding Carroll, who promptly convinced him to drop his briefcase and line up beside the four captive policemen.

The noisy alarm had been blaring a full fifteen minutes when Van Meter fired two shots into the ceiling, either as a signal to Carroll or simply to get the hostages moving. As they surged forward one bandit called out, "Everything okay out there?"

Carroll nodded and turned to his prisoners, ordering the officers to march ahead of them. Two robbers fired their Tommyguns into the air to clear the way through the crowds as the procession, comprising some twenty people, headed south toward the Packard.

❄ ❄ ❄

Sheriff Sells and his companion were hurrying through the hotel lobby when a voice cried, "They're coming out!" Realizing the bandits would reach their car before they could get to a window, the pair returned to the street. Sells figured that once the gang members were inside their vehicle they would release their captives and roar away. He snapped an ammunition drum onto his Thompson, then handed the riot gun and some shells to the reporter, saying, "Stick a couple loads in this."

Reaching the Packard four of the bandits scrambled inside. Carroll stood guard at the rear while Nelson singled out six hostages—teller Leo Olson, Alice Blegen, Emma Knabach, Bessie Dunne, Mary Lucas, and Mildred Bostwick—and instructed them to climb onto the car's running boards. Once Nelson and Carroll slipped into the back seat with Dillinger between them, the six prisoners took their places. Miss Dunne complained there was not room for her next to Olson and a woman on the driver's side. A voice within declared, "All right then, you can go."

She stepped off and the Packard pulled away, heading south along Main. The windows were open and several bandits reached out to take hold of the ladies' arms. "Don't be afraid," one said to the three women huddled on the passenger side. "We don't intend to hurt you."

Thwarted again when they saw the hostages clinging to both sides of the getaway car, Sells and the reporter jumped into the sheriff's car to follow the gang. Farther down the street Patrolman Harley Chrisman darted into a hardware store, reappearing with a high-powered rifle and a box of shells. Taking cover in a basement stairway, he quickly loaded the weapon, then rose up and carefully peppered the front of the Packard with slugs as it cruised past him. A bullet punctured the radiator.

Almost immediately a fountain of smoke and steam gushed from under the hood. A block later, barely 300 yards from the bank, the car heaved to a stop. Olson and the women heard the bandits arguing whether to abandon their vehicle and hijack another or continue in the smoking Packard for the moment to try to put some distance between them and the crowds and cops.

The latter course was finally agreed on, and the car lurched forward again, turning right on West 13th Street, then one block later left on Dakota Avenue.

The Packard never went faster than twenty-five mph and once slowed to a virtual crawl as it passed a horse-drawn milk wagon. Nevertheless, a bone-chilling wind whipped around the hatless, coatless captives huddled on the running boards, some feeling their hands and faces growing numb.

The Packard swung onto 29th Street, then took a left on South Minnesota Avenue. William Conklin, a service station attendant, spotted the vehicle moving sluggishly along the street, smoke pouring from the hood. Assuming the engine was on fire he dashed inside and returned with an extinguisher. As Conklin neared the car Van Meter, seated at the front passenger window, thrust his pistol past one of the female hostages and yelled, "Get back in there." The startled attendant, only now noticing the hood was pockmarked with bullet holes, swiftly retreated.

The gang spied a pair of cars following them. One contained Sheriff Sells and the reporter; in the other rode Deputy Sheriff Lawrence Green, Deputy U.S. Marshall Art Anderson, and Patrolman Chrisman with his borrowed rifle. Nearing the intersection with 41st Street the Packard drew to a stop beside the WNAX radio station. The hostages were ordered off the running boards as Nelson, Dillinger, and Carroll leapt out and scattered roofing tacks across the pavement. When they finished the robbers climbed back in and commanded their captives to resume their positions. "The girls are freezing," Olson complained.

"Come inside then," Carroll ordered as he and Nelson flung open the back doors.

"I told them I wasn't cold and I would rather ride outside," Emma Knabach recalled, "but it didn't do any good."

The four women crowded into the back seat and sat on the laps of the three gangsters. Olson was about to take his place on the running board, but the Packard pulled away, one bandit calling back, "Goodbye, Shorty, we don't need you anymore."

Leaving the city the damaged Packard gradually picked up speed as it headed south on U.S. 77. Four miles outside Sioux Falls the motor began to fail, and the outlaws parked the vehicle parked slantwise across the road at the top of a hill and ordered the women to get out. Within minutes Alfred Musch, a local farmer driving an old Dodge, came upon the scene and pulled onto the shoulder. Two men with machine guns marched over, one growling, "Get out of that car!" Musch was instructed to "start walking across that field" and "keep walking until we leave."

The pursuing vehicles, delayed by punctured tires, now approached from the north. At the sight of the four women standing in front of the Packard on the hilltop, the lawmen halted some 100 yards away. Nelson and Carroll suddenly appeared beside the women and started blasting with their machine guns. Most of their bullets ricocheted off the road, but several ripped into the front of Sells's car, shattering a headlight, and one punched through the windshield of the other vehicle. Fearing to return fire with the hostages arrayed across the highway, the officers withdrew out of range and waited.

As the bandits were transferring their loot, extra guns, and three 3-gallon cans of gas to the Dodge another automobile happened by. The woman at the wheel, on her way to visit relatives in Canton, saw the Packard blocking the road and stopped near the Dodge. Thinking an accident had occurred she rolled down her window and called to the quartet of shuddering ladies to warn them about standing in the cold without their coats. "The bank's been robbed," one girl replied.

A man appeared and leveled a machine gun at the driver, demanding to know how much gas was in her car. She answered there was less than half a tank. The gunman walked off, but when she attempted to back up and drive away he returned and threatened to shoot her if she tried to leave.

Ready to get under way, the bandits told the women they were being released and to start walking down the hill. The six gunmen squeezed into the Dodge and continued south along Highway 77. With lawmen in pursuit, the gang took the back roads, turning east toward Schnider, then crossing the Big Sioux River into Iowa near Granite and heading southeast toward Inwood. Each time the trailing cars closed in, one of the bandits would poke a machine gun through the Dodge's back window—smashed out by the men inside—and keep the lawmen at bay with sporadic bursts of bullets.

About noon the bandits turned north and raced for the Minnesota state line. Roadblocks were thrown up and two pilots from Soo Skyways took to the air hoping to spot the Dodge from above. One swooped down on a suspected vehicle, only to have an infuriated motorist leap from the car and shake his fist at the plane.

By zigzagging along miles of back roads the gang shook off its pursuers and vanished. At two o'clock Sheriff Sells phoned his office from a small town northeast of Luverne, Minnesota, and disheartenedly confessed, "I don't know which way to go now."

The bandits continued on an erratic northeasterly course, stopping once beside a haystack in a farmer's field near Tracy, about 150 southwest of Minneapolis. While one dumped two cans of spare fuel into the Dodge and tossed them aside, the others stood guard, littering the ground with more than a dozen cigarette butts.

Hours later they slipped back into the city under the cover of night. The money was divided at Green's apartment, with each man pocketing almost $8,000. As promised, Dillinger surrendered half his share to Nelson and Van Meter to reimburse them for the cash they had advanced to the East Chicagoans. Green vowed the next two scheduled holdups, both in Iowa, would be even bigger. Exhilarated and exhausted, the outlaws went their separate ways.

Back in Sioux Falls the entire city was buzzing over the daring bank robbery, the first in the city's history. Along with the excitement there was outrage and concern over the grave condition of Hale Keith, the patrolman shot down by Nelson. Whisked away by ambulance to Sioux Valley Hospital just minutes after the gang's departure, Keith was given two blood transfusions and attended by four physicians. The official prognosis provided by one doctor was "not good." Keith, however, fully recovered from his wounds.

The authorities questioned bank employees, customers, spectators, and anyone else who got a look at the six robbers to obtain detailed descriptions. But the results were often vague and conflicting, with many witnesses pointing out that when someone shoves a gun in your face, you tend to see little else but the gun.

There was, however, general agreement about two of the four gunmen who entered the bank, the pair guarding the assembled captives in the lobby. One was described as tall and slim with dark hair, dark eyes, and a thin black mustache. Witnesses referred to him as "the mouthy one" who used the most profanity and appeared the most menacing. Some got the impression he was the leader, or at least was trying to act as such.

His companion was described as short and chunky, about five-feet-four, 140 pounds, light complexioned and boisterous, with a round, chubby, smooth-shaven face. He was the one who "chirped with joy" after machine-gunning Keith.

Regarding their two cronies who looted the cages and vaults, one was said to be short and "very cool," the other slightly taller and clad in a brown overcoat and brown hat. It was this latter person who both bank President Clarke and teller Robert Dargen insisted was John Dillinger.

No one could provide much of a description of the sixth bandit, the one who had remained near the Packard. The other outside man, however, was closely observed by many as he guarded the bank's entrance, including the four policemen he captured. An *Argus-Leader* photographer even snapped several pictures as the outlaw waved his machine gun at the gathering crowds. Within hours a four-year-old Iowa mug shot of Tommy Carroll was singled out and identified by all four officers and several other witnesses.

While Carroll's involvement was uncontested, investigators swiftly rejected the idea that Dillinger was one of the robbers. Since he'd escaped from Crown Point just three days earlier, it seemed outlandish if not impossible that a criminal—even one of Dillinger's vaunted reputation—could have formed a new gang, selected a bank, and then robbed it in so short a span of time, especially considering the distances involved. It never seemed to occur to anyone that Dillinger had attached himself to an existing gang and participated in a holdup planned weeks ahead of time—they just assumed that the legendary outlaw must have done all the work himself.

Dillinger's fame had reached such staggering heights that people were claiming to see him everywhere, and almost every bank robbery on the North American continent was being attributed to him. The Sioux Falls holdup was treated as merely another "Dillinger sighting."

All agreed the answer to the identity of the bandits lay in the Twin Cities. The six outlaws had obviously fled there, and Carroll had a lengthy history in both Minneapolis and St. Paul. This gave investigators another reason to discredit the alleged presence of Dillinger since he was never known to be associated with either city or with any of the area's underworld characters, including Carroll.

One lawman not so quick to dismiss Dillinger's involvement was Special Agent Rufus C. Coulter of the FBI's St. Paul office. On March 7 the agent visited Sioux Falls and conferred with local officers. When asked about the bureau's interest in the case, Coulter pointed out that the Packard used in the holdup had been stolen in St. Paul, and transporting a stolen vehicle across state lines was a federal crime. In truth the St. Paul office, tapping into the underworld grapevine through paid informants, already suspected Dillinger was in the Twin Cities and had taken part in the robbery.

The FBI's entrance into the Dillinger case occurred just hours after his flamboyant exit from Crown Point, when he drove the sheriff's stolen Ford over the Illinois line into Chicago. Now that Dillinger was officially a federal fugitive, Uncle Sam and Director Hoover were justified in joining the massive manhunt to take their best shot a America's most celebrated and sought-after desperado.

This was the opportunity Hoover had waited for, and he fully intended to make the most of it. An edict was dispatched from Washington to every FBI office and agent throughout the nation. The director wanted a quick and decisive solution to the Dillinger case, one which would display the bureau's superiority over local law enforcement by succeeding were all others failed.

❋ ❋ ❋

The man at the center of the storm was gradually settling into his new surroundings at the Santa Monica Apartments. For the most part Dillinger rarely acted as if he was aware of the colossal effort to bring him to justice. In the days following the Sioux Falls holdup he and Billie spent their evenings at movie theaters, restaurants, and nightclubs around the Twin Cities, frequently in the company of his new band of criminal associates and their women. In the daytime they visited each other's apartments, Dillinger, Nelson and the other men often reading newspapers together.

Regarding the sensational coverage accorded him by the press, Dillinger seemed both pleased and puzzled. He enjoyed the attention. At Crown Point, standing beside the state prosecutor, he had struck a cocky, carefree pose and a crooked grin for photographers. Early in his criminal career he had vaulted over the counters or railings—as Nelson was prone to do—in an effort to show off or to impress witnesses with his agility. His entire approach to the business of bank robbery smacked of a deliberate effort to apply a daring yet cavalier style to his trade and capture the public's imagination in the process.

But despite his flair for showmanship, Dillinger regarded himself as a perfectly ordinary fellow with average tastes and rural Midwestern values. He savored the press coverage yet expressed genuine surprise over why he had been singled out and skyrocketed to gangster stardom. He considered himself a working-class criminal who associated with others of his kind out of necessity. He was never the leader of any gang; his affiliation with Nelson and the others was a partnership, and each man had a say in the decisions.

This is not the traditional picture painted of the so-called Second Dillinger Gang. Most accounts have depicted Dillinger as the leader and Nelson as little more than an insolent and unstable triggerman, someone Dillinger despised but was forced to tolerate. Nelson is usually portrayed as being envious of Dillinger's fame and perpetually attempting to usurp his authority.

However, there is remarkably little evidence to suggest anything of the sort. On the contrary, it appears that Dillinger and Nelson, at least in the early stages of their association, enjoyed each other's company and maintained a congenial working relationship. When Dillinger arrived in Minneapolis, Baby Face presented him with a gift to celebrate his escape—the .38 machine-gun pistol he had procured from Lebman. Both men enjoyed talking about their families and often traded jokes about policemen, who both viewed as inept and ignorant.. There was never any rivalry or struggle for power between them. Nelson's antics, notably his tendency to shoot first and talk about it later, were no more intolerable to Dillinger than were the excesses of Van Meter, or for that matter Pierpont or Makley. If Nelson harbored any animosity about his new partner's prominence in the media, he apparently kept it to himself.

For all his likable, even admirable qualities heralded by his partisans, the fact remains—though it is seldom mentioned—that Dillinger had a dark side. Slower to anger than the hair-triggered Nelson, once his temper flared Dillinger could be as prone to violence as many of the men around him, both in the heat of battle and in settling personal grudges. While Nelson was known to verbally swear vengeance against those who crossed him, Dillinger kept a personal death list containing the names of individuals, such as lawmen and informants, he intended to kill before he fled the country.

❀ ❀ ❀

Early Friday morning, March 9, Dillinger, Nelson, and Van Meter drove the 400 miles to Chicago, arriving about noon. Nelson contacted Jack Perkins with an order for more bulletproof vests while Dillinger arranged for Mary Kinder to receive $2,000 to help cover the legal fees for Pierpont, Makley, and Clark. Dillinger had another thousand dollars delivered to Piquett, leaving his share of the Sioux Falls loot almost depleted.

That evening they stopped at Louie's roadhouse before embarking on the long trip back to Minneapolis. All three ordered steak dinners for which they were charged twenty dollars apiece. Dillinger and Van Meter, consuming a pint of liquor between them with their meal, complained to Nelson about the inflated prices. "Maybe Fat Louie doesn't want our business anymore," Dillinger grumbled.

Nelson reproved the pair for "talking cheap," pointing out that Cernocky was taking a huge risk to serve them. "That's the price you pay for fame," he told them.

Back in Minneapolis, Dillinger, now almost broke, announced that he was eager to move on to their next score; the others all agreed. That weekend Van Meter and Green headed south to Mason City, Iowa. The pair checked into the YMCA and spent the next couple of days casing the quiet yet thriving community of 25,000. The main focus of their attention was the First National Bank, located in a mammoth seven-story building overlooking the square in the heart of Mason City's downtown. According to Green's information, the vault contained a quarter-million dollars.

Green spent most of his time studying the principal figures among the bank's more than thirty workers. Assistant Cashier Harold C. Fisher, one of the few hourly employees entrusted with the vault's combination, was relaxing after Sunday dinner when his wife alerted him that a stranger was "snooping around" their front porch. Fisher went to the door and discovered "a short fellow, mid-thirties, with a bad complexion" standing on his steps. "Something you want?" Fisher asked.

Green eyed the fifty-nine-year-old cashier as he explained he was looking for 1302 North Federal. When Fisher pointed toward the proper address, Green walked off in the opposite direction.

The next afternoon Carroll Mulcahy, owner of the Mulcahy Prescription Shop across the street from the bank, saw a slim young man with a thin mustache enter his store and ask a clerk for change. Mulcahy had spotted the stranger several times over the preceding few days, leisurely strolling past his windows. The man moved to a pay phone on the wall and started dropping in coins, obviously placing a long-distance call. The druggist had no idea that Homer Van Meter was notifying his partners back in Minneapolis that everything was set and the robbery could proceed as scheduled.

❋ ❋ ❋

March 13 was a bleak, blustery Tuesday. A thick carpet of clouds stretched across north-central Iowa spitting out snow flurries and a sharp, raw wind.

Around noon Van Meter and Green checked out of the YMCA, grabbed a quick lunch, then drove their large blue Plymouth to a quarry near the community of Hanford, four miles south of Mason City. Their five accomplices—Nelson, Dillinger, Carroll, Hamilton, and a bandit who was never identified, possibly Gannon or John Paul Chase—arrived in a Buick with Indiana plates, the glass in the rear window removed and its roomy back seat stocked with weapons and sacks of roofing nails. Van Meter and Green discussed the plan and each man's role as they strapped on their bulky steel-reinforced vests. Around two o'clock the seven bandits squeezed into the Buick, with Carroll taking the wheel.

H. C. Kunkleman, a local cameraman on a routine assignment, was shooting newsreel footage in and around the bank that afternoon. At 2:15 he was setting up his tripod on State Street when a large Buick double-parked near the south rear corner of the bank building. Six men stepped out looking like well-dressed salesmen—except that each carried a machine gun. "Hey you," one growled at Kunkleman. "If there's any shooting to be done, we'll do it. Get that damned thing out of here."

Carroll remained in the driver's seat, the barrel of his .351 rifle poking through the window. Nelson—attired in a blue suit, tie and vest, a camel-colored overcoat, dark gray cap, and black leather gloves—stationed himself beside the alley running behind the bank. Van Meter—wearing a black suit, gray topcoat, and gray Fedora—crossed the street and took up his post in front of Mulcahy's Prescription Shop.

Their four comrades marched up State, turned right on Federal Avenue, then burst inside the bank's front entrance waving their weapons and calling for the thirty-one employees and twenty-five customers to "hit the floor."

Willis Bagley, the bank's president, was at his desk when he heard the unexpected commotion, which he said later sounded as if "a raving maniac was yelling like a Comanche Indian. It's strange, the idea of a bank robbery never entered my mind." One bandit, described by Bagley as "a wild-looking sort of fellow" clad in a dark suit and a cap, glared at the banker and started toward him. Bagley leapt out of his chair and dashed into the closest office.

The gunman, John Hamilton, kept coming, following the president through the gate and managing to ram the barrel of his machine gun inside as Bagley slammed the door. Unable to push his way in, Hamilton wrestled his weapon free and snarled, "Come out of there, you son of a bitch!" Taking a step back, he fired through the door, the bullet missing Bagley "by about an inch." Cursing, Hamilton stomped across the lobby, entered the teller cages, and started emptying the drawers.

Dillinger strode directly into the accounting department at the rear of the building, warning everyone he passed to get on the floor and stay away from alarms. When he noticed some women were lying on their backs he barked, "I said on your faces, not on your backs. This is a stickup, not a directors' meeting."

171

The unidentified robber guarded the front while Green, in the role of center fielder, prowled the lobby's marble floor screaming for everyone to "stay down." In his meticulous casing of the bank Green had either overlooked or ignored a crucial security feature—a newly installed seven-foot steel cage equipped with a bulletproof glass window jutting from the overhead mezzanine, directly above the office where Bagley had taken sanctuary. Inside the cage, guard Tom Walters watched the opening moments of the robbery, first in surprise, then in disbelief. Grabbing his tear-gas gun, he aimed through the narrow horizontal gun slit and fired. The gas pellet struck Green square in the upper back. Behind the counter Hamilton yelled, "Get that son of a bitch with the tear gas!"

Green staggered but stayed on his feet, rage replacing his initial shock of the stinging impact and the fumes billowing around him. He yanked a customer off the floor to use as a shield, then sprayed the cage with a blast of his machine gun. The glass was chipped and scarred by the bullets but withstood the strafing; however, several slugs spat through the gun slit. Walters fell back with "bullet burns" on his jaw and right ear. He tried to reload the gas gun but discovered the expended shell was jammed in the chamber.

Tom Barclay, an assistant auditor, found a gas candle in an upstairs office. He ignited the fuse and tossed it into the lobby. It landed between a pair of sprawled customers. One man pushed the smoking candle away only to have the other bat it back toward him.

Still clutching his hostage, Green scanned the balcony for the man who threw the candle. He saw instead Margaret Johnson, the switchboard operator, standing at her desk, frozen in place as she watched the chaotic scene below. "I said everyone down," Green shrieked. "If you don't drop I'll drag you down."

"For God's sake," a co-worker shouted at her, "get down!"

Green fired a flurry of shots over the woman's head. Her daze broken, Margaret joined the others on the floor. She noticed Barclay and several others snaking their way across the balcony toward the offices. She started crawling with them, losing a shoe in the process. Reaching the safety of a storeroom, she got to her feet and rushed to a window overlooking State Street at the rear of the bank. A man bundled in a tan overcoat was loitering near the mouth of the alley right below her. Margaret opened the window, leaned out, and cried, "Hey, mister! Notify the police. The bank is being robbed!"

Baby Face Nelson turned and looked up at her, displaying his machine gun. "Lady," he called back, "you're telling me?"

❈ ❈ ❈

As was the case in Sioux Falls a week earlier, a throng of excited onlookers began to fill the streets around the bank. A rumor swept through the crowd—

no doubt started by those who had observed Kunkleman and his newsreel equipment minutes before—claiming that a mock robbery was being staged for the film camera. They pressed closer, some thinking they might see movie stars.

Van Meter, flashing what several witnesses afterward termed "a fiendish grin," decided to drive them back. He fired a burst into the air, producing a few screams and a minor stampede among some of the spectators. Moments later Nelson, not to be outdone by his fellow bandit, spotted a vehicle approaching from the opposite direction and loosed a quick volley of shots in that direction. "Get back!" he warned, stepping into the street. The frantic driver slammed on the brakes, shifted, and punched the accelerator, sending the auto hurtling backward down State at "an incredible speed."

Turning around, Nelson spied a crouching figure scurrying along the sidewalk toward Federal, an object clasped in his arms. Just seconds earlier Raymond L. James, secretary of Mason City's school board, had unknowingly walked into the midst of the action intending to enter the bank's rear door. Hearing gunfire and thinking *holdup!*, James started back the way he had come, stooping to keep his head below the windows.

Behind him Baby Face shouted "Stop!" But the hearing-impaired James claimed he never heard the command. Nelson fired low. Two bullets tore into James's right leg, a third passed through his trousers without touching him. He collapsed against the wall, then slumped to the sidewalk still clutching his portfolio.

Nelson strode over to the fallen man and tore the portfolio from his grasp. He looked inside, probably searching for a gun, but found only papers. "Stupid son of a bitch," he scolded the bleeding man. "I thought you were a cop."

"I'm not a cop," James groaned.

Across the street Van Meter hollered, "What's the matter with that fellow?"

"I thought he was a cop," Nelson threw back.

John James, the wounded secretary's son, was on the south side of State when he heard the shots and saw his father crumple. The high school sophomore started across the street but a blast of bullets from Van Meter chewed into a parked car near him—a warning, he surmised, to stay where he was.

❀ ❀ ❀

When the robbery began, Harry Fisher and another assistant cashier, Ralph Wiley, dropped to the floor near their station behind the counter. Several minutes passed before Green discovered the pair. Though it was evident to Wiley that the gunman was "extremely nervous," he "talked tougher than anyone I've ever seen." Cursing and coughing from the tear-gas fumes swirling around him, Green ordered them to stand. Fisher was turned over to Hamilton, who had finished looting the teller drawers and was ready to move to the vault. Fisher, eyes stinging from the fumes, led the way, with Hamilton, holding his machine gun in one hand and toting a huge money sack in the other, following. The robber complained that Fisher was moving too slowly and kicked him in the buttocks.

Wiley was added to a batch of almost a dozen hostages huddled near the front door and guarded by the seventh bandit. About this time Dillinger came from the accounting department herding several employees in front of him. The entire group was ordered outside. Wiley, lagging behind the others, heard one robber growl, "Get out there with the rest of them."

At first the captives were relieved to be outdoors, away from the choking, eye-burning effects of the tear gas. Within seconds, however, most were shivering in the near-freezing temperature. Dillinger—wearing a dark gray overcoat, Fedora, and striped scarf—ordered them to form a line on the sidewalk in front of the entrance, face the street, and keep their hands raised. During the next few minutes the unidentified bandit acted as a liaison between Dillinger and Green, darting back and forth through the front door.

Hamilton and Fisher, meanwhile, were at the vault. The bandit prodded him with his machine gun and threatened, "Now you open that and give us the money or we'll drill you full of holes." Fisher used his key to unlock the steel gate barring the way to the main safe. As the cashier stepped inside, Hamilton stopped to grab an almost worthless sack of pennies, allowing the gate to snap shut between them. "I can't open it from this side," Fisher lied.

The outlaw instructed him to pass the cash to him through the bars. Moving as slowly as he dared, Fisher began handing out wrapped stacks of one-dollar bills.

* * *

On State Street Nelson and Van Meter, watching the swelling crowd and anticipating the arrival of police before long, started to gather their own hostages.

Opal Koss and her eight-months-pregnant sister-in-law, coming from a nearby meat market, were walking by the rear of the bank when they turned a corner and encountered Nelson. The little gunman ordered the pair to drop their bags and stand beside the Buick. "You're gonna protect us," he declared.

Van Meter ducked into the pharmacy and returned with the druggist Mulcahy and another man at gunpoint. They were directed to the getaway car where Nelson, spouting obscenities and threats, forced both to climb onto the rear bumper. Mulcahy wore his customary white jacket, but his companion was coatless and trembled so badly from the cold, fear, or a combination of both that he had trouble complying. "He was shaking like a leaf," according to Opal, who watched the scene from the driver's-side running board. The man repeatedly pleaded, "I can't get on that bumper," but Nelson, unleashing more menacing curses, refused to set him free.

Seconds later a Studebaker came down the alley and turned onto State, braking directly behind the gang's double-parked vehicle. The occupants, Mrs. Ted Ransom and her daughter Dorothy, saw the people clinging to the back and sides of the Buick and assumed they must be a wedding party. Then the mother and daughter spotted the school secretary bleeding on the sidewalk—and a well-dressed young man carrying a machine gun moving toward them.

Nelson yanked open the passenger door. "Get out,' he demanded. "Get on the running board of that car over there." Mrs. Ransom immediately obeyed, but Dorothy, seated at the wheel, was too terrified to move. "C'mon, c'mon," he urged.

Thinking fast, she cried, "I can't get out. I'm lame."

Nelson frowned at her. "Okay then, you stay put."

Dorothy remained behind the wheel and watched as her mother climbed onto the side of the getaway car. She kept thinking, *They'll push them off or kill them or something!* Stepping from her vehicle she approached Nelson walking with an exaggerated limp. "You get back in the car," he told her.

"I want to get my mother off the running board," she begged. "Please don't take her. I need her to take care of me."

Nelson went to the Buick and brought Mrs. Ransom back to her daughter. "Now get back in your car," he ordered. "You sit there."

"So we sat there and watched everything," Dorothy recalled. Provided with a front-row seat to the spectacle, both women later commented on the "desperate appearance" of the gangster with the sardonic grin who patrolled the opposite side of the street. During Nelson's exchange with the two women, Van Meter either ran out of bullets or experienced a problem with his machine gun and exchanged it for Carroll's .351. He resumed shooting in "various directions," shattering a few store windows. Van Meter seemed to be enjoying himself, laughing maniacally whenever he fired his weapon.

❋ ❋ ❋

Around the corner on Federal Avenue Dillinger paced the sidewalk behind the line of human shields. He also expected police to arrive at any moment, and he was ready for them. He had a machine gun fitted with a leather strap slung over his right shoulder, a .380 automatic in his left hand, and carried a backup piece, a .38 revolver, in his shoulder holster. Extra clips for the .380 were pinned to his vest.

The throng of onlookers prevented lawmen from mounting any kind of organized response to the robbery. Officers reaching the scene were unable to get close or fire their weapons for fear of hitting hostages or bystanders. Deputy

Sheriff John Wallace, armed with a machine gun, huddled behind a Civil War monument in Central Park, directly across from the bank. Patrolman James Buchannan, carrying a sawed-off shotgun, took cover behind an ornamental boulder. Chief of Police E. J. Patton, unable to work his way through the crowd, entered the Weir Building and watched from the second-floor offices of the C. L. Pine Company.

Chief Patton wasn't the only one with an elevated view. Dozens of people in the building were at the windows looking down on the bank. In a doctor's office the physician and his patients were pressed against the glass, enthralled by the drama below. Directly above Dillinger and his hostages Judge John C. Shipley watched from his third-floor window in the bank building.

Things were beginning to heat up on the street. A motorist tried to move through the congestion of pedestrians and cars, horn blaring as he accelerated past the bank. Dillinger fired a shot into the vehicle's hood. Moments later the gangster spotted Patrolman Buchannan crouched beside the boulder in Central Park. He fired at the officer, driving him back to his cover. "Stand up and shoot it out like a man," Dillinger shouted to him.

"Move away from those people and I'll fight it out with you," Buchannan called back.

Shipley had seen enough. Grabbing an old pistol from his desk drawer, the middle-aged judge took careful aim at Dillinger, who had paused to re-load his .380, and fired. When he saw the bandit jump, Shipley ducked back inside. The slug caught Dillinger in the right shoulder and spun him around. He lifted his machine gun and loosed a quick burst at the windows, then ordered the hostages to squeeze in closer around him. When the unidentified robber reappeared at the bank door, Dillinger told him to tell the others it was time to leave.

The bandit relayed the message to Green, who in turn shouted the order to Hamilton at the vault. Despite the gangster's demand for "big bills," Fisher continued to dole out bundles of ones until they were all gone. The cashier had started surrendering five-dollar bills when Green poked his head into the vault and cried, "We're pulling out right now."

Hamilton grudgingly complied, leaving Fisher and nearly $157,000 behind. The seventh man was already out front with Dillinger. Green emerged clutching the same customer he earlier had used as a shield when firing at Walters. Hamilton followed, using teller Francis De Sart as his shield.

Dillinger yelled at the hostages to stay close and head toward State. As the procession moved along the sidewalk, Judge Shipley returned to his sniper's post, drew a bead on one bandit and squeezed the trigger. Hamilton, struck in the right shoulder, gasped, "I'm hit!" He continued to plod on with the others.

❋ ❋ ❋

About the same time Hamilton was being pried away from the vault, Van Meter, deciding the bandits needed more hostages, entered the Nichols and Green shoe store and ordered everyone out on the street. A few employees and customers discreetly slipped into the back room or basement, but nearly a dozen others, including a thirteen-year-old girl, obeyed the rifle-toting bandit. Seconds after Van Meter delivered the new captives to the Buick, Dillinger and the others rounded the corner and swarmed down State toward the getaway car. Surrounded by more than thirty citizens, the gang prepared to leave. Some hostages were either released or managed to slip away, including the shivering man perched on the back bumper. The customer serving as Green's shield complained that his eyes were still burning from the tear gas. "Okay, you've done your stuff," Green told him. "Goodbye."

Several women were ordered into the back seat. The rest were commanded to mount the outside of the vehicle and hang on. Ralph Wiley hesitated until one bandit barked, "Get on there, you bald-headed bastard, or I'll drop you."

Wiley climbed aboard the back bumper next to Mulcahy; three more bank employees—De Sart, Lydia Crosby, and Emmet Ryan—squeezed on beside them. In all at least fifteen people (some estimates run as high as twenty-six) covered the automobile. Van Meter and Green joined Carroll in the front seat while their four partners piled into the back.

The hundreds of onlookers lining the streets watched as the bandit's car creeped away at about ten mph. One spectator was Ruth De Sart, horrified to recognize her husband as one of the hostages clinging to the vehicle. As the Buick turned left on Federal, the police, hemmed in by the crowd, dared not open fire.

Within seconds of the car's departure, a policeman and several bystanders rushed to the aid of James. They carried the wounded man to the Ransom vehicle and gently placed him in the back seat. The officer climbed in with him, telling Dorothy, "Put you hand on the horn and don't stop for anything. Get this man to the hospital!"

❋ ❋ ❋

With Van Meter reading from a list of directions, Carroll swung the car west on Second Street, then south on Adams Avenue, then east on First Street. The vehicle briefly halted once to allow an elderly woman, frantically clinging to the passenger side, to step off, ironically in front of her home.

Traveling west on Fourth Street the bandits noticed a car trailing them and assumed it was the police. The occupants actually were a family—Clarence McGowan, his wife, and their five-year-old daughter. Finding themselves behind what seemed a raucous party on wheels, McGowan drew closer to get a better look. Suddenly a burst of gunfire spat from the Buick's back window. At least one round struck the vehicle and shattered, the fragments wounding McGowan in the abdomen and both knees.

Soon a real police car containing Chief Patton and two officers appeared but wisely remained a healthy distance behind the robbers. Nelson, now armed with a .351, and Dillinger, cradling his machine gun, poked the barrels of their weapons out the rear window and between the five hostages standing on the bumper. Mulcahy's white jacket was flapping in the breeze, and he heard one gunman warn, "If you don't button that thing, I'll have to shoot through it."

As the Buick reached the southwest outskirts of Mason City, leaving town on Highway 18, Carroll accelerated to about 25 mph. The wind whipping across the open countryside increased the misery of the hostages; many wondered how long they could continue to hold on. A sharp gust blew away the hat of Mrs. Jacob Leu, a shopper seized in the shoe store. Unable to endure the icy wind, she shoved her head inside the Buick and found herself looking into the face of Dillinger, who was still aiming his machine gun at the pursuing lawmen. "This is a fine police force you got here," he told her, cracking a smile. "They'd better quit following or we'll have to kill some of you."

A mile out of town the bandits stopped to release two more women. Nelson used the occasion to jump out and scatter a bag of tacks across the highway. Then, standing by the rear of the Buick with his rifle, he said, "Wait till they come over the hill and I'll pop 'em off."

When the police car appeared Nelson fired a series of booming shots, forcing the officers to turn onto a side road. Satisfied, Baby Face scrambled back inside, telling Carroll, "Let's roll."

Traveling gravel roads, Carroll steered east, then south, then east again. One outlaw noticed that a hostage—William Schmidt, a delivery boy captured by Van Meter—was clutching a large paper sack and snatched it away. The sack was filled with sandwiches and pickles Schmidt was taking to an office in the bank building. The bandits eagerly devoured the food, two of them munching sandwiches as they began counting the loot.

Three miles outside Mason City they crossed Highway 65, then continued a brief distance down a dirt road. Here, close to an hour after leaving State Street, Carroll pulled over and the captives were finally permitted to climb off the car. Teller Emmet Ryan studied the face of one gunman who bore a striking resemblance to photos of John Dillinger. The bandit noticed Ryan staring and grumbled, "Quit gawking at me, you asshole."

Nevertheless, it was Nelson the remaining hostages remembered as the most menacing, growling obscenities as he lined them up and forced them to keep their hands raised. Mulcahy later told reporters, "The big fellow [Dillinger] didn't seem so bad. That little bird was the mean one."

The outlaws conferred among themselves and decided to take one hostage along and set the rest free. Opal Koss was singled out and ordered back to the car. Her sister-in-law immediately spoke up; "If you take her, you have to take me, too."

One bandit shrugged, "I guess we can handle two women."

After traveling another mile of back roads with no further sign of the police, the gang deposited Opal and her loyal companion beside a country schoolhouse, then continued to the quarry. They abandoned the Buick, deliberately driving it into a ditch before piling into the waiting Plymouth and driving off.

❋ ❋ ❋

Shortly before eleven o'clock that evening Pat Reilly answered a knock at his door on Thomas Avenue in St. Paul and discovered an excited Eddie Green. The jug marker explained that Dillinger and Hamilton had been shot and needed immediate medical attention. Two cars waited at the curb. Reilly was instructed to drive the one containing Van Meter and the two wounded outlaws. Green joined Nelson, Carroll, and the seventh bandit in the other vehicle, which proceeded across the river into Minneapolis. Reilly drove south toward the Fairmount Avenue home of Dr. Nels Mortensen, a prominent Danish-born physician who, despite a respectable reputation in St. Paul, maintained close ties with Harry Sawyer and the Barkers.

Though he doubted Reilly's claim that the pair had been shot during a barroom brawl, Mortensen reluctantly agreed to treat their wounds. He became much more cooperative after noticing a poorly hidden machine gun beneath Van Meter's topcoat.

Despite their pain (Dillinger almost fainted when Mortensen cleaned his wound) and exhaustion, both bandits insisted on joining the others at Green's apartment. By the time they arrived the $52,000 collected by Hamilton had been divided into seven equal shares totaling $7,600 apiece.

The group was generally pleased with the haul. The one exception was the ever-solicitous Green who regretted not reaching "the big money" in the vault and blamed himself for the oversight of the guard's cage and tear-gas gun. "If I'd known they had that," he remarked, his eyes still red and sore from the fumes, "we would've skipped that job."

Their next target was the First National Bank in Newton, Iowa. All the preparations had been completed, but the robbers' wounds needed to heal before they proceeded. With plenty of cash in their pockets the gang members looked forward to several weeks of rest and relaxation in the security of the Twin Cities.

Nelson, however, had other things on his mind.

If there are two cities in America which need cleaning up,
they are St. Paul and Minneapolis.
— Homer S. Cummings,
U.S. Attorney General, 1933-39

CHAPTER 9

VANISHING ACT

THREE DAYS AFTER THE Mason City robbery Nelson, accompanied by Helen
and their son, stopped by Eddie Green's apartment to announce they were leaving town to visit relatives out west. Since Dillinger and Hamilton required several weeks to recover from their wounds, the Newton holdup was rescheduled
for April 4. Baby Face assured the jug marker he would be back by then.

Green envied the younger man's ability to hit the highway but felt the others needed him to stay in the area. He confided in Nelson that he, too, was
growing restless, mostly about having "Dillinger in my backyard." Just the day
before he had rented a new apartment on Marshall Avenue in St. Paul under
the name D. A. Stephens to distance himself from the most wanted man in
America. He and Bessie planned to move in a week or so.

The next morning, March 17, Nelson's entire entourage—his wife, son,
mother, and John Paul Chase—loaded their belongings into the Hudson and
headed west. A few days earlier Chase had turned over his Plymouth to Green,
who had traded it and two other vehicles to obtain a pair of "clean" cars for the
gang's use. Chase was compensated for the loss of his wheels, either by Nelson,
who had presented his pal with the Plymouth as a gift, or possibly from the
gang's emergency fund. Weeks later when FBI agents stumbled across the trans-
action—negotiated in part through St. Paul fixer Thomas Filbin—the
Plymouth was traced to a John P. Chase of Sausalito, leaving the G-Men

181

scratching their heads over the identity of Chase and how his California car had come to be in the possession of the Dillinger crowd.

After Nelson left the Twin Cities (probably for the last time) he and his companions passed almost a full month in total obscurity. Apparently they spent the greater part of the time with Leona in Bremerton, Washington. According to Mary Gillis, they proceeded directly from Minneapolis to Leona's home, a trip taking three days on the road. However, when the widow provided this information to Chicago agents in January 1935 she insisted that their departure had occurred two weeks earlier, thereby providing an alibi for her beloved son. After all, if Nelson had been with her and the others in the Pacific Northwest, he couldn't have robbed the Sioux Falls and Mason City banks, gunning down a policeman and a school board secretary in the process.

Despite the claims of Mary Gillis, who was either mistaken or deliberately misleading, the evidence indicates the troupe drove straight to Reno, arriving on March 19. The next day Nelson visited Frank Cochran to retrieve the Terraplane he'd left in storage with Cochran a month earlier, leaving his present vehicle, the Hudson, in its place. Once the switch was made, Cochran received his usual fifty-dollar tip for his trouble.

Over the next two days "Jimmie and Johnny" were observed around Reno. Then, either very late on the night of March 22 or in the pre-dawn hours of the 23rd, the two abruptly departed and were not to be seen again in the city for three and a half months.

❋ ❋ ❋

At age forty-five, Roy John Frisch—banker, bachelor, World War I veteran, and the government's key witness in the upcoming trial of Bill Graham and Red McKay—still lived in his family home at 247 Court Street with his mother, Barbara, and two sisters, Alice and Louisa. Just after 7:30 on the evening of March 22 he left the house, telling Alice he was going to a movie and adding that he would "be home early."

A number of people reported seeing Frisch strolling through downtown Reno that night. He was a familiar and generally well-respected member of the business community—a short, immaculately dressed figure with a ruddy complexion, jolly smile, invariably erect posture, and the beginning of a middle-age paunch. Though he was sighted in the vicinity of the Majestic Theater on First Street, which was showing *Gallant Lady* with Ann Harding, he must have changed his mind about the movie and headed home. The last person to see him was a friend, Harry Gorline, who chatted briefly with the banker near the county jail around ten o'clock. Bidding Gorline good night, he started up the Court Street hill.

Somewhere within the next two blocks before reaching his house, Roy Frisch vanished without a trace.

The next morning his mother, finding his bed empty and learning that he had not arrived at his office, notified the police. Lawmen and concerned citizens launched a countywide search for the missing banker. Volunteers, including National Guardsmen, Boy Scouts, college students, and Frisch's fellow veterans from the American Legion, combed the city and surrounding countryside. Sheriff Russell Traphen directed his men to drag the Truckee River and explore mine shafts throughout the region. Local businessmen posted a $1,000 cash reward.

In the weeks and months following Frisch's sudden disappearance, Reno was thick with rumors about his fate. A colleague revealed that Frisch had once spoken about suicide. Evidence was uncovered (or possibly planted) linking Frisch to the same swindles for which Graham and McKay were being tried, implying that the banker may have fled to escape prosecution. Some believed Frisch was paid to stage his own disappearance; others speculated that he wandered off with amnesia.

None of these theories satisfied the family or the authorities, all of whom expressed certainty that Frisch had been kidnapped and killed to silence his scheduled testimony. To learn more, lawmen tapped into Reno's underworld grapevine and discovered considerable talk alleging that Bill Graham's good friend and former employee Jimmie Burnell, aided by his pal Johnny from California, had taken the banker for a one-way ride.

Everyone had his favorite theory on how the pair had disposed of the body. The most popular was that Frisch's remains had been tossed into an abandoned mine shaft. Searchers found a bloody hat and three spent pistol shells at a mine near Hunter Creek Road southwest of Reno. More pistol casings and bloody rags were located at the Black Panther Mine north of the city. A Winnemucca prospector reported observing two cars and several men at the Adelaide Mine, owned by Graham-McKay associate George Wingfield, on the night Frisch vanished.

Alternate scenarios suggested that Nelson and Chase had weighted the corpse and dropped it into the depths of Lake Tahoe; the body had been driven to a desolate stretch of desert and either buried or simply left to the elements and scavengers; or perhaps Frisch had been abducted, taken to California, and then murdered and concealed somewhere in the Bay Area so familiar to Nelson and especially Chase. Certainly the most intriguing and disturbing possibility was the rumor claiming the banker had been killed and buried just a few yards from his home, in the backyard of Wingfield, whose house at 219 Court Frisch would have passed that night.

There were also varying opinions concerning Nelson's alleged involvement. Some maintained that he had agreed to eliminate the banker as a "paid hit" or as repayment to Graham. Others surmised he had taken care of Frisch strictly as a favor to his old bosses, perhaps without Graham or McKay knowing about the murder in advance. Another scenario suggested the two gambling czars had been the actual killers; Nelson and Chase had merely snatched Frisch off the street, delivered him to Graham and McKay, then disposed of the body for them. One Reno high roller, describing the pair as "old-time gamblers", declared, "If there's any shooting to be done, they'd do it themselves personally. They're not the type to hire someone to do it for 'em."

In short, there was an abundance of speculation and little evidence connecting Nelson to the fate of Roy Frisch. For many the very fact that the banker stepped into apparent oblivion on the same night Nelson and his companions made an evidently hasty exit from Reno was proof enough to conclude that Baby Face had performed a valuable service for his old friends.

More than two years later John Paul Chase, occupying a cell at Alcatraz, at last consented to speak about the Frisch affair. Instead of providing a final solution to the mystery, Chase only stirred up further controversy by repeatedly changing his story. One version was that Frisch had been taken to a garage and shot to death by Nelson. In another, Frisch supposedly had tried to escape by leaping out of their vehicle as they drove through Sparks, Nevada, and died of his injuries minutes after being placed back in the car.

While his description of the banker's death varied with each account, Chase remained consistent on two points: First, that Frisch was abducted on Court Street near his home and Nelson had forced him into their car at gunpoint. And second, the body had been buried in a valley outside Sparks, near Spanish Springs. Federal agents and local lawmen conducted a sweeping search of the area but failed to uncover any remains. Finally Chase was removed from the Rock and brought to Nevada to lead investigators to the gravesite—but the convict was suddenly unable to recall the exact spot.

❋ ❋ ❋

By sunrise on March 23 Nelson and his family were back on the road, driving along the jagged Pacific coastline toward their reunion with Leona. Chase turned up in San Francisco the same day. His first stop that Friday morning was reportedly the home of ex-Parente lieutenant Tony Moreno. According to an FBI report, Chase drove an old Buick caked with mud outside and telltale bloodstains inside. He allegedly left the vehicle with Moreno, asking him to dispose of it through a car agency he partly owned. Later, unable to sell the Buick, Moreno used a blowtorch to burn out the interior and then junked it.

Both Chase and Moreno vehemently denied the story, insisting there never had been any such vehicle. Chase claimed he was dropped off in San Francisco to visit his girlfriend Sally Bachman while Nelson continued up the coast to his sister's home.

Regardless of how Chase arrived, he had apparently left Reno in a hurry.

Later that day he met Fatso Negri at the Bank Buffet and asked the chubby bouncer for a favor. Negri was asked to go to Reno and contact Tex Hall in order to retrieve some clothes and personal effects Chase had left behind. Chase presented Negri with $100 for the service.

The next day, again according to FBI files, Chase met with Bill Graham at the Sir Francis Drake Hotel for about an hour. At 11 P.M. Negri returned to the Bank Buffet and found Chase sitting with Louis Tambini, another former Parente associate. Negri said the trip had gone smoothly, although Tex Hall had warned that Reno was "hot" and Johnny should stay away. Chase said he needed to reach Seattle, where he intended to rejoin Nelson.

Borrowing Tambini's car, Negri drove Chase to Sacramento the next morning. Failing to find any convenient departures for Seattle at the train station, the pair tried the airport, where Chase purchased a ticket for a flight later that night. With time to kill they visited the El Verano Inn, a resort in Sonoma County operated by a relative of Joe Parente. At Chase's request Negri made a side trip to San Raphael, returning with their mutual friend Eugene Mazet. The trio shared an early dinner and several hours of conversation before Chase was escorted back to Sacramento to catch his plane.

In Seattle Chase rode the ferry across Puget Sound to Bremerton and arrived at the home of Nelson's sister at 2119 Sixth Street. By this point Chase had been made to feel as if he were almost a member of the Gillis family. Leona, who had met her brother's best friend months earlier in California, refused to let him stay at a hotel. Chase was treated to home-cooked meals and spent the next few nights sleeping on the family sofa. About April 1 Nelson informed the others that it was time to leave. It was agreed among the women that Mary and Ronald would remain at the McMahon house until after a family reunion Leona was hosting in May. At first Nelson objected; Ronnie was just weeks away from his fifth birthday and he felt their son belonged with them, despite their often nomadic lifestyle. Eventually Helen and the others convinced him to allow the boy to stay.

As they prepared to depart, Nelson took Leona aside and handed her $500. He also wrote down the names of several individuals in the Bay Area who were holding money for him, and a series of numbers—a secret code—which would identify her. "I may need you to get some cash for me later," he told her, adding that if anything should happen to him, she was to retrieve the money and "spread it around the family."

Horrified to hear her baby brother implying that he might be killed or captured in the days to come, she tried to convince him to abandon his outlaw career. She pointed out that he had money and a family, and he was still young; he could buy land, maybe a ranch in the Northwest where the law would never look for him. "Think of Helen and the kids," she pleaded.

Nelson, as usual, dismissed her concern with a grin and a flippant attitude.

"You know how slippery I am, Lea. When are you women gonna stop fussing over me?"

When she persisted he declared, "Dillinger's getting all the attention!" Then, sounding torn between the comfort of his current criminal obscurity and his desire to achieve some kind of gangland glory, he boastfully added, "I can be as big as any of 'em if I wanted."

Ronald hugged his parents and waved goodbye as he watched them drive away with his "Uncle John." It was the last time the little boy would see his father alive.

❋ ❋ ❋

Back in the Twin Cities Nelson's partners in crime were finding it difficult to keep a low profile. The day after Nelson's departure Hamilton dropped by Dillinger's Minneapolis apartment. As the wounded gangster removed his overcoat, his pistol slipped from its shoulder holster and discharged upon hitting the floor. Dillinger and his lady hurriedly packed their bags and, according to Billie, were on their way out in less than ten minutes.

Deciding to switch cities, the couple registered as Mr. and Mrs. Carl P. Hellman at the Lincoln Court Apartments in a fashionable section of St. Paul the next day. Once the Hellmans were settled in Apartment 303, they began receiving frequent visits from Hamilton and Van Meter.

Green, however, kept his distance. His plan to separate himself from Dillinger's proximity by moving to St. Paul backfired when Dillinger unexpectedly relocated into his intended neighborhood. The jug marker decided to remain at the Charlou Apartments. He managed to unload his St. Paul apartment on Van Meter, who elected to make the move after his girl Mickey entered Samaritan Hospital for an operation. Unlike Green, Van Meter wanted to stay close to his old prison pal and was gradually becoming a dominant influence in Dillinger's life.

For the next ten days Green felt at ease knowing that America's most wanted man was no longer hiding out in his neighborhood. If lawmen happened to close in on Dillinger, as Green had feared since the beginning of their association, the jug marker was confident he was no longer in harm's way.

Green's anxiety about Dillinger proved prophetic. The landlady at the Lincoln Court grew curious about the couple in 303. While Mrs. Hellman was often seen out and about, no one ever caught a glimpse of her husband. The shades were kept drawn, and a veritable parade of visitors—mostly well-dressed, tough-looking men—came and went at all hours, usually by the rear entrance. On Friday, March 30, the landlady contacted the police.

The report was passed on to Special Agent Rufus Coulter who decided to stake out the apartment building that evening, accompanied by fellow agent

Rosser L. Nalls. About ten o'clock the next morning Coulter and St. Paul Police Detective Henry Cummings marched inside to question the couple, leaving Nalls to guard the front. Moments later a green Ford coupe pulled up. Nalls saw a slender, swarthy figure clad in a tan overcoat, checkered scarf, and dark hat step from the car and enter the building.

Dillinger and his mistress were still in bed when the lawmen knocked. Billie threw on a robe and opened the door a crack, peering past the chain lock at two strangers asking to speak with Carl Hellman. The groggy young women replied, "Carl who?"

The pair exchanged a glance, then repeated their request.

"He's just left," Billie stammered, suddenly remembering their current alias and realizing the men were law enforcement officers. "Come back this afternoon."

"We'll talk to you, then," said Cummings.

Billie said she needed to dress and closed the door. Scampering into the bedroom she cried, "Get up, Johnnie. It's cops."

Dillinger rolled out of bed. "Throw some clothes on, pack a bag, and stay calm," he said. "We're getting out of here."

Waiting in the hallway Coulter and Cummings noticed a man approaching. When he immediately slowed upon spotting them, Coulter stepped forward and demanded that he identify himself.

Van Meter managed an uneasy smile. "I'm a salesman."

When Coulter asked for proof, Van Meter invited the agent to follow him out to his car. As he led the way down the stairs the bandit discreetly unbuttoned his coat. Reaching the first floor Van Meter drew a pistol and turned on the agent. "You asked for it," he snarled. "Now I'm gonna give it to you."

Usually a crack shot, Van Meter missed with his first two bullets, allowing Coulter to dart past him and flee out the front door. The outlaw ran after him, firing. Nalls, hearing gunplay, started toward the building when he saw his fellow agent dash outside, chased by the thin man he had seen just minutes earlier. Coulter pulled his weapon and started shooting back at his pursuer. When Nalls also opened fire, Van Meter did an abrupt about-face and retreated inside.

Seconds after the gunfire erupted downstairs, Dillinger unlatched the apartment door, thrust the barrel of a submachine gun through the opening, and swept the hallway with a thundering barrage that drove Cummings into an alcove for cover. "Go!" the outlaw shouted to Billie, continuing to blast away as she darted down the hall toward the stairway. Despite bullets coming within inches of his face, Cummings emptied his revolver at the pair.

After disabling Van Meter's Ford by shooting a tire, Coulter and Nalls rushed up to the third floor. By that time Dillinger and his girl had escaped out the rear door and reached their Hudson sedan, leaving a trail of crimson dots in the snow; one of Cummings's slugs had struck the bank robber in the left leg.

Police reinforcements were arriving just as Hamilton, with Pat Cherrington and her sister Opal Long, approached the apartment building. The trio wisely kept walking. Hamilton made his way to the McCormick Restaurant in downtown St. Paul, one of the gang's favorite meeting places. He contacted Harry Sawyer to learn if Dillinger was in police custody.

A few blocks away Van Meter hijacked a garbage wagon and forced the driver and his assistant to take him into Minneapolis. Near the Charlou Apartments he left the terrified pair with a warning not to talk to police. Minutes later the lanky bandit reached Green's apartment. As he was in the middle of recounting his narrow escape, there was a knock on the door. It was Billie.

Green followed her to where Dillinger waited in the Hudson, the machine gun on his lap, his left hand clamped over a wound an inch below his left knee. "Cops raided us," he said. "I caught one in the leg, but it's not that bad. I just need a new place to hole up."

Earlier, when Dillinger and Hamilton had been wounded at Mason City, Green had decided against enlisting the aid of family friend Dr. Clayton E. May, fearing that if the physician were discovered tending Dillinger the trail would lead the law back to him. Now Green saw no choice. May was contacted and agreed to see a "special patient" at his private clinic on Park Avenue.

The "clinic" was actually a furnished apartment where May handled cases requiring extreme discretion—abortions, treatment for venereal disease, and the rare but inevitable gunshot wounds. May's association with the underworld was casual at best, but thanks to Green, who occasionally sent him special patients, it was sufficient to provide extra cash to supplement his conventional practice. The physician cleaned and bandaged the perforated leg, then informed Dillinger and his girl that they were welcome to remain at the apartment while he recovered. Green was hoping to get off cheap, but that evening May appeared at the jug marker's apartment wearing a wide grin. "You know that fellow you brought me today looked a lot like Dillinger. . . ."

A fee of $1,000 was agreed upon for the doctor's services. When arrested later, May claimed that he had been forced at gunpoint to treat Dillinger and never received a cent.

Green must have wondered how everything had soured so quickly. Over a seven-day span the gang had netted $100,000. The wounds suffered at Mason City were merely a minor setback, but now, just as his shoulder was almost healed, Dillinger had been incapacitated again while escaping a police trap in St. Paul, arguably the safest criminal haven in the nation. Green could only hope that it was no more than freakish happenstance, but in his comments to Bessie he implied that the damage to their Twin Cities sanctuary might be irreversible.

And things were about to get much worse.

❁ ❁ ❁

Prior to the March 31 Lincoln Court shootout there had been only suspicion and persistent rumors about Dillinger's presence in St. Paul. But on Easter Sunday, April 1, virtually every newspaper in the nation carried the story of the Indiana desperado blasting his way past the lawmen.

Any doubts that it was really Dillinger were dispelled once the G-Men searched Apartment 303 and collected eight itemized pages of belongings left behind by the couple. A set of Dillinger's fingerprints was lifted from a Listerine bottle. Amid the personal effects, agents discovered a bulletproof vest, a Remington rifle, "quite a few bullets," and a weapon none of them had ever seen—a .38 Colt super-automatic "converted into a small machine gun" and fitted with a vertical foregrip. A search of Van Meter's Ford yielded a machine gun with the stock removed, a spare 100-shell ammo drum, and a Winchester .351 rifle.

In particular the weapon dubbed "a baby machine gun" by the press aroused the most interest and indignation. Eager to determine the source of such an exotic piece of hardware, agents found the .38-caliber weapon's identification number obliterated from the frame but located the manufacturer's secret number (13585) on the firing pin. It would take almost a full month before the .38 was traced to the tiny San Antonio gun shop of H. S. Lebman.

Local newspapers referred to the machine-gun pistol as an example of how professional gangsters and thieves were better armed than law officers. A drive was started to raise funds for the St. Paul Police Department to buy machine guns. Federal agents appealed to their director for more modern and powerful weapons, as well as bulletproof vests.

Dillinger's abandoned arsenal was only part of the furor. The day before the gun battle a Ramsey County grand jury probe had concluded there was no substantial evidence to support allegations of an underworld existing in St. Paul. The *St. Paul Daily News* labeled the findings a "whitewash". The *Pioneer Press* called St. Paul a "happy hunting ground for kidnappers, thugs, thieves, and machine gunners . . . because gangsters have been given refuge here." An editorial charged that St. Paul Mayor William J. Mahoney, who had scoffed at reports that Dillinger was anywhere near his city, "insulted the intelligence" of the public.

From Washington J. Edgar Hoover fumed, "In the twenty-odd years of the existence of this division, no one has shot at any of our agents and got away with it." He vowed to nail Dillinger and "run down the entire gang." More than forty men, the majority from Chicago, were sent to St. Paul to aid in the investigation. The local FBI office, unequipped and unprepared for the deluge, was forced to set up cots in the Federal Courts Building for some of the out-of-towners. Headlines in the *St. Paul Dispatch* screamed, "Hoover Declares War on Gangs Here—U.S. Justice Bureau Chief Hurls Threat—Extra Forces to Run Down Entire Mob."

In personal memos to the St. Paul office Hoover raged over the fact that agents had Dillinger in their grasp and let him slip away. In the margin of one report he scribbled "See that leads of all evidence developed in this matter are promptly and vigorously pressed, J. E. H." He also expressed his "extreme displeasure" over the "atrocious bungling" by his men at the Lincoln Court. The director was notably infuriated that a policeman (Cummings) had been included in the raid and that newspapers had reported that one his agents (Coulter) was chased from the building by a gunman.

By Monday the publicity, public outrage, and police activity was enough to convince the gang members they needed to vacate the area; once Dillinger was able to travel they would pull up stakes and regroup in Chicago. Baby Face Nelson, the only absent member, was probably en route to Minneapolis when he learned of the shootout. It's possible he made a brief appearance in the city to confer with the others, but more likely he phoned Green while on the road. Either way he got the message and informed his partners he would meet them at Louie's roadhouse.

On April 2 Van Meter and Carroll brought Dillinger's Hudson to Clements Auto in Mankato for repainting and new taillights. While the pair waited, Carroll, who once had resided briefly in the southern Minnesota town, was recognized and his presence relayed to the chief of police. Federal agents were notified, but before they descended on the community Carroll was tipped off by friends and managed to flee with his companion.

It is doubtful either outlaw returned to the Twin Cities following this close call. Three days earlier Van Meter had picked up Mickey Conforti at the hospital, paid her bill, and deposited her at the home of Pat Reilly while she recuperated. Jean Crompton, Carroll's sweetheart and Reilly's sister-in-law, was also staying there. Reilly was entrusted by the outlaws to bring both women to Chicago the following week. Van Meter also phoned Green after their escapade in Mankato and requested that he retrieve some items from Van Meter's Marshall Avenue apartment.

Neither Van Meter nor Green was aware the apartment had come under FBI scrutiny. Sifting through evidence taken from the Lincoln Court, agents had found a phone number and traced it to the three-story red brick building at 2214 Marshall Avenue. At 11 P.M. four agents arrived at the address, prepared to intercept anyone entering or leaving the apartment.

The next morning, Tuesday, April 3, Werner Hanni, SAC of the St. Paul office, led a fresh team to the scene, obtaining a key from the janitor. The apartment was deserted except for clothes and personal items, most of them packed in cases. Though no weapons were found there were numerous indications of Van Meter's criminal trade. Among items the agents noted in their report were a shoulder holster, binoculars, two sets of license plates, several .45 clips, half a box of .380 ammunition, loose .45 and .38 shells, 16-gauge shotgun shells, a dynamite fuse, notebooks listing getaway routes, maps of Wisconsin and the Dakotas, fourteen silver dollars, and seven money wrappers.

After concluding their search, Hanni departed with his men, leaving Coulter, Nalls, and Special Agent George J. Gross—one of the reinforcements from Chicago—to stand guard and dust for fingerprints. Shortly before noon the agents heard footsteps outside the door, then a key opening the latch. Gross stood ready with a machine gun as the door swung open. A black woman entered and gasped when the agent pressed the muzzle into her stomach.

Once the woman calmed down she identified herself as Lucy Jackson. She explained that her sister Leona Goodman—at that moment waiting for her in the car—had given her the key and sent her in to clean up and collect some items. Gross went downstairs and brought Mrs. Goodman back to the apartment.

Under questioning Leona revealed that an hour earlier a white woman named Bessie and her husband had stopped at her home at 778 Rondo Avenue. She and Bessie had once worked together at a nightclub called The Alamo, Leona as a cook, Bessie a waitress. Over the years Bessie had arranged a number of jobs for Leona and Lucy. The pair had worked as maids for the Barkers and were employed on occasion by Harry Sawyer.

That morning Bessie and her "husband" had directed Leona to go to the apartment, giving her a key and a dollar. The husband had told her she would find at least ten silver dollars at the apartment and invited the women to keep them for their services. Leona was to take the belongings back to her house on Rondo where the husband would later collect them.

The sisters were brought to the St. Paul FBI office to recount their story. Inspector W. A. Rorer and SAC Hanni assigned Gross and five more agents to accompany Leona back to her home and set an ambush for the man. When the suspect arrived, she would meet him at the door, hand him the tan leather bag taken from the apartment (and filled with "Dillinger Wanted" circulars), then alert the agents lying in wait if it was the right man.

As the lawmen prepared to leave, Special Agent E. N. Notesteen spoke to Rorer to be sure he correctly understood their instructions. In a memo written that evening Notesteen reported that he "questioned Inspector Rorer particularly as to the exact procedure to be followed . . . and was advised that, if a man came to the house to call for the bag and the Negro maid advised that this was the man who had called at her home this morning and instructed her to get his effects from the Marshall Avenue apartment, that this man should be shot."

At three o'clock that afternoon the agents took their places around the Goodman house. Hanni and three men remained outside, in two cars strategically positioned to block any escape. Gross was stationed at a front-room window with his machine gun. Notesteen, toting a shotgun, waited with Leona in the kitchen. A third agent armed with a rifle watched from the bedroom.

During their vigil Notesteen phoned Rorer, inquiring what to do if the suspect attempted to enter. The inspector emphasized again, "If she says 'That's the man,' kill him."

At 5:45 a new Terraplane sedan parked on the opposite side of the street. A man in a dark overcoat stepped out, leaving the engine running and a lady inside. The agents watched him approach the side-porch door. When the visitor knocked, Notesteen directed Leona to answer. She quickly handed over the bag, then slammed the door in his face. "It's him," she cried.

"Let him have it!" Notesteen shouted.

Eddie Green—perhaps puzzled by Leona's abrupt behavior, possibly sensing danger—started back toward the car. Gross smashed out the windowpane with the barrel of his weapon. Green, hearing the glass break, might have glanced back or even turned, but only for a second. As he neared the sidewalk he quickened his pace.

Gross squeezed off a burst of five shots. One slug tore through the back of Green's skull, a second smashed into his right shoulder. The jug marker, still gripping the tan bag, dropped to his knees, then toppled forward onto his face.

Notesteen fired a blast at the Terraplane, blowing out a rear tire. The agent with the rifle put a bullet into the hood to disable the engine. Bessie, who had been reading a magazine and listening to the radio, heard none of the shots. Looking up, she saw her boyfriend sprawled on the patch of grass between the sidewalk and curb. She sprang from the car and ran to help him.

The agents quickly surrounded the pair. Kneeling beside her man Bessie clasped a handkerchief over his bleeding head.

"Don't shoot," she pleaded. "Don't shoot anymore. We're alone."

A police ambulance was summoned. Agents searched the crumpled figure for a gun that Gross insisted Green was reaching for, but they failed to find one. When the ambulance arrived, Green was loaded inside, two agents climbing in with him. Bessie sobbed, "Please, get Eddie a priest. He hasn't been to church in a long time and he needs one."

As Green was rushed to Ancker Hospital, agents took Bessie into custody. A search of the woman turned up $1,155—$105 in her purse and nine one-hundred-dollar bills and three fifties sown into the lining of her coat. She also surrendered two safety-deposit keys, leading agents to a pair of strongboxes containing more than $9,000.

The prisoner revealed her identity as Bessie Skinner, age thirty-six, divorced and the mother of a nineteen-year-old son. For the past two years she had lived with Green under a variety of aliases in a dozen different locations. Agents Coulter and Notesteen, using Bessie's keys, explored Apartment 207 at the Charlou and discovered a machine gun, a .351 rifle, a bulletproof vest, a .45 automatic pistol, a 16-gauge shotgun, and enough ammunition to start a small war. Coulter tallied all the weaponry in his report, adding the droll comment, "nice people."

The federal men were only now starting to learn about the man they had gunned down, including his real name. A check into Green's past disclosed his former association with Frank Nash and the Barkers, and his close ties with Harry Sawyer's St. Paul underworld. Obviously Green had recently joined the Dillinger gang. The agents realized there was a gold mine of information inside the gangster's shattered skull.

❋ ❋ ❋

The doctors attending Green assured the G-Men his head wound would certainly prove fatal. The .45 slug, still lodged beneath his scalp, had caused considerable damage to the right posterior section of the skull, sending bone fragments into the victim's brain. Semi-conscious and often delirious, Green could speak and at times respond to questions, alternating between rational statements and raving—an ideal situation for the agents to tap into his short-circuited mind.

Two agents were posted inside the hospital room twenty-four hours a day, one to "interview" the patient while the second recorded every word. Initially the only obstacle was the victim's family. When he began to blurt out names or details, Margaret Green, standing at her son's bedside with a bible, would interrupt by reading passages or calling on Eddie to pray with her. Green's brother Frank once cried, "Don't talk, Eddie." The G-Men had him barred from the hospital and threatened Mrs. Green with banishment if she interfered again.

At times the resourceful agents resorted to role-playing. Green thought one was a doctor, another a fellow gangster. He mistook a private nurse, hired by the bureau to monitor his condition, for Bessie. The dying man was repeatedly assured that no lawmen were present and was encouraged to speak freely.

Green once muttered, "Tell Tommy I will be over when I feel better." An agent asked, "Tommy who?" "Tommy Carroll," he replied. Pressed to reveal Carroll's location, Green mentioned several local addresses, then suddenly said Carroll was hiding in Wisconsin.

Asked about the Lincoln Court shootout, Green admitted that it was Dillinger who "opened up with the Tommy and then went out the back way." He added that Dillinger was wounded in the leg, and claimed that he, Green, had found a doctor and paid the bill himself. He refused to name Dr. May but blurted out his address on Park Avenue. The agents inquired if Green was the man who had arrived in the green Ford and fired at Coulter, but he denied that he was. When they demanded that he the name the gunman, Green replied, "Doc, you sure are a nosy follow. Give me a shot so I can sleep."

"I will if you tell me who drove the green Ford."

"What do you want to know that for?" was the response. "Doc, will you give me that shot?"

The lawmen wanted to hear more about Dillinger and asked Green where he had met the outlaw. "Downtown in St. Paul about three weeks ago, after he got out of Indiana." Green confessed that he was holding some keys for Dillinger and needed to return them. The agent promised to deliver the keys if Green revealed where Dillinger was. Green turned to the nurse, calling her Bess, and said, "You know, Dillinger doesn't like you." He added that he didn't care for Billie either because "she is too foul-mouthed."

Encouraged to play along, the nurse took over the questioning under the guidance of the agents. She asked what should be done the tan bag; Green told her to give it to Red. When she asked who Red was, he responded, "You know who Red is. I'll sock you."

Later she asked if he knew John Hamilton or Homer Van Meter. He glared at her and said, "What are you trying to do, get me in the penitentiary?"

The agents attempted to prod Green into speaking about holdups in which he had been involved, but he avoided specifics. He admitted participating in "five or six bank jobs" and revealed that the gang was planning to tackle a bank in Newton, Iowa. Eventually he acknowledged the Sioux Falls robbery, adding that "Wayne and Tommy were in on that one," and also the Mason City heist.

As the days dragged on Green's rambling responses grew more erratic and incoherent. At one point he pleaded for a gun; another time he screamed to be allowed to get out of a barber's chair. He called for his brothers and asked to be taken to the home of his Aunt Gladys. One moment he claimed to know Alvin Karpis, the next he denied ever hearing the name.

On the evening of April 10 Green slipped into unconsciousness for the final time. With his temperature approaching 105 and meningitis setting in, the patient became "comatose and unresponsive. Respiration became labored, rapid, and shallow . . ." doctors reported. At 12:55 P.M. on April 11, eight days after he was shot, Green was pronounced dead, leaving the FBI to decipher his recorded words.

Local officials and reporters made much of the fact that Green was unarmed and shot in the back, suggesting the G-Men had callously executed the outlaw. In order to absolve FBI agents of any wrongdoing and avoid what Hoover termed "adverse publicity," the agency cleverly reworded its reports on the Green shooting. A memo describing his attempt to escape was changed to say the suspect was "running in leaps" instead of the walking briskly. The "suspicious" turn Green had made was altered to a "threatening" or "menacing" gesture. An agent stationed outside claimed he shouted "Stop!" at the fleeing figure before the shots were fired. Thus the revised report read in part:

> "Disregarding the command to halt, he continued on his
> way, simultaneously reaching in the direction of his pocket with
> the apparent intention of drawing a weapon which he would use

in an effort to thwart his arrest. Having assumed this threatening attitude which was accompanied by a menacing gesture, indicating he intended doing bodily harm by the use of firearms to any so bold as to interrupt him, he was fired upon."

Despite the bureau's careful and colorful rephrasing of the incident, and its insistence that Green had reached for a gun he wasn't carrying, some remained convinced the shooting was unjustified. The *St. Paul Dispatch* demanded an inquest, and local police complained that instead of being trained lawmen, the agents were nothing more than a bunch of "lawyers armed with guns."

The top men at the St. Paul office—Assistant Director Hugh H. Clegg, Inspector Rorer, and SAC Hanni—did everything in their power to discourage an official probe into the Green matter, including refusing to name the agents involved in the Rondo Avenue ambush so none could be subpoenaed. (Hoover enthusiastically approved of this tactic and employed it in future cases since it stressed teamwork rather than singling out individual agents.) In the end the G-Men prevailed. No inquest was held, and the bureau's amended reports were accepted as the final word on Green's death.

Aside from the nagging controversy, the shooting of Green proved to be one of the luckiest breaks in FBI history. His deathbed rantings provided little illumination other than confirming his association with Dillinger. It did, however, pave the way for agents to squeeze some vital information from Bessie, who not only filled in the blanks left by her lover but also supplied pages of priceless insight into the Twin Cities underworld.

Initially she was reluctant to cooperate. Agents brought her to Chicago where she was personally interrogated by Melvin Purvis. Isolated and threatened with prosecution, Bessie broke down and confessed all in a series of progressively revealing admissions. She supplied valuable details about deceased hoodlums like Frank Nash and Verne Miller, and she revealed many of the activities and members of the Barker-Karpis gang. The bureau learned for the first time that the Barkers, not the Touhy mob, were responsible for the Hamm kidnapping and the more recent Bremer abduction. She also exposed the intimate connection between Harry Sawyer and Jack Peifer and the Barkers, along with their involvement in the kidnappings and the roles each played within the gangland scene of St. Paul.

She gave a full accounting of the Dillinger gang, including the bandits' addresses and the names of helpful individuals such as Dr. May and a man called Bill (Pat Reilly) who ran errands for them. Bessie made it clear that she didn't care much for Dillinger, blaming him for the tragedy that had befallen Eddie.

She declared there were six core members of the gang. In addition to Green and Dillinger, she was able to name Homer Van Meter, whom everyone called

Wayne or Van, and Tommy Carroll. There was also a man named Red, whom she immediately identified as John Hamilton when shown his photograph.

She described the final member, known to her only as Jimmie, as "small of stature, rather light hair and complexion, and is just a kid about 24 years old, last name unknown." Jimmie had a wife, Helen, two young children, and often traveled with his mother, a smallish, elderly woman who spoke with an accent Bessie mistook for either Polish or Bohemian. She said she had never encountered Helen without one or both of her children present and noted that she hadn't seen the little girl of late. Bessie said Helen was "very funny looking" and "acted very queer." She believed that Jimmie and his family were currently somewhere in California.

Agents checked every "Jimmie" in their files to find one with any known association to Dillinger or the Twin Cities underworld. They drew a blank, but several days later a report surfaced from a source within the Minnesota state police linking Carroll to the 1933 bank robbery in Brainerd. The report alleged one of Carroll's accomplices was a "young hood formerly known in Chicago as George Nelson, also called Baby Face or 'Blondie.' " The G-Men discovered that weeks earlier police in Sioux Falls and Mason City, acting on the same tip, had obtained copies of Nelson's 1931 police photos. Twelve witnesses in Sioux Falls identified Nelson as the little machine gunner who shot Patrolman Keith, and almost as many were positive that he was one of the bandits at Mason City. The authorities in both locations had failed to pass along the information to the bureau.

Nelson's photos were shown to Bessie, who said she was certain he was the young man she knew as Jimmie, the sixth member of the so-called Dillinger gang.

The one crucial detail Bessie was unable to share was the whereabouts of the outlaws. On April 1, the day after the Lincoln Court shooting, Green had confided that the entire gang was preparing to "blow town." Where the outlaws were headed she had no idea, but she was sure that by now they had all moved on.

❋ ❋ ❋

She was right.

The last of the gang members to leave the Twin Cities was Dillinger himself. Though his leg wound was still healing, the shooting of Green and capture of Bessie hastened his departure. After nightfall on April 4 Billie and her bank-robbing boyfriend vacated Dr. May's hideaway. Since they were several days early for the gang's weekend rendezvous in Chicago, the pair drove on to Indiana where they visited the desperado's relatives around the Dillinger farm in Mooresville, all the while playing hide-and-seek with federal agents keeping the farm under surveillance.

The rest of the gang, meanwhile, began arriving in Chicago, coincidentally at the same time and in the same city where Bessie was identifying them for Purvis. Nelson was apparently the first to reach his hometown. Assuming the role of arranger, as Green had in the Twin Cities, he visited gangland friends to secure safe havens for the others. Nelson and his wife also contacted the Fitzsimmons family in order to spend time with Darlene.

On Saturday, April 7, Nelson and Helen showed up at Louie's roadhouse. Caroline Corder, the young waitress who quit the previous September, had been re-hired only two days earlier. She was happy to see the diminutive couple she knew as Jimmie and Helen, who were always pleasant, talkative, and generous tippers. They were joined that evening by another couple—a handsome, dark-haired man and a buxom blond—introduced to her as "Tommy and Jean."

Cernocky visited the quartet at their table and over the course of the evening spent considerable time conversing with Nelson and Carroll. Nelson wanted Louie's permission to use the roadhouse as the primary meeting place for the gang during the next couple of weeks. Cernocky, knowing that Nelson never squawked over paying inflated prices, had no objections.

Dillinger and Billie reached Chicago late Sunday. Nelson found a place for them to spend the night on the West Side. The next day, April 9, the couple stopped at a North Side tavern to visit Larry Strong, a former boyfriend of Pat Cherrington's sister. Along with working as a bartender, cigar store clerk, and taxi driver, Strong had also been recruited recently as an FBI informer. A trap awaited Dillinger inside.

Billie entered first to make sure the coast was clear. After speaking with Strong and seeing nothing amiss, she strolled back to the entrance to signal Dillinger. The over-anxious agents, fearing she was leaving, immediately surrounded her. Unable to intervene, Dillinger drove off and phoned Art O'Leary. "The G's just picked up Billie," he said, telling O'Leary to contact Piquett at once and urge the attorney to do everything in his power to secure her release.

That evening Caroline Corder was working in the kitchen at the roadhouse. A man entered through the back door and warmly greeted Mrs. Cernocky, hugging the huge woman and calling her "Ma." He asked to wash his hands and get something to eat. As Mrs. Cernocky prepared a steak her husband walked in and welcomed the visitor. Telling Caroline the man was an old friend, Louie instructed her to serve him his meal in the kitchen instead of the dining area. It was only after hearing the man addressed as "John" that she realized she was waiting on Dillinger. After devouring his steak the desperado, clutching a quart of liquor brought to him by Louie, retired to one of the two basement bedrooms.

While Dillinger drowned his sorrows in a bottle at Fox River Grove, the woman he grieved over was subjected to a rigorous interrogation at the bureau's Chicago office on the 19th floor of the Bankers' Building. Billie later claimed she was denied food and sleep for forty-eight hours and was handcuffed to a chair with powerful lights blazing in her face. (Federal officials labeled the allegations "preposterous.") She cursed the agents and refused to reveal anything. Billie insisted that one interrogator, Special Agent Harold H. Reinecke, answered her stubbornness with frequent slaps across her face. Learning of the alleged abuse later, Dillinger vowed to kill Reinecke.

The next morning Nelson brought Dillinger to the Rainbo, where the Indiana outlaw spent the next two nights hidden away in one of Jimmy Murray's special second-story rooms. Billie's arrest and Strong's betrayal had left him sullen and shaken. He dyed his hair dark red and for the first time spoke about undergoing plastic surgery.

On April 12 the remaining members of the gang met at Van Meter's room in a North Side hotel, the first time all five had been together since the Mason City holdup. The absence of Eddie Green was sorely noted by all, and Nelson, Van Meter, and the usually affable Carroll were all bitterly vocal over the manner in which their unarmed comrade had been shot in the back. Dillinger, mourning the loss of Billie more than Green, readily agreed with the others about the less-than-honorable tactics employed by the federal agents. Nelson's personal assessment of the G-Men—expressed to Chase, Perkins, and others at this time—was that they were "a bunch of cowardly college bastards playing coppers," the gunning down of Green displaying "what kind of people we're up against."

The conversation eventually turned to their urgent need to replace the hardware left behind in the Twin Cities. Two submachine guns, a pair of bulletproof vests, three rifles, one of the machine-gun pistols, and a large quantity of ammunition had been lost. Nelson offered to arrange a buy through his sources, but both Dillinger and Van Meter, having discussed the matter earlier, declared they were tired of paying high prices to Nelson's pals.

The pair briefly returned to their native state. On the evening of Friday, April 13, they boldly walked into the police station at Warsaw, Indiana, where Van Meter pistol-whipped the officer on duty until he surrendered the keys to the arsenal. Unable to find any automatic weapons, the bandits settled for three bulletproof vests and two .38 revolvers.

In Chicago the next evening a car pulled up beside Art O'Leary. Dillinger, behind the wheel, invited him in. Two strangers, introduced by Dillinger as Red and Van, occupied the back seat. Hamilton extended his three-fingered hand to the investigator; Van Meter said nothing. When Dillinger asked for an update on Billie's situation, O'Leary said her bail had been set at $60,000 and she was scheduled to be sent to St. Paul to stand trial, with Bessie Skinner and Dr. May, for harboring the outlaw. Dillinger wanted to know all the details of the transfer and made it clear that he intended to liberate her. O'Leary privately thought he was crazy but promised to look into it.

That night, after dropping off Van Meter and picking up Hamilton's girl-friend, Dillinger reappeared at Louie's roadhouse where they met Nelson and Carroll and their women. The three couples feasted on a huge dinner while Dillinger withdrew to his room in the basement and was served a meal there by the bartender. When the girls retired for the evening, Nelson, Carroll, and Hamilton joined Dillinger downstairs and played cards until well past midnight.

In the morning the four desperados had a late breakfast with Cernocky and his wife. Hamilton said that he and Pat were leaving that afternoon to visit his sister Anna in Sault Ste. Marie, on the far northern tip of Michigan's Upper Peninsula. Cernocky mentioned that an old friend, Emil Wanatka, was currently operating a lodge in northern Wisconsin, just an hour's drive from the Michigan border. If the couple needed a safe place to stay or hide out in the vicinity, Cernocky assured them, Emil was a man who could be trusted to keep quiet.

Cernocky had spoken of the lodge a few nights earlier when Nelson had asked his host to recommend any out-of-the-way places where the gang could stay. At the time Baby Face had dismissed it as being too remote, but now that Chicago was once again the focus of the manhunt for Dillinger, Cernocky's description of Wanatka's resort as a safe retreat in the midst of a sparsely pop-ulated region sounded appealing. Carroll, more an outdoorsman than the city-bred Nelson, was especially interested and proposed that the entire gang meet there for a weekend in the woods. Dillinger not only endorsed Carroll's sug-gestion but also offered to join Hamilton on the ride to Sault Ste. Marie. Cernocky provided his guests with directions to the lodge—a straight shot up Highway 51—and they agreed to rendezvous there on the following Friday, April 20.

Once Dillinger, Hamilton, and Miss Cherrington were on their way, Nelson contacted John Paul Chase, who was currently staying at a boarding house on Jackson Boulevard under the name Earl Butler. Nelson called on him to pick up Father Coughlan, who had recently returned to the Chicago area and was resid-ing at his sister's home in Wilmette. That night, April 16, Coughlan and Chase attended a dinner party with Nelson, Helen, Carroll, and Jean at Louie's. When Chase was ready to leave, Nelson walked him outside and confided that the gang was "heading north" that weekend. He slipped Chase a wad of cash, instructing him to purchase a "clean car" while he was out of town. (Nelson at the time was driving a 1934 Ford V-8 deluxe sedan with 12,000 miles on it, stolen for him by Perkins and fitted with clean Kentucky plates provided by Lieder.) Father Coughlan, who reportedly drank more than his share during the festivities, was provided with a room for the night and driven back to his sister's the next day by Carroll.

Dillinger and his companions reached Sault Ste. Marie early on Tuesday, the seventeenth. It was a brief, bittersweet reunion for the usually quiet, mild-mannered Hamilton. After a roll of snapshots was taken in the back yard, the bandit had a few minutes alone with his sister and shared that he was certain the law would soon catch up to him and his outlaw associates. There simply wasn't any place left to hide.

Shortly after the trio departed on April 19 the local sheriff received a tip that Dillinger and Hamilton were hiding at the home of the latter's sister. The sheriff notified the FBI, and two planeloads of agents descended on the house that evening. A comprehensive search of the region failed to produce any trace of the outlaws, though they were probably not far away waiting to unite with their cronies in northern Wisconsin. When the G-Men discovered they had missed Dillinger again, they charged Anna with harboring a federal fugitive. Members of the community circulated a petition, ultimately signed by 1,500 citizens, to keep the former PTA president and mother of six out of jail. In the end, Anna would spend three months behind bars.

Late Thursday afternoon Van Meter and Mickey Conforti joined the others at Louie's. As the group dined together that evening they excitedly discussed the upcoming weekend getaway at the Wisconsin resort. Nothing was said in front of the women, but the outlaws had more practical objectives in mind for the retreat. If the lodge proved to be as remote and its owner as trustworthy as Cernocky claimed, the gang could use the place as a future hideout or meeting place. Carroll boasted that he knew the area and suggested casing some small-town banks.

Deciding a three-car caravan might attract attention, Van Meter obtained directions and left the roadhouse with Mickey that night. He planned to stop briefly in St. Paul to see Gannon and Reilly before making his way to the lodge.

At 8 A.M. April 20 Nelson and Helen departed in their Ford sedan, Carroll and Jean following in a Buick coupe purchased through Cernocky. Near the small town of North Leads, Wisconsin, less than halfway to their destination, Nelson's vehicle collided with a car driven by Jack Delany of Poynette. The damage to the Ford was extensive; its passenger side was smashed in. Badly shaken but uninjured, Helen climbed into the rumble seat of Carroll's coupe as her husband dealt with the other driver. Calling himself Robert Lane, Nelson told Delany he was from out of state and suggested, "Let's keep the cops out of this." Though the damage to Delany's car was not so severe, the outlaw handed him $300 to cover repairs.

With Carroll trailing him, Nelson drove the wrecked Ford another twenty miles to the Slinger Garage in Portage where he gave his name as R. L. Lane of Henderson, Kentucky, and paid to have the sedan stored. He told the attendant that a representative of the Oakley Auto Construction Company in Chicago would tow away the vehicle in a few days.

During the ride to Portage, Helen was unable to stop trembling. She managed to persuade Carroll to hand over his flask of whiskey, draining a fair amount of its contents before returning it. At the time she was happy to be alive. Later, reflecting on the incident with her in-laws, she decided the accident actually had been an omen, declaring, "Right then and there we should have turned around and headed back to Chicago."

Instead, once her husband squeezed into the rumble seat beside her, they resumed their journey toward Wanatka's lodge.

*Everyone seemed to have a good time, that is, until the
government men arrived and started shooting up the place.*
— Frank Traube

CHAPTER 10

WEEKEND AT EMIL'S

IN HIS PURSUIT OF the American dream Emil Wanatka learned to cut corners
and break a few laws. Born in Brumov, Bohemia, in 1888, he immigrated to the
United States as a skinny, spirited teenager in 1906, picking up English as he
worked on the docks and inside the sweatshops of New York. After several years
in a Brooklyn bakery he started moving about, briefly serving in the merchant
marine and operating a hotel in St. Louis.

Eventually he landed in Chicago, taking a job as a bartender. During
Prohibition he turned to bootlegging and invested his earnings in a North Side
restaurant. In 1923 he became the sole proprietor and renamed it Little
Bohemia. Business flourished, the patrons on any given night a mosaic of
prominent politicians, policemen, Cubs baseball players, prizefighters, and
mobsters. The restaurant became a favorite nightspot among members of the
North Side Gang. Thanks to powerful connections on both sides of the law,
Wanatka openly served beer to his most loyal clientele. His standing with the
local underworld was evidently strong. During an argument with mobster Terry
Druggan, Wanatka knocked him down a flight of stairs, a defiant act that might
have assured gangland retaliation, but Wanatka was never molested.

By 1930, however, he found his flashy lifestyle crumbling. The previous
year's St. Valentine's Day Massacre had left the North Side Gang virtually anni-
hilated, robbing Wanatka of some of his best customers and most of his underworld connections. His business was already hurting when the depression hit,
leaving him no choice but to sell the restaurant.

His wife, the former Nancy LaPorte, viewed the setback more as a blessing than a curse. Since the birth of their son, Emil Jr., in 1925 she had longed to return to her Wisconsin roots. She despised the noisy, crowded city life, but most of all she detested her husband's gangland pals. She repeatedly threatened divorce, especially after catching Emil one evening having a drunken party with a police inspector and a pair of young women.

After selling the restaurant and settling their debts, Nan insisted that they take what money was left and build a resort in the remote Wisconsin woodlands, where most of her relatives resided near the tiny community of Manitowish Waters, thirteen miles south of Mercer. Once resigned to his wife's will, Wanatka pursued the project with his characteristic gusto and energy, and within a year the Little Bohemia Lodge was completed.

The lodge itself was an Alpine-style, two-story structure built mostly of rustic timber. Along with the Wanatkas' living quarters, the upstairs had eight bedrooms. The ground floor contained a spacious dining area, a large kitchen, a parlor with a fireplace, and a bar, all adorned in rich wood paneling and sporting stuffed trophies of local wildlife.

The sign beside Highway 51, the main artery for traffic through the densely wooded region, read "Little Bohemia," with the words "Dine, Dance & Swim" above, "Steak, Duck & Chicken Dinners" below. A gravel driveway snaked through a thick cluster of pines to a wide unpaved parking area in front of the building. Directly behind the lodge, at the base of a steep bank, was a stretch of private beach along Little Star Lake, one of a chain of sparkling lakes dotting Iron County. (Wanatka had intended to add a pier and rental boats and canoes before money ran out.) Just north of the main building was a heated garage and several cabins to accommodate additional guests.

Full occupancy was a rare occurrence at Little Bohemia during its first three years, and it was the last thing its owner expected in late April. Although spring had officially begun a month before, temperatures rarely reached 50 during the day and at night plunged below freezing. Ice covered parts of the lake, and persistent patches of snow were still scattered across the landscape. Vacationers and travelers seldom descended on the area before Decoration (Memorial) Day.

Even at the peak of tourist season the lodge did a moderate business at best, barely enough to meet the oppressive mortgage payments. The Wanatkas' most faithful customers were locals, many from the Civilian Conservation Corps camp in Mercer, who dropped by for dinner and drinks. The infrequently overnight guests were mostly old Chicago acquaintances of Emil's whom Nan tolerated as long as they spent money. Wanatka managed to keep two full-time employees—George Bazo, age twenty-six, and Frank Traube, twenty-three—who took turns bartending and waiting on tables.

✳ ✳ ✳

At 2:30 Friday afternoon, April 20, a black Ford V-8 with Minnesota plates pulled into the lodge's parking area. Lloyd LaPorte, one of Nan's brothers, was just leaving, and the Ford stopped beside his car. A lanky figure stepped out, peered through the windshield at LaPorte, and asked, "Is this Emil's place?"

LaPorte nodded, noticing a young woman slip out the passenger side and a second, shorter man climb from the back seat. He watched the trio enter the main building. Not sure why, he took a moment to memorize the Ford's license before driving away.

Wanatka greeted the strangers in the vestibule between the bar and dining room. The tall man—Homer Van Meter—surprised the owner by addressing him as Emil and asking if they could get a late lunch. Mickey Conforti cradled a puppy, a black Boston bull terrier named Rex, in her tiny arms. Their companion was Pat Reilly, described by Wanatka as a pimply faced young man with bad teeth who seemed friendly but said little.

After a meal of pork chops, Van Meter asked Wanatka to show him around. As they strolled over the grounds the bandit, calling himself Wayne, explained they were traveling to Duluth and would be joined by a party of six to eight friends, one of which, Van Meter claimed, was bringing "a letter of introduction." He asked the owner if he could handle that many guests for the weekend. Elated at this unexpected surge in business, Wanatka instructed his wife and their employees to prepare the rooms. Van Meter kept checking his watch and glancing toward the road, obviously concerned about the delay of the others.

At 4:30 a Ford sedan carrying Dillinger, Hamilton, and Pat Cherrington arrived. A half-hour later Carroll's Buick coupe pulled in, bringing the group's total number to ten, six men and four women. One of the newcomers, a short, sandy-haired young man introducing himself as Jimmie, presented the owner with a short note signed by Louie Cernocky that said the bearers were friends and urged Emil to treat them well. Reading between the lines, Wanatka realized the visitors must be hoods of some importance to receive Cernocky's recommendation. He returned the letter to Nelson who tore it up and tossed the pieces into a wastebasket.

Wanatka's first impression of Nelson was a good one—Jimmie seemed by far the most talkative and personable of the group, the only one to take a few minutes to pet and play with the family's pair of collies, Shadow and Prince. After chatting about Cernocky and Chicago, Nelson inquired about the outside cabins. Wanatka showed him the largest one, which boasted two bedrooms and a sizable living room. Nelson and his wife decided to share the cabin with Carroll and Jean. The rest were provided with rooms upstairs, Dillinger and Reilly bunking together.

The task of bringing in the luggage fell to Bazo and Traube. Some of the cases were inexplicably heavy. "There must be lead in this one," Bazo complained as he passed Wanatka. "What are these guys, hardware salesmen?"

The tall, curly-haired Traube was already quite certain about the identity of the guests and claimed later that he'd recognized Dillinger "the minute he stepped into the room." Later Wanatka warned Traube to watch his step around the men. "These guys are all hoods and they're hot," he confided.

The seven late arrivals requested supper. About six o'clock Nan started grilling steaks. Helen and Jean offered to help. While Nelson's wife minced garlic for the steaks, Jean went to the bar and ordered drinks for the group. All ate ravenously and praised Mrs. Wanatka for her cooking. It was only after her husband revealed that the guests were "friends of Louie Cernocky" that Nan's attitude toward them cooled considerably.

After dinner the men wandered into the bar. Carroll, sitting at a table with Dillinger, called Wanatka over and asked if he played cards. "Sure, I play," he replied. "Mostly pinochle."

"We don't know that one," Carroll confessed. "How about some poker?"

Wanatka agreed to sit in if the stakes didn't climb too high. Eventually Nelson, who had been conversing with Traube and buying drinks for everyone, joined the game, as did Reilly. They soon switched from poker to hearts. The owner noticed all four of his opponents kept their jackets on, and at various times he spotted guns in shoulder holsters on everyone except Reilly. It was at this time, Wanatka later claimed, that he noticed the man with the odd reddish hair resembled newspaper photos of Dillinger.

A few regular customers drifted into the bar that evening. Whenever they spied a new face, Dillinger or Nelson asked Wanatka about them. When two women entered, the lodge owner identified them as his sister-in-law Ruth Voss and her teenage daughter Audrey. Dillinger insisted on buying drinks for the pair.

The game finally broke up about midnight. Wanatka, retiring upstairs with his two dogs, found Nan still awake and wanting to know more about the guests. When she persisted he whispered to her, "Don't say anything to anyone, but I think the fellow with the dyed red hair is Dillinger."

The remark left Nan so unnerved she slept only fitfully through the night. She swore she heard footsteps in the hallway, like someone on sentry duty, and doors opening and closing.

Wanatka rose early on Saturday and at six o'clock went down to let the dogs out. Carroll emerged from the cabin he shared with Jean and the Nelsons. "Good morning, Emil," he called, stretching his brawny arms. "Boy, did I sleep. How about breakfast?"

The owner told him to "get the gang up, and we'll eat." Carroll's companions, however, were not such early risers. It was after 9:30 before all ten visitors congregated in the dining area, the four women still in dressing gowns. As Mrs. Wanatka prepared breakfast some of the men helped set the table.

According to Wanatka, after the meal he asked Dillinger to step into his office. There he boldly informed the outlaw that he knew his identity and would not allow "a shooting match" at his place. "Everything I have to my name, including my family, is right here," he said. "And every policeman in America is looking for you."

Dillinger tried to put him at ease, promising to pay him well and guaranteeing there would be no trouble. "All we want is to eat and rest for a few days."

Exactly how accurate Wanatka's version of the confrontation was is difficult to say, or even if the meeting ever took place. It was never reported in his statements to the FBI or press, only in later accounts that made no mention of the Cernocky letter. In fact, when the story broke, Wanatka told outlandish tales claiming that the gang, openly brandishing their weapons, had taken over the lodge, holding the owner, his family, and his employees prisoners over the weekend. There is evidence that FBI publicists to some extent encouraged Wanatka to promote the portrait of innocent citizens preyed on by a band of desperate criminals. But those who knew of Wanatka's shady past suspected there was more to the story, some even suggesting that the owner knew in advance the gang was coming.

In either case Wanatka found himself caught in the middle of a very sticky situation. Since making the move to Wisconsin he had acted as a reformed character, at least for the sake of his wife and in-laws. His contacts back in Chicago still regarded him as a trusted friend of the underworld. During the past three years Emil occasionally had offered the hospitality of his remote lodge to visitors either on the run or looking to avoid embarrassing questions. Some were friends, others were sent there by gangland pals like Cernocky. It's likely that Wanatka considered the practice a low-risk method of augmenting his lodge's modest profits.

But he never envisioned the presence of anyone as nationally notorious as Dillinger, or calculated the cost of providing refuge to America's most wanted man. Still, he must have felt bound by his underworld ties to honor the desperado's request for temporary asylum. After all, the gang had been sent to Little Bohemia, and Cernocky had bestowed his seal of approval on Wanatka, pledging that the lodge owner would look after them.

Wanatka's private chat with Dillinger must have ended in some sort of arrangement, or at least an understanding, that the gang could remain with the owner's reluctant blessing. Dillinger's later remarks about Wanatka, and the fact that he added the lodge owner's name to his death list, indicate Dillinger felt betrayed by him, that he had been "ratted out" by someone obviously trusted as an underworld ally.

Dillinger's subsequent condemnation of Wanatka might have been too harsh. Emil was not entirely the captain of his own ship. Any deal struck between the lodge owner and Dillinger did not include Mrs. Wanatka.

Following breakfast Nan started upstairs to change the bedding, her arms filled with fresh linens. Nelson abruptly but politely halted her, explaining that the girls would attend to such matters. Nan quickly found her husband to complain about being "bossed around" in her own home and to convey her growing fear about the strangers. Emil, coming from his talk with Dillinger, did his best to calm her, having apparently determined to let the weekend quietly run its course with their guests.

Nelson, meanwhile, reported to Dillinger and Van Meter that he'd caught Mrs. Wanatka attempting to do some "snooping" in their rooms. Dillinger shrugged it off, confident that Emil would keep his wife in line, although he later bitterly remarked to Art O'Leary that "you couldn't whisper your own thoughts into your pillow without Mrs. Wanatka knowing about it." Van Meter, however, agreed that she posed a potential threat and decided to keep a watchful eye on her. From that moment on, any time Nan talked on the phone or spoke to people who stopped at the lodge, one of the gang was usually lurking close enough to eavesdrop.

A little later Pat Cherrington chatted with Nan while pressing some clothes. Mentioning her recent stay in the hospital, Pat asked if there was a local physician she could visit. Nan replied that the only doctor nearby was the one at the CCC camp in Mercer. When Pat went to the others to request a ride she learned that Van Meter was sending Reilly to St. Paul to retrieve some cash Tom Gannon was holding. Pat, who wanted to see a Twin Cities "specialist," asked to ride along. The pair left shortly after noon in the Ford V-8, expecting to return by nightfall on Sunday.

While the two Pats were preparing to leave, Frank Traube offered to show Nelson and Carroll around the outside of the lodge. At one point they heard gunshots echoing across the lake. "Probably squirrel hunters," Traube informed them. "Lotsa folks up here shoot their own suppers."

Nelson suggested doing some shooting of their own. Traube found a tin can and set it on a snowbank. Carroll took a few shots with his .38, nicking the target only once. Nelson drew a .45 and dazzled the young bartender by firing an entire clip into the can as it flopped across the ground.

Soon Wanatka, Dillinger, and Van Meter joined them. Moving back eighty yards all six took turns firing at the can with the lodge owner's .22 rifle until it jammed. "Go on, Van," Dillinger said, "get one of ours." Van Meter returned with a .351 and the shooting match resumed. Nelson was not so proficient with the rifle; only Wanatka and Van Meter scored hits.

The outlaws borrowed a softball from Emil Jr. and started tossing it around. Dillinger, a former semi-pro second baseman and rabid Cubs fan, displayed his skill before the others. The eight-year-old was allowed to play but quickly withdrew after Nelson fired the ball so hard it stung his hands.

Whether the action was intentional or not (Emil Jr. remains convinced to this day that Nelson deliberately tried to hurt him), the baby-faced bandit seemed to manifest a notably contentious mood that day. Later Van Meter stopped Wanatka to complain that the main building was too public and inquired if he could obtain a cabin for Mickey and himself. Wanatka spied Nelson loitering a few feet away, obviously trying to overhear their conversation. Once Van Meter departed, Nelson approached and asked, "What were you fellows talking about?"

After Wanatka told him about Van Meter's request, Nelson growled, "Listen, Emil, when he wants any cottages, you tell him to see me."

Nan, meanwhile, had devised a plan to get her son away from the lodge. George LaPorte, one of her brothers, was holding a birthday party for his son Cal at their home near Spider Lake, two miles from Little Bohemia. She marched Emil Jr. into the kitchen where her husband was talking to Dillinger and Van Meter. Announcing that her son was expected to attend the party and his absence "would look suspicious," she turned to Dillinger to ask for permission. The desperado replied, "Sure," and handed the youngster a quarter.

Wanatka's conversation with his guests at that moment concerned his recommendation of Maude Johnson, who, along with serving as town treasurer of Spider Lake, provided a laundry service at her home. Minutes later Emil Jr. climbed into the family's Chevy, sitting between his father at the wheel and Van Meter, the back seat loaded with sacks of the gang's clothing. After dropping off his son, Wanatka drove to the Johnson house. Surprised at the quantity and quality of the clothing, she jokingly remarked, "You haven't got Dillinger over there, have you?"

The comment obviously rattled the skinny bandit. On the ride back to Little Bohemia he threatened to return and silence the woman with a bullet. Wanatka convinced him it was only a harmless quip; everyone was talking about Dillinger.

Late that afternoon Wanatka and his wife discussed their situation in private. Nan insisted that something had to be done. By now Wanatka wanted to be rid of the gang as much as his wife. Between the unstable antics of Nelson and Van Meter he was certain one was going to shoot somebody, maybe each other. Even so, the owner did not dare alert the authorities. A raid on the lodge would lead to a shootout and inevitably some embarrassing questions.

To placate his wife and cover his own tracks in the event the gang's presence was disclosed, Wanatka agreed to write a letter to Edward A. Fisher, a Chicago friend who was an assistant district attorney. He knew the letter would not arrive before Monday, long after Dillinger and his pals had moved on.

Nan hid the letter in her corset and went downstairs to start dinner, trying to think of an excuse that would allow her to slip away and mail it. The three gang girls—who had spent most of the day sitting around, smoking, and playing rummy—offered to help. Nan said she wished she had accompanied her son to the party, and Helen, possibly reminded of her own children, urged her to go and leave the meal to them. Thanking Helen, Nan went to the bar where she found her husband and several of the gang starting a new card game. No one objected when she asked to leave.

A light snow was falling as Nan drove north on Highway 51. After a few miles she spotted a car behind her and grew certain that one of their guests was tailing her. In later accounts—perhaps to add a bit more drama and danger to her escapade—she claimed it was Baby Face Nelson, although in previous versions and statements to the FBI she had said she had been unable to see the driver clearly and never knew for sure if it was one of the gang.

Despite her fears she stopped at the home of her brother Lloyd and asked him to accompany her to Mercer. Along the way she blurted out the entire story. In town LaPorte hopped out and deposited the letter at the train station. When Nan asked him what to do next, he suggested that they go to the birthday party and discuss the matter with their brother-in-law Henry Voss.

Arriving at about 8 P.M., Nan and Lloyd called Voss into a bedroom to speak in private. There, Nan shared everything about the Dillinger gang staying at the lodge and the letter she sent to the Chicago D. A.'s office. Voss grimly shook his head. The letter, he pointed out, would not produce results for at least several days. "You could all be dead by then," he added.

They concluded the local sheriff's office and area constables would be no match for Dillinger and his crowd. Since the local phones offered no private lines, Voss volunteered to drive to Rhinelander, Wisconsin, that night and notify federal authorities in either Milwaukee or Chicago. Nan wanted to discuss the plan with Emil first, and so it was agreed that Lloyd would visit the lodge early in the morning and Nan would slip him a message containing her husband's decision.

George LaPorte and Ruth Voss were both curious about the conference in the bedroom. The former surmised it was some kind of domestic dispute and later told FBI agents that Emil and Nan "do not get along well together and are constantly having family quarrels." When the pair started asking questions Nan reluctantly retold her tale for the third time. Outraged to hear that gangsters had "taken over" Little Bohemia, George declared it was foolish to wait and proposed organizing a posse of local men to surround the lodge and storm it from all sides.

To the relief of the others, Voss wisely vetoed the idea by pointing out that Emil and his employees would probably be shot in the exchange. "We'll wait until the federal men get here," he told his in-laws, as long as Emil sanctioned their plan.

Nan returned to the lodge well after 10 P.M. and found her husband in the midst of another marathon card game with Dillinger, Nelson, Carroll, and Van Meter in the bar. Wanatka, who had lost seventeen dollars to his guests the previous night, this time walked away twenty-eight dollars richer when he finally retired upstairs.

Once the door was closed his wife excitedly told him of Voss's offer to call the government forces from Rhinelander. Wanatka must have been stunned to learn Nan had confided in her family about Dillinger's presence. To make matters worse his in-laws had hatched a scheme to help launch a federal raid on the lodge.

He realized he had no recourse but to go along with the plan. If he objected there would be questions and accusations, first from his in-laws, later from the law, charging him with protecting the fugitives. By cooperating no one could say he willfully harbored the gang. Besides, there might be a reward and the publicity could generate much-needed business for Little Bohemia.

At 7:15 Sunday morning, April 22, Lloyd appeared as planned, bringing his mother as an excuse to visit. They sat in the kitchen chatting while Nan, visibly nervous, prepared breakfast for their unwelcome guests. At one point LaPorte, diligently on watch for the outlaws, glanced out a window and spotted the tall fellow he'd briefly encountered on Friday. Van Meter approached LaPorte's car and suspiciously examined the vehicle, even opening the door to look over the interior. After a half-hour LaPorte announced they had to leave. Nan hugged her mother, then deftly slipped a pack of cigarettes to Lloyd as she said good-bye. Inside the pack was a note reading "Go ahead, Lloyd."

A few minutes later the gang gathered in the dining area. After breakfast Nelson and Dillinger walked outside and, observed by Wanatka, talked for some time in the parking lot. About nine o'clock Nelson and Carroll jumped into the latter's Buick coupe, Carroll teasingly telling Jean, "Me and Jimmie are going to church." Actually the pair drove toward the Michigan border to scout some banks around Hurley and Ironwood.

At the same moment Nelson and Carroll headed north on Highway 51, Lloyd LaPorte, Henry Voss, and Voss's son Lloyd were racing south on the road toward Rhinelander, arriving just before 10 A.M. From a pay phone Voss called a policeman he knew in Milwaukee. The officer recommended that he contact the U.S. Marshal in Chicago. Sending his brother-in-law and son running for change, Voss tried to reach the marshal at his office or at home but was unsuccessful. Finally, after placing several more calls, he managed to find the lawman. When Voss explained the situation, the marshal informed him the Justice Department was handling the Dillinger case.

Voss was losing patience. After two hours on the phone and using a fistful of coins, he started to wonder if the law really wanted Dillinger. He asked the marshal to call the agents and get back to him. The lawman jotted down the number, promising to pass it along to the right people.

❊ ❊ ❊

The man J. Edgar Hoover had placed in the key position of overseeing the Chicago field office was enjoying his first day off in weeks and was looking forward to a lazy Sunday afternoon lounging around his apartment. Melvin Henry Purvis looked more like a meek shoe salesman than a manhunter. He was thirty-two, diminutive and dapper, with narrow, furtive eyes and a squeaky, southern-accented voice. The product of a well-to-do South Carolina family, it took Purvis just five years to graduate with a law degree and a mere twenty months as a junior member of a Florence law firm to grow disillusioned with a career as a practicing attorney. On New Year's Day 1927 he took a train to Washington and applied for a job with the Justice Department.

He swiftly became a favorite of Hoover, a relationship evidently based on more than his efficiency as an agent. Rumors persisted that the director had a "crush" on Purvis, at the time a handsome young bachelor. Several of Hoover's personal letters to Purvis contain some thinly veiled attempts at homosexual flirting. Although aware of—but uninterested in—his boss's advances, Purvis did nothing to discourage Hoover from showing his favoritism. On December 17, 1932, he was promoted to Special Agent in Charge of the Chicago office, the most high-profile and critical outpost in the bureau's battle against the Midwestern crime wave.

Purvis excelled in the role, his diligent and tireless approach to crimefighting producing impressive results and an occasional headline for himself. Hoover was troubled by the latter but nevertheless stuck with Purvis even after some agents questioned his leadership abilities and complained about his excitability. (Behind his back a number of his men called him "Nervous Purvis.")

Since Dillinger's Crown Point escape seven weeks earlier, Purvis had worked day and night coordinating the efforts of his agents, running down leads, and interviewing hundreds of people. While the St. Paul office had been the center of most of the action, the trail led time and again back to Chicago, where Purvis, like Hoover, believed the major break in the manhunt would occur. Thus far the Chicago office had scored but one notable victory: the capture of Billie Frechette. But even that moment of triumph was tarnished by the fact that Dillinger, seated in a car right outside, had been allowed simply to drive away. Hoover's memos to Purvis grew increasingly intolerant of his failure to nail the bank robber.

About one o'clock that afternoon Purvis took a call from the U.S. Marshal informing him that a Mr. Voss in Rhinelander, Wisconsin, had some vital information regarding Dillinger's whereabouts. Purvis dialed the number.

"The man you want most is up here," Voss declared. Pressed for more details, Voss said that Dillinger, five of his pals, and several women were staying at a resort called Little Bohemia. Purvis asked the location of the nearest airport. "Here in Rhinelander," Voss replied. "A little over fifty miles from the lodge."

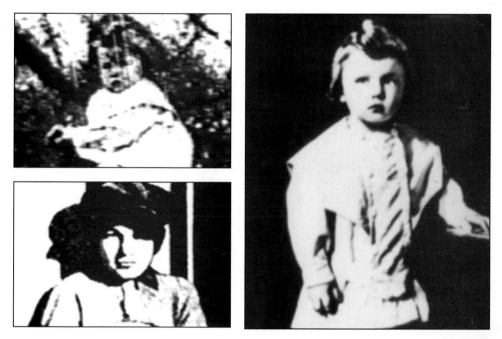

A handsome and intelligent child, Lester Joseph Gillis (above) would one day gain notoriety as public enemy Baby Face Nelson. The active and insatiably curious youngster was pampered and doted on by his siblings, father Joseph, and mother Mary, who gave birth to Lester on December 6, 1908, in the family's three-story red brick town house at 942 North California Avenue in Chicago (below, at left). By Lester's second birthday, Joseph had moved his family into a larger dwelling he had constructed on the lot next door at 944 North California (below, center).

Mary Gillis (left, behind eleven-year-old Lester) had high hopes for her son but was sorely tested by his penchant for truancy. Also shown are his sisters Leona (left) and Amy (right).

• Fifteen-year-old Lester was on leave from the state reformatory when he was photographed with his dog Brucie (below). Lester was kind to animals, and he often displayed a winning smile that served him well as he grew into young adulthood (above).

It was in *The Patch*, a triangle-shaped area on Chicago's Near West Side comprising nearly a dozen distinct European cultural communities, that young Lester Gillis first began running afoul of the law. Among his boyhood friends was John A. "Jack" Perkins, who later became a player in the Chicago crime scene. In the photo above, taken at Chicago's White City Amusement Park in 1932, Perkins (left) is joined by other gang members who honed their criminal skills in The Patch, including Anthony "Tough Tony" Capezio, Claude Maddox, and Louis Carzolli (third, fourth, and fifth from left).

In the spring of 1928, Lester fell in love with tiny, raven-haired Helen Wawrzyniak (above and right, with Gillis). The two were almost inseparable and eloped to Valparaiso, Indiana, where they were wed on October 30.

Helen was just fifteen when she and Lester were wed, but she added five years to her date of birth on their marriage certificate; Lester gave his age as twenty-one instead of nineteen. The newlyweds first lived with Mary Gillis but soon moved in with his sister Julie and her husband, Bob Fitzsimmons. On April 27, 1929, Helen gave birth to a son, Ronald Vincent Gillis. They appeared to be a loving family (left), but as Lester began to renew acquaintances and make new friends among Chicago's underworld, he and several partners embarked on a crime spree, plundering the homes of wealthy socialites. The additional income enabled Gillis to move his family into an apartment in Cicero, Illinois, buy a new car (below), and enjoy the finer things the Windy City had to offer.

Sentenced to serve one year to life in the Illinois State Prison at Joliet for the Hillside robbery, Gillis, now known as George "Baby Face" Nelson, entered the penitentiary in July 1931 as inmate 5437 (above). In February 1932, while returning to Joliet after being sentenced for the Itasca bank heist, Nelson staged a daring escape and headed west. In April 1933 Nelson returned to the Chicago area, where he met Eddie Bentz (right), a pioneer of modern bank robbery, who schooled Nelson in the art. Bentz helped Baby Face and his gang knock off the Peoples Bank in Grand Haven, Michigan, which grabbed headlines throughout the region (below).

THE GRAND HAVEN DAILY TRIBUNE

GRAND HAVEN, MICHIGAN, FRIDAY, AUGUST 18, 1933

FIVE SHOT AS PEOPLES BANK IS HELD UP; WOUND 1 BANDIT

PETER VAN LOPIK MAY BE SERIOUSLY HURT; KINKEMA IN HERO ROLE

One of Bandits Captured in Thrilling Fight As He Struggles with F. C. Bolt; Is Felled by Ed Kinkema

ARTHUR WELLING TURNS IN ALARM

Three Thugs Flee South in Bonema Car: Plenes, Pellegrom, Lindemulder Wounded; Loot Unknown

quickly agreed another car would be needed.

Four miles south of town the men noticed a Chrysler parked along the road near a farm house owned by Ernest Behm. The car, owned by Oscar Varneau of Grand Rapids, was occupied by Varneau's wife and son along with their dog Oscar was about 500 feet away purchasing berries.

Hearing his wife in distress, Oscar tried to stop the bandits but was covered by a sub-machine gun. Varneau asked the men to let his dog out of the car which they did He then watched helplessly as the men sped away.

In their excitement, the bandits left behind about $300 in the Chevy. They took the car and found to their chagrin it contained plenty of gasoline but the tires were almost bald. The car was later abandoned near Hudson after it developed a flat.

Meanwhile members of the police, coast guard

Sept. 9, Doyle pleaded guilty and was sentenced to life in prison. Doyle entered Southern Michigan Prison at Jackson at 11 a.m. Sunday, Sept. 10. The trial was to presumably keep crowds away.

Armed guards escorted Doyle to Jackson in a motorcade which left Grand Haven at 8 a.m.

Doyle appeared to be happy even after sentencing in Jackson. Doyle's leg was still in splints and he was on crutches. Ottawa County Sheriff Ben Kinkema called him a model prisoner.

According to a Tribune article, "Had the case come to trial, a jury there would have been little to it as Doyle had no counsel and could offer no defense.

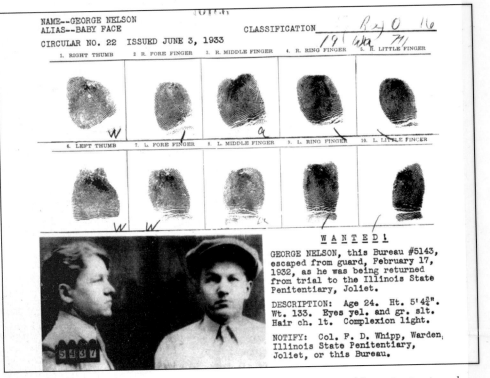

In June 1933 the Illinois State Bureau of Criminal Identification and Investigation issued a wanted poster for George Nelson, alias "Baby Face" (above). Authorities apparently were unaware that the bandit's real name was Lester J. Gillis. • Nelson arrived in St. Paul, Minnesota, in early September and began preparations to rob the First National Bank in Brainerd (below). The October 23 heist netted Baby Face and his gang $32,000.

Nelson *played a key role in arranging notorious John Dillinger's escape from the Crown Point, Indiana, jail in March 1934, on the condition that Dillinger join Baby Face's gang in the Twin Cities. Dillinger (far right, joking with prosecutor Robert Estill) was to use a smuggled gun to make his escape but ultimately bluffed his way to freedom with a wooden pistol. The photograph ended Estill's political career. • After his breakout from Crown Point, Dillinger worked with Nelson and his crew to pull off a $49,000 bank robbery at Sioux Falls, South Dakota, on March 6, 1934, and a $52,000 holdup at the First National Bank in Mason City, Iowa, (below) just one week later.*

Editorial cartoons such as the one above often depicted the nation's new "motorized bandits" as far more progressive than the U.S. justice system. Outlaws including John Dillinger, Baby Face Nelson, and the Barker-Karpis gang frequently carried more firepower and drove faster cars than the law enforcement officials trying to thwart them. • During the bungled FBI raid on the Little Bohemia Lodge near Rhinelander, Wisconsin, Nelson, Dillinger, and other gang members escaped, but their women were taken into federal custody (left). From left are Jean Crompton, Helen Gillis, and Mickey Conforti. • After Dillinger was slain by lawmen outside Chicago's Biograph Theatre on the night of July 22, 1934, newspapers wrongly assumed he had stashed considerable sums of cash (left, at bottom). The next afternoon J. Edgar Hoover announced that Baby Face Nelson had been designated the bureau's most wanted criminal, the nation's new public enemy number one.

WANTED

LESTER M. GILLIS,

aliases GEORGE NELSON, "BABY FACE" NELSON, ALEX GILLIS, LESTER GILES,
"BIG GEORGE" NELSON, "JIMMIE", "JIMMY" WILLIAMS .

On June 23, 1934, HOMER S. CUMMINGS, Attorney General of the United States, under the authority vested in him by an Act of Congress approved June 6, 1934, offered a reward of

$5,000.00

for the capture of Lester M. Gillis or a reward of

$2,500.00

for information leading to the arrest of Lester M. Gillis.

DESCRIPTION

Age, 25 years; Height, 5 feet 4-3/4 inches; Weight,
133 pounds; Build, medium; Eyes, yellow and grey
slate; Hair, light chestnut; Complexion, light; Occupation, oiler.

All claims to any of the aforesaid rewards and all questions and disputes that may arise
as among claimants to the foregoing rewards shall be passed upon by the Attorney General and
his decisions shall be final and conclusive. The right is reserved to divide and allocate
portions of any of said rewards as between several claimants. No part of the aforesaid rewards shall be paid to any official or employee of the Department of Justice.

If you are in possession of any information concerning the whereabouts of Lester M. Gillis,
communicate immediately by telephone or telegraph collect to the nearest office of the Division of Investigation, United States Department of Justice, the local offices of which are set
forth on the reverse side of this notice.

The apprehension of Lester M. Gillis is sought in connection with the murder of Special
Agent W. C. Baum of the Division of Investigation near Rhinelander, Wisconsin on April 23,
1934.

JOHN EDGAR HOOVER, DIRECTOR,
DIVISION OF INVESTIGATION,

*When the FBI issued this wanted poster for Baby Face Nelson in June 1934, the outlaw
was galled that the Justice Department had offered twice as much money for John Dillinger,
who teased him about the amount. For reasons never explained (or changed), the bureau
persisted in identifying Nelson as Lester M. Gillis, although his middle name was Joseph.*

The death of Homer Van Meter, slain while running from police in St. Paul, made headlines throughout the country. The bandit's sheet-covered body attracted a large crowd (above) before it was taken to the morgue, where an autopsy revealed his slender frame had been punctured by twenty-six buckshot slugs and a single machine-gun bullet—and that all of the entry wounds were in the back. • Nelson and his most faithful companion, John Paul Chase (left), looked like respectable businessmen while on the lam from the law. .

It was at the Lake Como Inn on Lake Geneva, Wisconsin, owned by Hobart Hermanson, that Nelson, Helen, and John Paul Chase (below left) encountered FBI agents, who initially mistook them for the returning Hermansons. The agents couldn't give chase because their car was in town, so they called their Chicago office, which dispatched two carloads of agents to intercept Nelson on the Northwest Highway, leading to the gun battle on the northern outskirts of Barrington, Illinois, in which Nelson and Chase killed FBI agents Herman Hollis (below center) and Samuel Cowley (below right). • Among the weapons used by Nelson during his criminal escapades was an Army Colt .45 automatic (right) with Thompson-type foregrip, compensator, and extended magazine, modified to fire full-automatic by San Antonio gunsmith Hyman Lebman.

The Ford sedan used by Nelson and John Paul Chase in the "battle of Barrington" attracted a large crowd of spectators (above). Many seemed to admire the bullet holes in the windshield made by Chase, who fired a Monitor rifle from the back seat at fleeing Special Agents William Ryan and Thomas McDade before agents Herman Hollis and Samuel Cowley pursued the outlaws' bullet-damaged vehicle to North Park, where Hollis was killed and Cowley and Nelson were mortally wounded. Newsreels of the day delighted in showing the site of the shootout (below), after which Nelson managed to transfer his weapons, wife, and Chase into the FBI car and reach the town of Wilmette, Illinois, where he died.

John Paul Chase drove
Nelson and Helen to a
house at 1627 Walnut
Street in Wilmette,
Illinois, (right), where
the baby-faced outlaw
died. Nelson's nude,
blanket-wrapped corpse
was found the morning
of November 28, 1934,
in a shallow ditch at the
southwest corner of
Niles Street and Long
Avenue in the Chicago
suburb of Niles Center
(now Wilmette) next to
St. Paul's Cemetery.

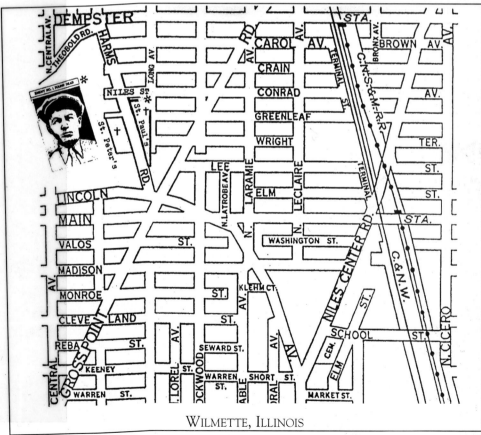

WILMETTE, ILLINOIS

Law enforcement officials were eager to be photographed with Nelson's body, which was taken to a mortuary in Niles Center (*above*) and was also briefly put on public display.
• Chicago newspapers trumpeted the news of Baby Face's demise (*right*), each taking a slightly different approach to the story. • While Nelson was lying in the morgue, his wife was being heralded by the press as the nation's first female public enemy (*below*).

On Saturday, December 1, 1934, more than 200 people crowded into Sadowski's funeral home, barely a third of them able to squeeze inside the chapel where Nelson was laid out in a silver-gray casket. Forty mourners braved the icy wind at St. Joseph's Cemetery (left), where the slain outlaw was interred beside his father in the Gillis family plot (above). Mary Gillis sobbed throughout the otherwise quiet service and at its conclusion collapsed into the arms of her son-in-law, Robert Fitzsimmons (left, with hat). At far left is mortician Phillip Sadowski.

• Melvin Purvis (below left) was hounded from the bureau in 1935 by Director J. Edgar Hoover because of the celebrity he achieved after the killing of Dillinger. Unable to find another job in law enforcement, he finally was hired to promote consumer products and regained prominence as the chief of the Post Toasties Junior G-Men.

Purvis immediately phoned his office and instructed his secretary, Doris Lockerman, to have all available agents report at once to the Bankers' Building. He also chartered two planes, specifying that they be fueled and ready to depart within the hour. Next Purvis spoke to his director in Washington. Hoover told him to contact the St. Paul office to arrange for additional manpower to meet them in Rhinelander.

The SAC dutifully followed orders, realizing that the call would ensure the presence of FBI Assistant Director Hugh Clegg and Inspector Rorer. Both outranked Purvis and would take command of the assault on the lodge. Twice before, Purvis had airlifted his agents while in pursuit of Dillinger. The first time took them to Pennsylvania, where they determined the lead was false. Just three days earlier the Chicago agents had flown to Sault Ste. Marie but had arrived too late. Hoover apparently felt Purvis needed all the help he could get on his latest mission.

After Purvis's call Clegg and Rorer organized their forces. SAC Hanni and three men departed by car for what would be a seven-hour trip, assuming the roads were in good shape and uncongested. Clegg, Rorer, and three agents proceeded to the airport, where they negotiated a charter rate of thirty-five cents for each of the 187 air miles to Rhinelander.

By the time the St. Paul agents were airborne, Purvis was just arriving at his office, the usually impeccably attired southerner entering with his tie and shoelaces unknotted. Most of the agents were similarly disheveled, having been pulled off stakeouts or summoned from home. Purvis briefed them as they gathered weapons, ammunition, steel-reinforced vests, and tear-gas equipment.

It took a full hour to reach the airport, where a pair of twin-engine aircraft awaited them. Told their destination, the two pilots confessed they had never before flown to Rhinelander and began checking road maps to plot their course. Each plane could accommodate just six passengers. The G-Men were allowed to carry their weapons but were forbidden to bring the tear-gas shells aboard. Purvis quickly chose eleven agents to accompany him and sent the rest, and the tear gas, by car.

Once they were off the ground Purvis checked his watch. It was after 3 P.M. The pilots estimated a three-hour flight, meaning the St. Paul agents would arrive a couple of hours ahead of them. Clegg could secure some vehicles and be ready when the Chicago planes landed. Hopefully Dillinger and his cronies at Little Bohemia—a ninety-minute drive from Rhinelander—would stay put until the government forces got there.

❋ ❋ ❋

Nelson and Carroll returned from their scouting expedition by mid-afternoon and found the lodge beginning to fill with local patrons. Each Sunday the

Wanatkas and their small staff served dinner for a dollar, usually handling between fifty and a hundred customers from 4 to 7 P.M. Nan's roast duck and liver dumpling soup was the overwhelming favorite with the crowd. Once their two comrades were back, the gang members sat down to an early supper and ordered steaks again.

Dillinger handed Wanatka $500, announcing that Nelson, Carroll, and their gals planned to spend the night. The rest, including himself, were preparing to leave that evening once Reilly returned. Wanatka relayed the news to his wife who, in turn, urgently shared it with Ruth Voss when she stopped by to check on her. Ruth quickly set out for Rhinelander to tell her husband of the change in plans.

After supper Nelson and his wife took a stroll through the woods. Later Baby Face joined Carroll in the bar, where they had spent more time than the other outlaws and were greatly appreciated by Bazo and Traube for their lavish tips. Traube, who was bartending that evening, had developed a special rapport with Nelson after telling the outlaw he was originally from River Grove. They discovered they knew some of the same people, including garage owner Howard Davis. Traube had briefly worked for the Touhys, driving trucks of bootleg beer for the brothers. "He (Nelson) had some bitter comments about the dirty tricks the feds were using to nail Tommy and Roger," Traube said later. "Most of the time he was easygoing, a very likable kind of guy. We talked for hours about cars."

Sharply attired as usual in a tan suede jacket, Nelson mixed freely with husky lumberjacks and CCC workers, drifting through the bar, buying drinks, trading jokes, and listening to stories of hunting and fishing. After a while he sat at a table and asked Bazo for a slice of Mrs. Wanatka's apple pie. He gobbled it down and ordered a second piece, handing the waiter a five-dollar tip. When Bazo brought him a third helping Nelson gave him another five dollars.

Hamilton, the most reclusive of the outlaws who was rarely seen except at meals, came into the bar and sat at a table alone. One patron, a burly tavern owner from Winchester, offered to buy him a drink. "Thank you," Hamilton replied, "but I don't drink."

The man grabbed the gangster by the arm and yanked him from his chair. Recalling his accident at the Santa Monica Apartments, Hamilton automatically clutched at his chest to prevent his pistol from slipping out of its holster. "Damn you," the man growled, "you'll drink with me or I'll pour it down your throat."

Observing the incident from the vestibule, a horrified Wanatka rushed over to calm the customer. Hamilton smiled and said, "This man is pretty tough. You'd better give me a small beer."

At the bar Hamilton bought a round of drinks for the man and his friends, then graciously purchased four tickets to a benefit dance the following Saturday. After several minutes and only a few sips of beer, he politely asked to be excused.

Dillinger and Van Meter entered and ordered drinks. The five outlaws briefly sat together, speaking in low voices. Nelson and Carroll decided to remain one more night so they could re-visit a local bank during business hours. Dillinger, however, didn't want to consider another robbery at the moment; he could only think about reaching St. Paul to free Billie. Although eager to set up their next score, neither Nelson nor Carroll pressed the matter.

About six o'clock Dillinger and Hamilton retired to the parlor, where the windows offered a better view of the parking area as they awaited Reilly's arrival. Behind the lodge the sun started to set over Little Star Lake.

※ ※ ※

About the time the gang was ordering dinner, the plane carrying the St. Paul agents touched down at Rhinelander. Hugh Clegg, the big, square-shouldered assistant director, was approached by three men who inquired if they were government officers. Once Clegg flashed his federal badge the group withdrew to a picnic area near the woods. Henry Voss recounted Nan's story claiming Dillinger and "a group of thugs" had taken over the resort and were holding the Wanatkas and their employees as virtual captives.

Inspector Rorer, smaller and more polished than Clegg, displayed photos of Dillinger and his known associates. LaPorte, who had seen only a couple of the guests (Van Meter twice and Reilly once), was unable to identify anyone. At Clegg's urging, Voss drew a rough diagram of the lodge showing the surrounding grounds and outside structures. Although trying to be thorough, Voss left out several key features, including a waist-high ditch to the south of the main building, a barbed wire fence on the north, and—most critical of all—the narrow stretch of shoreline below the steep bank at the rear. The omission led Clegg to believe that the close proximity of the lake would make any escape out the back of the lodge impossible. Voss also neglected to mention the Wanatkas' two dogs.

Clegg and two agents went into town to find vehicles. They spoke to the manager of a Ford dealership who said he wasn't licensed to rent cars. When Clegg explained they were federal officers on a crucial case and needed transportation, the manager asked, "You boys looking for Dillinger?"

"Well who isn't?" Clegg responded with a half-smile, adding that he wasn't at liberty to disclose their assignment. The manager conceded he had one coupe available at the moment, and two more currently being shown by salesmen would be available in a couple of hours.

By the time Clegg returned to the airfield the two planes from Chicago were approaching. It had been a torturous three-hour flight for the twelve agents, Purvis in particular. Choppy weather had tossed the aircraft so violently that even one of the pilots had become nauseous. Even so, the SAC, his stomach

215

churning and his shirt soaked with perspiration, had kept pressing for greater speed. When the plane carrying Purvis touched down in Rhinelander, a wheel brake failed, sending the aircraft into a dizzying spin across the landing strip. When it came to a halt, Purvis practically leapt from the plane, shaking and still sweating in the chilly Wisconsin twilight.

The strike force from the bureau's St. Paul and Chicago offices totaled seventeen men. As the agents unloaded their equipment, a few spectators gathered. The G-Men claimed they were part of a wedding party, a ruse that even Purvis admitted sounded absurd.

While the question of command was never discussed openly, Clegg took the lead in outlining the plan of attack on the lodge. Since the majority of the men were from Purvis's office, the assistant director allowed him a voice in all the decisions. It was agreed that the raiding party would carefully encircle the main building and that word would be sent through Voss to the Wanatkas and their employees instructing them to take cover in the basement at 4 A.M. The agents would storm the lodge at daybreak.

Voss, his son, and Special Agent Raymond Suran started back while LaPorte remained to serve as a guide for the others. Fifteen minutes later Voss reappeared, saying he had encountered his wife, daughter, and mother-in-law on the highway and had heard from them that Dillinger intended to leave shortly after supper.

The news sparked an uproar among the agents. It was already past 6:30 P.M., darkness and the temperature was falling, and Little Bohemia was fifty-five miles away. With a new sense of urgency the lawmen set about securing transportation. Purvis came across a young man named Isadore Tuchalski who had come to the airport in a souped-up Ford coupe capable of 103 mph. The SAC displayed his badge and commandeered the vehicle. The Ford dealer ultimately was able to supply the G-Men with four cars, two of them dilapidated jalopies he was unwilling to vouch for.

At seven o'clock the agents, needing a place to prepare, were allowed to gather in the Ford garage where they loaded their weapons and donned bullet-proof vests. Clegg once more went over the diagram of the resort and the plan of attack, which now called for the agents to launch their strike the moment they arrived and surrounded the place. One man was left at the airport to meet the carloads of agents coming from St. Paul and Chicago. The rest, grim and determined, piled into the five cars and at 7:20 headed for the highway.

❋ ❋ ❋

Back at Little Bohemia the supper crowd was thinning out. By 7:30 only a few customers remained, most of them congregating in the bar. Oblivious to the approaching danger, the outlaws continued to lounge about awaiting

Reilly's return. Helen and Jean, informed they would be staying another night, retired to their cabin and changed into evening wear. Mickey Conforti was upstairs packing and had donned a new green outfit for the long dark drive to St. Paul.

Nan Wanatka was heading upstairs when the phone rang. It was Ruth Voss, who had recently returned from her drive to Rhinelander. She first urged, then insisted that Nan join her at the Birchwood Lodge nearby. After promising to leave, Nan darted to her room and changed clothes. Back on the main floor, she spotted her husband talking to Eugene Boiseneau, a twenty-eight-year-old foreman at the CCC camp and native of nearby Mellen. Afraid one of the gang might overhear, Nan simply announced that she needed to visit her sister. It was exactly 8 P.M. when she drove away.

❋ ❋ ❋

The government caravan made good time over the bumpy, blacktopped two-lane highway until one of the older vehicles broke down just twenty miles from the lodge. The occupants and equipment were squeezed into the other cars. Five miles later another auto blew a tire, but Clegg, not daring to take more time or leave men behind to change the flat, ordered the eight agents to climb on the running boards of the remaining three vehicles. Once the procession resumed the men clinging to the sides of the cars, weighted down by their twenty-four-pound bulletproof vests, endured a frigid and jolting ride.

At 8:40 P.M. they halted outside the Birchwood Lodge, two miles south of Little Bohemia. Voss advised the agents that Mrs. Wanatka was safe inside his home. When she'd left a half-hour earlier, Dillinger and his pals were still at the resort. Asked to describe the remaining stretch of road, Voss said there were two curves just ahead, then almost a full mile of straight highway. The gravel entrance to the lodge was on the left.

Now within minutes of their target, Clegg ordered headlights and cigarettes extinguished. The three cars carrying the sixteen agents crept forward through the darkness.

❋ ❋ ❋

In his Washington office J. Edgar Hoover and his ever-present assistant, Clyde Tolson, awaited word of the impending raid. A small group of newsmen, all friends of the director, had joined the vigil as Hoover had coyly promised them a scoop about "a major development in the Dillinger case." Almost two hours earlier his agents had phoned from Rhinelander to report that they had obtained transportation and were set to proceed to the lodge. Brimming with confidence, Hoover confided to the cluster of journalists that his men had the Dillinger gang "trapped in a remote Wisconsin roadhouse." Confirmation of the outlaws' capture or demise should come at any moment.

❄ ❄ ❄

By 8:45 just three customers still lingered at Little Bohemia. Sitting in the bar with Eugene Boiseneau was John Morris, the fifty-nine-year-old camp cook. They had arrived earlier with a group of fellow CCC workers. After feasting on chicken dinners, the pair had wanted to remain when their companions were ready to leave. John Hoffman, a gas station operator from Mercer, had offered to provide a lift. Hoffman and Boiseneau were the same age and casual friends, having played some minor league baseball together. Boiseneau, in fact, was considered an exceptional ballplayer. All three were bachelors.

The gang members were scattered throughout the lodge. Nelson went to his cabin about the same time that his wife and Jean, growing bored and not yet ready to retire, pulled sweaters over their pajamas and scampered back to the main building, calling to Mickey to join them in a card game. Dillinger and Hamilton were upstairs. Van Meter walked into the bar and ordered a gin fizz. Carroll was either in the parlor or had possibly accompanied Nelson to the cabin.

It was almost 9 P.M. Van Meter finished his drink and was leaving the bar when Bazo and Traube noticed the two dogs tied out front were barking. No one paid much attention; the collies were always growling or yelping at something, it seemed, and even the gang had grown accustomed to the noise over the weekend.

Hoffman downed the last of his beer—just his second that night—and told his two riders it was time to shove off. Morris was the only one drinking heavily; the short, stocky cook waddled to the bar and handed Traube a whiskey flask to fill. The trio paid for their drinks and started for the door.

❄ ❄ ❄

Minutes earlier the three cars containing the G-Men had turned into the mouth of the long, snaky driveway leading to the lodge. Clegg ordered two vehicles parked in a V across the entrance to prevent any fleeing autos from reaching the highway. A pair of agents—one armed with a shotgun, the other with a rifle—took up positions at the barricade.

The rest moved on foot toward the lodge, its brightly lit exterior 500 yards in the distance visible through a cluster of stark narrow pines. The agents, their hands numb and breath frosty in the crisp evening air, attempted to move stealthily, but with almost every step their shoes crunched gravel, sticks, or brittle pine needles.

Seeing or sensing the figures creeping through the woods, Shadow and Prince went wild. Some agents halted in their tracks, certain the gang had been tipped off by the incessant barking. After a brief interlude of confusion and hushed discussion, Clegg ordered the men to proceed. Rorer led five men to the right, flanking the lodge on the north. Five agents fanned out left to cover the south side. Clegg, Purvis, and Special Agent W. Carter Baum approached the lodge head on, moving across the open parking area.

Suddenly three men emerged from the main entrance, walking briskly to one of the parked cars. The lawmen froze, assuming that members of the gang, alerted by the dogs, were trying to escape. Two more figures appeared in the doorway at the south end of the lodge: Bazo and Traube, concerned by the dogs' unusually persistent barking, had decided to investigate. As they stepped onto the small porch three agents covering the south side stepped out of the darkness, each aiming a submachine gun at the pair.

"Stick 'em up!" one shouted. The waiters instantly obeyed.

Clegg, Purvis, Baum, and several agents on the right began to close in on the first three men. But it was too late. With the collies still barking furiously behind them, the trio reached Hoffman's 1933 Chevrolet coupe. Hoffman slipped behind the wheel while Boiseneau climbed in beside him, followed by Morris. By the time the agents began yelling "Stop" and "Surrender" Hoffman had started the motor and switched on the radio, drowning out their shouts.

As the car began to move, Traube called out from the porch, "Don't shoot! Those are customers of ours!"

Hoffman had driven just a few yards when at least three agents with machine guns and one with a shotgun opened fire. "It was just like a big windstorm," Hoffman recalled. Windows exploded around the hapless occupants. Hoffman stomped on the brakes and threw himself out the door, clutching his right arm where a bullet had struck an inch above the elbow. His face and arms had been cut by glass and another bullet had gouged his right leg. The gas station operator ran for the woods north of the lodge, blindly bowling over an agent who stepped in his path.

Moments later Morris flung open the coupe's passenger door and tumbled out. Two machine gun slugs had smashed into his right shoulder and a pair of buckshot pellets were embedded in his right hip. He tried to stand, reeled drunkenly, then slumped back against the side of the Chevy. As Clegg watched, the man yanked an object from his back pocket. The AD was set to shoot until he saw Morris take a huge gulp from a metal flask.

Behind the wounded cook his fellow CCC worker lay motionless. With bullets in his chest and skull, Eugene Boiseneau had died instantly. The Chevy's motor continued to sputter, its headlights blazing and radio blaring.

Within seconds of the first shots, bursts of gunfire erupted all over the grounds. "The men were all out of control," one FBI memo stated. Convinced they were under attack by gangsters inside the lodge or attempting to escape through their ranks, some agents fired indiscriminately at shadows or figures (either real or imagined) behind the windows of the lodge.

Any actual exchange of gunfire between agents and outlaws was brief. In his book *American Agent*, penned two years later, Purvis claimed there had been intense, sustained gunfire from the lodge's roof and second-story windows. But Clegg, who was standing near or next to Purvis the entire time, made no mention of any such shooting in his official report submitted to Hoover three days after the raid. Wanatka, embittered by the actions of the "trigger-happy G-Men," later insisted that none of the gang had taken the time to do any shooting, at least not from inside his home. Once the fireworks started, "the boys cleared out right away."

Dillinger and Hamilton, armed only with pistols, slipped out a second-story window at the rear of the lodge. The pair scrambled over a small slanted roof above the dining room, then leapt into a three-foot-high snowbank. They were closely followed by Van Meter, who had grabbed the only machine gun available. (The gang's other six machine guns, along with their bulletproof vests and most of their possessions were packed in their two vehicles—another reason the outlaws didn't waste time shooting back.)

As Van Meter crawled across the roof he spotted two armed men—Inspector Rorer and another agent—coming around the right side of the building. The bandit paused to fire a few quick shots at the pair, driving them behind a tree. A moment later Rorer saw a shadowy figure jump from the roof. The inspector and his companion moved in, spraying the area with their Tommyguns. When they found no sign of Van Meter, Rorer mistakenly assumed the gangster had darted back into the lodge. Actually, he had slid down the steep embankment and joined Dillinger and Hamilton at the edge of the lake. The trio headed north over the icy rocks along the narrow strip of shoreline.

Baby Face Nelson was probably the only gang member not inside the main building when the raid began. The little desperado easily could have slipped away into the woods around his cabin—but evidently that wasn't his style, or at least not his initial reaction to the attack. Armed with his machine-gun pistol and a standard .45, he dashed out the cabin's front door blasting at the raiders.

Purvis was intently watching the main building when he suddenly realized he was being fired upon. A bullet struck the ground a yard from his right foot, and two more slugs chewed into a tree directly behind him. Spotting the muzzle flash of a weapon on his right, the agent turned and fired his machine gun at "a short, slender figure fleeing toward the woods." The weapon jammed after a quick burst, so Purvis dropped the machine gun, drew his .38, and frantically fired several shots.

At that moment Rorer, fresh from trading shots with Van Meter, was returning to the front lawn when he saw "one man running around the edge of one of the cabins and that the man was firing . . . in the direction of Mr. Purvis. . . ." Rorer opened up with his machine gun, strafing the ground near Nelson's feet. Finding himself under fire from both sides, Baby Face scrambled to the back of the lodge. This time the inspector was correct in assuming the gunman had taken cover inside.

Joining Purvis and Clegg in front of the lodge, Rorer reported the rear of the building was sealed off and that at least two gangsters were trapped inside. Actually, the south end wasn't covered—the agents assigned to flank the building on that side had toppled into the ditch while groping through the darkness and had withdrawn once the shooting began.

As the three lawmen discussed their next move, the wounded Morris, still clutching his flask, stood and staggered away from the Chevy. Agents ordered him to throw up his hands, identifying themselves as federal officers, but Morris either didn't hear or didn't believe them. His pace was so sluggish and awkward that Clegg, seeing the man was hurt or drunk or both, shouted at his men to hold their fire. The cook veered toward the garage where he sat down or fell, then took another swig of whiskey. Seconds later he rose again, this time lurching to the resort's main entrance and vanishing inside.

The instant the agents had unleashed their deadly attack on the Chevy, Bazo and Traube retreated into the lodge and, in Bazo's words, "ran like hell to the basement." They were joined there by Wanatka and the three gangster girls. Thinking it was a holdup, Bazo hid his wallet, fat with over fifty dollars in tips from the outlaws, in the coal bin. The girls, according to Wanatka, "were nervous and cried." Huddled in the darkened cellar the six listened to the roar of gunfire outside the lodge. About five minutes into the battle, they heard heavy footsteps on the floor above them, then a raspy voice speaking directly overhead. Morris had dragged himself to the kitchen phone and dialed Alvin Koerner, operator of the local telephone exchange.

"Alvin," the caller gasped. "It's Johnny Morris. I'm at Emil's. Somebody's held up the place. Boiseneau's dead and everybody's knocked out." He dropped the receiver and collapsed.

Wanatka heard the man fall and started upstairs. Still hearing "machine guns spraying," he returned and asked the others to help him with Morris. His two employees advised him to wait until the shooting stopped. One of the girls said, "If you want to give him help, you help him. We're staying here."

Morris, meanwhile, had staggered to his feet and was moving around the interior of the lodge. Removing the money from the cash register to save it from the "robbers," he hobbled into the men's room behind the bar. As he sagged against a wall beside the toilet, slipping in and out of consciousness, Morris noticed a young man peering down at him. The man said nothing, and the cook was too weak to speak. Later, when shown photos of the Dillinger gang, Morris picked out Nelson as the man he had glimpsed.

After shooting his way past the agents stationed at the north end of the lodge, Baby Face had managed to find a way inside the besieged building, probably hoping to link up with his comrades, possibly searching for Helen. Finding only the bleeding, semi-conscious cook, he realized that the others had fled and he was on his own. He quickly but quietly crept out the back. Knowing there were lawmen on the right, Nelson turned left and worked his way to the edge of the lake, the last of the five bandits to leave and the only one to make his escape to the south.

Carroll, like Nelson, was fleeing alone but heading the opposite way, no more than a minute or two behind Dillinger, Hamilton, and Van Meter. Carroll might have been with Nelson in the cabin when the agents arrived and, instead of charging out the front door like his friend, decided to make a more discreet exit out the rear. Or possibly he was in another part of the lodge—downstairs while the others were on the second floor.

Trotting along the lake, Carroll spied a figure at the water's edge and cautiously approached. Thinking it might be Hamilton, he called out, "Is that you, Red?"

It was John Hoffman, shot, scared, and still reeling from the attack and his mad dash through the timber, not sure what to say to the stranger. Receiving no answer, Carroll moved on.

While the main body of agents assaulted the lodge, the pair stationed at the blockade saw some action of their own. Reilly and his traveling companion, returning from their overnight trip to the Twin Cities and running late, had turned into the entrance just minutes after the shooting commenced. Reilly hit the brakes the instant he saw the obstructing vehicles and the two armed men bathed in his headlights.

Special Agent Samuel Hardy ordered the occupants to step out, hands in the air. Reilly threw the Ford into reverse, spraying the agents with dust and gravel. The lawmen opened fire. Buckshot shattered the window beside a shrieking Pat Cherrington while a rifle slug punctured the car's right rear tire. Reilly switched off the headlights as the Ford squealed away from the scene, heading back the way it had come.

Despite the flat, Reilly gunned the motor and drove on the rim all the way to Mercer where he pulled into a service station. The owner, Robert Collins, replaced the tire and filled the tank, the work taking more than a half-hour. The two Pats, both appearing nervous, drank soda pop and kept glancing down the highway—but the agents had not pursued them. After paying Collins and asking about the quickest route to St. Paul, the two drove off. Later that night their car bogged down on a washed out road and had to be pulled out by a farmer's tractor. When Reilly finally reached his home, almost twenty-four hours after the harrowing escape, he swore to his wife he was finished with the Dillinger gang.

Back at Little Bohemia, Clegg called a cease-fire. Since the opening volleys, the agents scattered throughout the grounds had fired sporadically for a full fifteen minutes, still believing the gang was cornered inside the lodge. Leaving Purvis to hold down the front, Clegg directed Rorer to inspect the guards to the south while the AD personally checked the men on the north, making certain the building was secured and completely surrounded.

Purvis, meanwhile, instructed Special Agent Jay C. Newman to drive to the Birchwood Lodge and phone the agent in Rhinelander. Newman was to relay details of the raid—that some gangsters had been shot, wounded and possibly killed, while the rest were trapped inside and unable to escape. (The agent in Rhinelander passed along Purvis's optimistic and unverified version to Hoover, prompting the director to prematurely boast to reporters that his men had successively smashed the Dillinger gang.) Newman also was to tell the agent to make sure the agents arriving by car received clear directions and urge them to proceed with great haste since nothing more could be done at the lodge until tear gas arrived. Almost as an afterthought, Newman was told to notify local law enforcement officials that federal agents were conducting a raid in their area.

A small, slim, devout Mormon who wore wire-framed glasses, Newman asked if an agent might accompany him. Baum volunteered to ride along. The pair left in Tuchalski's souped-up Ford coupe.

❋ ❋ ❋

Standing outside his home less than a mile from Little Bohemia, George LaPorte listened to the distant crackle of gunfire. He was anxious to act but promised his family not to get involved. Shortly after the shooting tapered off, his phone rang. It was Alvin Koerner excitedly reporting the desperate call from Morris claiming he had been shot by robbers at Wanatka's resort.

Grabbing a rifle, LaPorte jumped in his Ford sedan and raced to the CCC camp a quarter-mile north of his house. He told the camp physician, Dr. S. M. Roberts, and the stationmaster, C. J. Christianson, about the trouble at Little Bohemia and the likely need for medical aid. The pair looked skeptical at LaPorte's mention of Dillinger but agreed it was their duty to offer assistance. Christianson rode with LaPorte; the doctor followed in the camp ambulance.

As they drove south on Highway 51, LaPorte spotted a tall man on the side of the highway urgently waving his arms at the vehicles. Neither stopped, LaPorte remarking to Christianson that it was no time to pick up hitchhikers.

The tall man was Van Meter, hoping to flag down a motorist while Dillinger and Hamilton kept out of sight. Eventually they darted across the highway to a roadside resort owned by seventy-year-old Edward J. Mitchell. When the innkeeper's ailing wife answered their knock on the door, the three strangers pushed their way inside.

"I'm Dillinger," the leader announced as Hamilton ripped out the phone line. "The government is after me and I need your car." He was polite and apologetic, once rebuking Van Meter for using profanity, but he insisted the elderly couple accompany them outside. When Mitchell complained that his wife had influenza, Dillinger draped a blanket over her shoulders and promised the couple they would not be harmed.

The Mitchells' car was an old Model-A Ford that had not been started since the previous fall. The outlaws noticed a Ford coupe parked beside a cottage belonging to Robert Johnson, a young carpenter. The Mitchells were ordered to stand beside their house while the gunman pounded on Johnson's door until he answered. He was forced to drive the trio away and headed west on an old country road. Fifty miles later the outlaws gave Johnson seven dollars and set him free.

Meanwhile, Carroll had emerged from the woods farther north than the others. He walked along the highway to Manitowish Waters, more than a mile from Little Bohemia, before spying a Packard sedan parked by the Northern Lights Resort on the southwest tip of Rice Lake. Henry Kuhnert, owner of the lodge and the Packard, rushed outside upon hearing the vehicle start, evidently hot-wired by Carroll. After watching his car vanish into the night, Kuhnert went back inside and phoned the local constable.

It was now a few minutes past 10 P.M. and Nelson, tramping through the woods between Little Star Lake and Highway 51 in the opposite direction, was the only gang member still on foot.

❋ ❋ ❋

Forty minutes after Clegg ordered a cease-fire, the agents finally decided to investigate the Chevy, which had been idling in the parking lot since the agents' opening volley had torn into it. "Although quite dark," one report reads, "the Agents were able to dimly discern that the figure of the remaining occupant of the automobile did not move. . . . Inspector W. A. Rorer crept up to the car, examined the body of Boiseneau, found it to be dead, turned off the radio and motor of the automobile and returned."

Minutes later the car's owner reappeared from his hiding place in the forest, sheepishly calling out, "Is it all over?" Despite his painful, bleeding arm Hoffman was able to obey the command to raise his hands as agents surrounded him. He identified himself and insisted he was not a criminal. One agent gruffly frisked him and inquired, "Why did you run from us then?"

"Because you were shooting at me," Hoffman answered.

Only now did it begin to dawn on the G-Men that they had fired on a carload of innocent civilians. LaPorte and Christianson, followed by Dr. Roberts, arrived at the resort and were challenged by the two armed sentries to prove their identities before being allowed to pass. They immediately verified

Hoffman's claims, and as the doctor tended to the wounded man, LaPorte asked permission to go inside the lodge to check on his brother-in-law and anyone else who might need assistance. The agents refused.

The six people huddled in the cellar listened to the ominous silence for nearly a half-hour before Wanatka, this time joined by his two waiters, ventured upstairs. They found the dangling phone receiver, but Morris was nowhere in sight. Carefully avoiding the windows, Bazo and Traube followed a trail of crimson spatters into the restroom where they discovered the bloody, groaning cook beside the toilet. Traube fetched some bar rags, which they pressed against Morris's bullet-torn shoulder and hip.

Wanatka phoned Koerner but was interrupted by a third party claiming to be a federal officer. It was Special Agent Newman, in the process of making his calls from the Birchwood Lodge when he intercepted their conversation on the party line. He advised Wanatka to step outside at once with his hands raised.

After relaying the agent's instructions to the others, Wanatka led the way out, hands in the air and shouting to the G-Men to hold their fire. The waiters, supporting Morris on either side, followed. The agents kept the quartet "constantly covered" until they reached Purvis, who searched each one despite LaPorte's repeated assurances that he knew them.

Wanatka took an instant dislike to Purvis, who bombarded him with questions about the gangsters still inside: How many were there? What rooms were they holed up in? What were their names, physical characteristics, and how many guns did they have?

The lodge owner reported there were just three young women hiding in his basement. He was certain the gang had escaped.

"Did you see them run off?" Purvis asked.

"I was too busy running myself," was the reply.

"We know for a fact some of Dillinger's men are still in there," snapped Purvis, refusing to believe otherwise. When he insinuated the owner might be aiding the outlaws, Wanatka argued that it was he who was responsible—at least partially—for tipping off the government men.

❄ ❄ ❄

While making his calls to Rhinelander and the Vilas County Sheriff's department at Eagle River, Newman overheard another conversation. This time the owner of the Northern Lights resort was informing the local constable that his Packard had been stolen. After discussing the matter with Baum, both agreed the theft was likely the work of gangsters fleeing from Little Bohemia and decided to investigate.

The pair jumped in the Ford coupe and raced over the three miles of highway to the village, passing Little Bohemia along the way. They were directed to the home of Constable Carl C. Christensen, who had obtained a description and the license number of the Packard.

Newman and Baum took the constable into their confidence, telling him about the raid on the Wanatka resort and the possibility that several of the gang might have escaped from the lodge. They invited him along to help with local law officers in setting up roadblocks throughout the area.

"Hell, I'll ride along," he answered. A lanky, good-natured man of thirty-two, Christensen was a recently married carpenter from Racine who had moved to Manitowish Waters two years earlier and been elected constable just two weeks prior. He strapped on his shoulder holster containing a Smith & Wesson .38 revolver, then pulled on a sheepskin jacket as he squeezed into the coupe with the two agents. They headed back to the Birchwood Lodge. It was almost 10:40 P.M.

❋ ❋ ❋

When Baby Face Nelson finally found his way out of the dense woods as he neared Manitowish Lake, he had covered slightly over a mile in about ninety minutes. Looking to his right, he saw the lights of a lakeside house belonging to Mr. and Mrs. Paul W. Lang.

Normally on a Sunday evening after ten o'clock, the Langs would have been in bed. But the couple had heard the chatter of gunfire earlier from Little Bohemia, and when Lang, a big man with glasses, attempted to phone someone, he had overheard part of John Morris' frantic call to Koerner.

At 10:45 Lang looked up from a letter he was writing when their dog began to bark. A young man, well dressed and hatless, suddenly entered through the front door clutching a .45 automatic. "Now don't get excited," Nelson told the startled couple. "I won't harm you, but this is a matter of life and death. Do what I say and everything will be all right."

The intruder ordered them to put on their coats, saying they were all going for a ride. As Lang and his wife obeyed, Nelson put away his pistol and sat on the sofa, petting the dog. When Mrs. Lang began to cry, Baby Face fished a thick roll of bills from his pocket and declared, "I'm not gonna hurt either of you, and I'll pay you well. But I need your help to get away."

The woman continued to sob and made no move toward the door. Finally Nelson drew his pistol again and snarled, "Quit whining and start walking!"

He marched the couple out to their car, a 1932 Chevrolet, opened the back door for Mrs. Lang, and instructed her husband to drive. As Nelson hopped in beside him, Lang started the motor, but before they reached the highway the headlights flickered, faded, and then failed completely. Lang offered to check under the hood if allowed to return home for a flashlight. "Forget it!" Nelson snapped. "Just keep going."

Barely able to pick his way through the blackness, Lang swung his vehicle onto the highway, turning south at Nelson's command.

❋ ❋ ❋

While the government forces remained encamped around his lodge, Wanatka and his two waiters, all three hatless and in short sleeves, found themselves shivering. The owner asked permission to retrieve some jackets from the bar, but Purvis said that was "out of the question."

LaPorte offered to drive them to the Birchwood Lodge for some coats. As they piled into his car, Purvis hurried over to raise an objection. Tiring of the SAC's obstinacy and growing colder by the moment, Wanatka answered him with profanity. A heated argument erupted between the tiny G-Man with the squeaky southern drawl and the big Bohemian with the thick Germanic accent. Finally Purvis agreed but insisted that an agent take down the name and address of each individual before he could leave.

Once the information was recorded, Wanatka, trembling more from rage than from the cold, climbed in beside his brother-in-law. Christianson chose to ride along, joining Bazo and Traube in the back. Wanatka suggested that they stop first at Koerner's house, just a mile and a half away on the shore of Spider Lake. He was sure Koerner could provide some warm clothing, and he was eager to use Alvin's phone to contact the sheriff, intending to complain about Purvis and his army of G-Men.

❋ ❋ ❋

Creeping through the inky darkness without headlights at a ponderous yet perilous speed of 15 to 20 mph was hardly the style of escape Nelson would have preferred. The Langs' vehicle had traveled only a short distance when he noticed a brightly lit house on the left side of the highway. He ordered Lang to stop, then back up. "Who's house is that?" the outlaw asked.

"Alvin Koerner and his family live there," Lang replied.

Nelson instructed his hostage to pull onto the shoulder and park. The nervous couple were directed to get out. "You're going to get me inside," he announced, herding them across the highway with his .45. "Remember I'm keeping you covered."

The sound of the Langs' car drew Koerner and his wife to the front-room window of their white two-story house. Koerner immediately phoned the Birchwood Lodge hoping to catch the government man who had been there earlier. Newman, having just returned, took the call. Koerner anxiously reported that a suspicious vehicle without headlights had stopped along Highway 51 directly across from his home. He urged Newman to send a man at once to investigate.

227

Seconds after Koerner hung up there was a knock at the door. "It's a man and a woman," Mrs. Koerner observed, peering out the window. Her husband asked, "Who is it?"

The Langs identified themselves and asked to be admitted. When Koerner opened the door Nelson entered right behind the couple and sharply directed Koerner to step back, waving his pistol menacingly. The little gunman closed the door and ordered both couples to sit down.

❋ ❋ ❋

Special Agent Baum and Constable Christensen had remained in the coupe while Newman ran inside the Birchwood Lodge. He returned within minutes, "all fired up," according to Christensen, and told them of the mystery car lurking outside the Koerner home.

Newman slipped behind the wheel and they were off. It was a tight squeeze for the trio pressed shoulder to shoulder in the coupe's front seat, both agents still wearing their bulky steel-reinforced vests. Baum, seated in the middle, was a tall, husky, handsome man of twenty-nine who epitomized Hoover's ideal for his special agents. A graduate of George Washington University, Baum briefly had practiced law in Virginia before joining the bureau on June 30, 1930. He was transferred to the Chicago office two years later, bringing with him his wife, Mary, a preacher's daughter. When Purvis was appointed SAC six months later, Baum became his closest, most trusted agent—and a good friend.

"Everyone liked Carter Baum," recalled Doris Lockerman, Purvis's secretary, who described him as "a gentle giant." His soft-spoken, easygoing manner was refreshing in the often tense office, and his "infinite patience" allowed him to focus on tedious assignments, mountains of paperwork, and hours of interrogating suspects and witnesses that other agents could not handle. Since moving to Chicago Baum had become the father of two daughters—Margaret, age two, and Edith, eleven months.

As they sped down Highway 51 toward the Koerner house, Newman's excitement proved infectious. Christensen described the atmosphere inside the car as "hell-a-whooping." The constable twice had to caution Newman to slow down. Each man felt ready for action. All three wore sidearms—Newman, in fact, carried two, a .45 automatic and a .38 revolver. Baum held a machine gun.

❋ ❋ ❋

The desperate young man with the gun wanted Koerner and his wife to drive him away in their car. He claimed he needed to get to Woodruff, some thirty miles south on 51, and once he met his friends there he promised to release the couple unharmed.

The Koerners protested that their two children were upstairs asleep and refused to leave them. Unknown to Nelson, Flora Robbins, who operated the switchboard and roomed with the family, was at that moment behind a closed door a few feet away, listening to the stranger's demands. Baby Face advised the couple to calm down and allow the Langs to look after the children. He was suddenly interrupted by the sound of an approaching car. "Nobody move!" he warned, stepping to the nearest window.

LaPorte parked his sedan by the gate leading to the Koerners' front porch. Christianson remained in the back seat while the others—Wanatka and his two waiters following LaPorte—hurried toward the house. As LaPorte recalled, "We were all running on account of the cold. We barely reached the porch when the front door was opened and we all crowded inside." He saw "a short man with light brown hair" standing behind the door with a pistol. Bazo, entering right behind LaPorte, said, "Hi, Jimmie."

"Skip the bullshit and get in here," Nelson threw back. He gestured to the wall. "Line up over there where I can see you, and do it quick. I mean business."

Wanatka acted appalled. "What are you doing with these people, Jimmie? They're friends of mine."

Nelson didn't seem impressed. He asked if anyone else was in the car. In the excitement of the moment Wanatka forgot about Christianson and replied, "No one's out there."

"Are you sure there's no G-Men out there?"

"No, Jimmie, no one," the lodge owner insisted.

Addressing his eight hostages, Nelson said, "I want everybody to take it easy. I only want to get away. But don't think I won't kill anyone who doesn't do what I say."

He announced that he was taking the sedan and selected Wanatka and the Koerners to accompany him. When Mrs. Koerner cried, "I can't leave my children!" Nelson agreed to let her remain, then ordered her husband and Wanatka to lead the way. At the door Wanatka held back, complaining, "It's cold as hell out there and I got no coat."

Baby Face prodded him with the pistol. "I'm getting out of here and you're going with me."

Christianson still occupied the right side of the car's back seat, LaPorte's rifle resting near his right leg. He later recounted, "I saw three men come out . . . and recognized immediately the voice of Emil Wanatka. When they got to the car, Emil was ordered to get into the driver's seat and to start the car. . . . Koerner was ordered into the rear seat, where I was sitting. The man who did the commanding was dressed in a brown suede jacket. He went around to the front of the car and entered it on the right side and seated himself beside Wanatka, who was already behind the wheel. I heard Wanatka say to him, 'Jimmie, I have no keys for this car.'"

Christianson apparently drew no notice from Nelson, who was busy barking at Wanatka and jabbing him with the gun. The lodge owner, declaring he was nervous and unsure whether he could operate the vehicle, pleaded with Nelson to stop poking him.

"Put that switch on," Nelson directed. When the motor failed to turn over, Wanatka anxiously stomped on the gas pedal. Baby Face was livid. "You're flooding the damn thing!"

As he coped with the stubborn engine and the volatile Nelson, Wanatka spied a pair of headlights in the mirror. The car stopped along the highway near the Langs' Chevrolet. Christianson also noticed the vehicle, but while his left hand clutched the barrel of LaPorte's rifle, he was too terrified to raise the weapon.

❈ ❈ ❈

Newman eased the coupe onto the shoulder and examined the abandoned vehicle illuminated by its headlights. Christensen, who knew the Langs but not their car, said he didn't recognize it.

"Get your pencil and paper out," Newman told Baum. Once Baum had jotted down the license number, Newman turned into the Koerners' driveway. The house "was lit up like a church," Christensen recalled, "but we couldn't see a soul around anywhere. I thought that was damned funny."

By now Nelson had spotted the car, too. "Who are these guys?" he asked in an irritated hiss, glaring over his right shoulder as the coupe slowly drew closer. Wanatka and Koerner each swore they had no idea. At that moment Wanatka felt the gun removed from his ribs and assumed Baby Face was taking aim at the other vehicle. Actually Nelson, evidently smelling danger, was making a switch—slipping the .45 back into its shoulder holster and taking out the machine-gun pistol.

As the coupe's headlights swept across the sedan parked in front of the gate, Constable Christensen announced, "I think that's George LaPorte's car."

"Let's see," said Newman. Beside him Baum still held the pencil and paper, his machine gun resting on his lap with the safety on. Newman pulled alongside the sedan, rolled down his window, and called, "Hold on there. We're federal officers."

The words were still coming out of the agent's mouth when Nelson sprang from the car and shoved his weapon into the open window. "I know who you are," he snarled at the stunned trio. "A bunch of fucking government cops with vests on. I can give it to you bastards high and low."

"He was on us with the gun before we could move," Christensen said later. "The little jackrabbit flew right out of nowhere. Our car wasn't even stopped when his gun came through the window." In the next frantic few seconds

Christensen got a good look at the weapon, which he described as "a .45 Colt converted into a machine gun, with a long clip and a pistol grip."

As Nelson "cursed us horribly" Christensen attempted to draw his .38, but Baum was jammed so tightly against his left side that the weapon wouldn't budge. "We sat wedged in that coupe, hardly able to move, and he stood right beside the right-hand window. I tried to duck behind Baum, and he tried to duck behind Newman."

Nelson saw Newman's hand creep beneath his jacket and warned, "Don't touch that gun or I'll blow your brains out!"

Still spewing threats and profanity, Baby Face yanked open the door and growled, "Get out of that car." Newman obeyed, stepping onto the running board with his hands raised. "He talked to us and swore at us for what seemed like ages," Christensen recalled. "Then I guess some of us—I think it must have been Baum—made a move he must have thought was wrong."

Nelson's personal version of the shooting—overheard by Piquett and O'Leary a month later and told directly to Frank Cochran that summer—seemed to support Christensen's view. When "the driver" (Newman) climbed out, Nelson claimed to find himself staring into the barrel of a machine gun. "The big agent (Baum) had me cold," he later told Cochran. "I could never figure why he didn't pull the trigger on me. I should have been dead right there."

When Newman stepped out, Christensen managed to pull his revolver. But before he could use it, Nelson's weapon was booming. One of his first shots shattered the constable's right elbow, knocking the .38 from his grasp.

Newman later reported that he made a grab for the outlaw's gun the instant Nelson fired into the car. He felt a jolt of pain rocket through his skull, then lifted his head to discover he was lying in the gravel between the two cars. The agent concluded that Nelson had struck him over the head. Only later did he learn that he had been shot—the bullet, remarkably, just grazing his forehead above his right eye and traveling along his temple. Dazed, Newman began to crawl for cover, clawing inside his coat for one his pistols.

As Newman crumpled off the running board, Christensen shoved open the passenger door. Another slug from Nelson's gun slammed into his back as he spilled from the car. Baum's machine gun fell on top on him. The wounded constable rolled aside an instant before Baum himself tumbled out, landing on his own machine gun so hard that it cracked the stock. Shot in the throat, Baum tried to stand but was weighted down by his heavy vest. He finally rose, staggered several yards to the right of the coupe, then toppled sideways over a waist-high rail fence.

Christensen regained his feet and attempted to escape. "I started to run for a woodpile," he recalled, "but I was in the headlights. I was turning back when he caught me." Nelson fired a burst of slugs that spun the constable back into the ditch. He dragged himself to where Baum's machine gun lay but was unable to release the safety. "Nelson then got into the car and continued to fire at me while I lay in the ditch. I felt three or four more bullets hit me. . . . Nelson then backed the car away and Agent Newman opened fire. I was in the line of fire, and one of his bullets hit me in the foot."

Newman emptied his .45 at the coupe as it screeched out of the driveway with enough force to spatter the side of the Koerner house with gravel. The desperado almost smashed into the Lang vehicle, swerving at the last second before shifting gears and speeding away to the south. Once the car vanished into the night, Newman grasped his throbbing head, surprised to find his glasses still in place. He dropped the .45, drew his .38, and cautiously approached LaPorte's sedan.

While Nelson was confronting the lawmen, both Wanatka and Koerner had bailed out the left side, the latter scrambling back into his home while Emil leapt behind a snowbank near the southwest side of the house. Once the shooting stopped, Wanatka, who later insisted that a bullet fired by Nelson or Newman had narrowly missed him, ran down the dark highway toward his lodge.

C. J. Christianson stayed in the sedan until Newman ordered him out "at the point of his gun." The agent kept him covered although Constable Christensen, crumpled in the ditch with nine bullet wounds, called to him, vouching for the stationmaster. Newman told Christianson, "We're going in here and get assistance for the constable and Agent Baum."

But when the pair pounded on the front door and identified themselves, the frightened group within refused to admit them. Newman went to the window and lit a match to illuminate his federal badge. LaPorte and Traube advised opening the door, but the others argued against them. "The gangsters might have killed the officers and taken their badges," warned Mrs. Koerner.

Exasperated, Newman informed Christianson he was returning to the Birchwood Lodge to get help, "and you're going with me."

"The hell I am," he replied. "I'm staying right here."

The agent jammed his pistol into Christianson's stomach and, using language unbecoming a Mormon, demanded that he accompany him. The pair drove off in LaPorte's sedan, leaving Baum and Christensen lying in the cold, black night. After falling over the fence Baum had managed to crawl almost ten yards away. The constable heard him "gasping for breath" and valiantly attempted to reach him. But after creeping a few feet Christensen could go no farther. In a matter of minutes Baum's gasping stopped.

❄ ❄ ❄

At that moment—a few minutes past 11 P.M.—the vehicle containing SAC Hanni and three St. Paul agents was racing north toward the Birchwood Lodge where, they were told in Rhinelander, Clegg had set up a contact point. Less than a mile away they noticed a car approaching at "a rather high rate of speed." There was a frantic discussion among the agents that it might be "some of the Dillinger crowd" fleeing the area.

Nelson, the driver of the southbound car, had some suspicions of his own when he saw the speeding vehicle approaching from the opposite direction. Taking no chances he accelerated and switched on the coupe's spotlight, directing the powerful beam straight at the other car's windshield. The agent at the wheel, momentarily blinded, hit the brakes and fought for control. The coupe roared past before the driver could block the highway.

Eager to reach Clegg and the main body of men, Hanni elected not to pursue the coupe, having no idea the agents were allowing the slayer of one of their own to escape. Arriving at the Birchwood Lodge, they found Newman inside, his head wound being bandaged by Ruth Voss. Dazed and shaken, the agent, along with Christianson, provided a sketchy account of the shooting outside the Koerner house. Hanni, accompanied by the CCC man and Special Agent O. G. Hall, immediately set out for "the ambush site."

✸ ✸ ✸

Running almost the entire mile and a half to Little Bohemia, Wanatka—no longer complaining about the cold—arrived back at his lodge out of breath and unable to speak. As he lumbered into the yard, several agents turned their guns on him and barked, "Throw up your hands!"

"Don't shoot!" shouted Dr. Roberts. "It's Emil Wanatka."

Between heaving breathes Wanatka told the G-Men that "Jimmie," one of Dillinger's pals, had just gunned down some of their agents down the road. Purvis calmly took out his notepad and asked him to spell his name and Manitowish.

"Are you crazy?" Wanatka exploded. "I just told you all your men are dead over at Koerner's and you ask me how to spell Manitowish? Did you come here to get Dillinger or me?"

Another heated argument flared up in which the resort owner called Purvis "the stupidest son of a bitch who ever walked the earth" and an assortment of other names. Eventually Wanatka agreed to take a pair of agents to the Koerner house in his pickup truck. After tossing some blankets and hay in the back, Inspector Rorer and Special Agent John Brennan, both carrying machine guns, climbed into the cab with Wanatka.

They reached the scene only minutes before Hanni and his two companions pulled in. Wanatka backed his pickup into the yard where Baum was sprawled facedown and lifeless. Hanni parked near the wounded constable who was sitting upright beside the ditch. Since he was alert and able to speak, they assumed

Christensen's condition was not serious. Hanni and Christianson helped him onto the car's back seat.

On the opposite side of the fence, Wanatka, Brennan, and Hall attempted to lift Baum into the pickup, but the body, still clad in the twenty-four pound armored vest, proved too heavy. When Hall called on Rorer to lend a hand, the inspector complained that he had a kink in his back and was unable to assist. By that time Traube had emerged from the house and was offering to help. It took all four men to lift Baum off the ground. They laid the big agent on the hay in the bed of the pickup and draped a blanket over him. Wanatka then drove back to his besieged lodge where Dr. Roberts officially pronounced Baum dead.

Hanni returned to the Birchwood Lodge and picked up Newman, putting him in the back seat beside the constable. They stopped at Little Bohemia to drop off the tear gas equipment and then, guided by Wanatka in his pickup (which still contained Baum's body), Hanni drove thirty-five miles north to Ironwood, Michigan. There he delivered the two wounded men to the Twin City Hospital where they joined the night's earlier casualties, Morris and Hoffman.

Only then, more than an hour after he was shot, was Christensen's grave condition discerned. Dr. M. A. Gertz was astonished he was still alive, surmising that the constable's sheepskin jacket had kept him from bleeding to death. An inventory of the damage done by Nelson's weapon (excluding the final injury from Newman's gun) revealed "2 gunshot wounds, right anterior of chest; 1 gunshot wound, left posterior of chest; 1 gunshot wound, posterior surface of right chest; 1 gunshot wound over left hip; 1 gunshot wound middle of right arm; 1 gunshot graze on left leg; 1 gunshot graze on left arm; 1 gunshot wound right foot."

The constable appeared to be beyond hope. In addition to shattering bones in his foot, right arm, and left hip, bullets had punctured his liver and both lungs. Morris also was listed in critical condition because a shotgun pellet had torn through his kidneys. Both men recovered, although Christensen was hospitalized for a full year.

Once X-rays revealed that Newman had suffered only a mild concussion, he was released. Hoffman's wounds were largely superficial, inflicted more by glass than by gunfire. Though confined to the hospital for several days, he considered himself lucky. "There were twenty-eight holes in my car, one right behind where my head had been," he later recalled.

The body of Baum was removed from Wanatka's pickup and placed on a slab in the hospital morgue beside the corpse of Boiseneau.

❀ ❀ ❀

Speeding south at the wheel of a car capable of 103 mph, Nelson seemed guaranteed of a quick, clean escape from the region and the small army of agents he was rapidly leaving behind. With six hours before daylight he had plenty of time to get far away, even out of the state. He could look for a route west and slip into the sanctuary of St. Paul or preferably, with a bit more patience, continue due south to the more familiar territory of Chicago.

The desperado, however, had little time to consider his options. Just twelve miles from the Koerner house the coupe's right front tire blew. Nelson swung left onto a county road leading to Boulder Junction, six miles east of Highway 51.

About 11:30 farmer Ellert Engstrom heard a car approaching his house "at a high rate of speed and making a great deal of noise." He glanced out his window and saw a new Ford coupe listing slightly to the right. Engstrom watched the driver direct the vehicle's spotlight onto the family car parked in the yard. Evidently the would-be thief didn't like the looks of the vehicle, or he may have noticed the farmer peering at him from the window. Whatever the reason, he quickly drove off, the flat tire thumping loudly.

Less than two miles from Boulder Junction Nelson turned south on Old River Road, probably searching for a secluded spot to change the tire. Five hundred feet later the coupe became hopelessly mired in a patch of mud.

After repeated efforts to replace the flat failed, Nelson ransacked the car for anything he could take with him. On the right side floorboard he discovered Constable Christensen's revolver. He also found a suitcase and a leather satchel belonging to the federal men. He carried these to the front of the car and examined the contents in the glare of the headlights. He pocketed some ammunition and a road map, leaving behind a pair of gas masks, a camera, and binoculars.

A city boy armed with three weapons—the machine-gun pistol, his .45, and Christensen's .38—but no sense of direction, Nelson took to the woods.

❋ ❋ ❋

As the longest night of his life drew to an end, Emil Wanatka left the dead and wounded he helped deliver to Ironwood and wearily drove his pickup through the pre-dawn gloom to his lodge, dreading another confrontation with Purvis and the inevitable questions regarding how the Dillinger gang came to be his guests. Just as dawn was beginning to burn along the tree-shrouded horizon on his left, he arrived at Little Bohemia and was greeted by an almost carnival-like atmosphere.

Convinced that some of the gang were still trapped inside, the G-Men remained encamped around the lodge, their numbers augmented by fresh rein-forcements from St. Paul, Chicago, and elsewhere. Sheriff Dell McGregor had reached the scene with his deputies, and the county officers were mingling uneasily with the federal agents. Clegg later commented that the sheriff had acted "very cordial" in his presence but was overheard to make "some wise-cracks about the government coming in and making a raid without calling him in on it." Similarly, McGregor complained that Clegg and Purvis tried to take control of his men and "order them around."

In addition to the lawmen a horde of "special deputies" had arrived, mostly local residents mobilized by word of mouth to form a self-appointed posse armed with shotguns and hunting rifles. By sunrise spectators, including newsmen and their cameras, had begun to congregate nearby.

Forced to park his truck along the highway, Wanatka worked his way through the crowd and bumped into a local teenager holding a rifle. The youth exclaimed, "I'm gonna shoot Dillinger and get the reward."

"Go home," Wanatka told him.

The lodge owner found a group of agents and deputies clustered around Clegg, Purvis, Rorer, Hanni, and Sheriff McGregor, discussing various tactics to use in launching an assault on the main building. Wanatka was horrified to hear several advocate setting the structure afire while others favored rushing in and shooting anything that moved. The outraged owner marched over and vowed, "So help me, I'll clobber the next man who puts another bullet in my house. Dillinger left last night."

It was finally agreed that the best procedure would be to use the tear gas to flush out anyone still inside. Several gas shells were fired at windows but failed to break the glass and rebounded into the yard spewing fumes back toward the lawmen. A few deputies, ignoring Wanatka's warning and evidently looking for an excuse to shoot something, resolved the problem by blasting out a number of windowpanes.

Minutes after gas exploded inside the lodge a woman's voice cried, "We'll come out if you promise not to shoot."

After Clegg gave his word the three young women filed out the main door, their eyes puffy and cheeks streaked with tears. Helen, wearing a red sweater over her blue silky lounging pajamas, led the way, closely followed by Jean, also clad in pajamas, then Mickey with her puppy Rex clasped in her arms. The three were searched and turned over to the sheriff for safekeeping.

Six agents donned gas masks and stormed inside the deserted building, emerging shortly to confirm what Wanatka had been saying all night. The only consolation was that the gangsters had again left behind their possessions and the greater part of their arsenal. The raiders discovered a .351 Winchester rifle beneath the bed in Dillinger's room and a .45 automatic in the cabin occupied by Nelson and Carroll. Packed inside Carroll's Buick and Hamilton's Ford they found six submachine guns, two shotguns, a rifle, four pistols, a pair of revolvers, and five bulletproof vests.

At 6:30 A.M., with the siege of Little Bohemia officially over, Clegg and Purvis left Rorer and Hanni in charge of the cleanup. The two drove to the Birchwood Lodge where they phoned Hoover with the disappointing details of the raid.

The director was not pleased.

There was a mirror hanging on the wall, and I could tell by his face he
wasn't a "right" man. Every now and then he'd look in the mirror,
and I could tell by his eyes he wasn't honest. He wasn't acting right,
though he was nice and polite.
— Mary Schroeder

CHAPTER 11

ESCAPE FROM WISCONSIN

BY DAYBREAK MONDAY, APRIL 23, the press was pouring into northern Wisconsin, some aboard chartered planes that landed in farmers' fields. The invasion of reporters, photographers, and newsreel crews rapidly turned "the Dillinger gang's great escape" from Little Bohemia into the number-one news story in the nation, portraying it as a major battle between a band of modern-day outlaws and J. Edgar Hoover's G-Men. A typical account, from United Press, declared, "Machine guns flamed on both sides and several raiders fell as bullets ricocheted through the dark forest."

But however the story was played, the essential facts remained the same: Federal forces let the bad guys get away and in the process shot up a carload of civilians, killing one, while one of their agents was slain by a fleeing gangster. In Washington the botched raid ignited a barrage of criticism aimed at Hoover and his bureau. Several high-ranking Republicans insisted the director be demoted or fired outright.

"They fumbled it again," observed U.S. Sen. Royal S. Copeland of New York. The reason for the latest debacle, he charged, was "a pathetic failure of cooperation between federal, state and local authorities." Hoover's so-called agents were a joke, he said. "They brought up a lot of young lawyers from the Department of Justice and armed them and turned them loose."

The critics were everywhere, but humorist Will Rogers summed it up best:

239

"Well, they had Dillinger surrounded and was all ready to shoot him when he come out, but another bunch of folks come out ahead, so they just shot them instead. Dillinger is going to accidentally get with some innocent bystanders some time, then he will get shot."

A furious and thoroughly humiliated Hoover for once shunned newsmen and withheld his comments, permitting Attorney General Cummings to defend the agents' actions by asserting that the bureau was understaffed, underfunded, and in desperate need of more modern crimefighting equipment. For the duration of the furor, Hoover saved his verbal tirades for his men. He demanded a full accounting and "prepared statements from all Agents" on the scene, calling upon Assistant Director Harold Nathan in St. Paul and Inspector Samuel Cowley in Chicago to directly oversee and organize the confusing and often contradictory reports coming out of Wisconsin. "There doesn't seem to be a very strong degree of accuracy in the descriptions of what transpired," Hoover wrote to Nathan. "It is most important that we get to the bottom of this situation, and I want you to exert every effort to find out what the real facts were. . . ."

Among the matters Hoover wanted resolved was confirming which gangster had killed Special Agent Baum. He received word from Cowley that the gunman had been "identified pretty clearly . . . as George Nelson, alias Baby Face Nelson. He is listed on the Chicago police bulletin, and has been mentioned by Bessie at St. Paul who calls him Jimmy and he is known as Jimmy where the shooting occurred." Cowley added that Wanatka was shown photos of the gang and "unhesitatingly picked Jimmy's picture from a group without seeing the names."

The bureau had learned of Nelson's association with Dillinger just two weeks earlier. Agents had uncovered few details about the pint-sized bandit, assuming that, because of his youth or inexperience (his record revealed only a couple of minor bank holdups four years earlier), he had played an insignificant role within the gang. Now, identified as the murderer of a federal agent, Baby Face Nelson began to share the national spotlight with Dillinger. Press releases from the Justice Department vilified him as a cold-blooded killer, "John Dillinger's top trigger man," and "the gang's vicious machine gunner."

Nelson's overnight notoriety not only played well in the press but also served as a key element in the bureau's attempts at damage control. By heralding the loss of Baum as a fallen soldier in the government's war against crime, it diverted attention from the Little Bohemia fiasco and the fact that federal bullets had killed one innocent man and wounded two others.

Baum's body was embalmed at Ironwood on Monday, then returned to Chicago and from there flown to Washington where the slain agent would receive a hero's funeral at Rock Creek Cemetery. Almost no one noticed when, that same Monday, fifty-year-old widow Izelda Boiseneau appeared at Ironwood to claim the remains of her son.

✳ ✳ ✳

Amid all the controversy and criticism one of the largest manhunts in Wisconsin history was mounted. Lawmen throughout the state set up road-blocks and patrolled highways hoping to nab the fugitives. Since the outlaws had fled in three separate directions—Nelson speeding south in Tuchalski's coupe, Carroll north in a Packard, and Dillinger with the others heading west in a Ford coupe—police concentrated their efforts on guarding roads leading into Michigan's Upper Peninsula, Minnesota, Illinois, and Iowa. Descriptions of the vehicles and their license plates were broadcast across the Midwest.

Among the hundreds of officers on alert Monday morning were three Dakota County, Minnesota, deputies and a local policeman stationed at the Hastings Spiral Bridge leading into South St. Paul. Shortly past ten o'clock, six hours after their vigil had begun, they observed a Ford coupe with Wisconsin plates and three men crammed in the front seat. The officers, delayed by a cattle truck, missed their chance to stop the vehicle at the bridge's entrance. Crossing the Mississippi the quartet drew close enough to check the license and confirm they had the right car.

A high-speed chase ensued. When the outlaws started lobbing .45 slugs at the county car, the officers opened fire with a .30-30 rifle, pelting the Ford's rear with a dozen rounds. Hamilton was struck by a bullet that plowed into his lower back.

After several miles of trading shots at speeds up to 70 mph, the trio outdis-tanced their pursuers, then lost them by turning onto a side road. Three hours later the outlaws forced a Ford sedan to stop. The occupants—Roy Francis, his wife, and two-year-old son—were herded into the back seat at gunpoint. Once Hamilton, wrapped in a blanket, was loaded in front, Dillinger took the wheel as Van Meter climbed in beside the terrified family.

Near Mendota they stopped for gas. Hamilton pleaded for a drink. Dillinger bought two bottles of soda pop, one for his wounded friend, the other for the little boy. Back on the road, Van Meter asked Francis what he did for a living. He said he worked for a South St. Paul power company.

"You don't know how lucky you are," Van Meter commented wistfully. "You've got a good job and a nice family."

The bandits released the hostages near a farmhouse. Sticking to back roads Dillinger drove south into Iowa, stopping in Dubuque to purchase food, newspapers, and a first aid kit. They crossed into Illinois and headed for Chicago, hoping to find shelter and an underworld doctor before Hamilton bled to death.

✳ ✳ ✳

Early that Monday morning in a small, red frame, three-room cabin on the shore of Stearns Lake, Mary Schroeder, a full-blooded Chippewa, awoke to what sounded like a distant gunshot. The cabin, home of Mary's aunt and uncle, Maggie and Ollie Catfish, was located on the eastern edge of the Lac du Flambeau reservation, a full eighteen miles south of where Nelson's car had broken down the night before. With her husband, George, away trapping, Mary and her two daughters—Dorothy, age fifteen, and two-year-old Gertrude—were staying with the Catfishes, helping to make maple syrup. The previous day Ollie and Maggie, both in their mid-sixties, had embarked on an overnight visit to town and were expected back that evening.

Mary spent her morning doing laundry, a chore requiring her to carry water from the lake, which was still partially covered with ice. Her teenage daughter lent a hand, at the same time looking after her little sister and searching for the family dog, Geegans, who had inexplicably run off leaving her five puppies whining for food. Dorothy and Gertie tried to pacify the pups with some canned milk. In the afternoon Mary started baking bread while Dorothy went outdoors to hang the laundry to dry. The girl suddenly rushed inside and announced, "Ma, there's a man coming!"

Mary went to the window. "I looked out and could see a man's legs under the sheets," she later recalled. "Then he came around to the front door, and I said, 'Tell him to come around to the back.' Through the window Dorothy told him to go to the back, and he came in. He was very friendly, said, 'Hello, Mother, could I buy some lunch from you? Your baking smells good.'"

The stranger was "about five-six and slim." He was "well-dressed," wearing a light jacket and black oxfords, hardly the recommended attire for hiking through the Wisconsin woods in late April. Mary invited him to sit at the table and fixed fried eggs, bacon, fresh bread, and coffee. "He gave me two dollars—put it down on the table—and gave Dorothy a dollar." When he inquired about her husband, Mary told him he would be gone three or four days. "He asked me if we had any neighbors or a radio or a telephone. I said no. He said, 'Don't you get the papers, either?' And I said, 'No, we're in the sticks. We could be killed, and no one would know anything about it.'"

"Does your husband have any old clothes?" Baby Face Nelson asked.

"All we have is old clothes," Mary replied. She brought him a pair of khaki pants and a plaid shirt with the sleeves cut off. The outlaw pulled them on over his good clothes, then pointed to a cot along the wall. "Would you mind if I lay down for a while? I've been walking a long ways."

"I kept the kids out of the room," she remembered, "but he didn't really sleep, I don't think." Later Mary saw her aunt and uncle cutting across the ice-covered lake. When they entered the house, Ollie, speaking in Chippewa, told his niece, "An awful thing happened in town." Mary tried to motion them "not to talk too much." Noticing the figure lying on the cot in George's clothes, Ollie assumed that Mary's husband had returned and asked, "When did he come home?"

Nelson arose, walked over, and greeted the pair with an engaging smile. "Hello, Uncle and Auntie," he said, warmly shaking hands with them. Impressed by the young stranger's manners, Maggie laughed and asked Mary, "Who is that to come and be so friendly?"

While Mary and her aunt prepared supper, Catfish took their visitor outside. The two men sat on a woodpile attempting to communicate in Ollie's broken English and by writing in the dirt. The fugitive wanted to know how close they were to the highway and the nearest town, and the distance to Eagle River and Rhinelander. Catfish—tall and broad-shouldered, with iron-gray hair, a leathery face, and a jutting jaw—did his best to answer. Later, with Mary interpreting, he was able to provide more details.

Gradually Nelson came to understand exactly how secluded the family's home was—a blessing for him at present but it would be a major obstacle when he eventually decided to return to civilization. He inquired about cars, and Catfish replied that the only cars in the area were in town, a six-mile walk from the cabin. When Nelson asked if Catfish owned any guns, the old man informed him that he had four rifles but no ammunition.

The sun was setting by the time they sat down to supper. Nelson asked, "Would you mind if I stayed overnight? It's getting dark and I wouldn't be able to find my way."

Catfish voiced no objections, for he and the others had realized their guest was running from the law. In Lac du Flambeau Ollie and Maggie had heard sketchy reports about the shootout and deaths at Little Bohemia. And shortly before supper Dorothy had run to Mary, exclaiming, "Mommy, you should see the guns he has under his pillow!"

Later, when the visitor stepped out, Catfish took a peek at the three pistols Nelson had stashed in the cot. The old man briefly considered taking the weapons—but then what? The stranger might have another gun on him, and Catfish had no intention of endangering his family.

Before retiring Mary wrapped herself in a blanket and ventured outside to look again for Geegans. The dog had been missing all day, and one of the puppies had died. She repeatedly called and whistled, but all she heard was the howling of the wind and the rustling of the trees, nothing more. Mary returned to the cabin and told her aunt and uncle, "I don't know what's become of that dog."

❋ ❋ ❋

A few minutes past nine o'clock Monday evening the three young women captured at Little Bohemia arrived at the Dane County Jail in Madison. Agents

243

Sam Hardy and R. G. Gillespie, who with Sheriff McGregor and a pair of deputies had escorted "the molls" from Eagle River, told Dane County Sheriff Fred T. Finn the three were "federal prisoners" to be kept isolated from each other in separate cells and granted no privileges.

In other words, while the girls were held in the county lockup until their appearance in federal court, the sheriff and his staff were expected to provide only protection. Any actual contact, including looking after their needs, was reserved exclusively to the two G-Men. In gratitude for the sheriff's expected cooperation, Hardy presented Finn with a souvenir of the shootout—a cigar which, the agent claimed, had belonged to Dillinger.

Memos from Hoover reveal the director demanded that his men use any and all means to pry information from the women. One of Inspector Cowley's dispatches to Hoover mentions that "Hardy was advised not to give the girls anything to eat and not to let them sleep until they talked," and "that no privileges was to be granted newspaper men to interview or photograph the girls."

Cowley, apparently the chief architect of these tactics, often boasted that he had perfected the method of dealing with obstinate females, alleging "the success obtained at the Chicago office in questioning . . . women has been the result of holding them indefinitely and breaking down their resistance and obtaining from them, piece by piece, the story of their activities."

Thus far the women from Little Bohemia had revealed precious little about themselves or anything else. All three had provided fictitious names, admitted they were from Chicago, and insisted they knew nothing about their boyfriends being gangsters. Jean Crompton, described by reporters (who briefly glimpsed the trio during the transfer) as the prettiest and having a "Mae West chest," was using the name Ann Southern. Mickey Conforti, calling herself Rose Ancker, was the most talkative but no more helpful. Saying she had arrived in Wisconsin by train and met her boyfriend at the lodge, she shared some "off-color" jokes with the agents and repeatedly complained about being forced to leave her puppy, Rex, back in Eagle River with the wife of Sheriff McGregor.

Helen alone sported a wedding band, diamond-studded and obviously expensive. She had given her name as Marion Virginia Marr and claimed she had married a Chicago physician, Dr. Joseph D. Marr, two weeks earlier and their visit to Little Bohemia was just one stop on their honeymoon. The agents labeled her answers "absurd."

At midnight "a reliable source" notified the sheriff that the Dillinger gang was planning an assault on the jail to free the women. The girls were taken by a dozen armed guards to a church where they were hidden among the pews until dawn.

❊ ❊ ❊

Dillinger and his pals reached the outskirts of Chicago about 10 P.M. They visited several underworld hangouts, including the Seafood Inn in Elmhurst, but each time they were turned away, branded as "too hot." Finally, well past midnight, Dillinger convinced a sympathetic saloon owner to grant them temporary asylum in the back room of his establishment.

Hamilton, in constant agony and weak from loss of blood, needed immediate medical attention. Dillinger desperately sought a physician, but thanks to the publicity over Little Bohemia, no one was willing to help. Evidently it was more than fear of the police or G-Men that prevented Dillinger from finding aid; according to Alvin Karpis, the Chicago syndicate had taken "a hard stand with us common thieves." Hours after the Wisconsin gun battle local mob bosses had issued explicit orders forbidding any gangland affiliates to provide shelter or assistance to the Indiana bank robber and his pals. The fact that Baby Face Nelson had killed a government agent no doubt played a major role in the decision.

Ironically Nelson, whose Chicago contacts were numerous and extremely loyal, was probably one of the few who might have arranged medical treatment for Hamilton. In the past weeks the gang members had come to rely on their young confederate's intimacy with the Chicago underworld. Dillinger and Van Meter could only hope that Nelson would be able to evade the massive manhunt and make his way back to the city. In the meantime the pair did their best to comfort Hamilton and keep him alive.

❊ ❊ ❊

Ollie Catfish and his family were early risers. By 5 A.M., well before dawn, they were consuming a big breakfast before beginning the day's work. Nelson, offering to assist and probably intending to keep a watchful eye on his hosts, joined them as they hiked through the woods collecting sap from maple trees, at times carrying two-year-old Gertie on his shoulders.

When it came time to boil the sap, Ollie and Maggie built a huge fire in a shallow pit. Nelson quickly complained it was "too windy to make a fire." The old couple ignored him and continued to toss logs and branches into the roaring flames. "You'll burn up the whole woods!" Baby Face warned.

Taking matters into his own hands, Nelson dumped several barrels of sap into the pit, extinguishing the fire. Catfish glared at the stranger, muttering a few phrases in Chippewa that Mary chose not to translate. "It'll be all right," Nelson said, laughing at their scowling expressions. He pulled a roll of bills from his pocket and handed Catfish seventy-five dollars.

❊ ❊ ❊

That same day, Tuesday, April 24, the Mercer Lakelands Association, the region's civic council, drafted a petition calling for the suspension of Melvin Purvis. The document cited as grounds the "irresponsible conduct of federal officers" under his control while raiding the Wanatka resort "in such a stupid manner as to bring death to two men, and injuries to four others, none of whom were gangsters." The offenses included (1) "Failure to seek aid of persons familiar with . . . area who could have prevented escape of Dillinger gang over only highways leading from . . . Little Bohemia, merely by barricading three nearby bridges"; (2) "Wanton recklessness and disregard of human life in firing upon a car bearing three unarmed and respected citizens, killing one and wounding two"; and (3) "Criminal stupidity of two United States Agents acting evidently either with insufficient instructions or in disregard of orders for caution in approaching a suspicious car . . . as a result of which a lone bandit slew one agent, seriously wounded a constable, and injured another agent."

The petition's vehement language made Hoover livid. Rorer, instructed to give it his "full attention," reported that the petition was being circulated through five Wisconsin communities and sent the director a list with the name of every citizen who signed it. Rorer claimed he detected "no wave of resentment" among locals and was convinced "the whole thing was concocted for a newspaper story . . . a malicious attempt to embarrass Mr. Purvis." He was confident the petition "would die a natural death."

Hoover replied he was concerned, saying that "because of the manner in which this matter is played up in the press, the feeling of the public might be so aroused as to cause serious trouble." He wanted the reporters identified and, if possible, discredited, but he advised Rorer to "not try to suppress the petition or interfere with it."

At the same time, an inquest into the deaths of Baum and Eugene Boiseneau was conducted by the Vilas County coroner's office. Purvis and half a dozen agents were summoned to give their accounts of the shootout, and all did their utmost to justify the actions of the raiding party with carefully crafted answers.

When asked, "Did the agents act on their own responsibility without orders at any time?" each swore the officers had "acted under specific orders . . . other than, of course, firing when fired upon or at gun flashes." Clegg, Rorer, and Purvis had remained in command throughout the episode, they stated, and the "men were stationed under their direction and appeared to be closely and directly controlled during the entire time."

Concerning the shooting of Boiseneau and his companions, the agents told similar stories using remarkably similar wording. The three customers "were ordered to halt a number of times and disregarded these instructions." The G-Men claimed they had repeatedly identified themselves as federal officers and insisted the trio "ran" to their car and "attempted to flee." One agent testified that "the automobile immediately accelerated and an effort was made to drive through the agents." Purvis swore he had given a command only to "shoot the tires" of Hoffman's vehicle.

At that point, the lawmen said, the outlaws inside the lodge and the adjacent cabin had opened fire "in the direction of our agents and of the car containing the CCC men." The result, both implied and clearly stated by the government witnesses, was that the Hoffman car had been caught in the crossfire, and the causalities suffered by the occupants "most likely" were caused by the gangsters' guns.

The attempt to shift the guilt for the civilian injuries might have been more convincing had it not been for the testimony of Frank Traube. The young waiter took the stand and swore the only commands he had heard were "Halt!" and "Put up your hands!" Not once did he hear the agents identify themselves. Traube said that when he saw the armed men taking aim at Hoffman's car, he had shouted a warning that the occupants were customers of the lodge.

Moments later—as the car "only started" in motion—"machine guns in the hands of the government men opened fire on the three men," Traube stated. He distinctly recalled observing three separate bursts of fire, one from the south and two more from the north, which constituted one brief, ferocious volley that riddled the Chevy. None of the shots, he maintained, had come from the main building or the cabin.

Adding insult to injury, Traube spoke to newsmen as he exited the inquest. Wanatka and the G-Men had portrayed the Dillinger gang as a desperate, vicious band of hoods who had taken over the lodge and terrified the staff. But Traube told reporters the true situation was nothing like that. "No, they weren't hard to get along with," he was quoted as saying. "Nelson, in particular, has a nice personality, and Dillinger is likable although he doesn't talk much. We did some target shooting one day, and believe me, that Nelson can shoot."

His damaging testimony at the inquest was bad enough, but describing Baum's killer as "nice" while complimenting his shooting skills earned Traube special disfavor in FBI reports. One file listed him as "a contact and an acquaintance" of Nelson, someone the agents should watch.

In light of Traube's evidence, Purvis and his men were recalled and asked which agents had fired on the Chevrolet. Their answers produced a rather startling revelation. Purvis declared, "Baum was close by me at the time and I saw him fire in the direction of the car." Special Agent Newman, recovered from his head wound, also reported seeing Baum, who "stood a little to the right and in front of me," spray the Chevy with his machine gun. Two agents who testified they had spoken with Baum after shooting alleged that Baum confessed "he had fired directly into the car and he hoped he had not killed an innocent man."

In Chicago, Doris Lockerman heard the stories claiming Baum was responsible for the death of Boiseneau. "Carter Baum was a big, easygoing man," she later wrote. "He was too gentle ever to have become a killer. . . . If it were he who had shot at the innocent party under the misapprehension that they were fleeing gangsters, his subsequent mental anguish would have explained very well the momentary lowering of his guard, which permitted Nelson to murder him."

Baum's alleged remorse also reinforces Nelson's version of the shooting, indicating why the agent failed to fire when he had Baby Face in his sights. (An equally plausible explanation is that Baum attempted to shoot without realizing his weapon's safety was still on.)

Baum's culpability in Boiseneau's death as reported by his fellow agents was not without controversy. Surprisingly the director himself challenged the claims of his own men, suspecting that since they were unable to blame the gangsters, they had attempted to accuse the only member of the raiding party incapable of defending himself. But Hoover, always concerned with the bureau's image, had hoped to use the occasion of Baum's funeral to enshrine the slain agent as a national hero and martyr—and he knew that a lawman who mistakenly mowed down innocent citizens was not a good candidate for sympathy.

Actually the director had good reason to believe Baum was not one of the shooters. U.S. Assistant Attorney General Joseph B. Keenan provided information which Hoover summarized in a memo to Nathan:

> "In regard to the CCC man who was killed, the statement that Agent Baum killed this man is absolutely untrue for the reason that Agent Baum's gun, when found at the place where Mr. Baum was killed . . . was shown to have been locked, that no shot had been fired from it, and for that reason he did not fire his gun at the Little Bohemia shooting, but that Mr. Rorer was the man who killed the CCC man, it being understood and agreed among Clegg, Purvis, and Rorer that 'it would be fixed up another way.'"

Hoover instructed Nathan to "drop everything else . . . and give every attention to this matter," demanding that he "find out the exact condition of Mr. Baum's gun." The report Hoover received conceded that Baum's "machine gun was fully loaded and was on 'safety,' and Agent Brennan stated that the bolt was clean," indicating the weapon had not been fired earlier. It was pointed out, however, that "there was considerable shifting of guns during the Little Bohemia episode" and "Baum may have reloaded his gun, or at the time he met his death . . . may have been carrying an entirely different gun."

In the end, the inquest concluded that "Eugene Phillip Boiseneau, aged 28 years, came to his death accidentally on April 33, 1934, in the town of Spider Lake, State of Wisconsin, as a result of gun shot wounds inflicted by federal officers in the act of apprehending the Dillinger gang." The names of the agents participating in the raid, including any who might have fired the shots that killed the young CCC worker, were not disclosed.

Hoover refused to let his men off that easy, however, and continued to press for answers and explanations from his chief officers concerning their conduct. He demanded to know why, for instance, Rorer had refused to help lift Baum's body into Wanatka's pickup. The inspector responded that the bulletproof vest he wore that evening had aggravated a previous back injury. Hoover also expressed a furious disappointment with SAC Hanni's failure to stop the car containing Nelson. After looking into the matter on behalf of the director, Cowley reported that Hanni's actions were "inexcusable," insisting the SAC and his men had had "ample opportunity to block the road and be in a position to protect themselves."

Purvis grew tired of Hoover's inquiries. Reportedly distraught over Baum's death, and thoroughly humiliated by the Mercer petition and his subjugation to Cowley back in Chicago, he submitted his resignation. Hoover refused to accept it, telling Purvis he wanted results instead of whining.

Against the background of all the federal finger-pointing and bickering, the same inquest—after hearing testimony from Emil Wanatka, Alvin Koerner, Paul Lang, and Special Agent Newman—ruled that W. Carter Baum had died from gunshot wounds inflicted by one George "Baby Face" Nelson. A complaint charging murder was filed against him in Vilas County.

❋ ❋ ❋

Late Tuesday afternoon Mrs. Wilbur Alt, a school bus driver in Boulder Junction contacted Deputy Sheriff William Paquette to report an abandoned Ford coupe on Old River Road. County officers quickly determined it was the Tuchalski vehicle.

By daybreak another colossal manhunt was under way. Sheriff's departments in Eagle River, Hurley, and Rhinelander were alerted, and a force of federal agents, county officers, local police, and volunteers poured into the triangular, densely wooded region between the towns. Roads were blockaded and houses searched.

The coupe obviously had been abandoned Sunday night, and lawmen believed there was a good chance Nelson was still in the area, hopelessly lost or holed up in an unoccupied summer cabin. No cars had been reported stolen, and it was seriously doubted that the fugitive had managed to hike out of the area. A pair of agents joined local officers in a series of "raids" on houses and barns throughout the vicinity where Nelson could have walked. Rorer notified Hoover that if the young killer were still in the area he would be found.

❋ ❋ ❋

Wednesday morning Nelson noticed Mary Schroeder preparing to leave the cabin with a hatchet. "We don't got no wood," he observed, pulling on a mackinaw and a stocking cap. "I'd better go out and cut some."

Maggie wanted to come along, probably out of concern for her niece. Nelson told her, "No, we're younger than you."

As Mary showed him how to saw logs into "stove lengths," then split the wood with the hatchet, she spied an airplane overhead which "seemed to be following the railroad tracks and the roads." Mary noted, "That plane is flying low."

"Oh, they're just looking for somebody," Nelson replied.

As they returned with a few days' supply of firewood, the outlaw grew talkative. "He told me about himself and asked me where I went to school and what religion we had," Mary recalled. "I said, 'We're Catholics.' 'Oh,' he said, 'I was raised in a convent.' He said he was from Chicago. Said he walked in from the road, was lost. . . . Said something about 'I got to get to Eagle River and see whether my friends got there or not.' After a while he said, 'You're not as dumb as you let on you are. You know a lot, but you won't let on.'"

Despite Nelson's pleasant manner Mary could tell "by his face he wasn't a 'right' man." She was particularly bothered by his narcissistic habit of gazing into the mirror and the way his eyes squinted when he looked at her. After three days Ollie had grown annoyed at the stranger's preoccupation with cleaning his fingernails and the fact that he never seemed to sleep.

But aside from his brief outburst over the fire the previous day, Nelson had been "nice and polite" for the most part. "He was very friendly with the kids," Mary reported, "playing with them and joking with Dorothy." Now and then he slipped the teenager a dollar and teasingly warned, "Don't let your ma take that from you." Mary added, "He kept the guns hid all the time," although he was aware they knew he had them.

By Wednesday afternoon the outlaw began talking about leaving, pestering Catfish to lead him through the woods toward town. The old Indian, fearing he might not return if he accompanied the stranger, kept making excuses not to go throughout the rest of the day.

❋ ❋ ❋

Shortly after noon on Wednesday Helen, Mickey, and Jean were escorted under heavy guard to a seventh-floor courtroom in the Bank of Wisconsin Building in downtown Madison, where they were formally arraigned on charges of harboring federal fugitives John Dillinger and Tommy Carroll. All three pleaded not guilty. Bail for each was set at $50,000—although if found guilty, the fine would be only $5,000. Melvin Purvis proudly predicted, "The three women . . . are going to get the maximum sentence. They must be punished amply for assisting a man who is an enemy of the public."

Agents Hardy and Gillespie managed to bar the press from the hearing. Newsmen complained to Sheriff Finn, who explained that he wasn't allowed to see the girls either. In the courtyard of the Dane County Jail, Hardy spotted a *Capital Times* reporter snapping pictures as the prisoners were being hustled inside. The G-Man rushed over, demanding the photo plates. When the reporter refused, Hardy "physically assaulted" him by knocking him to the pavement, then kneeling on the newsman's throat as he pried the plates from his grasp. "I feel sorry for those girls," the reporter later commented. "Now I know how it feels to be 'questioned' by a federal agent."

By now the authorities had identified Marion Marr as Helen Gillis, twenty-one-year-old wife of Baby Face Nelson and mother of his two children. While Mickey and Jean were allowed meals together and provided with a deck of cards, Helen was kept in isolation, the marathon interrogations conducted by Hardy and Gillespie becoming more grueling. The agents threatened to put Helen behind bars for years and take away her children. Her husband, they gleefully told her, was at that moment being hunted down like a mad dog, to be shot on sight for murdering a federal officer.

Hardy noted in his report, "Every method of attack has been used by agents in an effort to get this woman to talk, but without avail. It was thought that possibly her weak point would be her children, which this agent brought into the picture at length. . . . On two occasions, when discussing her children, she broke down and wept at length, but would not give in."

❋ ❋ ❋

On Thursday, April 26, Nelson was growing restless and "getting kind of mad." At 5 P.M. Ollie Catfish, tired of their uninvited guest and grumbling about a shortage of food, finally agreed to guide him to the highway, a three-mile hike instead of the seven-mile trek to Lac du Flambeau.

Nelson asked Mary to pack a lunch for them. "I made some meat sandwiches and some strawberry jam ones and put them in a big sack. I think I took a couple of maple sugar cakes and put them in," she remembered. He gave her twenty dollars and said, "You're the one who got the meals. Was it their groceries or yours?" Mary said the food was hers and received another fifty dollars.

The two men started off but minutes later Catfish returned complaining, "I can't walk fast." Maggie told her niece it was her fault for first admitting the stranger into their home, saying, "If anything happens to your uncle, you'll be to blame for it."

Mary threw on a sweater and scarf. She handed the cash Nelson had given her over the last four days to Dorothy, telling her, "You keep it, in case I don't come back." The teenager began to cry. Mary said, "Things will come out all right—or let's hope they do."

She hurried down the trail to where Nelson waited. "Well, Mother," he called out, "you going with me?"

"I'll take you as far as the highway."

"All right," he said, following her deeper into the woods. Before long they heard Catfish shouting to them. The old man caught up and told Mary he would go with the man. Nelson glared impatiently at them. "You going to show me or is she?"

"I'll go," answered Catfish, ordering Mary to go back to the cabin. Turning to leave she noticed Nelson had drawn a pistol. "Walk fast," he growled, motioning with the gun. "It's getting late."

Mary returned to find both of her daughters in tears. The last of the five puppies had died. Mary suddenly recalled the gunshot that had woken her Monday morning and told her aunt about it. Maggie nodded grimly and said, "I bet you he killed that dog."

❄ ❄ ❄

It was after 8 P.M. and growing dark when Nelson and Catfish reached Highway 47. They walked half a mile along the road, then crossed to a trail leading down to the shores of Fence Lake. Nelson spotted a parked car. The owner, Herbert Ackley, and two friends, William Grunewald and Herman Weber, were catching suckers and at the moment were building a campfire. Nelson asked Catfish what they were doing. "Fishing," he replied.

The outlaw grinned. "Let's go fishing, too."

A few minutes later a blue Plymouth sedan pulled up beside Ackley's vehicle. The driver was Adolph Goetz, a postal worker and deputy sheriff from Merrill. His companion was Al Snow, a Lac du Flambeau police officer. Off duty and unarmed, the pair approached the camp calling out hellos to the men who were seated around the fire "like they were holding a pow-wow." Snow recognized Catfish, who was sitting beside a young, light-haired stranger. No one spoke until Nelson asked, "Whose car is that?"

"Mine," replied Goetz.

"I want the keys."

"Who are you?" Goetz demanded, thinking he was possibly a game warden. "What's your authority for this?"

Nelson uncrossed his hands, revealing a pistol. "Never mind. I want the keys to the car."

Keeping his distance, the bandit instructed all six men to line up around the fire. "I'm in trouble," he explained. "I need a car to get out of this country. I wanna get out right away."

252

"He wanted to know about the roads," Goetz said later. "We told him the roads were all right, none were blockaded. . . . I told him one agent had been killed at Little Bohemia, and the next question his voice kind of quivered, so I figured, 'Aha, you're the son of a gun that did it!'"

As he questioned the group, Nelson moved to Ackley's car and threw open the hood, ripping off the distributor cap and tossing it into the bushes.

"He was a nice guy to talk with, real polite," recalled Goetz. "He asked me for the title to the car; [he] wanted to buy it and pay cash, but I said I didn't have the title with me." Nelson asked if Goetz had insurance. When the deputy said he did, the little gunman remarked, "Well, you'll get paid for it then."

"Nelson told me, 'I'll give you twenty dollars to take you home.' I said all right. He peeled off a couple of tens and let them fall to the ground. I asked, 'You want me to start it for you?' He said, 'No, I know all about these cars.' I had the door locked and he couldn't open it. I reached in through the window and opened it."

Baby Face ordered Catfish into the Plymouth's passenger side. As he slipped behind the wheel Nelson called to the others, "I know you guys are gonna report this, but gimme a little time."

Driving into Lac du Flambeau, the outlaw stopped at a gas station and filled the tank, presenting the attendant with a ten-dollar bill for two dollars' worth of gas and telling him to keep the change. He headed south on a county road until he came to Highway 70. There he handed Catfish seventy-five dollars and said good-bye. After the aged Chippewa climbed out, the Plymouth turned west on Highway 70 and vanished into the night.

Catfish arrived back in Lac du Flambeau about the same time Goetz and Snow hiked in from Fence Lake. The news that Baby Face Nelson was still in their midst lit up switchboards across northern Wisconsin. By midnight a statewide effort was under way to track down the gangster. Roadblocks were erected on Highway 70 and other roads leading west, as the majority of lawmen agreed he appeared to be heading for the Minnesota state line.

But at dawn on Friday the strategy for catching Nelson abruptly changed. Officers received reports that the fugitive had turned north and was racing toward Duluth. Near Solon Springs, thirty miles southeast of Superior, Deputy George Johnson attempted to stop a suspicious vehicle containing two men and was fired on and wounded. Johnson shot back but lost the car when it veered east toward Ashland. Within two hours a 5,000-man posse was on the move combing three counties for the outlaw. Local papers boasted that Nelson was trapped in the region.

The lawmen, however, were looking in the wrong place. Nelson had turned south on Highway 13 and was confident that he could reach Illinois by sunrise. But once again an easy escape eluded him. Slightly more than 100 miles southwest of Lac du Flambeau the Plymouth burned a bearing, forcing Baby Face to leave the highway and prowl the rural roads for another vehicle.

Just before 5 A.M. his search brought him to a farmhouse near Greenwood. The owner, Joseph Gregorich, was doing his morning chores when Nelson appeared, still wearing the plaid jacket Mary Schroeder had given him. He introduced himself as Jim Lane, a CCC worker. Explaining that his car had broken down, he asked if the farmer would give him a ride into Marshfield thirty miles away and store his disabled vehicle over the weekend.

Gregorich—young and stocky, with a round face and clad in overalls—was reluctant at first, telling the stranger that he had a long day's work ahead and that the plates on his truck were expired. But when Nelson offered him twenty dollars for his time and trouble, Gregorich could hardly refuse. "I need to finish a few chores first," he said.

Nelson shrugged. "I'm in no hurry."

The farmer pointed to an old shed, telling Nelson he could park his car inside. Delighted to get the stolen Plymouth out of sight, the bandit pocketed the keys and took his tan jacket with him as he followed Gregorich into the barn. The farmer thought he might offer to help, but Nelson just stood idly by the door, jacket draped over his arm, while Gregorich fed and milked his cows. He later said he felt the stranger was "keeping an eye" on him.

Almost two hours later the pair got into the farmer's pickup and started for town. Gregorich asked how a young CCC worker could afford to be so generous with his cash. "I've been doing little bootlegging on the side," Nelson confided with a grin.

Near the outskirts of Marshfield, Nelson declared, "This'll be fine right here." He handed the farmer an extra ten dollars, "in case you get pinched." As he stepped out he shook hands with Gregorich and said, "Goodbye, Joe."

Nelson shed his old clothes, discarding them along the roadside before reaching town. At ten o'clock he entered the Marshfield Hardware and Auto Company and told salesman W. J. Smith that he needed "a car with a strong motor and good rubber." Smith had doubts about the customer, "He looked like a young kid," Smith later claimed, though he noticed that Nelson, unshaven for at least five days, displayed a faint trace of stubble. His pants and suede jacket appeared expensive but were spattered with mud.

Nelson showed no interest in the first car Smith recommended, a Plymouth. The salesman directed him to a black 1929 Chevrolet with more modern disk wheels. "I'll take it," Nelson said. "Never mind about the sticker. I don't think the police will bother me."

Smith left to retrieve the keys and paperwork. He returned to find Nelson seated behind the wheel "all eager to go," though "he didn't appear impatient or worried." The desperado gave his name on the bill of sale as "Harold Aaron, Box 177, Greenwood, Wis." He asked to make monthly payments but was informed it would take several days to perform a credit check. Smith thought he had blown the sale until the young man fished a roll of bills from his pocket and counted out the Chevy's full price in tens and twenties.

Resuming his southbound journey in the new vehicle, Nelson followed Highway 13 for another 100 miles before turning onto rural roads, zigzagging his way down the state through forests and rolling farmland. He was spotted only once—a Green County man passed him near New Glarus and jotted down the license number. By the time local authorities were alerted, Nelson was across the state line.

Caroline Corder was waitressing at Louie's roadhouse that night when she noticed the young man she knew as Jimmie enter. Usually dapper and neat, this evening he looked disheveled, his clothing dingy. "He appeared very nervous and remained upstairs most of the time," she later reported. The bartender brought him a meal and newspapers. Nelson learned for the first time his wife was in federal custody back in Wisconsin.

❋ ❋ ❋

John Hamilton was dying, and thus far there was nothing his friends could do for him. On Friday—about the time Nelson was leaving Marshfield—Dillinger visited Dr. Joseph Moran at his office in the Irving Park Hotel. The underworld physician had been working almost exclusively for the Barker-Karpis gang over the past year. Finding the most wanted man in the nation on his doorstep, Moran reacted with a mixture of indignation and horror, refusing to treat Hamilton. When Dillinger demanded some kind of assistance, the panicky doctor put him in touch with some of his Barker cronies.

The accounts vary, but one way or another Hamilton was transported to the apartment of Volney Davis at 415 Post Street in Aurora, forty miles southwest of Chicago. Since the Bremer kidnapping three months earlier, the Barkers had been laying low; half the gang, including Alvin Karpis and Freddie Barker, were hiding out in Ohio, dividing their time between underworld spots in Toledo and Cleveland. The rest, like Davis, were scattered throughout Chicago.

The presence of Dillinger, Van Meter, and the wounded Hamilton created an extra risk the Barkers could not afford at the moment. The following day agents nabbed John J. "Boss" McLaughlin, a former politician loosely connected with the gang. His subsequent interrogation placed them all in imminent peril.

Within hours of McLaughlin's arrest Doc Barker, Harry Campbell, and William Weaver joined Davis at his apartment. Despite the danger, they allowed Dillinger and his companions to remain, a gesture of camaraderie among thieves. While Hamilton, pumped full of painkillers, lay dying, the six outlaws took turns standing guard in the event that McLaughlin talked and the apartment was raided.

Nelson spent Saturday holed up at the roadhouse attempting to contact his array of allies by phone. He discovered, as Dillinger had, the full repercussions of the Little Bohemia affair and the death of Agent Baum. His two most reliable connections, Jack Perkins and Art Johnston, were vacationing in Florida, doing some deep-sea fishing and patronizing racetracks. The others Nelson tried to reach were either unavailable, made excuses, or refused outright to help. Finally he called upon his former criminal mentor Al Van de Houton, now a tavern owner. That night Van de Houton picked up Nelson and brought him back to the city.

It's not known exactly when or how Nelson re-established contact with Dillinger, or if—either through his ties to Dr. Moran or Volney Davis—he ever found his way to the latter's apartment. He later told Helen that he saw Hamilton after Little Bohemia but didn't specify whether he was alive or dead.

By the weekend Hamilton was beyond help. Gangrene had set in, and his condition was growing worse each day. Dillinger remained at his friend's bedside, reading Western novels while awaiting the end. Either late on April 30 or in the early morning hours of May 1, Hamilton succumbed to his week-old wound.

His body was taken to a gravel pit near Violet Patch Park in Oswego, Illinois. A shallow grave was dug and the corpse, its right hand with the telltale missing fingers amputated and disposed of separately, was placed inside. Dillinger sprinkled four cans of lye over Hamilton's face and the remaining hand to further prevent identification. Before shoveling the dirt over his friend, Dillinger, a dedicated (or desperate) believer in good-luck symbols, placed a horseshoe on Hamilton's chest.

Details of the burial were supplied to the FBI by Edna Murray, Davis's girlfriend, who claimed the four Barker-Karpis gangsters were present. Dillinger, in his statements to Art O'Leary, indicated that the scene at Hamilton's gravesite was a more intimate affair, attended only by himself, Van Meter, and Nelson.

✳ ✳ ✳

The investigative efforts of Hoover's G-Men, meanwhile, began to uncover a wide range of individuals connected to the so-called Dillinger gang through past associations with Baby Face Nelson.

The first to feel the heat was Hyman Lebman. The machine gun-pistol recovered at St. Paul was traced from Hartford, Connecticut, to a firearms company in San Francisco, then to a gun dealer in Fort Worth. Agents suspected the weapon ultimately found its way into the hands of the San Antonio gunsmith, who had been under scrutiny since December when Carroll killed Detective Perrow, but no direct link to Lebman was confirmed. A trace of serial numbers from the gang's abandoned arsenal at Little Bohemia disclosed that two of the six Thompsons had come from Texas, one trail leading again to Fort Worth, the other to El Paso.

At 8 P.M. on April 28 Lebman was arrested at his home by SAC Gus Jones and his men. After being interrogated through the night, Lebman was forced to accompany the agents while they searched his gun shop the next morning. Though he insisted that his business was primarily a saddlery and harness store, the raiders found an impressive inventory of weapons on the premises. As Jones noted in his report, there were "possibly 200 second-hand rifles and shotguns, approximately 50 second-hand pistols and approximately one dozen new pistols of assorted makes."

On Lebman's backroom workbench agents discovered a .45 automatic that had been partially dismantled and was "in the process of being converted into a machine gun." They also found pieces of a disassembled submachine gun concealed in various places within the store.

While Jones indignantly referred to Lebman as "the biggest liar and unprincipled human I have ever talked to," the gunsmith made a sincere effort to cooperate. He provided a detailed account of his casual friendship and business dealings with the young man known to him as Jimmie Williams who, in the company of his family and others, had visited San Antonio on three separate occasions the previous year. He readily identified Nelson's photo and admitted that he had shipped five machine guns to Jimmie at a Minneapolis address. The disassembled Thompson was a sixth weapon Nelson had returned for failing to fire "full auto."

Lebman maintained that he had never met or heard any mention of Dillinger. He did, however, identify a picture of Homer Van Meter as "Jimmie's pal Wayne Huttner." It was Wayne, he confessed, who had left the .45 with him to be modified into a machine-gun pistol. But the gunsmith claimed he had not heard from Jimmie, Wayne, or any of the others since Fisher was arrested.

On Monday, April 30, Lebman was arraigned in federal court on a charge of receiving stolen government property—a nickel-plated .45 automatic found in his shop was U.S. Army issue, though he insisted the weapon had been left with him for repairs. Bail was set at $2,000 and posted by his father, Samuel Lebman. The San Antonio press declared that "gangland nemesis Gus Jones" had captured the man who supplied "firearms to George ('Baby Face') Nelson, chief machine-gunner for the Dillinger mob, and to Homer Van Meter, Dillinger lieutenant."

None of these charges, including the federal one, held up in court. State authorities, however, looked at the evidence collected by the G-Men and indicted Lebman for violation of the recent Texas statute forbidding the sale, purchase, or possession of machine guns except by law officers. Lebman's shipment of the five Thompsons preceded the law's effective date, but the presence of the sixth machine gun, even though it was dismantled and not operational, constituted a breech of the law. Lebman faced a maximum sentence of ten years' imprisonment.

Back in the Midwest agents descended on Louie's roadhouse after learning from Emil Wanatka that it was Cernocky who had sent the gang to Little Bohemia. Wanatka had even mentioned the letter penned by Cernocky and presented by Nelson. No evidence was uncovered on the premises, and the agents had nothing, other than Wanatka's statements, to prove that Louie had ever harbored or assisted the outlaws. According to Caroline Corder, her employer had anticipated the raid and "repeatedly warned us not to say anything concerning Dillinger and his gang, and further stated that if anyone should ask any questions in this connection and should show us photographs . . . we were to answer such questions by stating that we had just started to work there and did not know anything."

Eddie Cernocky was even more blunt, warning Corder that if she ever talked about their notorious clientele, "I would be sorry for it, indicating possibly that some harm would come to me."

A check stub found in the handbag of Helen Gillis led agents to the Slinger garage in Portage where Nelson's wrecked Buick was stored. An attendant identified Nelson's photo and revealed that the desperado had said the Oakley Auto Construction Company in Chicago would retrieve his vehicle. The next day Special Agent James Metcalf visited the yellow brick garage on the northwest corner of Oakley and West Division. Clarence Lieder answered his questions and allowed a search. He freely admitted that he was a longtime friend of Nelson, at least "ten or twelve years," but never knew him by any name other than Lester Gillis. He insisted that the last time he had seen the man was "about three years ago when Gillis was driving a racing car at Robey Speedway." He claimed to know nothing about a wrecked vehicle in Portage and denied ever encountering any other members of the Dillinger gang.

There seemed to be no point in investigating further, for Lieder had no criminal record. A background check revealed that he had emigrated from Poland with his parents, becoming a naturalized U.S. citizen at the age of ten. He lived quietly with his wife, child, and parents a few doors down Division from his garage, in which his father, Julius, was part owner.

If the agents were startled to find Lieder, to all appearances a shining example of the American dream, they probably didn't know what to make of Father Phillip Coughlan. His card had turned up in Carroll's Buick at Little Bohemia. Two agents met him at his sister's home in Wilmette to sheepishly inquire about his relationship—if any—with the Dillinger gang. Coughlan professed to be shocked when informed his young friend Jimmie and Jimmie's pals were hoodlums. Like Lieder, he managed to tell the G-Men exactly what they wanted to hear, without really telling them anything. The priest promised to notify the bureau immediately if he had any further contact with the gangsters.

❋ ❋ ❋

On May 2 Roy Francis' stolen Ford was found on a residential street on Chicago's North Side, the passenger side of its front seat saturated with Hamilton's blood. An empty surgical kit, matchbooks imprinted with "Little Bohemia," and some .45 shells had been left inside. The discovery ignited a new round of police activity. Sergeant Reynolds and his forty-man Dillinger squad rushed to the site with machine guns and searched more than three dozen apartments in the neighborhood. Federal agents also poured into the area. Soon police officers and G-Men were bumping into one another or trying to beat their rivals to the scene of a new investigation. Each contingent complained that the other was withholding evidence and refusing to cooperate.

Focusing the authorities' attention on the North Side was probably what the outlaws had intended. Following Hamilton's burial, Nelson transported his two comrades to Lake County, Indiana, where Dillinger and Van Meter still had some trusted allies within the East Chicago underworld. Unfortunately the best their contacts were willing to do was provide "a small wooden shack" a few miles southeast of Gary. As Dillinger later told O'Leary, "It was in terrible condition, with windows broken or missing and a leaking roof." The desperate pair remained there for nearly a week, cold and miserable, Van Meter making sarcastic cracks about the glamour and excitement of a life of crime.

Nelson chose to take his chances back in the city, hoping to secure a more suitable hideout for himself and eventually his partners. Late that day he was reunited with Tommy Carroll, a recent arrival from the Twin Cities who manage to contact Nelson through Jimmy Murray. While his fellow outlaws had attracted all the attention in fleeing Wisconsin, Carroll, renowned for his unlucky breaks in evading lawmen, had pulled off the cleanest escape of all. After stealing the Packard in Mercer he had driven due north on County Trunk W until, twenty miles later, the car slid into a ditch. From there he'd hitchhiked to Minnesota. Aided by Reilly and Gannon he had hidden in St. Paul for a full week before coming to Chicago aboard a train.

Nelson wished he had better news to share about the gang's status. Carroll was informed of Hamilton's death, Dillinger and Van Meter's wilderness retreat, and the current state of siege by police and federal agents in Chicago. Nelson bitterly reported that many of his friends and contacts had come under FBI scrutiny, complaining that agents were even watching his sister Julie's home. Most of all he was infuriated over Helen's incarceration. He spoke incessantly of freeing her, through legal process if possible, by other means if necessary.

Cash wasn't a problem at the moment—each of the outlaws was either wearing a money belt or had grabbed one when the G-Men launched their raid on the lodge—but vehicles and weapons were. Nelson was driving a "borrowed" car, possibly Van de Houton's or one obtained through Lieder. Aside from the machine gun carried away by Van Meter and Nelson's machine-gun pistol, the four bandits possessed only a few handguns between them. Lebman's arrest ruled out another gun-buying expedition to Texas.

Shortly after Carroll rejoined him, Nelson managed to locate John Paul Chase, who had wisely withdrawn into obscurity in the wake of the furor over Little Bohemia. He expected his pal to present him with the "clean car" which he had instructed Chase to purchase before his departure. But Chase unhappily confessed that he'd made a tremendous blunder, using the name of Nelson's brother-in-law when buying a 1933 Essex Terraplane from a Chicago car dealer.

Nelson angrily declared the vehicle was useless to him, since he had no desire to cause trouble for his sister's family should the car be found in his possession. He directed Chase to contact Julie and present her with the Terraplane as a gift. In return he wanted Julie to make arrangements with Chicago attorney Harold Levy to represent Helen. Chase was to tell the lawyer that if he needed "cash up front," he could contact Nelson through Murray or Cernocky.

Once Chase had his instructions, Nelson and Carroll withdrew to the town of Wauconda, some 50 miles northwest of Chicago, where they were given the use of a cottage on Wilson Street belonging to Murray. Evidently the pair utilized the place as their principal hideaway through most of the month of May and enjoyed an infinitely more comfortable arrangement than Dillinger and Van Meter had. For the moment Nelson seemed unfazed by his new, notorious status in the media. He became a familiar figure to many merchants in Wauconda and nearby McHenry who knew the polite, well-dressed young man as "Mr. Cody."

Nelson and Carroll also visited Louie's, which was just a few miles southwest of Wauconda. Although G-Men reportedly were keeping a watchful eye on the roadhouse, Caroline Corder spotted the pair on three occasions, noting that they always avoiding the main dining area. Once she saw the two outlaws, along with Cernocky, son Eddie, and "an attorney by the name of Levy," holding a hushed conference in the kitchen. According to Miss Corder, Nelson and Carroll passed "quite a sum of money" to the lawyer.

On May 4 Harold Levy appeared before a federal judge in Madison asking to represent Helen Gillis. The judge denied the request, citing the fact that Levy's practice was in Illinois. Acting "on behalf of the Gillis family," Levy hired a local lawyer, Carl W. Hill, who by no coincidence was also an acquaintance of Cernocky. Hill's appointment was approved, but the judge refused to hear any motions on Helen's behalf until the attorney spent an "appropriate time" to familiarize himself with the case. Hearing of the latest legal delay, Nelson fumed that the courts were deliberately stalling in order to hold his wife and subject her to more relentless interrogation.

On May 5 the U.S. House of Representatives passed ten of the twelve anti-crime bills proposed by Attorney General Cummings. The laws, in effect, created a federal criminal code that placed investigations of an array of offenses (interstate flight, robbing a federal bank, assaulting or killing a federal officer) under the jurisdiction of the G-Men. Historians generally agree the new laws marked the birth of the modern FBI.

Critics of the bills complained that they gave too wide a range of powers to Hoover and his bureau. However, the slaying of Special Agent Baum by Nelson at the very moment the debate raged had compelled many opponents to approve the measures.

To underscore the importance of the new legislation President Roosevelt appealed to all citizens to join the fight against the depression desperados. He declared that according folk-hero status to men designated (by Hoover and Cummings) as public enemies was no longer acceptable and added that without public support the government's war against crime was destined to fail. "Law enforcement and gangster extermination," the president said, "cannot by effective while a substantial part of the public looks with tolerance upon known criminals, or applauds efforts to romanticize crime."

❋ ❋ ❋

Nelson and Carroll made several trips to Lake County, Indiana, that week to look in on their comrades and deliver food and supplies. They found Dillinger and Van Meter miserable, eager to abandon their wretched accommodations. Nelson had not yet found a safe place for the pair but suggested an unorthodox solution.

On May 7 a tall man using the name Addie James appeared at the Rimes Motor Company in East Chicago where he purchased a Ford V-8 Deluxe delivery truck. James, later identified by owner Herbert Rimes as John Paul Chase, paid cash for his new vehicle. Chase met Nelson near Gary and followed him to Dillinger's hideaway. While the outlaws were not excited by Chase's choice of color—fire engine red—they conceded it was a clever, if unusual way to keep a low profile. After all, who would suspect the nation's top public enemy of traveling the highways in a bright red delivery truck? A mattress was tossed in the back, turning the vehicle into a home on wheels for Dillinger and Van Meter.

For the next two weeks the pair stayed on the move, driving the back roads of Lake County and the outskirts of Chicago, taking turns sleeping in the back. A week spent in the damp, unheated shack followed by more nights in the drafty truck left Dillinger with a dreadful cold—at one point the outlaw's temperature soared to a feverish 104 degrees. Again they turned to Nelson for help. Baby Face convinced Clarence Lieder to let the two stay at his garage for a few nights to spare the ailing Dillinger from the chill of the early May evenings.

The arrangement came with conditions to satisfy Lieder, who was understandably cautious since agents had visited him two weeks earlier. They were to arrive at the garage after dark and be gone by dawn, and the truck was to be parked on the garage's elevator, which was to be raised, with Dillinger and Van Meter inside, halfway between floors to conceal it through the night.

During this period Dillinger met O'Leary three times. On each occasion, with Van Meter and his machine gun stationed at the truck's rear window, Dillinger drove over country roads as he spoke with Piquett's young assistant. O'Leary was told of Hamilton's demise and given an envelope to deliver to Pat Cherrington. Dillinger also spoke about acquiring the services of a plastic surgeon, a matter they had briefly discussed before. He was sick—literally—of his current nomadic existence. With a new face he could hide in plain sight and return to a more civilized lifestyle. O'Leary promised to make the arrangements.

Dillinger's chief concern at this time was his imprisoned sweetheart, whose trial was set for May 15. O'Leary reported that Piquett was in St. Paul preparing her defense and was optimistic about the outcome. The outlaw gave him a note to pass along to Billie and $600 for Piquett, promising—as always—that more was to come.

Nelson, meanwhile, was conducting a similar vigil, monitoring the legal action (or the lack thereof) surrounding Helen's case. With each passing day he became more infuriated.

At 10 P.M. on May 11 Bob Fitzsimmons answered a knock at his door and found a teenage boy on his porch. "Jimmie's out on the boulevard," the youth announced. "He wants to see his sister."

Fitzsimmons and Julie followed the teenager north to Garfield and turned west. A block later a dark sedan drew up to the curb. Nelson was at the wheel. Julie and her husband climbed in beside him while the youth slipped into the back next to Tommy Carroll.

Embracing her little brother, Julie related how worried the family was over the reports coming out of Wisconsin. "I'm glad to see you alive, Les," her husband added. Nelson "merely grinned and did not say anything," Fitzsimmons recalled, "evidently not caring to talk about previous events."

Driving east along Garfield, Nelson "immediately began talking about getting a writ for his wife." It was obvious "Lester was mad at the way the lawyer business had gone," especially since Levy's counsel had been rejected and the new attorney was being put off by the judge. Nelson asked the couple to go to Madison to visit Helen and offer encouragement. He also wanted them to let Hill know how "disgusted" he was. He told his sister to hire "a new lawyer and, if necessary, to get the best one in Wisconsin."

When Nelson asked if they planned to take their new Terraplane on the trip to Madison instead of the family's old Buick, Fitzsimmons revealed that Chase had not yet delivered it. The outlaw "raved about the stupidity of using my name in the purchase of the car" and vowed that they would get the vehicle as soon as he got back in touch with Chase. After about ten minutes Nelson dropped off the pair half a block from their home, and Julie assured her brother they would do everything possible to help Helen.

Two days later the couple and three of their children made the 140-mile drive to Madison, although Chase had still not turned over the Terraplane. Julie was startled to find her sister-in-law looking even thinner and paler than usual and noticed dark circles beneath her normally sparkling blue eyes. Without going into detail Helen admitted that she had not slept or eaten well while in custody.

Her spirit seemed equally drained. She wept while speaking of her children, whose latest birthdays she had missed. Ronald, now five, was still in Bremerton with Nelson's mother and sister Leona. Darlene, who had turned four just two days ago, was living with Julie's family. She desperately wanted to rejoin them and felt torn between her kids and remaining at her husband's side. When Julie told her she had seen Les and he was doing all he could to free her, Helen grew even more despondent. "They'll get him, you know," she said in an abruptly fatalistic tone. "It won't be long, either. I just want to spend all my time with him before the end comes." She then shocked Julie by talking about funeral arrangements for her outlaw husband.

Sitting in on the meeting, Attorney Carl Hill informed them the grand jury had been scheduled to reconvene on May 17, after which federal Judge Patrick T. Stone would determine the fate of Helen and her two co-defendants.

On May 19 the federal grand jury in Madison returned two sets of indictments. The first charged John Dillinger, Lester Gillis, Homer Van Meter, John Hamilton, Albert Reilly, Patricia Cherrington, Helen Gillis, Jean Crompton, and Marie Conforti with harboring and conspiracy to harbor Thomas Leonard Carroll, a federal fugitive. The second batch of indictments was virtually identical, although substituting Carroll's name for Dillinger's, and charged the same individuals with harboring the Indiana outlaw. Now armed with federal warrants, Hoover's agents possessed the legal clout to pursue Nelson and the rest of the gang.

Four days later Billie Frechette was found guilty and sentenced to two years at the women's federal prison in Milan, Michigan. Her conviction was viewed as another victory in the government's quest to smash the Dillinger gang. In the same St. Paul courtroom Bessie Skinner, despite providing crucial aid to the G-Men, received a fifteen-month sentence; Dr. May was given two years behind bars. Hoover announced that the convictions served notice to "all those who would give aid and shelter" to gangsters that the federal forces would show no leniency.

A similar verdict was expected for the three women in Madison. For a full week Mickey and Jean had been taken repeatedly to the federal courtroom to plead their case before Judge Stone. Helen's absence remained a mystery until it was finally revealed by Sheriff Finn's wife that she had grown so weak a physician had to be summoned to the jail. The young woman was diagnosed as malnourished and gravely anemic, and the doctor cautioned against subjecting her to any further forms of stressful questioning.

On May 25 all three women, having changed their pleas to guilty on the advice of Hill, were brought back to court for sentencing. Reporters for the first time were allowed a lengthy and close look at the trio as they waited in the corridor. Helen, described as "a comely brunette who appeared closer to eighteen than twenty-one," seemed plain and pallid beside her two companions. Mickey and Jean, wearing makeup and new clothes, beamed at the newsmen, while Helen hung her head and remained silent. Mickey chatted openly with reporters, although at one point she snapped, "Don't call us molls. We hate that!"

The defendants were escorted before the judge one at a time—Mickey first, then Helen, and finally Jean. Helen alone was provided with a chair. Imposing a sentence of eighteen months on each, Stone declared, "The court is satisfied that while these girls are technically guilty, they didn't do anything to aid in the concealment of Dillinger. It is doubtful a jury would have convicted these girls." He ordered the sentences suspended and placed each on a year's probation."

Helen smiled faintly as she left the courtroom. Her only comment was, "I'm happy to be going home to my little girl."

Hoover was furious. In light of his public crowing over the Frechette conviction the day before, the ruling by Judge Stone made him look foolish. He immediately directed his men to keep a tight surveillance on all three women, anticipating that they may lead agents to their boyfriends.

The girls' request to serve their probation in Chicago was granted, and with a couple hours to kill before their train departed, the trio, accompanied by a female reporter, went shopping. Mickey and Jean purchased clothes, perfume, and inexpensive jewelry; Helen bought a new hat and toothpaste. At lunch, while the others drank beer to celebrate their freedom, Helen picked at a salad and sipped hot chocolate topped with whipped cream. "I have to build up my health," she told the reporter. In spite of their ordeal each agreed Wisconsin's capital city was a great place. "Everyone in Madison has been very nice to us," Helen said. "The federal men are the only ones who acted rough."

Their train left at 3:35 that afternoon. As they got under way Helen gazed out a window and remarked to Jean, "If I never see Madison again, that'll be too soon."

Helen's conversation during the journey to Chicago was moody and often morbid. Reading newspaper accounts of the burials of Clyde Barrow and Bonnie Parker, who had been slain by officers in Louisiana three days earlier, she told her companions it was "romantic" that the pair had perished together. Jean later told agents, "They were very devoted to each other, and Helen wanted to die at the same time Jimmie died."

In Chicago they were met by Probation Officer William McGrath, who brought the women to his office and outlined their obligations. Each was required to contact him once a week by phone and once a month in person, forbidden to leave the state without written permission, and prohibited from associating with known criminals, especially any of the six men named in the indictments. Vowing she was "finished with Wayne," Mickey was allowed to move in with a friend on the North Side. When Jean confessed that she had no place to stay, Helen invited the blond to join her at the Fitzsimmons apartment.

The next day Julie and her family piled into the new Terraplane, which Chase had finally delivered a week earlier, and headed west for a visit with Mary Gillis and Leona in Bremerton. Darlene was left in the care of Nelson's eldest sister, Amy, who had recently moved into the household after separating again from her second husband. Happy to be reunited with her daughter, Helen took the little girl shopping and for walks around the neighborhood. Jean, who often accompanied them, recalled that Helen was always nervous and claimed to see agents tailing them everywhere.

It is entirely possible that Helen wasn't imagining the G-Men. Hoover's orders calling for surveillance of the women were evidently followed to some extent. However, the Chicago office was juggling a score of investigations and possessed neither the means nor the manpower to keep the trio under round-the-clock observation.

During her daily walks with Darlene, Helen kept a watchful eye for her husband who, she repeatedly told Amy and Jean, would soon come for her. She was unaware that Nelson had suddenly become a very busy man and was performing a series of services on Dillinger's behalf as the result of a tragic incident.

On the evening of May 24—the day after Billie's conviction and the day before Helen's court appearance—two East Chicago policemen, Lloyd Mulvihill and Martin O'Brien, left the station after reportedly telling a fellow officer that they had a tip on where to find Dillinger. Fifteen minutes later a night watchman on his way to work discovered their squad car sitting in the middle of a road along a desolate, marshy area outside Gary. In the front seat were Mulvihill and O'Brien, their bodies riddled with .45 slugs, their weapons still holstered.

Rumors and suspicions swirled around the investigation and all, to some degree, connected the crime to Dillinger. Both officers were deeply involved in the hunt for the bandits. Mulvihill, the father of six children, had been present at the East Chicago holdup and the death of Patrolman O'Malley. Some stories implied that the pair had been in the midst of learning the names of Dillinger's connections within the East Chicago underworld. One advocate of this theory was Captain Matt Leach, head of the Indiana State Police. He was convinced the officers had been set up for execution by Capt. Tim O'Neal and Sgt. Martin Zarkovich. Leach even believed that Zarkovich was the actual killer.

Dillinger's statements to O'Leary concerning the double murder also placed the blame on Zarkovich while revealing that the shooter was really Van Meter. It was Zarkovich, Dillinger insisted, who had deliberately sent out Mulvihill and O'Brien that night with orders to "shake down a couple of suspicious characters who were driving around in a red truck." According to the bank robber, the two officers "were getting to know too much and Zark was getting antsy." When the squad car pulled them over, Van Meter strafed the windshield with machine-gun fire.

The pair quickly fled to Chicago and called upon Nelson to find them temporary asylum. Reluctantly Murray agreed to provide them with rooms at the Rainbo. Nelson took the truck to Lieder's garage, where it was painted black and placed in storage.

The next evening Nelson received word that Murray needed to see him at once. The instant he pulled into the parking lot Murray rushed out to him. Dillinger, he complained, wasn't "behaving himself." Obviously invigorated and happy to be back among people after living in the truck, the most wanted man in America could not remain secluded in his room and made frequent appearances downstairs to socialize with customers and even flirt with the waitresses. Murray was shocked to hear several patrons comment that his guest resembled the notorious outlaw. After calming down his friend, Nelson went in to confront Dillinger.

While no record exists of their private chat, it is amusing to imagine Nelson, already portrayed in the press as tempestuous and unstable, lecturing Dillinger about self-control. Evidently whatever he said had little effect since Dillinger swiftly resumed fraternizing with the patrons and waitresses, even after Nelson had convinced Van Meter and then Piquett to talk to him.

Murray's dilemma was soon resolved by James Probasco, a seventy-six-year-old ex-teamster, ex-boxer, onetime veterinarian, and casual friend to both Murray and Piquett. Often arrested but never prosecuted, his underworld escapades included operating a speakeasy, fencing stolen goods, and suspicion of burglary. Murray spoke to Probasco about taking in Dillinger as a border. The idea of playing host to the nation's most celebrated criminal intrigued Probasco, who was looking to make some money in the hopes of purchasing a tavern.

On Sunday, May 27, Probasco informed Murray he would accept Dillinger as his houseguest. Piquett was called in to relay the suggestion to his client. The outlaw agreed to make the move, primarily due to Piquett's enthusiastic assurances that the house was not only an ideal hideout but also the perfect place for Dillinger to undergo his plastic surgery.

That evening Piquett and O'Leary arrived at Probasco's two-story cottage on Crawford Avenue. Dillinger was already there, pacing the sidewalk. After greeting them, the outlaw walked to a tan Hudson sedan that had been acquired by Carroll several days earlier. Dillinger conversed with the three occupants (most likely Carroll, Nelson and Van Meter) before grabbing his bags and Van Meter's machine gun, which was wrapped in a robe. The Hudson sped away as Dillinger rejoined the lawyer and his assistant.

The three men went inside where Dillinger was introduced to Probasco. They sat at the kitchen table discussing a fair price for his room and board. Probasco wanted fifty dollars a day but was persuaded to settle for thirty-five. Dillinger also presented Piquett with $3,000 as a down payment on his surgery. The operation was set for the next day.

Van Meter remained at the Rainbo while Nelson and Carroll continued to use Murray's Wauconda cottage. Baby Face learned at this time that Jack Perkins had returned from Florida. A late-night meeting was arranged. The boyhood pals warmly greeted each other, Nelson remarking how tanned and healthy Perkins looked. After sharing stories of recent adventures, Nelson said he needed to replenish his arsenal with as much firepower as Perkins could get his hands on—especially machine guns and high-powered rifles—as well as acquire bulletproof vests. Perkins asked for at least a week, claiming that most of his sources had dried up.

Helen, meanwhile, anxiously awaited word from her husband. Still weak and sickly, she was urged by Amy to visit a doctor. She scheduled an exam with Dr. William James of Oak Park for June 4. It was an appointment she would fail to keep.

After dark on May 29 "an unknown party"—probably the same teenager Nelson had used earlier—delivered a note instructing Helen to leave immediately and walk north on Marshfield. Two blocks from the apartment a car pulled alongside her. Nelson, wearing "a huge grin," was behind the wheel. For the next hour the couple drove around their old neighborhood. Nelson said that he and Carroll were in the process of securing a safe hideaway for all of them. Helen and Jean were to be ready to leave when he returned, which Nelson promised would be in no more than a couple days.

On May 31 Helen received a note providing directions on where to meet. That evening she and her husband stuffed as much of their belongings as they could into their handbags. Helen sat with her daughter until Darlene was asleep. At the appointed time both women told Amy farewell and left with their bulging purses. After a few blocks Helen whispered to Jean that she believed a man in a car was tailing them, but they agreed to stick to the plan.

They bought tickets at a movie theater and took seats in the last row. The instant the lights dimmed, they ducked out an exit, hurried along a dark alley, and emerged onto the street where they saw their ride. Helen joined her husband in the back as Carroll, with Jean nestled beside him, drove them away.

There were some of the Dillinger gang we would like to take alive, but Nelson wouldn't do us much good. . . . We aren't particular whether we take him alive or dead."
— Melvin Purvis

CHAPTER 12

CHICAGO CONFIDENTIAL

SINCE THE MID-1920S LAKE Geneva, Wisconsin, had been known as a resort haven for Chicago mobsters. Located twelve miles north of the Illinois border along Highway 12, the town played host to many of the Windy City's most notorious gangland figures, some of whom, including a brother of Al Capone, purchased palatial summer homes overlooking the spectacular lake.

For those who didn't rank among the underworld elite, or merely preferred a more secluded, low-profile place to stay, there was the Lake Como Inn three miles west of Lake Geneva. Access to the inn was gained by a quarter-mile gravel road leading from a county highway to a spacious clearing along the southwest shore of the smaller, unspoiled Lake Como. Fifty yards from the hotel was a two-story house at the edge of the water, the home of the inn's owner, Hobart "Hobe" Hermanson. On occasion rooms inside the house were used to handle extra guests, usually special friends of Hermanson or "hot" individuals who didn't wish to mingle with the other patrons.

Like almost everyone else who crossed paths with Baby Face Nelson, Hermanson was one of those gray characters who straddled the fence dividing the underworld from mainstream society—one foot planted in respectability while the other stepped precariously into criminal activities. He was a short, squat figure whose graying hair, potbelly, and ruddy complexion made him look older than his thirty-seven years. During Prohibition he had done well running the inn as a deluxe speakeasy and avoiding entanglements with the law. His intimacy with Chicago mobsters led to his marriage to Lucille Moran, ex-wife of Bugs Moran. One of Hermanson's principal contacts was Jimmy Murray, who no doubt played a major part in Nelson's choice to visit the inn.

Hermanson's official version, recited under the intimidating glare of federal agents, stated that on or about May 28 a tall, friendly man appeared at the hotel. He introduced himself as John Scott and confided that he "had been in the bootlegging business in California" and was presently on the lam after being charged with tax evasion. Scott—John Paul Chase—inquired about reserving some rooms for friends who would be arriving shortly. Hermanson was happy to accommodate the visitor. Late that night two men stopped in, met with Chase, and took time to look over the inn.

On June 1 two couples arrived and requested the rooms that had been reserved by Scott. One couple—described as a handsome man and an attractive blond—were given a room in the Hermanson house and were rarely seen. The other couple, calling themselves Jimmie and Jeanette, stayed in the main building and mingled frequently with other guests, giving the impression they were young newlyweds. Two days later Chase returned to the inn and was provided with a room near Nelson and his wife.

On June 5 Carroll and Jean announced they were leaving. Their destination was St. Paul, where Carroll was certain he could acquire some weapons. He also intended to case a few banks along the way.

That evening Nelson drove into Chicago for a scheduled rendezvous with Jack Perkins, who had managed to partially fill Nelson's request for "hardware" with one machine gun, two automatic rifles, and a quantity of ammunition. Perkins had placed an order for four steel-reinforced vests with "a syndicate friend" and promised delivery in a couple of weeks. He also revealed that he had found a source in New York looking to sell several Thompsons and a Monitor machine rifle, the commercial version of the army's Browning automatic rifle. Nelson was intrigued, even after learning the Monitor's asking price was $750, and urged his pal to make the trip to New York as soon as possible.

After leaving Perkins, Nelson arrived at Probasco's house about 9 P.M. and was greeted by Dillinger, Van Meter, Piquett, and O'Leary with a chorus of "Hello, Jimmie." Nelson had a present for his comrades—a fully loaded ammo drum for Van Meter's machine gun, which, he boasted, was a mere token of the arsenal he was presently accumulating for the gang.

Although glad to see Nelson and grateful for his gift, Dillinger and notably Van Meter were not in pleasant moods. By their own admission each looked frightful, like tortured subjects of some mad experiment. While Nelson and Carroll were relaxing with their women at Lake Como, the pair had subjected their faces and fingerprints to the scalpel of Dr. Wilhelm Loeser and an assistant, Dr. Harold Cassidy, a relative of O'Leary. Both were less-than-respectable members of the medical profession. Loeser, a Prussian immigrant in his late fifties, had served time in Leavenworth for peddling narcotics and had briefly fled to Mexico after parole to avoid paying his fine on the charge. Cassidy, an alcoholic abortionist, was being sought by police for giving perjured testimony on behalf of one of Piquett's clients.

Dillinger's first operation took place on May 28 and was followed by a facial touch-up and fingerprint removal five days later. On June 3 Van Meter underwent a similar treatment, the doctors attempting to cover a scar on his forehead, reshape his beak-like nose, reduce the size of his prominent lower lip, burn away the tattoo on his right forearm with acid, and obliterate his prints. The lanky bandit had also moved into the Probasco home, paying the required thirty-five dollars a day and $5,000 for his surgery.

For all their expense and days of excruciating pain, when the bandages were removed the outlaws studied their scarred, swollen faces and saw little actual change in their appearance. Despite Piquett's robust assurances that they had been transformed, Van Meter's dissatisfaction went from brooding to belligerent to ballistic. When Loeser stopped to check on his patients that day, Van Meter called him a "butcher" who had turned his face into "a fucking mess." He marched into the bedroom to retrieve his machine gun, threatening to "drill" the doctor, but discovered his fingers were too sore to grasp the weapon. Taking O'Leary's advice, Loeser discreetly fled shortly before Nelson's arrival. Van Meter was still complaining to Piquett about the surgery when Nelson took a seat with them in the front room. Baby Face listened to the grumbling with as ever-widening smile. "So you two decided to go out and buy yourselves a pair of new mugs," he said mockingly. "Well, maybe you needed them."

"At least I'll be able to go out on the street and get around now," Dillinger declared.

Nelson continued to tease Van Meter, telling him at one point to stop whining about his marred features because "you weren't all that pretty to begin with." Van Meter's comeback, laced with profanity, was to blame Nelson for having "turned up the heat" on all of them. "If you hadn't killed that fed, Johnnie and I wouldn't have had to get our faces cut."

Briefly describing the shooting outside the Koerner house, Nelson insisted Baum gave him "no choice." Due to all the publicity over the agent's death, Piquett suggested that he consider on operation as well. "No, thanks," the young outlaw replied, making it clear no "quack with a knife" would get near his face.

❋ ❋ ❋

While Nelson returned to Lake Como and Dillinger and Van Meter continued their recuperation at the Probasco home, Tommy Carroll and Jean Crompton were cruising through Iowa on a leisurely trek toward the Twin Cities. On the morning of June 7, after spending the night at the Evening Star tourist camp five miles outside Cedar Rapids as Mr. and Mrs. Leonard Murdock, their Hudson developed engine trouble, forcing them to stop at a garage in Waterloo. While servicing the car, a mechanic stumbled upon three sets of extra license plates—Illinois, Missouri, and Minnesota—hidden beneath the front floor mat and phoned the police.

The couple were gone by the time Detectives Emil Steffen and P. E. Walker arrived at the garage. Armed with a description of the car and the occupants, the pair searched the city for an hour before spotting the Hudson parked by an alley just half a block from the Waterloo police station. Steffen found the car locked and peered inside, spying what looked like a machine gun (later found to be an automatic rifle and 300 rounds of ammunition) hidden beneath a bathrobe on the back seat.

The detectives waited in their car a few yards away. At noon Carroll and Jean stepped out the rear door of a restaurant and strolled toward the Hudson. As the outlaw drew his keys to unlock the car, Walker approached him from behind, announcing, "I'm an officer and I'd like to talk to you a minute."

Carroll turned on the lawman, reaching for his pistol. Walker lunged at him and knocked the weapon from his grasp. As they scuffled, Steffen attempted to come to his partner's aid but was grabbed—almost tackled—by Jean. Carroll tore free from Walker, snatched up his gun, and dashed into the alley.

It was San Antonio all over again, only this time Carroll, perhaps fearing that he might hit Jean, fled without firing back. Steffen managed to throw Jean aside and joined Walker at the mouth of the alley, both men pulling their pistols. Five bullets fired between them smashed into the running figure and sent Carroll sprawling on the pavement.

The dying outlaw was rushed to the hospital, shot in the left armpit, chest, and three times in the lower back, shattering his spine. He lasted seven hours, admitting his identity but refusing to answer questions as he awaited the end. He had one request: "Take care of the little girl," he gasped. "She doesn't know what it's all about. I've got seven hundred dollars on me. Be sure she gets it."

Carroll's cash was actually closer to $600, but Jean never saw a cent of it. Arrested for parole violation, she was returned to Madison where, on June 11, she was brought before Judge Stone and sentenced to serve one year and a day in the Federal Industrial Institution for Women at Alderton, West Virginia.

The next day Judge Stone revoked the probation of Helen Gillis on being informed that she had dropped from sight and failed to report her whereabouts. He issued a bench warrant for her arrest.

❊ ❊ ❊

Nelson, Helen, and Chase were still at Lake Como when they heard of Carroll's death. Stunned, saddened, and shaken at the news, the trio checked out on June 8 for parts unknown. Of all his criminal companions over the past year, Nelson had grown closest to Carroll, a man he honestly admired and regarded as a true friend. Helen also bitterly mourned the loss of Jean who had been "like a sister" during the past three months.

In the wake of Carroll's demise the couple went underground so successfully that over the next six weeks no one, except for a select few, ever knew where they stayed. The fact that Nelson continued to make sporadic appearances around Chicago the entire time indicates they were laying low close to the Windy City. O'Leary reported overhearing Baby Face telling his fellow bandits that he stayed in tourist camps but never "two nights in the same place." He refused to "hole in" like the others.

Chase, along with Perkins and Murray, saw more of Nelson than did anyone else and took turns relaying messages. Baby Face also enjoyed once-a-week meetings with his sisters Amy and Julie, the latter having returned with her family on June 3 from their West Coast trip. Most of these get-togethers were held on back roads outside Chicago, usually after dark. Nelson grew so accustomed to this arrangement that he soon refused to make any more personal trips to the Probasco house, agreeing only to make late-night roadside rendezvous with Dillinger and Van Meter. The pair often returned from their nocturnal visits with "Jimmie" carting a fresh batch of weapons, which were stockpiled in Probasco's front bedroom.

According to O'Leary, Dillinger and Van Meter were also deeply affected by Carroll's death. Both lapsed into a daylong depression over the news, followed by a period of distinct anger. Dillinger, vowing to drive to Waterloo to "take care of those guys," added the names of Steffen and Walker to his "death list," which by now—in addition to Special Agent Harold Reinecke, Captain Matt Leach, Sergeant Frank Reynolds, and informer Art McGinnis—included Emil Wanatka, Purvis, and the four officers responsible for Hamilton's fatal wound. Dr. Loeser claimed he heard Van Meter boast that he intended to personally shoot the garage mechanic who tipped off the Waterloo police.

Instead of withdrawing into obscurity like Nelson, both outlaws—tired of their isolated existence at Probasco's and starting to believe Piquett's exhortations that the surgery had indeed altered their faces—began to venture into public. Dillinger made at least two trips back to Indiana to visit family and friends. He also attended an occasional Cubs game at Wrigley Field.

In the evenings Dillinger went to movies and jazz cabarets, usually escorting an attractive date. Though he continued to mourn the loss of Billie and, with Piquett appealing her conviction, still hoped to free her, Dillinger could no longer deny himself female companionship. He was keenly aware of the risk involved; Nelson, Van Meter, Piquett, and O'Leary all had warned him about his playboy antics. According to Perkins, Nelson once told Dillinger—probably during his flirtatious behavior at the Rainbo—that if he wasn't careful "your dick is going to do you in."

Most of Dillinger's dates were apparently arranged through Anna Sage, a former Gary madam and onetime mistress of Martin Zarkovich, who had relocated to Chicago. By late June Dillinger had settled into a steady relationship with one of Anna's girls, a pretty redhead named Polly Hamilton.

Eventually Van Meter, inspired by Dillinger's amorous excursions, decided to rekindle his romance with Mickey Conforti. In order to win her back, he figured he needed a place and a vehicle of his own. During one of his late-night sessions with Nelson, he appealed to the outlaw to help him acquire a new set of wheels.

On June 12 Clarence Lieder and Jack Perkins walked into an auto agency on North Damon Avenue and purchased a 1934 maroon Ford V-8 sedan. Lieder, who was known to the salesman, claimed he was buying the car for his friend Henry Adams, Van Meter's current alias—though Lieder implied that Perkins was actually Adams. That evening Perkins delivered the new Ford to Van Meter at Probasco's house.

Since her release almost three weeks earlier, Mickey, to all appearances, had acted as a model of reform. Agents had kept her under almost constant surveillance, especially after the May 31 disappearance of Helen and Jean. Mickey, however, displayed no hint of returning to her former role as Van Meter's mistress. Living quietly at a friend's apartment, she worked days as a clerk in a dime store and evenings as a waitress.

The young brunette knew she was being watched and no doubt maintained her impeccable behavior accordingly. The G-Men decided to take a chance, instructing Special Agent Al Muzzy to contact her without disclosing his identity in the hope that she might reveal some information about the gang. One day as Mickey walked to work Muzzy offered her a lift. "It's nice of you to give me a ride," she said, hopping in beside him. "I didn't know the federal government was supposed to do that for me."

Now that they knew she was on to them, the agents made their presence felt day and night in an attempt to press Mickey into service. "They took me on long rides trying to trap me into telling them about Baby Face Nelson," she said later. When Mickey complained that she knew nothing, the agents told her if she uncovered information for them they would leave her alone. She didn't have to betray Van Meter, or even talk about Dillinger. "It was Nelson they wanted the most," she said.

Mickey reluctantly gave in. A pair of agents drove her "all over Chicago" to businesses and residences where Nelson was suspected of having contacts. While the G-Men waited in the car, Mickey was directed to go in and "find out whatever I could." One stop was the Fitzsimmons apartment, where she told Julie that she needed to reach Helen to retrieve some of her clothes. In the end Mickey was unable to provide the bureau with any useful information. Confident she was at least cooperating, the agents eased away from their surveillance.

On the morning of June 13 Mickey was shocked to find her former boyfriend waiting outside her home. Refusing to take no for an answer, Van Meter coaxed her into his new Ford. As they drove, he gushed about how much he had missed her and wanted her back, promising "gifts and good times" in the days to come. Mickey said she needed time to consider his offer and warned him about the agents who were pestering her almost daily and trying to use her to obtain leads on Nelson. Van Meter told her not to worry, chuckling, "Jimmie is way too careful for those clowns to ever catch him."

Dropping Mickey off a block from her job, Van Meter vowed to return in a week—time enough for her to decide whether to join him and for him to find a suitable place to share. In the meantime agents continued to badger her, demanding that she accompany them on more fact-finding missions. When Van Meter returned for her on June 21, Mickey went with him.

"Why did I violate the probation?" she later told newsmen. "Because the federal men hounded me into it. . . . I got so I was afraid some of the boys would see me with the agents and think I was a squealer. So I went back to Homer Van Meter."

The two moved into an apartment in Calumet City as Mr. and Mrs. Henry Adams. Their rent was fifteen dollars a week, a bargain for Van Meter after doling out thirty-five dollars a day to Probasco.

❋ ❋ ❋

Shortly after their departure from Lake Como, Chase separated from Nelson to drive back west. His main goal was to lure their former rumrunning associate Fatso Negri back to Chicago as an ally of the gang. In the process Chase hoped to spend some time with his sweetheart, Sally Bachman.

He reached San Francisco June 14 and contacted Negri. "Are you ready for a little activity?" Chase inquired with a sly grin. He promised Negri would be "seeing some big money" if he joined them. "Jimmie wants you out there. He needs people he can trust right now."

Unemployed for the past few months and rapidly slipping into debt, Negri was easy to win over this time. The two men spent the day visiting old friends in the area. Chase, however, carefully avoided Sausalito after being warned that federal agents recently had been making inquiries about him.

That evening Sally received a phone call from Negri informing her that he would take her to see "Johnny." He arrived at her apartment on Turney Street in Sausalito an hour later. Just before midnight they reached the home of Gene

Mazet in San Raphael where Chase was waiting. Sally was happy to see her boyfriend but bewildered by all the precautions. Chase explained that while in Chicago he'd loaned his car to a friend who had accidentally killed a man with the vehicle. The authorities, tracing the license, were wrongfully seeking him for the crime. At daybreak Chase announced that he had to return to Chicago. After receiving Sally's pledge that she still cared for him, Chase vowed to be back by July 12, her twenty-seventh birthday.

Chase left a note with Mazet containing instructions for Negri. Fatso was to proceed to the Cal-Neva Lodge and ask for Tex Hall, who would provide some cash and a certain Hudson sedan. Negri was to drive to the Coolidge Hotel and wait to be contacted. "Where the hell is the Coolidge Hotel?" Negri asked.

"Must be Chicago," Mazet said. "That's where Johnny is."

Negri flew to Reno that day and met with Hall. In his office Tex handed Negri $100, then placed a phone call. He asked Fatso if he really wanted the Hudson. "Something wrong with it?" Negri inquired.

"That's the St. Paul Hudson," Hall answered. "You know about that shooting up there?"

Negri said he'd never heard about it. Saying there should be no problem as long as Negri was careful, Hall left and returned about ten minutes later with a stranger. "You go with this fellow, Fats," the manager told him. "He'll fix you up."

The stranger was Frank Cochran. He drove Negri to his home and led him into the garage where the Hudson was parked. "This car has been here so long I ought to be claiming it," Cochran grumbled. He said the tank was full, the oil had been changed, and the vehicle was ready to make the long drive to Chicago. Negri, however, confessed that he didn't know his way around Reno and had to be guided to the highway by Cochran.

Negri drove all night and reached Chicago late the next day, June 17. Following Chase's instructions he found the Coolidge Hotel on Jackson Boulevard and registered as Joseph Pasquale. The desk clerk told him that a man had asked for him earlier and said he would check back later. Negri went to his room, washed up, and changed, then returned to the lobby. About nine o'clock a small man with coal-black hair and dark, darting eyes walked directly to Negri and shook his hand, introducing himself as Clarey. "You bring the Hudson?" Lieder asked. When Negri replied that he had, Lieder said, "Let's go for a ride."

Lieder drove to the Rainbo and pulled into the drive-in service area. A teenage boy came out to take their order, and Lieder asked, "Have you seen Jimmie yet?" The youth said he hadn't, and Lieder and Negri ordered sandwiches and soft drinks. An hour later a Hudson coach containing Nelson, Helen, and Chase parked beside them. Baby Face warmly greeted his West Coast pal, asking him, "How do you like the big city?"

After a brief chat with Nelson, Lieder drove off in the sedan Negri had brought from Reno. ("I never saw it again," Negri later told the FBI.) The rest walked inside the Rainbo, where Fatso was introduced to Murray and his wife. When the restaurant closed, the entire group retired to Murray's house in Oak Park.

Negri soon settled into a routine that each day brought him back to the Rainbo, where he often passed time playing the slot machines until he was met by Chase or Lieder. Describing his role to government agents later, Negri revealed that he carried "messages to Clarey regarding automobiles, license plates, ammunition, making arrangements for the places to meet Jimmie, Johnnie, and Helen. I would go down to Clarey's [the Oakley garage] and deliver the messages, and then I would come back to Jimmie Murray's place and wait until Clarey picked me up."

Nelson, always in the company of his wife or Chase or both, met Negri after dark on out-of-the-way country roads. The locations varied, and they were often as far as thirty miles outside Chicago. Negri, who was unfamiliar with the area, later recalled pre-arranged meetings along Highways 16 and 62, Wolf Road, Meacham Road, Algonquin Road, and Holland Bend. One of their favorite rendezvous spots was behind a white frame schoolhouse on the west side of Highway 53 several miles south of Palatine, which offered an excellent view of all approaches.

On one occasion Nelson gave Fatso $200 to pay Lieder for a package; Negri was never told what was inside. Once Negri and Lieder delivered an automatic rifle, and the two often brought boxes of ammunition. Another time they presented Nelson with a burlap sack stuffed with license plates. Occasionally Nelson and Lieder exchanged cars—both drove almost identical Hudsons—and when Lieder had finished servicing the vehicle to Nelson's specifications they would switch back.

During one of their nocturnal sessions a maroon Ford appeared on the scene. When a lanky stranger stepped out, Negri asked, "Who's that?" Chase assured him it was all right. Nelson and the other man engaged in several minutes of quiet conversation before Baby Face waved Negri over. "Here's a friend of mine from California," Nelson announced. "Fatso, this is Wayne."

Negri offered a gregarious hello; Van Meter responded with a curt nod and a suspicious glare. Although Chase had described Wayne and Jimmie as best friends, Negri sensed there some kind of tension between them. Since Little Bohemia Dillinger and Van Meter had become virtually inseparable, the latter seeming to dominate his more celebrated companion. Dillinger reportedly had grown so mistrustful that he wouldn't make a move without consulting the faithful Van Meter. Over the past few weeks Nelson, made to feel excluded and subordinate to the pair, had gravitated closer to Carroll and then to Chase.

Adding to Nelson's disenchantment with his comrade was Van Meter's recently revived romance with Mickey Conforti. When he heard from his sisters and others that Mickey was aiding G-Men in their search for him, Nelson was predictably furious. His insistence that Van Meter either terminate the relationship or terminate Mickey inevitably drove the wedge deeper between the two outlaws.

A few days later Chase came to Negri's room looking pale and shaken. "Can you imagine, I just got away from the cops!" he said. He explained that he had just picked up a new Hudson from Lieder's garage when a squad car started after him. After a desperate high-speed chase through Chicago's West Side, he had managed to shake his pursuers.

Negri suggested that it might be wise to stay off the streets for a while. Chase, however, said there was an important meeting at the schoolhouse that night, promising Fatso a special treat. When they arrived, Nelson was already there conferring with Van Meter and a short man attired in a light gray suit. Chase whispered to Negri, "You know who that is, don't you?"

Negri shrugged. "No, who is it?"

"Never mind," Chase replied with an odd laugh as he left to join the others. As Negri waited in the car, it slowly dawned on him that the man in the gray suit was Dillinger, although he looked nothing like his photos. In addition to his recent face-lift the desperado had blackened his hair. He was only a couple inches taller than Nelson and slightly heavier. Returning to the car, Chase handed Negri a pistol and directed him to stand watch near the front of the school building. "If any cars pull in, you shoot," he said. When Fatso objected to using a gun, Chase argued, "You can fire a warning shot in the air, can't you?"

"I stood over there three or four hours," Negri said later. "They were talking all the time, Jimmie, Johnnie, Van Meter, and Dillinger." Finally Chase called him over. "You got a car?" Dillinger asked. Negri, who had been dependent on Chase, Lieder, and taxis since he hit town, replied that he didn't. "We'll have to get Fats some wheels," Nelson announced.

As they prepared to leave, Dillinger made a comment about the plates on Chase's Hudson. Negri, catching pieces of the conversation, gathered that Dillinger and Van Meter were complaining that Lieder had supplied Chase with either hot or suspicious plates. "No wonder they came after you," Van Meter growled, referring to Chase's narrow escape. When Nelson spoke up to defend Lieder, Dillinger snorted, "That little Jew has been making more money off our jobs than we are."

✳ ✳ ✳

On June 22, Dillinger's thirty-first birthday, Attorney General Homer Cummings designated the Indiana bank robber as the nation's top public enemy, a title unofficially bestowed on him by the media since his colorful exit from the Crown Point jail. The following day the government posted a $10,000 reward for the capture of John Dillinger and offered $5,000 for information leading to his arrest. A wanted bulletin was also issued for Baby Face Nelson, although the rewards were slashed in half—$5,000 for his arrest, $2,500 for information.

Dillinger read the news during one of Van Meter's visits. "Looks like my price is going up," he noted proudly. "Watch Jimmie burn when he finds out the feds put a cheaper price tag on him than on me. And you, Van, you don't rate at all."

That night Dillinger couldn't resist a little playful gloating over the difference in the rewards offered for himself and Nelson. Instead of the expected petulant display, Baby Face—according to Negri's earliest and most reliable account—actually chuckled over his cut-rate status. "Who's to say?" he said. "Someday I might be worth as much as you."

Negri had been in Chicago nearly a week but still was puzzled over what function he served other than relaying messages and standing guard during their night meetings. Nor had he seen any of the action or big money Chase had promised, or the car Nelson said he would receive.

Finally, one afternoon Chase visited Negri's hotel room and tossed a bundle of money onto the bed, telling him, "Count it out for me." Separating the bills into stacks of fives, tens, and twenties, Negri arrived at a total of $1,180. Chase never disclosed where the cash came from, leaving Negri to assume the gang had pulled off a robbery. (The money may have been cash that Nelson had deposited with underworld friends out west and was sent to him by his sister Leona.) "You keep the fives," Chase told Negri, who pocketed "around $300," the first cash he had received since his arrival.

Chase announced it was time to get Fatso more involved in the gang's affairs. Their primary objective at the moment, he said, was to case some banks in hopes of finding a low-risk score with a big payoff. The bandits had their eye on a number of possible targets, but Dillinger, Nelson, and Van Meter believed their faces—altered or not—were too well-known for them to do their own scouting. The trio looked to Nelson's trusted pals—Chase, Negri, Lieder, Perkins, and Johnston—to act as their jug markers.

One evening Nelson schooled Negri in the art of casing a bank. He stressed observing the layout of the interior, the number and positions of employees, the flow of customers, and any guards stationed inside. The next day Chase and Negri drove to a small town "about three hours out of Chicago." Chase handed his chunky friend a twenty-dollar bill and directed him to ask for singles as he surveyed the premises. Later Negri accompanied Lieder to a bank in Elgin, Illinois, which they diligently studied for the gang.

Neither bank generated much interest among the outlaws since the reports indicated that they didn't do enough business to be worth the trouble. The gang was also considering three banks in Platteville, Wisconsin, and Dillinger had even discussed robbing all three by staging a daring raid on the town. Piquett heard about the outlandish scheme and complained that Platteville was his hometown. "I'm telling you, Johnnie, you can't do this!" he squawked at his notorious client. "Everybody knows I'm your lawyer. If you go up to Platteville, it will look like I cased the banks and put my hometown on the spot."

The Platteville caper was also scrapped. In the end, Van Meter fingered the job which proved to be the gang's final robbery. Apparently this was the way Dillinger intended it. Recently he had confided to the people around him that he was tired of fugitive life and looking to get out once and for all.

It was the old outlaw dream of pulling off one last high-stakes score, then vanishing in a foreign land. Dillinger reportedly arranged for his exit from the States with a pilot who, for a hefty fee, agreed to fly him to Mexico. He even had a backup plan, paying an elderly Chicago couple to smuggle him across the border as their son should the other deal fall through. All he needed to make his flight into oblivion a reality was money.

Van Meter convinced Dillinger and Nelson that the Merchants' National Bank of South Bend, Indiana, was precisely what they were looking for. Over the past two weeks Van Meter, wearing disguises, had visited the college town, scrutinized the bank, and worked out a getaway route. The post office made daily deposits at the bank, which, he insisted, guaranteed a six-figure payoff—the huge haul that the jobs in Sioux Falls and Mason City had been expected to yield.

Perkins, acting as Nelson's emissary, made two trips to South Bend and confirmed there was plenty of business and little security at the bank. The only problem he noted was its location in the center of the town's busy business district. Van Meter suggested springing the holdup on a Saturday just before the noon closing, thus ensuring less traffic and more cash on hand.

His fellow thieves were probably unaware that Van Meter had personal reasons for choosing South Bend. Nine years earlier the outlaw, then a lanky teenager pulling chump-change stickups with his buddy Cal Livingston, had gotten into a gun battle with South Bend lawmen. Livingston was shot to death but Homer escaped, only to be hunted through northwest Indiana and arrested days later. Despite his supposedly professional assessment of the Merchants' National as the perfect bank to hit, Van Meter had his own private score to settle with South Bend.

The details of the robbery were worked out during their meetings beside the schoolhouse. Everything fell into place with one glaring exception: Dillinger, Nelson, and Van Meter could not do the job alone. The trio briefly considered Nelson's pals as possible recruits, but although Baby Face gave each one an enthusiastic endorsement, his partners apparently felt they needed a more seasoned veteran to join them in the holdup.

❋ ❋ ❋

A full year had passed since the Kansas City Massacre, and whether they had participated in the bloody ambush or not, Charley Floyd and his faithful sidekick Adam Richetti gradually had risen from the ranks of many to become the FBI's chief suspects in the case. Some claimed that J. Edgar Hoover had manipulated evidence and witnesses to create an excuse to pursue the celebrated Oklahoma outlaw.

In any event, with the authorities turning up the heat, Floyd and Richetti were forced to go underground. The pair fled first to Cleveland and then Buffalo, where they secluded themselves with two sisters, Rose and Juanita Baird, in a five-room, eighth-floor unit in the Amantus Apartments on 18th Street. As the months crawled by, the sisters complained of crushing boredom and cabin fever, but their boyfriends "remained in the apartment constantly," fearing they would be spotted if they ventured outside.

After hibernating from September to April, Pretty Boy and his pal "took a few trips," leaving the sisters behind. According to Rose, they would "be gone one or two days, sometimes two or three weeks." Once they returned with extra money.

On May 13—Mother's Day—Floyd and Richetti spent the morning with Pretty Boy's mother at a farm near Akins, Oklahoma. The Floyd family later revealed that Charley also had met with Clyde Barrow and Bonnie Parker at the home of Floyd's brother Bradley. Floyd always spoke disapprovingly of the pair, since their depredations tended to be small-time and bloody. Nevertheless, itching for action and in desperate need of funds, he agreed to accompany the pair on "a big job."

Nine days later Bonnie and Clyde were dead, putting an end to Floyd's hopes of joining them. On their way back to Buffalo, Floyd and Richetti stopped in Cleveland, where they learned that members of the Barker-Karpis gang were hiding out. Karpis, in fact, was the guest of a hood named James "Shinney" Patton, a part owner of the Harvard Club, a lucrative gambling den in suburban Newburgh Heights.

Karpis later recalled the evening he was informed two men wanted to see him in the club's parking lot. Floyd and Richetti sat in a dark 1934 Ford coupe with the motor running. Explaining that they "felt safer in the car," Floyd said he "wanted to get in with us guys," but Karpis regretfully informed him "there wasn't a chance." The Barkers had too many people and problems already. The outlaws "parted on good terms," Floyd telling Karpis that if he should change his mind or find they needed an extra gun for an upcoming heist, he could be reached through a mob contact in Canton.

Word circulated through the underworld grapevine that Floyd was looking to hook up with an established outfit. Dillinger and/or Van Meter probably heard about Pretty Boy's quest and managed to reach him in Buffalo. It is equally possible that Floyd, hearing from the Barkers about Hamilton's death and reading of Tommy Carroll's passing, sought out Dillinger and offered his services. Whichever side made the first move, the key mediator seems to have been Richetti. In 1928 Richetti had been arrested in Hammond, Indiana, for a mugging in which he stole a six-dollar ring and four dollars in cash. Convicted of petty theft, he spent the next two years in the Pendleton reformatory, where he became acquainted with both Dillinger and Van Meter.

✳ ✳ ✳

A full week before the South Bend robbery, FBI agents in Chicago heard gangland chatter that an alliance had been forged between Floyd and the Dillinger outfit. They paid little attention to the rumors. From the voluminous reports filed by the Chicago office in the month of June, it seems almost every lead and investigative effort pursued by the G-Men focused on the family, friends, and underworld associates of Nelson. This was not only by design, since the agents privately wanted Baby Face for Baum's murder more than Dillinger at this point, but also because the gang's trail continually led back to Nelson's people.

The work proved to be exhausting and exasperating, some memos complaining of an overload of leads and a shortage of manpower. From the many individuals interviewed or dragged in for interrogation, agents obtained another long list of names and places to be checked. At times the roll of Nelson's alleged pals read like a Who's Who of Chicago hoods, including such infamous figures as Jack McGurn and Tony Capezio. (McGurn's Oak Park home and Capezio's Hy-Ho Club and Western Avenue flower shop were all watched at times in the hope of spotting Nelson.)

More often the tips led to honest citizens who admitted past connections to the young man they knew as "Les" but professed they hadn't seen for years. When Al Van de Houton—who had provided Nelson with rides just two months earlier—was questioned, he spoke for hours about his past involvement with the desperado but insisted the last time he had seen Nelson was when he had accompanied Helen on a visit to Joliet almost three years ago. The agents asked him who, among all of Nelson's friends, was his closest. Van de Houton replied that, without a doubt, it was Jack Perkins.

Perkins's name repeatedly surfaced during the scores of interviews conducted by the G-Men, but he was the one friend of Nelson they couldn't locate, despite weeks of extensive efforts. The agents delved into his shady background, examined his lengthy police record, and squeezed their informants about him. They discovered that Perkins was employed by mobsters as a collector and that, despite having a wife and two children, "one great weakness Perkins has . . .

is women, and from this standpoint considerable information might be obtained if the cooperation of a clever and reliable woman could be obtained." Inspector Cowley heartily approved this strategy. The only problem was determining the whereabouts of the phantom-like Perkins.

One evening an excited informant notified agents that Perkins was at the Pioneer Restaurant. But by the time Special Agents William Ryan and Earl Richmond arrived at the scene, Perkins had vanished. Less than a week later Richmond, this time with Special Agent James Metcalf, spotted Perkins in the company of two young ladies at the Hy-Ho Club. Before they could tail them, however, the chubby hood and his woman managed to slip away.

On June 25 the bureau received a tip on Perkins from an unexpected source. The call came from Father Coughlan, who reported an encounter with Perkins. Coughlan's zeal to cooperate was no doubt generated by his Catholic superiors who continued to frown on his socializing with known criminals. To appease them and to dispel any growing suspicions agents might have about his veracity, the priest decided to play the role of responsible citizen.

The agent who arrived to interview Coughlan that evening was himself a devout Catholic and was possibly assigned this particular task for that reason. Herman Edward Hollis was born in Des Moines, Iowa, on January 27, 1903. He graduated from Drake University Law School in 1927 and two months later joined the bureau. Over the next seven years he was bounced across the map, assigned to field offices in Kansas City and Oklahoma City, then serving as SAC at New Orleans, Cincinnati, and Detroit. His request for transfer to the Chicago office a few months earlier had been a step down from his former supervisory positions. But Chicago was where the action was, and it was closer to his and his wife Genevieve's relatives in Iowa.

Called Eddie by friends, family, and fellow agents, Hollis was a mirror image of Purvis's quiet efficiency on the job and also had a nearly identical meek, unassuming appearance. Short and wiry, with a high forehead and small mouth, he possessed the kind of plain, nondescript features that no one seemed to notice. It was no surprise that his favorite assignments involved undercover work. He was a natural.

Hollis produced a photo of John Alfred Perkins, which Coughlan quickly identified. The priest said he'd first met Perkins the previous summer at Long Beach and had seen him numerous times since at Chicago nightclubs. (Coughlan apparently offered no explanation why a Catholic priest patronized nightclubs.) About 5:30 that afternoon, Coughlan stated, he had been driving on Dundee Road near Louie's roadhouse when he was flagged down by the driver of a Ford V-8 sedan. Perkins stopped, got out of his car, and walked over to speak with Coughlan, leaving a woman—the priest was unable to tell if it was Perkins's wife—waiting in the vehicle. Perkins mentioned that he was presently residing in Lake Zurich and was in daily contact with their mutual friend

Jimmie. In fact Perkins claimed to have just left Nelson, who asked him to pass along his regards to the priest. Coughlan was surprised Jimmie was in the area, having earlier heard from Eddie Cernocky that Nelson was hiding out in St. Paul—a fact Coughlan had reported to agents on June 8.

Hollis wondered—as did others in the Chicago office—if Coughlan was providing reliable information or deliberately feeding them false leads. As a test of the Father's good faith the agent invited Coughlan to accompany him on a tour of some of Nelson's known hangouts. "Certainly," Coughlan replied, sounding excited at the prospect of riding with a G-Man.

Their first stop was the River Grove garage of Howard Davis. The priest did all the talking and didn't introduce Hollis. He asked the garage owner if he had seen Jimmie lately, and Davis told him that his last contact with Nelson had been about six months ago. Hearing this, Hollis recalled that in a previous interview with agents Davis had insisted he hadn't seen the outlaw for well over three years. "The next time you see Jimmie," Coughlan told Davis, "have him get in touch with me."

The priest and the agent visited Louie's next, and again Coughlan made casual inquiries about Nelson among the staff and clientele while Hollis looked on and listened. The agent's cover was almost blown when he spotted Madison attorney Carl Hill, accompanied by a young woman, entering from the upstairs. Three years earlier Hollis had met Hill during a Prohibition case in Kansas City. While it was evident that "Hill at this time was pretty well under the influence of liquor," Hollis tried to avoid him.

As the evening wore on Eddie Cernocky introduced Coughlan and "his friend" to the lawyer. Hill referred to the young woman as "my girl" and boasted that he was "the Dillinger attorney" who had succeeded in getting the gang's three girls released on probation. He also revealed he had been a frequent visitor to the roadhouse over the past three years and regarded Louie as "a hell of a fine fellow." Hill and Coughlan spoke about the death of Tommy Carroll, the attorney saying that he "sure hated to see Carroll's girl have her probation revoked."

Later Hill called Hollis aside and asked, "Aren't you a federal man?" When Hollis denied he was, the tipsy lawyer remarked, "Yes, I guess I was mistaken. You'll have to excuse me."

Hollis's report on the evening ended by saying, "Father Coughlan will return to the tavern of Louis Cernocky and discreetly ascertain whether the identity of this agent has become known." Though virtually none of Coughlan's information—including the tip that Perkins was living in Lake Zurich—proved useful, the priest managed to convince at least Hollis that he was genuinely doing his best to assist in the investigation.

❋ ❋ ❋

At eight o'clock that same Monday evening six men arrived in three cars in front of a hotel on the western outskirts of Chicago. Perkins had a special delivery for the gang. After a brief conversation Nelson announced to everyone, "We're going out to the schoolhouse."

Nelson and Chase led the way in a Hudson, Perkins and Art Johnston following in a Plymouth, Lieder and Negri in the rear driving a Ford. Nelson called on Lieder to stand guard, then invited Negri to help him "check out the merchandise." From the Plymouth's back seat Perkins removed four bulletproof vests. Nelson studied them and selected one, which he propped against a tree. Taking out a high-powered rifle, he fired a rapid stream of slugs into the vest and diligently inspected the results.

"There was a little debate about the price," Negri recalled. Perkins asked for $300 apiece. Nelson—rarely known to haggle—offered $1,000 for all four. After settling the price, Nelson looked to Negri and inquired, "You want one of these, Fats?"

Negri was startled. "What do I want that thing for?"

The next night the gang met alongside a stretch of highway near some train yards instead of at their usual spot. Dillinger and Van Meter arrived in separate cars, while Nelson, Helen, Chase, and Negri rode together. Baby Face presented each of his partners with a vest. As the trio engaged in another hushed conversation a car suddenly appeared.

Two young men in a Ford, noticing the three vehicles parked along the road, stopped and asked if they needed help. The desperados immediately flashed their guns and ordered them out of their car. Negri said later, "I thought the boys were going to kill these two fellows." Instead they were frisked and told to turn around and stay put until everyone else departed. One young man acted "kind of funny" and kept looking back at the gunmen. Dillinger barked at Negri, "Go over there and tell that guy to quit gawking at us."

Fatso relayed the command, but the intruder, perhaps fearing he and his friend would be shot, continued to glare at the outlaws. Negri joined Helen in the Hudson. "That guy's crazy, Fats," she remarked. "I hope nothing happens."

Dillinger was the first to drive off. Van Meter stared at the two men as he walked to his car. When Nelson said, "I'll see you later," his skinny comrade declared, "I ought to hit that guy just for fun."

"Why don't you be smart?" Nelson advised.

Van Meter slipped behind the wheel and, according to Negri, "he deliberately put it in low gear and hit the guy with the bumper." Nelson was furious as he watched Van Meter drive away. "I really believe if Van Meter was standing there Jimmie would have shot him," Negri added.

Nelson and Negri helped the man to his feet, the victim evidently more shaken by Van Meter's rude departure than injured. At first Nelson angrily rebuked him for failing to "do what you're told." Then, Negri recalled, "Jimmie apologized and said don't tell anybody, and we went away in good spirits."

The next day, June 27, Pat Reilly was captured by agents in St. Paul and charged with harboring a federal fugitive. While the G-Men grilled him about his ties with the Dillinger crowd and his presence at Little Bohemia, Nelson, Van Meter, and Perkins visited South Bend for a final reconnaissance of the bank, returning via the getaway route drawn up by Van Meter.

Negri spent the day switching to a new hotel, the Fullerton. That evening he rode with Chase to the schoolhouse, finding Nelson and his two companions, back from their scouting expedition, already there. From the bits and pieces he had overheard, Fatso was certain a major holdup was in the works. With each night, however, he wondered if the disintegrating relationship between Nelson and Van Meter would tear the gang apart.

Before long the two outlaws were arguing again. Nelson screamed at Van Meter about his hit-and-run antics the previous night, his failure to share in the gang's expenses, and most of all his ongoing affair with Mickey Conforti. Finally Chase suggested, "Let's go for a walk," and with Perkins joining them they discreetly withdrew from the feuding bandits. Even at a distance Negri could still hear Nelson's angry words. At one point Baby Face growled that he was sick of Van Meter making excuses for Mickey. Nelson wanted her dead. "If you're not gonna bump her off, I can find somebody who will. Or maybe I'll just kill you instead," he threatened.

"The argument got so hot," Negri claimed, "I expected firecrackers [to] bust open any moment." Eventually the shouting subsided. Nelson and Van Meter apparently resolved their differences, or at least managed to forge a shaky truce for the sake of the South Bend job.

Two days later—Friday, June 29—Negri was "hanging around" the Rainbo, waiting to be contacted by the gang. A young carhop ran up, pointed to a vehicle that had just pulled in, and announced, "They want you there."

Inside the car were Dillinger, Van Meter, and "a heavy-set fellow" Negri had not seen before. The stranger, he noticed, "covered his face and he didn't want me to recognize him." Van Meter wanted to know if Negri could get in touch with Nelson. Fatso informed them that, unless he heard differently, he would see Nelson in a few hours at the schoolhouse. "Make sure you're out there," Van Meter said as they pulled away.

Using an old Ford loaned to him by Lieder, Negri arrived at the schoolhouse at the usual time. He spotted some cars parked in a cluster, all darkened, with no one in sight. Negri stepped out and approached the nearest vehicle, a Ford, spying several figures within. As he drew close to the driver's side, the large man he'd glimpsed earlier outside the Rainbo suddenly shoved a pistol through the open window into Fatso's face. "Don't go near that car!" either Nelson or Chase shouted behind him.

Negri backed away, his heart galloping. Nelson spoke to the men in the Ford, then walked over to Negri. "It's all right, Fats," he said soothingly. "Go ahead and take your post awhile."

As Negri performed the lonely duty of standing guard during the next two hours as Nelson and his confederates finalized their plans for the raid on the Merchants' National Bank. Baby Face, from all indications, was enthusiastic about the project but not overly thrilled with the people with whom he was working. He and Van Meter were close to killing each other, and his relationship with Dillinger, always affable and professional, was also starting to sour, thanks in large part to Van Meter's influence. Moreover, Nelson had generously used his own funds to replenish the gang's arsenal while Dillinger and Van Meter repeatedly exploited Nelson's friends, then complained about having to pay them.

Now they had invited Floyd in on the South Bend score. Baby Face and Pretty Boy, so the story goes, disliked and distrusted each other from the start. For his part Nelson was irritated by Floyd's inflated ego and paranoid behavior, especially after he pointed a gun at Negri. Richetti, Pretty Boy's henchman, was useless—over the past year he had deteriorated into an alcoholic who by noon on most days had trouble holding a beer bottle let alone a loaded weapon.

A fifth man was needed for the holdup. The bandits looked to Nelson's pals, considering both Perkins and Chase to fill the position. After some debate they settled upon Perkins, since he had twice visited the bank and was familiar with the layout. Chase would accompany them as driver of the gang's second car.

When the meeting ended Nelson spoke to Negri. "This is real important, Fats. Make sure you and Clarey are out here tomorrow night. Make it about six. Don't pull into the schoolyard. Just drive up and down the road until you see our car in here."

Negri and Lieder spent the next afternoon at a racetrack, killing time until their scheduled appearance at the schoolhouse. On leaving the track they heard a newsboy crying, "Bank robbery in South Bend! Dillinger strikes again!"

Snatching up a paper Negri scanned the details of the big story. "Oh, mother," he remarked, "it must be them."

Lieder, reading along with Negri, nodded grimly.

At this point we ain't headed nowhere. We just runnin' from.
— From the film *Bonnie and Clyde*

CHAPTER 13

THE FINAL SCORE

AT PRECISELY 11:30 A.M. Assistant Postmaster Robert Schnelle left the South Bend post office with the morning's deposits. As he walked down the west side of Michigan Street he was tailed by a pair of lawmen in a squad car. Detectives Edward McCormick and Harold Henderson had followed this routine the last few days after receiving a tip that the post office was to be robbed.

It was a hot, sunny Saturday, June 30; the beginning of an unprecedented heat wave which would broil the Midwest over the next several weeks. The intersection of Michigan and Wayne, the very heart of South Bend's downtown, was bustling with shoppers and clogged with traffic. The task of unsnarling occasional jam-ups while making sure pedestrians crossed safely—a feat complicated by the slow-moving trolley cars rumbling up and down Michigan—fell this day to Patrolman Howard Wagner, who was filling in for a vacationing officer due back on Monday. A big, broad-shouldered bachelor who had turned twenty-nine the previous month, Wagner had lived in South Bend all his life.

To the north and south of where Wagner stood, two more patrolmen performed similar traffic duty along Michigan. A fourth officer, Nels Hanson, had recently arrived to give each a fifteen-minute break. After spelling Wagner, the tall, Danish-born Hanson moved on to relieve the next officer at the corner of Jefferson Boulevard.

From inside their vehicle McCormick and Henderson watched Schnelle enter the Merchants' National Bank at 229 South Michigan, a few yards north of the Wayne Street intersection. Thinking their work was done, the two detectives continued south one block to grab lunch at a diner.

Neither Schnelle nor the two officers noticed a chubby young man wearing sunglasses standing beside the bank's entrance. Jack Perkins eyed the assistant postmaster as he passed, then looked north awaiting the return of the comrades who had dropped him off minutes earlier. When a caramel-colored Hudson sedan with Ohio plates cruised by, Perkins nodded to the men inside. The Hudson turned right onto Wayne. Finding the curb lined with cars, the driver double-parked in front of a jewelry shop.

Moments earlier Alex Slaby, a twenty-six-year-old amateur boxer, had taken the last parking space. He was about to step from his car when the Hudson stopped alongside. Four men piled out, leaving the motor running and a jazzy tune on the radio pouring through the open windows. Slaby noticed the quartet didn't look right; their shirts (because of the bulletproof vests they wore beneath them) seemed curiously puffy.

Two of the men marched to the sidewalk, passing directly in front of Slaby. The bigger man—Floyd—had a powerful build and wore a snap-brimmed Fedora pulled low over his eyes. His companion—Dillinger—sported a straw hat and tinted glasses. Each carried a bulky oblong object wrapped in white cloth that looked suspiciously like a machine gun. Dillinger peered into Slaby's car and gruffly advised, "You'd better scram."

Slaby was about to do as he was told when two more men stepped from the Hudson, neither attempting to conceal his weapon. Van Meter, dressed in overalls and a straw hat, held a .351 rifle. Nelson, wearing a brown cap, sunglasses, a light blue shirt, and dark trousers, cradled a machine gun in his arms.

As the four armed men headed east toward the intersection, Slaby leapt from his vehicle, took a moment to memorize the Hudson's license plate number (C-8016), then trotted across the street to a furniture store to phone the police. (Years later Slaby told author John Toland that he attempted to pluck the keys from the bandit car's ignition but was thwarted when Nelson, lagging behind the others, noticed him and asked what he was doing. Oddly, none of Slaby's previous accounts mentioned the incident.)

Nelson halted on the northwest corner of the busy intersection providing an excellent view of both streets, the Hudson to his right, the bank on his left. Van Meter walked on a few yards, stopping in front of the Nisely Shoe Store, two doors south of the Merchants' National. By the time Nelson and Van Meter assumed their positions, Dillinger and Floyd had joined Perkins at the entrance. Dillinger removed the two flour sacks covering his machine gun, handing one to Perkins, then led the way inside. Drawing a pistol, Perkins followed him through the doors. Floyd entered last, his Tommygun still sheathed in a pillowcase.

A dozen employees and fifteen customers were inside. Schnelle was at one of the teller windows where his deposit was counted as $7,900—far from the small fortune Van Meter had envisioned. When Dillinger walked in brandishing his machine gun, most assumed he was a plainclothes guard making a delivery. Described by witnesses as "perfectly calm," he stopped near the desk of the bank's vice president, Charles W. Coen, and shouted, "This is a holdup!"

The words sent a wave of fear sweeping through the lobby. A woman standing in line abruptly found herself alone, her fellow customers having retreated toward the rear. The elderly Coen ducked beneath his desk and remained hidden through the robbery. Two tellers, including the one who had tabulated the postal deposit, hid the cash they were handling when the bandits entered.

Irwin H. "Bruce" Bouchard, the young manager of the Radio Distributing Company, was walking out when Dillinger declared the gang's intentions. "I was just passing though the inner door to the bank when I noticed a heavy-set man by the drinking fountain on the right holding an object wrapped in white cloth. As he unwrapped it and I saw it was a machine gun I started to make my exit, but he ordered me to come in."

Tossing aside the pillowcase, Floyd moved a few steps into the lobby and barked out a command for everyone to lie on the floor. When only Bouchard obeyed, Pretty Boy fired a burst of six shots into the ceiling. Bouchard winced as one of the ricocheting slugs grazed his back.

Some dropped to the floor. Others, fearing they would be mowed down by the gunmen, joined the exodus toward the back of the bank. Ten people crowded into a restroom and locked the door. A few fled into offices hoping to escape through the windows but discovered that each was covered with bars.

As Floyd was shooting up the ceiling, his two companions casually strode through the swinging door on their left and entered the cages. Perkins, a cigar stub jutting from the corner of his mouth, began methodically ransacking the cash drawers. Dillinger moved with him, assisting by opening drawers, grabbing fistfuls of bills with his free hand, and placing the loot on the counter for his partner to collect. When Perkins filled the first flour sack, Dillinger handed him the other.

❋ ❋ ❋

The crackle of gunfire inside the bank alerted Patrolman Wagner, standing on the opposite side of the intersection. He swiftly started across the street, dodging several vehicles as he grabbed for the revolver on his hip.

A block away Officer Hanson also heard the shots and came running. He spotted Patrolman Sylvester Zell and shouted to him to follow. Nearing the scene Hanson saw Wagner darting over the trolley tracks in the middle of Michigan Street.

"I saw him reach for his gun," Hanson later reported. "Before he had a chance to pull it out, I heard someone open fire on him with a rifle. . . .

[Wagner] took hold of his chest with both hands. He staggered back across the tracks and stopped for a moment in the middle of the street, swaying. Then he backed up again, and as he got near the curb in front of the Star store, he clutched hard at his chest and fell down sideways on his left shoulder and head."

At first Hanson didn't see the shooter. By the time he spotted the gunman in front of the shoe store, Van Meter had turned his weapon in Hanson's direction. The officer threw himself behind a parked sedan and cried out, "Duck, Zell, that fellow's going to shoot at us." Bullets smashed into the vehicle as Zell took cover beside him.

Moments after Wagner collapsed with three slugs in his chest, Nelson decided to employ his favorite method of crowd control. He fired several quick bursts over the heads of the noonday shoppers, who at first were attracted by the shots—some thought they were early Fourth of July fireworks—then scattered in terror. Pedestrians ran into shops, hid behind parked cars, or dove around corners. A few brave but foolhardy souls stayed on the sidewalks watching the gunmen. Nelson's brief barrage shattered a pair of second-floor office windows and blasted holes in the marquee of the Strand Theater, which was advertising its current feature, *Stolen Sweets*, and admission prices—adults, fifteen cents; children, ten cents.

Harold F. Berg, proprietor of the Wayne Street jewelry shop, heard shots and screams, then saw a stream of people run past his display window. Snatching his .22 pistol, he charged outside and spotted a machine gunner on the corner, his weapon pointed menacingly at bystanders. Berg took careful aim and fired.

The bullet struck Nelson in his upper right back, glancing off his protective vest with enough impact to put a dent in the steel and send a jolt of pain rocketing through the diminutive gunman. He reeled dizzily before his startled expression turned furious. Berg squeezed off another shot—missing—as Nelson swung the barrel of his machine gun toward him. A hail of slugs disintegrated Berg's display window, driving the jeweler back inside. Jacob Solomon, a middle-aged customer, crumpled near the doorway, one of Nelson's bullets buried in his abdomen.

With his back turned to Michigan as he blasted Berg's storefront, Nelson did not see the approach of seventeen-year-old Joseph Pawlowski. When the shooting erupted the high school senior was sitting in his car parked in front of the Strand, affording him a front-row seat to the violent drama unfolding on the street. He watched Van Meter gun down Wagner, then saw Nelson fire recklessly about the intersection.

Pawlowski was astonished that no one was attempting to stop the gunmen, although he saw people running everywhere and two more patrolmen—Hanson and Zell—coming from the north. The youth jumped from his car shouting, "Shoot him! Grab him!" He boldly dashed across the street, and "I jumped on his shoulders."

Nelson, still smarting from the sting of Berg's .22 slug, suddenly found himself under attack by a teenager who was trying to wrestle him to the ground. He fought and twisted in a frantic attempt to dislodge his assailant. Finally, Pawlowski recalled, "As we were struggling somebody [Van Meter?] struck me a blow on the right side of my head and I was only semi-conscious."

Another version claims Nelson slammed the youth into a window of the Newmade Hosiery Company. As Pawlowski slumped to the sidewalk, the angry gangster smashed the plate glass with a burst of slugs. Pawlowski was later treated for a wound to his right hand, which had been either cut by glass or nicked by a bullet.

By this time Hanson and Zell were joined behind the now-riddled sedan by a third officer. Van Meter managed to keep all three pinned down, unloading an entire clip of .351 slugs into the vehicle with deliberate patience. Hanson held his cocked revolver in his hand but didn't dare to fire. While shooting at the policemen, Van Meter had grabbed several pedestrians, including a local musician, and ordered them to line up in front of him, their hands in the air.

After ejecting the empty clip from his weapon and snapping in a fresh one, Van Meter—described as "extremely cool" by one witness—evidently felt he needed more protection. He stalked into the shoe store and herded the terrified customers and employees outside. The captive musician took advantage of the bandit's brief absence and slipped away. But at the corner he was halted by Nelson and again forced to raise his hands and provide cover.

※ ※ ※

McCormick and Henderson were in the middle of lunch one block away when the shooting started. As the detectives, mouths full, looked at one another, a report came over the diner's radio calling all available officers to the Merchants' National. The pair hurried outside to their car, listening as the gunfire intensified. Almost immediately they were blocked in by the backed-up traffic (a recent city ordinance prohibited South Bend police from using sirens). Telling his partner, "I can run faster than you can drive," McCormick grabbed a double-barreled shotgun, jumped out of the car, and began zigzagging his way through the tangle of vehicles.

Dillinger and Perkins, meanwhile, completed their plundering of the cages. Carting two sacks of loot, they ordered a pair of prostrate employees to stand and walk ahead of them. One was bank director Perry Stahly; the other was Delos Coen, forty-eight-year-old head cashier and son of the bank's vice president. (Another son, Charles Jr., had fled into the back.) As the group moved to the front, Bouchard felt a gun muzzle poke his back. He glanced up to find Floyd smiling at him. "Let's go," the big bandit ordered. "You're coming with us."

McCormick reached the intersection just in time to see the three robbers emerge from the bank, each using a hostage as a shield. Looking for an alternate target, the detective chose Nelson, who was still guarding the corner and, from McCormick's position, exposed behind several captive pedestrians. As he raised his weapon an overly curious spectator stepped in front of him.

"Get the hell out of the way!" McCormick hollered, and fired. The blast blew out a window directly behind Baby Face. Infuriated and appalled at the resistance they were facing, Nelson spun to his right and sprayed the opposite side of the street with lead. An instant later Van Meter redirected his fire at the detective. McCormick and bystanders near him scrambled for cover, many flattening themselves on the pavement and crawling for safety. One bullet drilled through the windshield of a car, passing between the heads of the husband and wife inside. A splinter of glass cut the woman's left cheek.

When Van Meter began shooting toward McCormick, it allowed Hanson and his two companions to rise up behind the vehicle. The three robbers were moving with their hostages toward Wayne Street. Dillinger held Coen in front of him, Perkins walked behind Stahly, and Floyd, with Bouchard, brought up the rear.

"I picked out the big fellow who came out last," recalled Hanson, "and took careful aim and fired. I aimed for his shoulder because I figured that would knock the machine gun out of his hand. His shoulder kicked back, but he didn't even turn around. So I aimed for his head." Hanson's second shot evidently missed, because "he kept right on going."

The officers with Hanson also fired at the bandits. On the south side of the intersection two more policemen arrived, one toting a shotgun, the other a pistol. The pair joined McCormick and a store manager armed with a rifle. All four traded shots with the gangsters. A bullet struck Coen in the left leg just above the ankle, and the cashier immediately collapsed. Dillinger let him fall as he hustled toward the corner, firing sporadic bursts with one hand, a sack of money clenched in the other.

Stahly heard the pudgy robber behind him scream "Fuck!" as a bullet shrieked past their heads. Another flurry of slugs whipped past their legs, one tearing a hole through the director's trousers. Perkins, obviously rattled by the near misses, kept cursing and jabbing his pistol into Stahly's back, growling, "Move! Move! Move!"

As the group turned right onto Wayne Street, Nelson, Van Meter, and Dillinger kept up a steady suppressing fire, but the police bullets kept coming. At that moment Detective Henderson reached the chaotic scene, brazenly swinging his car onto Wayne and stopping in the very midst of the battle. He jumped out behind the vehicle and opened fire with his revolver.

With bullets and buckshot whistling around him, Bouchard decided he wasn't going any farther. "I voluntarily dropped to my stomach to avoid being hit," he said later, "and as I did so a bullet grazed the heel of my shoe, passed in one side of my pant leg and went out the other without touching my skin."

In that same instant a police slug slammed into Stahly's left side. "I'm shot!" he cried out, clutching the wound.

"Keep moving," Perkins snarled.

Stahly desperately tried to reason with his captor. "You've got the money. Why don't you leave without killing anyone?"

Receiving no answer, Stahly tore free and flung himself to the sidewalk. As he attempted to wiggle beneath a parked car, Perkins or one of his partners fired at Stahly's head. The slug passed close enough to burn a crease above his left ear.

Their human shields gone, the bandits broke into a mad dash for their getaway car. The police started pouring lead into the Hudson, and even Berg reappeared in his shop's doorway to empty his revolver at the fleeing gang.

Across the street Samuel Toth was seated in his car waiting for his friend Jacob Solomon, unaware that Solomon lay critically wounded inside the jewelry shop. As the exchange between cops and robbers continued, stray slugs began smashing into his automobile. When he attempted to drive out of danger a volley, most likely fired by police thinking it was a second getaway car, blasted through the windshield. Glass flew into Toth's face, cutting his forehead and cheek and barely missing his right eye. Despite his wounds Toth kept driving. A block away he pulled to the curb and passed out.

As Van Meter climbed into the driver's seat a bullet plowed across the right side of his skull, ripping a six-inch gash along his scalp. Dillinger swiftly shoved him to the side and took the wheel. A moment later Nelson, busy firing at police, also rushed up to the driver's side. "Move over!" he barked.

There was no time to argue. Dillinger pushed the sagging, semi-conscious Van Meter farther to the right and slid over as Nelson scrambled in, shifted gears, and stomped on the gas pedal. The Hudson roared off with Floyd firing from the left-hand window of the back seat and Perkins spilling tacks out of the right.

Unlike the gang's methodical, almost ponderous getaways from Sioux Falls and Mason City, Nelson drove through the streets of South Bend as if he were back on a dirt track. The Hudson made a screeching turn south onto Main Street, then swung right onto Western Avenue. By the time they reached the outskirts of town Nelson had the vehicle racing between 85 and 90 mph.

A pair of police cars that arrived just moments after the gang's departure attempted to pursue the bandits. One gave up the chase when two of its tires were punctured by tacks. The other, an old Studebaker, broke a fuel line, stranding the officers near the edge of town.

Motorcycle Patrolman Bert Olmstead spotted the Hudson hurtling south along U.S. 31. He sped after them at full throttle but after a few miles realized it was hopeless. "I was doing 80 miles an hour, all the motorcycle had," he stated, "and they just walked away from me." Olmstead kept pushing his machine until the cycle's engine burned out near Lakeville.

It is doubtful that Nelson's companions complained about his daredevil driving as he put distance between them and South Bend. Van Meter, blood spurting from his scalp wound, was in agony. Floyd and Perkins had sustained flesh wounds in their legs and had taken several stinging hits in their vests. Dillinger alone came out of the shootout miraculously unscathed.

Back in South Bend, the smoke was still clearing from the intersection of Michigan and Wayne when ambulances arrived to take away the wounded. Patrolman Wagner died ten minutes after reaching Epworth Hospital, his lungs torn by Van Meter's rifle slugs. Stahly, Coen, Toth, and Solomon were admitted as patients; Bouchard, Pawlowski, and two others were treated for minor wounds and released. Despite the tragic death of Wagner, all agreed it was a wonder the casualties were not higher. In the eight minutes from the moment the bandits first entered the bank to their blazing exit, more than 100 rounds were exchanged between the two sides.

❋ ❋ ❋

Slashing southwest across the state on back roads, the bandits suffered only one setback when their car developed a flat tire near Knox, Indiana. Four and a half hours after the robbery they stopped outside Goodland, 100 miles from South Bend and just fifteen miles east of the Illinois state line. A quartet of Newton County farm boys watched as the tan Hudson pulled off onto the road's shoulder. Four men climbed out as a smaller, darker Hudson (presumably driven by Chase) braked to a stop, then they squeezed inside and the vehicle sped away.

Summoned to the site by a call from the boys, police searched the abandoned car, whose windows had been perforated by two bullets and nineteen buckshot pellets. A check of the Hudson revealed that it had been stolen from a Chicago auto dealer on May 23. Its Ohio plates were reported missing by a Toledo man on May 2.

By the time the outlaws switched cars the loot had been counted—a disappointing $28,439. Nelson was furious with Van Meter that they had endured so much for so little after all his promises of a huge haul. Dillinger too was bitterly disgusted. His plans to escape into South American anonymity had to be put on hold until a bigger score could be arranged.

Van Meter's pitiful groans during the long journey did not make him a good candidate for criticism. Nelson found a substitute for his brooding anger. Sometime before they reached Goodland, Floyd separated from the others, probably meeting Richetti at a prearranged point along the route. Nelson was enraged by the husky outlaw's departure, either feeling that Floyd was running out on them at a critical time—perhaps when the tire blew—or, as one source hinted, because Pretty Boy skipped out with more than his share of the money.

❋ ❋ ❋

At the appointed hour Negri and Lieder made their first pass by the school-house and saw no one. Returning every twenty minutes over the next few hours, Fatso began to get an ominous feeling. The news coming out of South Bend sounded more like a Wild West shootout than a bank heist. Several reports alleged that at least two of the bandits had been shot. Scanning the papers that afternoon Lieder remarked it would be a shame if Nelson were killed. "He's one of the nicest guys I've ever known."

Shortly after 10 P.M. the pair spotted a car and pulled in, flashing their head-lights as a signal. They came upon a grim scene. Chase, holding a rifle, stood guard near the car, Dillinger and Perkins loitering close by. Two figures were sprawled atop blankets spread on the ground. Drawing closer, Negri recognized one as Van Meter, his hand clasping a handkerchief against his head. The other was Nelson, who complained of a "monster headache" that had been growing worse since the .22 bullet struck his vest.

Van Meter moaned and spat profanities. Noticing "a lot of blood," Negri was sure the outlaw was dying and suggested that Lieder "go out and get a doc-tor." Nelson swiftly vetoed the idea. "We don't want Clarey getting in trouble," he said. "We'll yaffle [kidnap] a doc if we have to."

Not seeing the large man who had pushed a pistol in his face, Negri inquired, "Where's that guy that was here last night?"

Van Meter, his teeth clenched in agony, said, "Go stand over there a little while, Fats."

It was obvious Negri had raised a sore subject. Forgetting his headache, Nelson leapt to his feet and stormed over to Dillinger. "What are we gonna do about that bastard? We gonna let him get away with that? Aren't we going after him?"

Dillinger told his impetuous partner to settle down. "He's a friend of Richetti. If we go after him, we'll have to take on both of them. We're not gonna do that."

"I'll go after him then," Nelson shot back.

There was a brief argument between them, with Van Meter, groaning con-stantly, managing to get a few words in. Negri heard Richetti referred to several more times, but even in their anger Nelson and the others were careful not to call Floyd by name.

Once his temper cooled, Nelson retrieved a briefcase from the car and handed it to Negri. "Take this and be careful with it," he said. "There's a lot of money in there. Go back to the hotel. You stay in the room until Johnny gets there. And put that grip some place where the maid won't mess with it."

Although he disliked Van Meter, Negri asked again about getting him medical attention. "We'll take care of him," Nelson replied, suddenly looking very tired. "Go home, Fats."

Dillinger brought his wounded pal back to the Probasco house, and Dr. Cassidy was summoned to treat the bandit. In the meantime—Cassidy took nearly twenty-four hours to arrive—Probasco used his veterinary skills to clean and patch Van Meter's bullet-torn scalp. Despite all his bleeding and suffering, Van Meter's wound proved not to be serious. The outlaw's anguish was soon replaced by anger. Newspapers credited Detective Henderson, the officer who had been closest to the bandit car, with firing the shots that produced the bloodstains found in the Hudson. Van Meter, however, claimed it was jeweler Harry Berg who had nailed him. "I was looking right at him when he came running out of his store," he told Dillinger. "We'll have to go back to South Bend in the next few days and take care of that little Jew."

"Sure we will, Van," Dillinger promised. "We can't afford to let a guy go on living that can shoot that straight."

❋ ❋ ❋

About 1:30 the next afternoon Chase showed up at Negri's room at the Fullerton. Fatso asked about Van Meter's condition and was told, "He's all right." Negri also wanted to know how the argument over the big man (Floyd) had turned out. Chase advised him to forget about it.

Their attention turned to the briefcase Nelson had placed in Negri's care. Chase opened it with a key and dumped the contents on the bed. Negri's eyes widened as the cash spilled out, much of it in thick stacks bound with wrappers. The two men started counting. The total, Negri recalled, was between $12,000 and $13,000, roughly a third of the South Bend take. Impressed, Negri commented, "I guess you guys did pretty good."

"It wasn't good at all," Chase corrected him, his expression grave. "Things got bloody. Jimmie nearly got killed. They shot him in the back—if he hadn't been wearing his vest we would have lost him. God saved him with that vest."

While putting the money back into the briefcase, Chase asked if Negri wanted to go back to California for a visit. Fatso had mentioned several times that he was homesick and hoped to take some cash back to his mother and sister in San Francisco.

Chase moved to the door, the briefcase under his arm. "See us tonight at Murray's," he said. "After dark."

That evening Negri met Chase at the Rainbo. They drove to a remote spot quite some distance from the city. On a dirt road beside a lake, they found

Nelson and Dillinger waiting for them. Negri stood off to the side while the others talked. Dillinger complained that Cassidy had charged $500 to tend Van Meter; Nelson still argued sullenly about settling his score with Floyd. ("No, we can't do it," Dillinger kept insisting.)

Eventually Negri became the topic of discussion. He overheard Nelson telling Dillinger, "We'll need Fats pretty soon. The rest of us got too much heat. He's so cool he can go and take care of all the angles. And he's getting more confident."

When Nelson finished singing Fatso's praises, Dillinger turned to Negri and presented him with two packets of cash. "This is from Van and me," he said. Negri tucked the bills in his pocket, discovering later that Dillinger had handed him $1,000. "It seems as though Jimmie forced them to give me that much money," Negri remembered.

Nelson winked at his friend and said, "Me and Johnny will fix you up later." After some more talk Nelson looked back at Fatso, asking, "Are you going to take that trip back home?"

Negri said he was seriously considering it. Nelson called Chase to the side and spoke to him for several minutes. Then Chase strolled over and announced, "Okay, Fats, let's go."

During the long drive back to Chicago, Chase pulled a thick stack of cash from his pocket and handed it to Negri. "This is for you," he said, "from Jimmie and me." Negri counted $1,500. "You don't have to worry about nothing," Chase promised. "You'll have more money than you can ever spend."

"You guys must have something big lined up."

"Bigger than any bank job, believe me. You'll see."

The next day, finding himself with $2,500—"more money than I ever had"—Negri decided to buy a car of his own. After purchasing a 1934 Oldsmobile sedan from Lieder's garage for $900, he drove to the Rainbo to show off his new vehicle. Murray's wife was the first to notice. "New car, huh?" she asked, taking a seat with him. "Were you there at the bank?"

Negri quietly denied anything to do with the robbery. Looking skeptical, she inquired, "Is everyone all right?" Before he could answer, Murray appeared, sat by his wife, and asked the same questions. "They're all fine," he assured the couple. "And I wasn't there. I just wanted you to see my car."

Later Negri was joined by Chase. Fatso proudly pointed out his new Olds, but when he mentioned that he had used his real name on the paperwork, Chase exclaimed, "Mother of Jesus! You never use your own name! If you got hot, they can check stuff like that."

Chase told Negri the gang needed him to be back in two weeks. The "big job" was scheduled before the end of the month, and Chase promised "a lot of work" for him. He asked Negri to pass along messages to two of his brothers and his ex-business partner, George Nerton. "Tell 'em I'm fine and doing well," Chase instructed. "And don't spend all your money."

The next day, July 3, Negri put his new car in storage. After buying a roundtrip ticket under a false name, as Chase had urged him to do, Negri boarded a plane for San Francisco. He slept well during the flight—better, in fact, than he had during any of the past sixteen nights he'd spent in Chicago.

❄ ❄ ❄

On July 2 the FBI's Chicago office received a telegram from the SAC in Portland advising that Mary Gillis, daughter Leona McMahon, Leona's infant son Timothy, and five-year-old Ronald Gillis were observed leaving Bremerton on Sunday evening aboard a train that was scheduled to arrive in Chicago at 9 A.M. July 4.

An agent met the train and followed Mary and her companions outside where they caught a taxi to the Fitzsimmons apartment. Two days earlier Bob Fitzsimmons had been summoned to the bureau and grilled about his outlaw brother-in-law. For the most part he answered their questions truthfully, even telling the lawmen about his recent meeting with Nelson near their home. Shortly after Mary and the others arrived, the phone rang. The agents asked to speak with Fitzsimmons again and to Mrs. McMahon as well.

The next evening Fitzsimmons, his wife, and sister-in-law visited the bureau's offices. Agents briefly interviewed Leona, who made it clear by her tone that she resented the polite interrogation. She flatly denied any recent contact with her brother or his wife. The skeptical agents asked why she had returned to Chicago at this particular time. Leona told them that aside from bringing her mother back home, her husband was presently at sea and she intended to find a cottage or apartment for about thirty-five dollars a month for herself, her infant son, her mother, and Lester's two children. When an agent requested that she notify them when she moved, Leona asked why, since she was obviously under surveillance. She also intimated that she knew the G-Men were intercepting her mail and monitoring her phone conversations. The agents vigorously insisted that was not true.

Fitzsimmons was then ushered in and privately "questioned in detail." He assured the lawmen that he had been completely truthful in all his previous statements, but the agents remained unconvinced. They were particularly interested in how he had acquired the Essex Terraplane, which investigators discovered had actually been purchased by Chase. Fitzsimmons reportedly gave "two fictitious stories" before admitting that Chase had given the car to him on instructions from Nelson. Although Fitzsimmons's name had been used to buy the vehicle, he denied having anything to do with the purchase and added that he knew nothing of the car's history before it came into his possession.

Two days later, on July 7, he was called back for further questioning, his third appearance in five days. This time he provided a statement in his own handwriting, detailing all he knew or had observed about Nelson over the past year. At the end he wrote, "I've told my story as best I can and will not withhold a thing pertaining to either Helen or Lester that may come my way in the future."

In his report Special Agent Virgil Peterson noted, "Fitzsimmons requested that Agents do not interview his wife along similar lines, or inform her that he had furnished this Office with information, as he felt that such action might tend to break up his home, or if such news became known to Lester Gillis it might be the reason for him receiving bodily harm."

That same week many Chicago agents were focusing on the South Bend robbery. There was a movement under way to deny that the raid was the work of the Dillinger gang. An Indiana police chief stated the holdup didn't resemble the bandit's style. "Dillinger works quietly; he doesn't enter a bank shooting," he said. There was also the word of Bruce Bouchard, who steadfastly denied that the lead bandit had been Dillinger. The man was heavier and darker, he said, adding, "He looked like none of the pictures of Dillinger I've ever seen."

But the G-Men had no doubts that the South Bend heist had been the work of Dillinger and his more trigger-happy associates. Delos Coen (Dillinger's shield), Perry Stahly, Charles Coen, Officer Hanson, and Detective Henderson all positively identified the outlaw as the first robber to enter the bank and the first to march back out. Agents also learned from an informant in Gary that Dillinger and five or six companions had been seen passing through that city in two cars, both Hudsons, on the morning of the holdup.

There was certainly no controversy over the identity of two of the bandits. Seven eyewitnesses selected the photograph of Baby Face Nelson, saying they were "absolutely certain" he had been the short, "excited" machine-gunner guarding the corner. Two individuals also swore it was Nelson who had shot and killed Patrolman Wagner since they had seen him firing at the instant the officer went down. Three others claimed it was the taller gunman standing closer to the bank who had fired at Wagner. Eleven persons identified Van Meter as the bandit in front of the shoe store. The discrepancy was resolved by the fact that the fatal bullets had been fired from a .351 rifle.

The real mystery facing investigators, both federal and local, was determining the identity of the pair of bandits who had entered the bank with Dillinger—the husky machine-gunner stationed inside the entrance and "the fat boy" (so dubbed by the South Bend police) who ransacked the cash drawers. The G-Men were certain one must have been John Hamilton. They were surprised when only two witnesses pointed to Hamilton's picture—a bank employee who said that Hamilton "looks something like" the stocky robber and a woman who claimed she had seen Hamilton outside the bank two days before the robbery.

Agents had learned through Father Coughlan's sporadic confessions about Nelson's association with Eddie Bentz at Long Beach the previous summer. After the South Bend witnesses failed to identify Bentz, the G-Men showed them photos of Eddie's half-brother Theodore. Amazingly, Stahly, Henderson, Hanson, and a teller were all positive that he was the portly robber. Lawmen were already hunting Ted in connection with the Grand Haven holdup, another crime he had no part in.

But one agent had a hunch about Jack Perkins, who resembled Ted Bentz and whose lengthy friendship with Nelson made him a much more viable suspect. One of the most damning pieces of evidence against Perkins was his love of cigars—he averaged twelve a day and was rarely seen without one. The witnesses all agreed the fat bandit had kept an unlit cigar stub clenched between his teeth during the holdup. Even so, the photos of Perkins received a lukewarm response; only two bank employees remarked that the young hood looked "very similar" to the chunky robber.

Even greater uncertainty surrounded the fifth bandit. His abrupt, menacing behavior—spraying the ceiling with machine-gun slugs—and the low manner in which he wore his hat had prevented anyone from getting a good look at his face. Of the three hostages who had been closer to the robber, both Stahly and Coen were positive the man was Pretty Boy Floyd. Bouchard—who described the bandit as heavy-set, five-foot-eight, and nearly 200 pounds—was less certain.

The government investigators were reluctant to believe that Floyd had been a member of the bandit team, but the press instantly embraced the idea and reported that the nation's three most notorious public enemies—Dillinger, Nelson, and Floyd—had joined forces to create a "super gang" poised to plunder banks throughout the United States. The lawmen had their doubts, for South Bend hardly seemed to be the work of a super gang. Nor was it a preview of things to come—in fact, it was to be the final score for all three outlaws.

❊ ❊ ❊

On July 4 John Dillinger, having spent more than a month in the house of James Probasco, moved to an apartment on North Halsted, which he shared with his latest sweetheart, Polly Hamilton, and her "good friend" Anna Sage.

Van Meter and Mickey continued to reside in Calumet City while Nelson and his wife remained in their unknown hideaway somewhere near Chicago. Dillinger divided his time between them, visiting Van Meter during daylight hours, then meeting Nelson after dark. The two were still feuding, each bouncing complaints about the other off Dillinger who patiently attempted to make peace between them.

If forced to choose, Dillinger would have favored Van Meter, whom he regarded as his best surviving friend and chief advisor, despite the disappointing South Bend score. But he also needed Nelson, and not merely for his Chicago contacts. The upcoming "big haul" was the brainchild of Jimmy Murray, whose chief allegiance was to Baby Face. In order to share in the loot, Dillinger had to remain in Nelson's good graces and find a way to keep him and Van Meter from killing each other.

With Van Meter recovering from his head wound, Negri in California, and Murray's heist several weeks away, the so-called Dillinger gang was in a state of limbo. Nelson continued to acquire weapons, both for his own personal arsenal and for Dillinger, who divided the hardware with Van Meter. Nelson also made a special request to Perkins, asking him to obtain some "soup." "Are you talking about nitro?" Perkins asked, appalled.

Baby Face explained they needed the explosive for their next job. When Perkins said he could score some dynamite, Nelson told him, "No good, Jack. Murray says its gotta be soup."

About this time Lieder, fronting for Nelson, purchased a new Hudson sedan through a Chicago auto dealer, trading in the pickup that he'd kept in storage for more than a month. On July 9 Chase, using the alias John Powers of 67 West Harrison Street, was issued Illinois plates for the vehicle.

The next day, equipped with a clean car and plates to match, Nelson announced that he planned to travel west for a few days. He promised to return by the weekend and scheduled a meeting with Perkins and Lieder for the following Sunday. It is not known if the trip was a spur-of-the-moment decision or a planned getaway. Chase had intended to visit Sally on her birthday and possibly appealed to Nelson to join him.

When told of their plans, Dillinger encouraged Baby Face to go, no doubt hoping the interlude might ease the tensions between Nelson and Van Meter. That night, prodded by Dillinger, the pair agreed to meet at one of their rendezvous spots outside the city. Once again a shouting match erupted. Nelson left fuming over a sum of money he insisted Van Meter owed him, swearing to kill his ex-pal the next time they locked horns.

In the days following Nelson's departure, Dillinger stuck to his routine of attending Cubs games and going to movies with Polly. He broke off his once close relationship with Piquett, angered when he learned the lawyer had pocketed money that Dillinger had entrusted him to give to others. Despite his grudge against Piquett, the outlaw remained on friendly terms with O'Leary.

On the evening of July 12 O'Leary provided his public-enemy pal with a ride to the Rainbo. O'Leary waited in the car as Dillinger went inside. Minutes later he reappeared with Van Meter, who was holding a half-eaten sandwich in one hand and a bottle of soda pop in the other, and as usual was whining. As Dillinger slipped back into the car, O'Leary was able to hear that the subject of their conversation was Nelson.

"I had it out with Jimmie," Van Meter grumbled to Dillinger through the window. "I told him I wasn't going to pay him any twenty-five hundred dollars. I never did care a hell of a lot about that guy, anyway."

"He was always complaining to me about you, too, Van," Dillinger pointed out.

"We had it pretty heavy there for a while. I thought we were going to draw guns on each other."

"Forget it, Van," Dillinger said, obviously tiring of the conversation and announcing that Nelson was "out of the gang."

By declaring that Nelson was henceforth excluded from their plans, Dillinger evidently hoped to placate his brooding friend for the moment. There was evidence he told Nelson the same thing about Van Meter. But privately Dillinger hoped to reconcile the two, if only for the duration of the upcoming robbery.

"It will be one of the biggest jobs in the world," Dillinger boasted to O'Leary as they drove away from the Rainbo. He provided a few teasing details before revealing the gang was "going to take a mail train." The plan was perfect, Dillinger crowed. "We also know how much money it will be carrying, and it's plenty. We'll have enough to last us the rest of our lives, and right after it's over we're lamming it out of the country."

Ten years after the Roundout train robbery, which had landed him in prison for five years, Murray was plotting to duplicate the crime with a fresh cast of characters. This time, with the Dillinger gang substituting for the Newton brothers, Murray hoped to achieve the success that previously had eluded him.

❄ ❄ ❄

That same evening Sally Bachman was celebrating her birthday without fanfare on her job at the ferry newsstand in San Francisco. Near sunset Louis Tambini stopped by to inform her that her beloved Johnny was back in town and wanted to see her.

When Sally finished her shift at 11 P.M. Tambini returned for her in his Plymouth sedan. The pair rode the ferry to Sausalito, then drove along Highway 101 to the Black Point cutoff between Vallejo and Sonoma. Tambini pulled off next to a black Hudson parked on the shoulder. Chase emerged from the Hudson's back seat and joined Sally in the Plymouth. Both vehicles proceeded to Sonoma, where Chase and his girlfriend spent the remainder of the night in a hotel.

The next morning, Friday the 13th, the couple checked out and started walking down the highway. Chase tried to convince Sally to return to Chicago with him, but she was reluctant to agree. At noon the black Hudson appeared, stopping beside them. Nelson was at the wheel, Helen snuggled beside him. The two couples spoke briefly before Nelson, obviously irritated by Sally's indecisiveness, announced he was eager to get under way. He drove off with Helen and returned an hour later. When Sally still remained uncertain what to do, Nelson conferred with his henchman. Chase walked back to his sweetheart and sadly informed her that Nelson was "not yet ready" to allow her to accompany them. Once Sally's return home was arranged with Tambini, Nelson and his companions started their long drive back east.

They reached Chicago late on July 15, a swelteringly hot Sunday. Though Nelson had done most of the driving over the past forty-eight hours, he was more concerned with making his scheduled rendezvous with his friends than grabbing some rest. Near midnight Perkins and Lieder arrived separately at the appointed spot to find Nelson and the others waiting for them. Helen sat in the Hudson's front seat reading a magazine by flashlight while the four men talked along the roadside.

An hour later two Illinois state troopers, Fred McAllister and Gilbert Cross, were driving north on Wolf Road. They were off duty but each night returned by way of backroads, on the lookout for stranded motorists or abandoned autos. McAllister, age thirty-two, spied several cars parked on a side road and alerted his partner. Cross, four years younger and due to be married the next weekend, agreed they should investigate.

As their headlights swept the scene the troopers saw there were three vehicles, all dark-colored new models, the lead one a black Ford V-8 sedan. Drawing closer they noticed a dark-haired young woman seated on the front passenger side of the rear car. Cross stopped the state car, and McAllister stepped out and called, "What's the trouble there?"

A man suddenly emerged from the darkness behind the rear Hudson. Seconds earlier, at the sight of the approaching Ford, Nelson had reached into his car's back seat and armed himself with his machine-gun pistol, then concealed himself behind the vehicle. "No trouble at all," he replied coolly.

Nelson swiftly raised his weapon and assumed a shooter's stance. Before McAllister could react, the gunman poured a stream of lead into the troopers' car. The impact of a .45 slug smashing into his right shoulder knocked McAllister into the ditch. Cross, literally a sitting target behind the wheel, was struck six times before he could manage to scramble out the passenger-side door and tumble into the weeds beside his partner.

McAllister caught "a fleeting glimpse" of the four men as they hurried into the three vehicles and roared off. Despite his damaged shoulder, he managed to drag Cross back to their car and lift him inside. Then, driving with one hand while looking through a windshield pockmarked by seven bullet holes, McAllister managed to reach Des Plaines Emergency Hospital.

Cross was immediately wheeled into surgery where his chances of survival were listed as "slim." The trooper had lost a tremendous amount of blood, and two slugs embedded in his chest lay perilously close to his heart. While his shoulder was patched, McAllister provided fellow lawmen with an account of the shooting. Unfortunately, he was able to supply only general details about the assailants and their vehicles. The shooter, he said, had worn a straw hat and light-colored shirt with the sleeves rolled up. An agent showed him photos of Helen Gillis and Mickey Conforti, but McAllister could not identify either woman. Nor had he noticed any license plate numbers.

Outraged over the savage, unprovoked attack upon the two officers, city, state, and county lawmen pledged a joint effort to bring the guilty parties to justice. Sergeant Frank Reynolds declared publicly that he had no doubts the shootings were the work of the Dillinger gang. McAllister's description of the weapon as "a large-caliber automatic pistol that fired like a machine gun," similar to the one that had been discovered in Dillinger's St. Paul apartment, lent considerable support to Reynolds's conviction.

It was hardly the kind of heat Dillinger and company needed as they prepared for what they hoped would be the biggest heist of their criminal careers. But they got lucky, and the furor subsided after a single day. Cross, miraculously, survived his wounds, and the investigators focused on a different set of suspects. Less than twenty-four hours after the incident, a team of county officers raided a farmhouse just 250 yards from the scene of the attack. Inside they discovered a bootlegging operation supplied by a 2,000-gallon still in a nearby barn. Eight people caught on the premises were arrested, one a dark-haired girl of nineteen matching McAllister's description of the young woman in the Hudson.

Lack of evidence ultimately prevented any prosecution for the assault on the troopers, but authorities nonetheless considered the case solved. Cross and McAllister obviously had interrupted the bootleggers (and perhaps some customers) at a critical moment, resulting in the gunplay. A county officer assured federal agents that he was "quite positive" the Dillinger gang was not involved. However, just a few months later Chase's confession would reveal that the shooting was in truth Baby Face Nelson's hair-trigger response to the arrival of the unfortunate officers.

✳ ✳ ✳

It was difficult for Negri to return to Chicago. Had he not given his word to come back, he would have remained in the Bay Area. But Nelson and the other gang members were not the kind of people one wanted to disappoint. And then, of course, there was the money—and the promise of much more to come.

Arriving by plane on Wednesday July 18, Negri retrieved his Oldsmobile and checked into the YMCA before driving to the Rainbo, where he met with Chase and Murray. Both spoke with great enthusiasm and anticipation of the "big train job" and gradually began sharing details with Negri.

In what sounded like a recital of the Murray-sponsored Roundout robbery, the gang—Nelson, Dillinger, Van Meter, Chase, possibly Perkins and others— intended to stop the train at a designated point outside the city and then blow the door to the mail car with nitro. "Murray had it all cased and set up for them," Negri later revealed. "He knew somebody on the inside. Because he knew what day the big shipment was and to what banks, and there was only a certain day good to knock off [the train]." According to Murray, who was to receive a sizable chunk of the proceeds, that day was less than a week away.

The more Fatso heard, the more fearful he became. On Saturday afternoon July 21 Negri and Chase had a late lunch at a North Side restaurant before attending an important meeting that night. During the meal Negri remarked, "You know, Johnny, I got that new Olds. If I was to drive it back to California, I could sell it for a pretty good price back there. So how is it with you if I drive home and stayed there?"

The question took Chase by surprise. Unsure how to respond, he told Negri they would discuss the matter with the others that night. Negri had been afraid he would say that.

When the two reached the meeting things were already turning sour. Nelson, Dillinger, and Murray were waiting for Van Meter, who was well over an hour late. According to Negri, "Murray was nervous" and Nelson was "going crazy" with rage. Only Dillinger remained calm, making excuses for his friend's failure to show. As the mood got uglier, Chase sprang the news that "Fats wants to go home."

To Negri's surprise, Nelson only shrugged and asked Chase for his opinion. When Chase voiced no objection, Baby Face agreed, "It's okay with me, too."

Overhearing the conversation, Dillinger's poised demeanor abruptly vanished. "Well, I don't know about that," he told Nelson and Chase. "Tell him we'll let him know tomorrow."

Almost in defiance of Dillinger, Nelson turned to Negri and said, "As far as Johnny and I are concerned, if you want to go, Fats, then you go ahead."

"He knows too much," Dillinger protested, approaching Negri and, for the first time, flashing his crooked grin at him. "Why not stay here and play ball? We'll make a lot of money," he said smoothly. "Then you can go home and go about your business, and no one will find you. You'll have some real dough in your pockets. I heard Johnny say your folks are poor. You can smother them in money when we're finished. You can do that, can't you, Fats?"

Negri found his head nodding. "Sure, I can stay," he conceded.

After another hour passed with no sign of Van Meter, the outlaws decided to call it a night. Dillinger promised to track down Van Meter and make sure he was present at the next meeting, which was scheduled for Monday night. Nelson's parting remark was to instruct Dillinger to give Van Meter a kick in his "skinny ass."

❄ ❄ ❄

Sunday night, July 22.

At first no one was certain if the reports were true. Negri was at the Rainbo when a news flash came over the radio announcing that Dillinger had been slain by federal officers outside a Lincoln Avenue theater. Murray immediately made a phone call and returned ashen-faced, probably realizing his dream to recreate the Roundout robbery had just evaporated. He sat by Fatso and croaked, "They got him all right."

Chase, who had been switching hotels every few days, happened to be staying at a North Side rooming house only a few blocks from the Biograph. A boarder rushed in, hurriedly telling everyone he encountered, "They've shot Dillinger over on Lincoln." Chase spent an hour mingling with the excited crowd gathering at the scene, learning all he could. At about midnight he drove to the schoolhouse, anticipating Nelson would want to discuss the gang's next move.

After a brief wait Nelson appeared. To Chase's amazement he acted neither shaken nor surprised by Dillinger's death. "This changes nothing," Nelson declared. "We go ahead with the train job with the men we got."

The next morning Nelson asked Lieder to contact Van Meter to arrange a meeting for that night. According to Negri, Nelson was even hopeful that with Dillinger gone, he might be able to work in harmony with Van Meter again. But Lieder returned with the news that the skinny bandit had vanished.

The previous night Mickey had heard a radio broadcast about the Biograph shooting and rushed to tell her boyfriend, who was asleep in the next room. Van Meter hurriedly dressed and departed. An hour later he was back, ordering Mickey to pack her things. They were on the road before daybreak, heading back to the former sanctuary in St. Paul.

Nelson cursed Van Meter, labeling him "a yellow dog" for running out on them. Now, with both Dillinger and Van Meter out of the picture, there was no choice but to scrap the train heist. Chase and Negri both advised their friend that the best strategy was to leave Chicago for the next couple of months and lay low in California. Baby Face was reluctant at first, suggesting they should wait in case Van Meter came to his senses and returned. Apparently Nelson, like Dillinger, had come to regard the train job as an ultimate, once-in-a-lifetime score that would make them all millionaires.

Late that afternoon J. Edgar Hoover announced that Baby Face Nelson had been designated the bureau's most wanted criminal, the nation's new public enemy number one. Nelson abruptly changed his mind about remaining in Chicago, and at 7 P.M. he stopped in at the Pioneer to find Perkins.

Two nights later, on July 25, Perkins arrived at the agreed rendezvous site on River Road where he found Nelson and Chase waiting for him. Perkins told the pair that after considerable discussion he and Grace had decided to join them on their westward junket. They agreed to bring along their three-year-old son, John Jr., but wanted to leave their daughter with relatives. Nelson said he would have Negri pick the couple up about noon the next day.

After their meeting with Perkins, Nelson and Chase drove back to River Grove and turned north. As they passed St. Joseph's Cemetery, Nelson slowed the car and gazed wistfully out the window. "I've got family there," he said without further elaboration.

CHAPTER 14

ENDLESS HIGHWAY

AT 3 P.M. ON July 26 the travelers assembled on a secluded road a mile west of
Dundee, a few miles west of Chicago. After briefly discussing their plans,
Nelson, Helen, and Chase led the way in the Hudson, with Perkins, his wife,
and son riding with Negri in his Oldsmobile. Both vehicles' trunks were packed
to capacity with luggage. Nelson's arsenal—three bulletproof vests, three rifles
(the Monitor, a .351, and a .22), a Thompson submachine gun, his machine-
gun pistol, five handguns, and a case of ammunition—occupied one side of the
Hudson's back seat, concealed under blankets and within easy reach.

They drove the entire night, Chase spelling Nelson at the wheel while
Perkins relieved Negri. Although the mood among them was generally carefree,
they observed caution at all times, stopping infrequently and avoiding public
places. When the Hudson needed gas, Chase would drop off Nelson a short distance away from the station, then pick him up when the tank was full. The
nation's new top public enemy again began to grow a mustache.

Late the following afternoon they pulled into a tourist camp in Wyoming
and spent the night. The next day they passed through Salt Lake City and the
Nevada towns of Elko and Reno, then turned south looking to enter California
on a back road. Near Lake Tahoe the Olds suffered a flat. While Negri changed
the tire, the others decided that two vehicles sporting Illinois plates might

appear suspicious crossing the state line together. Perkins and his family joined Nelson and Helen in the Hudson and headed for Sacramento.

The next morning, July 29, they arrived at the El Verano Inn, where they were welcomed by Gus Zappas, the manager, and provided with a pair of rooms. Chase and Negri showed up at about 4 P.M. and met the others in the dining area for an early supper.

Zappas's hospitality came at a stiff price, since he knew Nelson's true identity. After dinner Nelson told Negri he was looking for a safe location where he wouldn't be "sucked dry" of cash. Negri agreed to drive into San Francisco and look up their old friend Tony Moreno to arrange a place. Moreno seemed pleased to see Fatso until Negri announced, "Jimmie's in town and wants to know if you can set him up."

"He's too hot," Moreno protested. "Tell him I can't do a thing for him."

"Tell him yourself," Negri shot back. "He wants to see you."

Moreno followed Negri back to El Verano and spoke with Nelson. "Honest, Jimmie, I don't know any place," Moreno insisted. "Why don't you buy a trailer and go camp out in the country?"

"I'm tired of living like that," Nelson answered. "Haven't you got a ranch or something I can go to?"

But Moreno maintained there was nothing he could do. He suggested that Nelson and his friends head north for a few months.

Shortly after Moreno's departure Helen informed her husband she was unable to find her coat and concluded she must have left it at the inn in Sacramento the previous night. She couldn't remember if the pockets contained any identification. As Negri phrased it later, "I was nominated to go."

It was 3 A.M. when Negri returned with Helen's coat. He slept till noon, then joined the rest in the dining room, ordering breakfast while they ate lunch. When he noticed Chase was missing, Nelson told him, "Johnny's borrowed your Olds to go look for Sally."

As they were leaving the dining room Negri heard someone call, "Hey, Fats." The voice belonged to David J. Dillon, a San Francisco police officer Negri had known for years and considered a good friend. Dillon introduced his wife, explaining they were spending the weekend at the El Verano. "I haven't seen you much lately," the officer said. "You behaving yourself?"

After chatting with Dillon for several minutes Negri caught up to the group. Nelson asked, "Who is that guy?"

"He's okay," Fatso replied. "He's a cop from 'Frisco."

"What?" Nelson's eyes widened. "He's a cop? I thought you said he was okay!"

"He is. He's a nice fellow."

"Why didn't you tell me he was a cop?"

"I said he's okay. What's the big deal?"

Nelson called the others together. "Get packed," he said. "We're leaving."

Once the luggage was loaded in the Hudson, Nelson drove along a winding dirt road through the hills overlooking Sonoma. Nelson and Chase always had an alternate spot to meet in case one place became too hot. "We're waiting here for Johnny," he told his companions. Helen spread a blanket beneath a tree and turned the vigil into a picnic. Perkins decided, "We need some beer." As usual Negri was chosen to take the Hudson and get refreshments.

Negri was tiring of his errand-boy status and felt compelled "to kiss them all off." He toyed with the idea of finding Chase, trading cars, and driving off without looking back. Returning, Fatso told the group his sister was ill and he needed to leave a while. Nelson withheld his comments until Chase arrived. After consulting with his closest friend, Baby Face told Negri, "We won't know where we're going until we get there. As long as your sister is sick, you better go home." If Negri needed to reach them, Nelson added, he should get a message to Lieder in Chicago.

When Fatso reached his sister's home that afternoon, she saw his new car and exclaimed, "Holy shit, Joey! That's way too flashy for you. You ought to get rid of it. People will think you're a millionaire."

A few days later, on August 3, Negri traded his Olds for a black 1934 Plymouth coupe.

❋ ❋ ❋

The remaining six travelers, now squeezed into the Hudson, drove north along California's scenic coastline, stopping on subsequent nights in Caspar, Scotia, and then Eureka, where they spent the next three days. From there they headed inland and turned south, stopping each night at a new tourist camp in a new town—Weaverville, Redding, Red Bluff, and eventually back to Sacramento.

On August 9 the Nelson party visited Sausalito, then rode the ferry to San Francisco. While the others saw the sights, Nelson and Chase took a few hours to connect with Louis Tambini, who had obtained a pair of clean California license plates for them. Back on the road, the group ate supper in Salinas and spent the night at another tourist court near Stockton. In the morning they crossed back into Nevada, staying one night outside Carson City and the next at the Big Chief Auto Camp in Fallon.

Growing weary of their nomadic lifestyle after more than 2,000 miles and two weeks on the move, Nelson and his companions arrived at the Mount Grand Lodge at the southern tip of Walker Lake on August 12. It was an idyllic location, remote and peaceful, eighty miles southeast of Reno on the eastern edge of the Sierras. Chase introduced himself as John Powers to the middle-aged owners, John and Florence Benedict. He paid two weeks' rent in advance for three cabins.

"Baby Face and his friends seemed like a merry, carefree group," Flo Benedict recalled later. Nelson himself was polite and friendly in a quiet way, always smiling at her. Although they kept to themselves, they appeared to be typical tourists, swimming, relaxing, and soaking up the sun. Helen and Grace wore their bathing suits throughout most of the days, changing into lounging pajamas in the evenings. The men fished for hours, each morning frying their catch from the previous day for breakfast. The only trouble occurred one evening when a vacationing deputy sheriff and his wife in a nearby cabin complained that the six were playing their music too loud. Mrs. Benedict asked them to turn down the volume, mentioning that their neighbor was a lawman. The music stopped immediately.

Two days after the group arrived at Walker Lake, Chase declared that he wanted to see his sweetheart and bring her back to the lodge. Nelson still had doubts about Sally—both Negri and Tambini warned him that she would "talk her head off" if arrested—but he could hardly refuse Chase and risk alienating the man who had proved to be his most faithful friend. He agreed to drive Chase into San Francisco the next morning and specified a time and place near Sacramento where he would meet him on August 18.

The following day Chase managed to track down Negri and caught him coming out of the Andromeda Cafe. He appealed to Fatso to contact Sally and arrange a meeting for him. Negri agreed. Since separating from the others, the chunky hood had spent his money freely. "My bankroll is shot," he confessed.

Chase handed Negri $200, advising him that cash was tight at the moment. Nelson, Chase reported, was "sore as hell" at Van Meter for running off. "If Van had showed we could have pulled that train job," Chase lamented, "and had plenty of dough."

Sally Bachman finished work at the ferry newsstand at three o'clock that afternoon and found Negri waiting for her. "Wanna take a ride?" he asked, adding that he had "a surprise." They drove to the Cliff House near Seal Rock, where Chase was waiting. Negri dropped the couple at the El Capitano Hotel.

The next afternoon Negri stopped by the Andromeda. As he was leaving, two policemen walked in. "I thought to myself there was something wrong," Negri said later. He managed to slip out unseen while the officers spoke with owner Jim Griffen. After dinner Fatso returned to the Andromeda about 8 P.M. "You've been made, brother," Frankie Fields, the bartender, confided. "Two cops were in here looking for you." He suggested that Fatso call Hans Strittmatter.

Negri hurried across the street to a drugstore where he phoned Strittmatter at his Sausalito cigar store. "You're plenty hot, Fats, that's for sure," his former boss told him. Strittmatter's contacts among Bay Area police provided him with up-to-the-moment information. The big break in what was labeled "Baby Face Nelson's California connection" had occurred two weeks earlier when Officer David Dillon, just as Nelson feared, thought he'd recognized America's top public enemy at the El Verano in the company of a small-time hood and ex-con, Joseph Raymond "Fatso" Negri.

Acting on Dillon's tip, federal agents on the West Coast and in Chicago began to examine Negri's past and his recent movements. They discovered his association with the Parente mob where he worked with both Nelson and Chase, the latter already confirmed as a follower of Baby Face. The G-Men were able to place Negri in Chicago at the time of the South Bend holdup through his purchase of the Oldsmobile and his registration at the Fullerton from June 27 to July 3. They also learned that Negri had traded in his Olds for a Plymouth coupe on August 3 in San Francisco. "The feds are looking to tag you for the South Bend job," Strittmatter warned. "They got a description of your new car and your California plates."

Stunned, Negri lurched back across Columbus Avenue to the Andromeda. Griffen, Moreno, and Tambini were all there and called him into a back room. "You'd better get out of town," Griffen advised. "And don't tell a soul where you're going."

Negri explained that Chase was presently in the city. Tambini accompanied him to the El Capitano, where Chase and Sally were registered as Mr. and Mrs. Cooper. "Doc Bones" recommended that the couple abandon their love nest and follow him to a friend's house which was currently vacant.

The next morning, August 17, Sally announced that she wanted to return to the newsstand to finish her scheduled work for the day and tell her boss she was leaving. Chase and Negri spent the evening with Vince Marcovitch, another buddy from their bootlegging days. At midnight Marcovitch picked up Sally and delivered her to their meeting place on Highway 101 near Vallejo.

At two o'clock the next afternoon the trio reached the designated spot near Sacramento. Nelson, accompanied by Helen and Perkins, arrived on schedule. The desperado and his wife joined Negri in his Plymouth and returned to Walker Lake. Chase, Sally, and Perkins proceeded to Fallon, where a small trailer, purchased a week earlier and stocked with camping equipment and six gas cans filled with reserve fuel, was attached to the Hudson.

The group remained at the lodge another five days. Nelson and Helen stayed in one cabin, Chase and Sally in another, the Perkins family in a third, and Negri slept outdoors on a cot. While the others were at ease, enjoying the lake and perfect weather, Nelson anxiously scanned the newspapers each day to learn the latest developments in the nationwide search for him. Often he was amused, but at other times he was angered by what he read.

Nelson's reported presence in the west sparked a great deal of activity among local, state, and federal law enforcement agencies. Seven separate raids were conducted around the Bay Area and rounded up some of the bandit's alleged friends but failed to provide any significant leads. Sightings of Baby Face grew commonplace. One story claimed he had been identified while robbing a filling station in Salt Lake City and had fled the scene in a 16-cylinder Cadillac. Almost simultaneously Los Angeles police raided a Hollywood apartment and informed the press they had missed capturing Nelson by mere minutes. At the same time, reportedly while working with his old mentor Eddie Bentz, Nelson had pulled off a $470,000 robbery in New York.

On August 23 Nelson, Chase, and Perkins drove into Reno and visited Frank Cochran while the Hudson was serviced. The garage owner seemed unfazed by all the publicity surrounding his friend. Cochran reassured Nelson that whenever he needed anything, he would be glad to help out.

Back at Walker Lake that evening, Nelson heard over the radio that Homer Van Meter—once his trusted ally but more recently his sworn enemy—had been killed by police in St. Paul.

❋ ❋ ❋

After their hasty evacuation from Chicago, Van Meter and Mickey reached St. Paul on July 25 and immediately contacted Tom Gannon and his wife. Gannon made several inquiries about Nelson, but Van Meter, flashing a petulant smirk, made it clear that he had nothing to say about their former partner in crime. His chief concern was obtaining money and temporary sanctuary, both of which he was convinced he could find in the old gangster haven of the Twin Cities.

But times were rapidly changing. The shootout at the Lincoln Court Apartments four months earlier had cast the national spotlight on St. Paul's meticulously crafted system of local hoods, corrupt cops, and bribed officials working together to protect the likes of Van Meter. The furor triggered a massive reform movement throughout the Twin Cities. With the key gangland figures scrambling to cover their tracks, Van Meter's unexpected and undesirable presence threatened to ignite the already volatile situation.

To make matters worse, Van Meter had deposited $9,000, part of his take from the Sioux Falls and Mason City holdups, with Harry Sawyer for safekeeping. When the desperado sent word that he wanted to collect his cash, Sawyer—who had either spent the money or simply had no intention of parting with it—managed to stall Van Meter over the next few weeks.

Van Meter's principal contact was Thomas Franklin Kirwin, a short, gray-haired handyman who worked on Sawyer's farm north of St. Paul. In addition to relaying messages between the bandit and Sawyer, Kirwin took Van Meter to a resort on Bear Island in Leech Lake where the outlaw and Mickey, registered as Henry and Ruth Adams, enjoyed their longest respite from the road, from August 6 to 14. Van Meter fished during the day and at night slipped into St. Paul to visit friends in bars and bowling alleys along Rice Street.

A number of his Twin Cities pals, including Gannon, noticed a disturbing change in his behavior. Instead of the cocky, confident swagger he had possessed when boasting that John Dillinger was his closest friend, Van Meter now appeared jittery, erratic, and even forgetful. Rumors circulated that he had grown addicted to painkillers in the aftermath of his plastic surgery and had escalated to morphine after sustaining the head wound in South Bend.

With Mickey stashed at Bear Island, Van Meter spent some evenings in St. Paul in the amorous company of Opal Milligan, a twenty-one-year-old brunette who worked as a waitress, part-time prostitute, and occasional FBI informer. (Two months earlier she had helped lead G-Men to Pat Reilly.) There was considerable consternation within the St. Paul underworld over the company Van Meter was keeping, and what might happen in his unstable condition if he were to fall into federal hands.

When Van Meter and Mickey left the resort, their movements became more furtive and they moved frequently from place to place outside the Twin Cities. Obviously Van Meter was nervous about being spotted and increasingly anxious to recover his money. But while he was busy looking over his shoulder for the dreaded G-Men or local officers untainted by the underworld, his doom was being sealed in St. Paul by the very people he'd trusted to help him.

Precisely who was involved in the conspiracy to put Van Meter "on the spot"—and what the motives of those involved might have been—remains a matter of conjecture. There is no doubt, however, about the involvement of two persons: Sawyer, who engineered the plan, and Police Detective Thomas Brown, who handled the details and put the plan into motion.

At exactly 5:12 Thursday afternoon, August 23, the trap was sprung. A Chevrolet stopped in front of St. Paul Motors, an auto dealership near the intersection of University and Marion, just two blocks from the state Capitol. Van Meter—smartly attired in a blue serge suit, white shirt, black-and-white oxfords, and a straw hat—stepped from the passenger side carrying a small brown bag tucked under his arm. As the Chevy's driver (various accounts claim it was either Gannon or Kirwin) sped off, four men emerged from an unmarked police car parked a few yards away. Tom Brown and newly appointed Chief of Police Frank Cullen carried sawed-off shotguns; two young detectives, Jeff Dittrich and Thomas McMahon, were armed with machine guns.

Van Meter saw the quartet coming. Pulling a Colt .380 automatic, he darted across University Avenue, dodging traffic and pedestrians. Cullen later insisted that he shouted "Stick 'em up!" but no one else near the scene heard the command. The fugitive fled south down Marion, throwing two shots over his shoulder at his pursuers.

Near Aurora Avenue Van Meter made a fatal mistake when he darted left into a blind alley. He was desperately searching for a way out or some cover when the lawmen arrived at the mouth of the alley. From a distance of no more than forty feet they unleashed a furious fusillade that splattered Van Meter over much of the pavement.

The body was a hideous sight. Reports that Van Meter was riddled with fifty bullets were exaggerated; even so, the officers' excessive use of firepower was evident in the Ramsey County coroner's findings, which revealed the outlaw's thin frame had been perforated by twenty-six buckshot slugs and a single machine-gun bullet—and that all of the entry wounds were in the back. In his zeal to make sure that Van Meter never talked, Brown had emptied all five loads of his shotgun into the fugitive.

The amount of lead discovered in Van Meter was only part of the controversy surrounding his bloody demise. Hoover was livid that the St. Paul Police Department—which he and Attorney General Cummings had blasted for corruption—took all the credit for ridding society of Dillinger's right-hand man. The director criticized his agents for their "utter lack of aggressiveness" in not finding Van Meter first, and he instructed his men to conduct a thorough investigation into how the local police had beaten them.

Almost immediately certain facts arose to cast doubt on the official story, which claimed that "approximately five or ten minutes before the shooting" police had "received a tip that Van Meter was in the vicinity of University Avenue" and that while "cruising" the area, officers had spotted him standing on the corner.

Exactly who supplied the tip was the question everyone wanted answered, especially Hoover and the press. It was learned that "within minutes" of the ambush, Opal Milligan had been taken into custody by police and held on "an open charge," apparently to be intimidated into cooperation by Brown's men. Word leaked out alleging that Opal (or her family) had alerted police. Newsmen jumped on the rumor and reported that Van Meter, like Dillinger, had been betrayed by a woman and shot dead in an alley. Opal, however, refused to support the Police Department's claims. Forced to change their story, the officers revealed the tip actually had been provided by an employee of the auto dealership.

The manager of St. Paul Motors swore he had no idea what the police were talking about. In fact, while Chief of Police Cullen insisted that the tip had been received a mere "five or ten minutes" prior to the shooting, the manager reported that Tom Brown had visited the car lot a full five hours earlier. The detective had confided that a wanted man would arrive to purchase an automobile and that the lawmen intended to be on hand to arrest him. Describing the action that had taken place outside his window, the manager said that a "mystery man" in a Chevrolet had delivered Van Meter to within a few yards of the officers, who waited until the driver was out of the way before charging from their vehicle.

The auto dealer also mentioned that Van Meter was carrying a brown zippered bag when he was confronted by the lawmen. However, an inventory of the dead man's possessions at the morgue included his clothing, a pack of Lucky

Strike cigarettes, two boxes of matches, an extra clip for his .380, $923 in cash, and $1.18 in coins—no brown bag. The significance of the missing item was not realized until Mickey later revealed that the bag contained $6,000 and that her boyfriend was carrying another $2,000 on his person.

Two days after Van Meter was slain the *St. Paul Daily News* published a story identifying Harry Sawyer as "the underworld leader" who had fingered the skinny bandit for the police. What the account failed to uncover was the alliance between Sawyer and Brown that kept Van Meter from talking and his money in local pockets. Most of all the slaying made Brown and the St. Paul police look more efficient and less corrupt than they were. While Brown divided Van Meter's loot with others in the conspiracy, newspapers praised him as part of the city's new "fighting police force" which was "cleaning house" in St. Paul.

In the end, many in the local underworld benefited from Van Meter's death. Jack Peifer, whom Van Meter was scheduled to see that evening, was also linked to the setup and reportedly received a portion of the cash taken from the corpse. For his part, Tom Gannon was said to have received Van Meter's guns and avoided prosecution for crimes in the Twin Cities area.

❋ ❋ ❋

Baby Face Nelson didn't shed any tears over his onetime friend. In fact, according to Fatso Negri, "he seemed irritated because he wanted to kill Van Meter himself." The news also must have had a sobering effect on the young desperado. Of the six men who joined forces after Dillinger's escape from Crown Point to form an elite bank-robbing unit, Nelson was now the sole survivor.

It is not known whether Van Meter's death played a part in the decision, but the next day the group vacated the Mount Grand lodge. Nelson drove the Hudson with Helen beside him, the Perkins family in the back seat, and the trailer attached behind. Chase and Sally rode with Negri in his Plymouth. After spending the night in Gunnison, Colorado, they took a more scenic route through the Rockies and entered Kansas on August 27.

At one point in the journey John Jr. announced that he had to go and couldn't hold it. Nelson pulled to the side of the highway, saying he too was unable to wait for the next rest stop. While the outlaw and the little boy relieved their bladders at the bottom of a hill, they noticed a band of riders on horseback pounding across the plains in the distance. John Jr., certain they were wild Indians, scurried back to the safety of the Hudson and his mother's lap. His father, seated beside a canvas bag stuffed with Nelson's arsenal, laughed and assured the boy, "If they attack us, I think we're prepared."

After two more days on the road and two more nights in tourist camps in Nebraska and Iowa, the travelers arrived in East Burlington, Illinois, and rented cabins along the Mississippi River. Two days later, on August 31, Perkins spotted an item in the personals section of the *Chicago Tribune:* "Jack, Book going bad—Art."

"I gotta get back," Perkins told Nelson. The vacation was over. The boyhood chums talked privately for a while, then Perkins asked about his friend's plans. "We'll keep moving," Nelson said with a shrug. He spoke about getting "set up" someplace over the winter, then recruiting a new gang in the spring. He hinted that he had several people in mind.

Negri remembered that it was almost midnight when "Jimmie asked me to take Jack Perkins and his wife and child home, and Jimmie instructed me to contact Clarey Lieder." Nelson wanted to meet Lieder the next evening.

At the appointed time on September 1, the garage owner drove along Mannheim Road until he spotted Negri's signal, headlights flashing three times. Lieder followed the Plymouth—containing Negri, Perkins, and Art Johnston—to a hilltop affording an excellent view in every direction. Shortly after eight o'clock Nelson's Hudson, still pulling the trailer, approached after receiving an all-clear signal from the headlights. Helen and Sally remained in the car while the six men briefly talked. The entire group then proceeded to a country tavern where Nelson bought food and drinks for everyone.

At the table Lieder and Johnston took turns recounting events that had rocked Chicago over the past five weeks. Police and federal agents were turning up the heat on anyone even remotely connected to Nelson. Old pals like Al Van de Houton, Mike Juska, George Ackerman (presently in the Cook County jail for robbery), Frank Paska, and others were tracked down and interrogated. Johnston's girlfriend Jean Burke was detained and rigorously questioned. One person the lawmen were unable to locate was Hazel Doyle. While her husband remained behind bars at the Michigan State Prison, she had moved in with Harry Sherman, a night club owner. Hearing that agents were searching for her, Hazel, along with Harry and her Pekinese dogs, abandoned their Chicago apartment for the obscurity of a mobile home near her relatives in Missouri.

Two of Nelson's favorite hangouts were currently off limits. Jimmy Murray had sold the Rainbo, partly to help settle his mounting debts (which the gang's train robbery was meant to do) and partly to sever his ties with the underworld for the moment. Murray nevertheless had confided to Lieder that he was available if Nelson should need his help in the future. Louie's roadhouse was still open and operating, but Cernocky had withdrawn from the business because of poor health. (In fact, just three weeks later, he suffered a fatal heart attack.) Taking over for their father, sons Eddie and Louis Jr. made it clear that the roadhouse no longer catered to Baby Face and his kind.

The situation got worse. The Chicago syndicate's disdain for free-lancers like Nelson had grown stronger than ever. Word came down from the "big-shot dagos," as Johnston called them, leaving Accardo, Capezio, McGurn and his many other "connected" friends no choice but to turn their backs on their former pal from The Patch. Hearing this, Nelson remarked, "You boys better clear out while you can. I'm too damn dangerous to be around."

In the parking lot Nelson handed Lieder some money and asked him to put the trailer in storage. "I'm sick of hauling this thing all over the country," he declared as they disconnected it from the Hudson. "I wouldn't do too hot if I got chased by the cops."

Before leaving with Negri, Perkins asked if there was anything he could do. Nelson shook his head and said, "You've done enough." Helen, standing beside her husband, yearned to see her children but knew, at the moment, it was impossible. She requested that Perkins get word to the Warwick family and arrange a meeting. She particularly wanted to see her youngest sister, fourteen-year-old Wanda. Perkins promised to see to it.

❋ ❋ ❋

The day after Dillinger was slain outside the Biograph Theatre, Samuel Parkerson Cowley—the man Hoover credited with cracking the Dillinger case—celebrated his thirty-fifth birthday. He was a stocky figure with dark, somber eyes and a sagging face that made him look ten years older. Born into a middle-class Mormon family in Idaho, Cowley spent four years (1916 to 1920) doing missionary work in Hawaii. He then studied engineering and agriculture in Utah before developing a passion for law and earning a degree from George Washington University in 1928.

On March 11, 1928, Cowley joined the FBI and spent the next three years serving in field offices in Salt Lake City, Butte, Los Angeles, and Detroit. He was a bright, mercurial, tenacious investigator, a little older than the average agent (six months older than the director himself) and a natural to advance through the ranks. Transferred to the bureau's headquarters in Washington and promoted to inspector, he soon became one of Hoover's most trusted men. When Purvis kept missing Dillinger and his gang, Cowley was dispatched to oversee the Chicago office.

Although they were portrayed as friends in the press, Purvis and Cowley had little in common and barely managed to tolerate each other. Purvis resented the inspector's presence and was suspicious of him; Cowley had gained a reputation as one of Hoover's hatchetmen who never neglected to notify the director of any misconduct or failure by the agents around him, no matter how trivial the offense. Nor was the SAC particularly pleased with Cowley's often brutish style of interrogation. The inspector had no patience with a stubborn suspect who refused to cooperate; to obtain results he would "get tough," then gloat in his memos about his ability to "soften up" difficult subjects, especially females.

Since Cowley supervised all crucial interviews at this time, it was certainly he whom Doris Lockerman had in mind when she wrote: "Some of the agents did handle prisoners over-roughly. They had read about the 'third degree' and tried to use it without knowing how. Their attempts were stupid and useless."

After Dillinger's death the Cowley-inspired methods of extracting information at the Chicago office began to attract attention and some undesirable publicity. On July 24 Dr. Loeser was apprehended and subjected to an intense grilling. According to Anna Patkze, Loeser's common-law wife, the agents "smashed in his nose." The surgeon quickly cut a deal, naming Probasco, Piquett, O'Leary, and Cassidy as among those who had harbored Dillinger and Van Meter. Loeser swore he had been forced to perform the operations at gunpoint and claimed that Baby Face Nelson often marched through the house brandishing a machine gun.

On July 25 agents acting on Loeser's information arrested Probasco. Shortly after ten o'clock the next morning the interrogation of the sixty-nine-year-old suspect ended abruptly when he plunged to his death from one of the bureau's nineteenth-story windows. The official story—provided to the press by Cowley himself—alleged that during a break in Probasco's questioning, Special Agent Max Chaffetz had fingerprinted the old man and left the room for only an instant. Rather than face a prison sentence, Probasco evidently had chosen to take his own life by leaping out the open window. Cowley claimed that when Probasco was taken into custody, agents found a letter indicating "he was on the verge of committing suicide." Cowley insisted the suspect had not been mistreated in any way.

The inspector's version of Probasco's death might have gone unchallenged had it not been for the claims of John J. "Boss" McLaughlin. Less than three months earlier McLaughlin had publicly charged that while being interrogated about the Bremer kidnapping, agents had beaten him savagely enough to knock out his front teeth, then dangled him out the same window from which Probasco had "fallen" and threatened to drop him if he refused to talk.

Rumors circulated that Probasco had met his end during a similar interrogation. O'Leary confided to author Russell Girardin that while he was a federal prisoner he overheard agents discussing the incident: "From their conversation, it sounded like Cowley had been battering the old man around but was dissatisfied with his answers. Supposedly he said something along the lines of, 'I know how to make you talk,' and while holding Probasco over the the edge of the window lost his grip on the struggling man."

Another scenario suggested that in their zeal to make Probasco talk, the agents applied a bit too much force, either killing him outright or inducing a heart attack. Then, to cover their tracks and avoid the embarrassment of being caught with the battered corpse, they tossed Probasco out the window and concocted the suicide story. Cowley never produced the alleged suicide note, nor has it ever surfaced in any of the voluminous FBI files on the Dillinger case.

Hoover rebuked his men for their "extreme carelessness" in the handling of Probasco.

O'Leary was the next to fall into federal hands. On the evening of August 25 the young man and his wife and daughter walked out of an Evanston restaurant and found themselves surrounded by a dozen agents, most armed with machine guns. "Make a move and we'll blow you to pieces!" one warned.

During a marathon questioning at the bureau's offices over the next five days, O'Leary was kept handcuffed to a chair almost constantly. "One of you fellows jumped out a window," an agent explained, "and we don't want it to happen again."

O'Leary later said he was mostly treated well by the agents, the one exception being Cowley, who often resorted to "slapping me around." When O'Leary persisted in claiming that he was not a member of the gang, just an investigator employed by Piquett, Cowley grew belligerent and demanded that he sign a confession implicating himself in the South Bend holdup. When he refused, the inspector ordered O'Leary's handcuffs removed, then yanked him out of the chair, threw him to the floor, and repeatedly kicked him.

As part of his deal for a reduced sentence O'Leary testified against others on trial for harboring Dillinger. He denied under oath that he had been abused while in federal custody, despite the fact he was treated for six broken ribs after his arrest.

After Van Meter's death, Mickey Conforti fled back to Chicago, where she was nabbed by agents only three days later. At the same time O'Leary was being questioned, Mickey was undergoing a similar interrogation in the bureau's nineteenth-floor offices. Nearly four months passed before she spoke to reporters; Hoover had issued "very definite instructions" to his agents to prevent her from being interviewed and was furious when the "oversight" occurred. Mickey told newsmen that after her capture she was subjected to "torture" tactics, and once again Cowley was singled out as the main offender. "He chained me to a chair, and every few minutes he would ask, 'Where is Nelson?' Every time I said I didn't know, he slapped me and punched me."

O'Leary, Loeser, Probasco, Mickey Conforti—all were minor players in the Dillinger drama. Nelson was the only remaining marquee outlaw from the gang, and Cowley desperately wanted to nail him. "He's a runty little murderer," Cowley declared during an interview. "Wherever the trail leads our men will follow until Baby Face is behind bars or beneath the dirt where he belongs."

✾ ✾ ✾

On Labor Day, September 3, Nelson, Helen, Chase, and Sally arrived at the Lake Como Inn. They avoided the hotel, going directly to the Hermanson house and making themselves at home. Helen went to the icebox and made sandwiches while Chase stretched out on the sofa and took a nap. Nelson stayed outside conversing with Eddie Duffy, the Inn's chief caretaker.

A skinny six-footer with a freckled face and Brooklyn accent, the twenty-six-year-old Duffy had worked for Hermanson since Prohibition days and had seen his share of notorious guests at the resort, many of whom treated him with snobbish contempt or unwarranted suspicion. Though he later denied it to agents, Duffy was fully aware that he was speaking to America's most wanted man. He remembered Nelson from his previous visit and was greatly impressed with the young outlaw's easy, down-to-earth demeanor. He assured Baby Face he and his friends were welcome at the resort at any time.

That evening Nelson and Chase drove into Lake Geneva and spoke to Hermanson outside his tavern on Center Street. "We want to come back here after the season is closed and get you to put us up," Chase said. Knowing they would pay top dollar for temporary asylum, Hermanson agreed to the arrangement and set the date for "between Halloween and Thanksgiving."

Two days later Nelson and his companions returned to the western outskirts of Chicago. At this time, as Negri puts it, "Jimmie and Johnny had an argument over Sally." Nelson not only mistrusted her but also was angered that she did nothing to help with the group's chores, leaving Helen to do the majority of cooking and cleaning up. The two couples decided to split up for a while.

Chase and Sally were dropped off at the Kelly Hotel in Elgin, where they registered as Mr. and Mrs. Ed Burns. Over the next three days they lived like newlyweds, sleeping till noon and having their meals delivered to the room. One afternoon they rode the train into Chicago and spent the day shopping with Negri, who was staying at the Carlos Hotel.

Nelson and his wife, meanwhile, lived in auto camps around Kane County. They briefly came out of hiding on receiving word that Perkins had arranged a meeting with Helen's relatives at the Paris Cafe in Elgin. During the get-together Nelson was amused to hear a report on the radio that a squad of eight federal agents armed with machine guns and smoke grenades had raided a hotel in Atlantic City in an attempt to capture him.

On September 9 Nelson drove Chase and Sally to the Baker Hotel in St. Charles. He handed his friend an envelope containing $3,500 and announced that he was heading west again in the morning. When Chase was ready to re-join him, preferably without Sally, he was to place a personal ad in the *Reno Evening Gazette*.

The next day, as Chase and his sweetheart boarded a train for New York City, Nelson and Helen picked up Negri at the Carlos Hotel and departed in the Hudson. During the past eleven days, Fatso had run low on cash. Afraid Nelson or Chase would scold him if he asked for money, he sold his Plymouth coupe for $400.

Short of funds, the trio slept in the car along the highways. On September 19 they entered Reno. Nelson left Helen and Negri at a diner while he visited the Air Service Garage. Cochran could tell life on the road was taking its toll on the young desperado; Nelson looked haggard and drained. He seemed surprised when the garage owner reaffirmed his promise to help in any way he could.

Two nights later the three slipped back into the city and stopped at Cochran's house on March Avenue. Both Cochran and his wife seemed delighted to see the young couple and their friend. Invited inside, Nelson hesitated, sheepishly asking if Cochran thought his two children might recognize him as a notorious public enemy. Cochran assured him they wouldn't.

The friends sat and chatted for several hours. Nelson recalled some recent adventures and spoke at length about how the law had gunned down his former partners in crime—Green, Hamilton, Carroll, Dillinger, and Van Meter. He shared an interesting observation about their deaths: "They all got it in the back."

Anna remarked, "How lucky you are. All the rest of the gang are killed and you're the only one left alive."

Nelson said he didn't feel very lucky. Then, in words that would prove prophetic, he added, "They're not going to get me like that. I'll face 'em head-on and take a few of 'em with me."

Later he told Cochran about some repairs he wanted on the Hudson and asked to use another car while his was in the shop. Cochran offered his 1928 Buick sedan, and both cars were driven into the garage at the rear of the house. As the pair transferred weapons and luggage from one vehicle to the other, Cochran mentioned that he had a siren at his place of business, an item he had ordered for Reno's police chief before the work was cancelled. Nelson was intrigued. Hopping into the Buick, they drove to the Virginia Street garage. "I want it," Nelson declared. "Can you put it on the Hudson?"

Cochran quoted a price of fifty dollars for the siren and ten for installation. With that and all the other work ordered, the Hudson would be ready in "four or five days."

Nelson and his companions drove to Las Vegas, in those days a small, drab dot on the sprawling Nevada landscape, its major attraction the newly constructed Hoover Dam. They returned to Reno at nightfall on September 25 but the Cochrans were not at home. When Nelson saw his Hudson parked outside a movie theater, he became enraged. By the time the Cochrans returned, Nelson had cooled down but still told the garage owner it was unwise to drive his car in public.

Pulling the cars inside the garage, the men transferred the travelers' belongings back to the Hudson. Cochran presented his friend with a bill for $200, which Nelson paid on the spot, throwing in his customary fifty-dollar tip.

325

Then, leaving Helen and Negri sitting with Anna in the kitchen, the two men took a ride in the desert, testing the siren while streaking along a highway at 80 mph or better.

The next day the trio checked into the Big Chief auto camp in Fallon, sixty miles east of Reno, where Nelson and Helen had stayed six weeks earlier. Each evening they returned to the Cochrans for supper and socializing. Despite the garage owner's assurances that the group was safe in Reno, Nelson insisted on caution. They kept to back roads when approaching the city and always entered after sundown. Negri was sent ahead to knock on Cochran's door while Nelson and Helen circled the block. Once satisfied the coast was clear, the couple pulled into the driveway and used the back door. The visitors rarely came empty-handed, repaying the Cochrans' hospitality with gifts and groceries.

By September 28 Nelson's cash was almost depleted. That evening he spoke to Cochran about switching vehicles again. He explained that he had some money waiting for him in California but was reluctant to cross the state line in the Hudson. Cochran's Buick had a non-resident permit on the windshield that would exempt it from having to stop for an inspection at the California State Motor Vehicle Checking Station.

The Hudson was driven into the garage, and the arsenal was unloaded and stored in Cochran's basement. In the process Nelson showed his machine-gun pistol to Cochran. "I killed a man back east with this," he said matter-of-factly. The bandit briefly recounted his version of the shooting of Special Agent Baum during his frantic flight from Little Bohemia. "It was a case of him or me," he insisted. "I was a little faster."

Nelson, Helen, and Negri arrived at the Dogian Auto Camp in Vallejo the next afternoon. That night they visited Tobe Williams at his office in the Vallejo General Hospital. Nelson announced he needed some of the cash he had deposited with him, saying, "A G should tide us over."

Williams hobbled on his wooden leg to a bookcase and retrieved a strongbox hidden behind some medical volumes on the top shelf. Back at his desk the aged administrator counted out $1,000 for his young friend. "Anything else you need, Jimmie?" he inquired.

Nelson said he was eager to get in touch with "Ray and Freddie," referring to Karpis and Barker. "I don't have a lead on the boys at the moment," Williams told him. "If you can get back this way in the spring, I'll have a meeting set up."

After Nelson and his companions departed, a doctor took the administrator aside and declared, "That was Baby Face Nelson you had in your office."

"That was him," Williams confessed, proudly explaining that the most wanted man in America was a personal friend. The doctor was aghast and asked Williams if he wasn't afraid Nelson would reveal the names of people who aided him once he was captured. "He'd never talk," Williams assured the physician. "Besides, they'll never take him alive. Not in a million years."

The next day, September 30, Negri phoned Tony "Soap" Moreno and summoned him to the auto court in Vallejo. Soap was visibly edgy about calling on his old pals. Ever since Nelson had been spotted at the El Verano two months earlier, agents under Edward P. Guinane, SAC of the San Francisco office, had been relentless in their hunt for the notorious criminal. Many mutual friends, including Tambini, had been grilled about their association with Nelson. Police in San Francisco, Sausalito, and Oakland were aiding the G-Men in the search.

Nelson asked Moreno if he had heard from Chase recently. "Not a word," Soap said, adding that "Johnny is as hot as you are around here." He advised Nelson that the authorities had been tipped off about Sally Bachman's relationship with Chase. "They're on the lookout for her," he warned.

As Nelson and Moreno spoke, Negri overheard Soap refer to "that Buick," saying, "I was afraid to sell it and had it torched." When Negri later related this statement to FBI interrogators, the agents concluded that Moreno was telling Baby Face he had disposed of the Frisch car.

Nelson said he was low on ammunition and asked his friend to obtain some for him. Moreno refused. "You're too hot, Jimmie. I've always been your pal, but I'm not going to stop a bullet for you or end up in the joint. Get Fats to buy it."

The trio returned to Fallon that night. The next evening they drove to Cochran's house, swapped vehicles again and transferred the weapons back to the Hudson. The fugitives, as usual, were invited inside and spent the next three hours socializing. Nelson mentioned his dwindling supply of ammo, lamenting that he could no longer drive into the desert and keep his shooting skills sharp with target practice. Cochran revealed that his sister-in-law was married to a marine stationed at a base near Hawthorne, 100 miles southeast of Reno. "He's able to buy ammunition cheap through the Navy, though it might be old stuff. I'll see what I can do for you."

Nelson handed Cochran a few cartridges as a sample of what he needed. Apparently the garage owner came through for him. Negri reported that a few days later Nelson spent an entire afternoon in the wilderness blasting anything that moved. That evening he presented the Cochrans with five pheasants, a duck, and a mud hen, which Anna used to prepare a small feast.

By that time Nelson, Helen, and Negri had moved from Fallon to Walley's Hot Springs, halfway between Carson City and Minden. The desperado felt secure enough to pay three weeks' rent in advance. Each day Negri drove into Carson City to purchase supplies and newspapers. Nelson continued to read the almost daily accounts of himself—people were seeing Baby Face everywhere (usually in the company of Alvin Karpis or the late John Hamilton); crimes throughout the nation were attributed to him; and federal agents kept insisting they were hot on his trail and close to catching him. Nelson also scanned the personals section of the *Reno Evening Gazette*, searching for the message from his favorite henchman. Almost a full month had passed since Nelson and Chase went their separate ways.

On October 10 he spotted the ad he was waiting for. "Johnny's back," he told Negri. "We're going into Reno tonight."

❋ ❋ ❋

Arriving in New York on September 11, Chase and Sally moved into the St. Andrews Hotel, registering as Mr. and Mrs. John Madison of Boston. Over the course of their romantic getaway and sightseeing excursions, Chase took some time to shop for a vehicle and verification of his new identity. On September 26 he purchased an Air-flow DeSoto Town Sedan, obtaining New York license plates issued in the name of John Madison. Two days later he acquired a New York driver's license using the alias of Madison, a resident of the St. Andrews Hotel in Manhattan.

On September 30 he placed Sally aboard a plane for San Francisco, vowing to return for her by Christmas. Chase left that same day in his new DeSoto. On October 4 he reached Helena, Montana, and stayed four nights in three different hotels while visiting Arthur Pratt, an old friend and former Sausalito bartender currently working in his mother's jewelry shop.

Pratt's acquaintances were impressed by Chase during his brief sojourn in their midst. On one occasion he took Pratt and several friends for a long scenic drive in his new car, then treated them to a memorable dinner. They later described him as "a man of unusually pleasing personality, affable, and an interesting conversationalist." While Chase made a dazzling impact on many, there was one who had suspicions about the visitor. Otto Krieg was the proprietor of the AAA garage where "Mr. Madison" stored his DeSoto on his final two nights in the city. Chase told Krieg he was "a statistician connected with some federal bureau" and that he resided in Manhattan, unaware that Krieg was a native New Yorker. When they conversed, Chase seemed "strangely hazy" about common New York sites and happenings.

Shortly before leaving Helena on the morning of October 8, Chase asked his friend to hold some money for him. Pratt was stunned at the amount— $1,740 in twenties, tens, and fives, the major portion remaining of the $3,500 Nelson had given Chase a month earlier. Pratt placed the cash in a safe deposit box.

Within hours of Chase's departure, agents from the Butte office arrived in Helena searching for John Madison. The G-Men had been tipped (evidently by an informant) that Chase had spent most of September in New York and managed to track him to Montana. The trail led to Pratt, who profusely denied knowing that his old pal was wanted by the law. He immediately surrendered the keys to the safe deposit box and pledged his full cooperation.

A contingent of agents remained in Helena, prepared to pounce on Chase if he reappeared to collect his cash from Pratt. As badly as they wanted Nelson's enigmatic follower, the agents unanimously agreed that it was better they had missed Chase in Montana. They had a description of his vehicle—the Air-flow DeSoto was a distinctive automobile—and its New York plates, 4W324. They were confident the car would be spotted and that Chase might lead them to the present lair of Baby Face Nelson.

Chase arrived in Reno on October 9. His first stop was the Air Service Garage, where he spoke to Cochran about contacting their mutual friend. Cochran confessed he didn't know where Nelson was staying or how to get in touch with him, although he said the outlaw dropped by their home regularly—in fact, the outlaw, along with Helen and their friend Fatso, had visited the last three nights in a row. Chase left his car at the garage for servicing and obtained a room at a near by hotel. To let Nelson know he was in town, he placed an advertisement in the newspaper's personals section.

By the time the ad ran, lawmen were already aware of Chase's presence in the city. The FBI's San Francisco office received word that the DeSoto had been seen in Reno and tracked to the Air Service Garage at 241 South Virginia Street. The break came at a bad time for SAC Edward Guinane, a slim, bushy-haired man with glasses, who was at home nursing a severe cold when the report reached him. He immediately chartered a plane and chose ten agents to accompany him.

The eleven G-Men arrived shortly before noon on October 10. They were met at the airport by Reno's police chief, who told them the DeSoto was still at the garage and there had been no sign of the owner. A quick check revealed the president and principal stockholder of the Air Service Company was Franklin Bradford Cochran. The police chief vouched for Cochran as a reputable businessman with no criminal record.

Guinane and his men proceeded to the garage and searched the sedan, finding only an overcoat and a suit left in the back seat. The agents interviewed Cochran about the vehicle's owner. "I never saw him before," Cochran swore. "He must be a tourist. He said he would be back to pick up the car but didn't say when."

When agents showed Cochran a photo of Chase, he shook his head, saying the picture did not resemble the driver. The surprised lawmen displayed photos of Nelson, Negri, and Perkins, but Cochran repeatedly shook his head and denied ever having seen any of the men.

Knowing they had the right car and finding no reason for Cochran to lie, the agents took him into their confidence and counted on his cooperation. A trap was set for whoever showed up to claim the DeSoto. Two agents were posted inside the garage , awaiting a signal from Cochran to move in when the party arrived.

Once he was alone, Cochran phoned Chase at his hotel and warned him that the city was "crawling with government officers" searching for the owner of the DeSoto. Chase was stunned. He had been so careful; how could they have found him? "They showed me your picture," Cochran said. "Stay away from the garage."

Still reeling from the revelation, Chase revealed that he had placed an ad in the *Gazette* and expected Nelson to come to town. Cochran told him not to worry, they had a prearranged signal that would alert Nelson if there was any danger. "If Jimmie comes by my house and sees my car parked in the driveway instead of the garage, it'll warn him to keep away."

Eager to rejoin his pal, Nelson entered Reno earlier than usual, a good hour before sundown. As he, Helen, and Negri neared Cochran's home, all three noticed the Buick sitting in the driveway. "Let's get out of here," Fatso suggested from the back seat.

"He probably just forgot to put the car in," Nelson said.

Helen clasped her husband's arm. "Maybe something's wrong."

Nelson kept driving and told Negri to "put on one of those vests back there and go ring the doorbell." If there were any trouble, he was to run back to the Hudson. Nelson drew his .38 super automatic from its shoulder holster and placed it in his lap. "If anyone follows you out, I'll pick 'em off from here," he said.

Negri was not thrilled with the plan, but he dutifully strapped on a steel-reinforced vest as they again approached the house. Nelson parked a few yards down the street and sent Negri on his way. Fatso walked up the front steps and pressed the bell. The door opened immediately, revealing an angry Frank Cochran. "Get out of here quick, you dumbass," he hissed. "Didn't you see the signal to stay away? We're surrounded by government men."

"Jimmie wants to find Johnny," Negri said urgently.

"Johnny's all right. Tell him to drive out on the Geiger Road, and I'll bring Johnny out there."

Negri scurried back to the Hudson and relayed Cochran's message. As the sun was sinking behind the Sierras, Nelson drove ten miles south of the city. Near Mount Rose he turned up the Geiger Grade toward Virginia City and stopped, waiting in the. fading light along the highway. A half-hour later Cochran's Buick—containing the garage owner, his wife, and Chase—approached. Nelson called to them to follow him onto a side road. Several miles later Baby Face pulled over and sprang from the Hudson, glaring back down the road with a machine gun in his grasp.

Anna remained in the Buick while her husband and Chase went to speak to Nelson. Negri joining them between the two cars. Cochran told the bandits all he knew—the arrival of the agents by plane earlier that day, the trap laid at his garage, the photos they flashed. Nelson listened with mounting anger. He started pacing up and down the road's shoulder, the machine gun still clenched in his hand. "I'll go back there and get that car," he fumed. "And I'll blast the hell out of those government bastards if they try to stop me."

The others tried to settle him down. "Think about it, Jimmie," Cochran pleaded. "You'll only get yourself and other people killed."

"I don't care anymore," he snarled. "I'm sick of them hunting me and my wife like we were animals."

The group finally prevailed upon their hot-headed friend to abandon his reckless plans. Once Nelson's rage was defused, the quartet discussed what to do next. Baby Face refused to simply pack up and evacuate the region. "I'm through running," he told them. He agreed, however, that Reno would remain off limits for the time being. Cochran reluctantly consented to continue to play his double role. "Meet us here tomorrow night," Nelson told him. "Same time and place, and give us any more dope you can get on the G-Men."

Chase and Negri joined Helen in the Hudson as Nelson walked to the Buick with Cochran. "I'm sorry as hell I got you into this, Frank," the young outlaw said.

"Then for God's sake," Cochran pleaded, "stay out of Reno!"

Nelson and the others returned to the cabin at Walley's Hot Springs. Negri recalled that they stayed up the entire night listening to Chase talk about his recent travels. He was apologetic and still mystified over how the agents traced him to Reno. Nelson put him at ease, saying, "They're a clever bunch, not dumb like regular cops."

As arranged, they met Cochran the following night near the Geiger pass. He provided Nelson with a description and license plate numbers of two cars the G-Men were using and also shared the address of the Reno apartment house where they were staying. Nelson wrote down the information and later scrawled the license numbers on the wall of their cabin, probably to memorize them. One agent theorized that the outlaw, knowing that the lawmen would eventually learn about his stay at Hot Springs, was leaving a taunting and rather unnerving message for his pursuers to find.

Negri recalled that Nelson often glared at the numbers and spoke of "hitting" the agents. Once in Negri's presence he suggested to Chase, "We ought to go in there (Reno) single-handed and do away with a couple of those G's—wait for their car, see it parked, hijack the men, and do away with 'em and take 'em out and bury them like we did with Frisch. That'll keep 'em out of here. They'd be afraid to come down here around Reno then, and we'd have clear sailing."

Cochran met with them two more times. At the first rendezvous, on or about October 15, he reported that the agents were continuing their vigil at his garage. He also said the U.S. Attorney's Office had secured a court order allowing federal officers to take possession of the DeSoto once the stakeout was terminated. Cochran's original estimate of the work performed on the sedan was thirty-five dollars. "Make sure you jack up the price of your bill," Chase advised, bitter over the impending loss of his vehicle. "They'll pay any amount you ask when they take the car."

They met again a week later. Cochran mentioned that he'd recently noticed the G-Men's cars were always muddy. Nelson shook his head. "They're checking the auto camps and resorts in the area," he declared solemnly. "It's only a matter of time before they reach Hot Springs. We have to clear out." He shook hands with Cochran and thanked him. "If you end up getting burned because of this," Nelson pledged, "I'll make it up to you someday."

On the evening of October 22, as the group discussed their plans to leave, the radio blared out the news that Pretty Boy Floyd was dead, slain by federal agents on a farm outside East Liverpool, Ohio. Nelson's reaction was much the same as it had been when he learned of Van Meter's death. "I would've liked to have done the job myself," he remarked. "I guess that saves me the trouble."

Melvin Purvis had been on hand for the kill, summoned from Chicago to lead the manhunt for Floyd with local lawmen. Pretty Boy and his pal Richetti had been spotted after their car broke down along Ohio's eastern border. Richetti was captured but Floyd escaped into the woods and hid for the next three days. When he finally emerged, he made his way to a farmhouse seeking a hot meal and then a ride. Before he could arrange the latter, Purvis, tipped that the fugitive was in the vicinity, arrived on the scene with three agents and four police officers. Floyd attempted to flee across a field, but a volley of slugs brought him down—shot in the back like the rest of Nelson's recent confederates.

As he lay dying, Floyd admitted his identity. But when Purvis questioned him about the Kansas City Massacre, the outlaw answered with obscenities. After the fourth "Fuck you!" Purvis turned away, and moments later Floyd died from his wounds.

That remains the official version. However, decades later Chester Smith, a police marksman who was present, claimed the G-Men executed Floyd. According to Smith, Purvis responded to the wounded outlaw's profanity by ordering Special Agent Herman Hollis to finish him off. Hollis obeyed the command. Purvis reportedly told Smith, "Mr. Hoover, my boss, told me to bring him in dead."

The FBI denied Smith's account, citing as evidence the autopsy results— which claimed Floyd had been struck by three bullets, all fired from a distance—and the fact that Hollis was not present at the scene. In defense of Smith's story, the funeral record contained a cryptic notation, apparently scribbled by the undertaker, alluding to four gunshot wounds that were not mentioned by the coroner. And Hollis was one of the Chicago agents who accompanied Purvis to Ohio, although none of the accounts (except Smith's) place him at the farm where Pretty Boy died.

Whatever the circumstances, Floyd's death sparked a new intensity in the hunt for Nelson. Though designated by Hoover as the nation's most wanted man, Nelson—in the opinion of some—had shared the unofficial title of Public Enemy Number One with Floyd. With Pretty Boy eliminated, the spotlight fell on Nelson alone. Karpis and the Barkers were still at large, but aside from a couple of unprofitable holdups they had remained underground since the Bremer kidnapping. People kept spotting John Hamilton, but it was Nelson the G-Men focused on.

Two days after Floyd drew his last breath, Nelson and his companions drove to Las Vegas, where Chase, using the name Roy Meade, purchased a new gray Ford V-8 half-ton pickup and was issued 1934 Nevada plates. That evening back at Walley's Hot Springs, they packed their bags and prepared to leave at first light. The $1,000 obtained from Tobe Williams was already dwindling. Chase offered to contact Art Pratt to have him send his money, but Nelson advised against it, surmising—correctly—that the G-Men might have traced Chase to Helena and set a trap.

"We're going back to Chicago," Nelson decided. Once there, he added, they would "meet some people and pull some jobs."

At 10:30 the next morning, October 25, Cochran received a phone call at his house. The man on the line spoke in a thick accent, asking if the Air-flow DeSoto were ready. Cochran replied that it was. Unsure what to make of the call, the garage owner assumed Nelson had arranged for a third party to retrieve Chase's vehicle. He was unaware that just hours earlier the fugitives had departed from Hot Springs and were on their way back east.

It didn't occur to Cochran that after two weeks the agents watching his garage had grown suspicious and decided to test him, recruiting the local postmaster to disguise his voice and make the phone call. That afternoon Cochran made three anxious trips to his business, each time encountering the men on stakeout duty without ever mentioning the mysterious caller. Finally, a full eight hours after taking the call, when it was evident that no one was going to show, Cochran informed the agents about the stranger who had phoned his home. By that time the agents' doubts about the garage man's reliability had been confirmed.

Two days later Cochran was called in for questioning. With his permission agents examined the business records of the Air Service Garage over the past year. They were particularly interested in the account of one James Burnell who between December 18, 1933, and October 8, 1934, had servicing and repairs performed on seventeen separate occasions on five different vehicles. Cochran confessed his two-year acquaintance with the desperado, insisting that he knew the man only as Jimmie Burnell and had never imagined he was the notorious Baby Face Nelson until a week ago when, the garage owner claimed, the outlaw admitted his identity to him. "He was a family man with a wife and kids," Cochran pointed out. "Who would have thought he was a gangster?"

Cochran was allowed to go free pending further investigation and his pledge of future cooperation with the G-Men. Evidently word leaked out that the garage owner had been consorting with the nation's top criminal. A few days later Washoe County Sheriff Russell Traphen approached Cochran and asked him to put Baby Face "on the spot" so he could kill or capture him. The sheriff was hoping the publicity would help him win his bid for reelection. Cochran refused. A week later Traphen was defeated at the polls.

❋ ❋ ❋

By the time Cochran's duplicity was discovered, agents on the West Coast had scored a monumental break in the Nelson case. When Sally Bachman returned to San Francisco on October 2 she was met at the airport by Tambini, who warned her that "every cop and G-Man" in the Bay Area was looking for her. He deposited her in the Frisco Hotel and told her to stay put until other arrangements were made. But after four days Sally grew restless. On October 6 she rode the ferry to Sausalito, planning to make a quick visit to her apartment to retrieve some items. As she left the building two police detectives took her into custody.

The Sausalito authorities turned her over to the FBI. SAC Guinane and his men held Sally in "technical custody" as they pressured her to talk. For a full two weeks she remained silent. Guinane did not share Cowley's zeal to forcibly pry information from subjects. He employed a more subtle approach, wearing down the woman with time, infinite patience, and some persuasive counseling that it would be far better for her beloved Johnny if he were captured before Nelson got him into deeper trouble.

It was obvious Sally cared nothing for Nelson. In fact, she stated plainly, she despised him for "drawing Johnny into the outlaw life." Guinane worked this angle to convince her that she was Chase's only hope to "get him away from that kill-crazy punk." Still Sally was reluctant to cooperate. "He [Nelson] has got a lot of friends in the area," she told the agents. "They'd kill me if I ratted on the boys."

Finally, on October 22, after receiving promises of protection, Sally began to provide details about her three weeks of traveling with the Nelson party. The most intriguing part of her account was that the group had spent Labor Day at a certain hideout beside a lake a few hours' drive from Chicago. Sally said she had heard Nelson speaking to a young man named Eddie about returning to the place after it closed for the season.

It seemed a golden opportunity for the agents to get a step ahead of their prey for the first time, provided they could identify the location. Sally was unable to be specific, however. This was her first trip to the Midwest, and much of the time she was never certain what state they were in.

She gave agents a detailed description of the house and surrounding area. The hideout lay just outside a small town where the group had stopped at a restaurant with a bar in front, tables and booths in the back. Across the street from the restaurant was a small park divided into two sections. To reach the hideout Nelson had driven down an incline that wound through a patch of woods, across a set of railroad tracks, and at the bottom provided a breathtaking view of the lake. The house in question was on the left, and "a structure resembling a country club" was on the right. Sally drew a diagram of the layout. Studying Chicago-area maps with Guinane, she said she was reasonably certain it lay between Elgin, Illinois, and Elkhorn, Wisconsin.

Her statement and sketches were forwarded to Chicago. Calling it "the best lead we ever had on Baby Face," Cowley delegated the task of locating the hideout to Special Agent James Metcalf. The G-Man discovered almost every small town between Elgin and Elkhorn had at least one park and often several restaurant-bars operating near by. In Lake Geneva, however, he stumbled upon one similar to what Sally reported. Checking the outlying areas, Metcalf arrived at the Lake Como Inn and found everything—the approach through the woods, the house, hotel, and lake—exactly as Sally had described. An inquiry into the resort's owner revealed Hermanson's ties to the Chicago underworld. The agent also learned that Hermanson employed a young man named Eddie Duffy whose general appearance matched the "Eddie" in Sally's statement.

Metcalf reported his findings to Cowley on October 25, and that night Sally arrived from the West Coast by plane. The next day Metcalf and two agents drove her to Lake Geneva and asked her to confirm that the inn was where Nelson intended to spend part of the upcoming winter. She failed to recognize the restaurant, which had been remodeled and repainted since September, but she was absolutely certain about the Hermanson house. The agents and Sally cruised the town until they spotted Duffy's truck, then waited in the car until he appeared. Upon seeing Duffy, Sally nodded and said, "That's Eddie."

After a week of cautious surveillance and considerable discussion, it was decided on November 2 to question the subjects. Both Hermanson and Duffy expressed shock on being informed their former visitor and potential future guest was the infamous gangster. Each agreed to aid the G-Men in any way he could.

Several days later Cowley, Metcalf, Hollis, and two other agents visited Lake Como and toured Hermanson's house and its grounds. Cowley told the owner he wanted to leave a team of three agents to await Nelson's arrival. Eager to please the lawmen, Hermanson offered the use of a small cottage adjacent to the inn where the trio could bunk. The inspector was not pleased with the arrangement, saying his men needed better cover and the "best line of fire possible." He wanted to have them posted at the front upstairs bedroom window of the house. Knowing he had no choice, Hobe gave Cowley permission to move the agents into his home.

The stakeout began on November 8. Joining Metcalf in Hermanson's house were Special Agents C. E. McRae and Charles B. Winstead. While most operatives in the Chicago office were law school graduates and accountants, Winstead was a veteran peace officer, one of the "hired guns" Hoover had grudgingly infiltrated into the ranks of his squeaky-clean agents to ensure they got results. In defiance of the bureau's code of attire and choice of weaponry, Winstead wore cowboy boots and carried a long-barreled .357 Magnum. Fellow agents admired him for his maverick ways which Hoover was forced to tolerate. Most of all, he was revered for his marksmanship. He was reportedly one of the three agents who had fired at Dillinger outside the Biograph Theatre—the other two were said to have been Agents Hollis and Clarence Hurt. The unofficial word within the bureau was that Winstead had been responsible for the bandit's fatal head wound.

Winstead was the man Cowley wanted at the window when Nelson showed up. Armed with a pair of high-powered rifles equipped with scopes, his orders—unwritten but evident from Cowley's instructions—were to shoot the outlaw on sight. The Chicago agents felt they had, in Metcalf's words, "a personal score to settle" with Nelson for the death of Baum. Since the Little Bohemia shootout occurred before passage of the law designating the murder of an FBI agent as a federal crime, Nelson could only be prosecuted on state charges of homicide. Wisconsin had abolished the death penalty. It was up to the G-Men to make sure Baum's slayer received "appropriate justice."

It seemed the agents embraced Attorney General Cummings's charge to "Shoot to kill—then count to ten" in dealing with desperados such as Dillinger more than ever when it applied to Nelson.

It was just like Jimmy Cagney. I never seen nothing like it. That fellow
just kept a-coming right at them two lawmen, and they must have hit him
plenty, but nothing was going to stop that fellow.
— Robert Hayford

CHAPTER 15

BARRINGTON

IN THE EARLY MORNING hours of October 25 Nelson and his companions
vacated their Hot Springs hideaway, Baby Face and Helen riding in the
Hudson, Chase and Negri in the new Ford pickup. At the same moment Frank
Cochran was being tested by agents in Reno and Sally Bachman was being
flown to Chicago to identify the Hermanson house, the travelers drove south to
Las Vegas and crossed into southern Utah on a scenic route that took them
along the northern rim of the Grand Canyon and into Monument Valley.

Entering the Colorado Rockies the next day, Nelson stripped the Hudson's
transmission. Using the pickup they towed the vehicle to a garage in Durango,
where they were informed the repairs would take five days. Nelson and Chase
discussed abandoning the Hudson. "You're crazy!" Negri exclaimed. "I'll stay
here and wait for it."

Nelson left Negri with a roll of cash, a duffel bag containing his possessions,
two rifles, and a box of ammo. Everything else, including the siren Cochran had
installed, was removed from the Hudson and loaded into the pickup. "Contact
Clarey when you get to town," Nelson told him. "See you in about a week."

Due to unforeseen circumstances, however, it would be a full thirty days
before Negri reached Chicago. As a result, Nelson's movements during this
period are rather hazy.

According to Chase, the trio arrived in the Chicago area about November 1,
and each evening he was dropped off at a different hotel in a different small town.

337

Where Nelson and his wife spent their nights remains a mystery, although Chase later insisted he was never told but suspected the diminutive couple had, for the most part, camped out or slept in the truck. But with autumn setting in, and given Nelson's intolerance of cold weather, it seems unlikely they spent many nights outdoors.

The FBI later suspected the two were provided with a private hideout in the Chicago vicinity. The bureau never identified it, nor were they able to force Helen to reveal its whereabouts. One theory suggests that Jimmy Murray supplied Nelson with a list of "safe houses" where he could stay from time to time, and that one of these was a certain residence in Wilmette.

Nelson and Helen returned each morning to pick up Chase, and the three spent their days cruising backroads and small towns, wandering as far west as Bloomington and as far north as Milwaukee but never going more than a few hours' drive from Chicago. One evening they were stopped for speeding in an Illinois town. The patrolman failed to notice the cache of weapons hidden beneath a blanket. Nor did he or any fellow officers recognize Public Enemy Number One when he calmly followed the lawman back to the station and paid a five-dollar fine. "I told you they were dumb," Nelson said, sharing a laugh with Chase as they drove away.

Lieder was one of the few who saw Nelson during this time in a series of brief night meetings. He often conveyed messages to individuals like Murray. It appeared that a new Murray-engineered robbery was in the works, although Lieder never heard any details. Chicago police later reported that Nelson's "gang" intended to pull a daring daylight robbery of a major department store in Chicago's Loop. The store employed a messenger service to deliver deposits totaling up to $150,000 a day. The heist was scheduled for the week following Thanksgiving when Christmas shopping was at its peak and the deposits might be even greater.

✼ ✼ ✼

On Sunday, November 25, Negri finally reached Chicago and drove immediately to the Oakley Auto Company. Lieder was startled to see him. "We were all worried about you," he said. "Jimmie and Johnny thought you got picked up."

Negri explained that the Hudson's transmission, improperly repaired at Durango, had broken again, stranding him outside Marshalltown, Iowa. Eventually he had the vehicle towed into town and, dipping into his personal funds, scraped together enough cash to have an entirely new transmission installed. Leaving the Hudson with Lieder, Fatso checked into the Milshire Hotel on Milwaukee Avenue under the name George Pero.

Chase spent that night in a hotel in Morris, Illinois, some sixty miles southwest of Chicago. Monday morning Nelson and Helen were there to meet him as usual. "We're going into the city tonight," Nelson announced, complaining that he was tired of the pickup. Unaware that Negri had returned with the Hudson, Baby Face was determined to obtain a more conventional vehicle, even if it meant stealing it himself. In times past he would have paid Jack Perkins to swipe one for him, but at the moment he simply didn't have the cash to spare.

Toward dusk they cruised through Oak Park, gradually working their way toward the city. At 7 P.M. Nelson dropped off Helen near the corner of North Avenue and Campbell and encouraged her to take in a movie. Instead she strolled through their old neighborhood in the crisp evening air. She passed her father's home, hoping to glimpse some family members. Seeing no one, she walked a few blocks southeast to the Fitzsimmons apartment. For half an hour Helen loitered outside, staring wistfully at the windows, thinking about her two children inside. She toyed with the idea of stealing a brief visit with them, but in the end she didn't dare take the risk.

She was back at North and Campbell at 10 P.M., the time specified by her husband. Nelson and Chase showed up in a 1934 black Ford V-8 sedan, which they had stolen off West Grand Avenue. After transferring their weapons and baggage, the placed the pickup in storage in a West Side garage. An hour later they reached a secluded spot along a country road for a scheduled meeting with Lieder. At the sight of Negri with the garage owner, Nelson exclaimed, "Where the hell have you been, Fats?"

Negri re-told his story of the Hudson's second breakdown. "It took those hicks forever to get the work done," he grumbled, handing Nelson the repair bill. Nelson forked over fifty dollars with the comment, "Don't forget the bankroll is getting short."

The outlaw drew a claim check from a pocket of his suede jacket. "This is where we stashed the truck," he said, handing the slip to Lieder and requesting that he retrieve the vehicle. Nelson also asked Lieder to purchase a supply of ammunition, writing down the various calibers and quantities he needed and giving him $100 to cover his expenses. A meeting was set for 6 P.M. the following evening at the same location. Nelson planned to exchange the Ford for the Hudson at that time and he told Lieder he wanted the siren and "clean" Illinois plates installed on the Hudson.

Lieder and Negri appeared at the rendezvous at the agreed time and waited a full hour without any sign of Nelson and the others. It was the first time the outlaw had failed to show for one of their scheduled meets. "We talked about something being wrong," Negri recalled later. Lieder speculated it was most likely car trouble. "Probably nothing serious," he said as they returned to the city to await word from their friend.

❋ ❋ ❋

Tuesday turned into a pleasant, sun-drenched autumn day, almost balmy by Midwestern standards for November 27, two days before Thanksgiving. That afternoon temperatures along the state line soared to near 60 beneath a cloudless blue sky.

The three agents stationed inside the Hermanson house were approaching their third week of stakeout duty and had spent much of the past nineteen days battling the effects of boredom. Winstead, Metcalf, and McRae had grown to appreciate their hosts, who had graciously done their best to make them comfortable, kept them well fed and entertained in the evenings with card games.

The Hermansons had left on Saturday and not yet returned, leaving the lawmen to themselves the last three days. Adding to the agents' complaints of cabin fever on this unseasonably warm day, they realized they had thoughtlessly depleted the contents of the Hermanson ice box and kitchen shelves. Metcalf and McRae flipped a coin to decide who would drive into Lake Geneva to buy groceries to replace what they'd consumed. McRae won.

At 2:20 P.M., about a half-hour after McRae's departure, Winstead was cleaning one of his rifles when he glanced out the open window and noticed a dark-colored sedan approaching. He could see a woman on the passenger side, but the sun's glare on the windshield obscured his view of the driver. "Get ready," he called to the younger agent. "Here comes a car."

Metcalf was downstairs in his shirt sleeves and stocking feet. He was also unarmed, having observed Mrs. Hermanson's wishes that the lawmen leave their firearms upstairs. Peering out the screen door, Metcalf assumed it was Hobe's dark green Ford sedan. "Everything's okay," he shouted. "It's the Hermansons."

The agent stepped out on the porch expecting, as he had over the past weeks, to help Lucille carry in her packages. As the vehicle drew up to the house Metcalf realized his mistake. The Ford was black and its occupants were strangers. The driver had a round face and a light, neatly trimmed mustache. He wore a cap, wire-framed sunglasses, gray suit jacket, and white shirt. The petite young woman beside him had dark eyes and sharp features and wore a black cloth coat over a dark blue dress. She gave Metcalf a brief glance before returning to her magazine.

Baby Face Nelson never took his eyes off the short, shoeless figure on the porch. Unseen by Metcalf, the outlaw—either sensing a trap or habitually on guard—coolly slipped out his .38 Super automatic, concealing it beneath a newspaper on his lap. In a voice Metcalf later described as "smooth and pleasant," Nelson asked, "Is Hobe in?"

"No, he's not here now," the agent answered, carefully eyeing the couple. "He'll probably be back later today." At that moment Metcalf noticed a second man, wearing a cap and dark brown suede jacket, in the back seat. He leaned forward and gave Metcalf a menacing glare.

"Is Eddie still driving the truck?" Nelson inquired.

"Yeah," replied Metcalf, remaining outwardly calm as he began to realize to whom he was talking. "You might find him in town."

"Thanks," Nelson said as he backed up the Ford a few feet, then turned sharply and sped away.

The instant Nelson put the car in motion Winstead took aim at the driver. For a fleeting moment he had the desperado's left shoulder and the side of his face in the crosshairs of his scope. "Who is that?" he called down to Metcalf.

"That's Baby Face Nelson!" the agent exclaimed as he charged back inside. "I recognized his wife. It has to be him."

Winstead raised his rifle again. "By that time the car had reached the railroad tracks and turned south toward the main highway," the G-Man stated in his report (on which a scowling J. Edgar Hoover would scribble "very sloppy work") "and was too far away to be shot at with any likelihood of success."

"Tell me you got the license number," Winstead barked.

"Yeah, as they drove off," the excited Metcalf yelled back.

The senior agent ordered him to run to the hotel and place a call to Inspector Cowley to apprise him of the details of their brief encounter with Nelson and the embarrassing fact that they were without a car. "Give him a description of the auto, the folks inside, and the license number," he advised.

Winstead stayed at the window in the event the black Ford reappeared. This time he wouldn't hesitate to pull the trigger.

❋ ❋ ❋

As they pulled away Chase asked, "What do you make of that?"

"That bird was definitely a G," Nelson concluded, stuffing his automatic back into its holster. "He sure as hell didn't look right. I guess we must've caught him with his pants down."

Ignoring the protests of Helen and Chase, Nelson drove into Lake Geneva, determined to locate Eddie and find out what was going on. As they motored along the streets hoping to spot Duffy's truck, Helen said she saw men that looked like "officers" watching them. One might have been Special Agent McRae, who at that moment was preparing to return with the provisions. He claimed he recognized Nelson as the driver of a black sedan but was unable to maneuver his car in time to follow.

Before long Helen's paranoia spread to her husband. "You're right," he told her. "The town's probably crawling with G-Men." He left Lake Geneva by way of backroads to be sure they were not tailed. Satisfied there was no danger, Nelson worked his way to Highway 12, and within minutes they were across the

Illinois state line, speeding due south. Near Crystal Lake he turned onto the well-traveled Northwest Highway, which would bring them back in plenty of time for their 6 P.M. meeting with Lieder and Negri.

❋ ❋ ❋

The call from Lake Como reached Cowley at 2:30. He listened to Metcalf's account, jotting down all the information. The inspector instructed Metcalf to "stay put" at the Hermanson house, even after McRae returned with their car. There was a strong possibility that Nelson, whether he found Duffy or not, might come back. "I'm sending you some more men right away," he promised.

Cowley discovered, however, there were no available agents to send. He ordered his secretary, Mary Gray, to track down whoever she could and summon them to the office at once. Curiously, the inspector made no effort to contact Purvis. His oversight may have been intentional, possibly based on a private order from Hoover, who had grown resentful of "Little Mel" for being in the spotlight too much. It was better for the bureau if Purvis was excluded from what Cowley hoped to be the conclusion of the Nelson manhunt.

Only minutes after his conversation with Metcalf, the inspector took a call from Special Agent William Ryan, making a routine check-in from his assignment in a North Side apartment. Ryan and Special Agent Thomas McDade were monitoring an unproductive and tedious phone tap on the sister of a suspect in the Bremer kidnapping. Cowley told Ryan he wanted him and his partner to drive immediately to Lake Geneva. "We've got a tentative identification of Gillis traveling with another man and a woman," Cowley explained. He told Ryan to watch for a black Ford V-8 sedan bearing 1934 Illinois plates 639-578.

By 2:50 only three agents—Herman Hollis, John Madala, and C. R. LaFrance—had reached the bureau's office. Time was against them; it would soon be rush hour. Not daring to wait any longer, Cowley called the trio into his office and laid out the situation. Madala and LaFrance were to proceed north in one vehicle, Hollis and himself in another. In addition to their sidearms each man selected a heavier weapon on the way out. The inspector chose a Thompson submachine gun with a 50-round ammunition drum. Hollis took a Remington 12-gauge automatic shotgun with a sawed-off barrel.

Leaving the building, Cowley and his companion climbed into one of the government automobiles, a dark blue Hudson designated "Chicago Division Car No. 13." Hollis took the wheel and headed for the Northwest Highway. Madala and LaFrance chose an alternate route to Wisconsin.

❋ ❋ ❋

A few minutes past 3:30 P.M. Agents Ryan and McDade passed through Barrington, some thirty-five miles from Chicago, a good ten minutes ahead of Cowley and Hollis. The two were relieved to be out of the stuffy apartment on this sunny fall afternoon and were hoping for some excitement after the monotonous duty of eavesdropping on phone conversations. Ryan, an experienced veteran, had served in the Chicago office the past three years and was present at Little Bohemia and the Biograph Theatre. McDade, at the wheel of their Ford coupe, had been an agent for just two months and had yet to see any action. He was a tall, slim man of twenty-seven, affable and eager, already well-liked and appreciated by his fellow agents for his droll sense of humor.

Coming from their wire-tap surveillance, they were armed only with pistols. Ryan carried two, a pair of .38 Super automatics, while McDade wore a .38 revolver. Neither expected any trouble before they joined the others in Lake Geneva.

Five miles beyond Barrington they entered Fox River Grove. Ryan instructed the younger agent to slow down as they passed Louie's roadhouse, thinking Nelson might have stopped at his former hangout. But there were no cars present and the place appeared to be closed. Half a mile north of the village McDade noticed an oncoming black sedan, his eyes automatically looking to the license plate. As the two cars passed, McDade read the last three numbers and cried out, "Five-seven-eight."

"There's two men and a woman inside," Ryan observed. McDade hit the brakes, but his partner pointed ahead and said, "Keep going to that curve and turn around there."

Nelson noticed the staring faces inside the passing vehicle and commented, "What the hell are those guys looking at?" He watched the coupe in the rearview mirror as its brake lights flickered before continuing another 200 yards and performing a U-turn. "They're coming after us," he alerted the others.

Instead of stepping on the gas, as his wife and Chase expected, Nelson drew to the shoulder, then abruptly swung the sedan around. "Let's see who those birds are," he said.

"They've turned back," Ryan informed his partner. The two vehicles approached each other again. McDade was so focused on the license plate that he didn't notice the occupants. As the car streaked past, both agents shouted the entire plate number in unison.

Nelson quickly spun the wheel, the sedan's tires screeching as he made another U-turn back into the eastbound lane, putting them directly behind the coupe. "Get ready," he called to Chase. "I'm gonna take 'em."

Chase hefted the Monitor automatic rifle into his arms. "You think they're government boys?" he asked.

"Who else would they be?" Nelson threw back. Helen watched her husband take out his .38 and set it on his pants leg. His gaze was locked on the car ahead, but in a soft voice he warned her, "I don't know what's going to happen. Be ready to get your head down if I tell you."

"They've turned again," Ryan announced, staring intently through the coupe's back window. "They're right behind us."

McDade glanced anxiously at the trailing car in his rear-view mirror. "I think we ought to stay ahead of them."

"No, no," Ryan advised, "let them catch up to us so we can get a look at them."

McDade had doubts about the senior agent's strategy but held his tongue. The cars, traveling at about 40 to 45 mph, passed back through Fox River Grove. Ryan pulled one of his pistols and chambered a round.

Back on the open highway Nelson started honking the Hudson's horn. The agents watched the sedan veer into the opposite lane, then speed up until it was almost parallel with the government car. Nelson waved his arm and shouted, "Pull over!"

In the same instant both Ryan and McDade spotted the figure in the back seat taking aim at them with the Monitor. Ryan, hunched forward to see past his partner, suddenly pressed himself back into the seat and cried, "We've got to get out of here!"

McDade flattened the gas pedal. As the coupe surged ahead, Nelson clasped Helen's shoulder and pushed her down. "Let 'em have it!" he screamed.

Chase opened fire, his bullets punching ragged holes through the right side of the sedan's windshield. Accelerating to keep pace with the G-Men, Nelson snatched up his .38 with his left hand and began squeezing off shots at the coupe.

Ryan returned the fire, blasting out the coupe's back window, his shells ejecting into the side of McDade's face. The younger agent struggled to stay in control of the speeding vehicle while slumping down in his seat to keep his six-foot-four frame out of the line of fire. His heart was racing with the coupe's engine. "Where are they?" he asked his partner.

"Right behind us. Step on it."

For the first time McDade glanced at the speedometer and was startled to find the needle climbing toward 75 mph. They were rapidly overtaking a slow-moving milk truck. Ryan had fired a full clip—seven shots—at the sedan. Reaching for his second pistol he noticed Nelson's car was no longer riding their bumper. "They've fallen back," he said.

McDade had no time to think about what was occurring behind them. He swerved into the opposite lane to avoid slamming into the rear of the milk truck and was horrified to find a westbound car hurtling toward them. Facing a head-on collision, he made a split-second decision to keep going, passed the truck, and veered back in time to miss the oncoming vehicle.

Ryan continued to watch through the tattered glass of the back window. He saw the sedan maneuver around the milk truck 100 yards behind them, but the coupe continued to widen the gap. Even after the veteran declared, "I can't see 'em anymore," McDade kept the accelerator mashed underfoot as they roared back into Barrington. "Ease up," Ryan ordered. "There's a sharp right turn ahead. You'll have to slow down."

When McDade saw the turn he reduced speed—much too late. Unable to make the curve, the coupe bounced into a field and lurched to a stop. Both agents leapt out, pistols in hand, and took cover behind their vehicle. But the sedan never appeared.

"You know," McDade commented after five anxious minutes passed, "this isn't going to look too good. We're federal officers. Weren't we supposed to be chasing them?"

❄ ❄ ❄

Ryan and McDade were unaware that within moments of pulling away from Nelson, two more G-Men had arrived on the scene, turning their pursuers into the pursued. At some point along the five-mile stretch of highway between Fox River Grove and Barrington, Cowley and Hollis encountered the high-speed gun battle taking place in the opposite lane. (It is possible the car McDade almost hit while passing the milk truck was their Hudson.) Hollis immediately executed a U-turn and started after the sedan. The two men inside the milk truck watched the big blue Hudson streak around them, the third car to pass in a matter of seconds.

Smoke and steam began to gush from beneath the Ford's hood. "I can't get any speed," Nelson said. "Those guys must've hit the motor."

"We can't stay around here," Chase growled. "We gotta get off the highway."

Nelson was stomping furiously on the accelerator when he noticed the car behind them. "There's a Hudson back there," he said grimly. "It's gaining on us."

"I see it." Chase was perched at the rear window with the Monitor. He saw the man on the Hudson's passenger side awkwardly lean out into the whipping wind clutching a machine gun. "One of 'em has a sprayer," Chase warned.

"What are you waiting for? Blast 'em!"

With Chase firing through the back window, Nelson attempted to squeeze a few more miles out of their dying vehicle, its radiator punctured by one of Ryan's metal-jacketed slugs. Helen continued to crouch beside him, her head between her knees, her left hand clutching her husband's right knee.

Through the smoke belching from the damaged motor, Nelson saw they were entering the northwest edge of Barrington. As the Hudson continued to gain and was maneuvering to pull alongside them, Baby Face realized he had to make a drastic move. It was almost 4 P.M.

Three competing gas stations—a Standard, a Shell, then a Sinclair—lined the north side of the highway. Directly opposite—surrounded by mostly open field—was a gravel road leading to the town's North Side Park. Some 400 yards farther east houses began to appear on both sides of the road.

Nelson suddenly swerved into the park entrance, the tires slinging gravel as the Ford skidded to an abrupt stop. Hollis hit the brakes but the Hudson fishtailed, burning 75 feet of serpentine streaks into the asphalt. As they shot past the entrance, Cowley fired a burst of shots at Nelson's car.

"Out! Everyone out!" Nelson shouted, lunging from the driver's door. He scrambled around to the back of the vehicle as his wife and Chase exited the right side. "Run, Helen!" the outlaw yelled, reaching for a weapon in the back seat. "Get in that field and get down."

Helen dashed into the knee-high weeds between the road and the park's football field, dropping to her stomach as gunfire erupted. The first shots came from Chase, who was huddled near the front of the Ford with the Monitor's long barrel resting across the still-smoking hood. Seconds later Nelson, standing at the rear of the sedan with a machine gun, opened fire on the G-Men.

The Hudson had shrieked to a stop in the middle of the highway almost 120 feet away. Bullets smashed into the vehicle as Cowley bailed out the passenger-side door, taking cover at the rear of the car. Grabbing his shotgun, Hollis dove through the same door and crouched beside the front bumper.

For the next three minutes a furious gun battle raged, the combatants shielded behind their respective vehicles. Hidden in the weeds some twenty yards west of the Ford, Helen briefly raised her head once while the two sides threw lead at each other. "I saw Les jump and grasp his side," she later reported. "I knew then that was the end." She buried her face beneath her arms, not wanting to see any more.

❉ ❉ ❉

The majority of the more than thirty people who unexpectedly found themselves witnessing a dramatic life-and-death spectacle had been enjoying the final hours of golden sunlight on that gloriously warm fall day when their reverie was broken by the rapidly approaching sounds of squealing tires and a curious crackling noise. The chatter of machine-gun fire was familiar to Chicagoans but completely foreign to the residents of the quiet community. Residents and workers in the North Park vicinity of Barrington were drawn to their open doors or windows, and those already outside moved closer to the road and looked west as two cars roared down the highway toward the unsuspecting town.

Mrs. Frances Kramer and her twenty-one-year-old son, Harold, were operating the Standard station that day when they noticed a racket "like race cars backfiring." They hurried to the front windows in time to see the Hudson veer into the westbound lane and pull abreast of the lead car. The Ford's driver turned into the park entrance and braked, producing a spray of gravel. Tires screeching, the Hudson whirled almost completely around in its frantic attempt to stop. It came to rest across the middle of the highway, the driver's side facing the Ford, its front end pointing toward the gas station. Mother and son saw the occupants of both vehicles pile out. They briefly glimpsed a young woman run from the Ford and hide in the field.

"Then all hell broke loose," Harold Kramer recalled in later years. "Bullets were flying everywhere. It was like being in a bunker with a war going on right outside."

Kramer and his mother had a clear view of the two men behind the Ford firing automatic weapons at the Hudson. Midway through the battle they saw the shorter one grab his side and "crouch as if hit." He stumbled toward the other man, then sat on the running board. The two swapped weapons, and the taller one began firing the machine gun as his wounded comrade reloaded the rifle.

Harry Cooper, proprietor of the Shell station 150 yards east of the Standard, heard gunshots and raced outside thinking "a truck must have blown some tires." He saw the government car halted across the highway, then noticed the Ford stopped on the side road, with "two blazes of fire" coming from behind it. Unable to see the rear of the Hudson (where Cowley had taken cover) from his position, Cooper spotted only one figure behind the closest car—a slender man hunched near the headlights returning fire with a shotgun, its thunderous booms a distinct contrast to the brisk rattle of the automatic weapons. A stray bullet struck the gas pump beside him, prompting Cooper to retreat into the building.

Ten minutes before the shooting started, Highway Patrolman William Gallagher had stopped at the Sinclair station looking to sell tickets to the upcoming American Legion benefit. Inside he found the owner, Robert Malone, playing nickel blackjack with Francis Donlea and three friends while Malone's employee, Alfred Trestick, handled the pumps. Gallagher, in uniform but off duty and unarmed, joked that he would arrest them for gambling if they didn't purchase at least one ticket apiece.

The patrolman was saying goodbye to the group when they heard an odd "popping sound." Suddenly Trestick bolted through the door shouting, "Some gangsters are shooting it out up the road." Gallagher and the others ran outside. From a distance of nearly 300 yards they could see the two cars turned broadside to each another, puffs of smoke rising from each end of both vehicles. A spray of bullets pierced one of the station's swinging signs, driving the men back through the door.

Gallagher warned the others to "keep low," then asked Malone if he had a gun. The owner crept behind the counter and reappeared with a .22 rifle.

Gallagher took it and slipped out the rear door, with Donlea and several others following. Moments later a "bullet whizzed by my head," Donlea recalled. "I said, 'That's enough of that,' and ducked into the cellar until it was all over. I didn't see much but I heard one heckuva fight."

Paul Sherman, a car salesman traveling from Chicago to Cary, Illinois, had just passed through Barrington and was starting to accelerate in anticipation of the open highway ahead. He was stunned to find himself speeding toward a hail of lead and a Hudson partially blocking the road. Sherman hit the brakes but roared past the government car and turned into a field.

Once his vehicle bounced to a stop, Sherman jumped out and ran toward the gas stations. He saw one of the shooters at the rear of the Ford, later describing him as "a young person, short with light hair, and rather slight in build." At that point a barrage of slugs screamed past him. "The shots were terrific—they were buzzing and cracking all around my ears." He flattened himself in the mud and tried to pry a handkerchief from his pocket to wave as a white flag. He was certain the shots had come from the Hudson, where Cowley must have mistaken him for a gang member coming to Nelson's aid.

After crawling some twenty yards the salesman heard a lull in the gunfire. He leapt to his feet and "ran like hell," not stopping until he reached the rear of the Sinclair station, where he joined Gallagher and two others. When they asked if he was hurt, an out-of-breath Sherman croaked, "I don't know; I'm pretty shaken up. Those crazy sons of bitches were trying to kill me!"

Mrs. William Meister, whose home was 400 yards east of the park entrance, dashed into the back yard to grab her six-month-old son, then ran upstairs and hid in a bedroom. The house of Joseph Rowland, a state highway worker, was almost a quarter-mile away but offered an excellent, unobstructed view to the south. Rowland watched the entire battle from his back porch. A pair of preteen brothers, William and Robert Eiserman, were selling magazines door to door along the highway when the gun battle erupted. The boys hid in a ditch until the shooting was over.

Six men working construction near the bathhouse at the rear of the North Park swimming pool heard the staccato reports of machine-gun fire punctuated by the booming blasts of a shotgun. All six hurried toward the highway and halted abruptly near a clump of trees about 300 feet from the roadside. They arrived in time to witness the climax of the gunfight, a brief but appalling spectacle that looked like a scene straight out of a gangster film.

❋ ❋ ❋

Less than a minute into the battle, a .45 slug from Cowley's Thompson tore into Nelson's left side at the beltline, piercing his liver and pancreas before exiting through the lower-right portion of his back. Remarkably, considering all of his bullet-riddled escapades, it was the first time Nelson actually had been shot. The wound left him a walking dead man.

Doubled over and clasping his side with his left hand, the outlaw retreated to the running board and exchanged weapons with Chase, reloading the Monitor while his friend continued to fire at the lawmen. No words were spoken, according to Chase, who later swore he didn't even know Nelson had been wounded. When the machine gun was empty, Baby Face took it and handed the Monitor back to Chase.

Baby Face slipped a fresh drum into the Tommy and attempted to fire through the Ford's side window. Between shots Chase heard him complain that the weapon was jamming and saw him toss it aside. Nelson snatched a .351 rifle from the back seat and moved toward the rear of the vehicle. Chase assumed he was returning to his former position but soon discovered Nelson had stepped into the open and was advancing on the Hudson.

It is an image forever associated with Baby Face Nelson: The reckless desperado marching into a blizzard of bullets, his machine gun flaming at his hip— an act that enshrined him in the annals of gangster lore. But while tradition and more than a dozen witnesses insisted the baby-faced outlaw carried a machine gun when he strode toward the G-Men, Chase contended (and ballistics confirmed) that Nelson was actually shooting the .351 rifle, its rapid fire easily mistaken for a Thompson at a distance.

Most accounts imply that it was Nelson's sheer ferocity and intoxication with violence that drove him to charge into the open like an enraged bull. However, it is possible that the gut-shot bandit, realizing the severity of his wound, did what he had to in order to bring an end to the shootout, even at the risk of sustaining further injury. Or perhaps, sensing that he was mortally wounded, Nelson recalled his words to the Cochrans and decided to go out in a blaze of gangster glory, taking "a few of them with me."

Jack Perkins probably understood best why Nelson chose to step into the line of fire and take on his opponents face to face: He was still the tough, undersized kid from The Patch who would never consider backing down from a fight.

❄ ❄ ❄

Twenty-five-year-old Robert Hayford, one of the six construction workers, later provided a vivid description of what he observed. His attention was drawn first to the blue Hudson slanted across the road, with two figures huddled behind it firing at the Ford. The man at the back, closest to Hayford and his companions, appeared to be "somewhat stout," while his partner was taller and thinner.

Then Hayford spotted "a slender young man dressed in a dark suit" who was "halfway between the two cars, and was in the middle of the road . . . approaching the sedan . . . and as he kept approaching, he kept firing . . . " Nelson kept the lawmen at bay by sweeping his weapon back and forth, loosing a burst at one end of the arc, then the other.

The stout man suddenly abandoned his position and darted left toward the south side of the highway, where he hopped—or fell—into the ditch. Rising to his knees, he attempted to shoot but the machine gun failed to fire. Nelson sent a blast of slugs in his direction. Cowley crumpled onto his left side.

A split second later Hollis leaned out and fired his shotgun. The impact seemed to tear the legs out from under Nelson. Hayford saw the young man hit the ground, then immediately leap to his feet and continue to march forward. Baby Face fired at Hollis, turned to throw several more shots at the downed Cowley, then again sprayed the front of the Hudson.

Now Hollis tried to retreat. He ran toward a telephone pole on the north side of the road directly between the Standard and Shell stations, facing his attacker in an apparent effort to fire back. But his shotgun, like Cowley's weapon, refused to work. The agent's movements, Hayford observed, appeared erratic and wobbly, as though he was already wounded.

Nearing the telephone pole he dropped the shotgun and drew his .38 Super automatic, but before he could fire, Nelson's bullets caught him. The gangster kept coming, firing several more shots as Hollis slumped against the pole, then fell facedown beside the highway.

Hayford and the other horrified onlookers watched Nelson draw closer to the sprawled figure. For a long chilling moment he stood over the body, his weapon poised to fire again. Evidently satisfied, he turned and plodded toward the agents' Hudson. Hayford noticed for the first time that the young man was dragging his left leg, his limp growing more pronounced with each step.

❋ ❋ ❋

Nelson eased his bleeding body behind the Hudson's wheel and pulled up behind the disabled Ford as he shouted for Helen.

Chase, little more than a spectator during the final minute of the battle, gathered their weapons when he saw his comrade climb into the Hudson. Arms full, he trotted over to where Nelson was parked and sat calling for his wife. Upon seeing Chase, Baby Face groaned, "Drop everything and get me to the priest."

"Let me grab our cases," Chase said, tossing the guns into the back seat.

"Forget that stuff." Nelson yelled for Helen again, then tried to crawl to the passenger side, leaving a crimson smear on the seat. "You'll have to drive," he told Chase. "I'm hit pretty bad."

Chase opened the door and leaned in to help Nelson slide over. The outlaw's left pant leg was darkening with splotches of blood that extended from mid-thigh to his ankle. There was still no sign of Helen as Chase took the wheel and asked, "Where is she?"

Nelson shook his head. "We'll have to catch her later."

As the vehicle lurched into motion Chase suddenly spied Helen running toward them. He reached back and flung open the rear door. The young woman jumped inside, and Chase hit the gas, pointing the vehicle west, back toward Fox River Grove.

Helen sat behind her wounded husband, cradling his head in her arms. Nelson looked back at her and gasped, "I'm done for."

❊ ❊ ❊

Patrolman Gallagher waited a full minute after the shooting ceased before leaving his hiding place behind the Sinclair station. Several others, including Sherman, the shaken motorist, followed him out. Reaching the highway as the Hudson roared away, the officer raised the .22 rifle and fired six shots, hoping to hit a tire. The car kept going, and both Helen and Chase later admitted they were unaware they were fired upon.

Once the Hudson disappeared, Gallagher and the others rushed to where the lawmen lay, coming first to Hollis, It was immediately obvious there was little hope for the man. As one witness recalled, the entire back of his skull "looked crushed."

Gallagher handed the .22 to Trestick before removing the unfired .38 from the agent's grasp and picking up the empty shotgun lying beside him. (A count of the ejected shells collected on the road revealed that Hollis had fired at least ten times.) He gently turned Hollis on his side and spotted the badge pinned on his vest. Up to this point Gallagher and the other bystanders all had assumed they were witnessing a gun battle between rival gangsters. The agent's eyes blinked at the faces above him, but when Gallagher spoke to him, he received only a "heavy groan" in response.

Crossing the highway toward the second victim, Gallagher saw Mrs. Meister coming out of her parents' house and shouted to her to phone for an ambulance. Inside the Standard station, Mrs. Kramer had already phoned the Barrington police. The dispatcher notified the Lake County Sheriff's Department.

Cowley was lying in the ditch, the right side of his face covered in blood, his hands clasped over a wound in the left side of his abdomen. At the sight of the uniformed Gallagher approaching with Hollis' shotgun in one hand and the pistol clenched in the other, the inspector raised his right arm and cried out, "Don't shoot, I'm a federal officer."

Sherman pushed past Gallagher, grabbed the injured man by the coat collar, and cursed him. "What makes you think you can shoot at innocent people?" the motorist growled.

Gallagher ordered Sherman to stand back. The patrolman took a moment to examine Cowley's machine gun. Like the shotgun, it too was out of ammunition, indicating that the inspector had emptied the weapon's entire fifty-round drum during the battle. Gallagher bent down to question him, but Cowley did most of the talking. "I knew he was some kind of boss the way he spoke to me," the officer later remarked.

Cowley instructed him to write down a phone number—Randolph 6226. "That's the Chicago Division office," he said. "Call them and let them know what happened here. Then get in touch with my wife and tell her I won't be home for supper. Better just tell her I was called out of town."

After providing a description of the government car in which the gangsters escaped, he asked, "Was Hollis hurt?" Gallagher nodded. "Be sure he gets taken care of before me," Cowley said.

Gallagher returned to the north side of the road where a number of people were clustered around Hollis. A blanket was draped over the fallen agent. Another man appeared with a first-aid kit but had no idea what to do. "Half this fellow's head is blown off," he whispered to Gallagher.

When several minutes passed with no sign of the ambulance, Gallagher flagged down a passing motorist. Hollis, wrapped in the blanket, was delicately placed in the vehicle's back seat. Gallagher climbed in and directed the driver to the Barrington Central Hospital at Lincoln Avenue and Hough Street, a few blocks south of the shooting. Dr. D. F. Brooke and a single nurse, Nellie Berghorn, were present when the agent was carried in. Most emergencies treated at the small-town facility consisted of broken bones or women in labor. One look at Hollis convinced Dr. Brooke that his only chance to save the agent's life was to halt the bleeding and hope the victim survived the trip to a better-equipped hospital.

Hollis had suffered three gunshot wounds. One bullet had plowed through the left side of his stomach and a second entered his lower back—neither would have proved fatal. But the third wound was devastating: the slug had struck Hollis near the top of his forehead and literally exploded out the back of his skull. The physician did what he could, but the effects of shock and hemorrhage were too great. The patient went into cardiac arrest, and the injection of a heart stimulate failed to bring him back. Ten minutes after his arrival Hollis was pronounced dead.

Among the personal items collected from his pockets Nurse Berghorn found a rosary and handed it to Gallagher. "We should call a priest for this man," she said.

Minutes after Hollis was taken from the highway the ambulance arrived with a second local physician, Dr. Kenneth Fisk. He tended to Cowley, placing a bandage over his abdominal wound. The doctor also wiped the blood from the victim's face and examined his right cheek where a bullet fragment had lodged. Once Cowley was lifted into the ambulance, Fisk instructed the driver to proceed to Sherman Hospital in Elgin, fourteen miles away.

Gallagher returned to the site of the shootout a few minutes after 4:30. Sunlight was fading, but the crowd of curious onlookers had grown markedly. Many were youngsters recently dismissed from school who had been attracted by the sirens and the reports of a gunfight on the edge of their once peaceful community. County officers had arrived and were doing their best to preserve the crime scene while a garage owner prepared to tow away the abandoned Ford. Some spectators, young and old alike, were pocketing shell casings that littered the highway. Gallagher observed one youth using his pocketknife to dig out a slug imbedded in a telephone pole.

✱ ✱ ✱

With the wind whistling through the Hudson's bullet-pierced windshield, Chase tried to stay focused on the road, but it was difficult and he had no idea where to go. Nelson was slumped against the passenger door, drawing deep breaths while Helen wept and continued to hold her husband's sagging head.

Nelson did his best to direct his friend. Three miles west of Barrington he told him to turn right on Kelsey Road, then right again on Route 22. They were now headed east again, passing two miles north of Barrington and speeding toward Lake Zurich. Between towns Chase kept his foot on the accelerator, averaging 85 mph. Within half an hour they reached Highland Park. Growing weaker each minute, Nelson instructed his pal to head south on Skokie Road. Entering Wilmette, they made their way to 1155 Mohawk Road, the home of Father Coughlan's sister.

It was approximately 4:45 when the family maid notified Father Coughlan there was a young woman rapping on the back-door window and asking to see him. The priest went to the kitchen and found Helen Gillis standing in the doorway. "Jimmie's been shot!" she said frantically. "You have to help us. He's in the car."

Coughlan grabbed his hat and coat and followed her. Chase had pulled into the garage and helped Nelson out, hoping to bring his wounded friend into the house. When Helen returned with Coughlan, the two men were standing at the rear of the Hudson, with Nelson—hatless, pale, and barely able to raise his head—supported by Chase's arms. At the sight of the priest he managed to mutter a faint "Hello."

Helen pleaded with Coughlan to provide her husband with refuge, but the priest refused. It was his sister's home, he protested; her eight-year-old son was inside and she was hosting her bridge club later that evening. There was no way he could allow a desperately wounded public enemy to be brought in. "But he's dying," Helen sobbed. "He's got to go someplace where he can lie down."

Coughlan offered to lead them to a safe location, although, he later asserted, he really had no specific place in mind, his immediate objective being

353

simply to steer them away from his sister's neighborhood. Helen suggested they all ride together in the priest's car, but Coughlan again objected. "You can't leave that here," he complained, pointing to the bullet-scarred Hudson. "You follow in your car. We won't be going far."

Chase eyed him suspiciously and spoke for the first time. "You wouldn't try to fool us, would you, Father?"

Coughlan assured them he had every intention of helping. As Helen returned to the Hudson's back seat, the priest helped Chase maneuver Nelson back into the passenger seat. Once the outlaw was situated, Coughlan felt a warm, sticky wetness on his right hand, and pulling it back, he discovered it was covered with blood.

The priest slipped into his Ford coupe and backed onto the street. With the Hudson following, he turned north on Ashland Avenue, then west on Skokie Road. Two blocks later he noticed the Hudson make an abrupt U-turn and accelerate quickly in the opposite direction. Coughlan swung around and attempted to catch them, but he lost the vehicle in traffic near Lake Street. He later confessed that he was relieved but also saddened, concluding that his friend must have feared "I was leading them into a trap."

According to Helen and Chase, that is exactly what Nelson surmised. After about ten minutes of driving behind the priest, he told the others in a feeble voice, "I don't like the way he's acting. He seems wrong. Lose him."

Nelson, it seems, already had an alternate destination in mind. Once again he directed Chase, every so often raising his head to say, "Turn here" or "Go this way." They gradually moved south, keeping to mostly residential streets as they left Wilmette and entered Winnetka. At one point Nelson appeared to pass out, and Chase stopped in an alley to await further instructions. Within a minute Nelson snapped back with an exasperated groan and said, "C'mon, I've got to get to a bed."

On Sixteenth Street the outlaw told Chase to slow down. Pointing out a narrow alley running behind Walnut Street, he said, "Pull in there." Chase made the turn and drove down the alley to a red two-car garage at the rear of a light gray stucco cottage facing Walnut. He drove into the garage, parked, and asked, "Who lives here?"

"Friends," Nelson replied weakly. "Go in there and tell the fellow inside to come help me."

Chase walked to the front door and knocked. A tall, dark-complexioned man in his late thirties answered. "There's someone out here who needs you," Chase said.

The man accompanied Chase to the garage where "he instantly recognized Jimmie," Chase recalled later. The two men, with Helen following, carried Nelson into the cottage. As Chase—who swore he'd never been to the house before—later described it, they entered by a side door and passed through the kitchen. Along the way Chase glimpsed an older man in his late sixties and a young woman who appeared "rather frightened" at the sight of the wounded desperado. They turned left into a small bedroom, where they placed Nelson on a large white iron bed. The younger man walked out, leaving Nelson in the care of his wife and Chase.

"All three of us knew that Les was dying," Helen recounted days later. "But there was nothing we could do."

They did their best to make him comfortable and stop the bleeding. Provided with scissors and other supplies, Helen cut the bloody clothing from her husband's body, noting that his white shirt was stained almost completely crimson. She stuffed cotton into the bullet hole in his stomach and the gaping exit wound in his back, then covered both wounds by wrapping his waist with a long strip of cloth torn from the bedsheet. Helen cleaned his buckshot-punctured legs, then covered him with a blanket after he complained he was cold.

"That's better," Nelson muttered. He told them his pain was gone, replaced by a spreading numbness. Helen clenched his hand and waited for the end.

❊ ❊ ❊

The switchboard at the Chicago FBI's office was flooded with calls about the gun battle on the Northwest Highway. Gradually they pieced together what happened. Hollis was dead; Cowley, gravely wounded, was being taken to a hospital in Elgin; and Nelson and his companions had escaped in the government car. Purvis dispatched a squad of agents to conduct an investigation at Barrington, then selected three men to accompany him to Elgin, where he hoped to obtain a firsthand account from Cowley.

Just minutes after Purvis departed, Genevieve Hollis and her four-year-old son, Edward, appeared. The pair had been waiting in the downstairs lobby; Hollis, who had celebrated his seventh wedding anniversary the previous weekend, had promised to take his family out for dinner and early Christmas shopping after work. It was not unusual for him to be running late; Genevieve had come up to the nineteenth floor expecting to hear that her husband had been called away on an important assignment. Noticing the gallery of grim, saddened, and stunned expressions greeting her, she knew something dreadful had occurred. Mary Gray and Doris Lockerman escorted her into a private office and broke the news that "Eddie" had fallen in the line of duty.

❊ ❊ ❊

The ambulance carrying Cowley reached Sherman Hospital at 4:50 P.M. Dr. Morgan Carpenter, the staff surgeon, ordered x-rays and an immediate operation to halt any internal hemorrhaging. At 5:15, minutes before the inspector was to be wheeled into surgery, the hospital was notified that "representatives of the government" were en route to Elgin and needed to speak to the patient before he was anaesthetized. Carpenter agreed to a ten-minute delay; any longer, he stated emphatically, would endanger Cowley's hopes for survival.

Within five minutes Purvis arrived. He was led into Cowley's room and told by the doctor to keep the conversation brief. "I'm glad you made it," Cowley told the agent.

"You just rest easy and everything will be fine," Purvis assured him.

"Is there really any doubt about that?"

Purvis promised the doctors would do their best for Cowley. He then stepped closer and asked, "What happened, Sam?"

"I emptied a Tommy at them."

"Who was it?"

"It was Nelson and Chase."

Cowley briefly recounted the battle, telling the SAC "I think we got" Nelson but admitting, with a bewildered look, that the diminutive gunman "wouldn't go down." At that point Dr. Carpenter insisted the operation had to proceed at once.

On his way into surgery Cowley was informed that his condition was "very serious" and there was a chance he night not survive the operation. "Is there any information you want us to pass along?" he was asked.

The inspector shook his head. "Purvis knows it all."

Despite the bleak outlook, Cowley remained stubbornly confident that he would pull through. He told one of the nurses, "I'll be okay as long as the bullet wasn't loaded."

But it was.

Ironically, Cowley's wound was almost identical to the injury he had inflicted upon Nelson, the slug ripping through his abdomen left to right. There were two notable differences, however. The bullet entering the inspector's side had traveled at a more downward angle since, as witnesses reported, he was on his knees when hit. Also, in the phraseology of Dr. Carpenter, the .351 slug "blew up" inside the victim, shattering two ribs and tearing open intestines up to four inches in some spots. The largest fragment of the shattered bullet had exited through a gaping hole in Cowley's right hip. Most of the internal damage, Carpenter noted, was irreparable.

❋ ❋ ❋

About an hour after Nelson and his companions arrived at the house on Walnut Street, the man who had helped carry the wounded desperado inside came to the bedroom door and "began to holler about moving the car out of the garage." Chase agreed to dispose of the bullet-riddled government vehicle, but Nelson raised his head and pleaded, "Don't leave me now."

Minutes later the man was back, demanding that the Hudson be removed. Nelson again appealed to his friend to remain at his side. Chase repeated his promise to stay, but he could see Nelson was "getting weaker and weaker all the time," drifting in and out of consciousness. Before long Chase "quietly slipped out the back door" and drove off, insisting later that he intended to return once he ditched the car. He was, however, unfamiliar with the area and soon became lost. Attempting to head south for the city, he ended up veering north and found himself back in Winnetka. When the Hudson ran out of gas, he abandoned it near some railroad tracks. By then Chase had resolved to concentrate on getting away, knowing that he could no longer help his pal. He managed to catch a train into Chicago.

Helen was left alone with her dying husband. Shortly after Chase's departure Nelson suddenly grew talkative, as if realizing he had little time left. He asked Helen to "say goodbye to mother." She recalled later that "he mentioned all the family," his sisters and brother, nieces and nephews, and in-laws. "When he came to our own children, he cried. A few minutes later, Les said, 'It's getting dark, Helen. I can't see you anymore.'"

She noticed at that point that "his eyes were glazed." Moments later his breathing became shallow and raspy, then abruptly stopped. The young widow remembered glancing at her watch. It was 7:35 P.M.

*He won't be captured alive. If they get him, they'll take him
to the morgue and not a cell."*
— Juliette Fitzsimmons

CHAPTER 16

THE WAGES OF SIN

INSPECTOR COWLEY OUTLIVED HIS killer by almost seven hours, dying at 2:18 A.M. His wife, Lavon, and one of their two sons, eight-month-old Sam Jr., were present to comfort him during his sporadic periods of consciousness following surgery. So was Melvin Purvis. When the SAC left the hospital after Cowley's death, reporters swarmed around him asking for a statement. "If it's the last thing I do," Purvis swore, "I'll get Baby Face Nelson."

Throughout the long night the agents of the Chicago office did their best to track down the desperado who had now slain three of their brethren. They were convinced Nelson was holed up in or around the city, possibly wounded, and almost certainly seeking the aid of his family or—more likely—his underworld pals. Most were exhausted and bleary-eyed, having had little or no sleep since receiving the first reports of the late-afternoon gun battle at Barrington. (Special Agent McDade, who along with his partner Ryan first learned of the shootout while phoning the office after their wild flight from Nelson on the Northwest Highway, later claimed that he had only "a vague recollection of going out that night with a party of agents searching buildings in the city.") Even so, the G-Men participated in a series of raids in conjunction with local police, hoping to catch the baby-faced killer.

Among the places targeted were the apartments of Nelson's sister Julie and Helen's father. Each location was searched, then placed under surveillance by a team of men. Two agents accompanied by police detectives converged on the

359

home and business of Clarence Lieder. The garage owner was brought to the FBI office, where he was photographed and fingerprinted before being subjected to several hours of interrogation. According to bureau records, the man who was to have rendezvoused with Nelson the previous evening once again "denied that he had any recent information concerning Gillis, stating he had not seen Gillis for over three years." The bureau also brought in Al Van de Houton for questioning after raiding his residence and tavern. He too insisted he'd had no new contact with the public enemy. Both Lieder and Van de Houton maintained that if Nelson were in the city, the man he would look to for help was Jack Perkins. As before, neither could provide any clues that would lead the lawmen to Perkins.

Another pair of agents, assisted by nineteen police officers, stormed the Oak Park home of Jimmy Murray but found only Murray's three daughters inside. The terrified girls said their parents had gone out for the evening. The lawmen searched diligently for the couple, even raiding the home of Murray's father. The fact that Murray's whereabouts during the early morning hours of November 28 could not be determined would prove intriguing in light of later evidence.

The final raid before sunrise was conducted at 5:15 A.M. on Murray's cottage in Wauconda, just a few minutes' drive from Barrington. Ten agents broke into the dwelling but found the place deserted. Interestingly, they discovered fifteen beds in the four-room cottage, which added credibility to the claims that Murray used the location to shelter individuals on the lam from the law.

In Washington, Director Hoover received hourly updates on the progress of the Nelson manhunt. By morning, however, he was reportedly more enraged by Purvis's remarks to the press than by the loss of Cowley and Hollis or Nelson's apparent escape. An article in the *Chicago American* spotlighting the SAC referred to him as the bureau's "ace manhunter" and declared that Cowley had been Purvis's "right-hand man." The man the media credited with nailing Dillinger and Pretty Boy Floyd had now taken "a blood oath" to be the personal avenger of his slain comrades.

Hoover could tolerate no more. Determined to get Purvis off the streets and out of the headlines, he dispatched Assistant Director Clegg and Inspector Earl J. Connelley to take command of the Chicago office. While Purvis remained the nominal SAC (removing him outright would create a storm of bad publicity for the bureau), he was yanked off the case and forced to perform a series of low-profile "inspection tours." When the press demanded to speak to Purvis, Clegg informed them he was on "sick leave." Within a few months Purvis, tiring of the monotonous duties and his exile from Chicago, re-submitted his resignation. This time Hoover accepted it.

❋ ❋ ❋

A rainstorm spattered the city at 1:30 A.M. and ended abruptly a half-hour later. Helen remained with her husband's body in the tiny bedroom of the Walnut Street cottage. "I didn't know what to do," she said later, "so I sat there hour after hour with him." Not long after the rain stopped, a man came into the room and told her, "We'll have to take him out."

"I'd like to take him to the undertaker's," Helen said.

After wrapping Nelson in an old green-red-and-black imitation Navajo blanket, Helen and the man carried the body outside, placing it in the back seat of an Oldsmobile parked in the drive-way. She climbed in beside her husband, cradling him in her arms as the man slid behind the wheel. They drove south into Niles Center (now Skokie). When Helen sheepishly inquired if they were heading for the funeral home, he told her bluntly, "No, we're not going to the undertaker's. We have to put him out around here."

"This fellow had a funny, queer look," she said later, adding that she was afraid of the man. At the southwest corner of Niles (now Conrad) and Long Avenues, they reached St. Paul's Cemetery. Helen decided "that was the best place to leave Les's body," and the driver pulled to the curb.

"We didn't dump him in the ditch like they said.," Helen insisted. "When we stopped, I put my arms under Les's shoulders and the other man took his feet. It was too much for me, though, and I fell down, hurting my knee on the pavement. We lifted him out and put him down on the grass." She took a moment to tuck the blanket around her husband's naked, bloody body. "I wanted Les to be comfortable. . . . He always hated the cold."

A few blocks away, just south of Howard Avenue, Helen tossed the blood-stained clothing out the window. The driver continued south until they reached the city's North Side. When he inquired, "This okay?" Helen said that it was, although she had no idea where she was or where to go. Before stepping out of the vehicle, she asked the man a favor, then provided him with the name of the mortician who had handled the funerals of her mother and sister. He promised to notify the undertaker where to pick up Nelson's body.

Helen wandered the unfamiliar pre-dawn streets for over an hour. About 5 A.M. she spotted a taxi and slipped into the back seat, mostly to escape the chilly temperatures, which had dropped almost thirty degrees from the previous day. Asked for her destination, she told the cabbie to "just drive on."

❋ ❋ ❋

At 6:45 A.M. the automobile every lawman in the Midwest was looking for was discovered by a Winnetka milk man who notified a patrolman. Federal agents arrived within an hour and conducted a diligent on-the-spot examination. In addition to thirty bullet holes, the Hudson had "numerous large clots of blood

361

on the floor at approximately the place they would drop from the left leg of a person sitting on the right-hand side. . . . There was considerable blood on the back of the front seat on the right. . . . This blood was about the width of a man's back and about four inches in height."

About 7:30 Phillip Sadowski, owner of a funeral parlor on North Hermitage Avenue, answered his phone. A "rough voice" on the line informed him that the body of a man named Gillis was lying near a graveyard in Niles Center, a block away from Harms Road. "And I want you to go get it."

"I can't do that." Sadowski, a stocky man with a beefy face and thinning white hair, protested that he was in the midst of preparing a funeral that was to start in an hour. Besides, he added, morticians do not recover bodies from the street. "I'd have to notify the coroner."

"Go ahead and notify anybody, but I want you to handle it."

Sadowski reported the anonymous call to the Chicago coroner's office and was advised to contact the Niles Center police. Acting on the undertaker's information, Captain Axel Stolberg and a Niles Center patrolman proceeded to the area specified by the unknown caller. Sadowski, however, failed to mention the cemetery, and the searchers were unable to locate the body.

Shortly after the pair returned to the police station, Stolberg took a call from a Niles Center resident who claimed to have found a bundle of bloody clothing in a ditch near the area the officers had just searched. The clothes were recovered and proved to be a pair of gray trousers, part of a white shirt, underwear, a pair of blue socks, a money belt, and a pillow case. Each item was ripped or cut and soaked with blood. The money belt had been sliced open and emptied. The pants displayed a number of small holes where buckshot had chewed through the fabric before tearing through Nelson's stubby legs.

News of the discovery was relayed to the federal men who had spent the morning focusing their investigation around Winnetka. Four agents arrived to assist Stolberg and his men in a second attempt to locate the body. It was almost noon when the group began its sweep of the area. Within minutes Special Agent Sam McKee signaled that he had found the remains of America's most wanted man.

Nelson's body lay on the grass, with his head resting on the curb. His face, turned slightly to the left, wore what might have been a grin or a grimace. Beneath the blanket his naked (except for the cloth strip around his waist) body was, in Stolberg's words, "a crimson mess." The outlaw's right arm was draped across his chest, the left hand frozen claw-like directly above his stomach wound. His feet were crossed, the right atop the left. Nelson obviously had been dead for a while—rigor mortise had set in.

The FBI report stated, "In order that a crowd would not be attracted the body was immediately wrapped in the blanket and placed in the rear seat of the automobile of Captain Stolberg and driven to an undertaking establishment. . . . "

Clegg, Connelley, and Agents Peterson and Chaffetz, arrived at the mortuary to make the identification official. Fingerprints—still bearing the scars from his attempt to obliterate them almost two years earlier—confirmed that the corpse was Lester Joseph Gillis.

The body was photographed and examined. The press reported the little desperado had been shot seventeen times, but the actual total was nine. Aside from the fatal stomach wound, six buckshot pellets had blasted through Nelson's left leg and two more were imbedded in his right.

By mid-afternoon the story of Nelson's death was sweeping through the city. Newsmen flocked to the Fitzsimmons apartment, hoping to glean some comments from the outlaw's family. At one point the door opened, revealing a tiny aged figure in a gray gingham dress and a huge apron. Several reporters cried out that Nelson's body had been found.

"You're not telling me anything I don't already know," Mary replied. "We heard the news over the radio."

When they clamored for a statement the old woman declared, "It is terrible what they say about my son. He didn't do all those things they say he did. I know he didn't. My son is dead now, and there is nothing left to talk about. Any information we have we will give to the federal government."

The reporters continued to hurl questions at Mary until her daughter appeared. Julie, who previously had boasted to the press that her brother was "a clever kid" who could always "take care of himself," glared at the newsmen and slammed the door shut.

Early that evening the body was transported to the Cook County Morgue, where it was placed on the same slab Dillinger had occupied four months earlier, then briefly placed on public display. More than 2,000 morbidly curious individuals filed past the dead outlaw, barely half the number that had viewed Dillinger.

❀ ❀ ❀

Once Nelson was confirmed dead, the massive manhunt for the killers of Cowley and Hollis shifted to his two companions at the battle of Barrington. No doubts existed that the woman observed there had been Nelson's twenty-one-year-old wife. The press concluded that their "unidentified male companion" must have been John Hamilton or possibly Alvin Karpis. The G-Men, however, knew exactly who they were looking for and were keeping the suspect's name confidential. Both Special Agent McDade and the dying Cowley had positively identified Nelson's confederate as John Paul Chase.

With little cash and no car, Chase had checked into the Garfield Arms, a downtown hotel, and sequestered himself in his room, going out only to buy newspapers while hoping the furor over the Barrington shootout would subside before long. Chase soon devised a novel way to escape the city by answering a newspaper ad looking for drivers to deliver automobiles to the West Coast. Using the name Elmer Rockwood, Chase applied and was accepted. He received a paycheck for driving a Studebaker to Seattle, and upon his arrival there he quickly went his own way.

Fatso Negri found himself in a similar predicament: trapped in Chicago with no means or money to leave. On Thanksgiving evening he managed to locate Lieder at the Town Club in Cicero, and over drinks they discussed their situations now that Nelson was dead. Lieder, fresh from his latest FBI grilling, was eager to sever all his connections to Baby Face, and Negri was one of them. Agreeing that it would be "advisable" for Fatso to get out of town, the garage owner handed him fifty dollars and the keys to a 1934 Chevrolet coach. He warned Negri the car was hot (it had been stolen ten days earlier from a North Side street) and urged him to ditch it once he reached California. Negri departed that night.

While Chase, Negri, Lieder, and many others fretted over the long arm of the law, it was Helen who drew the most publicity. When Hoover ordered his agents to "find the woman and give her no quarter," the press interpreted his words to mean she was to be shot on sight. Some news stories even suggested that Helen had replaced her husband as Public Enemy Number One. The headlines of the Chicago *Herald Examiner* declared "KILL WIDOW OF BABY-FACE!" U.S. ORDERS GANG HUNTERS. The accompanying story stated that she had been "named as the nation's first woman public enemy" and that "orders were issued to capture her at any cost, to show her no mercy. In other words—'Shoot to kill!'"

Even worse was a United Press story that labeled Helen "the Tiger Woman" and painted her as a "ruthless gun moll of the Bonnie Parker type, leading her cohorts in bank raids and in battles with officers of the law." For the most part, the story contended, "she remained much in the background, directing the mob's activities—the brains of the gang." It was Helen who prodded her pint-sized husband into a life of crime; "the Tiger Woman made him." By "doing her bidding," Nelson went from "a small-time hood" to "the outstanding terror of the Middle West." The account claimed that during the shootout at Barrington, Helen loaded the guns for her husband and his friend.

The G-Men soon began to believe the outlandish tales. "I'd hate to shoot a woman," an agent was quoted as saying, "but I'm not following Cowley and Hollis because of ideas over a woman like that."

Assistant Director Clegg echoed the same sentiments when he was asked about the government's procedure in apprehending Helen. "From now on," he told newsmen, "mercy goes by the boards."

❀ ❀ ❀

On Thanksgiving morning, November 29, Helen Gillis—America's latest public enemy, "the Tiger Woman"— resumed her aimless trek through the city streets after sleeping most of the night in the doorway of an abandoned building. Her wandering that morning brought her to her old neighborhood where, from a safe distance, she watched her father leave for work with a small crowd in his wake. As she suspected, some were agents and the rest were reporters. Asked if he had any statement for his daughter, Vincent Warwick made a plea that was published the next day: "Come home. Surrender and give up alive or you'll be mowed down by machine guns. Remember your babies."

Helen moved on and spent the remainder of the day around Humbolt Park, feeling more forsaken than hunted. She considered calling her sister-in-law Julie but was certain the Fitzsimmons phone was tapped. (It was.) As evening approached she dreaded the thought of spending another night on the streets. Near Lafayette school she stopped a teenage girl and paid her a dollar to deliver a hastily scribbled note to Julie's apartment.

At that moment, Julie's husband was on the phone, as he had been for most of the day. This time he was speaking with Special Agent McKee, who had called to inquire about the time and place of Nelson's funeral. According to Helen's wishes, the body was turned over to Sadowski's funeral home, but the arrangements were still being discussed.

An FBI report noted, "At the time of this conversation Agent McKee informed Mr. Fitzsimmons that if he or the Gillis family would get in touch with Mrs. Gillis and endeavor to have her surrender herself, that they might avoid her being killed. It was stated to him that in the event she was found in the company of the individual who had been with Gillis on the afternoon of November 27, 1934, that she would no doubt be killed. He stated that the family had been talking of this situation all day and had agreed that it would be the best thing for her to give herself up. He also said the entire family felt that since Gillis was dead she would return to her children. . . . He promised to do his best to have the family try to contact her and said that in the event they were successful, that he would arrange to have Agents take her into custody in a quiet manner for the purpose of avoiding as much publicity as possible."

Just minutes after Fitzsimmons hung up, the girl arrived with Helen's note. Bob and Julie, accompanied by Leona, immediately departed. Once they were satisfied they were not being tailed, they drove to the school, where they found Helen sitting in the shadows on the front steps. The young widow joined them in the car. For the next hour they rode around while Helen told them about Les's final hours, how he had died in her arms, and about her own lonesome odyssey over the last thirty-six hours. Saying she would have surrendered sooner but feared she might be shot, Helen added that she was hopeful a deal could be arranged with the federal men that would allow her to attend her husband's funeral.

At 10:25 P.M. Fitzsimmons phoned the FBI office and was put in touch with Special Agent Virgil Peterson. When he admitted he had "succeeded in meeting Helen," the agent wanted to know the widow's whereabouts. "She's with me right now," Fitzsimmons replied.

He said the Gillis family had a request: Helen would voluntarily give herself up and cooperate fully with the federal men if she was permitted to remain with the family until the funeral. Peterson said such an arrangement "could not possibly be complied with, and it was demanded that she be turned over to Agents of the Division immediately." Fitzsimmons tried to strike a compromise, asking that Helen be allowed a brief, private visit to the funeral home. The agent answered that he was "unable to make any definite promises" and emphasized that "it would be in the best interests of Helen Gillis" if she surrendered first.

It was apparent the G-Men were in no mood to bargain. Fitzsimmons took a moment to urge Helen to heed their advice. When the widow nodded, he told Peterson, "We'll meet you on the southwest corner of Jackson and Halsted."

Peterson and five agents leapt into two cars and raced to the intersection. Upon their arrival, Fitzsimmons escorted Helen to the curb and she was placed in the lead car's back seat beside Peterson. Special Agent Max Chaffetz stepped from the second vehicle and spoke briefly with Fitzsimmons, telling him "the division would appreciate your cooperation" in not letting it be known Helen was in federal custody. Fitzsimmons promised he would say nothing to the press.

At the Bankers' Building Helen, surrounded by the six G-Men, was hustled in through the rear entrance. Chaffetz and another agent proceeded to the nineteenth floor ahead of the rest, making certain no newsmen were present and that the doors to the outer hallway were closed. The prisoner was led into the main office through a little-used passage cutting through a supply room.

For the next five days Helen's "capture" was kept secret while she was "questioned persistently" by the federal men. "I instructed Mr. Connelley to 'work on her' constantly and not let her get any sleep . . . ," Hoover noted in a memo. "I stressed the point that she should be made to talk."

But Connelley, stepping into the SAC's shoes of the phased-out Purvis, was no Cowley. When Nelson gunned down the inspector he unknowingly and quite probably spared his wife a more grueling interrogation. "Mr. Connelley was very, very nice," Helen later acknowledged, adding that "he treated me well."

Reluctantly she talked, sharing an abundance of information while carefully avoiding the mention of any crucial names. Chase, Perkins, Negri, Murray, and the like were referred to as "friends of Les" whose names she either could not recall or was never told. Their companion at Barrington, Helen said, had been "a fellow named George.")

While Helen was compelled to talk about her entire history with her husband, especially their movements during the past two years, the agents were particularly interested in Nelson's final hours. They were determined to discover where the desperado had gone to die and who had offered him help along the way.

Helen's answers were evasive at first, and she insisted that Les had been conscious and directed "George" the whole time. Nelson guided his companions through the northern suburbs and eventually brought them to a house that Helen claimed (as Chase would later) never to have seen before and that was occupied by individuals completely unknown to her. FBI records reveal that when she was pressed for more details, "Mrs. Gillis described the place . . . as being a one-story cottage, gray in color, with an attic, a front porch which covered the entire front portion of the cottage, and contained the front door on the left side of the porch. There was a double garage in the rear of this cottage. The cottage was described as being the second cottage from a corner and a having a vacant lot or open space between it and the building next nearest the corner. The people residing in this cottage were described as poor people. The woman's given name was furnished as MARY, and she was said to have a twelve-year-old daughter and a son around 15 years of age."

The agents were not satisfied until Helen led them, block by block, then turn by turn, to Wilmette and ultimately to Walnut Street. There they discovered the bungalow at 1627 was an exact match of the residence described by the young widow.

An immediate and rather extensive investigation was launched. With the cooperation of neighbors, Special Agents Ryan and LaFrance set up an around-the-clock surveillance from the house at 1621 Walnut, a few yards west of 1627, chosen by the G-Men because "one can see into the windows of the cottage . . . and can also observe anyone who enters the house by way of the garage in the rear, as well as the front door."

Over the next several weeks the agents noted the comings and goings of its occupants and their visitors. They also spoke to neighbors, checked license numbers, consulted police and public records, and even enlisted the aid of the local postman. The principal members of the household were Raymond J. Henderson, an unemployed truck driver currently receiving relief checks; his wife Marie; a son, age fourteen; and a daughter, age twelve. The agents' report states that "Henderson's reputation was not very good in Wilmette," especially among his neighbors. Police had been called to the bungalow numerous times to quell disorderly conduct and domestic scrabbles. At a former residence, the report noted, "Mrs. Henderson stole a diamond ring from her landlady" and was "forced to return it by Police."

But certainly the most interesting discovery about the Hendersons was that they were not alone at 1627. According to the postman, at least several individuals used the place as a mailing address and, from time to time, lived there. The part-time residents included one Guy McDonald, a known hood and onetime business associate of Jimmy Murray. Agents learned that McDonald had first become linked with the bungalow the previous fall. Over the summer he had left a forwarding address in Wauconda which proved to be Murray's cottage, a fact already known to the G-Men. Recently McDonald had returned to the Henderson house. Ryan and LaFrance often observed McDonald and his car, an old Packard, at the bungalow. They also heard neighborhood chatter claiming Mrs. Henderson had boasted that McDonald was one of her lovers.

The Hendersons and their houseguests were eventually brought in and questioned. All were allegedly adamant in their denial that Baby Face Nelson had visited their home on the day of his death or on any previous occasion. And there, to all appearances, the FBI probe into 1627 Walnut unexpectedly ended. If the Henderson interrogations produced any usable information or surprising revelations, they were not recorded in the usually meticulous reports of the G-Men. Nor is there any mention that Helen was called upon to identify any of the individuals mentioned.

The fact that no arrests were made and no charges were filed was no doubt due to a lack of evidence. But that hardly explains the abrupt closing of the case, especially since Hoover's memos to his men repeatedly exhorted them to uncover the identities of everyone involved and have them prosecuted.

Today, the circumstances surrounding Nelson's death and precisely who was present still remains a most intriguing mystery. At its core is a question that was never satisfactorily answered: What connection did Nelson have to 1627 Walnut and the persons residing there prior to November 27? Helen and Chase both swore that they had never been there before and knew none of the people, but it is more likely—since Nelson rarely traveled without one or the other or both—that neither told the truth. Neither Helen nor Chase mentioned the Henderson children being present that evening, yet in her statement she speaks of them and knows their approximate ages.

The FBI case file on 1627 Walnut contains only two subsequent memos, both of which provide some tantalizing clues about the events of November 27. The first was the report by one of the bureau's confidential informants, a man named Walsh who told agents in March 1935 that the man who assisted Helen in removing Nelson's body was not Chase, Henderson, or even McDonald, but none other than Jimmy Murray. (Murray's whereabouts that evening were never determined.) If Walsh's rmation was correct, someone (most likely McDonald) may have ned him to the bungalow either to aid the dying Nelson or oversee the clean-up after the desperado's death. Walsh also mentioned that Murray was presently attempting to sell Nelson's guns, but the weapons were "too hot" and he was having a difficult time.

The second was a report filed two years later, in March 1937. By that time, it was noted, both Ray Henderson and Guy McDonald were dead. Marie was living in a house on Wilmette Avenue but was on the verge of being evicted. One of her neighbors was Sergeant W. R. Sumner, a policeman in the North

Shore suburb of Kenilworth. Sumner contacted the bureau to advise that Mrs. Henderson often dropped by to chat and "has been doing considerable talking and bragging." Among information Sumner said she shared with him and his wife were details about the death of Baby Face Nelson. Marie allegedly told the couple they would be surprised if they knew where the bandit actually had died and who was with him at the end.

Sumner tried to learn more without appearing to be too interested and thus alarming Marie. Once he claimed "to have been reading in a magazine about the Baby Face Nelson episode" and stated "how wrong the article was," thus prodding her into talking.

In the course of their conversations, Marie gradually revealed more pieces of the puzzle. She said she was aware that "agents were watching her home from her neighbor's house" before she was brought in for questioning. Her husband was interrogated "very thoroughly" but, she insisted, Ray actually had no knowledge of the Nelson incident and no information to share. As a result, the agents "assumed she did not know anything and did not question her very much."

If her husband had not been present at the bungalow at the time of Nelson's death, then who was? Sumner had a tough time coaxing information from Marie and only managed to obtain a few helpful hints. She revealed that Murray, McDonald, and "some other man" (perhaps Chase) were the principal figures on hand that evening. She also mentioned the name of Leo Heinz who, it turned out, was a member of the Niles Center Board of Trustees and rumored to have an interest in local gambling activities. Marie indicated that Heinz had some connection with her house and, perhaps, with Nelson's reason for going there. She also told Sumner that a certain Father Coughlan had given agents "misleading information" in his official statement—the implication being that the priest himself had helped deliver Nelson to the bungalow. (The FBI later reported an unverified story alleging that Coughlan took time to administer the last rites to his dying friend in the Hendersons' bedroom.) Saying that Coughlan was "a very heavy drinker," Marie claimed the priest had had a long association with Murray, one that pre-dated even the 1924 Roundout robbery.

But by far the most astonishing revelation Marie shared with her neighbor was, in Sumners's words, "that Gillis died at the home of someone who was either an agent or informant, as someone who had the confidence of the Chicago Field Division, as the person in whose home Gillis died had been providing Gillis with information as to the Division's activities, and Gillis figured that this would be the last place where the bureau would search for him."

While this bombshell only serves to deepen the mystery surrounding 1627 Walnut Street, it does offers a plausible explanation as to why the bureau decided to drop the matter and dig no further, at least officially. If true, Marie Henderson's allegations cast doubt on much of the accepted record, including the statements of Helen, Chase, and Father Coughlan concerning the events of that evening. There are indications that the agents suspected the trio knew more than they revealed and, at times, had trouble keeping their stories straight. (Helen, for instance, changed at least several key points of her version to match Chase's confession after his arrest.)

By the spring of 1937, when Sumner began reporting Marie's conversations, further inquiry into Nelson's death could only hurt the bureau's image, and further prosecution of the principals seemed pointless. Helen had served her time and returned to her children, vowing publicly to sin no more. Chase was in Alcatraz serving a life sentence. Coughlan was either persuaded or forced to cooperate—but even if the agents suspected he had withheld certain information, there was no way the bureau would risk the inevitable negative publicity by prosecuting a priest.

Nor did the FBI have any intention of charging the mysterious individual linked to the Henderson house, who must have been some kind of paid informant, trusted by agents but all the while supplying Nelson with intelligence on the bureau's efforts to catch him. Public disclosure would prove embarrassing, indicating that the FBI, rather than pursue the matter, actually might have helped cover up the original cover-up. While Murray appears the most likely candidate, the identity of the informant and his (or her) relationship with the bureau was evidently concealed, the name blotted out on existing records.

The final report on 1627 Walnut ends by noting that on March 25, 1937, Sergeant Sumner phoned the bureau and "advised that Mrs. Henderson had visited him again, and had reiterated that the place where Gillis had died was the home of someone who had the confidence of the Chicago Field Division." She also said that Nelson's cache of weapons—consisting of a machine gun, the Monitor rifle, and a sawed-off shotgun—as well as "one or more bulletproof vests" had been stashed somewhere in Niles Center and were still for sale, or at least they had been two months earlier.

No further entries ever appeared. One can only conclude that the agents either had no desire to unravel the mystery—or they already knew the answers.

❄ ❄ ❄

At 10 A.M. on Saturday, December 1, nearly 200 people crowded into Sadowski's funeral home, barely a third of them able to squeeze inside the chapel where the slain outlaw was laid out in a silver-gray casket. The deceased was attired in a brown suit and his mustache shaved and his wavy blond hair combed in a neat pompadour. A six-foot mound of chrysanthemums and roses surrounded him. A floral wreath of forget-me-nots was labeled "To Our Dear Son," and another, composed of yellow and red roses, contained the banner "To Our Loving Husband and Father." A third bore the inscription "From Sisters, Wife, and Brother." Carved on the inside of the casket's lid were the words "At Rest."

The service was brief. There was no priest, no music, no eulogy, no candles, no crucifixes. Sadowski led the mourners in a succession of six short prayers, concluding with the benediction "May the grace of our Lord always remain with us." A woman among the spectators cried out, "And deliver us from all evil. Amen."

Six unidentified men, said to be the desperado's relatives and friends from his old neighborhood, acted as pallbearers. The casket was loaded into a hearse for the long drive to River Grove. Two vehicles packed with reporters and cameramen joined the caravan. Also following was Special Agent Ray Suran, who had been delegated to watch the crowd for wanted criminals.

At St. Joseph's Cemetery a brisk, icy wind greeted the mourners, their number now reduced to about forty souls. The coffin was placed on a trap above the open grave directly beside his father's headstone. Sadowski stood at the head of the casket, and to his left stood Mary Gillis, supported between Julie and her husband Bob. Her sobbing and pitiful moans were the only sounds in the graveyard until the mortician led the shivering spectators in the pater noster, followed by three repetitions of "Hail Mary."

Nelson's mother collapsed into the arms of her son-in-law.

Over the next few days Mary dealt with her grief by writing a series of melancholy articles about her youngest son which were eventually published in the *Chicago Daily Times*. She extolled her boy's virtues while glossing over his sins. In the process she blasted the pals who lured him into crime as a youth, the corrupt cops who "hounded" him as a young man, and especially the press, which vilified and exploited him as a public enemy.

Most of all Mary remembered him as the bright, precocious youngster he had been before "they" twisted his life into the brief, violent saga it became. An incident that repeatedly came to mind as she left the grave that chilly December day was one of eleven-year-old Lester's "adventurous excursions" with his dog Brucie and a neighborhood pal. The trio ended up in Crystal Lake, some twenty miles northwest of Chicago, where they fell into the hands of the local police. Notified that their son was in custody, Mary and Joseph drove to the police station, where they found Lester and Brucie sitting in a cell. Mary never forgot "the forlorn look" of both her boy and his dog. The incident typified most of her memories of her son—the youngster who couldn't keep out trouble, pleading for her help with his eyes, but too proud to speak the words, too stubborn to conform.

In the end even Mary admitted that her boy's death was the proper, inevitable conclusion to his tempestuous life. "Perhaps it is better so for his children and the rest of the family," she later wrote. "Life had made him a thing hunted like wild animals and there could have been nothing but agonizing suspense for those who loved him."

EPILOGUE

On December 4 word leaked to the press that Helen Gillis had been in federal custody since Thanksgiving evening. The next morning Assistant Director Clegg faced newsmen and confessed that the bureau had "apprehended" Nelson's widow. A *Chicago American* reporter asked if Helen had been captured or had surrendered; Clegg refused to speak about "the specifics of the arrest."

The AD was equally evasive about Helen's fate, indicating that while she had been "cooperative" under questioning, the government was still contemplating prosecuting her for complicity in the deaths of Cowley and Hollis. (Since many of the Barrington witnesses had stated they saw Helen hide in the field before the first shots were fired, the charge would have been difficult to prove.) The bureau wanted to hold her longer for further interrogation, but once her "capture" became known, they were forced to proceed with the only legal recourse available. A few hours after Clegg's news conference two agents arrived at the Fitzsimmons apartment and were admitted by Mary Gillis. The pair reappeared with a suitcase packed with Helen's clothing.

At 6 A.M. on December 6 four agents delivered Helen to the Dane County Jail in Madison, where she was placed in the same cell she had occupied seven months earlier. The next morning she was taken to Judge Stone's chambers for a ninety-minute conference before her court appearance. Stone wanted to know why she had violated her probation. "What about your two children?" he asked. "You love them, don't you?"

"Yes, very much."

"Your husband was an outlaw who was certain to be caught. If you loved your children, how could you leave them behind with relatives and follow your husband around?"

"I knew Les didn't have long to live, and I wanted to be with him as long as I could," she said.

More than 150 spectators jammed the courtroom for the official hearing. Helen stood before the bench looking tiny and frail, a white handkerchief clasped in one hand. In a voice barely audible past the front row, she admitted violating her probation. Stone commented, "I believe you have a little more respect for the Department of Justice now than when you were placed on probation in May."

Helen nodded.

Stone sermonized that Hoover's bureau "has convinced you and others that there is but one end to that kind of life: death or prison. It ought to teach a lesson to you and others who are similarly inclined toward crime." He went on the praise the G-Men for their record of efficiency which "surpasses anything done by the mounted police or any other similar department anywhere."

He ordered Helen's probation revoked. She was to be taken immediately to serve her sentence of a year and a day at the Women's Correctional Farm at Milan, Michigan.

❋ ❋ ❋

On December 24 a police detective in Portland, Oregon, notified agents that he had information "concerning a San Francisco Italian known as 'Fat,' who was supposed to have . . . some connection with Baby Face Nelson." Acting on the tip, G-Men staked out the Herman Apartments in Portland on Christmas morning. At 9:15 P.M. a stocky young man living under the name John Novo emerged from the building, accompanied by a pretty brunette. Agents swiftly surrounded them and relieved Novo of a German Luger. The pair were hustled into a bureau car and whisked away to the Portland office.

Novo confessed that he was actually Joseph Raymond Negri but was "reluctant to talk or discuss his connection" with Nelson. However, "he soon changed his attitude and commenced to make a complete "statement." Thirty-eight pages later, the agents had the inside story on much of Nelson's movements and activities over the preceding six months, along with the names, dates, and places to aid their efforts to identify anyone associated with the outlaw's flight from justice. Negri's companion, a local girl named Betty Morgan, was released. Fatso was taken to San Francisco to assist federal prosecutors in assembling evidence against those suspected of having been Nelson's friends.

❋ ❋ ❋

On December 26 John Paul Chase celebrated his thirty-third birthday by hitchhiking to Mount Shasta and visiting the fish hatchery where he had worked five years earlier. He spoke with several old friends, including the foreman, confessing that he was "flat broke" and hoping to borrow a few dollars.

The next morning the foreman, hearing talk that Chase was wanted by the law, notified Mount Shasta police that the fugitive had mentioned he was staying in town at the Park Hotel. When Police Chief Al Roberts and a deputy sheriff arrived at the hotel they discovered their suspect had just left. A few blocks away they spotted Chase walking along the street and quietly arrested him. Although attired in an expensive blue suit, his pockets contained less than five dollars, a tube of shaving cream, a razor, toothbrush, and toothpaste. He had no luggage or weapons.

Chase was turned over to federal agents who took him to San Francisco for several days of questioning. He admitted that he had been Nelson's faithful traveling companion for nearly a year but denied ever taking part in any holdups or gun battles—except for the Barrington shootout, in which he insisted he had fired only in self-defense and was not responsible for the deaths of either federal agent.

Guarded by six agents, Chase was taken by train to Chicago on New Year's Eve. U.S. District Attorney Dwight Green recalled the federal grand jury from holiday recess to issue an indictment against Chase for the murder of Inspector Cowley. Under the new law passed after Nelson's slaying of Special Agent Baum, the killing of a government agent was a federal offense, punishable by death on the gallows. Chase was the first to be indicted on the charge, and his scheduled trial would be the first murder case tried in a federal court since 1893.

❄ ❄ ❄

While Chase awaited his court date, Hoover's G-Men continued to round up individuals they suspected of providing aid and shelter to Nelson over the course of his criminal career, arresting almost two dozen persons in Chicago, Reno, and San Francisco's Bay Area. Federal prosecutors decided to charge each with conspiracy to harbor a federal fugitive and place them on trial together in San Francisco.

The most significant arrest occurred in Chicago at 1:15 A.M. on January 26, 1935. Acting on an informer's tip, Special Agents LaFrance and McDade stopped at the Sheridan Restaurant and flashed a photo of Jack Perkins. The night manager pointed to a table where a chunky young man sat scribbling in a small red notebook containing a record of recent wagers. The man who (aside from Chase) was allegedly Nelson's most trusted friend, and had been the object of an intensive FBI investigation over the past nine months, surrendered quietly.

The agents discovered that Perkins was more talkative and cooperative "during somewhat casual conversation with him, inasmuch as direct questioning tended to anger him, resulting in his refusal to answer any questions whatever." They obtained a sworn statement from him in which he recounted his six-week summer road trip with Nelson, acknowledging that he was aware his pal was a wanted man who "constantly carried a pistol with him." Perkins, however, was careful about what he said and whom he implicated. He refused to admit selling guns or bulletproof vests to Nelson or anyone else. He said he had met Dillinger and Van Meter on only two occasions and was never "closely associated with either." He claimed his acquaintance with Clarence Lieder "was of a casual nature" and that he "never had any dealings with him." Perkins insisted that he didn't know and in fact had never met Jimmy Murray.

Most crucial of all, Perkins denied any knowledge of the Merchants' National Bank robbery in South Bend. The bureau agents and Indiana lawmen threatened to prosecute him and did their best to build a case. No official deal was recorded, but their attempts to link Perkins to the holdup immediately ceased once the bookie agreed to arrange for his wife's surrender, then consented to their extradition to San Francisco to face harboring charges.

Perkins's one complaint while in FBI custody was that newsmen were allowed access to him and had hounded him for interviews and pictures. Once, when a U.S. marshal was escorting him from the Bankers' Building, a reporter closed in and attempted to snap a photo. The handcuffed prisoner cursed him and tried to kick the camera from his grasp.

Unlike any of his fifteen co-defendants in San Francisco, Perkins pleaded guilty to the charges. On March 2 he was sentenced to two years' imprisonment and fined $1,000.

❋ ❋ ❋

On March 18 the trial of John Paul Chase opened in the U.S. district court in Chicago. The prosecution was prepared to call fifty-five witnesses to testify that the defendant had been Baby Face Nelson's henchman or to identify him as a participant in the slayings of Cowley and Hollis. The list included Helen Gillis and Melvin Purvis, but neither was summoned to the courtroom; the evidence against Chase was already overwhelming.

Among the witnesses who took the stand was Father Coughlan, who had been recalled from a sabbatical in Oklahoma to tell how Helen and Chase had brought the dying desperado to him seeking his help. Special Agents Ryan and McDade recounted their harrowing escapade on the Northwest Highway and told how Chase had opened fire on their car with an automatic rifle.

Defense Attorney W. W. O'Brien's two-pronged strategy was (1) to portray his client as an innocent pawn who came under Nelson's evil influence, and (2) to question the integrity and tactics of the G-Men. Cross-examining Ryan he asked, "Weren't you under instructions to shoot to kill Nelson and anyone in his company?" The agent vigorously denied ever receiving such orders, but O'Brien, for the jury's sake, repeatedly referred to the "shoot first" command issued by Attorney General Cummings.

While questioning the glib McDade, O'Brien attempted to show that the agents never bothered to identify themselves, leaving Nelson and Chase to assume they could be rival gangsters. "Did you and Ryan tell Nelson and the others in his car that you were agents when they drove up beside you?"

"I wouldn't be here today if I'd done that," was McDade's reply.

Instead of stopping to arrest the suspects, O'Brien pointed out, "You and Ryan drove away from Nelson's party as quickly as you could, didn't you?"

"You would too," McDade answered, producing a roar of laughter from the spectators.

The only witness for the defense was Chase himself, who swore he had no idea the men were federal agents and insisted that they had fired first. He admitted firing several shots during the chase on the highway but only at the vehicle, not the occupants. In the gun battle with Cowley and Hollis, he confessed that he had fired his rifle "not over six times" but claimed most of his shots were directed into the air since Nelson had marched into the open directly between him and the agents.

On March 25 the jury found Chase guilty and recommended leniency. He was sentenced to life imprisonment at Alcatraz.

By the time Chase began his sentence on "the Rock," the trial of Nelson's friends was under way in San Francisco. The charges against Anna Cochran, Arthur Pratt, Ralph Rizzo, William Schivo, and several others were dismissed, leaving nine defendants to face the court. Fatso Negri was the star witness for the prosecution. A parade of upstanding citizens testified on behalf of the accused. A Reno minister and a Nevada judge appeared as character witnesses for Frank Cochran. A petition signed by 119 Vallejo residents, including many city officials, was presented to call for clemency for Tobe Williams and described him as "a man of sterling character, charitable to the needy, and fair to his fellow man."

On April 5, following a twelve-day trial, Grace Perkins, Louis Tambini, Gene Mazet, Frankie Fields, and Vince Marcovitch were acquitted. Williams was sentenced to eighteen months in prison and fined $5,000. Cochran and Tex Hall each received a year and a day and a $2,000 fine. Tony Moreno was ordered to serve six months. The sentences of Williams and Hall were later reduced by six months because of their age and ill health.

Clarence Lieder managed to fight extradition to San Francisco for three months. Finally, on May 23, he pleaded guilty to the charge of harboring Nelson and was fined $1,000 and given a term of a year and a day behind bars. The day after Lieder's sentencing, Negri was placed on five years' probation and released. He immediately returned to Portland and married Betty Morgan.

The last of Nelson's associates to come to trial was actually the first to be indicted. More than a year passed before San Antonio gunsmith Hyman Lebman was tried on the state charge of violating the Texas machine-gun law. On August 2, 1935, he was found guilty, and one week later he was sentenced to five years in the state penitentiary at Huntsville. His conviction was appealed, and the decision was reversed on May 27, 1936. Six months later Lebman was re-tried on the same charge, but that trial ended in a hung jury.

The state considered calling for a third trial, prompted, at least in part, by a series of letters from Hoover to the state District Attorney's Office demanding that Lebman be prosecuted as "an aid [sic] and associate of bandit gangs." However on February 5, 1941, the indictment against the gunsmith was dismissed. Evidently Lebman learned his lesson from his seven-year legal ordeal—he re-established himself as a reputable merchant in San Antonio and remained an honest citizen until his death in 1990.

❋ ❋ ❋

Although it cost two lives to extinguish one, the battle of Barrington was viewed as another decisive victory in Hoover's "War On Crime." The Public Enemy Era continued, but aside from the spectacular shootout in Florida on January 16, 1935, in which G-Men killed Freddie Barker and his mother, the excitement and thrills of the depression desperados was over.

John Hamilton succeeded Nelson as the nation's Public Enemy Number One. People kept spotting the outlaw and lawmen reported chasing him until his badly decomposed remains were unearthed on August 28, 1935. The bandit was identified through dental records.

By that time the only prominent outlaw of the era still at large was Alvin Karpis, and Hoover designated him the nation's most wanted man. Karpis managed to evade capture for another eight months, pulling off a couple of major holdups in the process. On May 1, 1935, the public learned that Karpis had been arrested in New Orleans by Hoover himself, a fitting way for the saga of the G-Men's gang-busting crusade to end. Four decades passed before Karpis claimed to set the record straight by revealing that it was actually a squad of agents led by Clarence Hurt who had nabbed him. Once he was in custody and found to be unarmed, he said, Hoover appeared from his "hiding place" behind a building and took credit for personally capturing Karpis.

The golden age of the Midwest bandit gangs was over. The folk-hero image that had surrounded the depression-era outlaws had been successfully smashed. In 1931 James Cagney electrified audiences as gangster Tommy Powers in *Public Enemy*; in 1935 moviegoers applauded Cagney as a dashing young federal agent in Warner Brothers' *G-Men*, which glorified the exploits of Hoover's bureau. Baby Face Nelson and his criminal contemporaries became an integral part of FBI lore, transformed into villains who were more formula than fact, their photos adorning the targets on the FBI's shooting range at Quantico, Virginia.

In the introduction to his book *G-Men*, author Richard Gid Powers wrote, "A half century ago Franklin D. Roosevelt, Homer Cummings, J. Edgar Hoover, John Dillinger, Pretty Boy Floyd, and Baby Face Nelson collaborated with Warner Brothers, James Cagney, *G-Men Magazine* . . . and the American Press to create a new American legend, a myth that was so exciting and so satisfying that for nearly forty years we kept J. Edgar Hoover under glass, feeding his vanity, tolerating his foibles, excusing his failures."

In later years, when his bureau was besieged with criticism for its civil rights record and charges of national espionage, Hoover invariably invoked the names of Nelson, Dillinger, Floyd, Kelly, Karpis, and Ma Barker in an attempt to dredge up "all those old cases of the thirties" as proof of the FBI's prestige and a reminder of the debt the nation owed him.

❋ ❋ ❋

While many of Nelson's closest friends and confederates remained actively involved in crime, few came to violent ends. The most notable exception was Machine Gun Jack McGurn, who was shot to death in a Chicago bowling alley by unknown assassins on February 15, 1936.

The Two Tonys—Accardo and Capezio—continued to rise into the upper echelon of Chicago gangdom. Capezio's prominence ended abruptly when he was struck and killed by lightning on a golf course, prompting more than one lawman to remark that "there is a God." With the downfall of Frank Nitti and other high-ranking mobsters by the 1940s, Accardo established himself as overlord of the Chicago outfit. He died of natural causes in 1992 at the age of eighty-six.

Despite the fact that he was implicated in at least a dozen confessions connected with the Nelson case, Jimmy Murray somehow managed to escape prosecution and continued to be a highly touted friend of the underworld and freelance criminals. But whatever special protection Murray enjoyed suddenly vanished when FBI agents learned he was involved in the $85,000 holdup of a Pennsylvania bank in 1938. On June 6, 1939, he was sentenced to twenty-five years behind bars. He served his first six months at Atlanta, the next seven years at Alcatraz, and seven more years at Leavenworth. He was paroled on February 22, 1954. The Jimmy Murray who returned to Chicago in his late sixties was no longer the same shrewd player of the Public Enemy Era but a doddering figure with Alzheimer's. Yet even in his twilight years he continued to run afoul of the law. He was repeatedly caught shoplifting but each time was released into the care of his family. He died January 20, 1963.

Bill Graham and Jim McKay, Nelson's protectors in Reno, were brought to trial three times. Without the testimony of the vanished Roy Frisch, the first two trials ended in hung juries. But in 1937 the two were convicted in a third trial, and each was sentenced to nine years' imprisonment and fined $11,000. After six years in Leavenworth they were paroled and resumed control of their lucrative enterprises in Reno and Lake Tahoe. McKay died on June 20, 1962, and Graham followed his partner to the grave on November 5, 1965.

In 1941 Frisch was declared legally dead. His body has never been found.

On March 13, 1936, federal agents finally caught up to Eddie Bentz, capturing the legendary bank robber in a Brooklyn hotel. While in custody he reportedly told lawmen, "I hope they send me to Alcatraz. All my friends are there."

He got his wish and was sentenced to twenty-five years on the Rock for the 1935 holdup of a Vermont bank. Although he pleaded guilty to the charge, he refused to name his accomplices or supply any details. In fact, for obvious reasons, the only robbery he talked about openly was the Grand Haven heist. In the summer of 1934 his half-brother Ted was arrested and sentenced to life imprisonment for the crime. Eddie's detailed confession to the FBI and a vividly recounted article published in *Argosy* made it clear that Ted had no part in the holdup other than helping to dispose of some stolen bonds. In 1955 Ted was finally pardoned after twenty-five years behind bars.

Eddie was paroled in 1949 but was immediately claimed by authorities in Massachusetts and charged with a bank robbery committed at Turners Falls. He was sentenced to five to eight years. Upon his release, Wisconsin successfully petitioned to have Bentz delivered for prosecution on another holdup. He enjoyed a few years of freedom before his death in 1965.

Like Murray and Bentz, most of Nelson's partners in crime paid with prison time. Earl Doyle, the only person other than Ted Bentz to be convicted for the Grand Haven robbery, was paroled in 1948 after serving fourteen years. Chuck Fisher was an inmate at Leavenworth until his release on New Year's Eve 1942. Remarkably, Tom Gannon managed to dodge the law for nearly a decade before Wisconsin indicted him in 1943 for the Amery holdup. Forty-two years old and completely deaf, Gannon raged throughout his four-day trial that he had been framed and repeatedly threatened to kill the judge and prosecutor. On April 20, 1944, he was found guilty and sentenced to fifteen to forty years in the state prison at Waupon.

❋ ❋ ❋

Following his release from Leavenworth, Jack Perkins returned to his family in Chicago. He and his wife had three more children and eventually moved to a house in Oak Park. Over the years Perkins always seemed to have at least several sources of income, some of them legal, including a tool and die operation in the 1940s. But his principal profession remained crime, primarily overseeing the mob's gambling action in Cicero.

His notorious past resurfaced only once, in 1955 when Perkins, traveling with "an unidentified woman," crashed his car and was arrested for driving while intoxicated. An officer at the police station either recognized him or saw his record, and a reporter was tipped off that a former confederate of Baby Face Nelson had been caught driving drunk with a woman other than his wife. When the newsman arrived and attempted to snap a photo, Perkins slammed a fist into his face. After spending a few days in jail and paying a hefty fine, Perkins was set free.

In 1970 he suffered a stroke. With his health deteriorating, he spent his final years reminiscing with family and close friends about his days as a young hood and part-time outlaw, most of the stories centering around his "best friend Jimmie." On February 2, 1973, Perkins was drinking coffee at the apartment of a friend, a Chicago policeman, when he suffered a massive heart attack and died. He was buried in St. Joseph's Cemetery in River Grove, his grave only a brief walk away from the Gillis plot.

✳ ✳ ✳

There were many misconceptions among guards and convicts about John Paul Chase when he entered Alcatraz. The general opinion was that the former adjutant of Baby Face Nelson would be an insolent, dangerous inmate.

Chase proved to be nothing of the sort. He was, in fact, a model, almost docile prisoner, well liked by both the staff and his fellow cons. During his nineteen years on the Rock, the only hint of trouble occurred in 1937 when prison officials suspected (but never proved) that he had conspired with two inmates who attempted an escape. As it turned out, the cons had befriended Chase to take advantage of his familiarity of the Bay Area; Chase was happy to advise them but never contemplated participating in the break.

Over the years he developed a passion for painting and was regarded by many as an accomplished artist. He also became close friends with the prison chaplain, who helped Chase acquire painting materials and sold some of his artwork for him in San Francisco.

In 1955 Chase became eligible for parole. The chaplain was one of his strongest advocates, claiming the convicted killer of a G-Man was a reformed character who could be a useful part of society. Hoover learned of the chaplain's crusade on Chase's behalf and immediately launched a counter-campaign to ensure the convict remained at Alcatraz. At the bottom of a memo he directed his agents, "Watch closely & endeavor to thwart efforts of this priest who should be attending to his own business instead of trying to turn loose on society such mad dogs."

Two years later Hoover was horrified to learn that one of his former agents supported Chase's bid for freedom. Tom McDade, one of the targets of Chase's gunfire on the Northwest Highway, wrote the Alcatraz chaplain saying he had no objection to Chase's release. The FBI director branded McDade, in retirement, a traitor to the bureau.

On September 21, 1954, Chase was transferred to Leavenworth, and seven months later he received his first parole hearing. He discovered that federal prosecutors, prodded by Hoover, stood ready to indict him for the murder of Herman

Hollis if he were set free. Hoover had used his agents and the FBI's resources to track down about a dozen witnesses to testify against Chase, including a feeble Father Coughlan, who was living out his last days in a retirement home in Jasper, Indiana. Chase filed a petition in federal court charging that the government had deliberately withheld the twenty-year-old murder charge in order to block his application for parole at this time. A federal judge ruled to dismiss the indictment, stating that the idea of prosecuting a man on a charge that had been shelved for two decades "shocks the imagination and the conscious."

Undeterred, Hoover continued to fire off letters of protest and make phone calls voicing his opposition to the parole board. Finally, on October 31, 1966, Chase was released. He moved to Palo Alto, California, where he lived a quiet, prosaic life working as a custodian and performing odd jobs until his death on October 5, 1973, from colon cancer.

❋ ❋ ❋

Despite her model behavior behind bars, Helen Gillis served almost the entire year of her sentence inside the women's prison at Milan. On December 6, 1935, FBI agents escorted her to San Francisco, where she was met and placed under arrest by a U.S. marshal. Later that day she was arraigned in federal court on the charge of harboring her late husband, then placed in a cell to await trial.

Assistant U.S. Attorney R. B. McMillan, the man delegated to prosecute Helen, wrote a letter to Attorney General Cummings complaining that the twenty-two-year-old widow was clearly no threat to society and appeared so pathetic that further prosecution seemed pointless. He also was concerned that some "blubbering brothers" might portray the Justice Department as mean-spirited. Hoover received a copy of the letter and dismissed McMillan as "a blubbering brother himself." He insisted the wife of Baby Face Nelson belonged in a cell, declaring that any sympathy the public had for her would be better directed toward the widows of Baum, Cowley, and Hollis.

On December 9 Leona McMahon, her husband, William, and six-year-old Ronald arrived in San Francisco and visited Helen. It was the first time Ronnie had seen his mother in over a year. Later that day Leona obtained a lawyer for her sister-in-law and spoke to the press. "Helen wants to get it all over as quickly and quietly as possible," she told them. She explained that both Ronnie and Darlene were presently living with her in Long Beach, California, where he husband served aboard the Coast Guard cutter Astoria. Helen hoped to be released and move in with them.

Helen's day in court arrived on December 13. As she was escorted from the jail a black woman in a neighboring cell pressed a rabbit's foot into her hand and said, "This is Friday the Thirteenth, honey. You take this. It'll bring you some luck."

With her lawyer at her side and the rabbit's foot dangling from her tiny fist, the young woman who had married Lester Gillis seven years earlier and become the constant companion of Baby Face Nelson, timidly pleaded guilty and applied for probation. "She is guilty of being a faithful wife to a misguided husband," her attorney stated. "She has been through a hell on earth. She was never a criminal herself."

To everyone's surprise (and Hoover's chagrin) McMillan added his recommendation to her plea for probation, citing her record of excellent behavior over the past year in federal custody. "I believe you've been punished enough," the judge declared. "I want you to lead a good life and be a good mother to your children."

Helen was ordered to serve one year's probation, with the provision that she reside with the McMahon family and "not write any articles regarding her life or her husband's life" during that time.

"I'm very happy," she told newsmen, flashing the brightest smile anyone had seen her manage over the past two years. She said it was "wonderful" to be returning to her children and looked forward to spending Christmas with them. After making sure the rabbit's foot was returned, she boarded a bus with Leona for the ride to Long Beach.

❋ ❋ ❋

"I loved Les," Helen told a writer in one of the rare interviews she later granted. "When you love a guy, you love him. That's all there is to it."

There was a flicker of defiance in her big blue eyes, along with a hint of loss, as she explained that she had no regrets about her decisions. "If I had my life to live over again, I'd do it just as I did. I'd stick to my husband any time, any place, no matter what he did."

And with that said, Helen got on with her life. In 1937 she returned to Chicago with her children and spent the next fifty years shunning publicity and even recognition as the widow of the infamous outlaw, although—oddly—she used the name Helen Nelson on occasion at some of her jobs. She kept in close contact with the Gillis family, especially her mother-in-law, until Mary's death in 1961 at the age of ninety-two. By then her children had married and moved away, Ronald to LaFox, Illinois, Darlene to southern Wisconsin. Helen was a frequent visitor at both homes and in her later years lived with Ronald.

She never remarried. One week after suffering a cerebral hemorrhage, she died on July 3, 1987, in a hospital in St. Charles. According to her request, she was buried beside her husband in the Gillis family plot at St. Joseph's Cemetery.

ACKNOWLEDGMENTS

THE LIST OF THE many individuals whose time, information, and expertise contributed to the shape and substance of this book begins with the late Joe Pinkston, a pioneer in the revisionist research on the Dillinger gang and for many years a staunch advocate for a serious work to be written on Nelson's life.

The authors are particularly grateful to Jim Perkins for sharing his stories and personal recollections of his father and, on occasion, serving as our guide through The Patch; Paul Maccabee for his time and generous help with our research in the Twin Cities; Dr. David Seibold for providing his unpublished manuscript "Historic Grand Haven" and other materials which became the cornerstone of our research of the Grand Haven holdup; Terry Harrison, archivist/historian at the Mason City Library, who supplied us with his interviews of Opal (Koss) Graham, Dorothy (Ransom) Crumb, and Margaret (Johnson) Gieson contained in the Lee P. Loomis Archive of Mason City History; Neal Frantzen (son of Raymond Frantzen) and Emma (Droegemueller) Plass for their vivid recounting of the Itasca bank robbery; and Alta Johnson, who shared valuable information about her uncle Theodore Kidder.

In addition, our thanks goes out to Ann Diestal at the Federal Bureau of Prisons, Becky Fargo at the *Grand Haven Tribune*, Rise Larson at Towers Productions in Chicago, Russ Lewis at the Chicago Historical Society, John Palmer at the St. Joseph Library in South Bend, Marie Thomas at the Barrington Area Library, Tom and Paula Peterson (our hosts and part-time guides while we were in the Twin Cities), Jim Adams, DeWayne Alexander, Ed Baumann, Jeanette Calloway, Rick Cartledge, Don Costello, Phillip Earl, Art Fischbeck, Bob Fischer, Gordon Herigstad, Tom Hollatz, Sandy Jones, Lori Hyde, Jeff King, Richard Lindberg, Rick Mattix, Jeff Maycroft, Jack Melcher, Ellen Poulsen, Clarence Pool, and Larry Sax. There were also certain individuals, including members of the Gillis family, who generously contributed to this book but wish to remain anonymous.

Our search for the real Baby Face Nelson took us through a dozen different states. The establishments and institutions utilized, and the newspapers consulted, include:

In California—San Francisco Public Library and Sausalito Police Department; *Oakland Tribune, Sacramento Union, San Francisco Call-Bulletin, San Francisco Chronicle, San Francisco News.*

In Illinois—Barrington Area Library, Chicago Crime Commission, Chicago Historical Society, Chicago Pubic Library, Archives Department of the Cook County Circuit Court, Illinois Department of Corrections, Illinois Division of Vital Records, and Newberry Library; *Barrington Courier, Chicago American, Chicago News, Chicago Daily Times, Chicago Tribune, Chicago Herald Examiner.*

In Indiana—Long Beach Realty Company, Porter County Courthouse, and St. Joseph Public Library in South Bend; *Indianapolis News, Indianapolis Star, South Bend Tribune.*

In Iowa—Mason City Public Library; *Des Moines Tribune, Mason City Globe-Gazette.*

In Michigan—Loutit Library in Grand Haven; *Detroit Free Press, Grand Rapids Press, Muskegon Chronicle.*

In Minnesota—Hennepin County Sheriff's Department, Minneapolis *Public Library, Minnesota Historical Society in St. Paul; Brainerd Daily Dispatch, Brainerd Journal, Minneapolis Journal, St. Paul Daily News, St. Paul Dispatch, St. Paul Pioneer Press.*

In Nevada— Nevada Historical Society in Reno; *Nevada State Journal, Reno Evening Gazette.*

In South Dakota—Siouxland Libraries; *Aberdeen Evening News, Sioux Falls Argus-Leader.*

In Texas—Texana/Genealogy Department at San Antonio's Central Library; *San Antonio Evening News, San Antonio Express, San Antonio Light.*

In Wisconsin—French Country Inn (formerly Lake Como Inn), Hedberg Public Library, Little Bohemia Lodge, State Historical Society of Wisconsin in Madison; *Antigo Daily Journal, Capital Times, Janesville Gazette, Manitowoc Herald-Times, Marshfield News-Herald, Menominee Herald Leader, Milwaukee Sentinel, Portage Daily Register, Wisconsin State Journal.*

In Washington D. C.— Federal Bureau of Prisons, J. Edgar Hoover Reading Room at the Federal Bureau of Investigation, Library of Congress, National Archives; *Washington Daily News, Washington Evening Star, Washington Post.*

At the core of our research were the FBI's declassified files—more than 100,000 pages of which were scrutinized for this book. The majority of these papers bear the names of Special Agents Virgil Peterson (in Chicago), D. L. Nicholson (St. Paul), and William Ramsey (San Francisco), who transcribed and recapitulated most of the data collected in their respective cities. Also included in the files were many of Director Hoover's personal memos to his men and numerous reports written by Assistant Director Hugh Clegg, Inspector Samuel Cowley, Inspector W. A. Rorer, SAC Edward Guinane, SAC Werner Hanni, SAC Gus Jones, SAC Melvin Purvis, and Special Agents Rufus

Coulter, Thomas Dodd, Samuel Hardy, Herman Hollis, Thomas McDade, James Metcalf, Jay Newman, E. N. Notesteen, William Ryan, Raymond Suran, and Charles Winstead.

The most useful and illuminating information in these files often came from recorded statements and interviews. These included Nelson family members Juliette Fitzsimmons, Robert Fitzsimmons, Helen Gillis, Mary Gillis, Fred Kenniston, and Leona McMahon; his friends and part-time companions Eddie Bentz, John Paul Chase, Jean Delany Compton, Mickey Conforti, Father Phillip Coughlan, Clarence Lieder, Joseph Negri, Art O'Leary, and Bessie Skinner; and witnesses (at Barrington) Harry Cooper, Patrolman William Gallagher, Robert Hayford, Mrs. Frances Kramer, and Paul Sherman; (at Lake Como) Eddie Duffy and Hobe Hermanson; (at Little Bohemia) George Bazo, Constable Carl Christensen, C. J Christianson, John Hoffman, Alvin Koerner, Paul Lang, George LaPorte, Lloyd LaPorte, John Morris, Frank Traube, and Emil and Nan Wanatka; and (at Louie's roadhouse) Eddie Cernocky and Caroline Corder.

SELECTED BIBLIOGRAPHY

A VAST LIBRARY OF published works exists on the Public Enemy era, the depression years, and the Midwest bandit gangs, the roads they followed, and the cities in which they stayed. Many were consulted for this book, but few were actually helpful. Among the most valuable books and articles, some less for their accuracy than for their reflections on the era and insights into Hoovers FBI, were:

Books

Cooper, Courtney Ryley. *Here's to Crime.* Boston: Little, Brown and Company, 1937.

———. *Ten Thousand Public Enemies.* Boston: Little, Brown and Company, 1935.

Cromie, Robert and Joseph Pinkston. *Dillinger: A Short and Violent Life.* New York: McGraw-Hill, 1962.

Edge, L. L. *Run the Cat Roads: The True Story of Bank Robbers in the '30s.* New York: Dember Books, 1981.

Gentry, Curt. *J. Edgar Hoover: The Man and the Secrets.* New York: Norton, 1991.

Girardin, G. Russell, with William Helmer. *Dillinger: The Untold Story.* Bloomington: Indiana University Press, 1994.

Godwin, John. *Alcatraz: 1868-1963.* Garden City, N. Y.: Doubleday, 1963.

Hollatz, Tom. *Gangster Holidays: The Lore and Legends of the Bad Guys.* St. Cloud, Minn.: North Star Press, 1989.

Hoover, J. Edgar. *Persons in Hiding.* Boston: Little, Brown and Company, 1938.

Karpis, Alvin, with Bill Trent. *The Alvin Karpis Story.* New York: Coward, McCann and Geoghegan, 1971.

Karpis, Alvin, with Robert Livesey. *On the Rock.* Don Mills, Ontario: Musson Book Company, 1980.

King, Jeffery S. *The Life and Death of Pretty Boy Floyd.* Kent, Ohio: Kent State University Press, 1998.

Maccabee, Paul. *John Dillinger Slept Here: A Crook's Tour of Crime and Corruption in St. Paul, 1920-1936.* St. Paul: Minnesota Historical Press, 1995.

Powers, Richard Gid. *G-Men: Hoover's FBI in American Popular Culture.* Carbondale: Southern Illinois University Press, 1983.

———. *Secrecy and Power: The Life of J. Edgar Hoover.* New York: Free Press, 1987.

Purvis, Melvin. *American Agent.* Garden City, N. Y.: Doubleday, Duran and Company, 1936.

Summers, Anthony. *Official and Confidential: The Secret Life of J. Edgar Hoover.* New York: G. P. Putnam's Sons, 1993.

Toland, John. *The Dillinger Days.* New York: Random House, 1963.

Wallis, Michael. *Pretty Boy: The Life and Times of Charles Arthur Floyd.* New York: St. Martin's Press, 1992.

Articles

Bentz, Edward. "I, Edward Bentz, being sworn , depose and say . . ." *Argosy,* Jan. 1951.

Courson, George. "How G-Men Trapped Ed Bentz." *True Detective Mysteries,* Feb. 1937.

Earl, Phillip I. "The Disappearance of Roy Frisch." *Nevada Magazine,* Aug. 1998.

Foster, Ralph. "Baby Face Nelson's Crimson Career." *Startling Detective Adventures,* Nov. 1934.

Negri, "Fatso," with Bennett Williams. "In the Hinges of Hell: How G-Men Ended Crime's Reddest Chapter." *True Detective Mysteries,* Dec. 1940, Jan., Feb., Mar., Apr., May, July, Aug. 1941.

Zirpoli, A. J., with Dean S. Jennings. "The G-Men Strike!" *Famous Detective Cases,* Sept. 1935.

INDEX